The Western Heritage
to 1715

VOLUME I

The Western Heritage
to 1715

Donald Kagan / Steven Ozment / Frank M. Turner
YALE UNIVERSITY HARVARD UNIVERSITY YALE UNIVERSITY

Third Edition

Macmillan Publishing Company
New York

NOTE:
The dates cited for monarchs and popes are generally the years of their reign rather than of their births and deaths.

Printed in the United States of America

MACMILLAN PUBLISHING COMPANY
866 Third Avenue, New York, New York 10022

Collier Macmillan Canada, Inc.

Library of Congress Cataloging-in-Publication Data

Kagan, Donald.
The Western heritage.

Includes bibliographies and indexes.
Contents: v. 1. To 1715—v. 2. Since 1648.
1. Civilization, Occidental. I. Ozment, Steven E.
II. Turner, Frank M. (Frank Miller),
III. Title.
CB245.K28 1987b 909'.09821 86-5224
ISBN 0-02-363210-0

Printing: 1 2 3 4 5 6 7 8 Year: 7 8 9 0 1 2 3 4 5 6

Preface

THIS THIRD EDITION of *The Western Heritage,* while retaining the fundamental character, structure, and outlook of its earlier versions, has made several significant changes in response to needs expressed by readers and to important trends in the teaching of the history of western civilization in colleges and universities. Since the second edition we have further condensed the narrative and reduced the number of chapters dedicated to the ancient world. We have incorporated substantial coverage of the Byzantine Empire in Chapter Six. Colonial Latin America and its struggle for independence from Spain and Portugal are examined in depth in Chapters Ten, Sixteen, and Twenty. In addition to these changes, we have updated the material on the post-World War II era.

We have also tried to improve the style and organization wherever we saw the need. Once again, we have sought fresh historical documents and illustrations, changing about a third of each. The text is now divided into six sections. Each part is introduced with a brief essay, which gives an overview of major trends, influences, and events in each era.

Taking note of the continuing interest in social history among both professors and students, we have added new sections throughout the work dealing with that aspect of the human experience from ancient times to our own era. We believe that this new material adds depth, perspective, and interest by telling more about the private lives and concerns of men and women; at the same time, we hope that our account of larger events and institutions gives meaning to the experiences of individuals. This new emphasis will also be found in many of the new documents and illustrations. Notably, the full-color section from the second edition has been transformed into a pictorial essay entitled "Cities and Their People." We have also revised the bibliographies at the end of each chapter, referring to important new works while retaining the most important ones previously included.

This revision has gained much from the advice and teaching experience of our colleagues across the country, many of whom sent us advice and suggestions. We read and considered them all with care and made many changes and corrections as a result. We are especially grateful to the following readers who were good enough to criticize and evaluate the previous edition and early drafts of our revision:

David Applebaum, *Glassboro State College*
William Arnett, *West Virginia University*
Marc Baer, *Hope College*
James Barringer, *Hillsborough Community College*
Paul Chardoul, *Grand Rapids Junior College*
Walter Fraser, *Georgia Southern College*
W. Kent Hackman, *University of Idaho*
Louise Hoffman, *Pennsylvania State University—Capitol Campus*
Frayda Hoffnung, *California State University—Long Beach*
John Kesler, *Lakeland Community College*
Theodore Koditschek, *University of California—Irvine*
R. Michael Mase, *Golden West College*
Dean O'Donnell, *Virginia Polytechnic Institute*
Ann Quartararo, *United States Naval Academy*
Roger Schlosser, *Grand Rapids Junior College*

We benefitted greatly from their work, and we hope that this edition reflects their contributions.

The third edition is accompanied by several ancillaries designed to assist both the instructor and the student. Perry Rogers of the Ohio State University has authored the Instructor's Manual; the Study Guide was written by Anthony Brescia of Nassau Community College. Delta Software, in conjunction with Macmillan Publishing Company and the authors, is producing a computerized testing disk. Twenty-four color transparencies of maps from the text are also available.

Our intention in producing this revision has been to provide a text that is clear, informative, interesting, and easy to teach. Just as the revision of a textbook is a joint effort between authors and readers, so the use of a textbook is a joint effort between teachers and students—a relationship that we hope this volume will enhance and enliven.

D.K.
S.O.
F.M.T.

New Haven and Cambridge

Contents

20 Restoration, Reaction, and Reform (1815–1832)

21 Economic Advance and Social Unrest (1830–1850) 721

Toward the Modern World 760

22 The Age of Nation-States 763

Documents

Maps

Illustrations in Color: Cities and Their People

Some Prominent Emperors, Kings, and Popes

ROMAN EMPIRE

Augustus	27 B.C.–A.D. 14	Trajan	98–117	Severus Alexander	222–235
Tiberius	14– 37	Hadrian	117–138	Philip the Arab	244–249
Caligula	37– 41	Antoninus Pius	138–161	Decius	249–251
Claudius	41– 54	Marcus Aurelius	161–180	Valerian	253–260
Nero	54– 68	Commodus	180–193	Gallienus	260–268
Vespasian	69– 79	Septimius Severus	193–211	Aurelian	270–275
Titus	79– 81	Caracalla	211–217	Diocletian	284–286
Domitian	81– 96	Elagabalus	218–222		

West		East		West		East	
Maximian	286–305	Diocletian	284–305	Gratian	375–383		
Constantius	305–306	Galerius	305–311	Valentinian II	383–392		
		Maximimus	308–313	Theodosius	394–395	Theodosius	379–395
		Licinius	308–324	Honorius	395–423	Arcadius	393–408
Constantine	308–337	Constantine	324–337			Theodosius II	408–450
Maxentius	307–312			Valentinian III	425–455	Marcian	450–457
Constantine II	337–340					Leo	457–474
Constans	337–350			Romulus	475–476	Zeno	474–491
Constantius II	351–361	Constantius II	337–361			Anastasius	491–518
Julian	360–363	Julian	361–363			Justin	518–527
Jovian	363–364	Jovian	363–364			Justinian	527–565
Valentinian	364–375	Valens	364–378				

CAROLINGIAN KINGDOM

Pepin, Mayor of the Palace	680–714
Charles Martel, Mayor of the Palace	715–741
Pepin the Short, Mayor of the Palace	741–751
Pepin the Short, King	751–768
Charlemagne and Carloman, Joint Kings	768–771
Charlemagne, King	771–814
Charlemagne, Emperor	800–814
Louis the Pious, Emperor	814–840

West Franks

Charles the Bald	840–877
Louis II the Stammerer	877–879
Louis III	879–882
Carloman	879–884

Lotharingia

Lothar	840–855
Louis II	855–875
Charles	855–863
Lothar II	855–869

East Franks

Louis the German	840–876
Carloman	876–880
Louis	876–882
Charles the Fat	884–887

HOLY ROMAN EMPIRE

Saxons

Henry the Fowler	919–936
Otto I	962–973
Otto II	973–983
Otto III	983–1002

Salians

Conrad II	1024–1039
Henry III	1039–1056
Henry IV	1056–1106
Henry V	1106–1125
Lothar II	1125–1137

Hohenstaufens

Frederick I Barbarossa	1152–1190
Henry IV	1190–1197
Philip of Swabia	1198–1208
Otto IV (*Welf*)	1198–1215
Frederick II	1215–1250
Conrad IV	1250–1254

Luxemburg, Hapsburg, and Other Dynasties

Rudolf of Hapsburg	1273–1291
Adolph of Nassau	1292–1298
Albert of Austria	1298–1308
Henry VII of Luxemburg	1308–1313
Ludwig IV of Bavaria	1314–1347
Charles IV	1347–1378
Wenceslas	1378–1400
Rupert	1400–1410
Sigismund	1410–1437

Hapsburgs

Frederick III	1440–1493
Maximilian I	1493–1519
Charles V	1519–1556
Ferdinand I	1556–1564
Maximilian II	1564–1576
Rudolf II	1576–1612
Matthias	1612–1619
Ferdinand II	1619–1637
Ferdinand III	1637–1657
Leopold I	1658–1705
Joseph I	1705–1711
Charles VI	1711–1740
Charles VII	1742–1745
Francis I	1745–1765
Joseph II	1765–1790
Leopold II	1790–1792
Francis II	1792–1806

THE PAPACY

Leo I	440– 461
Gregory I	590– 604
Nicholas I	858– 867
Silvester II	999–1003
Leo IX	1049–1054
Nicholas II	1058–1061
Gregory VII	1073–1085
Urban II	1088–1099
Paschal II	1099–1118
Alexander III	1159–1181
Innocent III	1198–1216
Gregory IX	1227–1241
Boniface VIII	1294–1303
John XXII	1316–1334
Gregory XI	1370–1378
Martin V	1417–1431
Eugenius IV	1431–1447
Nicholas V	1447–1455
Pius II	1458–1464
Alexander VI	1492–1503
Julius II	1503–1513
Leo X	1513–1521
Adrian VI	1522–1523
Clement VII	1523–1534
Paul III	1534–1549
Paul IV	1555–1559
Pius V	1566–1572
Gregory XIII	1572–1585
Pius VII	1800–1823
Gregory XVI	1831–1846
Pius IX	1846–1878
Leo XIII	1878–1903
Pius X	1903–1914
Benedict XV	1914–1922
Pius XI	1922–1939
Pius XII	1939–1958
John XXIII	1958–1963
Paul VI	1963–1978
John Paul I	1978
John Paul II	1978–

ENGLAND

Anglo-Saxons

Alfred the Great	871– 900
Ethelred the Unready	978–1016
Canute (*Danish*)	1016–1035
Harold I	1035–1040
Hardicanute	1040–1042
Edward the Confessor	1042–1066
Harold II	1066

Normans

William the Conqueror	1066–1087
William II	1087–1100
Henry I	1100–1135
Stephen	1135–1154

Angevins

Henry II	1154–1189
Richard I	1189–1199
John	1199–1216
Henry III	1216–1272
Edward I	1272–1307
Edward II	1307–1327
Edward III	1327–1377
Richard II	1377–1399

Houses of Lancaster and York

Henry IV	1399–1413
Henry V	1413–1422
Henry VI	1422–1461
Edward IV	1461–1483
Edward V	1483
Richard III	1483–1485

Tudors

Henry VII	1485–1509
Henry VIII	1509–1547
Edward VI	1547–1553
Mary I	1553–1558
Elizabeth I	1558–1603

Stuarts

James I	1603–1625
Charles I	1625–1649
Charles II	1660–1685
James II	1685–1688
William III and Mary II	1689–1694
William III alone	1694–1702
Anne	1702–1714

Hanoverians (from 1917, Windsors)

George I	1714–1727
George II	1727–1760
George III	1760–1820
George IV	1820–1830
William IV	1830–1837
Victoria	1837–1901
Edward VII	1901–1910
George V	1910–1936
Edward VIII	1936
George VI	1936–1952
Elizabeth II	1952–

FRANCE

Capetians

Hugh Capet	987– 996
Robert II the Pious	996–1031
Henry I	1031–1060
Philip I	1060–1108
Louis VI	1108–1137
Louis VII	1137–1180
Philip II Augustus	1180–1223
Louis VIII	1223–1226
Louis IX	1226–1270
Philip III	1270–1285
Philip IV	1285–1314
Louis X	1314–1316
Philip V	1316–1322
Charles IV	1322–1328

Valois

Philip VI	1328–1350
John	1350–1364
Charles V	1364–1380
Charles VI	1380–1422
Charles VII	1422–1461
Louis XI	1461–1483
Charles VIII	1483–1498
Louis XII	1498–1515
Francis I	1515–1547
Henry II	1547–1559
Francis II	1559–1560
Charles IX	1560–1574
Henry III	1574–1589

Bourbons

Henry IV	1589–1610
Louis XIII	1610–1643
Louis XIV	1643–1715
Louis XV	1715–1774
Louis XVI	1774–1792

Post 1792

Napoleon I, Emperor	1804–1814
Louis XVIII (*Bourbon*)	1814–1824
Charles X (*Bourbon*)	1824–1830
Louis Philippe (*Bourbon-Orléans*)	1830–1848
Napoleon III, Emperor	1851–1870

ITALY

Victor Emmanuel II	1861–1878
Humbert I	1878–1900
Victor Emmanuel II	1900–1946
Humbert II	1946

SPAIN

Ferdinand and	1479–1516	**Hapsburgs**		**Bourbons**			
Isabella	1479–1504	Philip I	1504–1506	Philip V	1700–1746	Ferdinand VII (restored)	1814–1833
		Charles I (Holy Roman Emperor as Charles V)	1506–1556	Ferdinand VI	1746–1759	Isabella II	1833–1868
		Philip II	1556–1598	Charles III	1759–1788	Amadeo	1870–1873
		Philip III	1598–1621	Charles IV	1788–1808	Alfonso XII	1874–1885
		Philip IV	1621–1665	Ferdinand VII	1808	Alfonso XIII	1886–1931
		Charles II	1665–1700	Joseph Bonaparte	1808–1813	Juan Carlos I	1975–

AUSTRIA AND AUSTRIA-HUNGARY

(Until 1806 all except Maria Theresa were also Holy Roman Emperors.)

Maximilian I, Archduke	1493–1519	Maximilian II	1564–1576	Leopold I	1658–1705	Leopold II	1790–1792
Charles I (Emperor as Charles V)	1519–1556	Rudolf II	1576–1612	Joseph I	1705–1711	Francis II	1792–1835
Ferdinand I	1556–1564	Matthias	1612–1619	Charles VI	1711–1740	Ferdinand I	1835–1848
		Ferdinand II	1619–1637	Maria Theresa	1740–1780	Francis Joseph	1848–1916
		Ferdinand III	1637–1657	Joseph II	1780–1790	Charles I	1916–1918

PRUSSIA AND GERMANY

Hohenzollerns

Frederick William the Great Elector	1640–1688	Frederick II the Great	1740–1786	William I	1861–1888
Frederick I	1701–1713	Frederick William II	1786–1797	Frederick III	1888
Frederick William I	1713–1740	Frederick William III	1797–1840	William II	1888–1918
		Frederick William IV	1840–1861		

RUSSIA

Ivan III	1462–1505	**Romanovs**			
Basil III	1505–1533	Michael	1613–1645	Elizabeth	1741–1762
Ivan IV the Terrible	1533–1584	Alexius	1645–1676	Peter III	1762
Theodore I	1584–1598	Theodore III	1676–1682	Catherine II the Great	1762–1796
Boris Godunov	1598–1605	Ivan IV and Peter I	1682–1689	Paul	1796–1801
Theodore II	1605	Peter I the Great alone	1689–1725	Alexander I	1801–1825
Basil IV	1606–1610	Catherine I	1725–1727	Nicholas I	1825–1855
		Peter II	1727–1730	Alexander II	1855–1881
		Anna	1730–1740	Alexander III	1881–1894
		Ivan VI	1740–1741	Nicholas II	1894–1917

The Foundations of Western Civilization in the Ancient World

The roots of Western civilization may be found in the experience and culture of the Greeks, but Greek civilization itself was richly nourished by older, magnificent civilizations to the south and east, especially in Mesopotamia and Egypt. In the valley of the Tigris and Euphrates rivers (Mesopotamia) and soon after in the valley of the Nile in Egypt, human beings moved from a life in agricultural villages, using tools of wood, bone, shell, and stone, into a much richer and more varied social organization that we call *civilization*. The use of irrigation in the rich alluvial soil vastly increased the supply of food, thereby permitting a growth in population and even a surplus to support specialists: artisans, merchants, priests, and soldiers. For the first time, people lived in cities, complex centers of government, religion, metallurgy and advanced crafts, and commerce. The need for organizing this new and varied activity and for keeping records led to the invention of writing. The wealth acquired through more effective agriculture, better tools, the specialization of function, commerce, and conquest permitted the development of unprecedented skills. Great advances took place in the arts and the sciences, in literature, and in the development of complex religious ideas and organizations.

The new style of life required firm, efficient management and soon produced governments that were centralized and powerful. The kings' power rested on their capacity to manage the economy and to collect taxes. This capacity, in turn, permitted them to train and support armies, which imposed control over their subjects and also engaged in wars of expansion against their neighbors. The rulers' legitimacy was guaranteed by religion, for in Mesopotamia the kings were accepted as the representatives of the gods, and in Egypt they were themselves regarded as divine. The resulting combination of political, military, economic, and religious power produced societies that were rigidly divided into social classes: slaves, free commoners, priests, and aristocrats, as well as the divine or semidivine monarchs. There was almost no social mobility and little individual freedom; only a handful of people took part in government. The great power controlled by these rulers led the stronger of them to dominate kingdoms and empires that grew ever larger and more powerful.

The struggle between great empires sometimes permitted smaller city-states and kingdoms to survive and flourish in the spaces between them. Among these, two were especially important for the civilization that would some day arise in the West. The cities of Phoenicia, in what is now Lebanon, produced great sailors and traders who came into early and frequent contact with the Greeks. Through the Phoenicians, among other Eastern peoples, the Greeks learned the art of writing and were powerfully influenced by the art, technology, and mythology of the earlier cultures. Absorbed, transformed, and transmitted by the Greeks, the civilizations of Mesopotamia and Egypt, very indirectly, became part of the Western heritage. Neighbors of the Phoenicians, called Hebrews or Israelites, would have a more direct influence on the civilization of the West. They conceived a religion based on belief in a single all-powerful God who ruled over all peoples and the entire universe and made strong ethical demands on human beings. This religion of the Jews, as they came to be called from the name of their kingdom of Judah, became the basis of two later religions of great importance: Christianity and Islam.

Greek civilization arose after the destruction of the Bronze Age cultures on Crete and the Greek mainland before 1000 B.C. It took a turn sharply different from its predecessors in Egypt and western Asia. It was based on the independent existence of hundreds of city-states called *poleis* that retained their autonomy for hundreds of years before being incorporated into larger units. These cities attained a degree of self-government, broad political participation, and individual freedom never achieved before that time. They also introduced a new way of thinking that looked on the world as the product of natural forces to be understood by means of the senses and human reason, unaided by reference to supernatural forces. The result was the invention of science and philosophy as we know them. This approach led the Greeks to focus their attention on the life of human beings on earth, and a humanistic concern about accurate and realistic depiction of people came to characterize their art. In the same way their literature placed humankind at the center of its concerns, adapting and inventing a great variety of literary genres, from epic, lyric, and dramatic poetry, to history, philosophy, rhetoric, and fiction in prose. The Greeks' way of thinking, their forms of art and literature, and their commitment to self-government and political freedom became and have remained central to Western civilization.

The Greeks also developed ways of fighting on land and sea that enabled them to plant cities from Spain to the Black Sea and to defeat repeated attacks by the vast and powerful Persian Empire. At last, continued quarrels and wars between the *poleis* so weakened the Greeks that they fell under the control of their Macedonian cousins to the north. Alexander the Great of Macedon, using Greek troops as well as his own, swiftly conquered the Persian Empire, establishing Greek and Macedonian rule over the lands that had made up the great Eastern empires. After his death in 323 B.C. this vast territory was divided among his successors to form three great kingdoms. We call the new world that resulted and the culture that grew up in it *Hellenistic,* for it was different from the earlier culture of the independent *poleis* that we call *Hellenic.* Hellenistic culture was a mixture of Greek elements combined with some from the native peoples. It was without the particularism of the Hellenic world, and anyone speaking Greek could move comfortably from city to city and find a familiar and common culture. This was the world that succumbed to the Roman conquest in the last two centuries before the Christian era.

The Romans were tough farmers who began as inhabitants of a small town on the Tiber river in west-central Italy. After deposing their king in about 500 B.C., they invented a republican constitution and a code of law that provided a solid foundation for a stable and effective political order. Constantly at war with their neighbors, the Romans achieved military discipline and skills that allowed them to fight off attacks and to gain control of most of Italy by about 270 B.C. They developed an ingenious organization of the conquered lands whereby the conquered peoples came to be allies and even fellow citizens rather than subjects. In this way Rome expanded its military resources as well as its control when it gained new territory, and it acquired an army whose numbers could not be matched. From 264 until well into the first century B.C., the Romans extended their conquests overseas until they had conquered the Carthaginians in the west and defeated all the great Hellenistic powers, dominating the shores of the Mediterranean and lands well beyond. The Romans were fine engineers and road builders, but in art, literature, and philosophy they had barely made a start when they came into contact with the advanced Greek civilization of the Hellenistic world. In these areas the Romans became eager students, and as the Roman poet Horace put it, "Captive Greece took Rome captive." The Romans took the Greek poets and prose writers as their models, but in time they adapted them to suit their own experience and cast of mind. Educated Romans came to be bilingual, and Roman culture passed on the legacy of the Greeks both directly and indirectly, transformed by passing through Roman hands.

The conquest of most of the known world created many problems for a republican constitution designed to govern only a small collection of farmers. Competition for eminence, power, and wealth within the Roman aristocracy led to struggles and civil wars that ravaged Italy and the empire as well. Finally, Gaius Julius Caesar defeated his opponents, put an end to the republic, and established himself as dictator for life. Rumor had it that he meant to be installed as king. An aristocratic plot put an end to these plans, but from the civil wars that followed Caesar's assassination in 44 B.C., his nephew Octavian, later called Augustus, emerged as the commander of all of Rome's armed forces and as the effective ruler of the Roman Empire. His new constitution tried to conceal the death of the republic and its replacement by what was really an imperial monarchy, but it is correct to place the birth of the Roman Empire at the time of Augustus' victory at Actium in 31 B.C. Augustus' disguised monarchy flourished for almost two centuries, but after the death of the emperor Marcus Aurelius in 180 A.D., Rome's decline became obvious. Pressure from barbarian tribes on the frontiers, economic troubles at home, weak and incompetent emperors, and civil wars—all strained Rome's resources, human and material. By the fifth century A.D., the Roman Empire in the west had collapsed and was shared out among different Germanic tribes, although the eastern portion of the empire, with its capital at Constantinople, survived for a thousand years more. Before Rome's fall the empire had abandoned paganism and had adopted Christianity as its official religion. The heritage that the ancient world passed on to its medieval successor in western Europe was a combination of cultural traditions including those coming from Egypt, Mesopotamia, Israel, Greece, Rome, and the German tribes that destroyed the Roman Empire.

An eighth-century B.C. *alabaster relief of Gilgamesh, the god-like hero of an ancient Sumerian epic poem. The sculpture was found in the ruins of the palace of the Assyrian king Sargon II and is now in the Louvre.* [*EPA*]

1

The World Before the West

HISTORY, IN ITS TWO SENSES—as the events of the past that make up the human experience on earth and as the written record of those events—is a subject of inescapable interest and importance. We are naturally interested in how we came to be what we are and in how the world we live in came to be what it is. In addition, we need to know the record of the past and to try to understand the people and forces that shaped it; whatever changes in the human condition may have occurred since the emergence of our species, the study of human experience through history remains the best aid to understanding present human behavior. We must, therefore, examine the life of people on this planet from the earliest times.

Early Human Beings and Their Culture

Scientists estimate that the earth may be as many as six billion years old, that creatures very much like humans may have appeared three to five million years ago, and that our own species of human being goes back at least fifty thousand years. Humans are different from other animals in that they are capable of producing and passing on a culture. Culture may be defined as the ways of living built up by a group and passed on from one generation to another. It may include behavior, material things, ideas, institutions, and beliefs. The source of humanity's creation of material culture is the hands. We can touch the balls of our fingers with the ball of the thumb, and so we can hold and make tools. The source of our ability to create ideas and institutions is in our capacity to speak, and this is what allows us to transmit our culture to future generations. Whether our ability to make a material culture is more important than our ability to speak, and therefore to think abstractly, is an interesting question, but clearly both abilities are needed for the development of human culture.

The anthropologist designates early human cultures by their tools. The earliest period is the Paleolithic (from Greek, "old stone") Age. In this immensely long period (from perhaps 600,000 to 10,000 B.C.), people were hunters, fishers, and gatherers, but not producers, of food. They learned to make and use tools of stone and of perishable materials like wood, to make and control fire, and to pass on what they learned in language. In the regions where civilization ultimately was born, people depended on nature for their food and were very vulnerable to attacks from wild beasts and to natural disasters. Because their lives were often "solitary, poor, nasty, brutish, and short," as Thomas Hobbes put it, their responses to troubles and dangers were filled with fear. Their minds endowed all the objects they met with life or spirit, and they tried their best to put themselves in the right relationship to all these forces. They trusted magic, incantations, and ritual. Evidence of this Paleolithic culture has been excavated or found in caves in widely scattered areas of Europe, Asia, and Africa.

The style of life and the level of technology of the Paleolithic period could support only a sparsely settled society. If hunters were too numerous, game would not suffice. In Paleolithic times, people were subject to the same natural and ecological constraints that today maintain a balance between wolves and deer in Alaska.

But human life in the Paleolithic Age easily lent itself to division of labor by sex. The men engaged in hunting, fishing, making tools and weapons, and fighting against other families, clans, and tribes. The women, less mobile because of frequent childbearing, smaller in stature, and less strong and swift than the men, gathered nuts, berries, and wild grains; wove baskets; and made clothing. Women gathering food probably discovered how to plant and care for seeds. This knowledge eventually made possible the Age of Agriculture—the Neolithic Revolution.

Paleolithic cave painting of bulls and horses from the Dordogne valley of southern France. The animals, which were hunted by prehistoric humans, are depicted with remarkable realism. [*Ronald Sheridan's Photo Library*]

Of early Paleolithic societies only a few developed into Neolithic or New Stone Age agricultural societies, and anthropologists disagree on why that revolutionary development occurred. In many areas, right into our own time, some isolated portions of humankind have been content to continue to live in the "Stone Age" unless compelled by more advanced cultures to change; why toil in fields, on a South Sea island, if fruit, vegetables, and fish are plentiful and free, the weather is wonderful, and there's a party on the beach? The reasons for the shift to agriculture by late Paleolithic groups are unclear. In the past, some scientists thought that climatic change—a drop in temperature and rainfall—forced people to be inventive and to seek new ways of acquiring food, but newer evidence suggests that there was little climatic variation in Neolithic times. Other theories focus on the human element: a possible growth in population, an increased sense of territoriality, and a resulting interference with the pursuit of herds for hunting.

However it happened, some ten thousand years ago parts of what we now call the Middle East began to shift from a hunter–gatherer culture to a settled agricultural one. People began to use precisely carved stone tools, so we call this period the Neolithic (from Greek, "new stone") Age. Animals as well as food crops were domesticated. The important invention of pottery made it possible to store surplus liquids, just as the invention of baskets had earlier made it possible to store dry foods. Cloth came to be made from flax and wool. Crops required constant care from planting to harvest, so the Neolithic people built permanent buildings, usually in clusters near the best fields.

The agricultural revolution may not have produced an immediate population explosion. Anthropologists suggest that village living produced a much greater incidence of disease, there being no provision for the disposal of human and animal waste. The Neolithic villages also provided attractive targets for raiders. Still, agriculture provided a steadier source of food and a greater production of food in a given area. It thus provided the basis for a denser population over time. It was a major step in human control of nature, and it was a vital precondition for the emergence of civilization. The earliest Neolithic societies appeared in the Near East about 8000 B.C., in India about 3600 B.C., and in China about 4000 B.C. The Neolithic revolution in the Near East and India was based on wheat and in China, on millet and rice; in Meso-America, several millennia later, it would be based on corn.

Neolithic villages and their culture, gradually growing from and replacing Paleolithic culture, could be located in almost any kind of terrain. But about four thousand years before the Christian era, people began to move in large numbers into the river-watered lowlands of Mesopotamia and Egypt. This shift evolved into a new style of life: an urban society and civilization. The shift was accompanied by the gradual introduction of new technologies and by the invention of writing.

Again, we do not know why people first chose to live in cities, with their inherent disadvantages: overcrowding, epidemics, wide separation from sources of food and raw materials, and the concentration of wealth that permitted organized warfare. Perhaps cities were created because, to quote the Greek philosopher Aristotle, "Man is by nature a political animal"; perhaps they arose merely because they offered more possibilities for amusement, occupational choice, and enrichment than had the Neolithic villages. In any event, by about 3000 B.C., when the invention of writing gave birth to history, urban life was established in the valleys of the Tigris and Euphrates rivers in Mesopotamia (modern Iraq) and of the Nile in Egypt. Somewhat later, urban life arose in the Indus valley of India and the Yellow River basin of China. The development of urban centers by no means meant the disappearance of numerous outlying peasant agricultural villages. Nevertheless, with the coming of cities, writing, and metals, humankind had attained civilization.

Neolithic pots found in what is today Israel. The invention of pottery made it possible to store surplus liquids, such as water and cooking oil, just as the invention of baskets had earlier made it possible to store dry foods. [Ronald Sheridan's Photo Library]

Early Civilizations to About 1000 B.C.

Civilization, then, is a form of human culture in which many people live in urban centers, have mastered the art of smelting metals, and have developed a method of writing. The rich alluvial plains where civilization began made possible the production of unprecedented surpluses of food—but only if there was an intelligent management of the water supply. Proper flood control and irrigation called for the control of the river by some strong authority capable of managing the distribution of water. This control and management required careful observation and record keeping. The first use of writing may have been to record the behavior of the river and the astronomical events that gave clues about it. It was also used by the powerful individuals (the kings) who dominated the life of the river valleys to record their possessions, by priests to record omens, by merchants and artisans to record business transactions, and by others to record acts of the government, laws, and different kinds of literature.

This widely varied use of writing reflects the complex culture of the urban centers in the river valleys. Commerce was important enough to support a merchant class. Someone discovered how to smelt tin and copper to make a stronger and more useful material—bronze—which replaced stone in the making of tools and weapons; the importance of this technological development is reflected in the term *Bronze Age*. The great need for record keeping created a class of scribes, because the picture writing and complicated scripts of these cultures took many years to learn and could not be mastered by many. To deal with the gods, great temples were built, and many priests worked in them. The collection of all these people into cities gave the settlements an entirely new character. Unlike Neolithic villages, they were communities established for purposes other than agriculture. The city was an administrative, religious, manufacturing, entertainment, and commercial center.

The logic of nature pointed in the direction of the unification of an entire river valley. Central control would put the river's water to the most efficient use, and the absence of central control would lead to warfare, chaos, and destruction. As a result, these civilizations produced unified kingdoms under powerful monarchs who came to be identified with divinity. The typical king in a river-valley civilization was regarded either as a god or as the delegate of a god. Around him developed a rigid class structure. Beneath the monarch was a class of hereditary military aristocrats and a powerful priesthood. Below them were several kinds of freemen, mostly peasants, and at the bottom were many slaves. Most of the land was owned or controlled by the king, the nobility, and the priests. These were traditional, conservative cultures of numerous peasant villages and urban centers of administration, commerce, and religious and military activity. Cultural patterns took form early and then changed only slowly and grudgingly.

MAP 1-1 *Two ancient river valley civilizations: While Egypt early was united into a single state, Mesopotamia was long divided into a number of city states.*

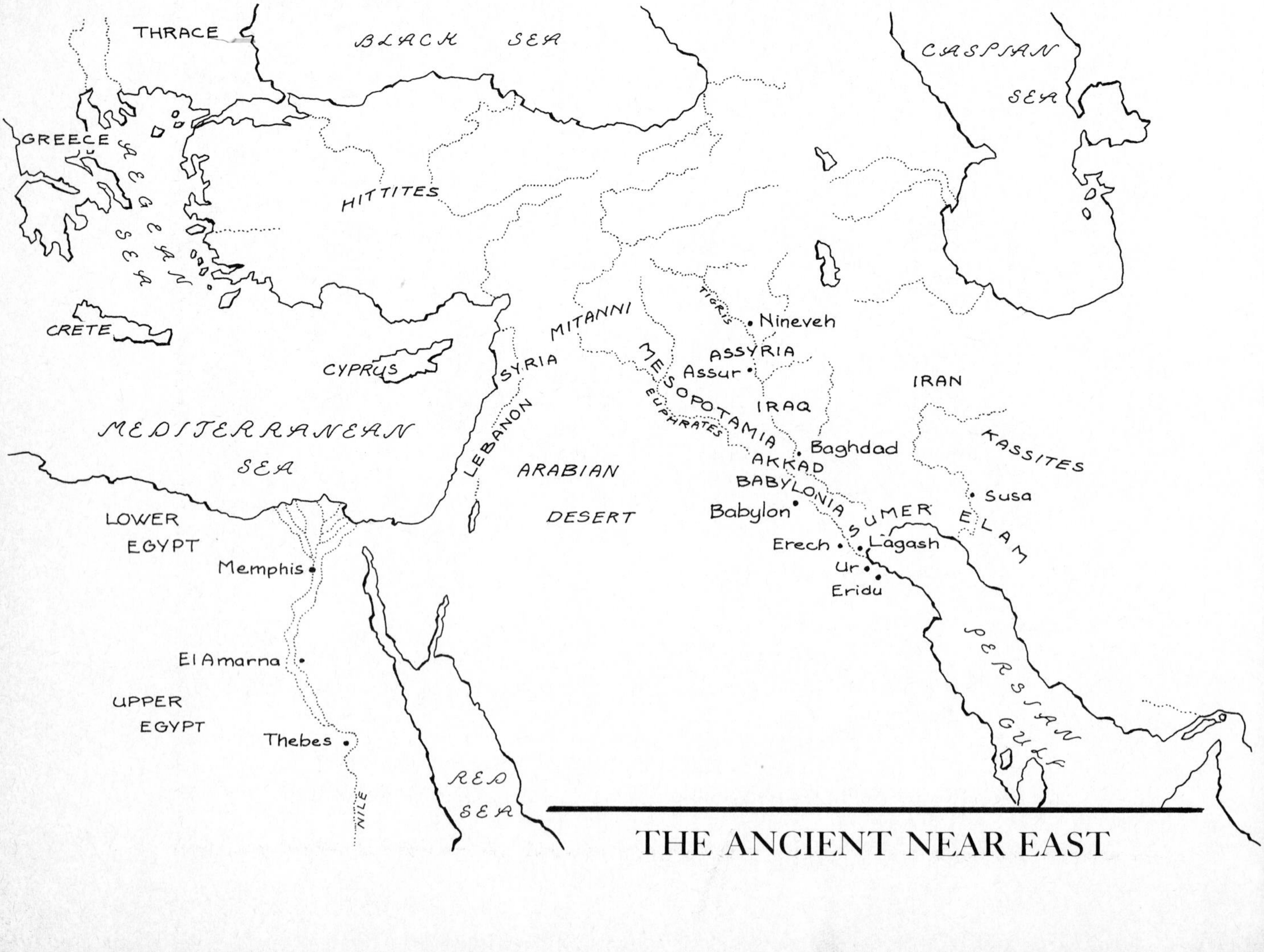

Mesopotamian Civilization

The first civilization appears to have arisen in the valley of the Tigris and Euphrates rivers, Mesopotamia (the land "between the rivers" from the Greek). Its founders seem to have been a people called Sumerians, who controlled the southern part of the valley (Sumer) close to the head of the Persian Gulf by the dawn of history, around 3000 B.C. (see Map 1.1). At first, city-states about one hundred square miles in size dotted the landscape. Ur, Erech, Lagash, and Eridu are examples of such cities that archaeologists have revealed to us. Quarrels over water rights and frontiers led to incessant fighting, and in time, stronger towns conquered weaker ones and expanded to form larger units, usually kingdoms. While the Sumerians were fighting with their neighbors and among themselves for supremacy in the south, a people from the Arabian Desert on the west called Semites had been moving into

The Reforms of a Sumerian King

Urukagina ruled the Sumerian city-state of Lagash from about 2415 to 2400 B.C. The following selections describe reforms that he claimed to have enacted, in the process revealing some of the social and economic problems of the time.

Formerly, from days of yore, from (the day) the seed (of man) came forth, the man in charge of the boatmen seized the boats. The head shepherd seized the donkeys. The head shepherd seized the sheep. The man in charge of the fisheries seized the fisheries. The barley rations of the guda-*priests were measured out (to their disadvantage) in the Ashte (presumably the storehouse of the* ensi*). The shepherds of the wool-bearing sheep had to pay silver (to the* ensi*) for (the shearing of) the white sheep. The man in charge of field surveyors, the head* gala*, the* agrig*, the man in charge of brewing, (and) all of the* ugula*'s had to pay silver for the shearing of the* gaba-*lambs. The oxen of the gods plowed the onion patches of the* ensi*, (and) the onion (and) cucumber fields of the* ensi *were located in the god's best fields. The* birra-*donkeys (and) the prize oxen of the* sanga*'s were bundled off (presumably as taxes for the* ensi*). The attendants of the* ensi *divided the barley of the* sanga*'s (to the disadvantage of the* sanga*'s). The wearing apparel (here follows a list of fifteen objects, principally garments, most of which are unidentifiable) of the* sanga*'s were carried off as a tax (to the palace of the* ensi*). The* sanga *(in charge) of the food (supplies) felled the trees in the garden of the indigent mother and bundled off the fruit.*

. . . .

These were the (social) practices of former days.

(But) when Ningirsu, the foremost warrior of Enlil, gave the kingship of Lagash to Urukagina, (and) his (Ningirsu's) hand had grasped him out of the multitude (literally, "36,000 men"); then he (Ningirsu) enjoined upon (literally, "set up for") him the (divine) decrees of former days.

He (Urukagina) held close to the word which his king (Ningirsu) spoke to him. He banned (literally, "threw off") the man in charge of the boatmen from (seizing) the boats. He banned the head shepherds from (seizing) the donkeys and sheep. He banned the man in charge of the fisheries from (seizing) the fisheries. He banned the man in charge of the storehouse from (measuring out) the barley ration of the guda-*priests. He banned the bailiff from (receiving) the silver (paid for the shearing) of the white sheep and of the* gaba-*lambs. He banned the bailiffs from the tax of (that is, levied on) the* sanga*'s which (used to be) carried off (to the palace).*

He made Ningirsu king of the houses of the ensi *(and) of the field of the* ensi*. He made Bau queen of the houses of the (palace) harem (and) of the fields of the (palace) harem. He made Shulshaggana king of the houses of the (palace) nursery (and) of the fields of the (palace) nursery. From the borders of Ningirsu to the sea, there was no tax collector.*

Trans. by S. N. Kramer, *The Sumerians* (Chicago: University of Chicago Press, 1963), pp. 317–319.

Mesopotamia north of Sumer. Their language and society were different from those of the Sumerians, but they soon absorbed Sumerian culture and established their own kingdom, with its capital at Akkad, near a later city known to us as Babylon. The most famous Akkadian king was Sargon, who conquered Sumer and extended his empire in every direction. Legends grew up around his name, and he is said to have conquered the "cedar forests" of Lebanon, far to the west near the coast of the Mediterranean Sea. He ruled about 2340 B.C. and established a family, or dynasty, of Semitic kings that ruled Sumer and Akkad for two centuries.

External attack and internal weakness destroyed Akkad. About 2125 B.C. the city of Ur in Sumer revolted and became the dominant power, and this Third Dynasty of Ur established a large empire of its own. About 2000 B.C., however, it was swept aside by another Semitic invasion, which ended Sumerian rule forever. Thereafter Semites ruled Mesopotamia, but the foundations of their culture were Sumerian. The Semites changed much of what they inherited; but in law, government, religion, art, science, and all other areas of culture, their debt to the Sumerians was enormous.

The fall of the Third Dynasty of Ur (ca. 2100–2000 B.C.) put an end to the Sumerians as an identifiable group. The Sumerian language survived only in writing, as a kind of sacred language known only to priests and scribes, preserving the cultural heritage of Sumer. For about a century after the fall of Ur, dynastic chaos reigned, but about 1900 B.C. a Semitic people called the Amorites gained control of the region, establishing their capital at Babylon. The high point of this Amorite, or Old Babylonian, dynasty came more than a hundred years later under its most famous king, Hammurabi (ca. 1792–1750 B.C.). He is best known for the law code connected with his name. Codes of law existed as early as the Sumerian period, and Hammurabi's plainly owed much to earlier models, but it is the fullest and best-preserved legal code we have from ancient Mesopotamia. The code reveals a society strictly divided in class: there were nobles, commoners, and slaves, and the law did not treat them equally. In general, punishments were harsh, literally applying the principle "an eye for an eye, a tooth for a tooth." The prologue to the code makes it clear that law and justice came from the gods through the king.

About 1600 B.C. the Babylonian kingdom fell apart under the impact of invasions from the north and east by the Hittites and the Kassites. The Hittites were only a raiding party who plundered what they could and then withdrew to their home in Asia Minor. The Kassites stayed and ruled Mesopotamia for five centuries.

Key Events and People in Mesopotamian History

Sumerians arrive	ca. 3500 B.C.
Sumerian city-states early dynastic period	ca. 2800–2340 B.C.
Sargon establishes Semitic dynasty at Akkad	ca. 2340 B.C.
Third Dynasty of Ur	ca. 2125–2027 B.C.
Amorites at Babylon	ca. 1900 B.C.
Reign of Hammurabi	1792–1750 B.C.
Invasion by Hittites and Kassites	ca. 1600 B.C.

Government. From the earliest historical records it is clear that the Sumerians were ruled by monarchs in some form. Some scholars have thought they could detect a "primitive democracy" in early Sumer, but the evidence, which is poetic and hard to interpret, shows no more than a limited check on royal power even in early times. The first historical city-states had kings or priest-kings who led the army, administered the economy, and served as judges and as intermediaries between their people and the gods. At first, the kings were thought of as favorites and representatives of the gods; later, on some occasions and for relatively short periods, they instituted cults that worshiped them as divine. This union of church and state (to use modern terminology) in the person of the king reflected the centralization of power typical of Mesopotamian life. The economy was managed from the center by priests and king and was planned very carefully. Each year the land was surveyed, fields were assigned to specific farmers, and the amount of seed to be used was designated. The government estimated the size of the crop and planned its distribution even before it was planted.

This process required a large and competent

staff, the ability to observe and record natural phenomena, a good knowledge of mathematics, and, for all of this, a system of writing. The Sumerians invented the writing system known as *cuneiform* (from the Latin *cuneus,* "wedge") because of the wedge-shaped stylus with which they wrote on clay tablets; the writing also came to be used in beautifully cut characters in stone. Sumerians also began the development of a sophisticated system of mathematics. The calendar they invented had twelve lunar months. To make it agree with the solar year and to make possible accurate designation of the seasons, they introduced a thirteenth month about every three years.

Religion. The Sumerians and their Semitic successors believed in gods in the shape of humans who were usually identified with some natural phenomenon. They were pictured as frivolous, quarrelsome, selfish, and often childish, differing from humans only in their greater power and their immortality. They each appear to have begun as local deities. The people of Mesopotamia had a vague and gloomy picture of the afterworld. Their religion dealt with problems of this world, and they used prayer, sacrifice, and magic to achieve their ends. Expert knowledge was required to reach the perfection in wisdom and ritual needed to influence the gods, so the priesthood flourished. A high percentage of the cuneiform writing we now have is devoted to religious texts: prayers, incantations, curses, and omens. It was important to discover the will and intentions of the gods, and the Sumerians sought hints in several places. The movements of the heavenly bodies were an obvious evidence of divine action, so astrology was born. They also sought to discover the divine will by examining the entrails of sacrificial animals for abnormalities. All of this religious activity required armies of scribes to keep great quantities of records, as well as learned priests to interpret them.

Religion, in the form of myth, played a large part in the literature and art of Mesopotamia. In poetic language, the Sumerians and their successors told tales of the creation of the world, of a great flood that almost destroyed human life, of an island paradise from which the god Enki was expelled for eating forbidden plants, of a hero named Gilgamesh who performed many great feats in his travels, and many more.

Religion was also the inspiration for the most interesting architectural achievement in Mesopotamia: the ziggurat. The ziggurat was an artificial stepped mound surmounted by a temple. Neighbors and successors of the Sumerians adopted the style, and the eroded remains of many of these monumental structures, some partly restored, still dot the Iraqi landscape.

A clay model of a liver inscribed with omens and magical texts. Such model livers were used to help predict events and determine the will of the gods. [*Courtesy of the Trustees of the British Museum*]

Society. We have a very full and detailed picture of the way people in ancient Mesopotamia conducted their lives and of the social conditions in which they lived during the reign of Hammurabi. More than fifty royal letters, many business contracts, and especially the Code of Hammurabi are the sources of our knowledge. We find that society was legally divided into three classes: nobles, commoners, and slaves. Punishment for crimes committed against freemen was harsher than for those against slaves, and crimes committed against nobles were more serious than those against commoners.

Hammurabi Creates a Code of Law in Mesopotamia

Hammurabi's Babylonian empire stretched from the Persian Gulf to the Mediterranean Sea. Building on earlier laws, Hammurabi compiled one of the great ancient codes. It was discovered about seventy-five years ago in what is now Iran. Hammurabi, like other rulers before and after, represented himself and his laws as under the protection and sponsorship of all the right gods. Property was at least as sacred as persons, and the eye-for-an-eye approach characterizes the code. Here are a few examples from it.

LAWS

If a son has struck his father, they shall cut off his hand.
If a seignior has destroyed the eye of a member of the aristocracy, they shall destroy his eye.
If he has broken another seignior's bone, they shall break his bone.
If he has destroyed the eye of a commoner or broken the bone of a commoner, he shall pay one mina of silver.
If he has destroyed the eye of a seignior's slave or broken the bone of a seignior's slave, he shall pay one-half his value.
If a seignior has knocked out a tooth of a seignior of his own rank, they shall knock out his tooth.
If he has knocked out a commoner's tooth, he shall pay one-third mina of silver. . . .

EPILOGUE

I, Hammurabi, the perfect king,
was not careless (or) neglectful of the black-headed (people),
whom Enlil had presented to me,
(and) whose shepherding Marduk had committed to me;
I sought out peaceful regions for them;
I overcame grievous difficulties; . . .
With the mighty weapon which Zababa and Inanna entrusted to me,
with the insight that Enki allotted to me,
with the ability that Marduk gave me,
I rooted out the enemy above and below;
I made an end of war;
I promoted the welfare of the land;
I made the peoples rest in friendly habitations; . . .
The great gods called me,
so I became the beneficent shepherd whose scepter is righteous. . . .

James B. Pritchard, *Ancient Near Eastern Texts,* 3rd ed. (Princeton: Princeton University Press, 1969), pp. 164–180.

Slaves were chiefly captives from wars, although some native Babylonians might be enslaved for committing certain crimes, such as kicking one's mother or striking an elder brother. Parents could sell their children into slavery or pledge themselves and their entire family as surety for a debt. In case of default, they would all become slaves of the creditor for a stated period of time. Some slaves worked for the king and the state, others for the temple and the priests, and still others for private citizens. Their tasks varied accordingly. Most of the temple slaves appear to have been women, who were probably used to spin and weave and grind flour. The royal slaves did the heavy work of building palaces, canals, and fortifications. Private owners used their slaves chiefly as domestic servants. Some female slaves were used as concubines. Laws against fugitive slaves or slaves who denied their masters were harsh, but in some respects, Mesopotamian slavery appears enlightened compared to other slave systems in history. Slaves could engage in business and, with certain restrictions, hold property. They could marry free men or women, and the resulting children would be free. A slave who acquired the necessary wealth could buy his or her own freedom. Children of a slave by the master might be allowed to share in his property after his death.

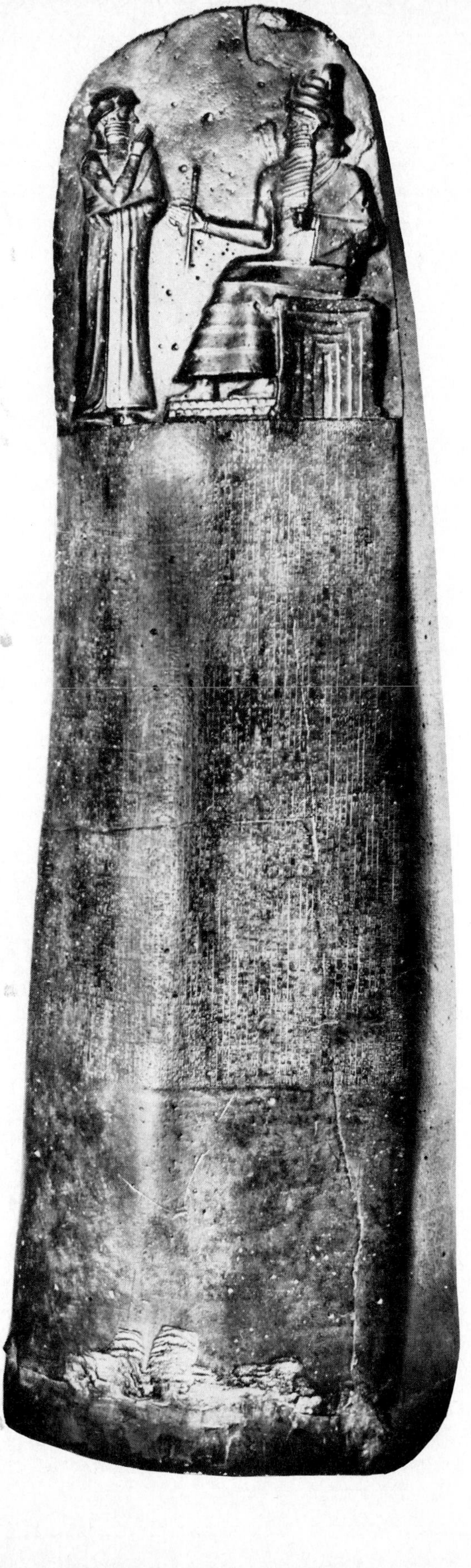

The code of Hammurabi. In the relief at the top, Hammurabi (ca. 1792–1750 B.C.*) receives the law, which is inscribed below, from the sun god. [The Oriental Institute, University of Chicago]*

Nevertheless, slaves, of course, were property, were subject to the will of their masters, and had little legal protection.

The Code of Hammurabi consists of 282 sections, and we may learn something of the society it governed by noticing where it placed the greatest emphasis. The second largest category deals with land tenure, as is not surprising in a society based so heavily on agriculture, but right behind this category comes the category relating to commerce. This position reveals how important and sophisticated trade and commercial life had become, for much is said about debts, rates of interest, security, and default. There are also sections dealing with the regulation of builders, surgeons, and other professionals, but the largest category relates to the family and its maintenance and protection.

Marriages were arranged by the parents, and the betrothal was followed by the signing of a marriage contract. The husband-to-be made a bridal payment, and the father of the bride-to-be agreed to a dowry for his daughter. Marriage was originally monogamous, but if the

A Sumerian husband and wife (ca. 2600 B.C.*). The statuette seems to convey a sense of real affection and dependence. [The Oriental Institute, University of Chicago]*

wife were ill for a long time or childless, the husband could take a second wife. Extramarital relations between the husband and concubines, female slaves, and prostitutes were common and acceptable. The wife did not have similar privileges. She was, in fact, the legal property of her husband in theory, but in practice, she seems to have been treated as an individual with rights protected by the law. Divorce was relatively easy and not entirely inequitable. Women divorced by their husbands without good cause received their dowry back. A woman seeking divorce could also recover her dowry if her husband could not convict her of wrongdoing. On the other hand, a woman's place was thought distinctly to be in the home. One law states that if a wife "has made up her mind to leave in order to engage in business, thus neglecting her house and humiliating her husband, he may divorce her without compensation."

Egyptian Civilization

While a great civilization arose in the valley of the Tigris and Euphrates, another, no less important, emerged in Egypt. The center of Egyptian civilization was the Nile River. From its source in central Africa the Nile runs north some 4,000 miles to the Mediterranean, with long navigable stretches broken by several cataracts. Ancient Egypt included the 750 miles of the valley from the First Cataract to the sea and was shaped like a funnel with two distinct parts. Upper (southern) Egypt was the stem, consisting of the narrow valley of the Nile. The broad, triangular delta, which branches out about 150 miles from the sea, was Lower Egypt (see Map 1.1). The Nile alone made life possible in the almost rainless desert that surrounded it. Each year the river flooded and covered the land, and when it receded, it left a fertile mud that could produce two crops a year. The construction and maintenance of irrigation ditches to preserve the river's water, with careful planning and organization of planting and harvesting, produced agricultural prosperity unmatched in the ancient world.

The Nile also served as a highway connecting the long, narrow country and encouraging its unification. Upper and Lower Egypt were, in fact, already united into a single kingdom at the beginning of our historical record, about 3100 B.C. Nature helped protect and isolate the ancient Egyptians from outsiders. The cataracts, the sea, and the desert made it difficult for foreigners to reach Egypt for either friendly or hostile purposes. Egypt knew far more peace and security than Mesopotamia. This security, along with the sunny, predictable climate, gave Egyptian civilization a more optimistic outlook than the civilizations of the Tigris–Euphrates, which were always in fear of assault from storm, flood, earthquake, and hostile neighbors.

The more than three-thousand-year span of ancient Egyptian history is traditionally divided into thirty-one royal dynasties, from the first, founded by Menes, the unifier of Upper and Lower Egypt, to the last, established by Alexander the Great, who conquered Egypt (as we shall see in Chapter 3) in 332 B.C. The dynasties are conventionally arranged into periods (see table). The unification of Egypt was vital, for even more than in Mesopotamia, the entire river valley required the central control of irrigation. By the time of the Third Dynasty, the king had achieved full supremacy and had imposed internal peace and order, and his kingdom enjoyed great prosperity. The capital was at Memphis in Upper Egypt, just above the delta. The king was no mere representative of the gods but a god himself. The land was his own personal possession, and the people were his servants.

Nothing better illustrates the extent of royal power than the three great pyramids built as tombs by the kings of the Fourth Dynasty. The largest, that of Khufu, was originally 481 feet high and 756 feet long on each side; it was made up of 2,300,000 stone blocks averaging 2.5 tons each. It was said by the much later Greek historian Herodotus to have taken 100,000 men twenty years to build. The pyramids are remarkable not only for the technical skill that was needed to build them but even more for what they tell us of the royal power. They give evidence that the Egyptian kings had enormous wealth, the power to concentrate so much effort on a personal project, and the confidence to undertake one of such a long duration. There were earlier pyramids and many were built later, but those of the Fourth Dynasty were never surpassed.

THE OLD KINGDOM. In the Old Kingdom royal power was absolute. The pharaoh, as he was later called (the term originally meant "great house" or "palace"), governed his kingdom through his family and appointed officials removable at his pleasure. The peasants were carefully regulated, their movement was lim-

The great pyramids of Egypt. These colossal tombs are at Giza, near Cairo. From left to right, they are the tombs of Menkaure, Khafre, and Khufu, three pharaohs of the Fourth Dynasty (ca. 2620–2480 B.C.). *The smaller tombs in the foreground may have been those of the pharaohs' wives and courtiers.* [*Egyptian Museum*]

ited, and they were taxed heavily, perhaps as much as one fifth of what they produced. Luxury accompanied the king in life and death, and he was raised to a remote and exalted level by his people. Such power and eminence cannot be sustained long by force alone. The Egyptians worked for the king and obeyed him because he was a living god on whom their life, safety, and prosperity depended. He was the direct source of law and justice, so no law codes were needed.

In such a world, government was merely one aspect of religion, and religion dominated Egyptian life. The gods of Egypt had many forms: animals, humans, and natural forces. In time, Re, the sun god, came to have a special dominant place, but for centuries there seems to have been little clarity or order in the Egyptian pantheon. Unlike the Mesopotamians, the Egyptians had a rather clear idea of an afterlife. They took great care to bury their dead properly and supplied the grave with things that the departed would need for a pleasant life after death. The king and some nobles had their bodies preserved as mummies. Their tombs were beautifully decorated with paintings; food was provided at burial and even after. Some royal tombs were provided with full-sized ships for the voyage to heaven. At first, only kings were thought to achieve eternal life; then nobles were included; finally, all Egyptians could hope for immortality. The dead had to be properly embalmed, and the proper spells had to be written and spoken. Later on, a moral test was added.

The Egyptians developed a system of writing not much later than the Sumerians. Though the idea may have come from Mesopotamia, the script was independent. It began as picture writing and later combined pictographs with sound signs to produce a difficult and compli-

PERIODS IN ANCIENT EGYPTIAN HISTORY (DYNASTIES IN ROMAN NUMERALS)

Early Dynastic Period (I–II)	ca. 3100–2700 B.C.
Old Kingdom (III–VI)	2700–2200 B.C.
First Intermediate Period (VII–X)	2200–2052 B.C.
Middle Kingdom (XI–XII)	2052–1786 B.C.
Second Intermediate Period (XIII–XVII)	1786–1575 B.C.
Hyksos invasion	ca. 1700 B.C.
New Kingdom (or Empire) (XVIII–XX)	1575–1087 B.C.
Post-Empire (XXI–XXXI)	1087–30 B.C.

Pharaoh Menkaure and his queen (*ca.* 2550 B.C.). *Menkaure built the smallest of the great pyramids at Giza. The frontality of the two figures and the extension of their left feet are typical of Egyptian sculpture.* [*Museum of Fine Arts, Boston*]

cated script that the Greeks called *hieroglyph* ("sacred carvings"). Though much of what we have is preserved on wall paintings and carvings, most of Egyptian writing was done with pen and ink on a fine paper made from the papyrus reed found in the delta. Egyptian literature was more limited in depth and imagination than the Mesopotamian writings. Hymns, myths, magical formulas, tales of travel, and "wisdom literature," or bits of advice to help one get on well in the world, have been preserved. But nothing as serious and probing as the story of Gilgamesh was produced in the happier and simpler world of Egypt.

THE MIDDLE KINGDOM. The power of the kings of the Old Kingdom waned as priests and nobles gained more independence and influence. The governors of the regions of Egypt called *nomes* gained hereditary claim to their offices, and their families acquired large estates. About 2200 B.C. the Old Kingdom collapsed and gave way to the decentralization and disorder of the First Intermediate Period (ca. 2200–2052 B.C.). Finally, the nomarchs (governors) of Thebes in Upper Egypt gained control of the country and established the Middle Kingdom, about 2052 B.C. The rulers of the Twelfth Dynasty restored the pharaoh's power over the whole of Egypt, though they could not completely control the nobles who ruled the nomes. Still, they brought order, peace, and prosperity to a troubled land. They encouraged trade and extended Egyptian power and influence northward toward Palestine and southward toward Ethiopia. Though they moved the capital back to the more defensible site at Memphis, they gave great prominence to Amon, a god especially connected with Thebes. He became identified with Re, emerging as Amon-Re, the main god of Egypt. The kings of this period seem to have emphasized their role in doing justice. In their statues they are often shown as burdened with care, presumably concern for their people. Tales of the period place great emphasis on the king as interested in right and in the welfare of his people. Much later, in the New Kingdom, ethical concerns appeared, as they had in the law codes of Mesopotamia, but the divine status of the kings gave them a novel place in religion as well.

The New Kingdom (The Empire). The Middle Kingdom disintegrated in the Thirteenth Dynasty with the resurgence of the power of the local nobility. About 1700 B.C. Egypt suffered an invasion. Tradition speaks of a people called the Hyksos who came from the east and conquered the Nile Delta. They seem to have been a collection of Semitic peoples from the area of Palestine and Syria at the eastern end of the Mediterranean. Egyptian nationalism reasserted itself about 1575 B.C., when a dynasty from Thebes drove out the Hyksos and reunited the kingdom. In reaction to the humiliation of the Second Intermediate Period, the pharaohs of the Eighteenth Dynasty, the most prominent of whom was Thutmose III (1490–1436 B.C.), created an absolute government based on a powerful army and an Egyptian empire extending far beyond the Nile valley (see Map 1.2).

From the Hyksos the Egyptians learned new

MAP 1-2 *About* 1400 B.C. *the Near East was divided among four empires. Egypt went south to Nubia and north through Palestine and Phoenicia. Kassites ruled in Mesopotamia, Hittites in Asia Minor, and Mitanni in Assyrian lands. In the Aegean the Mycenaean kingdoms were at their height.*

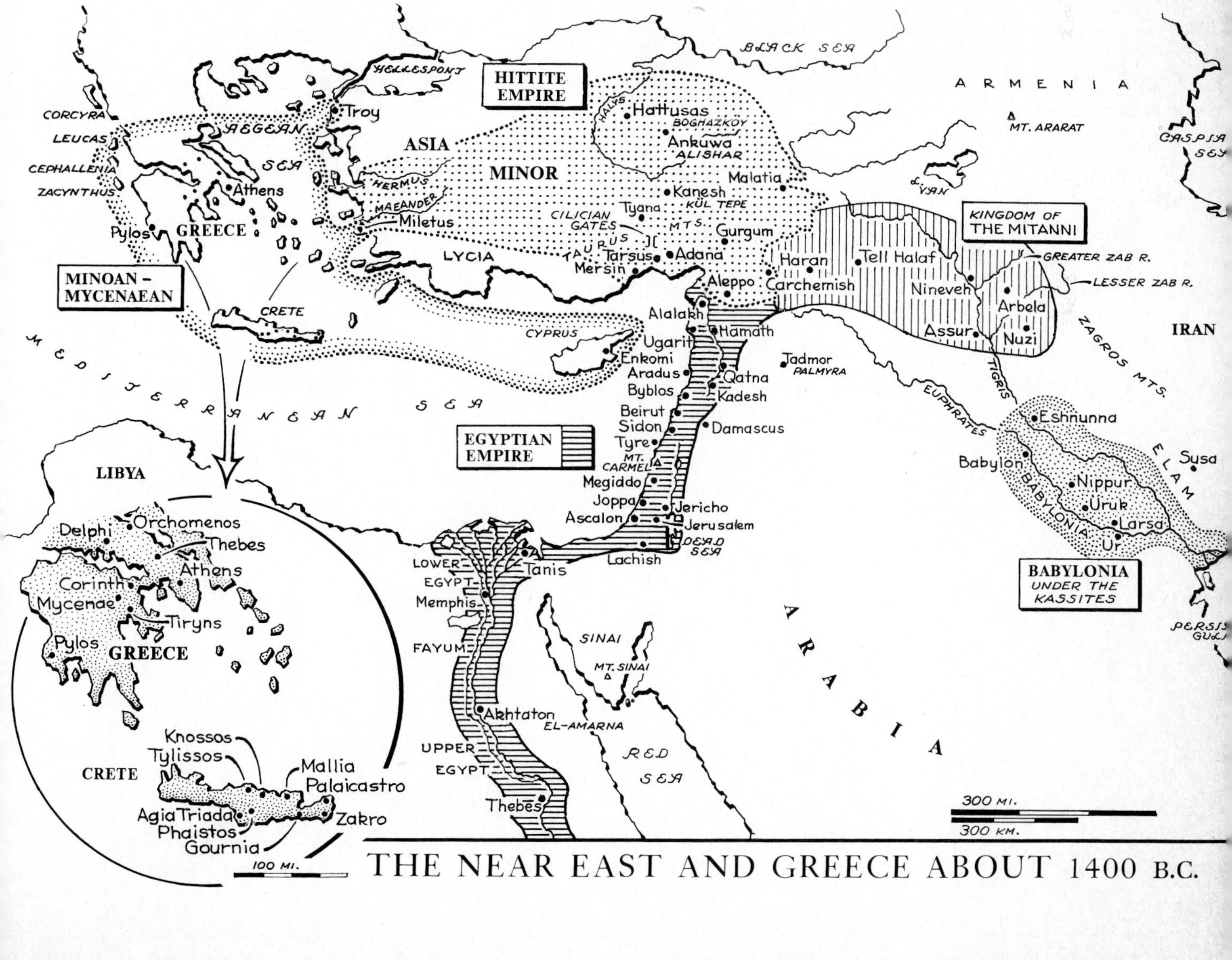

A wall painting depicting agricultural labor, ca. 1425 B.C. from the tomb of Menna, a noble of Thebes. As Menna watches from the upper left, his peasants harvest grain, herd cattle, and punish an unsatisfactory worker. [*Peter Clayton*]

The great hall of the Temple of Amon at Karnak, near Thebes. Embellished by pharaoh after pharaoh, Karnak was for centuries the largest, richest, and most magnificent temple in Egypt.

military techniques and obtained new weapons. To these they added determination, a fighting spirit, and an increasingly military society. They pushed the southern frontier back a long way and extended Egyptian power farther into Palestine and Syria and beyond to the upper Euphrates River. They were not checked until they came into conflict with the powerful Hittite empire of Asia Minor. Both powers were weakened by the struggle, and though Egypt survived, it again became the victim of foreign invasion and rule, as one foreign empire after another took possession of the ancient kingdom.

The Eighteenth Dynasty, however, witnessed an interesting religious change. One of the results of the successful imperial ventures of the Egyptian pharaohs was the growth in power of the priests of Amon and the threat it posed to the position of the king. When young Amenhotep IV (1367–1350 B.C.) came to the throne before the middle of the fourteenth century B.C., he apparently determined to resist the priesthood of Amon. He was supported by his family and advisers and ultimately made a clean break with the worship of Amon-Re. He moved his capital from Thebes, the center of Amon worship, and built an entirely new city about three hundred miles to the north at a place now called El Amarna. Its god was Aton, the physical disk of the sun, and the new city was called Akhtaton. The king changed his own name to Akhnaton, "It pleases Aton." The new god was different from any that had come before him, for he was believed to be universal, not merely Egyptian. Unlike the other gods, he had no cult statue but was represented in painting and relief sculpture as the sun disk.

The universal claims for Aton led to religious intolerance of the worshipers of the other gods. Their temples were shut down and the name of Amon-Re was chiseled from monuments on which it was carved. The old priests, of course, were deprived of their posts and privileges, and the people who served the pharaoh and his god were new, sometimes even foreign. The new religion, moreover, was more remote than the old. Only the pharaoh and his family worshiped Aton directly, and the people wor-

This unflattering portrayal of Akhnaton, the revolutionary pharaoh, is characteristic of the unusually realistic art of his reign (1367–1350 B.C.). [*Egyptian Museum*]

Akhnaton Intones New Hymns to Aton, the One God

These hymns were composed in the reign of Amenhotep IV (1367–1350 B.C.), or Akhnaton, as he called himself after instituting a religious revolution in Egypt.

Thou makest the Nile in the Nether World,
Thou bringest it as thou desirest,
To preserve alive the people of Egypt
For thou hast made them for thyself,
Thou lord of them all, who weariest thyself for them;
Thou lord of every land, who risest for them.
Thou Sun of day, great in glory,
All the distant highland countries,
Thou makest also their life,
Thou didst set a Nile in the sky.
When it falleth for them,
It maketh waves upon the mountains,
Like the great green sea,
Watering their fields in their towns.

How benevolent are thy designs, O lord of eternity!
There is a Nile in the sky for the strangers
And for the antelopes of all the highlands that go about upon their feet.
But the Nile, it cometh from the Nether World for Egypt.

Thou didst make the distant sky in order to rise therein,
In order to behold all that thou hast made,
While thou wast yet alone
Shining in thy form as living Aton,
Dawning, glittering, going afar and returning.
Thou makest millions of forms
Through thyself alone;
Cities, villages, and fields, highways and rivers.
All eyes see thee before them,
For thou art Aton of the day over the earth,
When thou hast gone away,
And all men, whose faces thou hast fashioned
In order that thou mightest no longer see thyself alone,
[Have fallen asleep, so that not] one [seeth] that which thou hast made,
Yet art thou still in my heart.

REVELATION TO THE KING

There is no other that knoweth thee
Save thy son Akhnaton.
Thou hast made him wise
In thy designs and in thy might.

UNIVERSAL MAINTENANCE

The world subsists in thy hand,
Even as thou hast made them.
When thou hast risen they live,
When thou settest they die;
For thou art length of life of thyself,
Men live through thee.

The eyes of men see beauty
Until thou settest.
All labour is put away
When thou settest in the west.
When thou risest again
[Thou] makest [every hand] to flourish for the king
And [prosperity] is in every foot,
Since thou didst establish the world,
And raise them up for thy son,
Who came forth from thy flesh,
The king of Upper and Lower Egypt,
Living in Truth, Lord of the Two Lands,
Nefer-khepru-Re, Wan-Re [Akhnaton],
Son of Re, living in Truth, lord of diadems,
Akhnaton, whose life is long;
[And for] the chief royal wife, his beloved,
Mistress of the Two Lands, Nefer-nefru-Aton, Nofretete,
Living and flourishing for ever and ever.

James H. Breasted, *The Dawn of Conscience* (New York: Charles Scribners' Sons, 1933, 1961), p. 137.

shiped the pharaoh. Akhnaton's interest in religious reform apparently led him to ignore foreign affairs, which proved disastrous. The Asian possessions of Egypt fell away, and this imperial decline and its economic consequences presumably caused further hostility to the new religion. When the king died, a strong counterrevolution swept away the work of his lifetime. His chosen successor was soon put aside and replaced by Tutankhamon (1347–1339 B.C.), the young husband of one of the daughters of Akhnaton and his beautiful wife, Nefertiti. The new pharaoh restored the old religion and wiped out as much as he could of the memory of the worship of Aton. He restored Amon to the center of the Egyptian pantheon, abandoned El Amarna, and returned the capital to Thebes. There he and his successors built his magnificent tomb, which remained remarkably intact until its discovery in 1922. The end of the El Amarna age restored power to the priests of Amon and to the military officers. A general named Horemhab became king (1335–1308? B.C.), restored order, and recovered much of the lost empire. He referred to Akhnaton as "the criminal of Akhtaton" and erased his name from the records. Akhnaton's city and memory disappeared for over three thousand years, to be rediscovered only by chance about a century ago.

For the rest of its independent history, Egypt returned to its traditional culture, but its mood was more gloomy. The Book of the Dead, a product of this late period, was a collection of spells whereby the dead could get safely to the next world without being destroyed by a hideous monster. Egypt itself would soon be devoured by powerful empires no less menacing.

Ancient Near Eastern Empires

In the time of the Eighteenth Dynasty in Egypt, new groups of peoples had established themselves in the Near East: the Kassites in Babylonia, the Hittites in Asia Minor, and the Mitannians in northern Mesopotamia. They all spoke languages in the Indo-European group, which includes Greek, Latin, Sanskrit, Persian, Celtic, and the Germanic languages and is thought to have originated in the Ukraine (now the southwestern Soviet Union) or to the east of it. The Kassites and Mitannians were warrior peoples who ruled as a minority over more civilized folk and absorbed their culture without changing it. The Hittites arrived in Asia Minor about 2000 B.C., and by about 1500 B.C. they had established a strong, centralized government with a capital at Hattusas (near Ankara, the capital of modern Turkey). Between 1400 and 1200 B.C. they contested Egypt's control of Palestine and Syria and were strong enough to achieve a dynastic marriage with the daughter of the powerful Nineteenth Dynasty pharaoh, Ramses II, about 1265 B.C. By 1200 B.C. the Hittite kingdom was gone, swept away by the arrival of new, mysterious Indo-Europeans. However, Neo-Hittite centers flourished in Asia Minor and Mesopotamia for a few centuries longer.

A Hittite war chariot. The Hittites were among the first to use iron weapons and war horns. Here, a pair of eighth-century B.C. Hittite warriors trample the defeated enemy.

In most respects the Hittites reflected the influence of the dominant Mesopotamian culture of the region, but their government resembled more closely what we know of other Indo-European cultures. Their kings did not claim to be divine or even to be the chosen representatives of the gods. In the early period the king's power was checked by a council of nobles, and the assembled army had to ratify his succession to the throne. The Hittites appear to have been responsible for a great technological advance, the smelting of iron. They also played an important role in transmitting the ancient cultures of Mesopotamia and Egypt to the Greeks, who lived on their frontiers.

The fall of the Hittites was followed shortly by the formation of empires that dominated the Near East's ancient civilizations and even extended them to new areas. The first of these empires was established by the Assyrians, whose homeland was in the valleys and hills of northern Mesopotamia on and to the east of the Tigris River. They had a series of capitals, of which the great city of Nineveh is perhaps best known (modern Mosul, Iraq). They spoke a Semitic language and, from early times, were a part of the culture of Mesopotamia. Akkadians, Sumerians, Amorites, and Mitannians had dominated Assyria in turn. The Hittites' defeat of Mitanni liberated the Assyrians and prepared the way for their greatness from earlier than 1000 B.C. By 665 B.C. they had come to control everything from the southern frontier of Egypt, through Palestine, Syria, and much of Asia Minor, down to the Persian Gulf in the southeast. They succeeded in part because they made use of iron weapons. Because iron was more common than copper and tin, it was possible for them to arm more men more cheaply. The Assyrians were also fierce, well disciplined, and cruel. Their cruelty was calculated, at least in part, to terrorize real and potential enemies, for the Assyrians boasted of their brutality.

Unlike earlier empires, the Assyrian Empire systematically and profitably exploited the area it held. The Assyrians used different methods of control, ranging from the mere collection of tribute, to the stationing of garrisons in conquered territory, to removing entire populations from their homelands and scattering them elsewhere, as they did to the people of the kingdom of Israel. Because of their military and administrative skills, they were able to hold vast areas even as they absorbed the teachings of the older cultures under their sway.

As these two reliefs from royal palaces show, the Assyrians boasted about their cruelty. The Assyrian kings used a policy of calculated terror to hold their empire together and to discourage revolt by subject peoples and attack by foreign foes. Above, the decapitated heads of enemies are being carefully counted by royal scribes as part of the spoils of victory. Below, the army of Ashurbanipal sacks the city of Hamanu in Syria. [Werner Forman]

In addition to maintaining their own empire, the Assyrians had to serve as a buffer of the civilized Middle East against the barbarians on its frontiers. In the seventh century B.C. the task of fighting off the barbarians so drained the overextended Assyrians that the empire fell because of internal revolution. A new dynasty in Babylon joined with the rising kingdom of Media to the east (in modern Iran) to defeat the Assyrians and destroy Nineveh in 612 B.C. The successor kingdoms, the Chaldean or Neo-Babylonian and the Median, did not last long; they were swallowed, by 539 B.C., by yet another great eastern empire, that of the Persians. We shall return to the Persians in Chapter 2.

KEY EVENTS IN THE HISTORY OF ANCIENT NEAR EASTERN EMPIRES

Hittite Empire	ca. 1400–1200 B.C.
Rise of Assyrian power	ca. 1100 B.C.
Assyrian conquest of Palestine–Syria	732–722 B.C.
Assyrian conquest of Egypt	671 B.C.
Destruction of Assyrian capital at Nineveh	612 B.C.
Neo-Babylonian (Chaldean) Empire	612–539 B.C.

Palestine

None of the powerful kingdoms we have described has had as much influence on the future of Western civilization as the small stretch of land on the eastern shore of the Mediterranean between Syria and Egypt, the land called Palestine for much of its history. The three great religions of the modern world outside the Far East—Judaism, Christianity, and Islam—trace their origins, at least in part, to the people who arrived there a little before 1200 B.C. and the book that recounts their experiences, the Old Testament of the Bible.

Canaanites and Phoenicians

Before the Israelites arrived in their promised land, it was inhabited by groups of people speaking a Semitic language called Canaanite.

A Phoenician ship from a sarcophagus found in Beirut, Lebanon. [*Roger Wood*]

Two seals of Hebrew officials from the late seventh or eighth centuries B.C. *The top seal is inscribed ''Belonging to Migneyaw, the Servant of Yahweh.'' The bottom seal, which is inscribed with an heraldic emblem, a fighting cock, belonged to Ya'azanyahu, a high royal official.* [*Bruce Zuckerman, West Semitic Research Project*]

The Canaanites lived in walled cities and carried on a version of Mesopotamian culture that included the worship of many gods. The arrival of the Israelites probably forced them northward to settle among similar people who inhabited the coastal land of Phoenicia. The Phoenicians were an important commercial people from a very early time. They seem to have developed a simplified system of writing that lacked only vowel signs to be a true alphabet. They founded colonies as far west as Spain, though their most famous was Carthage, near modern Tunis in north Africa. Sitting astride all trade routes, the Phoenician cities were important sites for the transmission of culture and knowledge from east to west.

The Israelites

The history of the Israelites must be pieced together from various sources. They are mentioned only rarely in the records of their neighbors, so we must rely chiefly on their own account, the Old Testament. It is not intended as a history in our sense but is a complicated collection of historical narrative, wisdom literature, poetry, law, and religious witness. Scholars of an earlier time tended to discard it as a source for historians, but the most recent trend is to take it seriously while using it with caution.

We need not reject the tradition that the patriarch Abraham came from Ur in Mesopotamia about 1900 B.C., and wandered west to tend his flocks in the land of the Canaanites. Some of his people settled there and others wandered into Egypt, perhaps with the Hyksos. By the thirteenth century B.C., led by Moses, they had left Egypt and wandered in the desert until they reached Canaan. They established a united kingdom that reached its peak under David and Solomon in the tenth century B.C. The sons of Solomon could not maintain the unity of the kingdom, and it split into two parts: Israel in the north and Judah, with its capital at Jerusalem, in the south. The rise of the great empires brought disaster to the Israelites. The northern kingdom fell to the Assyrians in 722 B.C., and its people were scattered and lost forever. These were the "ten lost tribes." Only the kingdom of Judah remained, and hereafter we may call the Israelites Jews.

In 586 B.C. Judah was defeated by the Babylonian king Nebuchadnezzar II. He destroyed the great temple built by Solomon and took thousands of hostages off to Babylon. When

MAP 1-3 *The Hebrews established a unified kingdom in Palestine under Kings David and Solomon in the tenth century* B.C. *After the death of Solomon, however, the kingdom was divided into two parts—Israel in the north and Judah, with its capital Jerusalem, in the south. North of Israel were the great commercial cities of Phoenicia.*

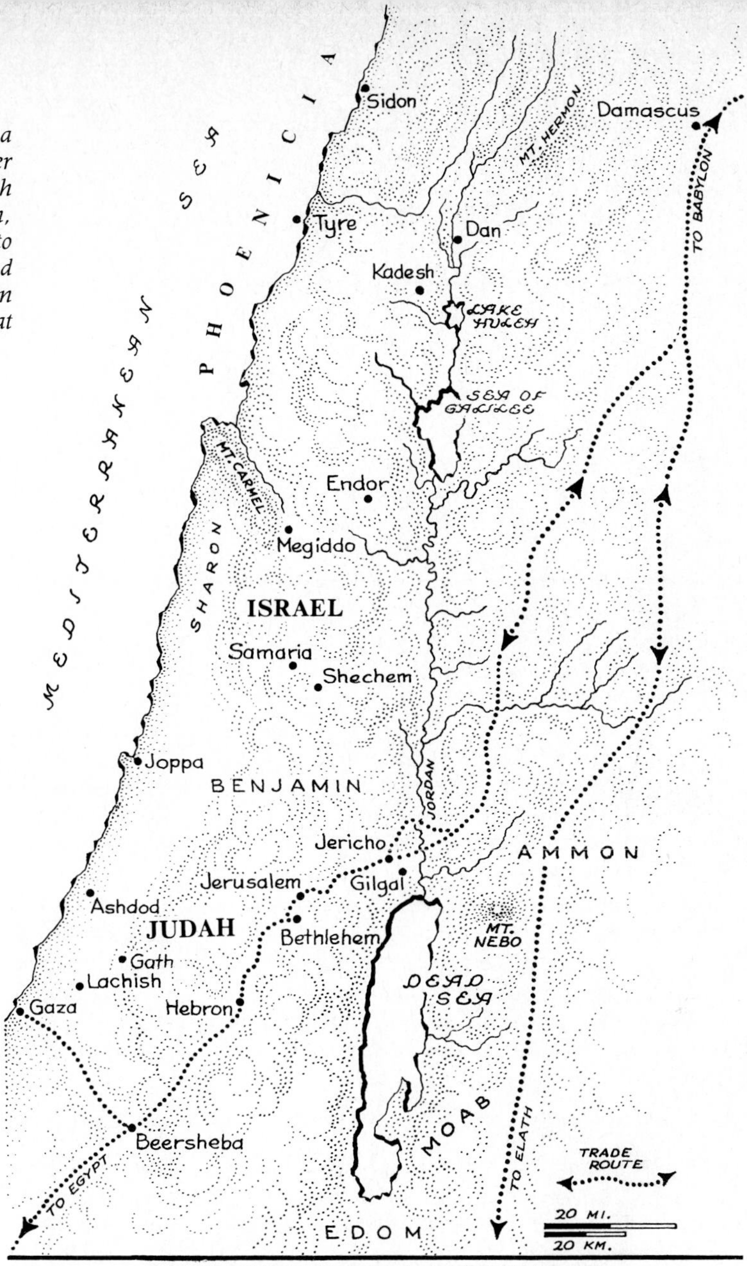

ANCIENT PALESTINE

The Israelites

Reign of King David	ca. 1000–961 B.C.
Reign of King Solomon	ca. 961–922 B.C.
Assyrian conquest of Israel (northern kingdom)	722 B.C.
Destruction of Jerusalem; fall of Judah (southern kingdom); Babylonian Captivity	586 B.C.
Restoration of temple; return of exiles	539 B.C.

The Second Isaiah Defines Hebrew Monotheism

The strongest statement of Hebrew monotheism is found in these words of the anonymous prophet whom we call the Second Isaiah. He wrote during the Hebrew exile in Babylonia, 597–539 B.C.

42

5 Thus says God, the LORD,
who created the heavens and stretched them out,
who spread forth the earth and what comes from it,
who gives breath to the people upon it and spirit
to those who walk in it:
6 "I am the LORD, I have called you in righteousness,
I have taken you by the hand and kept you;
I have given you as a covenant to the people,
a light to the nations,
7 to open the eyes that are blind,
to bring out the prisoners from the dungeon,
from the prison those who sit in darkness.
8 I am the LORD, that is my name;
my glory I give to no other,
nor my praise to graven images.
9 Behold, the former things have come to pass,
and new things I now declare;
before they spring forth I tell you of them."

44

6 Thus says the LORD, the King of Israel and his Redeemer, the LORD of hosts:
"I am the first and I am the last; besides me there is no god.
7 Who is like me? Let him proclaim it,
let him declare and set it forth before me.
Who has announced of old the things to come?
Let them tell us what is yet to be.
8 Fear not, nor be afraid;
have I not told you from of old and declared it?
And you are my witnesses!
Is there a God besides me?
There is no Rock; I know not any."

49

22 Thus says the Lord GOD:
"Behold, I will lift up my hand to the nations,
and raise my signal to the peoples;
and they shall bring your sons in their bosom,
and your daughters shall be carried on their shoulders.
23 Kings shall be your foster fathers,
and their queens your nursing mothers.
With their faces to the ground they shall bow down to you,
and lick the dust of your feet.
Then you will know that I am the LORD;
those who wait for me shall not be put to shame."

24 Can the prey be taken from the mighty, or the captives of a tyrant be rescued?
25 Surely, thus says the LORD:
"Even the captives of the mighty shall be taken,
and the prey of the tyrant be rescued,
for I will contend with those who contend with you
and I will save your children.
26 I will make your oppressors eat their own flesh,
and they shall be drunk with their own blood as with wine.
Then all flesh shall know
that I am the LORD your Savior,
and your Redeemer, the Mighty One of Jacob."

Revised Standard Version of the Bible (New York: Division of Christian Education, National Council of Churches, 1952).

the Persians defeated Babylonia, they ended this Babylonian Captivity of the Jews and allowed them to return to their homeland. After that, the area of the old kingdom of the Jews in Palestine was dominated by foreign peoples for some twenty-five hundred years until the establishment of the State of Israel in A.D. 1948.

Religion

The fate of this small nation would be of little interest were it not for its unique religious achievement. The great contribution of the Jews is the idea of monotheism, the existence of one universal God, the creator and ruler of the universe. This idea may be as old as Moses, as the Jewish tradition asserts, but it certainly dates as far back as the prophets of the eighth century B.C. The Jewish God is neither a natural force nor like human beings or any other creatures; He is so elevated that those who believe in Him may not picture Him in any form. The faith of the Jews is given special strength by their belief that God made a covenant with Abraham that his progeny would be a chosen people who would be rewarded for following God's commandments and the law He revealed to Moses.

A novelty of Jewish religious thought is the powerful ethical element it introduced. God is a severe but just judge. Ritual and sacrifice are not enough to achieve His approval. People must be righteous, and God Himself appears to be bound to act righteously. The Jewish prophetic tradition was a powerful ethical force. The prophets constantly criticized any falling away from the law and the path of righteousness. The prophets placed God in history, blaming the misfortunes of the Jews on God's righteous and necessary intervention to punish them for their misdeeds, but the prophets also promised the redemption of the Jews if they repented. The prophetic tradition expected the redemption to come in the form of a Messiah who would restore the house of David. The Christians eventually seized on this tradition and believed that Jesus of Nazareth was that Messiah.

Jewish religious ideas influenced the future development of the West, both directly and indirectly. The Jews' belief in an all-powerful creator, righteous Himself and demanding righteousness and obedience from humankind, a universal God who is the father and ruler of all peoples, is a critical part of the Western heritage.

General Outlook of Near Eastern Cultures

Our very brief account of the history of the ancient Near East so far reveals that the various peoples and cultures were different in many ways, yet the distance between all of them and the emerging culture of the Greeks, to whom we shall turn our attention in Chapter 2, is striking. We can see this distance best by comparing the approach of the other cultures to several fundamental human problems with the way some Greeks treated the same problems. The great questions are these: What is the relationship of humans to nature? to the gods? to other humans? These questions involve attitudes toward religion, philosophy, science, law, justice, politics, and government in general.

For the peoples of the Near East there was no simple separation between humans and nature or even between animate creatures and inanimate objects. Humanity was part of a natural continuum, and all things partook of life and spirit. These peoples imagined the universe to be dominated by gods more or less in the shape of humans, and the world they ruled was irregular and unpredictable, subject to divine whims. The gods were capricious because nature seemed capricious.

One Egyptian text speaks of humans as "the cattle of god." The Babylonian story of creation makes it clear that humanity's function is merely to serve the gods. The creator Marduk says,

> I will create Lullu "man" be his name,
> I will form Lullu, man.
> Let him be burdened with the toil of the gods,
> that they may freely breathe.[1]

In a world ruled by powerful deities of this kind, human existence was precarious. Even disasters that we would think human in origin they saw as the product of divine will. So a Babylonian text depicts the destruction of the city of Ur by invading Elamites as the work of the gods, carried out by the storm god Enlil:

> Enlil called the storm.
> The people mourn.
> Exhilarating winds he took from the land.
> The people mourn.

[1] Henri Frankfort et al., *Before Philosophy* (Baltimore: Penguin, 1949), p. 197.

Good winds he took away from Sumer.
  The people mourn.
He summoned evil winds.
  The people mourn.
Entrusted them to Kingaluda, tender of storms.
He called the storm that will annihilate the land.
  The people mourn.
He called disastrous winds.
  The people mourn.
Enlil—choosing Gibil as his helper—
Called the (great) hurricane of heaven.
  The people mourn.[2]

The helpless position of humankind in the face of irrational divine powers is clearly shown in both the Egyptian and the Babylonian versions of the story of the flood. In one Egyptian tale, Re, the god who had created humans, decided to destroy them because of some unnamed evil that the god had suffered. He sent the goddess Sekhmet to accomplish the deed, and she was in the midst of her task, enjoying the work and wading in a sea of blood, when Re changed his mind. Instead of ordering a halt, he poured seven thousand barrels of blood-colored beer in Sekhmet's path. She quickly became drunk, stopped the slaughter, and preserved humanity. In the Babylonian story, the motive for the destruction of humanity is more obvious: "In those days the world teemed, the people multiplied, the world bellowed like a wild bull, and the great god was aroused by the clamour. Enlil heard the clamour and he said to the gods in council, 'The uproar of mankind is intolerable and sleep is no longer possible by reason of the babel.' So the gods in their hearts were moved to let loose the deluge."[3] The gods repented to a degree and decided to save one family, Utnapishtim and his wife, but they seem to have chosen him whimsically, for no particular reason.

In such a universe humans could not hope to understand nature, much less control it. At best, they could try by magic to use some mysterious forces against others. An example of this device is provided by a Mesopotamian incantation to break a sorcerer's spell. The sufferer tried to use the magical powers inherent in ordinary salt to fight the witchcraft, addressing the salt as follows:

O Salt, created in a clean place,
For food of gods did Enlil destine thee.
Without thee no meal is set out in Ekur,
Without thee god, king, lord, and prince do not
  smell incense.
I am so-and-so, the son of so-and-so,
Held captive by enchantment,
Held in fever by bewitchment.
O Salt, break my enchantment! Loose my spell!
Take from me the bewitchment!—and as my
  Creator
I shall extol thee.[4]

Human relationships to the gods were equally humble. There was no doubt that they could destroy humankind and might do so at any time for no good reason. Humans could—and, indeed, had to—try to win the gods over by prayers and sacrifices, but there was no guarantee of success. The gods were bound by no laws and no morality. The best behavior and the greatest devotion to the cult of the gods were no defense against the divine and cosmic irrationality.

In the earliest civilizations, human relations were guided by laws, often set down in written codes. The basic question about law concerned its legitimacy: Why, apart from the lawgiver's power to coerce obedience, should anyone obey the law? For the Egyptians the answer was simple: the law came from the king and the king was a god. For the Mesopotamians the answer was almost the same: they believed that the king was a representative of god, so that the laws he set forth were equally divine. The prologue to the most famous legal document in antiquity, the Code of Hammurabi, makes this plain,

I am the king who is preeminent among kings;
my words are choice; my ability has no equal.
By the order of Shamash, the great judge of
  heaven and earth,
may my justice prevail in the land;
by the word of Marduk, my lord,
may my statutes have no one to rescind them. . . .[5]

The Hebrews introduced some important new ideas. Their unique God was capable of great anger and destruction, but He was open to persuasion and subject to morality. He was therefore more predictable and comforting, for all the terror of His wrath. The biblical version of the flood story, for instance, reveals the great

[2]Frankfort et al., p. 154.
[3]*The Epic of Gilgamesh,* trans. by N. K. Sandars (Baltimore: Penguin, 1960), p. 105.
[4]Frankfort et al., p. 143.
[5]James B. Pritchard, *Ancient Near Eastern Texts,* 2nd ed. (Princeton: Princeton University Press, 1955), pp. 164–180.

difference between the Hebrew God and the Babylonian deities. The Hebrew God was powerful and wrathful, but He was not arbitrary. He chose to destroy His creatures for their moral failures: for the reason that "the wickedness of man was great in the earth, and that every imagination of the thought of His heart was evil continually . . . the earth was corrupt in God's sight and the earth was filled with violence."[6] When He repented and wanted to save someone, He chose Noah because "Noah was a righteous man, blameless in his generation."[7]

That God was bound by His own definition of righteousness is neatly shown in the biblical story of Sodom and Gomorrah. He had chosen to destroy these wicked cities but felt obliged first to inform Abraham because of God's covenant with him.[8] In this passage Abraham calls on his Lord to abide by His own moral principles, and the Lord sees Abraham's point. In such a world there is the possibility of order in the universe and on this earth. There is also the possibility of justice among human beings, for the Hebrew God had provided His people with law. Through his prophet Moses, He had provided humans with regulations that would enable them to live in peace and justice. If they would abide by the law and live upright lives, they and their descendants could expect happy and prosperous lives. This idea was quite different from the uncertainty of the Babylonian view, but like it and its Egyptian partner, it left no doubt of the centrality of the divine. Cosmic order, human survival, and justice were all dependent on God.

Toward the Greeks and Western Thought

Different approaches and answers to many of the same concerns were offered by ancient Greek thought. Calling attention, even this early, to some of those differences will help to point up the distinctive outlook of the Greeks and of the later cultures of Western civilization that have drawn heavily on it.

Greek ideas had much in common with the ideas of earlier peoples. The gods of the Greeks had most of the characteristics of the Mesopotamian deities; magic and incantations played a part in their lives; and their law was usually connected with divinity. Many, if not most, Greeks in the ancient world must have lived their lives with notions not very different from those held by other peoples. But the surprising thing is that some Greeks developed ideas that were strikingly different and, in so doing, set a part of humankind on an entirely new path. As early as the sixth century B.C. some Greeks living in the Ionian cities of Asia Minor raised some questions and suggested some answers about nature that produced an intellectual revolution. In speculating about the nature of the world and its origin, they made guesses that were completely naturalistic and made no reference to supernatural powers. One historian of Greek thought put the case particularly well:

> In one of the Babylonian legends it says: "All the lands were sea . . . Marduk bound a rush mat upon the face of the waters, he made dirt and piled it beside the rush mat." What Thales did was to leave Marduk out. He, too, said that everything was once water. But he thought that earth and everything else had been formed out of water by a natural process, like the silting up of the Delta of the Nile. . . . It is an admirable beginning, the whole point of which is that it gathers together into a coherent picture a number of observed facts without letting Marduk in.[9]

Thales was the first Greek philosopher. His putting of the question of the world's origin in a naturalistic form as early as the sixth century B.C. may have been the beginning of the unreservedly rational investigation of the universe, and so the beginning of both philosophy and science.

The same relentlessly rational approach was used even in regard to the gods themselves. In the same century as Thales, Xenophanes of Colophon expressed the opinion that humans think that the gods were born and have clothes, voices, and bodies like themselves. If oxen, horses, and lions had hands and could paint like humans, they would paint gods in their own image; the oxen would draw gods like oxen and the horses like horses. Thus black people believed in flat-nosed, black-faced gods, and the Thracians in gods with blue eyes and red hair.[10] In the fifth century B.C. Protagoras of Abdera went so far in the direction of agnosticism as to say, "About the gods I

[6] Genesis 6:5–11.
[7] Genesis 6:9.
[8] Genesis 18:20–33.

[9] Benjamin Farrington, *Greek Science* (London: Penguin, 1953), p. 37.
[10] Frankfort et al., pp. 14–16.

can have no knowledge either that they are or that they are not or what is their nature."[11] This rationalistic, skeptical way of thinking carried over into practical matters as well. The school of medicine led by Hippocrates of Cos (about 400 B.C.) attempted to understand, diagnose, and cure disease without any attention to supernatural forces or beings. One of the Hippocratics wrote of the mysterious disease epilepsy: "It seems to me that the disease is no more divine than any other. It has a natural cause, just as other diseases have. Men think it divine merely because they do not understand it. But if they called everything divine which they do not understand, why, there would be no end of divine things."[12] By the fifth century B.C., too, it was possible for the historian Thucydides to analyze and explain the behavior of humans in society completely in terms of human nature and chance, leaving no place for the gods or supernatural forces.

The same absence of divine or supernatural forces characterized Greek views of law and justice. Most Greeks, of course, liked to think in a vague way that law came ultimately from the gods. In practice, however, and especially in the democratic states, they knew very well that laws were made by humans and should be obeyed because they represented the expressed consent of the citizens. Law, according to the fourth century B.C. statesman Demosthenes, is "a general covenant of the whole State, in accordance with which all men in that State ought to regulate their lives."[13]

The statement of these ideas, so different from any that came before the Greeks, opens the discussion of most of the issues that appear in the long history of Western civilization and that remain major concerns in the modern world: What is the nature of the universe and how can it be controlled? Are there divine powers, and if so, what is humanity's relationship to them? Are law and justice human, divine, or both? What is the place in human society of freedom, obedience, and reverence? These and many other problems were either invented or intensified by the Greeks. We now need to see whether there was something special in the Greeks' experience that made them raise these questions in the way that they did.

[11]Hermann Diels, *Fragmente der Vorsokratiker,* 5th ed., ed. by Walter Kranz (Berlin: Weidmann, 1934–1938), Frg. 4.

[12]Diels, Frgs. 14–16.

[13]*Against Aristogeiton,* 16.

Suggested Readings

W. F. ALBRIGHT, *From the Stone Age to Christianity* (1957). An original and interesting interpretive study.

W. F. ALBRIGHT, *Archaeology of Palestine* (1960). A study of the physical remains by a great scholar.

CYRIL ALDRED, *Akhenaten, Pharaoh of Egypt: A New Study* (1968). A judicious and critical biography of the enigmatic pharaoh.

J. H. BREASTED, *Ancient Egyptian Religion* (1961). An illuminating study by one of the great Egyptologists.

V. GORDON CHILDE, *What Happened in History* (1946). A pioneering study of human prehistory and history before the Greeks from an anthropological point of view.

HENRI FRANKFORT, *Ancient Egyptian Religion: An Interpretation* (1948). A brief but masterful attempt to explore the religious conceptual world of ancient Egyptians in intelligible and interesting terms.

HENRI FRANKFORT, *Birth of Civilization in the Near East* (1968). A good brief study of the transition to civilization.

HENRI FRANKFORT et al., *Before Philosophy* (1949). A brilliant examination of the mind of the ancients from the Stone Age to the Greeks.

ALAN GARDINER, *Egypt of the Pharaohs* (1961). A sound narrative history.

O. R. GURNEY, *The Hittites* (1954). A good general survey.

W. W. HALLO and W. K. SIMPSON, *The Ancient Near East: A History* (1971). A fine survey of Egyptian and Mesopotamian history.

JACQUETTA HAWKES, *Prehistory and the Beginning of Civilization* (1963).

THORKILD JACOBSEN, *The Treasures of Darkness: A History of Mesopotamian Religion* (1976). A superb and sensitive re-creation of the spiritual life of Mesopotamian peoples from the fourth to the first millennia B.C.

D. C. JOHNSON and M. R. EDEY, *Lucy: The Beginnings of Mankind* (1981).

SAMUEL N. KRAMER, *The Sumerians: Their History, Culture and Character* (1963). A readable general account of Sumerian history.

S. MOSCATI, *Ancient Semitic Civilizations* (1960). A general survey of the ancient Semites.

A. T. OLMSTEAD, *History of Assyria* (1923). A good narrative account.

H. M. ORLINSKY, *Ancient Israel* (1960). Chiefly a political survey.

JAMES B. PRITCHARD (Ed.), *Ancient Near Eastern Texts Relating to the Old Testament* (1969). A good collection of documents in translation with useful introductory material.

CHARLES L. REDMAN, *The Rise of Civilization* (1978). An attempt to use the evidence provided by anthropology, archaeology, and the physical sciences to illuminate the development of early urban society.

G. Roux, *Ancient Iraq* (1964). A good recent account of ancient Mesopotamia.

Samuel Sandmel, *The Hebrew Scriptures* (1963). An examination of the Bible's value as history and literature.

K. C. Seele, *When Egypt Ruled the East* (1965). A study of Egypt in its imperial period.

Roland de Vaux, *Ancient Israel: Its Life and Institutions* (1961). A fine account of social institutions.

John A. Wilson, *Culture of Ancient Egypt* (1956). A fascinating interpretation of the civilization of ancient Egypt.

The "Trojan Horse," as depicted on a seventh-century B.C. *Greek vase. Note the wheels on the horse and the Greek soldiers holding weapons and armor who are hiding inside it.* [*German Archaeological Institute of Athens*]

2

The Rise of Greek Civilization

ABOUT 2000 B.C. Greek-speaking peoples settled the lands surrounding the Aegean Sea and established a style of life and formed a set of ideas, values, and institutions that spread far beyond the Aegean corner of the Mediterranean Sea. Preserved and adapted by the Romans, Greek culture powerfully influenced the society of western Europe in the Middle Ages and dominated the Byzantine Empire in the same period. The civilization emerging from this experience spread across Europe and in time crossed the Atlantic to the Western Hemisphere.

At some time in their history, the Greeks of the ancient world founded cities on every shore of the Mediterranean Sea, and pushing on through the Dardanelles, they placed many settlements on the coasts of the Black Sea in southern Russia and as far east as the approaches to the Caucasus Mountains. The center of Greek life, however, has always been the Aegean Sea and the islands in and around it. This location at the eastern end of the Mediterranean very early put the Greeks in touch with the more advanced and earlier civilizations of the Near East: Egypt, Asia Minor, Syria–Palestine, and the rich culture of Mesopotamia. A character in one of Plato's dialogues says, "Whatever the Greeks have acquired from foreigners they have, in the end, turned into something finer."[1] This proud statement indicates at least that the Greeks were aware of how much they had learned from other civilizations.

The Bronze Age on Crete and on the Mainland to About 1150 B.C.

The Minoans

One source of Greek civilization was the culture of the large island of Crete in the Mediterranean. With Greece to the north, Egypt to the south, and Asia to the east, Crete was a cultural bridge between the older civilizations and the new one of the Greeks. The Bronze Age came to Crete not long after 3000 B.C., and in the third and second millennia B.C. a civilization arose that powerfully influenced the islands of the Aegean and the mainland of Greece. This civilization has been given the name *Minoan,* after Minos, the legendary king of Crete.

[1] *Epinomis,* 987 d.

A Minoan goddess brandishing snakes with a lion perched on her head. The statuette was found in the ruins of the palace at Cnossus on Crete and is about a foot high. [*Giraudon/Art Resource*]

On the basis of pottery styles and the excavated levels where the pottery and other artifacts are found, scholars have divided the Bronze Age on Crete into three major divisions with some subdivisions. Dates for Bronze Age settlements on the Greek mainland, for which the term *Helladic* is used, are derived from the same chronological scheme.

During the Middle and Late Minoan periods in the cities of eastern and central Crete, a civilization developed that was new and unique in its character and its beauty. Its most striking feature is presented by the palaces uncovered at such sites as Phaestus, Haghia Triada, and, most important, Cnossus. These palaces were built around a central court with a labyrinth of rooms surrounding it. Some sections of the palace at Cnossus were as much as four stories high. The basement contained many storage rooms for oil and grain, apparently paid as taxes to the king. The main and upper floors contained living quarters as well as workshops for making pottery and jewelry. There were sitting rooms and even bathrooms, to which water was piped through excellent plumbing. The ceilings were supported by lovely columns, which tapered downward, and many of the walls carried murals showing landscapes and seascapes, festivals, and sports. The palace design and the paintings show the influence of Syria, Asia Minor, and Egypt, but the style and quality are unique to Crete.

Along with palaces, paintings, pottery, jewelry, and other valuable objects, writing of three distinct kinds was found, and one of these proved to be an early form of Greek. The script was written on clay tablets like those found in Mesopotamia. They were preserved accidentally, being hardened in a great fire that destroyed the palace. They reveal an organization centered on the palace, in which the king ruled and was served by an extensive bureaucracy that kept remarkably detailed records. This sort of organization is typical of what we find in the Near East but nothing like what we will see among the Greeks; yet the inventories were written in a form of Greek. Why should Minoans, who were not Greek, write in a language not their own? This question raises the larger one of what the relationship was between Crete and the Greek mainland in the Bronze Age and leads us to an examination of mainland, or Helladic, culture.

The Mycenaeans

In the third millennium B.C. most of the Greek mainland, including many of the sites of later Greek cities, was settled by people who used metal, built some impressive houses, and traded with Crete and the islands of the Aegean. The names they gave to places, names that were sometimes preserved by later invaders, make it clear that they were not Greeks and spoke a language that was not Indo-European.

Not long after the year 2000 B.C., many of the Early Helladic sites were destroyed by fire, some were abandoned, and still others appear to have yielded peacefully to an invading people. This invasion probably signaled the arrival of the Greeks.

The invaders succeeded in establishing control of the entire mainland, and the shaft graves cut into the rock at the royal palace-fortress of Mycenae show that they prospered and sometimes became very rich. At Mycenae and all over Greece, there was a smooth transition between the Middle and Late Helladic periods. At Mycenae the richest finds come from the period after 1600 B.C. The city's wealth and power reached their peak during this time, and the culture of the whole mainland during the Late Helladic period goes by the name *Mycenaean.*

The excavation of Mycenaean sites reveals a culture influenced by, but very different from, the Minoan culture. Mycenae and Pylos, like Cnossus, were built some distance from the sea. It is plain, however, that defense against attack was foremost in the minds of the founders. Both cities were built on hills in a position commanding the neighboring territory. The Mycenaean people were warriors, as their art, architecture, and weapons reveal. The success of their campaigns and the defense of their territory required strong central authority, and all available evidence shows that the kings provided it. Their palaces, in which the royal family and its retainers lived, were located within the walls; most of the population lived outside the walls. The palace walls were usually covered with paintings, like those on Crete, but instead of peaceful scenery and games, the Mycenaean murals depicted scenes of war and boar hunting.

About 1500 B.C. the already impressive shaft graves were abandoned in favor of *tholos* tombs. They were large, beehivelike chambers cut into the hillside, built of enormous, well-cut, and fitted stones, and approached by an unroofed passage (*dromos*) cut horizontally into the side of the hill. The lintel block alone of one of these tombs weighs over a hundred tons. Only a strong king whose wealth was great, whose power was unquestioned, and who commanded the labor of many men could undertake such a project. His wealth came from plundering raids, piracy, and trade. Some of this trade went westward to Italy and Sicily, but most of it was with the islands of the Aegean, the coastal towns of Asia Minor, and

Periods of the Aegean Bronze Age

Early Minoan, 2900–2100 B.C.	Early Helladic, 2900–1900 B.C.
Middle Minoan, 2100–1575 B.C.	Middle Helladic, 1900–1580 B.C.
Late Minoan, 1575–1150 B.C.	Late Helladic, 1580–1150 B.C.
Late Minoan I, 1575–1500 B.C.	Late Helladic I, 1580–1500 B.C.
Late Minoan II, 1500–1400 B.C.	Late Helladic II, 1500–1425 B.C.
Late Minoan III, 1400–1150 B.C.	Late Helladic III, 1425–1150 B.C.

The Lion Gate to the citadel of Mycenae. It dates from the 13th century B.C. *and is so massive that later Greeks believed it to be the work of giants.* [*Alison Frantz*]

A Linear B tablet from Pylos, dated about 1200 B.C. *First discovered in the late 19th century, Linear B was only deciphered in 1952 by a brilliant young Englishman, Michael Ventris, who demonstrated that it was an early Greek dialect. This tablet is part of a palace inventory listing vases. It survived because it was baked when the palace at Pylos was destroyed by invaders.* [*TAP - Art Reference Bureau/Athens Museum*]

the cities of Syria, Egypt, and Crete. The Mycenaeans sent pottery, olive oil, and animal hides in exchange for jewels and other luxuries.

Tablets containing Mycenaean writing have been found all over the mainland; the largest and most useful collection was found at Pylos. These tablets, written in a script called by the excavators *Linear B,* reveal a world very similar to the one shown by the records at Cnossus. The king, whose title was *wanax,* held a royal domain, appointed officials, commanded servants, and kept a close record of what he owned and what was owed to him. This evidence confirms all the rest: the Mycenaean world was made up of a number of independent, powerful, and well-organized monarchies.

Although their dating is still controversial, the Linear B tablets at Cnossus seem to belong to Late Minoan III, so that the great "palace period" at Cnossus came after an invasion by Mycenaeans in 1400 B.C. These Greek invaders inhabited a flourishing Crete until the end of the Bronze Age, and there is good reason to believe that at the height of Mycenaean power (1400–1200 B.C.), Crete was part of the Mycenaean world.

These were prosperous and active years for the Mycenaeans. Their cities were enlarged, their trade grew, and they even established commercial colonies in the east. They are mentioned in the archives of the Hittite kings of Asia Minor. They are named as marauders of the Nile Delta in the Egyptian records, and sometime about 1250 B.C. they probably sacked the city of Troy on the coast of northwestern Asia Minor, giving rise to the epic poems of Homer, the *Iliad* and the *Odyssey* (see Map 2.1). Around the year 1200 B.C., however, the Mycenaean world showed signs of great trouble, and by 1100 B.C. it was gone: its palaces were destroyed, many of its cities abandoned, and its art, its pattern of life, its system of writing buried and forgotten. How was the Mycenaean world destroyed?

Modern scholars have suggested theories explaining the destruction of Mycenaean civilization by means of a natural disaster. Some believe that the destruction of Cnossus and the Minoan culture was caused about 1400 B.C. by the volcanic explosion of the Aegean island of Thera (modern Santorini), which blackened and poisoned the air for many miles around and sent a monstrous tidal wave to destroy the great palace civilization. Others think that the explosion took place about 1200 B.C. and caused the destruction of Bronze Age culture throughout the Aegean. This explanation has the convenient consequence of ending the Minoan and the Mycenaean civilizations with one blow, but the evidence does not support it. The Mycenaean towns were not destroyed at one time; many fell around 1200 B.C., but some flourished for another century, and the Athens of the period was never destroyed or abandoned.

No theory of natural disaster holds, and we are left to seek less dramatic explanations. One suggestion is that piratical sea-raiders may have been responsible for the destruction of Pylos and, perhaps, other sites on the mainland. The Greeks themselves believed in a legend that told of the Dorians, a rude people from the north who spoke a Greek dialect different from that of the Mycenaean peoples. The Dorians joined with one of the Greek tribes, the Heraclidae, in an attack on the southern Greek peninsula of Peloponnesus, which was repulsed. One hundred years later they returned and gained full control. This legend of "the return of the Heraclidae" has been identified by modern historians with the Do-

THE AEGEAN AREA IN THE BRONZE AGE

MAP 2-1 *The Bronze Age in the Aegean area lasted from about* 1900 *to about* 1100 B.C. *Its culture on Crete is called Minoan and was at its height about* 1900–1400 B.C. *Bronze Age Helladic culture on the mainland flourished from about* 1600 *to* 1200 B.C.

rian invasion, the incursion from the north into Greece by a less civilized Greek people speaking the Dorian dialect.

Archaeology has failed to provide material support for a single Dorian invasion or a series of them. In the present state of the evidence, certainty is impossible, but the chances are good that the end of the Bronze Age in the Aegean came about gradually over the century between 1200 B.C. and 1100 B.C. as a result of internal conflict among the Mycenaean kings and because of continuous pressure from outsiders, who raided, infiltrated, and eventually dominated Greece and its neighboring islands.

Cnossus, Mycenae, and Pylos were abandoned, their secrets to be kept for over three thousand years.

The Greek "Middle Ages" to About 750 B.C.

The immediate effects of the Dorian invasion were disastrous for the inhabitants of the Mycenaean world. The palaces and the kings and bureaucrats who managed them were destroyed. The wealth and organization that had supported the artists and the merchants were likewise swept away by a barbarous people who did not have the knowledge or social organization to maintain them. Many villages were abandoned and never resettled. Some of their inhabitants probably turned to a nomadic life, and many perished.

An eighth-century B.C. *bronze statuette of a lyre player, found on Crete.* [*Heraklion Archaelogical Museum*]

Another result of the invasion was the spread of the Greek people eastward from the mainland to the Aegean islands and the coast of Asia Minor. The Dorians themselves, after occupying most of the Peloponnesus, swept across the Aegean to occupy the southern islands and the southern part of the Anatolian coast.

These migrations made the Aegean a Greek lake, but trade with the old civilizations of the Near East was virtually ended by the fall of the advanced Minoan and Mycenaean civilizations, nor was there much trade between different parts of Greece. The Greeks were forced to turn inward, and each community was left largely to its own devices. This happened at a time when the Near East was also in disarray, and no great power arose to impose its ways and its will on the helpless people who lived about the Aegean. These circumstances allowed the Greeks time to recover from their disaster and to create their unique style of life.

This period in Greek history is dark, for our knowledge of it rests on very limited sources. Writing disappeared after the fall of Mycenae, and no new script appeared until after 750 B.C. so we have no contemporary author to shed light on this period. Excavation reveals no architecture, sculpture, or painting until after 750 B.C.

The Age of Homer

For a picture of society in these "dark ages," the best source is Homer. His epic poems, the *Iliad* and the *Odyssey,* tell of the heroes who captured Troy, men of the Mycenaean age, but the world described in those poems clearly is a different one. Homer's heroes are not buried in *tholos* tombs but are cremated; they worship gods in temples, whereas the Mycenaeans had no temples; they have chariots but do not know their proper use in warfare. The poems of Homer are the result of an oral tradition that went back into the Mycenaean age. Through the centuries bards sang tales of the heroes who fought at Troy, using verse arranged in rhythmic formulas to aid the memory. In this way some very old material was preserved until the poems were finally written, no sooner

Odysseus Addresses Nobles and Commoners: Homeric Society

The *Iliad* was probably composed about 750 B.C. In this passage Odysseus is trying to stop the Greeks at Troy from fleeing to their ships and returning to their homes. The difference in his treatment of nobles and commoners is striking.

Whenever he found one that was a captain and a man of mark, he stood by his side, and refrained him with gentle words: ''Good sir, it is not seemly to affright thee like a coward, but do thou sit thyself and make all thy folk sit down. For thou knowest not yet clearly what is the purpose of Atreus' son; now is he but making trial, and soon he will afflict the sons of the Achaians. And heard we not all of us what he spake in the council? Beware lest in his anger he evilly entreat the sons of the Achaians. For proud is the soul of heaven-fostered kings; because their honour is of Zeus, and the god of counsel loveth them.''

But whatever man of the people he saw and found him shouting, him he drave with his sceptre and chode him with loud words: ''Good sir, sit still and hearken to the words of others that are thy betters; but thou art no warrior, and a weakling, never reckoned whether in battle or in council. In no wise can we Achaians all be kings here. A multitude of masters is no good thing; let there be one master, one king, to whom the son of crooked-counselling Kronos hath granted it. . . .''

Homer, *The Iliad,* trans. by A. Lang, W. Leaf, and E. Myers (New York: Random House, n.d.), pp. 24–25.

than the eighth century B.C., but the society these old oral poems describe seems to be that of the tenth and ninth centuries B.C.

In the Homeric poems the power of the kings is much smaller than that of the Mycenaean rulers. The ability of the kings to make important decisions was limited by the need to consult the council of nobles. The nobles felt free to discuss matters in vigorous language and in opposition to the king's wishes. In the *Iliad,* Achilles does not hesitate to address Agamemnon, the ''most kingly'' commander of the Trojan expedition, in these words: ''thou with face of dog and heart of deer . . . folk devouring king.'' Such language may have been impolite, but it was not treasonous. The king, on the other hand, was free to ignore the council's advice, but it was risky to do so.

The right to speak in council was limited to noblemen, but the common people could not be ignored. If a king planned a war or a major change of policy during a campaign, he would not fail to call the common soldiers to an assembly, where they could listen and express their feelings by acclamation, even though they could not take part in the debate. The evidence of Homer shows that even in these early times the Greeks, unlike their predecessors and contemporaries, practiced some forms of limited constitutional government.

Homeric society, nevertheless, was sharply divided into classes, the most important division being the one between nobles and commoners. We do not know the origin of the distinction, but we cannot doubt that at this time Greek society was aristocratic. Birth determined noble status, and wealth usually accompanied it. Below the nobles were the peasants, the landless laborers, and the slaves. We cannot tell whether the peasants owned the land they worked outright and so were free to sell it or if they worked a hereditary plot that belonged to their clan and was therefore not theirs to dispose of as they chose. It is clear, however, that the peasants worked hard to make a living.

Far worse was the condition of the hired agricultural laborer. The slave, at least, was attached to a family household and so was protected and fed. In a world where membership in a settled group gave the only security, the free laborers were desperately vulnerable.

Slaves were few in number and were mostly women, who served as maids and concubines. Some male slaves worked as shepherds. Few, if any, worked in agriculture, which depended on free labor throughout Greek history.

The Homeric poems hold up a mirror to this society, and they reflect an aristocratic code of values that powerfully influenced all future Greek thought. In classical times Homer was the schoolbook of the Greeks. They memorized his text, settled diplomatic disputes by citing passages in it, and emulated the behavior and cherished the values they found in it. Those values were physical prowess, courage; fierce protection of one's family, friends, and property; and above all, one's personal honor and reputation. Returning home after his wanderings, Odysseus ruthlessly kills all the suitors of his wife because they have used up all his wealth, wooed his wife, scorned his son, and so dishonored him. Speed of foot, strength, and, most of all, excellence at fighting in battle are what make a man great, yet Achilles leaves the battle and allows his fellow Greeks to be slain and almost defeated because Agamemnon has wounded his honor by taking away his battle prize. He returns not out of a sense of duty to the army but because his dear friend Patroclus has been killed. In each case the hero seeks to display the highest virtue of Homeric society, *arētē*—manliness, courage in the most general sense, and the excellence proper to a hero.

This quality was best revealed in a contest, or *agon*. Homeric battles are not primarily group combats but a series of individual contests between great champions. One of the prime forms of entertainment is the athletic contest, and the funeral of Patroclus is celebrated by such a contest. The central ethical idea in Homer can be found in the instructions that the father of Achilles gives to his son when he sends him off to fight at Troy: "Always be the best and distinguished above others." The father of another Homeric hero has given his son exactly the same orders and has added to them the injunction "do not bring shame on the family of your fathers who were by far the best in Ephyre and in wide Lycia." Here in a nutshell we have the chief values of the aristocrats of Homer's world: to vie for individual supremacy in *arētē* and to defend and increase the honor of the family. They would remain prominent aristocratic values long after Homeric society was only a memory.

The *Polis*

The characteristic Greek institution was the *polis.* The attempt to translate that word as "city-state" is misleading, for it says both too much and too little. All Greek *poleis* began as little more than agricultural villages or towns, and many stayed that way, so the word *city* is inappropriate. All of them were states, in the sense of being independent political units, but they were much more than that. The *polis* was thought of as a community of relatives; all its citizens, who were theoretically descended from a common ancestor, belonged to subgroups, such as fighting brotherhoods (*phratries*), clans, and tribes, and worshiped the gods in common ceremonies.

Aristotle argued that the *polis* was a natural growth and that the human being was by nature "an animal who lives in a *polis*." Humans alone have the power of speech and from it derive the ability to distinguish good from bad and right from wrong, "and the sharing of these things is what makes a household and a *polis*." Humans, therefore, who are incapable of sharing these things or who are so self-sufficient that they have no need of them are not humans at all, but either wild beasts or gods. Without law and justice human beings are the worst and most dangerous of the animals. With them humans can be the best, and justice exists only in the *polis.* These high claims were made in the fourth century B.C., hundreds of years after the *polis* came into existence, but they accurately reflect an attitude that was present from the first.

Development of the Polis

Originally the word *polis* referred only to a citadel, an elevated, defensible rock to which the farmers of the neighboring area could retreat in case of attack. The Acropolis in Athens and the hill called Acrocorinth in Corinth are examples. For some time such high places and the adjacent farms comprised the *polis.* The towns grew gradually and without planning, as the narrowness and the winding, disorderly character of their streets show. For centuries they had no city walls. Unlike the city-states of the Near East, they were not placed for commercial convenience on rivers or the sea, nor did they grow up around a temple to serve the needs of priests and to benefit from the needs of worshipers. The availability of farmland and of a natural fortress determined their location. They were placed either well inland or far enough away from the sea to avoid piratical raids. Only later and gradually did the *agora* appear. It grew to be not only a marketplace but also a civic center and the heart of the Greeks' remarkable social life, which was distinguished by conversation and argument carried on in the open air.

Some *poleis* probably came into existence early in the eighth century B.C. The institution was certainly common by the middle of the century, for all the colonies that were established by the Greeks in the years after 750 B.C. took the form of the *polis.* Once the new institution had been fully established, true monarchy disappeared. Vestigial kings survived in some places, but they were almost always only ceremonial figures without power. The original form of the *polis* was an aristocratic republic dominated by the nobility through its council of nobles and its monopoly of the magistracies.

The Hoplite Phalanx

A new military technique was crucial to the development of the *polis.* In earlier times the brunt of the fighting had been carried on by small troops of cavalry and individual "champions" who first threw their spears and then came to close quarters with swords. Toward the end of the eighth century B.C., however, the hoplite phalanx came into being. It remained the basis of Greek warfare thereafter.

The hoplite was a heavily armed infantryman who fought with a sword and a pike about nine feet long. These soldiers were formed into a phalanx in close order, usually at least eight ranks deep. So long as the hoplites fought bravely and held their ground, there would be few casualties and no defeat, but if they gave way, the result was usually a rout. All depended on the discipline, strength, and courage of the individual soldier. At its best the phalanx could withstand cavalry charges and defeat infantries not as well protected or disciplined. Until defeated by the Roman legion, it was the dominant military force in the eastern Mediterranean.

The usual hoplite battle in Greece was between the armies of two *poleis* quarreling over a piece of land. One army invaded the territory of the other at a time when the crops were almost ready for harvest. The defending army had no choice but to protect its fields. If the army was beaten, its fields were captured or destroyed and its people might starve. In every way the phalanx was a communal effort that relied not on the extraordinary actions of the individual but on the courage of a considerable portion of the citizens. The phalanx and the *polis* arose together, and both heralded the decline of the kings. The phalanx, however, was not made up only of aristocrats. Most of the hoplites were farmers working relatively small holdings. The immediate beneficiaries of the royal decline were the aristocrats, but because the existence of the *polis* depended on the small farmers, their wishes could not for long be wholly ignored. The rise of the hoplite phalanx created a bond between the aristocrats and the peasants who fought in it, and this bond helps explain why class conflicts were muted for some time. It also guaranteed, however, that the aristocrats, who dominated at first, would not always be unchallenged.

The hoplite phalanx. This vase is the earliest surviving depiction of the close-order, heavily armed infantry that the Greeks adopted in the late eighth century B.C. *Note the large shields, plumed helmets, body armor, raised spears, and the close order of the soldiers. The music of their flutist helped the soldiers to march in step.* [*Hirmer Fotoarchive, Munich*]

Importance of the Polis

The Greeks looked to the *polis* for peace, order, prosperity, and honor in their lifetime. They counted on it to preserve their memory and to honor their descendants after death. Some of them came to see it not only as a ruler, but as the molder of its citizens. It is easy to understand the pride and scorn that underlie the comparison made by the poet Phocylides between the Greek state and the capital of the great and powerful Assyrian Empire: "A little *polis* living orderly in a high place is stronger than a block-headed Nineveh."

Expansion of the Greek World

From the middle of the eighth century B.C. until well into the sixth, the Greeks vastly expanded the territory they controlled, their wealth, and their contacts with other peoples in a burst of colonizing activity that placed *poleis* from Spain to the Black Sea. A century earlier a few Greeks had established trading posts in Syria. There they had learned new techniques in the arts and crafts and much more from the older civilizations of the Near East. About 750 B.C. they borrowed a writing system from one of the Semitic scripts and added vowels to create the first true alphabet. The new Greek alphabet was easier to learn than any earlier writing system and made possible the widely literate society of classical Greece.

Syria and its neighboring territory were too strong to penetrate, so the Greeks settled the southern coast of Macedonia and the Chalcidic peninsula (see Map 2.2). These regions were sparsely settled, and the natives were not well enough organized to resist the Greek colonists. Southern Italy and eastern Sicily were even more inviting areas. Before long there were so many Greek colonies in Italy and Sicily that the Romans called the whole region *Magna Graecia* ("Great Greece"). The Greeks also put colonies in Spain and southern France. In the seventh century B.C. Greek colonists settled the coasts of the northeastern Mediterranean, the Black Sea, and the straits connecting them. About the same time they established settlements on the eastern part of the northern African coast. The Greeks now had outposts throughout the Mediterranean world.

The Greeks did not lightly leave home to join a colony. The voyage by sea was dangerous and uncomfortable, and at the end of it were uncertainty and danger. Only powerful pressures like overpopulation and land hunger drove thousands of Greeks from their homes to found new *poleis*. The Greek word for "colony" was *apoikia*, literally, "away home." The colony, though sponsored by the mother city, was established for the good of the colonists rather than for the benefit of those who sent it out. The colony often copied the constitution from

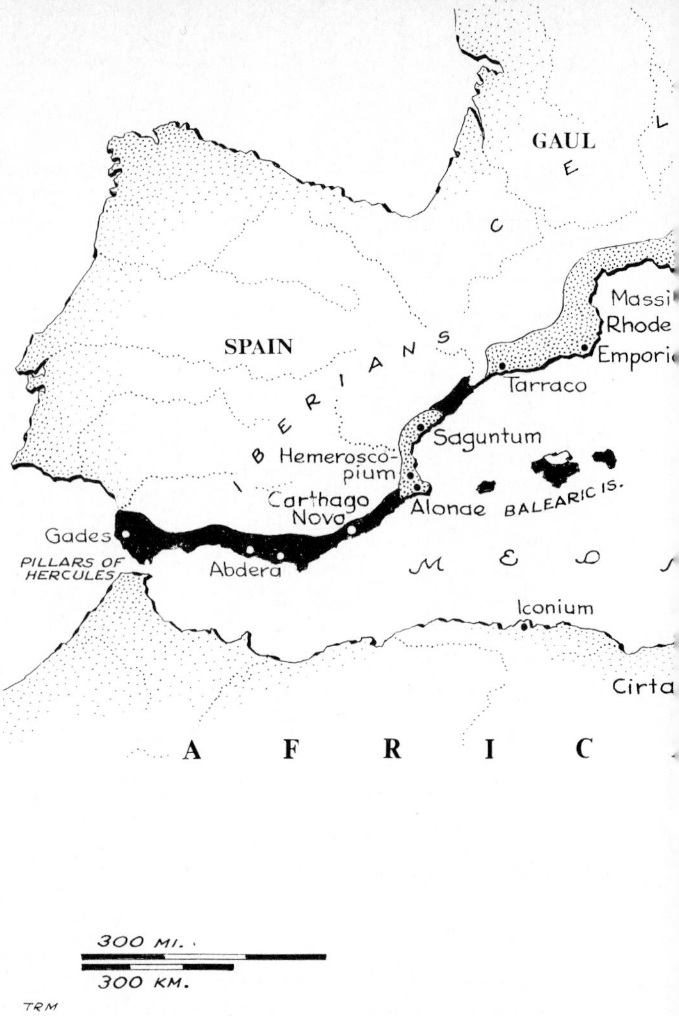

PHOENICIAN AND GREEK

MAP 2-2 *Most of the coast line of the Mediterranean and Black Seas was populated by Greek or Phoenician colonies. The Phoenicians were a commercial people who planted their colonies in North Africa, Spain, Sicily, and Sardinia chiefly in the ninth century* B.C. *The height of Greek colonization came later, between about 750 and* 550 B.C.

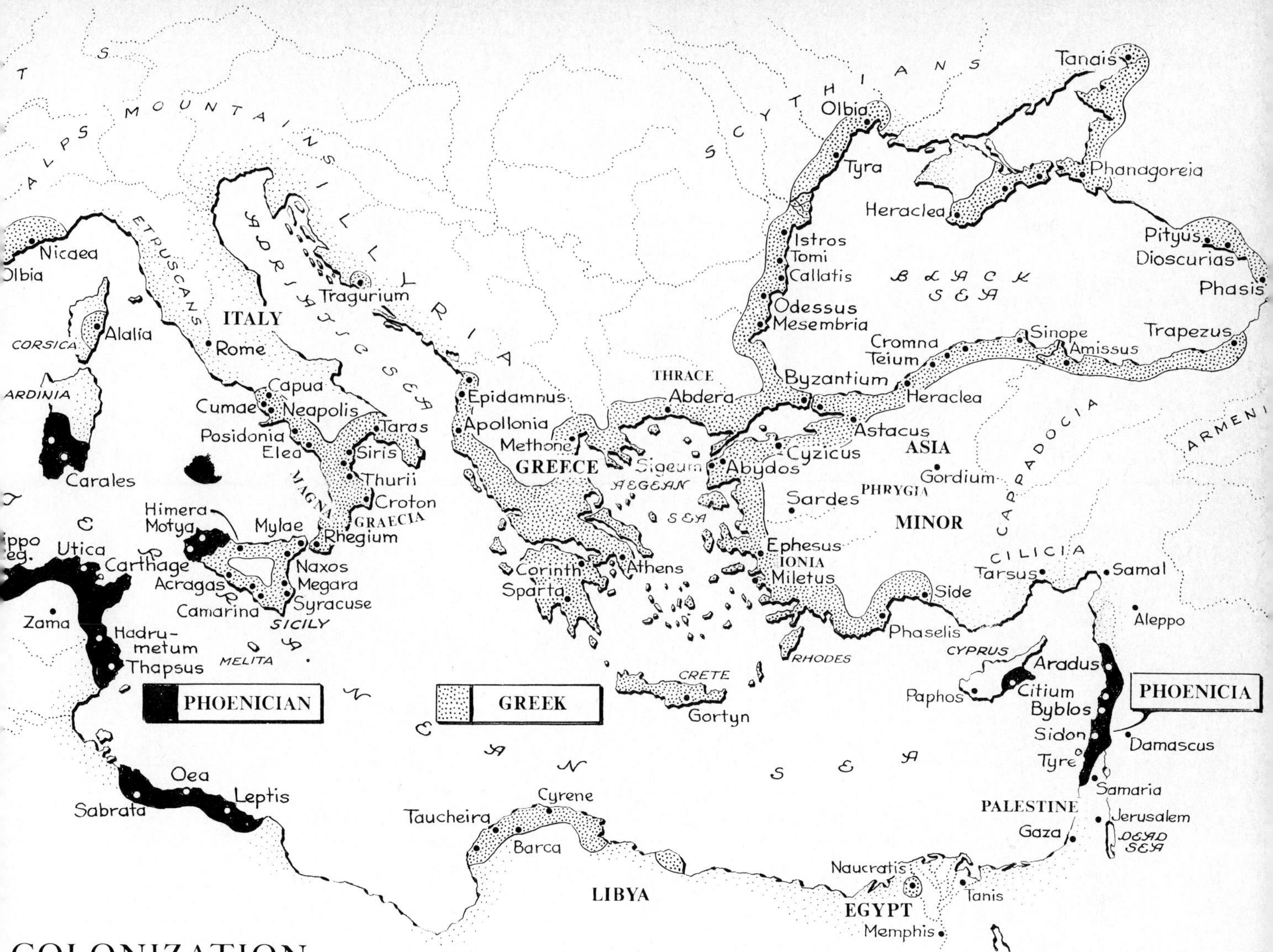

COLONIZATION

home, worshiped the same gods at the same festivals in the same way, and carried on a busy trade with the mother city. Most colonies, though independent, were friendly with their mother cities. Each might ask the other for aid in time of trouble and expect to receive a friendly hearing, although neither was obliged to help.

Colonization had a powerful influence on Greek life. By relieving the pressure of a growing population, it was a safety valve that allowed the *poleis* to escape civil wars. By emphasizing the differences between the Greeks and the new peoples they met, colonization gave the Greeks a sense of cultural identity and fostered a Panhellenic ("all-Greek") spirit that led to the establishment of a number of common religious festivals. The most important

Chronology of the Rise of Greece

Minoan period	ca. 2900–1150 B.C.
Probable date of the arrival of the Greeks on the mainland	ca. 1900 B.C.
Mycenaean period	ca. 1600–1150 B.C.
Sack of Troy (?)	ca. 1250 B.C.
Destruction of Mycenaean centers in Greece	ca. 1200–1150 B.C.
Dark Ages	ca. 1100–750 B.C.
Major period of Greek colonization	ca. 750–500 B.C.
Probable date of Homer	ca. 725 B.C.
Probable date of Hesiod	ca. 700 B.C.
Major period of Greek tyranny	ca. 700–500 B.C.

The temple of Hera at Paestum in southern Italy (sixth century B.C.). *It is considered the finest surviving example of Doric architecture.* [*Hirmer Fotoarchive, Munich*]

ones were at Olympia, Delphi, Corinth, and Nemea.

Colonization also encouraged trade and industry. The influx of new wealth from abroad and the increased demand for goods from the homeland stimulated a more intensive use of the land and an emphasis on crops for export, chiefly the olive and the wine grape. The manufacture of pottery, tools, weapons, and fine artistic metalwork as well as perfumed oil, the soap of the ancient Mediterranean world, was likewise encouraged. New opportunities allowed some men, sometimes outside the nobility, to become wealthy and important. The newly enriched became a troublesome element in the aristocratic *poleis,* for they had an increasingly important part in the life of their states but were barred from political power, religious privileges, and social acceptance by the ruling aristocrats. These conditions soon created a crisis in many states.

The Tyrants (About 700–500 B.C.)

The crisis produced by the new economic and social conditions usually led to or intensified factional divisions within the ruling aristocracy. In the years between 700 and 550 B.C., the result was often the establishment of a tyranny.

A tyrant was a monarch who had gained power in an unorthodox or unconstitutional but not necessarily wicked way and who exercised a strong one-man rule that might well be beneficent and popular.

The founding tyrant was usually a member of the ruling aristocracy who either had a personal grievance or led an unsuccessful faction. He often rose to power because of his military ability and support from the hoplites. He generally had the support of the politically powerless group of the newly wealthy and of the

Herodotus Relates the Tyranny of the Cypselids of Corinth

Herodotus (ca. 490–425 B.C.), "the father of history," was a Greek born in the city of Halicarnassus in Asia Minor. In this story he tells of the Cypselid tyrants of Corinth, who ruled from about 650 to about 585 B.C.

Having thus got the tyranny, he [Cypselus] showed himself a harsh ruler—many of the Corinthians he drove into banishment, many he deprived of their fortunes, and a still greater number of their lives. His reign lasted thirty years, and was prosperous to its close; insomuch that he left the government to Periander, his son. This prince at the beginning of his reign was of a milder temper than his father; but after he corresponded by means of messengers with Thrasybulus, tyrant of Miletus, he became even more sanguinary. On one occasion he sent a herald to ask Thrasybulus what mode of government it was safest to set up in order to rule with honour. Thrasybulus led the messenger without the city, and took him into a field of corn, through which he began to walk, while he asked him again and again concerning his coming from Corinth, ever as he went breaking off and throwing away all such ears of corn as overtopped the rest. In this way he went through the whole field, and destroyed all the best and richest part of the crop; then, without a word, he sent the messenger back. On the return of the man to Corinth, Periander was eager to know what Thrasybulus had counselled, but the messenger reported that he had said nothing; and he wondered that Periander had sent him to so strange a man, who seemed to have lost his senses, since he did nothing but destroy his own property. And upon this he told how Thrasybulus had behaved at the interview. Periander, perceiving what the action meant, and knowing that Thrasybulus advised the destruction of all the leading citizens, treated his subjects from this time forward with the very greatest cruelty.

Herodotus, *The Histories,* trans. by George Rawlinson (New York: Random House, 1942), p. 414.

poor peasants as well. When he took power, he often expelled many of his aristocratic opponents and divided at least some of their land among his supporters. He pleased his commercial and industrial supporters by destroying the privileges of the old aristocracy and by fostering trade and colonization.

The tyrants presided over a period of population growth that saw an increase especially in the number of city dwellers. They responded with a program of public works that included improvement of the drainage systems, care for the water supply, the construction and organization of marketplaces, the building and strengthening of city walls, and the erection of temples. They introduced new local festivals and elaborated the old ones. They were active in the patronage of the arts, supporting poets and artisans with gratifying results. All this activity contributed to the tyrant's popularity, to the prosperity of his city, and to his self-esteem.

In most cases the tyrant's rule was secured by a personal bodyguard and by mercenary soldiers. An armed citizenry, necessary for an aggressive foreign policy, would have been dangerous, so the tyrants usually pursued a program of peaceful alliances with other tyrants abroad and avoided war.

End of the Tyrants

By the end of the sixth century B.C. tyranny had disappeared from the Greek states and did not return again in the same form or for the same reasons. The last tyrants were universally hated for the cruelty and repression they employed. They left bitter memories in their own states and became objects of fear and hatred everywhere. Apart from the outrages committed by individual tyrants, there was something about the very concept of tyranny that was inimical to the idea of the *polis.* The notion of the *polis* as a community to which every member must be responsible, the connection of justice with that community, and the natural aristocratic hatred of monarchy all made tyranny seem alien and offensive. The rule of a tyrant, however beneficent, was arbitrary and unpredictable. Tyranny came into being in defiance of tradition and law and governed without either. Above all, the tyrant was not answerable in any way to his fellow citizens.

From a longer perspective, however, it is clear that the tyrants made important contributions to the development of Greek civilization. They put an end for a time to the crippling civil wars that threatened the survival of the aristocratic *poleis.* In general, they reduced the warfare between the states. They encouraged the economic changes that were necessary for the future prosperity of Greece. They increased the degree of communication with the rest of the Mediterranean world and made an enormous contribution to the cultivation of crafts and technology, as well as of the arts and literature. Most important of all, they broke the grip of the aristocracy and put the productive powers of the most active and talented of its citizens fully at the service of the *polis.*

This scene on an Attic jar from late in the sixth century B.C. *shows how olives, one of Athens's most important crops, were harvested.* [*Courtesy of the Trustees of the British Museum*]

Peasants and Aristocrats: Styles of Life in Archaic Greece

As the "dark ages" came to an end, the features that would distinguish Greek society thereafter took shape. The role of the artisan and the merchant grew more important as contact with the non-Hellenic world became easier, but the great majority of people continued to make their living from the land. Wealthy aristocrats with large estates, powerful households, families, and clans, however, led very different lives from those of the poorer peasants and the independent farmers who had smaller and less fertile fields.

Peasants rarely leave a record of their thoughts or activities, and we have no such record from ancient Greece. The poet Hesiod (ca. 700 B.C.), however, who presented himself as a small farmer was certainly no aristocrat. From his *Works and Days* we get some idea of the life of such a farmer. The crops included grain, chiefly barley but also wheat; grapes for the making of wine; olives for food, but chiefly for oil, used for cooking, lighting, and washing; green vegetables, especially the bean; and some fruit. Sheep and goats provided milk and cheese. The Homeric heroes had great herds of cattle and ate lots of meat, but by Hesiod's time land fertile enough to provide fodder for cattle was needed to grow grain. He and small farmers like him tasted meat chiefly from sacrificial animals at festivals.

These farmers worked hard to make their living. Although Hesiod had the help of oxen and mules and one or two hired helpers for occasional labor, his life was one of continuous toil. The hardest work came in October, at the start of the rainy season, the time for the first plowing. The plow was light and easily broken, and the work of forcing the iron tip into the earth was back-breaking, though Hesiod had a team of oxen to pull his plow. Not every farmer was so fortunate, and the cry of the crane that announced the time of year to plow "bites the heart of the man without oxen." Autumn and winter were the time for cutting wood, building wagons, and making tools. Late winter was the time to tend to the vines, May the time to harvest the grain, July to winnow and store it. Only at the height of summer's heat did Hesiod allow for rest, but when September came, it was time to harvest the grapes. No sooner was that task done than the cycle started again. The work went on under the burning sun and in the freezing cold. Hesiod wrote nothing of pleasure or entertainment. Less austere farmers than Hesiod gathered at the blacksmith's shop for warmth and companionship in winter, and even he must have taken part in religious rites and festivals that were accompanied by some kind of entertainment, but the life of the peasant farmers was hard and their pleasures few.

Most aristocrats were rich enough to employ many hired laborers, sometimes sharecroppers and sometimes even slaves, to work their extensive lands and were therefore able to enjoy leisure for other activities. The center of aristocratic social life was the drinking party, or *symposion.* This activity was not a mere drinking bout, meant to remove inhibitions and produce oblivion. The Greeks, in fact, almost always mixed their wine with water, and one of the goals of the participants was to drink as much as the others without becoming drunk. The *symposion* was a carefully organized occasion, with a "king" chosen to set the order of events and to determine that night's mixture of wine and water. Only men took part, and they ate and drank as they reclined on couches

Hesiod's Farmer's Almanac

Hesiod was a farmer and poet who lived in a village in Greece about 700 B.C. His poem *Works and Days* contains wisdom on several subjects, but its final section amounts to a farmer's almanac, taking readers through the year and advising them on just when each activity is demanded. Hesiod painted a picture of a very hard life for Greek farmers, allowing rest only in the passage that follows.

But when House-on-Back, the snail, crawls from the ground up
the plants, escaping the Pleiades, it's no longer time for vine-digging;
time rather to put an edge to your sickles, and rout out your helpers.
Keep away from sitting in the shade or lying in bed till the sun's up
in the time of the harvest, when the sunshine scorches your skin dry.
This is the season to push your work and bring home your harvest;
get up with the first light so you'll have enough to live on.
Dawn takes away from work a third part of the work's measure.
Dawn sets a man well along on his journey, in his work also,
dawn, who when she shows, has numerous people going their ways; dawn who puts the yoke upon many oxen.
But when the artichoke is in flower, and the clamorous cricket
sitting in his tree lets go his vociferous singing, that issues
from the beating of his wings, in the exhausting season of summer,
then is when goats are at their fattest, when the wine tastes best,
women are most lascivious, but the men's strength fails them
most, for the star Seirios shrivels them, knees and heads alike,
and the skin is all dried out in the heat; then, at that season,
one might have the shadow under the rock, and the wine of Biblis,
a curd cake, and all the milk that the goats can give you,
the meat of a heifer, bred in the woods, who has never borne a calf,
and of baby kids also. Then, too, one can sit in the shadow
and drink the bright-shining wine, his heart satiated with eating
and face turned in the direction where Zephyros blows briskly,
make three libations of water from a spring that keeps running forever
and has no mud in it; and pour wine for the fourth libation.

Works and Days, trans. by Richmond Lattimore, (Ann Arbor: 1959), University of Michigan Press, pp. 87, 89.

along the walls of the room. The sessions began with prayers and libations to the gods. Usually there were games, such as dice or *kottabos,* in which wine was flicked from the cups at different targets. Sometimes dancing girls or flute girls offered entertainment. Frequently the aristocratic participants provided their own amusements with songs, poetry, or even philosophical disputes. Characteristically these took the form of contests, with some kind of prize for the winner, for aristocratic values continued to emphasize competition and the need to excel, whatever the arena.

This aspect of aristocratic life appears in the athletic contests that became widespread early in the sixth century. The games included running events; the long jump; the discus and javelin throws; the *pentathlon,* which included all of these; boxing; wrestling; and the chariot race. Only the rich could afford to raise, train, and race horses, so the chariot race was a special preserve of aristocracy. Wrestling, however, was also especially favored by the nobility, and the *palaestra* where they practiced became an important social center for the aristocracy. The contrast between the hard, drab life of the peasants and the leisured and lively one of the aristocrats could hardly be greater.

An Athenian foot race ca. 530 B.C. *Athletics were an important part of Greek culture. The gods were honored with athletic games, and physical training was part of the essential education of all young men.* [*The Metropolitan Museum of Art, Rogers Fund,* 1914]

Sparta and Athens

Generalization about the *polis* becomes difficult not long after its appearance, for though the states had much in common, some of them developed in unique ways. Sparta and Athens, which became the two most powerful Greek states, had especially unusual histories.

Sparta

At first Sparta seems not to have been strikingly different from other *poleis,* but about 725 B.C. the pressure of population and land hunger led the Spartans to launch a war of conquest against their western neighbor, Messenia. The First Messenian War gave the Spartans as much land as they would ever need, and the reduction of the Messenians to the status of serfs, or Helots, meant that the Spartans need not even work the land that supported them. The turning point in Spartan history came with the Second Messenian War, a rebellion of the Helots, assisted by Argos and some other Peloponnesian cities, about 650 B.C. The war was long and bitter and at one point threatened the existence of Sparta. After the revolt had been put down, the Spartans were forced to reconsider their way of life. They could not expect to keep down the Helots, who outnumbered them perhaps ten to one, and still maintain the old free-and-easy habits typical of most Greeks. Faced with the choice of making drastic changes and sacrifices or abandoning their control of Messenia, the Spartans chose to introduce fundamental reforms that turned their city forever after into a military academy and camp.

The reforms are attributed to the legendary

Xenophon Tells How Lycurgus Encouraged Obedience at Sparta

Xenophon (ca. 430–354 B.C.) was an Athenian who was exiled and lived much of his life in the Peloponnesus. He was one of those rare foreigners who knew Sparta from his own observation.

We are all aware that there is no state in the world in which greater obedience is shown to magistrates, and to the laws themselves, than Sparta. But, for my part, I am disposed to think that Lycurgus could never have attempted to establish this healthy condition, until he had first secured the unanimity of the most powerful members of the state. I infer this for the following reasons. In other states the leaders in rank and influence do not even desire to be thought to fear the magistrates. Such a thing they would regard as in itself a symbol of servility. In Sparta, on the contrary, the stronger a man is the more readily does he bow before constituted authority. And indeed, they pride themselves on their humility, and on a prompt obedience, running, or at any rate not crawling with laggard step, at the word of command. Such an example of eager discipline, they are persuaded, set by themselves, will not fail to be followed by the rest. And this is precisely what has taken place. It is reasonable to suppose that it was these same noblest members of the state who combined to lay the foundation of the ephorate, after they had come to the conclusion themselves that of all the blessings which a state, or an army, or a household can enjoy, obedience is the greatest. Since, as they could not but reason, the greater the power with which men fence about authority, the greater the fascination it will exercise upon the mind of the citizen, to the enforcement of obedience.

Accordingly the ephors are competent to punish whomsoever they choose; they have power to exact fines on the spur of the moment; they have power to depose magistrates in mid career, nay, actually to imprison and bring them to trial on the capital charge. Entrusted with these vast powers, they do not, as do the rest of states, allow the magistrates elected to exercise authority as they like, right through the year of office; but, in the style rather of despotic monarchs, or presidents of the games, at the first symptom of an offense against the law they inflict chastisement without warning and without hesitation.

Xenophon, *Constitution of the Spartans,* trans. by H. G. Dakyns, in *The Greek Historians,* Vol. 2 (New York: Random House, 1942), p. 667.

figure Lycurgus. The new system that emerged late in the sixth century B.C. exerted control over each Spartan from birth, when officials of the state decided which infants were physically fit to survive. At the age of seven the Spartan boy was taken from his mother and turned over to young instructors who trained him in athletics and the military arts and taught him to endure privation, to bear physical pain, and to live off the country, by theft if necessary. At twenty the Spartan youth was enrolled in the army and lived in barracks with his companions until the age of thirty. Marriage was permitted, but a strange sort of marriage it was, for the Spartan male could visit his wife only infrequently and by stealth. At thirty he became a full citizen, an "equal." He took his meals at a public mess in the company of fifteen comrades. His food, a simple diet without much meat or wine, was provided by his own plot of land, which was worked by Helots. Military service was required until the age of sixty; only then could the Spartan retire to his home and family.

This educational program extended to the women, too. They were not given military training, but female infants were examined for fitness to survive in the same way as males. Girls were given gymnastic training, were permitted greater freedom of movement than among other Greeks, and were equally indoctrinated with the idea of service to Sparta. The

Tyrtaeus Describes Excellence: Code of the Citizen Soldier

The military organization of citizen soldiers for the defense of the *polis* and the idea of the *polis* itself, which permeated Greek political thought, found echoes in Greek lyric poetry. A major example is this poem by Tyrtaeus, a Spartan poet who wrote about 625 B.C. It gives important evidence on the nature of warfare in the phalanx and the values taught by the *polis*.

I would not say anything for a man nor take account of him
for any speed of his feet or wrestling skill he might have,
not if he had the size of a Cyclops and strength to go with it,
not if he could outrun Bóreas, the North Wind of Thrace,
not if he were more handsome and gracefully formed than Tithónos,
or had more riches than Midas had, or Kinyras too,
not if he were more of a king than Tantalid Pelops,
or had the power of speech and persuasion Adrastos had,
not if he had all splendors except for a fighting spirit.
For no man ever proves himself a good man in war
unless he can endure to face the blood and the slaughter,
go close against the enemy and fight with his hands.
Here is courage, mankind's finest possession, here is
the noblest prize that a young man can endeavor to win,
and it is a good thing his city and all the people share with him
when a man plants his feet and stands in the foremost spears
relentlessly, all thought of foul flight completely forgotten,
and has well trained his heart to be steadfast and to endure,
and with words encourages the man who is stationed beside him.
Here is a man who proves himself to be valiant in war.
With a sudden rush he turns to flight the rugged battalions
of the enemy, and sustains the beating waves of assault.
And he who so falls among the champions and loses his sweet life,
so blessing with honor his city, his father, and all his people,
with wounds in his chest, where the spear that he was facing has transfixed
that massive guard of his shield, and gone through his breastplate as well,
why, such a man is lamented alike by the young and the elders,
and all his city goes into mourning and grieves for his loss.
His tomb is pointed out with pride, and so are his children,
and his children's children, and afterward all the race that is his.
His shining glory is never forgotten, his name is remembered,
and he becomes an immortal, though he lies under the ground,
when one who was a brave man has been killed by the furious War God
standing his ground and fighting hard for his children and land.
But if he escapes the doom of death, the destroyer of bodies,
and wins his battle,and bright renown for the work of his spear,
all men give place to him alike, the youth and the elders,
and much joy comes his way before he goes down to the dead.
Aging he has reputation among his citizens. No one
tries to interfere with his honors or all he deserves;
all men withdraw before his presence, and yield their seats to him,
and youth, and the men of his age, and even those older than he.
Thus a man should endeavor to reach this high place of courage
with all his heart, and, so trying, never be backward in war.

Greek Lyrics, trans. by Richmond Lattimore (Chicago: University of Chicago Press, 1949, 1950, 1955), pp. 14–15.

A four-horse chariot racing at full speed. The chariot race was the main event at the Olympic Games, held every four years, and its winner was the most celebrated of the victors. Kings often sponsored drivers and sometimes raced themselves. [*Courtesy of the Trustees of the British Museum*]

entire system was designed to change the natural feelings of devotion to wife, children, and family into a more powerful commitment to the *polis*. Privacy, luxury, and even comfort were sacrificed to the purpose of producing soldiers whose physical powers, training, and discipline made them the best in the world. Nothing that might turn the mind away from duty was permitted. The very use of coins was forbidden lest it corrupt the desires of Spartans. Neither family nor money was allowed to interfere with the only ambition permitted to a Spartan male: to win glory and the respect of his peers by bravery in war.

SPARTAN GOVERNMENT. The Spartan constitution was mixed, containing elements of monarchy, oligarchy, and democracy. There were two kings, whose power was limited by law and also by the rivalry that usually existed between the two royal houses. The origins and explanation of this unusual dual kingship are unknown, but both kings ruled together in Sparta and exercised equal powers. Their functions were chiefly religious and military. A Spartan army rarely left home without a king in command.

The oligarchic element was represented by a council of elders consisting of twenty-eight men over sixty, who were elected for life, and the kings. These elders had important judicial functions, sitting as a court in cases involving the kings. They also were consulted before any proposal was put before the assembly of Spartan citizens. In a traditional society like Sparta's, they must have had considerable influence.

The Spartan assembly consisted of all males over thirty. Theoretically they were the final authority, but because, in practice, debate was carried on by magistrates, elders, and kings alone, and because voting was usually by acclamation, the assembly's real function was to ratify decisions already taken or to decide between positions favored by the leading figures. In addition, Sparta had a unique institution, the board of ephors. This consisted of five men elected annually by the assembly. Originally they appear to have been intended to check the power of the kings, but gradually they acquired other important functions. They controlled foreign policy, oversaw the generalship of the kings on campaign, presided at the assembly, and guarded against rebellions by the Helots. The whole system was remarkable both for the way in which it combined participation by the citizenry with significant checks on its power and for its unmatched stability. Most Greeks admired the Spartan state for this quality and also for its ability to mold its citizens into a single pattern of men who subordinated themselves to an ideal. Many political philosophers, from Plato to modern times, have based utopian schemes on a version of the Spartan education and constitution.

By about 550 B.C. the Spartan system was well established, and its limitations were made plain. Suppression of the Helots required all the effort and energy that Sparta had. The Spartans could expand no further, but they could not allow unruly independent neighbors to cause unrest that might inflame the Helots. When the Spartans defeated Tegea, their northern neighbor, they imposed an unusual peace. Instead of taking away land and subjecting the defeated state, Sparta left the Tegeans their land and their freedom. In exchange they required the Tegeans to follow the Spartan lead in foreign affairs and to supply a fixed number of soldiers to Sparta on demand. This became the model for Spartan relations with the other states in the Peloponnesus, and soon Sparta was the leader of an alliance that included

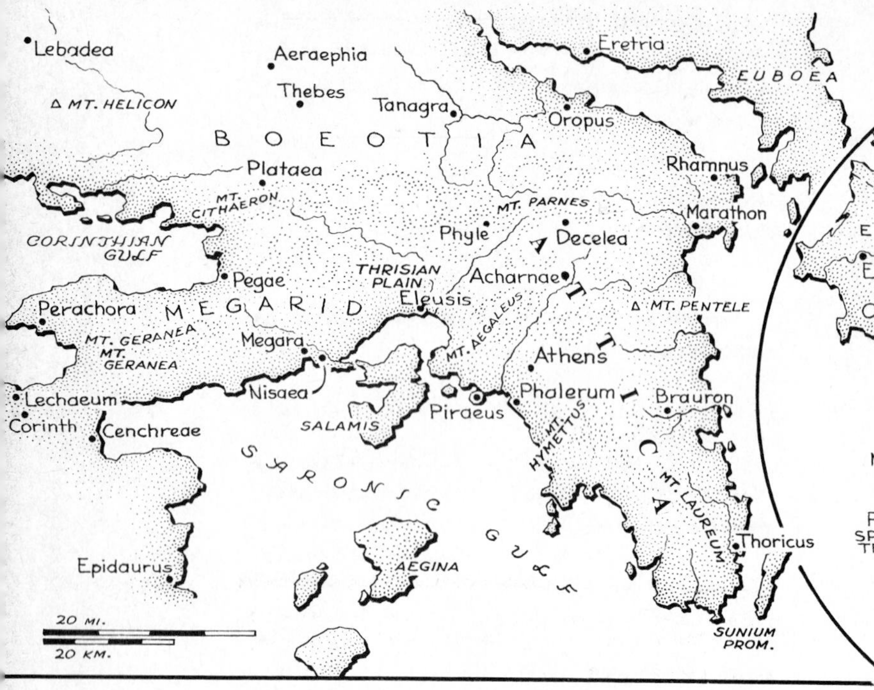

ATTICA AND VICINITY

MAPS 2-3, 2-4 *Citizens of all towns in Attica were also citizens of Athens. Sparta's region, Laconia, was in the Peloponnesus. Near-by states were members of the Peloponnesian League under Sparta's leadership.*

every Peloponnesian state but Argos; modern scholars have named this alliance the Peloponnesian League. It provided the Spartans with the security they needed, and it also made Sparta the most powerful *polis* in Hellenic history. By 500 B.C. Sparta and the league had given the Greeks a force capable of facing mighty threats from abroad.

Athens

Athens was slow to come into prominence and to join in the new activities that were changing the more advanced states, in part because Athens was not situated on the most favored trade routes of the eighth and seventh centuries B.C., in part because its large area (about one thousand square miles) allowed population growth without great pressure, and in part because the unification of the many villages and districts into a single *polis* was not completed until the seventh century B.C.

In the seventh century B.C. Athens was a typical aristocratic *polis*. The people were divided into four tribes and into a number of clans and brotherhoods (phratries). The aristocrats held the most and best land and dominated religious and political life. There was no written law, and decisions were rendered by powerful nobles on the basis of tradition and, most likely, self-interest. The state was governed by the Areopagus, a council of nobles deriving its name from the hill where it held its sessions. Annually the council elected nine magistrates, who joined the Areopagus after their year in office. Because they served for only a year, were checked by their colleagues, and looked forward to a lifetime as members of the Areopagus after their terms were ended, it is plain that the aristocratic council was the true master of the state.

In the seventh century B.C. the peaceful life of Athens experienced some disturbances, which were caused in part by quarrels within the nobility and in part by the beginnings of an agrarian crisis. In 632 B.C. a nobleman named Cylon attempted a coup to establish himself as tyrant. He was thwarted, but the unrest continued.

In 621 B.C. a man named Draco was given

special authority to codify and publish laws for the first time. In later years the penalties were thought to be harsh, hence the saying that Draco's laws were written in blood. We still speak of unusually harsh penalties as Draconian. Draco's work was probably limited to laws concerning homicide and was aimed at ending blood feuds between clans, but the precedent was important. The publication of law strengthened the hand of the state against the local power of the nobles.

The root of Athens' troubles was agricultural. Many Athenians worked family farms, from which they obtained most of their living. It appears that they planted wheat, the staple crop, year after year without rotating fields or using sufficient fertilizer. In time this procedure exhausted the soil and led to bad crops. To survive, the farmer had to borrow from his wealthy neighbor to get through the year. In return he promised one sixth of the next year's crop. The arrangement was marked by the deposit of an inscribed stone on the entailed farm. Bad harvests persisted, and soon the debtor had to pledge his wife and children and himself as surety for the loans needed for survival. As bad times continued, many Athenians defaulted and were enslaved. Some were even sold abroad. Revolutionary pressures grew among the poor, who began to demand the abolition of debt and a redistribution of the land.

Key Events in the Early History of Sparta and Athens

First Messenian War	ca. 725–710 B.C.
Second Messenian War	ca. 650–625 B.C.
Cylon tries to establish a tyranny at Athens	632 B.C.
Draco publishes legal code at Athens	621 B.C.
Solon institutes reforms at Athens	594 B.C.
Sparta defeats Tegea: Beginning of Peloponnesian League	ca. 560–550 B.C.
Pisistratus reigns as tyrant at Athens (main period)	546–527 B.C.
Hippias, son of Pisistratus, deposed as tyrant of Athens	510 B.C.
Clisthenes institutes reforms at Athens	ca. 508–501 B.C.

Solon. The circumstances might easily have brought about class warfare and tyranny, but the remarkable conciliatory spirit of Athens intervened. In the year 594 B.C., as tradition has it, the Athenians elected Solon as the only archon, with extraordinary powers to legislate and revise the constitution. Immediately he attacked the agrarian problem by canceling current debts and forbidding future loans secured by the person of the borrower. He helped bring back many Athenians enslaved abroad as well as freeing those in Athens enslaved for debt. This program was called the "shaking off of burdens." It did not, however, solve the fundamental economic problem, and Solon did not redistribute the land. In the short run, therefore, he did not put an end to the economic crisis, but his other economic actions had profound success in the long run. He forbade the export of wheat and encouraged that of olive oil. This policy had the effect of making wheat more available in Attica and encouraging the cultivation of olive oil and wine as cash crops. By the fifth century B.C. this form of agriculture had become so profitable that much Athenian land was diverted from grain production to the cultivation of cash crops, and Athens became dependent on imported wheat. Solon also changed the Athenian standards of weights and measures to conform with those of Corinth and Euboea and the cities of the East. This change also encouraged commerce and turned Athens in the direction that would lead her to great prosperity in the fifth century. He also encouraged industry by offering citizenship to foreign artisans, and his success is reflected in the development of the outstanding Attic pottery of the sixth century. Solon also significantly changed the constitution. All male adults whose fathers were citizens were citizens, too, and to their number he added those immigrants who were offered citizenship. All these Athenian citizens were divided into four classes on the basis of wealth, measured by annual agricultural production. Men whose property produced 500 measures were called 500-measure men, and those producing 300 measures were called cavalry; these two classes alone could hold the archonship, the chief magistracy in Athens, and sit on the Areopagus. Producers of 200 measures were called owners of a team of oxen; these were allowed to serve as hoplites. They could be elected to the council of 400 chosen by all the citizens, 100 from each tribe. Solon seems to have meant this council to serve as a check on the Areopagus and to prepare any business that

Solon Discusses the Virtues of Good Government

The Athenians appointed Solon to revise their constitution in the year 594–593 B.C. He explained and defended his policies in excellent verse. In the following selection he made the most powerful claims for the benefits of a well-ordered city-state governed by good laws.

Thus the public Ruin invades the house of each citizen,
and the courtyard doors no longer have strength to keep it away,
but it overleaps the lofty wall, and though a man runs in
and tries to hide in chamber or closet, it ferrets him out.
So my spirit dictates to me: I must tell the Athenians
how many evils a city suffers from Bad Government,
and how Good Government displays all neatness and order,
and many times she must put shackles on the breakers of laws.
She levels rough places, stops Glut and Greed, takes the force from Violence;
she dries up the growing flowers of Despair as they grow;
she straightens out crooked judgments given, gentles the swollen
ambitions, and puts an end to acts of divisional strife;
she stills the gall of wearisome Hate, and under her influence
all life among mankind is harmonious and does well.

Greek Lyrics, trans. by Richmond Lattimore, (Chicago: University of Chicago Press, 1960), p. 21.

needed to be put before the assembly. The last class, producing less than 200 measures, were the *thetes.* They voted in the popular assembly for the archons and the council members and on any other business brought before them by the magistrates. They also sat on the new popular court established by Solon. At first, it must have had little power, for most cases continued to be heard in the country by local barons and in Athens by the aristocratic Areopagus. But the new court was recognized as a court of appeal, and by the fifth century B.C. almost all cases came before the popular courts.

PISISTRATUS. Solon's efforts to avoid factional strife failed. Within a few years contention reached such a degree that no archons could be chosen. Out of this turmoil emerged the first Athenian tyranny. Pisistratus, a nobleman, faction leader, and military hero, briefly seized power in 560 B.C. and again in 556 B.C., but each time his support was inadequate and he was driven out. At last, in 546 B.C. he came back at the head of a mercenary army from abroad and established a tyranny that lasted beyond his death, in 527 B.C., until the expulsion of his son Hippias in 510 B.C. In many respects Pisistratus resembled the other Greek tyrants. His rule rested on the force provided by mercenary soldiers. He engaged in great programs of public works, urban improvement, and religious piety. Temples were built and religious centers expanded and improved. New religious festivals were introduced, such as the one dedicated to Dionysus, the god of fertility, wine, and ecstatic religious worship imported from Phrygia in Asia Minor. Old ones, like the Great Panathenaic festival, were amplified and given greater public appeal. Poets and artists were supported to add cultural luster to the court of the tyrant.

Pisistratus aimed at increasing the power of the central government at the expense of the nobles. The festival of Dionysus and the Great Panathenaic festival helped fix attention on the capital city, as did the new temples and the reconstruction of the Agora as the center of public life. Circuit judges were sent out into the country to hear cases, another feature that weakened the power of the local barons. All this time Pisistratus made no formal change in the Solonian constitution. Assembly, councils,

Aristogeiton and Harmodius. These Athenian aristocrats were slain in 514 B.C. *after assassinating Hipparchos, brother of the tyrant Hippias. After the overthrow of the Pisistratids in* 510 B.C., *the Athenians erected a famous statue to honor their memory. This is a Roman copy.* [*Naples, National Museum—Alinari/Art Resource*]

and courts met; magistrates and councils were elected; Pisistratus merely saw to it that his supporters were chosen. The intended effect was to blunt the sharp edge of tyranny with the appearance of constitutional government, and it worked. The rule of Pisistratus was remembered as popular and mild. The unintended effect was to give the Athenians more experience in the procedures of self-government and a growing taste for it.

INVASION BY SPARTA. Pisistratus was succeeded by his oldest son, Hippias, who followed his father's ways at first. In 514 B.C., however, his brother Hipparchus was murdered as a result of a private quarrel. Hippias became nervous, suspicious, and harsh. At last one of the noble clans exiled by the sons of Pisistratus, the Alcmaeonids, won favor with the influential oracle at Delphi and used its support to persuade Sparta to attack the Athenian tyranny. Led by their ambitious king, Cleomenes I, the Spartans marched into Attica in 510 B.C. and deposed Hippias, who went into exile to the Persian court. The tyranny was over.

The Spartans must have hoped to leave Athens in friendly hands, and indeed Cleomenes' friend Isagoras held the leading position in Athens after the withdrawal of the Spartan army, but he was not unopposed. Clisthenes of the restored Alcmaeonid clan was his chief rival but lost out in the political struggle among the noble factions. Isagoras seems to have tried to restore a version of the pre-Solonian aristocratic state. As part of his plan he carried through a purification of the citizen lists, removing those who had been enfranchised by Solon or Pisistratus and any others thought to have a doubtful claim. Clisthenes then took an unprecedented action by turning to the people for political support and won it with a program of great popular appeal. In response Isagoras called in the Spartans again; Cleomenes arrived and allowed the expulsion from Athens of Clisthenes and a large number of his supporters. But the Athenian political consciousness, ignited by Solon and kept alive under Pisistratus, was fanned by the popular appeal of Clisthenes. The people would not hear of an aristocratic restoration and drove out the Spartans and Isagoras with them. Clisthenes and his allies returned, ready to put their program into effect.

CLISTHENES. A central aim of Clisthenes' reforms was to diminish the influence of traditional localities and regions in Athenian life, for these were an important source of power for the nobility and of factions in the state. He made the deme, the equivalent of a small town in the country or a ward in the city, the basic unit of civic life. It was a purely political unit that elected its own officers. Henceforth enrollment in the deme replaced enrollment in the phratry (where tradition and noble birth dominated) as evidence of Athenian citizenship.

Clisthenes immediately enrolled the disenfranchised who had supported him in the struggle with Isagoras. The demes, which ultimately reached about 175 in number, were divided into ten new tribes that replaced the traditional four. The composition of each tribe guaranteed that no region would dominate any of them. Because the tribes had common religious activities and fought as regimental units, the new organization would also increase devotion to the *polis* and diminish regional divisions and personal loyalty to local barons.

A new council of 500 was invented to replace the Solonian council of 400. Each tribe elected 50 councilors each year, and no one could serve more than twice. The council's main responsibility was to prepare legislation for discussion by the assembly, but it also had important financial duties and received foreign emissaries. Final authority in all things rested with the assembly composed of all adult male Athenian citizens. Debate was free and open; any Athenian could submit legislation, offer amendments, or argue the merits of any question. In practice political leaders did most of the talking, and we may imagine that in the early days the council had more authority than it did after the Athenians became more confident in their new self-government. It is fair to call Clisthenes the father of Athenian democracy. He did not alter the property qualifications of Solon, but his enlargement of the citizen rolls, his diminution of the power of the aristocrats, and his elevation of the role of the assembly, with its effective and manageable council, all give him a firm claim to that title.

As a result of the work of Solon, Pisistratus, and Clisthenes, Athens entered the fifth century B.C. well on the way to prosperity and democracy, much more centralized and united than it had been, and ready to take its place among the major states that would lead the defense of Greece against the dangers that lay ahead.

Aspects of Culture in Archaic Greece

Religion

Like most ancient peoples, the Greeks were polytheists, and religion played an important part in their lives. A great part of Greek art and literature was closely connected with religion,

The temple of Apollo at Delphi, the oldest and holiest site in Greece. For centuries, pilgrims came from all over the Mediterranean to consult Appllo's oracle at Delphi. [*Alinari-Scala/Art Resource*]

as was the life of the *polis* in general. The Greek pantheon consisted of the twelve gods who lived on Mount Olympus: Zeus, the father of the gods; his wife, Hera; his brother, Poseidon, god of the seas and earthquakes; his sisters, Hestia, goddess of the hearth, and Demeter, goddess of agriculture and marriage; and his children—Aphrodite, goddess of love and beauty; Apollo, god of the sun, music, poetry, and prophecy; Ares, god of war; Artemis, goddess of the moon and the hunt; Athena, goddess of wisdom and the arts; Hephaestus, god of fire and metallurgy; and Hermes; messenger of the gods and connected with commerce and cunning.

On the one hand, these gods were seen as behaving very much as mortals behaved, with all the human foibles, except that they were superhuman in these as well as in their strength and immortality. On the other hand, Zeus, at least, was seen as being a source of human justice, and even the Olympians were understood to be subordinate to the Fates. Each *polis* had one of the Olympians as its guardian deity and worshiped the god in its own special way, but all the gods were Panhellenic. In the eighth and seventh centuries B.C. common shrines were established at Olympia for the worship of Zeus, at Delphi for Apollo, at the Isthmus of Corinth for Poseidon, and at Nemea once again for Zeus. Each held athletic contests in honor of its god, to which all Greeks were invited and for which a sacred truce was declared.

Besides the Olympians, the Greeks also worshiped countless lesser deities connected with local shrines and even heroes, humans real or legendary who had accomplished great deeds and had earned immortality and divine status. The worship of these deities was not a very emotional experience. It was a matter of offering prayer, libations, and gifts in return for protection and favors from the god during the lifetime of the worshiper. There was no hope of immortality for the average human and little moral teaching. Plato, in fact, at a later date, suggested that the poets be banned from the state because the tales they told of the gods were immoral and corrupting for humans. Most Greeks seem to have held to the commonsense notion that justice lay in paying one's debts; that civic virtue consisted of worshiping the state deities in the traditional way, performing required public services, and fighting in defense of the state; and that private morality meant to do good to one's friends and harm to one's enemies. In the sixth century B.C. the influence of the cult of Apollo at Delphi and of his oracle there became very great. The oracle was the most important of several that helped satisfy human craving for a clue to the future. The priests of Apollo preached moderation; their advice was exemplified in the two famous sayings identified with Apollo: "Know thyself" and "Nothing in excess." Humans needed self-control (*sophrosynē*). Its opposite was arrogance (*hubris*), which was brought on by excessive wealth or good fortune. *Hubris* led to moral blindness and finally to divine vengeance. This theme of moderation and the dire consequences of its absence was central to Greek popular morality and appears frequently in Greek literature.

The somewhat cold religion of the Olympian

The god Dionysus dancing with two female followers. The vase was painted in the sixth century B.C. *[Bibliotheque Nationale, Paris]*

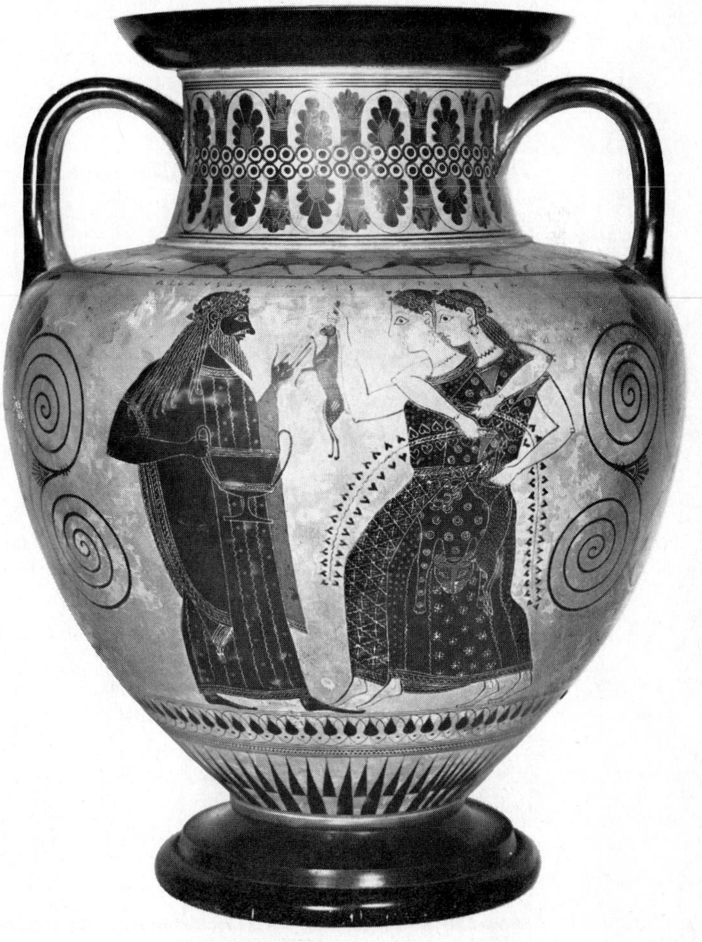

gods and of the cult of Apollo did little to attend to human fears, hopes, and passions. For these needs the Greeks turned to other deities and rites. Of these the most popular was Dionysus, a god of nature and fertility, of the grape vine and drunkenness and sexual abandon. In some of his rites the god was followed by maenads, female devotees who cavorted by night, ate raw flesh, and were reputed to tear to pieces any creature they came across.

Poetry

The great changes sweeping through the Greek world were also reflected in the poetry of the sixth century B.C. The lyric style, whether sung by a chorus or by one singer, predominated. Sappho of Lesbos, Anacreon of Teos, and Simonides of Cos composed personal poetry, often speaking of the pleasure and agony of love. Alcaeus of Mytilene, an aristocrat driven from his city by a tyrant, wrote bitter invective. Perhaps the most interesting poet of the century from a political point of view was Theognis of Megara. He was an aristocrat who lived through a tyranny, an unusually chaotic and violent democracy, and an oligarchy that restored order but ended the rule of the old aristocracy. Theognis was the spokesman for the old, defeated aristocracy of birth. He divided everyone into two classes, the noble and the base; the former were the good, the latter bad. Those nobly born must associate only with others like themselves if they were to preserve their virtue; if they mingled with the base, they became base. Those born base, on the other hand, could never become noble. Only nobles could aspire to virtue, and only nobles possessed the critical moral and intellectual qualities, respect or honor and judgment. These qualities could not be taught; they were innate. Even so they had to be carefully

Theognis of Megara Gives Advice to a Young Aristocrat

Theognis was born about 580 B.C. and lived to see his native city Megara torn by social upheaval and civil war. His poems present the political and ethical ideas of the Greek aristocracy.

Do not consort with bad men, but always hold to the good. Eat and drink with them, whose power is great, sit with them and please them. You will learn good from good men, but if you mingle with the bad you will lose such wisdom as you already have. Therefore consort with the good and one day you will say that I give good advice to my friends.

We seek thoroughbred rams, asses, and horses, Cyrnus, and a man wants offspring of good breeding. But in marriage a good man does not decline to marry the bad daughter of a bad father, if he gives him much wealth. Nor does the wife of a bad man refuse to be his bedfellow if he be rich, preferring wealth to goodness. For they value possessions and a good man marries a woman of bad stock and the bad a woman of good. Wealth mixes the breed. So do not wonder, son of Polypaus, that the race of your citizens is obscured since bad things are mixed with good.

It is easier to beget and rear a man than to put good sense into him. No one has ever discovered a way to make a fool wise or a bad man good. If God had given the sons of Asclepius the knowledge to heal the evil nature and mischievous mind of man, great and frequent would be their pay. If thought could be made and put into a man, the son of a good man would never become bad, since he would obey good counsel. But you will never make the bad man good by teaching.

The best thing the gods give to men, Cyrnus, is judgment, judgment contains the ends of everything. O happy is the man who has it in his mind; it is much greater than destructive insolence and grievous satiety. There are no evils among mortals worse than these—for every evil, Cyrnus, comes out of them.

Trans. by Donald Kagan in *Sources in Greek Political Thought,* ed. by D. Kagan (New York: Free Press, 1965), pp. 39–40.

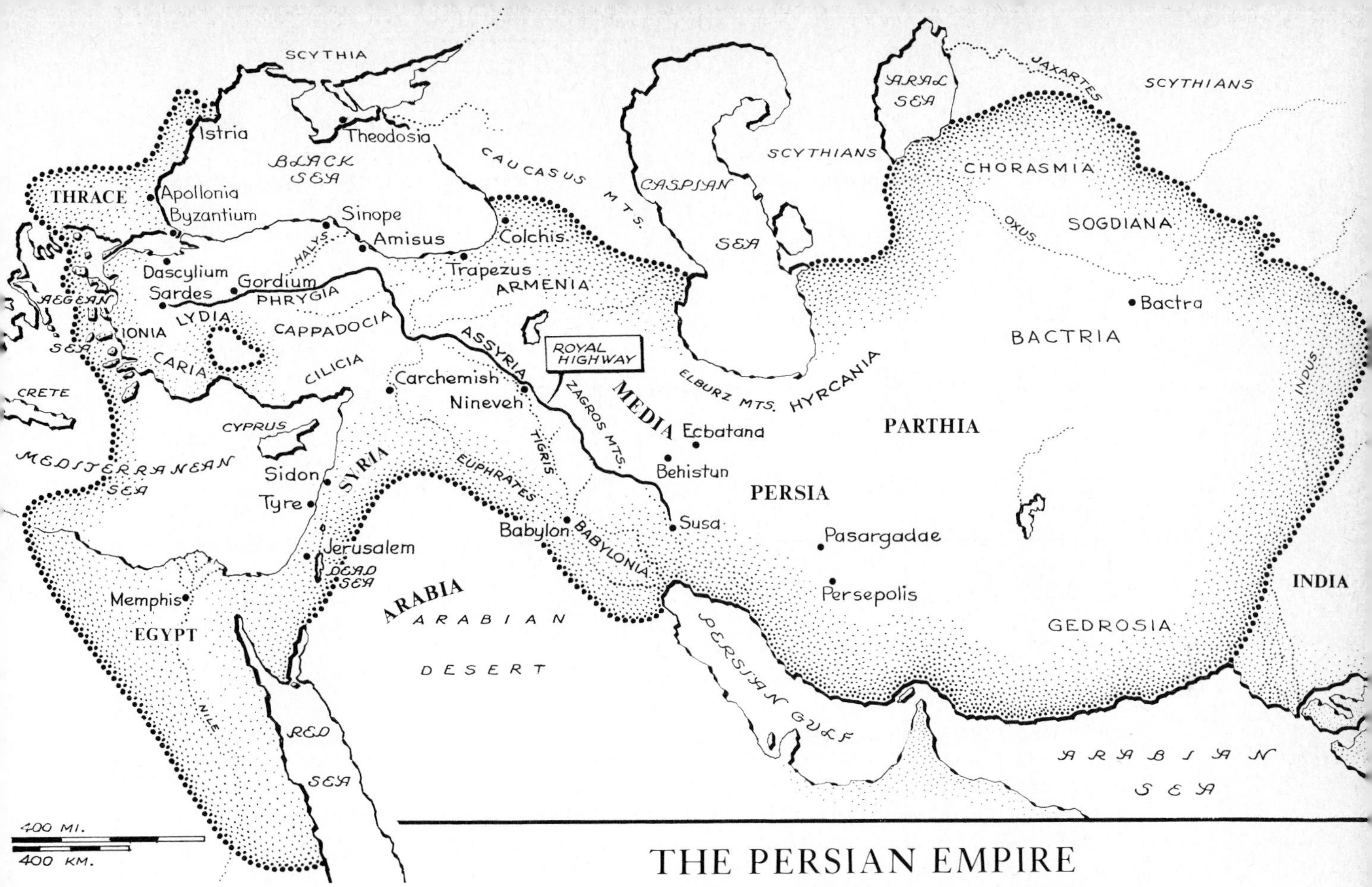

THE PERSIAN EMPIRE

MAP 2-5 *The empire created by Cyrus had fullest extent under Darius when Persia attacked Greece in* 490 B.C. *It reached from India to the Aegean—and even into Europe—including the lands formerly ruled by Egyptians, Hittites, Babylonians, and Assyrians.*

guarded against corruption by wealth or by mingling with the base. Intermarriage between the noble and the base was especially condemned. These were the ideas of the unreconstructed nobility, whose power had been destroyed or reduced in most Greek states by this time. These ideas remained alive in aristocratic hearts throughout the next century and greatly influenced later thinkers, Plato, again, among them.

The Persian Wars

The Greeks' period of fortunate isolation and freedom at last came to an end. They had established colonies along most of the coast of Asia Minor from as early as the eleventh century B.C. The colonies maintained friendly relations with the mainland but developed a flourishing economic and cultural life, independent of their mother cities and of their Oriental neighbors. In the middle of the sixth century B.C., however, these Greek cities of Asia Minor came under the control of Lydia and its king, Croesus (ca. 560–546 B.C.). The Lydian rule seems not to have been very harsh, but the Persian conquest of Lydia in 546 B.C. brought a subjugation that was less pleasant. The Persian Empire had been created in a single generation by Cyrus the Great. In 559 B.C. he came to the throne of Persia, then a small kingdom well to the east of the lower Mesopotamian valley; unified Persia under his rule; made an alliance with Babylonia; and led a successful rebellion toward the north against the Medes, who were the overlords of Persia (see Map 2.5). In succeeding years he expanded his empire in all directions, in the process defeating Croesus and occupying Lydia. Most of the Greek cities

The Rise of Persia	
Reign of Cyrus the Great	559–530 B.C.
Persians conquer Lydia	546 B.C.
Reign of Cambyses	530–522 B.C.
Civil war in Persia	522–521 B.C.
Reign of Darius	521–485 B.C.
Reign of Xerxes	485–465 B.C.

of Asia Minor sided with Croesus and resisted the Persians. By about 540 B.C., however, they had all been subdued. The western part of Asia Minor was divided into three provinces, each under its own satrap, or governor.

The Persians required their subjects to pay tribute and to serve in the Persian army. They ruled the Greek cities through local individuals, who governed their cities as "tyrants." The Ionians had been moving in the direction of democracy and were not pleased with monarchical rule, but most of the "tyrants" were not harsh, the Persian tribute was not excessive, and there was general prosperity. Neither the death of Cyrus fighting on a distant frontier in 530 B.C. nor the suicide of his successor, Cambyses, nor the civil war that followed it in 522–521 B.C. produced any disturbance in the Greek cities. Darius found Ionia perfectly obedient when he emerged as Great King in 521 B.C.

The Ionian Rebellion

The private troubles of the ambitious tyrant of Miletus, Aristagoras, started the rebellion. He had urged a Persian expedition against the island of Naxos; when it failed, he feared the consequences and organized the Ionian rebellion of 499 B.C. To gain support, he overthrew the tyrannies and proclaimed democratic constitutions. Then he turned to the mainland states for help. As the most powerful Greek state, Sparta was naturally the first stop, but the Spartans would have none of Aristagoras' promises of easy victory and great wealth. Sparta had no close ties with the Ionians and no national interest in the region, and the thought of leaving an undefended Sparta to the Helots while the army was far off for a long time was terrifying.

Aristagoras next sought help at Athens, and there the assembly agreed and voted to send a fleet of twenty ships to help the rebels. The Athenians were Ionians and had close ties of religion and tradition with the rebels. Besides, Hippias, the deposed tyrant of Athens, was an honored guest at the court of Darius, and the Great King (as the Persian rulers styled themselves) had already made it plain that he favored the tyrant's restoration. The Persians,

Persian nobles paying homage to King Darius, from the treasury at Persepolis. Darius is seated on the throne; his son and successor Xerxes stands behind him. Darius and Xerxes are carved in larger scale to indicate their royal status. [Courtesy of the Oriental Institute, University of Chicago]

Greek hoplite attacking a Persian soldier. The contrast between the Greek's metal body armor, large shield, and long spear and the Persian's cloth and leather garments indicates one reason the Greeks won. This Attic vase was found on Rhodes and dates from ca. 475 B.C. [*The Metropolitan Museum of Art, Rogers Fund,* 1906]

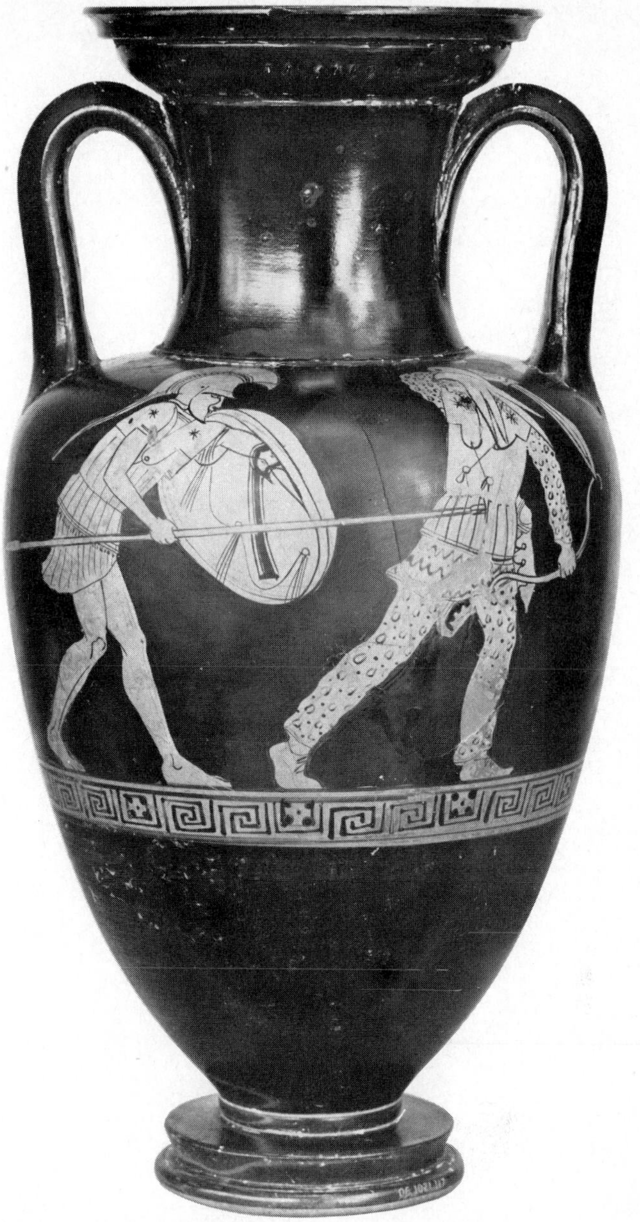

moreover, controlled both sides of the Hellespont, the route to the grain fields beyond the Black Sea, which were increasingly vital to Athens. Perhaps some Athenians already feared that a Persian attempt to conquer the Greek mainland was only a matter of time. The Athenian expedition was strengthened by five ships from Eretria in Euboea, which participated out of gratitude for past favors.

In 498 B.C. the Athenians and their allies made a swift march and a surprise attack on Sardis, the old capital of Lydia and now the seat of the satrap, and burned it. This action caused the revolt to spread throughout the Greek cities of Asia Minor outside Ionia, but the Ionians could not follow it up. The Athenians withdrew and took no further part, and gradually the Persians imposed their will. In 495 B.C. they defeated the Ionian fleet at Lade, and in the next year they wiped out Miletus. Many of the men were killed, others were transported to the Persian Gulf, and the women and children were enslaved. The Ionian rebellion was over.

The War in Greece

In 490 B.C. the Persians launched an expedition directly across the Aegean to punish Eretria and Athens, to restore Hippias, and to gain control of the Aegean Sea (see Map 2.6). The force of infantry and cavalry under the command of Datis and Artaphernes landed first at Naxos and destroyed it for its successful resistance in 499 B.C. Then they destroyed Eretria and deported its people deep into the interior of Persia.

The Athenians chose to risk the fate of Eretria rather than submit to Persia and restore the hated tyranny. The resistance was led by Miltiades, an Athenian and an outstanding soldier who had fled from Persian service after earning the anger of Darius. His knowledge of the Persian army and his distaste for submission to Persia made him an ideal leader. He led the army to Marathon and won a decisive victory. The battle at Marathon (490 B.C.) was of

THE GREEK WARS AGAINST PERSIA

Greek cities of Asia Minor conquered by Croesus of Lydia	ca. 560–546 B.C.
Cyrus of Persia conquers Lydia and gains control of Greek cities	546 B.C.
Greek cities rebel (Ionian rebellion)	499–494 B.C.
Battle of Marathon	490 B.C.
Xerxes' invasion of Greece	480–479 B.C.
Battles of Thermopylae, Artemisium, and Salamis	480 B.C.
Battles of Plataea and Mycale	479 B.C.

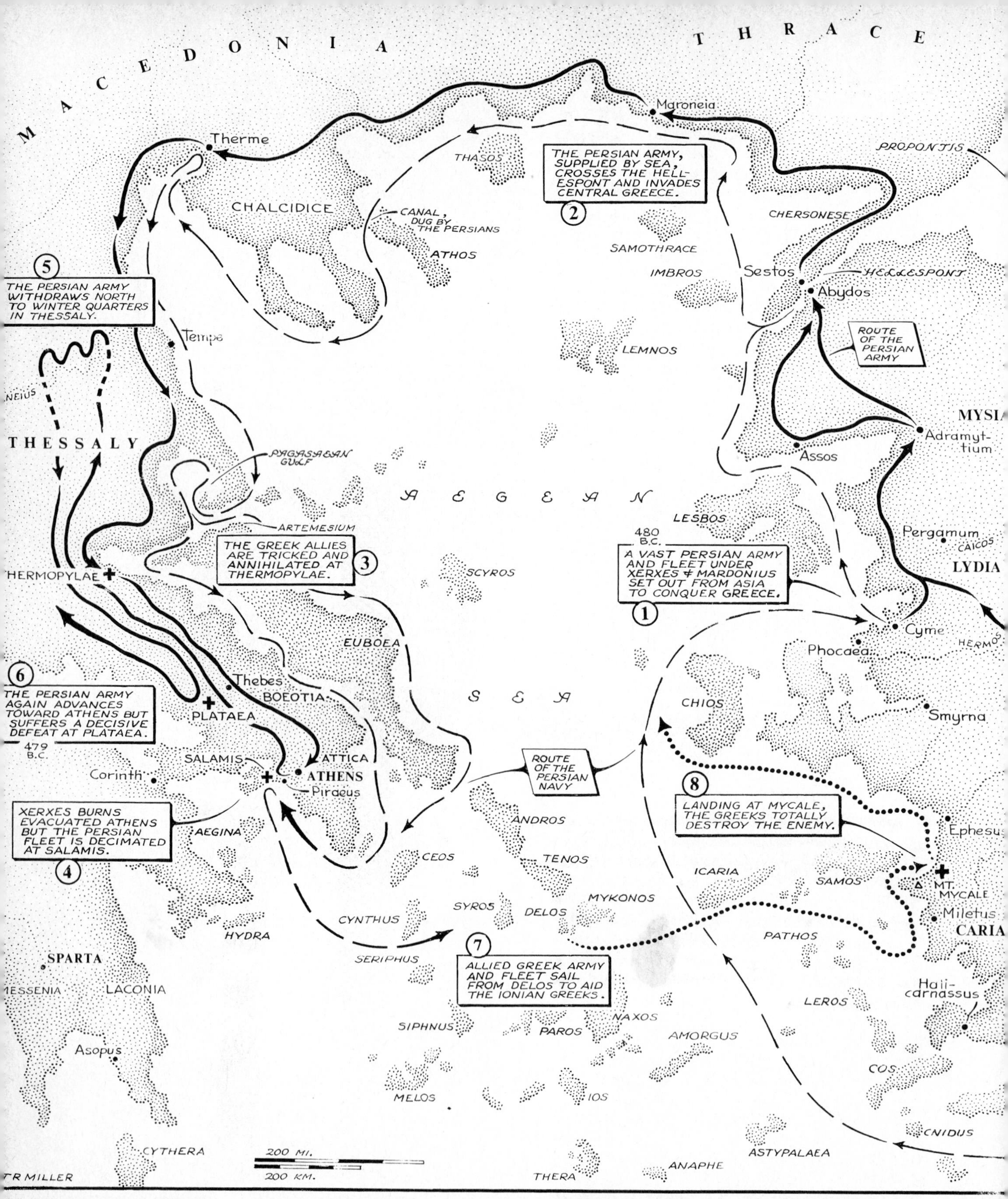

THE PERSIAN INVASION OF GREECE

MAP 2-6 *This map traces the route taken by the Persian King Xerxes in his invasion of Greece in 480* B.C. *The solid lines show movements of his army, the broken lines of his fleet.*

enormous importance to the future of Greek civilization. A Persian victory would have destroyed Athenian freedom, and the conquest of all the mainland Greeks would have followed. The greatest achievements of Greek culture, most of which lay in the future, would have been impossible under Persian rule. The Athenian victory, on the other hand, made a positive contribution to those achievements. It instilled in the Athenians a sense of confidence and pride in their *polis,* their unique form of government, and themselves.

For the Persians Marathon was only a small and temporary defeat, but it was annoying. Internal troubles, however, prevented swift revenge. In 481 B.C. Darius' successor, Xerxes, gathered an army of at least 150,000 men and a navy of more than six hundred ships for the conquest of Greece. The Greeks did not make good use of the delay, but Athens was an exception. Themistocles had become its leading politician, and he had always wanted to turn Athens into a naval power. The first step was to build a fortified port at Piraeus during his archonship in 493 B.C. A decade later the Athenians came upon a rich vein of silver in the state mines, and Themistocles persuaded them to use the profits to increase their fleet. By 480 B.C. Athens had over two hundred ships, the backbone of the navy that defeated the Persians.

As the Persian army gathered south of the Hellespont, only thirty-one Greek states out of hundreds were willing to fight. They were led by Sparta, Athens, Corinth, and Aegina. In the spring of 480 B.C. Xerxes launched his invasion. The Persian strategy was to march into Greece, destroy Athens, defeat the Greek army, and add the Greeks to the number of Persian subjects. The huge Persian army needed to keep in touch with the fleet for supplies. If the Greeks could defeat the Persian navy, the army could not remain in Greece long. Themistocles knew that the Aegean was subject to sudden devastating storms. His strategy was to delay the Persian army and then to bring on the kind of naval battle he might hope to win.

The Greek League, founded specifically to resist this Persian invasion, met at Corinth as the Persians were ready to cross the Hellespont. They chose Sparta as leader on land and sea and sent a force to Tempe to try to defend Thessaly. Tempe proved to be indefensible, so the Greeks retreated and took up new positions at Thermopylae (the "hot gates") on land and off Artemisium at sea. The opening between the mountains and the sea at Thermopylae was so narrow that it might be held by a smaller army against a much larger one. The Spartans sent their king, Leonidas, with three hundred of their own citizens and enough allies to make a total of about nine thousand. The Greeks may have intended to hold only long enough to permit the Athenians to evacuate Athens, or to force a sea battle, or they may have hoped to hold Thermopylae until the Persians were dis-

A bronze helmet dedicated to Zeus by Miltiades to commemorate the Athenian victory over the Persians in 490 B.C. [*German Archaelogical Institute, Athens*]

These potsherds from fifth-century B.C. *Athens are inscribed with the names of two famous Athenian statesmen, Themistocles, son of Neocles, and Aristides, son of Lysimachus. At different times each man was banished from Athens for ten years.* [*Agora Excavations, American School of Classical Studies at Athens*]

couraged enough to withdraw. Perhaps they thought of all these possibilities, for they were not mutually contradictory.

Severe storms wrecked a large number of Persian ships while the Greek fleet waited safely in their protected harbor. Then Xerxes attacked Thermopylae, and for two days the Greeks butchered his best troops without serious loss to themselves. On the third day, however, a traitor showed the Persians a mountain trail that permitted them to come on the Greeks from behind. Many allies escaped, but Leonidas and his three hundred Spartans died to the last man. At about the same time the Greek and Persian fleets fought an indecisive battle, and the fall of Thermopylae forced the Greek navy to withdraw.

If an inscription discovered in 1959 is authentic, Themistocles had foreseen this possibility, and the Athenians had begun to evacuate their homeland and move to defend Salamis. The fate of Greece was decided in the narrow waters to the east of the island. Themistocles persuaded the reluctant Pelopon-

The Athenian Assembly Passes Themistocles' Emergency Decree

The following is a translation of a portion of the Themistocles decree.

The Gods

Resolved by the Council and the People

Themistocles, son of Neokles, of Phrearroi, made the motion:

To entrust the city to Athena the Mistress of Athens and to all the other Gods to guard and defend from the Barbarian for the sake of the land. The Athenians themselves and the foreigners who live in Athens are to send their children and women to safety in Troizen, their protector being Pittheus, the founding hero of the land. They are to send the old men and their movable possessions to safety on Salamis. The treasurers and priestesses are to remain on the acropolis guarding the property of the gods.

All the other Athenians and foreigners of military age are to embark on the 200 ships that are ready and defend against the Barbarian for the sake of their own freedom and that of the rest of the Greeks along with the Lakedaimonians, the Korinthians, the Aiginetans, and all others who wish to share the danger. . . .

When the ships have been manned, with 100 of them they are to meet the enemy at Artemision in Euboia, and with the other 100 they are to lie off Salamis and the coast of Attica and keep guard over the land. In order that all Athenians may be united in their defense against the Barbarian those who have been sent into exile for ten years are to go to Salamis and to stay there until the People come to some decision about them, while those who have been deprived of citizen rights are to have their rights restored. . . .

Trans. by M. H. Jameson in "Waiting for the Barbarian," *Greece and Rome,* Second Series, Vol. 8 (Oxford: Clarendon Press, 1961), pp. 5–18.

nesians to stay by threatening to remove all the Athenians and settle anew in Italy; the Spartans knew that they and the other Greeks could not hope to win without the aid of the Athenians. The Greek ships were fewer, slower, and less maneuverable than those of the Persians, so the Greeks put soldiers on their ships and relied chiefly on hand-to-hand combat. The Persians lost more than half their ships and retreated to Asia with a good part of their army, but the danger was not over yet. The Persian general Mardonius spent the winter in central Greece, and in the spring he unsuccessfully tried to win the Athenians away from the Greek League. The Spartan regent, Pausanias, then led the largest Greek army up to that time to confront Mardonius in Boeotia. At Plataea, in the summer of 479 B.C., Mardonius died in battle and his army fled toward home.

Meanwhile the Ionian Greeks urged King Leotychidas, the Spartan commander of the fleet, to fight the Persian fleet at Samos. At Mycale, on the coast nearby, Leotychidas destroyed the Persian camp and its fleet offshore. The Persians fled the Aegean and Ionia. For the moment, at least, the Persian threat was gone.

Suggested Readings

A. ANDREWES, *Greek Tyrants* (1963). A clear and concise account of tyranny in early Greece.

A. ANDREWES, *The Greeks* (1967). A thoughtful general survey.

JOHN BOARDMAN, *The Greeks Overseas* (1964). A study of the relations between the Greeks and other peoples.

A. R. BURN, *The Lyric Age of Greece* (1960). A discussion of early Greece that uses the evidence of poetry and archaeology to fill out the sparse historical record.

J. B. BURY and R. MEIGGS, *A History of Greece*, 4th ed. (1975). A thorough and detailed one-volume narrative history.

E. R. DODDS, *The Greeks and the Irrational* (1955). An excellent account of the role of the supernatural in Greek life and thought.

V. EHRENBERG, *The Greek State* (1964). A good handbook of constitutional history.

V. EHRENBERG, *From Solon to Socrates* (1968). An interpretive history that makes good use of Greek literature to illuminate politics.

J. V. A. FINE, *The Ancient Greeks* (1983). An excellent survey that discusses historical problems and the evidence that gives rise to them.

M. I. FINLEY, *World of Odysseus*, rev. ed. (1965). A fascinating attempt to reconstruct Homeric society.

M. I. FINLEY, *Early Greece* (1970). A succinct interpretive study.

W. G. FORREST, *The Emergence of Greek Democracy* (1966). A lively interpretation of Greek social and political developments in the archaic period.

W. G. FORREST, *A History of Sparta*, 950–192 B.C. (1968). A brief but shrewd account.

P. GREEN, *Xerxes at Salamis* (1970). A lively and stimulating history of the Persian wars.

C. HIGNETT, *A History of the Athenian Constitution* (1952). A scholarly account, somewhat too skeptical of the ancient sources.

C. HIGNETT, *Xerxes' Invasion of Greece* (1963). A valuable account, but too critical of all sources other than Herodotus.

S. HOOD, *The Minoans* (1971). A sketch of Bronze Age civilization on Crete.

D. KAGAN, *The Great Dialogue: A History of Greek Political Thought from Homer to Polybius* (1965). A discussion of the relationship between the Greek historical experience and political theory.

G. S. KIRK, *The Songs of Homer* (1962). A discussion of the Homeric epics as oral poetry.

H. D. F. KITTO, *The Greeks* (1951). A personal and illuminating interpretation of Greek culture.

H. L. LORIMER, *Homer and the Monuments* (1950). A study of the relationship between the Homeric poems and the evidence of archaeology.

H. MICHELL, *Sparta* (1952). A study of Spartan institutions.

O. MURRAY, *Early Greece* (1980). A lively and imaginative account of the early history of Greece to the end of the Persian War.

A. T. OLMSTEAD, *History of the Persian Empire* (1960). A thorough survey.

D. L. PAGE, *History and the Homeric Iliad*, 2nd ed. (1966). A well-written and interesting, if debatable, attempt to place the Trojan War in a historical setting.

G. M. A. RICHTER, *Archaic Greek Art* (1949).

CARL ROEBUCK, *Ionian Trade and Colonization* (1959). An introduction to the history of the Greeks in the east.

B. SNELL, *Discovery of the Mind* (1960). An important study of Greek intellectual development.

A. M. SNODGRASS, *The Dark Age of Greece* (1972). A good examination of the archaeological evidence.

C. G. STARR, *Origins of Greek Civilization* 1100–650 B.C. (1961). An interesting interpretation based largely on archaeology and especially on pottery styles.

C. G. STARR, *The Economic and Social Growth of Early Greece*, 800–500 B.C. (1977).

EMILY VERMEULE, *Greece in the Bronze Age* (1972). A study of the Mycenaean period.

A. G. WOODHEAD, *Greeks in the West* (1962). An account of the Greek settlements in Italy and Sicily.

W. J. WOODHOUSE, *Solon the Liberator* (1965). A discussion of the great Athenian reformer.

Apollo, detail of a statue of the god found at the temple of Zeus at Olympia, ca. 460 B.C. *To the Greeks, Apollo was the radiant spirit of order, clarity, and reason.* [*Hirmer Fotoarchive, Munich*]

3

Classical and Hellenistic Greece

The Delian League

THE UNITY OF THE GREEKS had shown strain even in the life-and-death struggle against the Persians. Within two years of the Persian retreat it gave way almost completely and yielded to a division of the Greek world into two spheres of influence, dominated by Sparta and Athens. The need of the Ionian Greeks to obtain and defend their freedom from Persia and the desire of many Greeks to gain revenge and financial reparation for the Persian attack brought on the split.

Sparta had led the Greeks to victory, and it was natural to look to the Spartans to continue the campaign. But Sparta was ill suited to the task, which required a long-term commitment far from the Peloponnesus and continuous naval action.

The emergence of Athens as the leader of a Greek coalition against Persia was a natural development. Athens had become the leading naval power in Greece, and the same motives that had led her to support the Ionian revolt moved her to try to drive the Persians from the Aegean and the Hellespont. The Ionians were at least as eager for the Athenians to take the helm as the Athenians were to accept the responsibility and opportunity.

In the winter of 478–477 B.C. the islanders, the Greeks from the coast of Asia Minor, and some other Greek cities on the Aegean met with the Athenians on the sacred island of Delos and swore oaths of alliance. As a symbol that the alliance was meant to be permanent, they dropped lumps of iron into the sea; the alliance was to hold until these lumps of iron rose to the surface. The aims of this new Delian League were to free those Greeks who were under Persian rule, to protect all against a Persian return, and to obtain compensation from the Persians by attacking their lands and taking booty. League policy was determined by a vote of the assembly, in which each state, including Athens, had one vote. Athens, however, was clearly designated leader.

From the first the league was remarkably successful. The Persians were driven from Europe and the Hellespont, and the Aegean was cleared of pirates. Some states were forced into the league or were prevented from leaving. The members approved coercion because it was necessary for the common safety. In 467 B.C. a great victory over the Persians at the Eurymedon River in Asia Minor routed the Persians and added a number of cities to the league.

CLASSICAL GREECE
THRACE
MACEDONIA
PAEONIA
ILLYRICUM
Epidamnus
Apollonia
Pella
Philippi
Abdera
Maronea
Amphipolis
Eion
Thessalonica
Stagira
THASOS
CHALCIDICE
Methone
Pydna
Olynthus
Potidaea
Torone
Scione
MT. ATHOS
MT. OLYMPUS
SAMOTHRACE
IMBROS
Elaeus
Sestos
Cardia
Pactye
Lampsacus
Abydos
GRANICUS
Troy
TROAD
PHRYG
LEMNOS
EPIRUS
Dodona
PENEIUS
Larisa
CORCYRA
THESSALY
MT. PELIUM
Pherae
Thysalus
Ambracia
Anactorium
Sollium
ACARNANIA
LEUCAS
AETOLIA
THERMOPYLAE
Heraclae
Elatea
LOCRIS
Oreus
ARTEMESIUM
PEPARETHUS
SKYROS
Amphissa
MT. PARNASSUS
Naupactus
DELPHI
Chaeronea
BOEOTIA
Coronea
Delium
Chalcis
Eretria
EUBOEA
Thespiae
Thebes
Oropus
Leuctra
Plataea
GULF OF CORINTH
CEPHALLENIA
ELIS
Elis
ACHAEA
Sicyon
Megara
ATHENS
Decelea
Carystus
Corinth
SALAMIS
Piraeus
Thoricus
Laureum
ATTICA
ANDROS
ZACYNTHUS
Olympia
ARCADIA
Nemea
Cleonae
Argos
Mantinea
AEGINA
Megalopolis
Tegea
MT. DIDYMA
Epidaurus
Hermione
KEOS
SYROS
TENOS
Messene
LACONIA
MESSENIA
SPARTA
PELOPONNESUS
CYNTHOS
DELOS
MYKONOS
Pylos
MT. TAYGETUS
SERIPHOS
SIPHNOS
PAROS
NAXOS
IONIAN SEA
Gythium
MELOS
SIKINOS
IOS
PHOLEGANDROS
AMORGUS
CAPE TAENARUS
CAPE MALEA
CYTHERA
AEGEAN SEA
Methymna
AEOLIS
Adramyttium
MY
CAICUS
Atarneus
Mytilene
LESBOS
LYD
Phocaea
Cyme
HERM
Magnesia
CHIOS
Chios
Smyr
Clazomenae
Teos
Erythrae
Colophon
Notium
Ephesus
SAMOS
Prie
Miletus
ICARIA
Halicarnassus
COS
ASTYPALAEA
CNIDUS
CRETAN SEA
CARPATHOS
Cnossus
Tylissus
CRETE
Gortyna
MEDITERRANEAN SEA
100 MI.
100 KM.

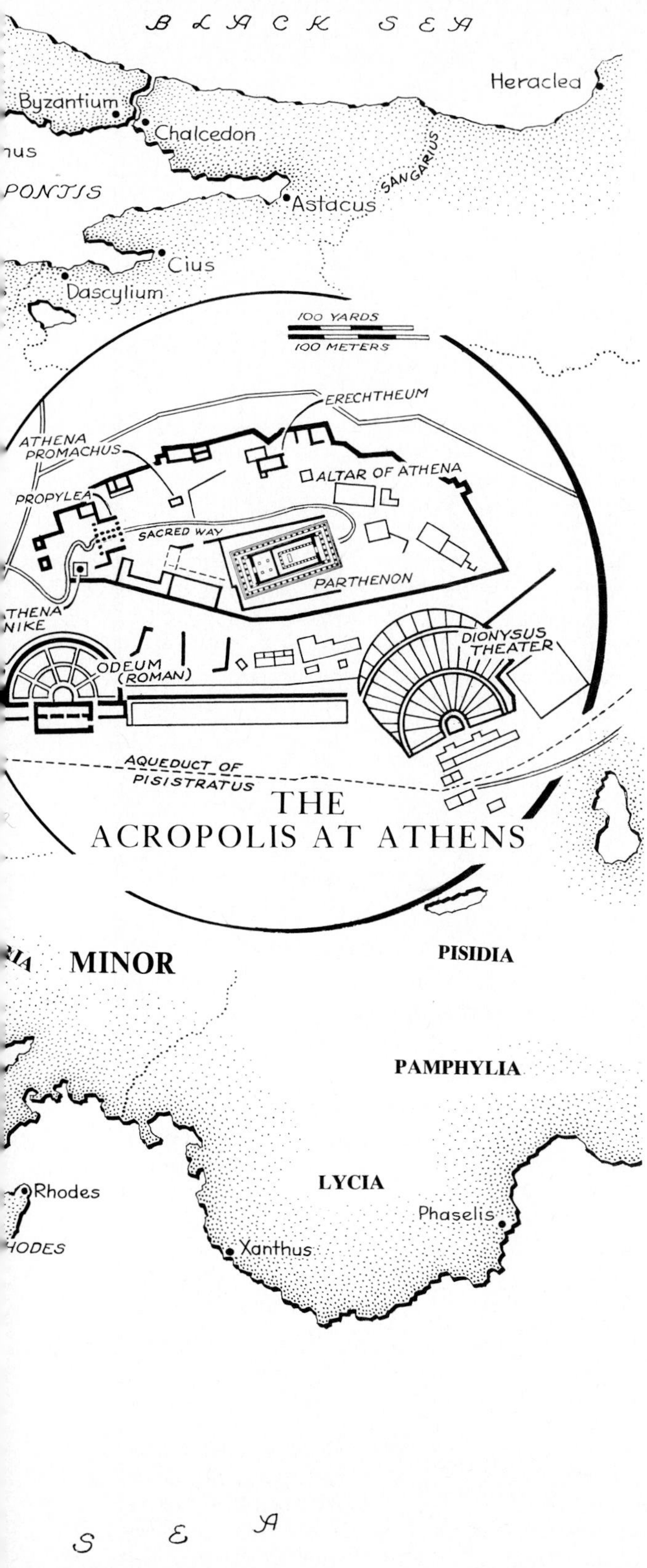

MAPS 3-1, 3-2 *Greece in the classical period* (*ca.* 480–338 B.C.) *centered on the Aegean Sea. Although there were important Greek settlements in Italy, Sicily, and all around the Black Sea, the area shown in this general reference map embraced the vast majority of Greek states. The inset shows the location of the major monuments still visible on the Athenian Acropolis of the classical period.*

Cimon, son of Miltiades, the hero of Marathon, became the leading Athenian soldier and statesman soon after the Persian war. Themistocles appears to have been driven from power by a coalition of his enemies. Ironically the author of the Greek victory over Persia of 480 B.C. was exiled and ended his days at the court of the Persian king. Cimon, who was to dominate Athenian politics for almost two decades, pursued a policy of aggressive attacks on Persia and friendly relations with Sparta. In domestic affairs Cimon was conservative. He accepted the democratic constitution of Clisthenes, which appears to have become somewhat more limited after the Persian war. Defending this constitution and this foreign policy, Cimon led the Athenians and the Delian League to victory after victory, and his own popularity grew with success.

The First Peloponnesian War

In 465 B.C. the island of Thasos rebelled from the league, and Cimon put it down after a siege of more than two years. The revolt of Thasos had an important influence on the development of the Delian League, on Athenian politics, and on relations between Athens and Sparta. It is the first recorded instance in which Athenian interests alone seemed to determine league policy, a significant step in the evolution of the Delian League into the Athenian Empire. When Cimon returned to Athens from Thasos, he was charged with taking bribes not to conquer Macedonia, although that was not part of his assignment, but he was acquitted. The trial was only a device by which his political opponents tried to reduce his influence. Their program at home was to undo the gains made by the Areopagus and to bring about further changes in the direction of democracy; abroad, the enemies of Cimon wanted to break with Sparta and to contest its claim to leadership over the Greeks. They intended at least to establish the independence of Athens and its

Athens Takes the Lead

After the defeat of the Persians at Plataea and Mycale in 479 B.C., many Greek states wanted to continue the war against Persia. At first, the Spartans continued to provide the leadership, sending their general Pausanias to conduct the campaign. Very soon, however, the Greeks rejected him and turned to the Athenians. In the following selection, Plutarch tells us how this came about.

. . . Well disposed as the Hellenes were toward the Athenians on account of the justice of Aristides and the reasonableness of Cimon, they were made to long for their supremacy still more by the rapacity of Pausanias and his severity. The commanders of the allies ever met with angry harshness at the hands of Pausanias, and the common men he punished with stripes, or by compelling them to stand all day long with an iron anchor on their shoulders. No one could get bedding or fodder or go down to a spring for water before the Spartans, nay, their servants armed with goads would drive away such as approached. On these grounds Aristides once had it in mind to chide and admonish him, but Pausanias scowled, said he was busy, and would not listen.

Subsequently the captains and generals of the Hellenes, and especially the Chians, Samians, and Lesbians, came to Aristides and tried to persuade him to assume the leadership and bring over to his support the allies, who had long wanted to be rid of the Spartans and to range themselves anew on the side of the Athenians. He replied that he saw the urgency and the justice of what they proposed, but that to establish Athenian confidence in them some overt act was needed, the doing of which would make it impossible for the multitude to change their allegiance back again. So Uliades the Samian and Antagoras the Chian conspired together, and ran down the trireme of Pausanias off Byzantium, closing in on both sides of it as it was putting out before the line. When Pausanias saw what they had done, he sprang up and wrathfully threatened to show the world in a little while that these men had run down not so much his ship as their own native cities; but they bade him be gone, and be grateful to that fortune which fought in his favour at Plataea; it was because the Hellenes still stood in awe of this, they said, that they did not punish him as he deserved. And finally they went off and joined the Athenians.

Plutarch, *Aristides* 23, trans. by Bernadotte Perrin (London and New York: Loeb Classical Library, William Heinemann, 1928).

alliance. The head of this faction was Ephialtes. His supporter, and the man chosen to be the public prosecutor of Cimon, was Pericles, a member of a distinguished Athenian family. He was still a young man, and his defeat in court did not do lasting damage to his career.

When the Thasians began their rebellion, they asked Sparta to invade Athens the next spring, and the ephors agreed. An earthquake, accompanied by a rebellion of the Helots that threatened the survival of Sparta, prevented the invasion. The Spartans asked their allies, the Athenians among them, for help. In Athens Ephialtes urged the Athenians "not to help or restore a city that was a rival to Athens but to let Sparta lie low and be trampled underfoot," but Cimon persuaded them to send help. The results were disastrous. The Spartans sent the Athenian troops home for fear of "the boldness and revolutionary spirit of the Athenians." While Cimon was in the Peloponnesus, helping the Spartans, Ephialtes stripped the Areopagus of almost all its power. In the spring of 461 B.C. Cimon was ostracized, and Athens made an alliance with Argos, Sparta's traditional enemy. Almost overnight Cimon's domestic and foreign policies had been overturned.

The new regime at Athens was confident and ambitious. When Megara, getting the worst of a border dispute with Corinth, withdrew from the Peloponnesian League, the Athenians accepted the Megarians as allies. This alliance gave Athens a great strategic advantage, for Megara barred the way from the Peloponnesus to Athens. It also brought on the First Peloponnesian War, for Sparta resented the defection of Megara to Athens. The early years of the war brought Athens great success. The Athenians conquered Aegina and gained control of Boeotia. At one moment Athens was supreme and invulnerable, controlling the states on her borders and dominating the sea (see Map 3.1.).

About 455 B.C., however, the tide turned. A disastrous defeat struck an Athenian fleet that had gone to aid an Egyptian rebellion against Persia. The great loss of men, ships, and prestige caused rebellions in the empire, forcing Athens to make a truce in Greece in order to subdue her allies in the Aegean. In 449 B.C. the Athenians ended the war against Persia. In 446 B.C. the war on the Greek mainland broke out again. Rebellions in Boeotia and Megara removed Athens' land defenses and brought a Spartan invasion. Rather than fight, Pericles, the commander of the Athenian army, agreed to a peace of thirty years by the terms of which he abandoned all Athenian possessions on the continent. In return, the Spartans gave formal recognition of the Athenian Empire. From then on Greece was divided into two power blocs: Sparta and its alliance on the mainland and Athens ruling her empire in the Aegean.

KEY EVENTS IN ATHENIAN HISTORY BETWEEN THE PERSIAN WAR AND THE GREAT PELOPONNESIAN WAR

Delian League founded	478–477 B.C.
Cimon leading politician	ca. 474–462 B.C.
Victory over Persians at Eurymedon River	467 B.C.
Rebellion of Thasos	465–463 B.C.
Ephialtes murdered; Pericles rises to leadership	462 B.C.
Cimon ostracized	461 B.C.
Reform of Areopagus	461 B.C.
First Peloponnesian War begins	ca. 460 B.C.
Athens defeated in Egypt; crisis in the Delian League	454 B.C.
Peace with Persia	449 B.C.
Thirty Years' Peace ends First Peloponnesian War	445 B.C.

The Athenian Empire

After the Egyptian disaster the Athenians moved the Delian League's treasury to Athens and began to keep one sixtieth of the annual revenues for themselves. Because of the peace with Persia there seemed no further reason for the allies to pay tribute, so the Athenians were compelled to find a new justification for their empire. They called for a Panhellenic congress to meet at Athens to discuss rebuilding the temples destroyed by the Persians and to consider how to maintain freedom of the seas. When Spartan reluctance to participate prevented the congress, Athens felt free to continue to collect funds from the allies, both to maintain her navy and to rebuild the Athenian temples. Athenian propaganda suggested that henceforth the allies would be treated as colonies and Athens as their mother city, the whole to be held together by good feeling and common religious observances.

There is little reason, however, to believe that the allies were taken in or truly content with their lot. Nothing could cloak the fact that Athens was becoming the master and her allies mere subjects. By 445 B.C. only Chios, Lesbos, and Samos were autonomous and provided ships. All the other states paid tribute. The change from alliance to empire came about because of the pressure of war and rebellion and in large measure because the allies were unwilling to see to their own defense. Although the empire was not universally unpopular and had many friends among the lower classes and the democratic politicians, it came to be seen more and more as a tyranny. But the Athenians had come to depend on the empire for their prosperity and security. The Thirty Years' Peace of 445 B.C. had recognized their empire, and the Athenians were determined to defend it at any cost.

Athenian Democracy

Even as the Athenians were tightening their control over their allies at home, they were evolving the freest government the world had ever seen. This extension of the Athenian democracy took place chiefly under the guidance of Pericles, who succeeded to the leadership of the democratic faction after the assassination of Ephialtes in 462 B.C. Legislation was passed making the hoplite class eligible for the archonship, and in practice no one was thereafter prevented from serving on the basis of property class. Pericles himself proposed the law introducing pay for jury members, opening that important duty to the poor. Circuit judges were reintroduced, a policy making swift impartial justice available even to the poorest residents in the countryside. Finally, Pericles himself introduced a bill limiting citizenship to those who had two citizen parents. From a modern perspective this measure might be seen as a step away from democracy, and, in fact, it would have barred Cimon and one of Pericles' ancestors. In Greek terms, however, it was quite natural. Democracy was defined in terms of those who held citizenship, and because citizenship had become a valuable commodity, the decision to limit it must have won a large majority. Participation in government in all the Greek states was also denied to slaves, resident aliens, and women.

Within the citizen body, however, the extent of the democracy was remarkable. Every decision of the state had to be approved by the popular assembly, a collection of the people, not their representatives. Every judicial decision was subject to appeal to a popular court of not fewer than 51 and as many as 1,501 citizens, chosen from an annual panel of jurors widely representative of the Athenian population. Most officials were selected by lot without regard to class. The main elected officials, such as the generals and the imperial treasurers, were generally nobles and almost always rich men, but the people were free to choose otherwise. All public officials were subject to scrutiny before taking office, could be called to account and removed from office during their tenure, and were held to compulsory examination and accounting at the end of their term. There was no standing army, no police force, open or secret, and no way to coerce the people. If Pericles was elected to the generalship fifteen years in a row and thirty times in all, it was not because he was a dictator but because he was a persuasive speaker, a skillful politician, a respected general, an acknowledged patriot, and a man patently incorruptible. When he lost the people's confidence, they did not hesitate to depose him from office. In 443 B.C., however, he stood at the height of his power. He had been persuaded by the defeat of the Athenian fleet in the Egyptian campaign and the failure of Athens' continental campaigns that its future lay in a conservative policy of retaining the empire in the Aegean and living at peace with the Spartans. It was in this

MAP 3-3 *The Empire at its fullest extent shortly before 450* B.C. *We see Athens and the independent states that provided manned ships for the imperial fleet but paid no tribute, dependent states who paid tribute, and states allied to but not actually in the Empire.*

An Athenian tribute list. In 454 B.C., *the Athenians moved the treasury of the Delian League to Athens and began to keep one-sixtieth of the allies' annual contribution for themselves. On stones like this, which were displayed on the Acropolis, they recorded the annual assessment of each ally. This stone records the assessment for 432–431* B.C., *the first year of the Peloponnesian War.* [*TAP—Art Reference Bureau*]

THE ATHENIAN EMPIRE ABOUT 450 B.C.

The Delian League Becomes the Athenian Empire

In the years following its foundation in the winter of 478–444 B.C., the Delian League gradually underwent changes that finally justified calling it the Athenian Empire. In the following selection, the historian Thucydides explains why the organization changed its character.

The causes which led to the defections of the allies were of different kinds, the principal being their neglect to pay the tribute or to furnish ships, and, in some cases, failure of military service. For the Athenians were exacting and oppressive, using coercive measures towards men who were neither willing nor accustomed to work hard. And for various reasons they soon began to prove less agreeable leaders than at first. They no longer fought upon an equality with the rest of the confederates, and they had no difficulty in reducing them when they revolted. Now the allies brought all this upon themselves; for the majority of them disliked military service and absence from home, and so they agreed to contribute a regular sum of money instead of ships. Whereby the Athenian navy was proportionally increased, while they themselves were always untrained and unprepared for war when they revolted.

Thucydides, *The Peloponnesian War,* trans. by Benjamin Jowett, Vol. 2, ed. by F. R. B. Godolphin in *The Greek Historians,* (New York: Random House, 1942), p. 609.

Pericles on Athenian Democracy

Pericles (ca. 495–429 B.C.) delivered this speech after the first campaigning season of the Great Peloponnesian War, probably late in the winter of 431 B.C. It is the most famous statement of the ideals of the Athenian imperial democracy.

Our constitution does not copy the laws of neighbouring states; we are rather a pattern to others than imitators ourselves. Its administration favours the many instead of the few; this is why it is called a democracy. If we look to the laws, they afford equal justice to all in their private differences; if to social standing, advancement in public life falls to reputation for capacity, class considerations not being allowed to interfere with merit; nor again does poverty bar the way, if a man is able to serve the state, he is not hindered by the obscurity of his condition. The freedom which we enjoy in our government extends also to our ordinary life. There, far from exercising a jealous surveillance over each other, we do not feel called upon to be angry with our neighbour for doing what he likes, or even to indulge in those injurious looks which cannot fail to be offensive, although they inflict no positive penalty. But all this ease in our private relations does not make us lawless as citizens. . . . Our public men have, besides politics, their private affairs to attend to, and our ordinary citizens, though occupied with the pursuits of industry, are still fair judges of public matters; for, unlike any other nation, regarding him who takes no part in these duties not as unambitious but as useless, we Athenians are able to judge at all events if we cannot originate, and instead of looking on discussion as a stumbling-block in the way of action, we think it an indispensable preliminary to any wise action at all. . . .

In short, I say that as a city we are the school of Hellas; while I doubt if the world can produce a man, who where he has only himself to depend upon, is equal to so many emergencies, and graced by so happy a versatility as the Athenian.

Thucydides, *The Peloponnesian War,* trans. by Richard Crawley (New York: Random House, 1951), pp. 104–106.

direction that he led Athens' imperial democracy in the years after the First Peloponnesian War.

The Women of Athens

Greek society, like most all over the world throughout history, was dominated by men. This was true of the democratic city of Athens in the great days of Pericles, in the fifth century B.C., no less than in other Greek cities, but just what was the position of women in classical Athens has been the subject of much controversy. The bulk of the evidence, coming from the law, from philosophical and moral writings, and from information about the conditions of daily life and the organization of society shows that women were excluded from most aspects of public life. They could not vote, take part in the political assemblies, hold public office, or take any direct part in politics at all. This was especially important in one of the few places in the ancient world where male citizens of all classes had these public responsibilities and opportunities.

The same sources show that in the private aspects of life women were always under the control of a male guardian: a father, a husband, or, failing these, an appropriate male relative. Women married young, usually between the ages of twelve and eighteen, whereas their husbands were typically over thirty, so in a way, they were always in a relationship like that of a daughter to a father. Marriages were arranged; the woman normally had no choice of husband, and her dowry was controlled by a male relative. Divorce was difficult for a woman to obtain, for she needed the approval of a male relative who was then willing to serve as her guardian after the dissolution of the marriage. In case of divorce, the dowry re-

The porch of the maidens on the Erechtheum on the Athenian Acropolis near the Parthenon. Built between 421 *and* 409 B.C., *the Erechtheum housed the shrines of three different gods. In place of the usual fluted columns, the porch uses the statues of young girls taking part in a religious festival.* [*Greek National Tourist Office*]

turned with the woman but was controlled by her father or the appropriate male relative.

The main function and responsibility of a respectable Athenian woman of a citizen family was to produce male heirs for the household (*oikos*) of her husband. If, however, her father's *oikos* lacked a male heir, the daughter became an *epikleros,* the "heiress" to the family property. In that case, she was required by law to marry the next of kin on her father's side in order to produce the desired male offspring. In the Athenian way of thinking, women were "lent" by one household to another for purposes of bearing and raising a male heir to continue the existence of the *oikos.*

Because the pure and legitimate lineage of the offspring was important, women were carefully segregated from men outside the family and were confined to the women's quarters in the house. Men might seek sexual gratification outside the house with prostitutes of high or low style, frequently recruited from abroad, but respectable women stayed home to raise the children, cook, weave cloth, and oversee the management of the household. The only public function of women was an important one in the various rituals and festivals of the state religion. Apart from these activities, Athenian women were expected to remain home out of sight, quiet and unnoticed. Pericles told the widows and mothers of the Athenian men who died in the first year of the Peloponnesian

War only this: "Your great glory is not to fall short of your natural character, and the greatest glory of women is to be least talked about by men, whether for good or bad."

The picture derived from these sources is largely accurate, but it does not fit well with what we learn from the evidence of the pictorial art, the tragedy and comedy, and the mythology of the Athenians, which often shows women as central characters and powerful figures in both the public and the private spheres. The Clytemnestra in Aeschylus' tragedy *Agamemnon* arranges the murder of her royal husband and establishes the tyranny of her lover, whom she dominates. The terrifying and powerful Medea negotiates with kings. We are left with an apparent contradiction clearly revealed by a famous speech in Euripides' tragedy *Medea.* (See the accompanying document.)

The picture that Medea paints of women subjected to men accords well with much of the evidence, but we must take note of the fact that the woman who complains of women's lot is the powerful central figure in a tragedy bearing her name, produced at state expense before most of the Athenian population, and written by a man who was one of Athens' greatest poets and dramatists. She is a cause of terror to the audience and, at the same time, an object of their pity and sympathy as a victim of injustice. She is anything but the creature "least talked about by men, whether for good or for bad." There is reason to believe that the role played by Athenian women may have been more complex than their legal status might suggest.

Medea Bemoans the Condition of Women

In 431 B.C. Euripides (ca. 485–406 B.C.) presented his play *Medea* at the Dionysiac festival in Athens. The heroine is a foreign woman and has unusual powers, but in the speech that follows, she describes the fate of women in terms that appear to give an accurate account of the condition of women in fifth-century Athens.

Of all things which are living and can form a judgment
We women are the most unfortunate creatures.
Firstly, with an excess of wealth it is required
For us to buy a husband and take for our bodies
A master; for not to take one is even worse.
And now the question is serious whether we take
A good or bad one; for there is no easy escape
For a woman, nor can she say no to her marriage.
She arrives among new modes of behavior and manners,
And needs prophetic power, unless she has learned at home,
How best to manage him who shares the bed with her.
And if we work out all this well and carefully,
And the husband lives with us and lightly bears his yoke,
Then life is enviable. If not, I'd rather die.
A man, when he's tired of the company in his home,
Goes out of the house and puts an end to his boredom
And turns to a friend or companion of his own age.
But we are forced to keep our eyes on one alone.
What they say of us is that we have a peaceful time
Living at home, while they do the fighting in war.
How wrong they are! I would very much rather stand
Three times in the front of battle than bear one child.

Euripides, *Medea* in *Four Tragedies,* trans. by Rex Warner, (Chicago: University of Chicago Press, 1955), pp. 66–67.

The Great Peloponnesian War and Its Aftermath

THE GREAT PELOPONNESIAN WAR	
Civil war at Epidamnus	435 B.C.
Sparta declares war on Athens	432 B.C.
Peloponnesian invasion of Athens	431 B.C.
Peace of Nicias	421 B.C.
Athenian invasion of Sicily	415–413 B.C.
Battle of Aegospotami	405 B.C.
Athens surrenders	404 B.C.

In the decade after the Thirty Years' Peace of 445 B.C., the willingness of each side to respect the new arrangements was tested and not found wanting.

About 435 B.C., however, a dispute arose in a remote and unimportant part of the Greek world, plunging the Greeks into a long and disastrous war that shook the foundations of their civilization. Civil war broke out at Epidamnus, a Corcyraean colony on the Adriatic, causing a quarrel between Corcyra and her mother city and traditional enemy, Corinth.

Corinth's threat to the Corcyraean fleet, second in size only to Athens', led the Athenians to make an alliance with the previously neutral Corcyra. Athens could not run the risk of having Corcyra's navy fall under Corinthian control, thus changing the balance of power at sea and seriously threatening Athenian security. That alliance angered Corinth and led to a series of crises in the years 433–432 B.C. that threatened to bring the Athenian Empire into conflict with the Peloponnesian League.

In the summer of 432 B.C. the Spartans met to consider the grievances of their allies. They were persuaded by their allies, and chiefly the Corinthians, that Athens was an insatiably aggressive power that aimed at enslaving all the Greeks, and they voted for war. The treaty of 445 B.C. specifically provided that all differences be submitted to arbitration, and Athens repeatedly offered to arbitrate any question. Pericles insisted, however, that the Athenians refuse to yield to threats or commands and that they uphold the treaty and the arbitration clause. Sparta refused to arbitrate, and in the spring of 431 her army marched into Attica, the Athenian homeland.

The Spartan strategy was traditional: to invade the enemy's country and threaten the crops, forcing the enemy to defend them in a hoplite battle. Such a battle the Spartans were sure to win because they had the better army and they outnumbered the Athenians at least two to one. Any ordinary *polis* would have yielded or fought and lost, but Athens had an enormous navy, an annual income from the empire, a vast reserve fund, and long walls that connected the fortified city with the fortified port of Piraeus.

The Athenians' strategy was to allow devastation of the land to prove that Athens was invulnerable. At the same time the Athenians launched seaborne raids on the Peloponnesian coast to show that the allies of Sparta could be hurt. Pericles expected that within a year or two, three at most, the Peloponnesians would become discouraged and make peace, having learned their lesson. If the Peloponnesians held out, Athenian resources were inadequate to continue for more than four or five years without raising the tribute in the empire and running an unacceptable risk of rebellion. The plan required restraint and the leadership only a Pericles could provide.

The first year of the war went as planned, with no result. In the second year a terrible plague broke out in Athens (it eventually killed a third of the population), and the demoralized Athenians removed Pericles from office and fined him heavily. They asked for peace, but the angry Spartans refused. In 429 B.C. the Athenians, recognizing their error and their need for his leadership, returned Pericles to office, but he died before the year was over. His strategy had gone wrong and all he had worked for was in danger.

After Pericles' death there was no one in Athens with his ability to dominate the scene and hold the Athenians to a consistent policy. Two factions vied for influence: one, led by Nicias, wanted to continue the defensive policy, and the other, led by Cleon, preferred a more aggressive strategy. In 425 B.C. the aggressive faction was able to win a victory that changed the course of the war. Four hundred Spartans surrendered, and Sparta offered peace at once to get them back. The great victory and the prestige it brought Athens made it safe to raise the imperial tribute, without which Athens could not continue to fight. And the Athenians wanted to continue, for the Spartan

Thucydides Describes the Moral Degeneration Caused by the Great Plague at Athens

In the second year of the Great Peloponnesian War (430 B.C.), a terrible plague broke out in Athens that ultimately carried off a third of the population. Thucydides described the effects on Athenian society caused by this experience:

The bodies of dying men lay one upon another, and half-dead creatures reeled about the streets and gathered round all the fountains in their longing for water. The sacred places also in which they had quartered themselves were full of corpses of persons that had died there, just as they were; for as the disaster passed all bounds, men, not knowing what was to become of them, became utterly careless of everything, whether sacred or profane. All the burial rites before in use were entirely upset and they buried the bodies as best they could. Many from want of the proper appliances, through so many of their friends having died already, had recourse to the most shameless sepultures: sometimes getting the start of those who had raised a pile, they threw their own dead body upon the stranger's pyre and ignited it; sometimes they tossed the corpse which they were carrying on the top of another that was burning, and so went off.

Nor was this the only form of lawless extravagance which owed its origin to the plague. Men now coolly ventured on what they had formerly done in a corner, and not just as they pleased, seeing the rapid transitions produced by persons in prosperity suddenly dying and those who before had nothing succeeding to their property. So they resolved to spend quickly and enjoy themselves, regarding their lives and riches as alike things of a day. Perseverance in what men called honour was popular with none, it was so uncertain whether they would be spared to attain the object; but it was settled that present enjoyment, and all that contributed to it, was both honourable and useful. Fear of gods or law of man there was none to restrain them. As for the first, they judged it to be just the same whether they worshipped them or not, as they saw all alike perishing; and for the last, no one expected to live to be brought to trial for his offences, but each felt that a far severer sentence had been already passed upon them all and hung over their heads, and before this fell it was only reasonable to enjoy life a little.

Thucydides, *The Peloponnesian War*, trans. by Richard Crawley (New York: Random House, 1951), pp. 112–113.

peace offer gave no adequate guarantee of Athenian security.

In 424 B.C. the Athenians undertook a more aggressive policy: they sought to make Athens safe by conquering Megara and Boeotia. Both attempts failed, and defeat helped discredit the aggressive policy, leading to a truce in 423 B.C. Meanwhile, Sparta's ablest general, Brasidas, took a small army to Thrace and Macedonia. He captured Amphipolis, the most important Athenian colony in the region. Thucydides, the historian of the Great Peloponnesian War, was in charge of the Athenian fleet in those waters and was held responsible for the city's loss. He was exiled and was thereby given the time and opportunity to write his history. In 422 B.C. Cleon led an expedition to undo the work of Brasidas. At Amphipolis both he and Brasidas died in battle. The removal of these two leaders of the aggressive factions in their respective cities paved the way for peace. The Peace of Nicias, named for its chief negotiator, was ratified in the spring of 421 B.C.

The peace was for fifty years and guaranteed the status quo with a few exceptions. Neither side carried out all its commitments, and several of Sparta's allies refused to ratify the peace. Corinth urged the Argives to form a new alliance as a separate force and encouraged the war party in Sparta. In Athens Alcibiades emerged as the new leader of the aggressive faction and was able to bring about an alliance with Argos.

In 415 B.C. Alcibiades persuaded the Atheni-

Greek fighting Greek: the siege of a Greek city in Asia Minor during the Great Peloponnesian War. [*Michael Holford*]

ans to attack Sicily to bring it under Athenian control. The undertaking was ambitious and unnecessary, but if it had succeeded, it would have deprived the Peloponnesians of all hope of western support in future wars and would have provided Athens with plenty of money for both military and domestic uses.

In 413 B.C. the entire expedition was destroyed. The Athenians lost some two hundred ships, about forty-five hundred of their own men, and almost ten times as many allies. It was a disaster perhaps greater than the defeat of the Athenian fleet in the Egyptian campaign some forty years earlier. It shook Athenian prestige, reduced the power of Athens, provoked rebellions, and brought the wealth and power of Persia into the war on Sparta's side.

It is remarkable that the Athenians were able to continue fighting in spite of the disaster. They survived a brief oligarchic coup in 411 B.C. and won several important victories at sea as the war shifted to the Aegean. As their allies rebelled, however, and were sustained by fleets paid for by Persia, the Athenians saw their financial resources shrink and finally disappear. When their fleet was caught napping at Aegospotami in 405 B.C., they could not build another. The Spartans, under Lysander, a clever and ambitious general who was responsible for obtaining Persian support, cut off the food supply through the Hellespont, and the Athenians were starved into submission. In 404 B.C. they surrendered unconditionally; the city walls were dismantled, Athens was permitted no fleet, and the empire was gone. The Great Peloponnesian War was over.

The Hegemony of Sparta

The collapse of the Athenian Empire created a vacuum of power in the Aegean and opened the way for Spartan leadership, or hegemony. Fulfilling the contract that had brought them the funds to win the war, the Spartans handed the Greek cities of Asia Minor back to Persia. Under the leadership of Lysander the Spartans went on to make a complete mockery of their promise to free the Greeks by stepping into the imperial role of Athens in the cities along the European coast and the islands of the Aegean. In most of the cities Lysander installed a board of ten local oligarchs loyal to him and supported them with a Spartan garrison. Tribute brought in an annual revenue almost as great as that the Athenians had collected.

Limited population, the Helot problem, and traditional conservatism all made Sparta less than an ideal state to rule a maritime empire. Some of Sparta's allies, especially Thebes and Corinth, were alienated by the increasing arro-

The trireme was the dominant Greek warship in the fifth and fourth centuries B.C. *Its superior speed and maneuverability swept the seas of competition. Previous naval warfare had relied on grappling and boarding, which made naval battles resemble land battles. The trireme, however, rammed the enemy at great speed with a metal prow, like a torpedo. The side view drawing (top) shows only the top of three rows of oarsmen. The cross section drawings from the front (left) show how the oars and rowers were arranged and how the oars struck the water and managed not to run afoul of one another. The two views of a trireme model from the front and top (right) show the positions of the three tiers of rowers.* [*Line drawings: J. D. Morrison and R. T. Williams:* Greek Oared Ships, 900–322 B.C. (*Cambridge University Press,* 1968), *plates 25 and 31. Photographs: J. S. Morrison, Cambridge University*]

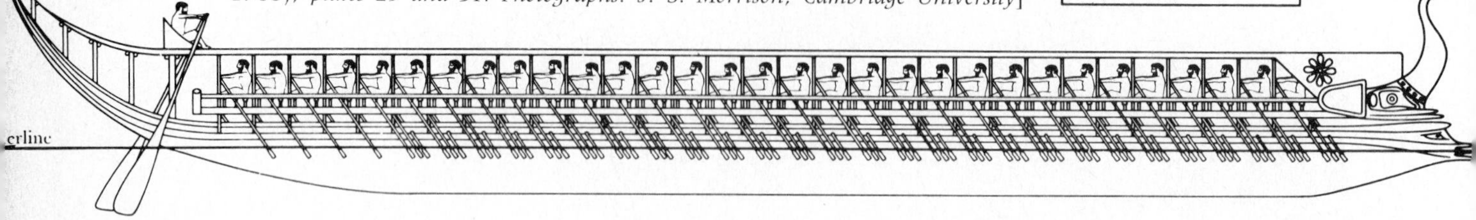

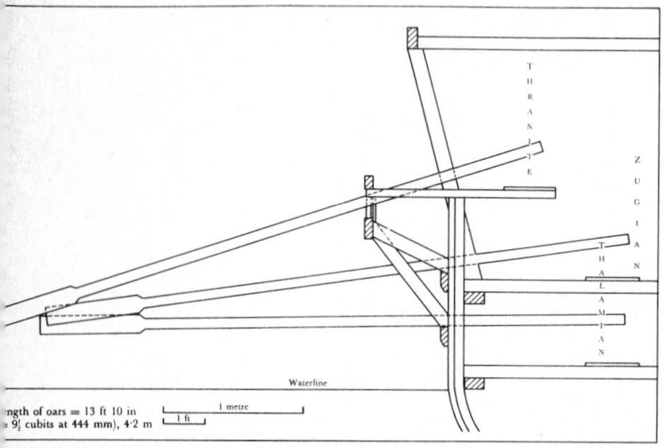

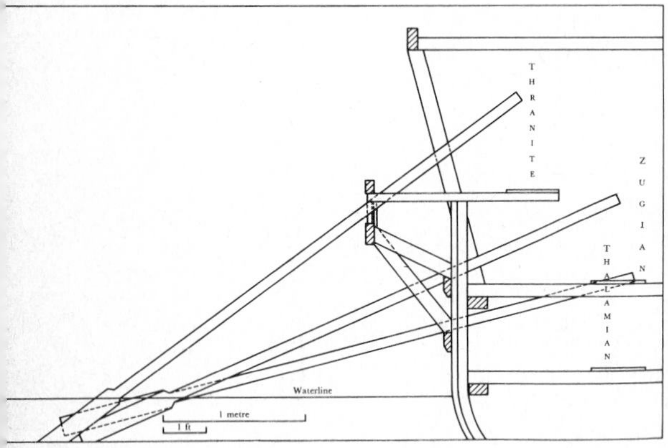

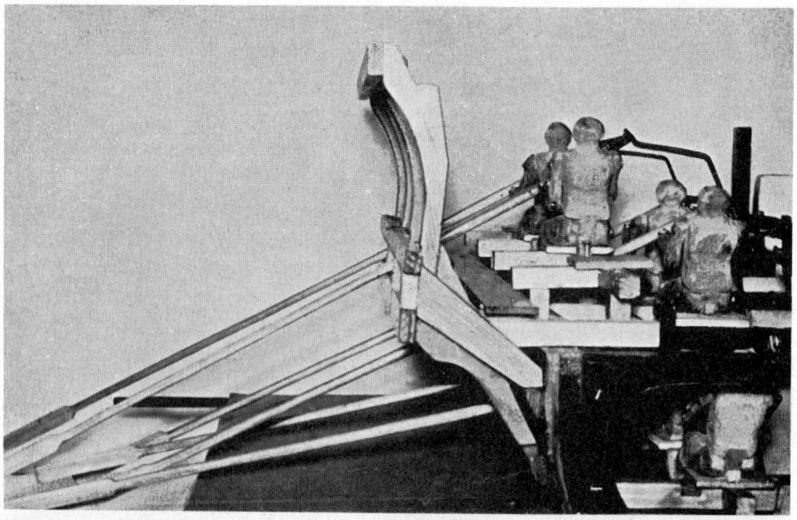

gance of Sparta's policies. In 404 B.C. Lysander installed an oligarchic government in Athens whose outrageous behavior earned them the title "Thirty Tyrants." Democratic exiles took refuge in Thebes and Corinth and created an army to challenge the oligarchy. Sparta's conservative king, Pausanias, replaced Lysander, arranging a peaceful settlement and ultimately the restoration of democracy. Thereafter Athenian foreign policy remained under Spartan control, but otherwise Athens was free.

In 405 B.C. Darius II of Persia died and was succeeded by Artaxerxes II. His younger brother, Cyrus, contested his rule and received Spartan help in recruiting a Greek mercenary army to help him win the throne. They marched inland as far as Mesopotamia, where they defeated the Persians at Cunaxa in 401 B.C., but Cyrus was killed. The Greeks were able to march back to the Black Sea and safety; their success revealed the potential weakness of the Persian Empire.

The Greeks of Asia Minor had supported Cyrus and were now afraid of Artaxerxes' revenge. The Spartans accepted their request for aid and sent an army into Asia, attracted by the prospect of prestige, power, and money. In 396 B.C. the command was given to Sparta's new king, Agesilaus. His personality and policy dominated Sparta throughout its period of hegemony and until his death in 360 B.C. Hampered by his lameness and his disputed claim to the throne, he seems to have compensated for both by always advocating aggressive policies and providing himself with opportunities to display his bravery in battle.

Agesilaus collected much booty and frightened the Persians. They sent a messenger with money and promises of further support to friendly factions in all the likely states. By 395 B.C. Thebes was able to organize an alliance that included Argos, Corinth, and a resurgent Athens. The result was the Corinthian War (395–387 B.C.), which put an end to Sparta's Asian adventure. In 394 the Persian fleet destroyed Sparta's maritime empire. Meanwhile the Athenians took advantage of events to rebuild their walls, to enlarge their navy, and even to recover some of their lost empire in the Aegean. The war ended when the exhausted Greek states accepted a peace dictated by the Great King of Persia.

The Persians, frightened by the recovery of Athens, turned the management of Greece over to Sparta. Agesilaus broke up all alliances except the Peloponnesian League. He interfered with the autonomy of other *poleis* by using the Spartan army, or the threat of its use, to put friends in power within them. Sparta reached a new level of lawless arrogance in 382 B.C., when it seized Thebes during peacetime without warning or pretext. In 379 a Spartan army made a similar attempt on Athens. That action persuaded the Athenians to join with Thebes, which had rebelled from Sparta a few months earlier, to wage war on the Spartans. In 371 B.C. the Thebans, led by their great generals Pelopidas and Epaminondas, defeated the Spartans at Leuctra. The Thebans encouraged the Arcadian cities of the central Peloponnesus to form a federal league, freed the Helots, and helped them found a city of their own. They deprived Sparta of much of its farmland and of the people who worked it and hemmed it in with hostile neighbors. Sparta's population had shrunk so that it could put fewer than two thousand men into the field at Leuctra. Sparta's aggressive policies had led to ruin. The Theban victory brought the end of Sparta as a power of the first rank.

The Spartan and Theban Hegemonies

Thirty Tyrants rule at Athens	404–403 B.C.
Expedition of Cyrus, rebellious prince of Persia: Battle of Cunaxa	401 B.C.
Spartan War against Persia	400–387 B.C.
Reign of Agesilaus at Sparta	398–360 B.C.
Corinthian War	395–387 B.C.
Sparta seizes Thebes	382 B.C.
Second Athenian Confederation founded	378 B.C.
Thebans defeat Sparta at Leuctra; end of Spartan hegemony	371 B.C.
Battle of Mantinea; end of Theban hegemony	362 B.C.

The Hegemony of Thebes; The Second Athenian Empire

Victorious Thebes had a democratic constitution, control over Boeotia, and two outstanding and popular generals. These were the basis for Theban power after Leuctra. Pelopidas died in a successful attempt to gain control of Thessaly. Epaminondas consolidated his work, and Thebes was soon dominant over all Greece

Xenophon Recounts How Greece Brought Itself to Chaos

Confusion in Greece in the fourth century B.C. reached a climax with the inconclusive battle of Mantinea in 362. The Theban leader Epaminondas was killed, and no other city or person emerged to provide the needed general leadership for Greece. Xenophon, a contemporary, pointed out the resulting near chaos in Greek affairs—tempting ground for the soon-to-appear conquering Macedonians under their king Philip.

The effective result of these achievements was the very opposite of that which the world at large anticipated. Here, where well-nigh the whole of Hellas was met together in one field, and the combatants stood rank against rank confronted, there was no one who doubted that, in the event of battle, the conquerors this day would rule; and that those who lost would be their subjects. But god so ordered it that both belligerents alike set up trophies as claiming victory, and neither interfered with the other in the act. Both parties alike gave back their enemy's dead under a truce, and in right of victory; both alike, in symbol of defeat, under a truce took back their dead. And though both claimed to have won the day, neither could show that he had thereby gained any accession of territory, or state, or empire, or was better situated than before the battle. Uncertainty and confusion, indeed, had gained ground, being tenfold greater throughout the length and breadth of Hellas after the battle than before.

Xenophon, *Hellenica,* trans. by H. G. Dakyns in *The Greek Historians,* ed. by F. R. B. Godolphin (New York: Random House, 1942), p. 221.

north of Athens and the Corinthian Gulf. The Thebans challenged the reborn Athenian Empire in the Aegean. All this activity provoked resistance, and by 362 B.C. Thebes faced a Peloponnesian coalition as well as Athens. Epaminondas once again led a victorious Boeotian army into the Peloponnesus at Mantinea but he died in the fight, and the loss of its two greater leaders ended Thebes' dominance.

Athens had organized the Second Athenian Confederation in 378 B.C. It was aimed at resisting Spartan aggression in the Aegean, and its constitution was careful to avoid the abuses of the Delian League. But the Athenians soon began to repeat those abuses, although this time they did not have the power to put down resistance. When the collapse of Sparta and Thebes and the restraint of Persia removed any reason for voluntary membership, Athens' allies revolted. By 355 B.C. Athens had had to abandon most of the empire. After two centuries of almost continuous warfare, the Greeks returned to the chaotic disorganization of the time before the founding of the Peloponnesian League.

The Culture of Classical Greece

The repulse of the Persian invasion released a flood of creative activity in Greece rarely, if ever, matched anywhere at any time. The century and a half between the Persian retreat and the conquest of Greece by Philip of Macedon (479–338 B.C.) produced achievements of such quality as to justify that era's designation as the Classical Period. Ironically we often use the term *classical* to suggest calm and serenity, but the word that best describes the common element present in Greek life, thought, art, and literature in this period is *tension.* It was a time in which conflict among the *poleis* continued and intensified as Athens and Sparta gathered most of them into two competing and menacing blocs. The victory over the Persians brought a sense of exultation in the capacity of humans to accomplish great things and of confidence in the divine justice that brought arrogant pride low. But these feelings conflicted with a sense of unease as the Greeks recognized that the fate

MAP 3-4 *This sketch locates some of the major features of the ancient city of Athens that have been excavated and are visible today. It includes monuments ranging in age from the earliest times to the period of the Roman Empire. The geographical relation of the Acropolis to the rest of the city is apparent, as is that of the Agora, the Areopagus (where the early council of aristocrats met), and the Pnyx (site of assembly for the larger, more democratic meetings of the entire people).*

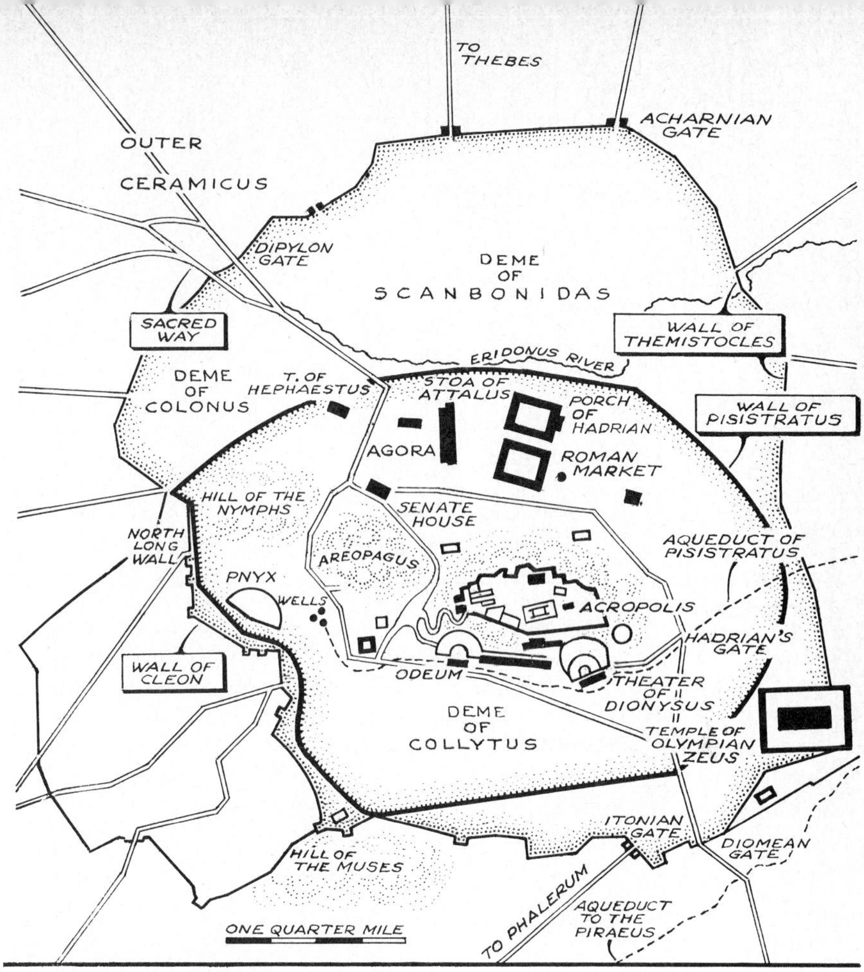

This vase painting, ca. 470 B.C., *depicts instruction in music and grammar in an Attic school. For the Greeks, music was always intimately bound up with literature, drama, and the dance.* [*State Museums, Berlin*]

The theater at Epidaurus. Epidaurus, a city in the eastern Peloponnesus, was the site of a famous sanctuary to Asclepius, the god of healing. Thousands of the sick and crippled went there to be cured. The religious festivals held there included theatrical performances and athletic contests that drew vast crowds. [*Alison Frantz*]

that had met Xerxes awaited all those who reached too far. Another source of tension was the conflict between the soaring hopes and achievements of individuals and the claims and limits put on them by their fellow citizens in the *polis*. These forces were at work throughout Greece, but we know them best and they had the most spectacular results in Athens in its Golden Age, the time between the Persian and the Peloponnesian wars.

Attic Tragedy

Nothing reflects these concerns better than the appearance of Attic tragedy as a major form of Greek poetry in the fifth century B.C. The tragedies were presented as part of public religious observations in honor of the god Dionysus. The whole affair was very much a civic occasion. Each poet who wished to compete submitted his work to the archon. Each offered three tragedies, which might or might not have a common subject, and a satyr play (a comic choral dialogue with Dionysus) to close. The three best competitors were each awarded three actors and a chorus. The actors were paid by the state, and the chorus was provided by a wealthy citizen selected by the state to perform this service as *choregos*, for the Athenians had no direct taxation to support such activities. Most of the tragedies were performed in the theater of Dionysus on the south side of the Acropolis, and as many as thirty thousand Athenians could attend. Prizes and honors were awarded to the author, the actor, and the *choregos* voted best by a jury of Athenians chosen by lot. On rare occasions the subject of the play might be a contemporary or historical event, but almost always it was chosen from mythology. Before Euripides it always dealt solemnly with serious questions of religion, politics, ethics, morality, or some combination of these.

Architecture and Sculpture

The great architectural achievements of Periclean Athens, just as much as Athenian tragedy, illustrate the magnificent results of the union and tension between religious and civic responsibilities on the one hand and the transcendent genius of the individual artist on the other. Beginning in 448 B.C. and continuing down to the outbreak of the Great Peloponnesian War, Pericles undertook a great building program on the Acropolis. The funds were provided by the income from the empire. The buildings were temples to honor the city's gods and a fitting gateway to the temples. Pericles' main purpose seems to have been to represent visually the greatness and power of Athens, but in such a way as to emphasize her intellectual and artistic achievement, her civilization rather than her military and naval power. It was as though these buildings were tangible proof of Pericles' claim that Athens was "the school of Hellas," that is, the intellectual center of all Greece.

Philosophy

Tragedy, architecture, and sculpture are all indications of the fifth century's extraordinary emphasis on human beings: their capacities, their limits, their nature, their place in the universe. The same concern is clear in the development of philosophy. Parmenides of Elea and his pupil Zeno, to be sure, carried on the theoretical debate about the nature of the cosmos.

In opposition to Heraclitus, they argued that change was only an illusion of the senses. Reason and reflection showed that reality was fixed and unchanging because it seemed evident that nothing could be created out of nothingness. Such fundamental speculations were carried forward by Empedocles of Acragas, who spoke of four basic elements: fire, water, earth, and air. Like Parmenides he thought that reality was permanent but not immobile, for the four elements were moved by two primary forces, Love and Strife, or, as we might be inclined to say, attraction and repulsion.

This theory is clearly a step on the road to the atomic theory of Leucippus of Miletus and Democritus of Abdera. They believed that the world consisted of innumerable tiny, solid particles that could not be divided or modified and that moved about in the void. The size of the atoms and the arrangement in which they were joined with others produced the secondary qualities that the senses could perceive, such as color and shape. These qualities, unlike the atoms themselves, which were natural, were merely conventional. Anaxagoras of Clazomenae, an older contemporary and a friend of Pericles, had previously spoken of tiny fundamental particles called *seeds,* which were put together on a rational basis by a force called *nous,* or "mind." Thus Anaxagoras suggested a distinction between matter and mind. The atomists, however, regarded "soul," or mind, as material and believed that everything was guided by purely physical laws. In the arguments of Anaxagoras and the atomists we have the beginning of the philosophical debate between materialism and idealism that has continued through the ages.

These discussions interested very few, and, in fact, most Greeks were suspicious of such speculations. A far more influential debate was begun by a group of professional teachers who emerged in the mid-fifth century B.C. and whom the Greeks called *Sophists.* They traveled about and received pay for teaching practical techniques such as rhetoric, a valuable skill in democracies like Athens. Others claimed to teach wisdom and even virtue. They did not speculate about the physical universe but applied reasoned analysis to human beliefs and institutions. This human focus was characteristic of fifth-century thought, as was the central problem that the Sophists considered: they discovered the tension and even the contradiction between nature and custom, or law. The more traditional among them argued that law itself

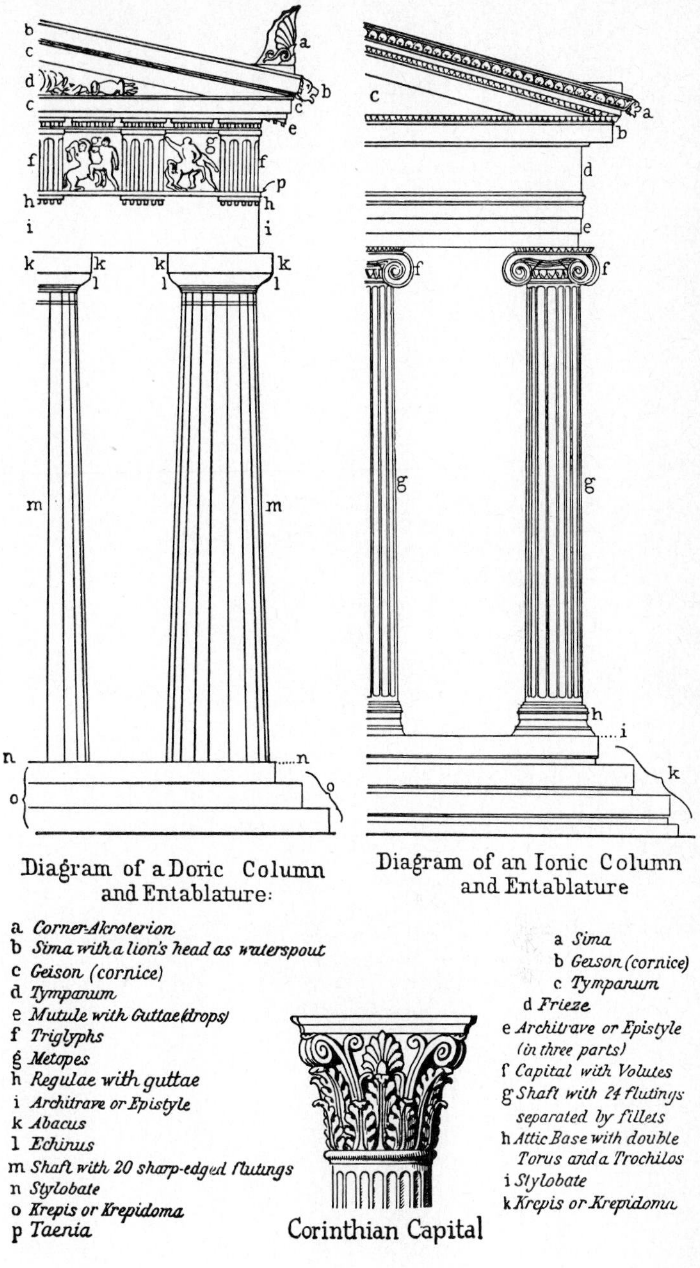

The three orders of Greek architecture: Doric, Ionic, and Corinthian. These three orders have enormously influenced Western architecture.

was in accord with nature, and this view fortified the traditional beliefs of the *polis.*

Others argued, however, that laws were merely conventional and not in accord with nature. The law was not of divine origin but merely the result of an agreement among peo-

(*Above*) *The Acropolis was both the religious and civic center of Athens. In its final form it is the work of Pericles and his successors in the late fifth century* B.C. *This photograph shows the Parthenon and to its left the Erechtheum.* [*Greek National Tourist Office*]

The temple of Victory on the Athenian Acropolis. This small temple was built in the Ionic order about 423 B.C. [*Greek National Tourist Office*] ple. It could not pretend to be a positive moral force but merely had the negative function of preventing people from harming each other. The most extreme Sophists argued that law was contrary to nature, a trick whereby the weak control the strong. Critias, an Athenian oligarch and one of the more extreme Sophists, went so far as to say that the gods themselves had been invented by some clever person to deter people from doing what they wished. Such ideas attacked the theoretical foundations of the *polis* and helped provoke the philosophical responses of Plato and Aristotle in the next century.

Plato Reports the Claims of the Sophist Protagoras

Plato (ca. 429–347 B.C.) remains to many the greatest of the ancient philosophers. Protagoras, the famous Sophist from Leontini in Sicily, came to Athens in 427 B.C. and created great excitement. In the following passage from the dialogue *Protagoras,* Plato's spokesman, Socrates, introduces a young man who wishes to benefit from Protagoras' skills.

When we were all seated, Protagoras said: Now that the company are assembled, Socrates, tell me about the young man of whom you were just now speaking.

I replied: I will begin again at the same point, Protagoras, and tell you once more the purport of my visit: this is my friend Hippocrates, who is desirous of making your acquaintance; he would like to know what will happen to him if he associates with you. I have no more to say.

Protagoras answered: Young man, if you associate with me, on the very first day you will return home a better man than you came and better on the second day than on the first, and better every day than you were on the day before.

When I heard this, I said: Protagoras, I do not at all wonder at hearing you say this; even at your age, and with all your wisdom, if any one were to teach you what you did not know before, you would become better no doubt: but please to answer in a different way—I will explain how by an example. Let me suppose that Hippocrates, instead of desiring your acquaintance, wished to become acquainted with the young man Zeuxippus of Heraclea, who has lately been in Athens, and he had come to him as he has come to you, and had heard him say, as he has heard you say, that every day he would grow and become better if he associated with him: and then suppose that he were to ask him, "In what shall I become better, and in what shall I grow?" Zeuxippus would answer, "In painting." And suppose that he went to Orthagoas the Theban, and heard him say the same thing, and asked him, "In what shall I become better day by day?" he would reply, "In flute-playing." Now I want you to make the same sort of answer to this young man and to me, who am asking questions on his account. When you say that on the first day on which he associates with you he will return home a better man, and on every day will grow in like manner,—in what, Protagoras, will he be better? and about what?

When Protagoras head me say this, he replied: You ask questions fairly, and I like to answer a question which is fairly put. If Hippocrates comes to me he will not experience the sort of drudgery with which other Sophists are in the habit of insulting their pupils; who, when they have just escaped from the arts, are taken and driven back into them by these teachers, and made to learn calculation, and astronomy, and geometry, and music (he gave a look at Hippias as he said this); but if he comes to me, he will learn that which he comes to learn. And this is prudence in affairs private as well as public; he will learn to order his own house in the best manner, and he will be able to speak and act for the best in the affairs of the state.

Plato, *Protagoras,* trans. by Benjamin Jowett in *The Dialogues of Plato,* Vol. 1 (New York: Random House, 1937), pp. 88–89.

History

The fifth century produced the first prose literature in the form of history. Herodotus, born shortly before the Persian wars, deserves his title of "the father of history," for his account of the Persian wars goes far beyond all previous chronicles, genealogies, and geographical studies and attempts to explain human actions and to draw instruction from them. Although his work was completed about 425 B.C. and shows a few traces of Sophist influence, its spirit is that of an earlier time. Herodotus accepted the evidence of legends and oracles, although not uncritically, and often explained human events in terms of divine intervention. Human arrogance and divine vengeance are key forces that help explain the defeat of Croesus by Cyrus as well as Xerxes' defeat by the Greeks. Yet the *History* is typical of its time in celebrating the crucial role of human intelligence as revealed by Miltiades at Marathon and Themistocles at Salamis. Nor was Herodotus unaware of the importance of institutions. There is no mistaking his pride in the superiority of the Greek *polis* and the discipline it inspired in its citizen soldiers and his pride in the superiority of the Greeks' voluntary obedience to law over the Persians' fear of punishment.

Thucydides, the historian of the Peloponnesian War, was born about 460 B.C. and died a few years after the end of the Great Peloponnesian War. He was very much a product of the late fifth century, reflecting the influence of the scientific attitude of the Hippocratic school of medicine as well as the secular, human-centered skeptical rationalism of the Sophists. Hippocrates of Cos was a contemporary of Thucydides who was part of a school of medical writers and practitioners. They did important pioneer work in medicine and scientific theory, placing great emphasis on the need to combine careful and accurate observation with reason to make possible the understanding, prognosis, treatment, and cure of a disease. In the same way Thucydides took great pains to achieve factual accuracy and tried to use his evidence to discover meaningful patterns of human behavior. He believed that human nature was essentially unchanging, so that a wise person equipped with the understanding provided by history might accurately foresee events and thus help to guide them. He believed, however, that only a few had the ability to understand history and to put its lessons to good use. He thought that even the wisest could be foiled by the intervention of chance, which played a great role in human affairs. Thucydides focused his interest on politics, and in that area his assumptions about human nature do not seem unwarranted. His work has proved to be, as he hoped, "a possession forever." Its description of the terrible civil war between the two basic kinds of *polis* is a final and fitting example of the tension that was the source of both the greatness and the decline of classical Greece.

The Fourth Century B.C.

Historians often speak of the Peloponnesian War as the crisis of the *polis* and of the fourth century as the period of its decline. But the Greeks of the fourth century B.C. did not know that their traditional way of life was on the verge of destruction. Thinkers could not avoid recognizing that they lived in a time of troubles, but they responded in different ways. Some looked to the past and tried to shore up the weakened structure of the *polis;* others tended toward despair and looked for new solutions; and still others averted their gaze from the public arena altogether. All of these responses are apparent in the literature, philosophy, and art of the period.

Drama

The tendency of some to avert their gaze from the life of the *polis* and to turn inward to everyday life, the family, and their own individuality is apparent in the poetry of the fourth century B.C. Tragedy proved to be a form whose originality was confined to the fifth century. No tragedies written in the fourth century have been preserved, and it was common to revive the great plays of the previous century. Some of the late plays of Euripides, in fact, seem less like the tragedies of Aeschylus and Sophocles than forerunners of later forms such as the New Comedy. Plays of Euripides like *Helena, Andromeda,* and *Iphigenia in Tauris* are more like fairy tales, tales of adventure, or love stories than tragedies. Euripides was less interested in cosmic confrontations of conflicting principles than in the psychology and behaviour of individual human beings. His plays, which rarely won first prize when first produced for Dionysian festival competitions, became increasingly popular in the fourth century and after.

Comedy was introduced into the Dionysian festival early in the fifth century B.C. Such poets as Cratinus, Eupolis, and the great master of the genre called Old Comedy, Aristophanes (ca. 450–ca. 385 B.C.), the only one from whom we have complete plays, wrote political comedies filled with scathing invective and satire against such contemporary figures as Pericles, Cleon, Socrates, and Euripides. The fourth century, however, produced what is called Middle Comedy, which turned away from political subjects and personal invective toward a comic-realistic depiction of daily life, plots of intrigue, and mild satire of domestic situations. Significantly the role of the chorus, which in some way represented the *polis,* was very much diminished. These trends all continued and were carried even further in the New Comedy, whose leading playwright, Menander (342–291 B.C.), completely abandoned mythological subjects in favor of domestic tragicomedy. His gentle satire of the foibles of ordinary people and his tales of lovers temporarily thwarted before a happy and proper ending would not be unfamiliar to viewers of modern situation comedies.

Sculpture

The same movement away from the grand, the ideal, and the general and toward the ordinary, the real, and the individual is apparent in the development of Greek sculpture. To see these developments, one has only to compare the statue of the *Striding God of Artemisium* (ca. 460 B.C.), thought to be either Zeus on the

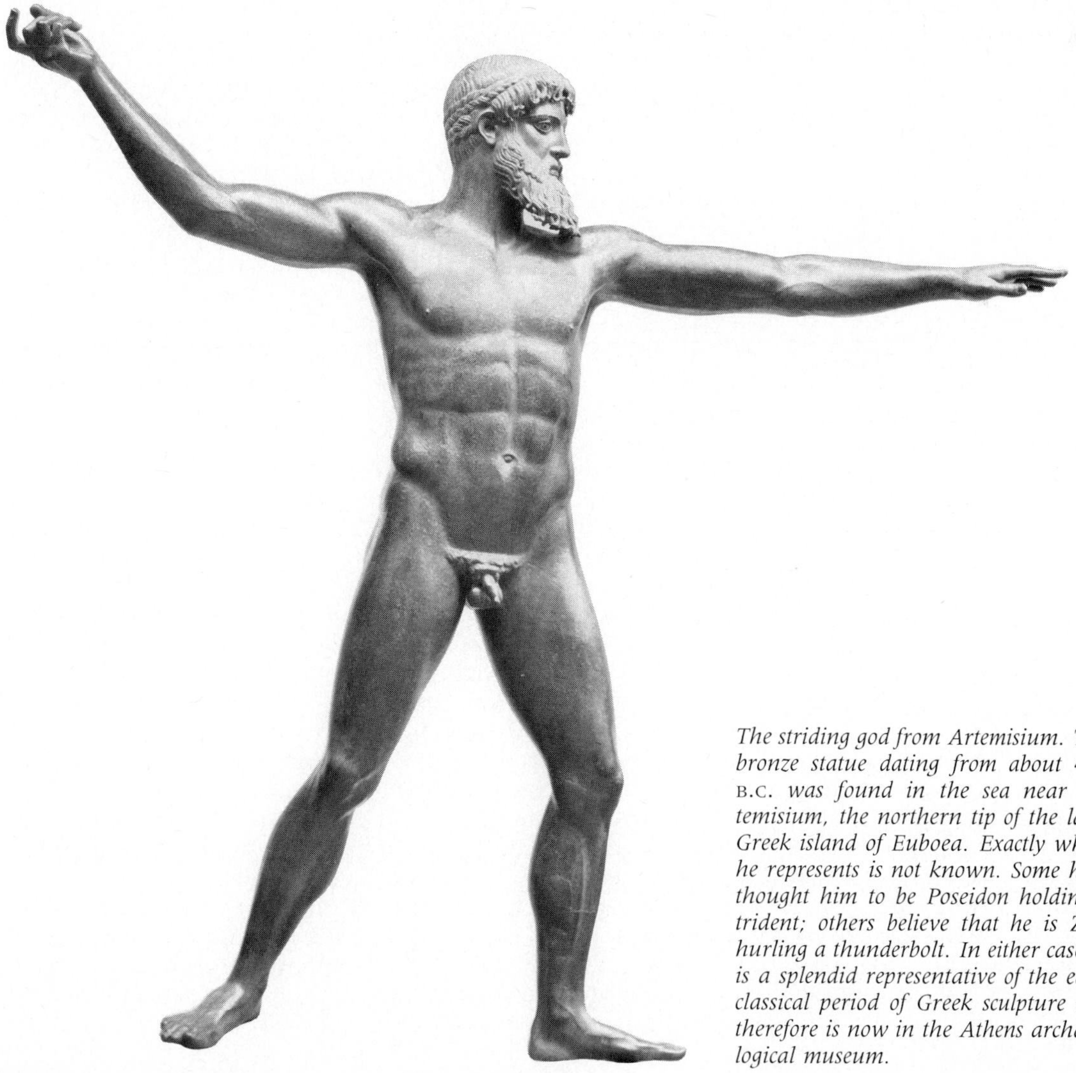

The striding god from Artemisium. This bronze statue dating from about 460 B.C. *was found in the sea near Artemisium, the northern tip of the large Greek island of Euboea. Exactly whom he represents is not known. Some have thought him to be Poseidon holding a trident; others believe that he is Zeus hurling a thunderbolt. In either case he is a splendid representative of the early classical period of Greek sculpture and therefore is now in the Athens archaeological museum.*

point of releasing a thunderbolt or Poseidon about to throw his trident, or the *Doryphoros* of Polycleitus (ca. 450–440 B.C.) with the *Hermes* of Praxiteles (ca. 340–330 B.C.) or the *Apoxyomenos* attributed to Lysippus (ca. 330 B.C.).

Philosophy

SOCRATES. Probably the most complicated response to the crisis of the *polis* may be found in the life and teachings of Socrates (469–399 B.C.). Because he wrote nothing, our knowledge of him comes chiefly from his disciples Plato and Xenophon and from later tradition. Although as a young man he was interested in speculations about the physical world, he later turned to the investigation of ethics and morality; as Cicero put it, he brought philosophy down from the heavens. He was committed to the search for truth and for the knowledge about human affairs that he believed could be discovered by reason. His method was to go among men, particularly those reputed to know something, like craftsmen, poets, and politicians, to question and cross-examine them. The result was always the same: those he questioned might have technical information and skills but seldom had any knowledge of the fundamental principles of human behavior. It is understandable that Athenians so exposed should be angry with their examiner, and it is not surprising that they thought Socrates was undermining the beliefs and values of the *polis.* Socrates' unconcealed contempt for democracy, which seemingly relied on ignorant amateurs to make important political decisions without any certain knowledge, created further hostility. Moreover, his insistence on the primacy of his own individualism and his determination to pursue philosophy even against the wishes of his fellow citizens reinforced this hostility and the prejudice that went with it.

But Socrates, unlike the Sophists, did not accept pay for his teaching; he professed ignorance and denied that he taught at all. His individualism, moreover, was unlike the worldly hedonism of some of the Sophists. It was not wealth or pleasure or power that he urged people to seek, but "the greatest improvement of the soul." He differed also from the more radical Sophists in that he denied that the *polis* and its laws were merely conventional. He thought, on the contrary, that they had a legitimate claim on the citizen, and he proved it in the most convincing fashion. In 399 B.C. he was condemned to death by an Athenian jury on the charges of bring new gods into the city and of corrupting the youth. His dialectical inquiries had angered many important people, and his criticism of democracy must have been viewed with suspicion, especially as Critias and Charmides, who were members of the Thirty Tyrants, and the traitor Alcibiades had been among his disciples. He was given a chance to escape, but in Plato's *Crito* we are told of his refusal because of his veneration of the laws. Socrates' career set the stage for later responses to the travail of the *polis*; he recognized its difficulties and criticized its shortcomings, and he turned away from an active political life, but he did not abandon the idea of the *polis.* He fought as a soldier in its defense, obeyed its laws, and sought to put its values on a sound foundation by reason.

THE CYNICS. One branch of Socratic thought—the concern with personal morality and one's own soul, the disdain of worldly pleasure and wealth, and the withdrawal from political life—was developed and then distorted almost beyond recognition by the Cynic school. Antisthenes (ca. 455–ca. 360 B.C.), a follower of Socrates, is said to have been its founder, but its most famous exemplar was Diogenes of Sinope (ca. 400–ca. 325 B.C.). Socrates disparaged wealth and worldly comfort, so Diogenes wore rags and lived in a tub. He performed shameful acts in public and made his living by begging, in order to show his rejection of convention. He believed that happiness lay in satisfying natural needs in the simplest and most direct way. Because actions to this end, being natural, could not be indecent, they could and should be done publicly.

Socrates questioned the theoretical basis for popular religious beliefs; the Cynics ridiculed all religious observances. As Plato said, Diogenes was Socrates gone mad. Beyond that, the way of the Cynics contradicted important Socratic beliefs. Socrates, unlike traditional aristocrats like Theognis, believed that virtue was a matter not of birth but of knowledge and that people do wrong only through ignorance of what is virtuous. The Cynics, on the contrary, believed that "Virtue is an affair of deeds and does not need a store of words and learning,"[1] Wisdom and happiness come from pursuing the proper style of life, not from philosophy.

[1] Diogenes Laertius, *Life of Antisthenes.*

They moved even further from Socrates by abandoning the concept of the *polis* entirely. When Diogenes was asked about his citizenship, he answered that he was *kosmopolites,* a citizen of the world. The Cynics plainly had turned away from the past, and their views anticipated those of the Hellenistic Age.

PLATO. (429–347 B.C.) was by far the most important of Socrates' associates and is a perfect example of the pupil who becomes greater than his master. He was the first systematic philosopher and therefore the first to place political ideas in their full philosophical context. He was also a writer of genius, leaving us twenty-six philosophical discussions, almost all in the form of dialogues, which somehow make the examination of difficult and complicated philosophical problems seem dramatic and entertaining. Plato came from a noble Athenian family and looked forward to an active political career until he was discouraged by the excesses of the Thirty Tyrants and the execution of Socrates by the restored democracy. Twice he made trips to Sicily in the hope of producing a model state at Syracuse under the tyrants Dionysius I and II, but without success. In 386 B.C. he founded the Academy, a center of philosophical investigation and a school for training statesmen and citizens that had a powerful impact on Greek thought and lasted until it was closed by the Emperor Justinian in the sixth century A.D.

Like Socrates, Plato firmly believed in the *polis* and its values. Its virtues were order, harmony, and justice, and one of its main objects was to produce good people. Like his master, and unlike the radical Sophists, Plato thought that the *polis* was in accord with nature. He accepted Socrates' doctrine of the identity of virtue and knowledge and made it plain what that knowledge was: *epistēmē,* science, a body of true and unchanging wisdom open to only a few philosophers, whose training, character, and intellect allowed them to see reality. Only such people were qualified to rule; they themselves would prefer the life of pure contemplation but would accept their responsibility and take their turn as philosopher kings. The training of such men required a specialization of function and a subordination of the individual to the community even greater than that at Sparta. This specialization would lead to Plato's definition of justice: that each man should do only that one thing to which his nature is best suited. Plato saw quite well that the *polis* of his day suffered from terrible internal stress, class struggle, and factional divisions. His solution, however, was not that of some Greeks, that is, conquest and resulting economic prosperity. For Plato the answer was in moral and political reform. The way to harmony was to destroy the causes of strife: private property, the family—anything, in short, that stood between the individual citizen and devotion to the *polis.*

Concern for the redemption of the *polis* was at the heart of Plato's system of philosophy. He began by asking the traditional questions: What is a good man, and how is he made? The goodness of a human being belonged to moral philosophy, and when it became a function of the state, it became political philosophy. Because goodness depended on knowledge of the good, it required a theory of knowledge and an investigation of what the knowledge was that was required for goodness. The answer must be metaphysical and so required a full examination of metaphysics. Even when the philosopher knew the good, however, the question remained how the state could bring its citizens to the necessary comprehension of that knowledge. The answer required a theory of education. Even purely logical and metaphysical questions, therefore, were subordinate to the overriding political questions. In this way Plato's need to find a satisfactory foundation for the beleaguered *polis* contributed to the birth of systematic philosophy.

ARISTOTLE. Aristotle (384–322 B.C.) was a pupil of Plato's and owed much to the thought of his master, but his very different experience and cast of mind led him in some new directions. He was born at Stagirus in the Chalcidice, the son of the court doctor of neighboring Macedon. As a young man he went to Athens to study at the Academy, where he stayed until Plato's death. Then he joined a Platonic colony at Assos in Asia Minor, and from there he moved to Mytilene. In both places he carried on research in marine biology, and biological interests played a large part in all his thoughts. In 342 B.C. Philip, the king of Macedon, appointed him tutor to his son, the young Alexander (see the following section). In 336 he returned to Athens, where he founded his own school, the Lyceum, or the Peripatos, as it was also called from the covered walk within it. In later years its members were called *Peripatetics.* On the death of Alexander in 323 B.C., the Athenians rebelled from Macedo-

Aristotle (383–322 B.C.). *This is believed to be an ancient copy of an actual portrait of the philosopher.* [*Kunsthistorische Museum, Vienna*]

nian rule, and Aristotle found it wise to leave. He died at Chalcis in Euboea in the following year.

The Lyceum was a very different place from the Academy. Its members took little interest in mathematics and were concerned with gathering, ordering, and analyzing all human knowledge. Aristotle wrote dialogues on the Platonic model, but none survive. He and his students also prepared many collections of information to serve as the basis for scientific works, but of these only the *Constitution of the Athenians,* one of 158 constitutional treatises, remains. Almost all of what we possess is in the form of philosophical and scientific studies, whose loose organization and style suggest that they were lecture notes. The range of subjects treated is astonishing, including logic, physics, astronomy, biology, ethics, rhetoric, literary criticism, and politics. In each field the method is the same. Aristotle began with observation of the empirical evidence, which in some cases was physical and in others was common opinion. To this body of information he applied reason and discovered inconsistencies or difficulties. To deal with these, he introduced metaphysical principles to explain the problems or to reconcile the inconsistencies. His view on all subjects, like Plato's, was teleological; that is, both Plato and Aristotle recognized purposes apart from and greater than the will of the individual human being. Plato's purposes, however, were contained in ideas, or forms, transcendental concepts outside the experience of most people, whereas for Aristotle the purposes of most things were easily inferred by observation of their behavior in the world. Aristotle's most striking characteristics are his moderation and his common sense. His epistemology finds room for both reason and experience; his metaphysics gives meaning and reality to both mind and body; his ethics aims at the good life, which is the contemplative life, but recognizes the necessity for moderate wealth, comfort, and pleasure.

All these qualities are evident in Aristotle's political thought. Like Plato he opposed the Sophists' assertion that the *polis* was contrary to nature and the result of mere convention. His response was to apply the teleology he saw in all nature to politics as well. In his view matter existed to achieve an end, and it developed until it achieved its form, which was its end. There was constant development from matter to form, from potential to actual. Therefore human primitive instincts could be seen as the matter out of which the human's potential as a political being could be realized. The *polis* made individuals self-sufficient and allowed the full realization of their potentiality. It was therefore natural. It was also the highest point in the evolution of the social institutions that serve the human need to continue the species—marriage, household, village, and finally, *polis.* For Aristotle the purpose of the *polis* was neither economic nor military but moral. "The end of the state is the good life" (*Politics* 1280b), the life lived "for the sake of noble actions" (1281a), a life of virtue and morality.

Characteristically Aristotle was less interested in the best state—the utopia that required philosophers to rule it—than in the best state practically possible, one that would combine justice with stability. The constitution for that state he called *politeia,* not the best constitution, but the next best, the one most suited to and most possible for most states. Its quality was moderation, and it naturally gave power to neither the rich nor the poor, but to the middle class, which must also be the most numerous. The middle class possessed many virtues: because of its moderate wealth it was free of the arrogance of the rich and the malice of the poor. For this reason it was the most stable class. The stability of the constitution also came from its being a mixed constitution, blending in some way the laws of democracy and of oligarchy. Aristotle's scheme was unique because of its realism and the breadth of its vision. All the political thinkers of the fourth century B.C. recognized that the *polis* was in danger, and all hoped to save it. All recognized the economic and social troubles that threatened it. Isocrates, a contemporary of Plato and Aristotle, urged a program of imperial conquest as a cure for poverty and revolution. Plato saw the folly of solving a political and moral problem by purely economic means and resorted to the creation of utopias. Aristotle combined the practical analysis of political and economic realities with the moral and political purposes of the traditional defenders of the *polis.* The result was a passionate confidence in the virtues of moderation and of the middle class and the proposal of a constitution that would give it power. It is ironic that the ablest defense of the *polis* came soon before its demise.

Emergence of the Hellenistic World

The term *Hellenistic* was coined in the nineteenth century to describe the period of three centuries during which Greek culture spread far from its homeland to Egypt and far into Asia. The new civilization formed in this expansion was a mixture of Greek and Oriental elements, although the degree of mixture varied from time to time and place to place. The Hellenistic world was larger than the world of classical Greece, and its major political units were much larger than the city-states, though these persisted in different forms. The new political and cultural order had its roots in the rise to power of a Macedonian dynasty that conquered Greece and the Persian Empire in the space of two generations.

The Macedonian Conquest

The quarrels among the Greeks brought on defeat and conquest by a new power that suddenly rose to eminence in the fourth century B.C., the kingdom of Macedon. The Macedonians inhabited the land to the north of Thessaly, and through the centuries they had unknowingly served the vital purpose of protecting the Greek states from barbarian tribes further to the north. By Greek standards Macedon was a backward, semibarbaric land. It had no *poleis* and was ruled loosely by a king in a rather Homeric fashion. He was chosen partly on the basis of descent, but the acclamation of the army gathered in assembly was required to make him legitimate. Quarrels between pretenders to the throne and even murder to achieve it were not uncommon. A council of nobles checked the royal power and could reject a weak or incompetent king. Hampered by constant wars with the barbarians, internal strife, loose organization, and lack of money, Macedon played no great part in Greek affairs up to the fourth century B.C. The Macedonians were of the same stock as the Greeks and spoke a Greek dialect, and the nobles, at least, thought of themselves as Greeks. The kings claimed descent from Heracles and the royal house of Argos. They tried to bring Greek culture into their court and won acceptance at the Olympic games. If a king could be found with the ability to unify this nation, it was bound to play a greater part in Greek affairs.

PHILIP OF MACEDON. That king was Philip II (359–336 B.C.), who, while still under thirty, took advantage of his appointment as regent to overthrow his infant nephew and make himself king. Like many of his predecessors, he admired Greek culture. Between 367 and 364 B.C. he had been a hostage in Thebes, where he learned much about Greek politics and warfare under the tutelage of Epaminon-

THE RISE OF MACEDON

Reign of Philip II	359–336 B.C.
Battle of Chaeronea; Philip conquers Greece	338 B.C.
Founding of League of Corinth	338 B.C.
Reign of Alexander III, the Great	336–323 B.C.
Alexander invades Asia	334 B.C.
Battle of Issus	333 B.C.
Battle of Gaugamela	331 B.C.
Fall of Persepolis	330 B.C.
Alexander reaches Indus Valley	327 B.C.
Death of Alexander	323 B.C.

das. His natural talents for war and diplomacy and his boundless ambition made him the ablest king in Macedonian history. Using both diplomatic and military means, he was able to pacify the tribes on his frontiers and make his own hold on the throne firmer. Then he began to undermine Athenian control of the northern Aegean. He took Amphipolis, which gave him control of the Strymon valley and of the gold and silver mines of Mount Pangaeus. The income allowed him to found new cities, to bribe politicians in foreign towns, and to reorganize his army into the finest fighting force in the world.

THE MACEDONIAN ARMY. Philip put to good use what he had learned in Thebes and combined it with the advantages afforded by Macedonian society and tradition. His genius created a versatile and powerful army. The infantry was drawn from Macedonian farmers as well as from the hill people, who so frequently proved rebellious. In time these were integrated to form a loyal and effective national army. The infantry was armed with pikes that were thirteen feet long instead of the usual nine. They stood in a more open formation, which depended less on the weight of the charge than on the skillful use of the weapon. This tactic was effective because the phalanx was meant not to be the decisive force but merely to hold the enemy until the winning blow was struck by a massed cavalry charge on the flank or into a gap. The cavalry was made up of Macedonian nobles and clan leaders, who were called Companions and who lived closely with the king and developed a special loyalty to him. In addition Philip employed mercenaries who knew the latest tactics used by mobile light-armed Greek troops as well as the most sophisticated siege machinery known to the Greeks. The native Macedonian army might be as large as forty thousand men and could be expanded by drafts from the allies and by mercenaries.

THE INVASION OF GREECE. So armed, Philip turned south toward central Greece. Since 355 B.C. the Phocians had been fighting against Thebes and Thessaly. Philip gladly accepted the request of the Thessalians to be their general, defeated Phocis, and treacherously took control of Thessaly. Swiftly he turned northward again to Thrace and gained domination over the northern Aegean coast and the European side of the straits to the Black Sea. This conquest threatened the vital interests of Athens, which still had a formidable fleet of three hundred ships.

The Athens of 350 B.C. was not the Athens of Pericles. It had neither imperial revenue nor allies to share the burden of war on land or sea, and its own population was smaller than in the fifth century. The Athenians, therefore, were reluctant to go on expeditions themselves or even to send out mercenary armies under Athenian generals, for they must be paid out of taxes or contributions from Athenian citizens.

The leading spokesman against these tendencies and the cautious foreign policy that went with them was Demosthenes (384–322 B.C.), one of the greatest orators in Greek history. He was convinced that Philip was a dangerous enemy to Athens and the other Greeks and spent most of his career urging the Athenians to resist Philip's encroachments. He was right, for beginning in 349 B.C., Philip attacked several cities in northern and central Greece and firmly planted Macedonian power in those regions. The king of "barbarian" Macedon was elected president of the Pythian Games at Delphi, and the Athenians were forced to concur in the election.

In these difficult times it was Athens' misfortune not to have the kind of political leadership that Cimon or Pericles had offered a century earlier, which allowed for a consistent foreign policy. Many, perhaps most, Athenians accepted Demosthenes' view of Philip, but few were willing to run the risks and make the sacrifices necessary to stop his advance. Others, like Eubulus, an outstanding financial official and conservative political leader, favored a cautious policy of cooperation with Philip in the hope that his aims were limited and no real threat to Athens. Isocrates (436–338 B.C.), the head of an important rhetorical and philosophical school in Athens, looked to Philip to provide the unity and leadership needed for the Panhellenic campaign against Persia that he and other orators had been urging for some years. Isocrates saw the conquest of Asia Minor as the solution to the economic, social, and political problems that had brought poverty and civil war to the Greek cities ever since the Peloponnesian War. Finally, there seem to have been some Athenians who were in the pay of Philip, for he used money lavishly to win support in all of the cities.

The years between 346 B.C. and 340 B.C. were spent in diplomatic maneuvering, each side trying to win strategically useful allies. At

Demosthenes Denounces Philip of Macedon

Demosthenes (384–322 B.C.) was an Athenian statesman who urged his fellow citizens and other Greeks to resist the advance of Philip of Macedon (ca. 359–317 B.C.). The following is from the speech we call the First Philippic, delivered probably in 351 B.C.

Do not imagine, that his empire is everlastingly secured to him as a god. There are those who hate and fear and envy him, Athenians, even among those that seem most friendly; and all feelings that are in other men belong, we may assume, to his confederates. But now they are cowed, having no refuge through your tardiness and indolence, which I say you must abandon forthwith. For you see, Athenians, the case, to what pitch of arrogance the man has advanced, who leaves you not even the choice of action or inaction, but threatens and uses (they say) outrageous language, and, unable to rest in possession of his conquests, continually widens their circle, and whilst we dally and delay, throws his net all around us. When then, Athenians, when will ye act as becomes you? In what event? In that of necessity, I suppose. And how should we regard the events happening now? Methinks, to freemen the strongest necessity is the disgrace of their condition. Or tell me, do ye like walking about and asking one another:—is there any news? Why, could there be greater news than a man of Macedonia subduing Athenians, and directing the affairs of Greece? Is Philip dead? No, but he is sick. And what matters it to you? Should anything befall this man, you will soon create another Philip, if you attend to business thus. For even he has been exalted not so much by his own strength, as by our negligence.

Demosthenes, *The Olynthiac and Other Public Orations of Demosthenes,* trans. by C. R. Kennedy (London: George Bell and Sons, 1903), pp. 62–63.

last, Philip attacked Perinthus and Byzantium, the life line of Athenian commerce, and in 340 he besieged both cities and declared war. The Athenian fleet saved both, so in the following year Philip marched into Greece. Demosthenes performed wonders in rallying the Athenians and winning Thebes over to the Athenian side, but in 338 Philip defeated the allied forces at Chaeronea in Boeotia in a great battle whose decisive blow was a cavalry charge led by the eighteen-year-old son of Philip, Alexander.

THE MACEDONIAN GOVERNMENT OF GREECE. The Macedonian settlement of Greek affairs was not as harsh as many had feared, although in some cities the friends of Macedon came to power and killed or exiled their enemies. Demosthenes continued to be free to engage in politics, and Athens was not attacked on the condition that it give up what was left of its empire and follow the lead of Macedon. The rest of Greece was arranged in such a way as to remove all dangers to Philip's rule. To guarantee his security, Philip placed garrisons at Thebes, Chalcis, and Corinth; these came to be known as the fetters of Greece. In 338 B.C. Philip called a meeting of the Greek states to form the federal League of Corinth. The constitution provided for autonomy, freedom from tribute and garrisons, and suppression of piracy and civil war. The league delegates would make foreign policy, in theory without consulting their home governments or Philip. All this was a facade; not only was Philip of Macedon president of the league, he was its ruler. The defeat at Chaeronea was the end of Greek freedom and autonomy. Though its form and internal life continued for some time, the *polis* had lost control of its own affairs and the special conditions that had made it unique.

Philip's choice of Corinth as the seat of his new confederacy was not made out of convenience or by accident. It was at Corinth that the Greeks had gathered to resist a Persian invasion almost 150 years earlier, and it was there in 337 B.C. that Philip announced his intention to invade Persia in a war of liberation and revenge as leader of the new league. In the spring of 336 B.C., as he prepared to begin the campaign, Philip was assassinated.

In 1977 a mound was excavated at the Mac-

Democracy crowns the people of Athens in this carving from 336 B.C. By that date Athens had already been forced to accept the hegemony of Philip of Macedon, and the era of the independent, democratic city-state was ending. [*American School of Classical Studies, Athens*]

edonian village of Vergina. The extraordinarily rich finds and associated buildings have led many scholars to conclude that this is the royal tomb of Philip II. If they are right, and the evidence seems persuasive, Philip richly deserved so distinguished a resting place. He found Macedon a disunited kingdom of semibarbarians, despised and exploited by the Greeks; at his death Macedon was a united kingdom, master and leader of the Greeks, rich, powerful, and ready to undertake the invasion of Asia. The completion of this task was left to Philip's first son, Alexander III (356–323 B.C.), later called Alexander the Great, who came to the throne at the age of twenty.

Alexander the Great

THE CONQUEST OF PERSIA AND BEYOND. Along with his throne, the young king inherited his father's plan to invade Persia. The idea was daring, for Persia's empire was vast and its resources were enormous, but the usurper Cyrus and his Greek mercenaries had shown its vulnerability by penetrating deep into the Persian Empire at the beginning of the fourth century B.C. Its size and disparate nature also made it hard to control and exploit. There were always troubles on some of its far-flung frontiers and intrigues within the royal palace. Throughout the fourth century B.C. the Persian king called on Greek mercenaries to put down trouble. In 336 B.C. Persia was ruled by a new and inexperienced king, Darius III, but it remained formidable because of its huge army, its great wealth, and a navy that ruled the sea.

In 334 B.C. Alexander crossed the Hellespont into Asia. His army consisted of about thirty thousand infantry and five thousand cavalry; he had no navy and little money. These facts determined his early strategy: he must seek quick and decisive battles to gain money and supplies from the conquered territory. He must move along the coast so as to neutralize the Persian navy by depriving it of ports. Memnon, the commander of the Persian navy, recommended the perfect strategy against this plan: to retreat, to scorch the earth and deprive Alex-

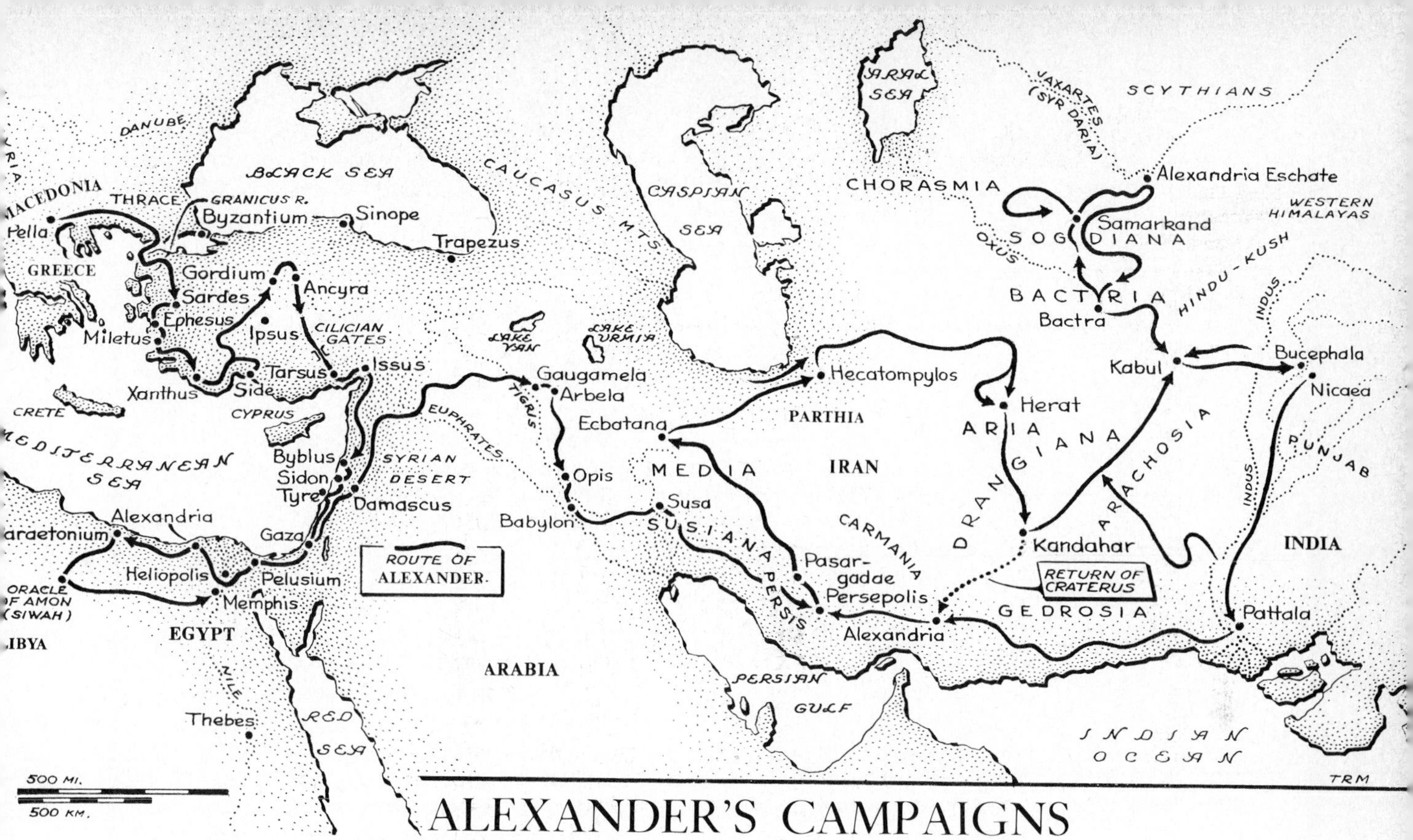

ALEXANDER'S CAMPAIGNS

MAP 3-5 *The route taken by Alexander the Great in his conquest of the Persian Empire, 334–323* B.C. *Starting from the Macedonian capital at Pella, he reached the Indus valley before being turned back by his own restive troops. He died of fever in Mesopotamia.*

ander of supplies, to avoid battles, to use guerrilla tactics, and to stir up rebellion in Greece, but he was ignored. The Persians preferred to stand and fight; their pride and courage were greater than their wisdom.

Alexander met the Persian forces of Asia Minor at the Granicus River, where he won a smashing victory in characteristic style (see Map 3.5). He led a cavalry charge across the river into the teeth of the enemy on the opposite bank, almost losing his life in the process and winning the devotion of his soldiers. That victory left the coast of Asia Minor open, and Alexander captured the coastal cities, thus denying them to the Persian fleet.

In 333 B.C. Alexander marched inland to Syria, where he met the main Persian army under King Darius at Issus. Alexander himself led the cavalry charge that broke the Persian line and sent Darius fleeing into central Asia Minor. He continued along the coast and captured previously impregnable Tyre after a long and ingenious siege, putting an end to the threat of the Persian navy. He took Egypt with little trouble and was greeted as liberator, pharaoh, and son of Re (an Egyptian god whose Greek equivalent was Zeus). At Tyre, Darius sent Alexander a peace offer, yielding his entire empire west of the Euphrates River and his daughter in exchange for an alliance and an end to the invasion. But Alexander aimed at conquering the whole empire and probably whatever lay beyond that.

In the spring of 331 B.C. Alexander marched into Mesopotamia. At Gaugamela, near the ancient Assyrian city of Nineveh, he met Darius, ready for a last stand. Once again Alexander's tactical genius and personal leadership carried the day. The Persians were broken and Darius fled once more. Alexander entered Babylon, again hailed as liberator and king. In January of 330 B.C. he came to Persepolis, the Persian capital, which held splendid palaces and the royal treasury. This bonanza ended his financial troubles and put a vast sum of money into circulation, with economic consequences that lasted for centuries. After a stay of several months Alexander burned Persepolis to dramatize the completion of Hellenic revenge for the Persian invasion and the destruction of the native Persian dynasty.

The new regime could not be secure while Darius lived, so Alexander pursued him eastward. Just south of the Caspian Sea he came

Arrian Describes Alexander's Actions at a Tragic Drinking Party

Arrian lived in the second century A.D., almost five hundred years after Alexander the Great, but his *Anabasis* is the best ancient source of information about Alexander's career. In 328 B.C. Alexander's expedition had reached Samarkand. By now he had adopted a number of Persian customs and had begun to reduce the distinction between Macedonians and Persians. The older Macedonians, in particular, were resentful, and in the following passage is described a drinking bout in which a quarrel arose between Alexander and one of the most distinguished Macedonian veterans.

When the drinking-party on this occasion had already gone on too long (for Alexander had now made innovations even in regard to drinking, by imitating too much the custom of foreigners), and in the midst of the carouse a discussion had arisen about the Dioscuri, how their procreation had been taken away from Tyndareus and ascribed to Zeus, some of those present, in order to flatter Alexander, maintained that Polydeuces and Castor were in no way worthy to compare with him and his exploits. Such men have always destroyed and will never cease to ruin the interests of those who happen to be reigning. In their carousal they did not even abstain from comparing him with Heracles, saying that envy stood in the way of the living receiving the honours due to them from their associates. It was well known that Clitus had long been vexed at Alexander for the change in his style of living in excessive imitation of foreign customs, and at those who flattered him with their speech. At that time also, being heated with wine, he would not permit them either to insult the deity or, by depreciating the deeds of the ancient heroes, to confer upon Alexander this gratification which deserved no thanks. He affirmed Alexander's deeds were neither in fact at all so great or marvellous as they represented in their laudation; nor had he achieved them by himself, but for the most part they were the deeds of the Macedonians. The delivery of this speech annoyed Alexander; and I do not commend it, for I think, in such a drunken bout, it would have been sufficient if, so far as he was personally concerned, he had kept silence, and not committed the error of indulging in the same flattery as the others. But when some even mentioned Philip's actions without exercising a just judgment, declaring that he had performed nothing great or marvellous, they herein gratified Alexander; but Clitus being then no longer able to contain himself, began to put Philip's achievements in the first rank, and to depreciate Alexander and his performances. Clitus being now quite intoxicated, made other depreciatory remarks and even vehemently reviled him, because after all he had saved his life, when the cavalry battle had been fought with the Persians at the Granicus. Then indeed, arrogantly stretching out his right hand, he said, "This hand, O Alexander, preserved you on that occasion." Alexander could now no longer endure the drunken insolence of Clitus; but jumped up against him in a great rage. He was however restrained by his boon companions. As Clitus did not desist from his insulting remarks, Alexander shouted out a summons for his shield-bearing guards to attend him; but when no one obeyed him, he said that he was reduced to the same position as Darius, when he was led about under arrest by Bessus and his adherents, and that he now possessed the mere name of king. Then his companions were no longer able to restrain him; for according to some he leaped up and snatched a javelin from one of his confidential body-guards; according to others, a long pike from one of his ordinary guards, with which he struck Clitus and killed him.

Arrian, *The Anabasis of Alexander,* trans. by E. J. Chinnock in *The Greek Historians,* Vol. 2, ed. by F. R. B. Godolphin (New York: Random House, 1942), pp. 507–508.

upon the corpse of Darius, killed by his relative Bessus. The Persian nobles around Darius had lost faith in him and had joined in the plot. The murder removed Darius from Alexander's path, but now he had to catch Bessus, who proclaimed himself successor to Darius. The pursuit of Bessus (who was soon caught), a great curiosity, and a longing to go as far as he could and see the most distant places took Alexander to the frontier of India.

Near Samarkand, in the land of the Scythians, he founded the city of Alexandria Eschate ("Furthest Alexandria"), one of the many cities bearing his name that he founded as he traveled. As part of his grand scheme of amalgamation and conquest, he married the Bactrian princess Roxane and enrolled thirty thousand young Bactrians into his army. These were to be trained and sent back to the center of the empire for use later.

In 327 B.C. Alexander took his army through the Khyber Pass in an attempt to conquer the lands around the Indus River (modern Pakistan). He reduced its king, Porus, to vassalage but pushed on in the hope of reaching the river called Ocean that the Greeks believed encircled the world. Finally, his weary men refused to go on. By the spring of 324 B.C. the army was back at the Persian Gulf and celebrated in the Macedonian style, with a wild spree of drinking.

A gold medallion bearing a portrait of Alexander the Great (356–323 B.C.). [*State Museums, Berlin*]

The Death of Alexander and Its Aftermath. Alexander was filled with plans for the future: for the consolidation and organization of his empire; for geographical exploration; for building new cities, roads, and harbors; perhaps even for further conquests in the west. There is even some evidence that he asked to be deified and worshiped as a god, although we cannot be sure if he really did so or what he had in mind if he did. In June of 323 B.C. he was overcome by a fever and died in Babylon at the age of thirty-three. His memory has never faded, and he soon became the subject of myth, legend, and romance. From the beginning, estimates of him have varied. Some have seen in him a man of grand and noble vision who transcended the narrow limits of Greek and Macedonian ethnocentrism and aimed at the brotherhood of humankind in a great world state. Others have seen him as a calculating despot, given to drunken brawls, brutality, and murder.

The truth is probably in between. Alexander was one of the greatest generals the world has seen; he never lost a battle or failed in a siege, and with a modest army he conquered a vast empire. He had rare organizational talents, and his plan for creating a multinational empire was the only intelligent way of proceeding. He established many new cities—seventy, according to tradition—mostly along trade routes. These cities had the effect of encouraging commerce and prosperity as well as of introducing Hellenic civilization into new areas. It is hard to know if the vast new empire could have been held together, but Alexander's death proved that only he had a chance to succeed.

Nobody was prepared for Alexander's sudden death in 323 B.C., and affairs were further complicated by a weak succession: Roxane's unborn child and Alexander's weak-minded half-brother. His able and loyal Macedonian generals at first hoped to preserve the empire for the Macedonian royal house, and to this end they appointed themselves governors of the various provinces of the empire. However, the conflicting ambitions of these strong-willed men led to prolonged warfare among various combinations of them, in which three of the original number were killed, and all of the direct members of the Macedonian royal house were either executed or murdered. With the murder of Roxane and her son in 310 B.C., there was no longer any focus for the enormous empire, and in 306 and 305 the surviving governors proclaimed themselves kings of their various holdings.

Three of these Macedonian generals founded dynasties of significance in the spread of Hellenistic culture:

Ptolemy I, 367?–283 B.C.; founder of the Thirty-first Dynasty in Egypt, the Ptolemies, of whom Cleopatra, who died in 30 B.C., was the last.

Seleucus I, 358?–280 B.C.; founder of the Seleucid dynasty in Mesopotamia.

Antigonus I, 382–301 B.C.; founder of the Antigonid dynasty in Asia Minor and Macedon.

For the first seventy-five years or so after the death of Alexander, the world ruled by his successors enjoyed considerable prosperity. The vast sums of money that he and they put into circulation greatly increased the level of economic activity. The opportunities for service and profit in the east attracted many Greeks and relieved their native cities of some of the pressure of the poor. The opening of vast new territories to Greek trade, the increased demand for Greek products, and the new availability of things wanted by the Greeks, as well as the conscious policies of the Hellenistic kings, all helped the growth of commerce. The new prosperity, however, was not evenly distributed. The urban Greeks, the Macedonians, and the hellenized natives who made up the upper and middle classes lived lives of comfort and even luxury, but the rural native peasants did not. During prosperous times these distinctions were bearable, although even then there was tension between the two groups. After a while, however, the costs of continuing wars, inflation, and a gradual lessening of the positive effects of the introduction of Persian wealth all led to economic crisis. The kings bore down heavily on the middle classes, who, however, were skilled at avoiding their responsibilities. The pressure on the peasants and the city laborers became great, too, and they responded by slowing down their work and even by striking. In Greece economic pressures brought clashes between rich and poor, demands for the abolition of debt and the redistribution of land, and even, on occasion, civil war.

These internal divisions, along with the international wars, weakened the capacity of the Hellenistic kingdoms to resist outside attack, and by the middle of the second century B.C. they were all gone, except for Egypt. The two centuries between Alexander and the Roman conquest, however, were of great and lasting importance. They saw the formation into a single political, economic, and cultural unit of the entire eastern Mediterranean coast and of Greece, Egypt, Mesopotamia, and the old Persian Empire. The period also saw the creation of a new culture that took root, at least in the urban portions of that vast area, one that deserves to be differentiated from the earlier one of the Greek city-states: Hellenistic culture.

Hellenistic Culture

The career of Alexander the Great marked a significant turning point in the thought of the Greeks as it was represented in literature, philosophy, religion, and art. His conquests and the establishment of the successor kingdoms put an end once and for all to the central role of the *polis* in Greek life and thought. Scholars disagree about the end of the *polis*. Some deny that Philip's victory at Chaeronea put an end to its existence; they point to the continuance of *poleis* throughout the Hellenistic period and even see a continuation of them in the Roman *municipia*, but these are only a shadow of the vital reality that had been the true *polis*.

Deprived of control of their foreign affairs, their important internal arrangements determined by a foreign monarch, the postclassical cities lost the kind of political freedom that was basic to the old outlook. They were cities, perhaps—in a sense, even city-states—but not *poleis*. As time passed, they changed from sovereign states to municipal towns merged in military empires. Never again in antiquity would there be either a serious attack on or a defense of the *polis*, for its importance was gone. For the most part, the Greeks after Alexander turned away from political solutions for their problems and sought instead personal responses to their hopes and fears, particularly in religion, philosophy, and magic. The confident, sometimes arrogant, humanism of the fifth century B.C. gave way to a kind of resignation to fate, a recognition of helplessness before forces too great for humans to manage.

Philosophy

These developments are noticeable in the changes that overtook the established schools of philosophy as well as in the emergence of two new and influential groups of philosophers, the Epicureans and the Stoics. Athens' position as the center of philosophical studies was reinforced, for the Academy and the Lyceum continued in operation, and the new schools were also located in Athens. The Lyceum turned gradually away from the universal investigations of its founder, Aristotle, even from his scientific interests, to become a center chiefly of literary and especially historical studies.

The Academy turned even further away from its tradition. It adopted the systematic Skepticism of Pyrrho of Elis, and under the leadership of Arcesilaus and Carneades, the Skeptics of the Academy became skilled at pointing out fallacies and weaknesses in the philosophies of the rival schools. They thought that nothing could be known and so consoled themselves and their followers by suggesting that nothing mattered. It was easy for them, therefore, to accept conventional morality and the world as it was. The Cynics, of course, continued to denounce convention and to advocate the crude life in accordance with nature, which some of them practiced publicly to the shock and outrage of respectable citizens. Neither of these views had much appeal to the middle-class city dweller of the third century B.C., who sought some basis for choosing a way of life now that the *polis* no longer provided one ready-made.

Epicurus of Athens (342–271 B.C.) *taught that the goal of philosophy was not knowledge, but happiness, which could be achieved through a reasonable and moderate way of life.* [*Metropolitan Museum, Roger Fund,* 1911]

THE EPICUREANS. Epicurus of Athens (342–271 B.C.) formulated a new teaching, which was embodied in the school he founded in his native city in 306. His philosophy conformed to the new mood in that its goal was not knowledge but human happiness, which he believed could be achieved if one followed a style of life based on reason. He took sense perception to be the basis of all human knowledge. The reality and reliability of sense perception rested on the acceptance of the physical universe described by the atomists, Democritus and Leucippus, in which atoms were continually falling through the void and giving off images that were in direct contact with the senses. These falling atoms could swerve in an arbitrary, unpredictable way to produce the combinations seen in the world; Epicurus thereby removed an element of determinism that existed in the Democritean system. When a person died, the atoms that composed the body dispersed so that the person had no further existence or perception and therefore nothing to fear after death. Epicurus believed that the gods existed but that they took no interest in human affairs. This belief amounted to a practical atheism, and Epicureans were often thought to be atheists.

The purpose of Epicurean physics was to liberate people from their fear of death, of the gods, and of all nonmaterial or supernatural powers. Epicurean ethics were hedonistic, that is, based on the acceptance of pleasure as true happiness. But pleasure for Epicurus was chiefly negative: the absence of pain and trouble. The goal of the Epicureans was *ataraxia,* the condition of being undisturbed, without trouble, pain, or responsibility. Ideally a man should have enough means to allow him to withdraw from the world and avoid business and public life; Epicurus even advised against marriage and children. He preached a life of genteel, restrained selfishness, which might appeal to intellectual men of means, but it was not calculated to be widely attractive.

THE STOICS. Soon after Epicurus began teaching in his garden in Athens, Zeno of Citium in Cyprus (335–263 B.C.) established the Stoic school, which derived its name from the *Stoa Poikile,* or Painted Portico, in the Athenian Agora, where Zeno and his disciples walked and talked beginning about 300 B.C. From then until about the middle of the second century B.C., Zeno and his successors preached a philosophy that owed a good deal to Socrates, by way of the Cynics, and was fed also by a stream of Eastern thought. Zeno, of course, came from Phoenician Cyprus; Chrysippus, one of his successors, came from Cilicia; and other early Stoics came from such places as Carthage, Tarsus, and Babylon.

Like the Epicureans, the Stoics sought the happiness of the individual. Quite unlike them, the Stoics held a philosophy almost indistinguishable from religion. They believed that humans must live in harmony within themselves and in harmony with nature; for the Stoics god and nature were the same. The guiding principle in nature was divine reason (Logos), or fire. Every human had a spark of this divinity, and after death it returned to the eternal divine spirit. From time to time the world was destroyed by fire, from which a new world arose. The aim of humans, and the definition of human happiness, was the virtuous life, life lived in accordance with natural law, "when all actions promote the harmony of the spirit dwelling in the individual man with the will of him who orders the universe."[2] To live such a life required the knowledge possessed only by the wise, who knew what was good, what was evil, and what was neither, but "indifferent." Good and evil were dispositions of the mind or soul: prudence, justice, courage, temperance, and so on were good, whereas folly, injustice, cowardice, and the like were evil. Life, health, pleasure, beauty, strength, wealth, and so on were neutral, morally indifferent, for they did not contribute either to happiness or to misery. Human misery came from an irrational mental contraction, from passion, which was a disease of the soul. The wise sought freedom from passion (*apatheia*), because passion arose from things that were morally indifferent.

Politically the Stoics fit well into the new world. They thought of it as a single *polis* in which all people were children of god. Although they did not forbid political activity, and many Stoics took part in political life, withdrawal was obviously preferable because the usual subjects of political argument were indifferent. Because the Stoics aimed at inner harmony of the individual, their aim was a life lived in accordance with the divine will, their attitude fatalistic, and their goal a form of apathy, they fit in well with the reality of post-Alexandrian life. In fact, the spread of Stoicism made simpler the task of creating a new political system that relied not on the active participation of the governed, but merely on their docile submission.

Literature

The literature of the Hellenistic period reflects the new intellectual currents and, even more, the new conditions of literary life and the new institutions created in that period. The center of literary production in the third and second centuries B.C. was the new city of Alexandria in Egypt. There the Ptolemies, the kings of Egypt during that time, founded the museum, a great research institute where scientists and scholars were supported by royal funds, and the library, which contained almost half a million volumes, or papyrus scrolls. In the library were the works making up the great body of past Greek literature of every kind, a great deal of which has since been lost. The Alexandrian scholars saw to it that what they judged to be the best works were copied; they edited and criticized these works from the point of view of language, form, and content and wrote biographies of their authors. Much of their work was valuable and is responsible for the preservation of most of ancient literature. Some of it is dry, petty, quarrelsome, and simply foolish. At its best, however, it is full of learning and perception.

The scholarly atmosphere of Alexandria naturally gave rise to work in the field of history and its ancillary discipline, chronology. Eratosthenes (ca. 275–195 B.C.) established a chronology of important events dating from the Trojan War, and others undertook similar tasks. Contemporaries of Alexander, such as Ptolemy I, Aristobulus, and Nearchus, wrote what were apparently sober and essentially

[2]Diogenes Laertius, *Life of Zeno* 88.

factual accounts of his career. Most of the work done by Hellenistic historians is known to us only in fragments cited by later writers, but it seems in general to have emphasized sensational and biographical detail rather than the rigorous impersonal analysis of a Thucydides.

Architecture and Sculpture

The opportunities open to architects and sculptors were greatly increased by the advent of the Hellenistic monarchies. There was plenty of money, the royal need for conspicuous display, the need to build and beautify new cities, and a growing demand from the well-to-do for objects of art. The new cities were usually laid out on the gridiron plan introduced in the fifth century by Hippodamus of Miletus. Temples were built on the classical model, and the covered portico, or *stoa,* became a very popular addition to the *agoras* of the Hellenistic towns.

Sculpture reflected the cosmopolitan nature of the Hellenistic world, for leading sculptors accepted commissions wherever they were attractive, and the result was a certain uniformity of style, although Alexandria, Rhodes, and the kingdom of Pergamum in Asia Minor developed their own characteristic styles. For the most part Hellenistic sculpture carried forward the tendencies of the fourth century B.C., moving away from the balanced tension and idealism of the fifth century toward a sentimental, emotional, and realistic mode. These qualities are readily apparent in the marble statue called the *Laocoon* which was carved at Rhodes in the second century B.C. and afterwards taken to Rome, and one of a drunken old woman in bronze cast in the second century B.C.

The drunken old woman. A Roman copy of a second century B.C. *bronze. It is marked by a stark realism very different from the classic serenity of the fifth-century* B.C. *Apollo pictured at the beginning of the chapter. [State Museum of Antiquities and Sculpture, Munich]*

A Roman copy of one of the masterpieces of Hellenistic sculpture, the Laocoon. *In the* Iliad, *Laocoon was a priest who warned the Trojans not to take the wooden horse within their city. This sculpture depicts his punishment: Great serpents sent by the goddess Athena, who was on the side of the Greeks, devoured Laocoon and his sons before the horrified people of Troy. [German Archaelogical Institute, Rome]*

Mathematics and Science

Among the most spectacular and remarkable intellectual developments of the Hellenistic age were those that came in mathematics and science. The burst of activity in these subjects drew from several sources. The stimulation and organization provided by the work of Plato and Aristotle should not be ignored. To these was added the impetus provided by Alexander's interest in science, evidenced by the scientists he took with him on his expedition and the aid he gave them in collecting data. The expansion of Greek horizons geographically and the consequent contact with the knowledge of Egypt and Babylonia were also helpful. Finally, the patronage of the Ptolemies and the opportunity for many scientists to work with one another at the museum at Alexandria provided a unique opportunity for scientific work. It is not too much to say that the work done by the Alexandrians formed the greater part of the scientific knowledge available to the Western world until the scientific revolution of the sixteenth and seventeenth centuries A.D.

Euclid's *Elements* (written early in the third century B.C.) remained the textbook of plane and solid geometry until just recently. Archimedes of Syracuse (ca. 287–212 B.C.) made further progress in geometry, as well as establishing the theory of the lever in mechanics and inventing hydrostatics. The advances in mathematics, when added to the availability of Babylonian astronomical tables, allowed great progress in the field of astronomy. As early as the fourth century Heraclides of Pontus (ca. 390–310 B.C.) had argued that Mercury and Venus circulate around the sun and not the Earth, and he appears to have made other suggestions leading in the direction of a heliocentric theory of the universe. Most scholars, however, give credit for that theory to Aristarchus of Samos (ca. 310–230 B.C.), who asserted that the sun, along with the other fixed stars, did not move and that the Earth revolved around the sun in a circular orbit and rotated on its axis while

Plutarch Cites Archimedes and Hellenistic Science

Archimedes (ca. 287–211 B.C.) was one of the great mathematicians and physicists of antiquity. He was a native of Syracuse in Sicily and a friend of its king. Plutarch discusses him in the following selection and reveals much about the ancient attitude toward applied science.

Archimedes, however, in writing to King Hiero, whose friend and near relation he was, had stated that given the force, any given weight might be moved, and even boasted, we are told, relying on the strength of demonstration, that if there were another earth, by going into it he could remove this. Hiero being struck with amazement at this, and entreating him to make good this problem by actual experiment, and show some great weight moved by a small engine, he fixed accordingly upon a ship of burden out of the king's arsenal, which could not be drawn out of the dock without great labour and many men; and, loading her with many passengers and a full freight, sitting himself the while far off, with no great endeavor, but only holding the head of the pulley in his hand and drawing the cords by degrees. . . . Yet Archimedes possessed so high a spirit, so profound a soul, and such treasures of scientific knowledge, that though these inventions had now obtained him the renown of more than human sagacity, he yet would not deign to leave behind him any commentary or writing on such subjects; but, repudiating as sordid and ignoble the whole trade of engineering, and every sort of art that lends itself to mere use and profit, he placed his whole affection and ambition in those purer speculations where there can be no reference to the vulgar needs of life. . . .

Plutarch, "Marcellus," in *Lives of the Noble Grecians and Romans,* trans. by John Dryden, rev. by A. H. Clough (New York: Random House, n.d.), pp. 376–378.

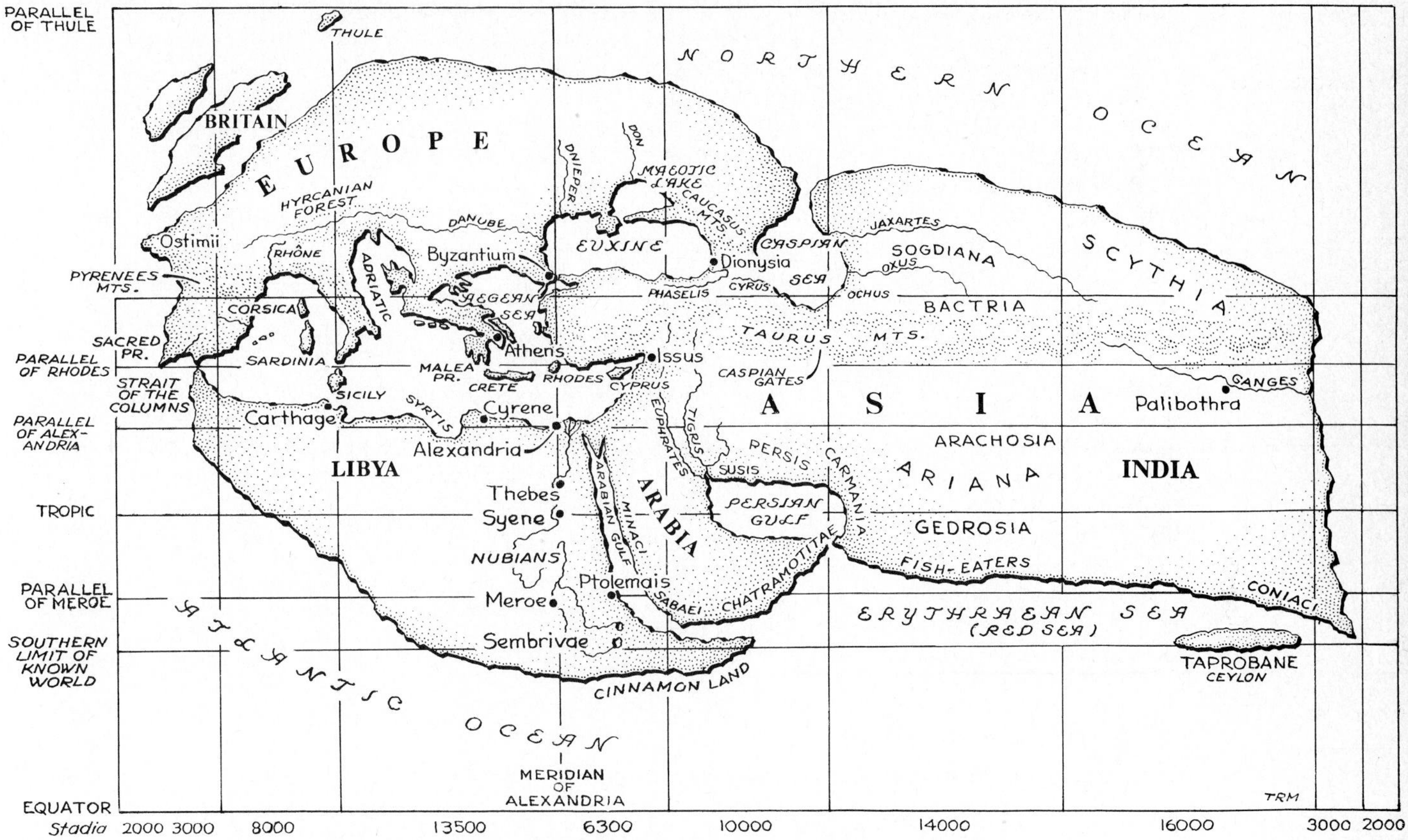

THE WORLD ACCORDING TO ERATOSTHENES

MAP 3-6 *Eratosthenes of Alexandria (ca. 275–195* B.C.*) was a Hellenistic geographer. His map, reconstructed here, was remarkably accurate for its time. The world was divided by lines of "latitude" and "longitude," thus anticipating our global divisions.*

doing so. The heliocentric theory ran contrary not only to the traditional view codified by Aristotle but to what seemed to be common sense. Besides, Hellenistic technology was not up to proving the theory, and, of course, the planetary orbits are not circular. The heliocentric theory did not, therefore, take hold. Hipparchus of Nicaea (born ca. 190 B.C.) constructed a model of the universe on the geocentric theory, employing an ingenious and complicated model that did a very good job of accounting for the movements of the sun, the moon, and the planets. Ptolemy of Alexandria (second century A.D.) adopted Hipparchus' system with a few improvements, and it remained dominant until the work of Copernicus, in the sixteenth century A.D.

Hellenistic scientists made progress in mapping the earth as well as the sky. Eratosthenes of Cyrene (ca. 275–195 B.C.) was able to calculate the circumference of the earth within about two hundred miles and wrote a treatise on geography based on mathematical and physical reasoning and the reports of travelers. In spite of the new data that were available to later geographers, Eratosthenes' map (see Map 3.6) was in many ways more accurate than the one that was constructed by Ptolemy and that became standard in the Middle Ages.

The Hellenistic Age made little contribution to the life sciences. Biology, zoology, and even medicine made little progress. Even the sciences that had such impressive achievements to show in the third century B.C. made little progress thereafter. In fact, to some extent, there was a retreat from science. Astrology and magic became the subjects of great interest as scientific advance lagged. The question has often been asked why science did not progress further in the ancient world: Why, for instance, was there no scientific and industrial revolution in the Hellenistic period? Many answers have been suggested, for example, the lack of an adequate base in technology and the absence of refined instruments of observation and measurement. Another explanation offered is that the deterrent effect of slavery on invention, the sharp class distinctions in ancient society, and the contemptuous attitude of the upper classes toward work separated the intellectual scientist from the practical application of any discoveries. All of these conditions may have played some role, but the wrong question seems to have been asked. To ask it in the usual way is to assume that anyone understands why the scientific and industrial revolutions took place when and where they did, but that assumption is unfounded. Perhaps when historians have solved the modern problem, they may more successfully approach the ancient one.

The Achievement of the Hellenistic Age

The Hellenistic Age speaks to us less fully and vividly than that of classical Greece or of the Roman Republic and Empire, chiefly because it had no historian to compare with Herodotus and Thucydides or Livy and Tacitus. We lack the continuous, rich, lively, and meaningful narrative without which it is difficult to get a clear picture. This deficiency should not obscure the great importance of the achievements of the age. The literature, art, scholarship, and science of the period deserve attention in their own right, but in addition the Hellenistic Age performed a vital civilizing function. It spread the Greek culture over a remarkably wide area and made a significant and lasting impression on much of it. Greek culture also adjusted to its new surroundings to a degree, unifying and simplifying its cultural cargo so as to make it more accessible to outsiders. The various Greek dialects gave way to a version of the Attic tongue, the *koinē* or common language. In the same way, the scholarship of Alexandria established canons of literary excellence and the scholarly tools with which to make the great treasures of Greek culture understandable to later generations. The syncretism of thought and belief introduced in this period also made understanding and accord more likely among peoples who were very different. When the Romans came into contact with Hellenism, they were powerfully impressed by it, and when they conquered the Hellenistic world, they became, as Horace said, captives of its culture.

To Rome and the Romans we must now turn.

Suggested Readings

E. Barker, *Political Philosophy of Plato and Aristotle* (1959). A sober and reliable account.

H. I. Bell, *Egypt from Alexander the Great to the Arab Conquest* (1948).

Max Cary, *History of the Greek World from* 323 *to* 146 B.C. (1968). The major part is devoted to political history.

G. Cawkwell, *Philip of Macedon* (1978). A brief but learned account of Philip's career.

W. R. Connor, *The New Politicians of Fifth-Century Athens* (1971). A study on changes in political style and their significance for Athenian society.

J. K. Davies, *Democracy and Classical Greece* (1978). Emphasizes archaeological evidence and social history.

V. Ehrenberg, *The People of Aristophanes* (1962). A study of Athenian society as revealed by the comedies of Aristophanes.

J. R. Ellis, *Philip II and Macedonian Imperialism* (1976). A study of the career of the founder of Macedonian power.

J. Ferguson, *The Heritage of Hellenism* (1973). A good survey.

W. S. Ferguson, *Hellenistic Athens* (1970). Reprint of an old but still valuable study.

J. R. Lane Fox, *Alexander the Great* (1973). An imaginative account that does more justice to the Persian side of the problem than is usual.

A. French, *The Growth of the Athenian Economy* (1964). An interesting examination of economic developments in Athenian history.

M. Grant, *From Alexander to Cleopatra* (1982). A general account of the Hellenistic period.

Peter Green, *Alexander the Great* (1972). A lively biography.

W. K. C. Guthrie, *The Sophists* (1971). A fine volume in an excellent history of Greek philosophy.

N. G. L. Hammond and G. T. Griffith, *A History of Macedonia,* Vol. 2, 550–336 B.C. (1979). A thorough account of Macedonian history that focuses on the careers of Philip and Alexander.

C. M. Havelock, *Hellenistic Art* (1971). A fine interpretive study.

W. Jaeger, *Demosthenes* (1938). A good biography of the Athenian statesman.

A. H. M. Jones, *The Greek City from Alexander to*

Justinian (1940). A fine study of the significance and spread of urban life.

D. KAGAN, *The Outbreak of the Peloponnesian War* (1969). A study of the period from the foundation of the Delian League to the coming of the Peloponnesian War that argues that war could have been avoided.

D. KAGAN, *The Archidamian War* (1974). A history of the first ten years of the Peloponnesian War.

D. KAGAN, *The Peace of Nicias and the Sicilian Expedition* (1981). A history of the middle period of the Peloponnesian War.

H. D. F. KITTO, *Greek Tragedy* (1966). A good introduction.

B. M. W. KNOX, *The Heroic Temper: Studies in Sophoclean Tragedy* (1964). A brilliant analysis of tragic heroism.

J. A. O. LARSEN, *Greek Federal States* (1968). Emphasis on the federal movements of the Hellenistic era.

G. E. R. LLOYD, *Greek Science After Aristotle* (1974).

A. A. LONG, *Hellenistic Philosophy: Stoics, Epicureans, Sceptics* (1974).

R. MEIGGS, *The Athenian Empire* (1972). A fine study of the rise and fall of the empire, making excellent use of inscriptions.

J. J. POLLITT, *Art and Experience in Classical Greece* (1972). A scholarly and entertaining study of the relationship between art and history in classical Greece with excellent illustrations.

M. I. ROSTOVTZEFF, *Social and Economic History of the Hellenistic World,* 3 vols. (1941). A masterpiece of synthesis by a great historian.

W. W. TARN, *Alexander the Great,* 2 vols. (1948). The first volume is a narrative account, the second a series of detailed studies.

W. W. TARN AND G. T. GRIFFITH, *Hellenistic Civilization* (1961). A survey of Hellenistic history and culture.

A. E. TAYLOR, *Socrates* (1953). A good, readable account.

V. TCHERIKOVER, *Hellenistic Civilization and the Jews* (1970). A fine study of the impact of Hellenism on the Jews.

F. W. WALBANK, *The Hellenistic World* (1981).

T. B. L. WEBSTER, *Hellenistic Poetry and Art* (1961). A clear survey.

A. E. ZIMMERN, *The Greek Commonwealth* (1961). A study of political, social, and economic conditions in fifth-century Athens.

The "Old Republican," a portrait bust of a Roman senator from ca. 75 B.C.

4

Rome: From Republic to Empire

THE ACHIEVEMENT of the Romans was one of the most remarkable accomplishments in human history. The descendants of the inhabitants of a small village in central Italy ruled the entire Italian peninsula, then the entire Mediterranean coastline. They conquered most of the Near East and finally much of continental Europe. They ruled this vast empire under a single government that provided considerable peace and prosperity for centuries. At no time before the Romans or since has that area been united, and rarely, if ever, has it enjoyed a stable peace. But Rome's legacy was not merely military excellence and political organization. The Romans adopted and transformed the intellectual and cultural achievements of the Greeks and combined them with their own outlook and historical experience. They produced that Graeco-Roman tradition in literature, philosophy, and art that served as the core of learning for the Middle Ages and the inspiration for the new paths taken in the Renaissance. It remains at the heart of Western civilization to this day.

Prehistoric Italy

The culture of Italy developed late. Paleolithic settlements gave way to the Neolithic mode of life only about 2500 B.C. The Bronze Age came about 1500 B.C., and about 1000 B.C. Italy began to be infiltrated by bands of new arrivals coming from across the Adriatic Sea and around its northern end. The invaders were warlike people who imposed their language and social organization on almost all of Italy. Their bronze work was better than their predecessors', and soon they made weapons, armor, and tools of iron. They cremated their dead and put the ashes in tombs stocked with weapons and armor. Before 800 B.C. people living in this style occupied the highland pastures of the Apennines. These tough mountain people—Umbrians, Sabines, Samnites, Latins, and others—spoke a set of closely related languages we call *Italic.*

They soon began to challenge the earlier settlers for control of the tempting western plains. Other peoples lived in Italy in the ninth century B.C., but the Italic speakers and three peoples who had not yet arrived—the Etruscans, the Greeks, and the Celts—would shape its future.

The Etruscans

The Etruscans exerted the most powerful external influence on the Romans. Their civilization arose in Etruria (now Tuscany), west of the Apennines between the Arno and Tiber rivers, about 800 B.C. (see Map 4.1). Their origin is far from clear, but their tomb architecture, resembling that of Asia Minor, and their practice of divining the future by inspecting the livers of sacrificial animals point to an eastern origin.

ANCIENT ITALY

MAP 4-1 *This map of the Italian peninsula and its neighbors in antiquity shows the major cities and towns, as well as a number of geographical regions and the locations of some of the Italic and non-Italic peoples of the area.*

The Etruscans brought civilization with them. Their settlements were self-governing, fortified city-states, of which twelve formed a loose religious confederation. At first these cities were ruled by kings, but they were replaced by an aristocracy of the agrarian nobles, who ruled by means of a council and elected annual magistrates. The Etruscans were a military ruling class that dominated and exploited the native Italians, who worked their land and mines and served as infantry in their armies. This aristocracy accumulated considerable wealth through agriculture, industry, piracy, and a growing commerce with the Carthaginians and the Greeks.

The Etruscans' influence on the Romans was greatest in religion. They imagined a world filled with gods and spirits, many of them evil. To deal with such demons, the Etruscans evolved complicated rituals and powerful priesthoods. Divination by sacrifice and omens in nature helped discover the divine will, and careful attention to precise rituals directed by priests helped please the gods. After a while the Etruscans, influenced by the Greeks, worshiped gods in the shape of humans and built temples for them.

The Etruscan aristocracy remained aggressive and skillful in the use of horses and war chariots. In the seventh and sixth centuries B.C. they expanded their power in Italy and across the sea to Corsica and Elba. They conquered Latium (a region that included the small town of Rome) and Campania, where they became neighbors of the Greeks of Naples. In the north they got as far as the Po valley. These conquests were carried out by small bands led by Etruscan chieftains who did not work in concert and would not necessarily aid one another in distress. As a result, the conquests outside Etruria were not firmly based and did not last long. Etruscan power reached its height some time before 500 B.C. and then rapidly declined. About 400 B.C. the Celts broke into the Po valley, drove out the Etruscans, and settled their conquered land so firmly that the Romans thereafter called it Cisalpine Gaul (Gaul on this side of the Alps). Thereafter even Etruria lost its independence and was incorporated into Roman Italy. The Etruscan language was forgotten and Etruscan culture gradually became only a memory, but its influence on the Romans remained.

Clay statue of Apollo from the Etruscan city of Veii in central Italy, ca. 500 B.C. *It is evidence of the considerable influence of Greek culture on Etruscan civilization.* [*German Archaelogical Institute, Rome*]

Royal Rome

Rome was an unimportant town in Latium until its conquest by the Etruscans, but its location gave it several advantages over its Latin neighbors. Its site was on the Tiber River, fifteen miles from its mouth, at the point where the hills on which Rome was situated made further navigation impossible. The island in the Tiber southwest of the Capitoline hill made the river fordable, so that Rome was naturally a center for communication and trade, both east–west and north–south.

Government

In the sixth century B.C. Rome came under Etruscan control. Led by their Etruscan kings, the Roman army, equipped and organized like the Greek phalanx, gained control of most of Latium. They achieved this success under an effective political and social order that gave extraordinary power to the ruling figures in both public and private life. To their kings the Romans gave the awesome power of *imperium,* the right to issue commands and to enforce them by fines, arrests, and corporal or even capital punishment. The kingship was elective and the office appears to have tended to remain in the same family. The Senate, however, had to approve the candidate, and the *imperium* was formally granted by a vote of the people in assembly. The basic character of Roman government was already clear: great power was granted to executive officers, but it had to be approved by the Senate and was derived ultimately from the people.

In theory and law the king was the commander of the army, the chief priest, and the supreme judge. He could make decisions in foreign affairs, call out the army, lead it in battle, and impose discipline on his troops, all by virtue of his *imperium.* In practice the royal power was much more limited. The second branch of the early Roman government was the Senate. Tradition says that Romulus, Rome's legendary first king, chose 100 of Rome's leading men to advise him. Later the number rose to 300, where it stayed through

Like the Egyptians, the Etruscans also believed that a person's spirit would continue to live well after death if a tomb were properly equipped. In this tomb, all the tools and utensils a person might need in the afterlife are carved on the walls. [*Alinari/Art Resource*]

most of the history of the republic. Ostensibly the Senate had neither executive nor legislative power; it met only when summoned by the king and then only to advise him. In reality its authority was great, for the senators, like the king, served for life. The Senate, therefore, had continuity and experience, and as it was composed of the most powerful men in the state, it could not lightly be ignored.

In early Rome citizenship required descent from Roman parents on both sides. All citizens were organized into the third branch of government, the curiate assembly made up of thirty groups. It met only when summoned by the king; he determined the agenda, made proposals, and recognized other speakers, if any. For the most part the assembly was called to listen and approve. Voting was not by head but by group; a majority within each group determined its vote, and the decisions were made by majority vote of the groups. Group voting was typical of all Roman assemblies in the future.

The Family

The center of Roman life was the family. At its head stood the father, whose power and authority within the family resembled those of the king within the state. Over his children he held broad powers analogous to *imperium* in the state, for he had the right to sell his children into slavery, and he even had the power of life and death over them. Over his wife he had less power; he could not sell his wife or kill her. As the king's power was more limited in practice than in theory so it was with the father. His power to dispose of his children was limited by consultation with the family, by public opinion, and, most of all, by tradition. The wife could not be divorced except for stated serious offenses, and even then she had to be convicted by a court made up of her male blood relatives. The Roman woman had a respected position and the main responsibility for managing the household. The father was the chief priest of the family. He led it in daily prayers to the dead that reflected the ancestor worship central to the Roman family and state.

Clientage

Clientage was one of Rome's most important institutions. The client was "an inferior entrusted, by custom or by himself, to the protection of a stranger more powerful than he, and rendering certain services and observances in return for this protection."[1] The Romans spoke of a client as being in the *fides,* or trust, of his patron, so that the relationship always had moral implications. The patron provided his client with protection, both physical and legal; he gave him economic assistance in the form of a land grant, the opportunity to work as a tenant farmer or a laborer on the patron's land, or simply handouts. In return the client would fight for his patron, work his land, and support him politically. These mutual obligations were enforced by public opinion and tradition. When early custom was codified in the mid-fifth century B.C., one of the twelve tablets of laws announced: "Let the patron who has defrauded his client be accursed." In the early history of Rome, patrons were rich and powerful whereas clients were poor and weak, but as time passed it was not uncommon for rich and powerful members of the upper classes to become clients of even more powerful men, chiefly for political purposes. Because the client–patron relationship was hereditary and was sanctioned by religion and custom, it was to play a very important part in the life of the Roman Republic.

Patricians and Plebeians

In the royal period, Roman society was divided in two by a class distinction based on birth. The upper class was composed of the patricians, the wealthy men who held a monopoly of power and influence. They alone could conduct the religious ceremonies in the state, sit in the Senate, or hold office, and they formed a closed caste by forbidding marriage outside their own group. The plebeians must originally have been the poor and dependent men who were small farmers, laborers, and artisans, the clients of the nobility. As Rome and her population grew in various ways, families that were rich but outside the charmed circle gained citizenship. From very early times, therefore, there were rich plebeians, and incompetence and bad luck must have produced some poor patricians. The line between the classes and the monopoly of privileges remained firm, nevertheless, and the struggle of the plebeians to gain equality occupied more than two centuries of republican history.

A patrician with portraits of his ancestors. Roman patricians took great pride in their lineage and would not marry outside their own group. [*German Archaeological Institute, Rome*]

[1] E. Badian, *Foreign Clientelae* (264–70 B.C.) (Oxford, 1958), p. 1.

The Republic and Its Constitution

Roman tradition tells us that the republic replaced the monarchy at Rome suddenly in 509 B.C. as the result of a revolution sparked by the outrageous behavior of the last kings and led by the noble families.

The Consuls

The Roman constitution was an unwritten accumulation of laws and customs that had won respect and the force of law over time.

The lictors, such as those pictured here, attended the chief Roman magistrates when they appeared in public. Note that one lictor carries an axe, while two others bear a bundle of wooden staffs. This symbolizes the power and the limits on the power of Roman magistrates to inflict corporal punishment on Roman citizens. Within the boundaries of the city of Rome, no citizen could be punished without a trial. To symbolize this the lictors in Rome carried bound-up staffs. Outside of the city, however, magistrates had the authority as commanders of the army to put anyone to death without a trial. This power was symbolized by their lictors bearing an axe. [*Alinari/Art Resource*]

The Romans were a conservative people, so they were never willing to deprive their chief magistrates of the great powers exercised by the monarchs. They elected two patricians to the office of consul and endowed them with *imperium.* They were assisted by two financial officials called *quaestors,* whose number ultimately reached eight. Like the kings, the consuls led the army, had religious duties, and served as judges. They retained the visible symbols of royalty—the purple robe, the ivory chair, and the *lictors* (minor officials) bearing rods and axe who accompanied them—but their power was limited legally and institutionally as well as by custom.

The vast power of the consulship was granted not for life but only for a year. Each consul could prevent any action by his colleague by simply saying no to his proposal, and the religious powers of the consuls were shared with others. Even the *imperium* was limited, for though the consuls had full powers of life and death while leading an army, within the sacred boundary of the city of Rome the citizens had the right to appeal to the popular assembly all cases involving capital punishment. Besides, after their one year in office, the consuls would spend the rest of their lives as members of the Senate. It was a most reckless consul who failed to ask the advice of the Senate or who failed to follow it when there was general agreement.

The many checks on consular action tended to prevent initiative, swift action, and change, but this was just what a conservative, traditional, aristocratic republic wanted. Only in the military sphere did divided counsel and a short term of office create important problems. The Romans tried to get around the difficulties by sending only one consul into the field or, when this was impossible, allowing the consuls sole command on alternate days. In really serious crises, the consuls, with the advice of the Senate, could appoint a single man, the *dictator,* to the command and could retire in his favor. The *dictator's* term of office was limited to six months, but his own *imperium* was valid both inside and outside the city without appeal. These devices worked well enough in the early years of the republic, when Rome's battles were near home, but longer wars and more sophisticated opponents revealed the system's weaknesses and required significant changes.

Long campaigns prompted the invention of the proconsulship in 325 B.C., whereby the term of a consul serving in the field was ex-

Polybius Summarizes the Roman Constitution

Polybius (ca. 203–120 B.C.) was a Greek from the city of Megalopolis, an important member of the Achaean League. As a hostage in Rome he became a friend of influential Romans and later wrote a history of Rome's conquest of the Mediterranean lands. He praised the Roman constitution as an excellent example of a "mixed constitution" and as a major source of Roman success.

As for the Roman constitution, it had three elements, each of them possessing sovereign powers: and their respective share of power in the whole state had been regulated with such a scrupulous regard to equality and equilibrium, that no one could say for certain, not even a native, whether the constitution as a whole were an aristocracy or democracy or despotism. . . .

. . . .

The result of this power of the several estates for mutual help or harm is a union sufficiently firm for all emergencies, and a constitution than which it is impossible to find a better. For whenever any danger from without compels them to unite and work together, the strength which is developed by the State is so extraordinary, that everything required is unfailingly carried out by the eager rivalry shown by all classes to devote their whole minds to the need of the hour, and to secure that any determination come to should not fail for want of promptitude; while each individual works, privately and publicly alike, for the accomplishment of the business in hand. Accordingly, the peculiar constitution of the State makes it irresistible, and certain of obtaining whatever it determines to attempt. . . . For when any one of the three classes becomes puffed up, and manifests an inclination to be contentious and unduly encroaching, the mutual interdependency of all the three, and the possibility of the pretensions of any one being checked and thwarted by the others, must plainly check this tendency: and so the proper equilibrium is maintained by the impulsiveness of the one part being checked by its fear of the other. . . .

Polybius, *Histories*, Vol. 1, trans. by E. S. Shuckburgh (Bloomington: Indiana University Press, 1962), pp. 468, 473–474.

tended. This innovation contained the seeds of many troubles for the constitution.

The introduction of the office of *praetor* also helped provide commanders for Rome's many campaigns. The basic function of the praetors was judicial, but they also had *imperium* and served as generals. By the end of the republic, there were eight praetors, whose annual terms, like the consuls', could be extended for military commands when necessary.

At first, the consuls classified the citizens according to age and property, the bases of citizenship and assignment in the army. After the middle of the fifth century B.C., two censors were elected to perform this duty. They conducted a census and drew up the citizen rolls, but this was no job for clerks. The classification fixed taxation and status, so that the censors had to be men of reputation, former consuls. The censors soon acquired additional powers. By the fourth century they compiled the roll of senators and could strike senators from that roll not only for financial reasons but for moral reasons as well. As the prestige of the office grew, it came to be considered the ultimate prize of a Roman political career.

The Senate and the Assembly

The end of the monarchy increased the influence and power of the Senate. It became the single continuous deliberative body in the Roman state. Its members were leading patricians, often leaders of clans and patrons of many clients. The Senate soon gained control of finances and of foreign policy. Its formal advice was not lightly ignored either by magistrates or by popular assemblies.

The most important assembly in the early republic was the centuriate assembly. In a sense, it was the Roman army acting in a political capacity, and its basic unit was the century, theoretically 100 fighting men classified according to their weapons, armor, and equipment. Because each man equipped himself, this meant that the organization was by classes according to wealth.

The assembly met on the Campus Martius, the drill field of the Roman army, convened by a military trumpet. Voting was by century and proceeded in order of classification from the cavalry down. The assembly elected the consuls and several other magistrates, voted on bills put before it, made decisions of war and peace, and also served as the court of appeal against decisions of the magistrates affecting the life or property of a citizen. In theory it had final authority, but the Senate exercised great, if informal, influence.

The Struggle of the Orders

The laws and constitution of the early republic clearly reflected the class structure of the Roman state, for they gave to the patricians almost a monopoly of power and privilege. Plebeians were barred from public office, from priesthoods, and from other public religious offices. They could not serve as judges, they could not even know the law, for there was no published legal code. The only law was traditional practice, and that existed only in the minds and actions of patrician magistrates. Plebeians were subject to the *imperium* but could not exercise its power. They were not allowed to marry patricians. When Rome acquired new land by conquest, patrician magistrates distributed it in a way that favored patricians. The patricians dominated the assemblies and the Senate. The plebeians undertook a campaign to achieve political, legal, and social equality, and this attempt, which succeeded after two centuries of intermittent effort, is called the *struggle of the orders.*

The most important source of plebeian success was the need for their military service. Rome was at war almost constantly, and the patricians were forced to call on the plebeians to defend the state. According to tradition, the plebeians, angered by patrician resistance to their demands, withdrew from the city and camped on the Sacred Mount. There they formed a plebeian tribal assembly and elected plebeian tribunes to protect them from the arbitrary power of the magistrates. They declared the tribune inviolate and sacrosanct, and anyone laying violent hands on him was accursed and liable to death without trial. By extension of his right to protect the plebeians, the tribune gained the power to veto any action of a magistrate or any bill in a Roman assembly or the Senate. The plebeian assembly voted by tribe, and a vote of the assembly was binding on plebeians. They tried to make their decisions binding on all Romans but could not do so until 287 B.C.

The next step was for the plebeians to obtain access to the laws, and by 450 B.C. the Twelve Tables codified early Roman custom in all its harshness and simplicity. In 445 B.C. plebeians gained the right to marry patricians. The main prize was consulship. The patricians did not yield easily, but at last, in 367 B.C., the Licinian–Sextian Laws provided that at least one consul could be a plebeian. Before long plebeians held other offices, even the dictatorship and the censorship. In 300 B.C. they were admitted to the most important priesthoods, the last religious barrier to equality. In 287 B.C. the plebeians completed their triumph. They once again withdrew from the city and secured the passage of a law whereby decisions of the plebeian assembly bound all Romans and did not require the approval of the Senate.

It might seem that the Roman aristocracy had given way under the pressure of the lower class, but the victory of the plebeians did not bring democracy. An aristocracy based strictly on birth had given way to an aristocracy more subtle, but no less restricted, based on a combination of wealth and birth. The significant distinction was no longer between patrician and plebeian but between the *nobiles*—a relatively small group of wealthy and powerful families, both patrician and plebeian, whose members

The Rise of the Plebeians to Equality in Rome

Kings expelled; republic founded	509 B.C.
Laws of the Twelve Tables published	450–449 B.C.
Plebeians gain right of marriage with patricians	445 B.C.
Licinian–Sextian Laws open consulship to plebeians	367 B.C.
Plebeians attain chief priesthoods	300 B.C.
Laws passed by Plebeian Assembly made binding on all Romans	287 B.C.

attained the highest offices in the state—and everyone else. The absence of the secret ballot in the assemblies enabled the *nobiles* to control most decisions and elections by a combination of intimidation and bribery. The leading families, although in constant competition with one another for office, power, and prestige, often combined in marriage and less formal alliances to keep the political plums within their own group. In the century from 233 to 133 B.C., for instance, twenty-six families provided 80 per cent of the consuls and only ten families accounted for almost 50 per cent. These same families dominated the Senate, whose power became ever greater. It remained the only continuous deliberative body in the state, and the pressure of warfare gave it experience in handling public business. Rome's success brought the Senate prestige, increased control of policy, and confidence in its capacity to rule. The end of the struggle of the orders brought domestic peace under a republican constitution dominated by a capable, if narrow, senatorial aristocracy. This outcome satisfied most Romans outside the ruling group because Rome conquered Italy and brought many benefits to its citizens.

The Conquest of Italy

Not long after the fall of the monarchy in 509 B.C., a coalition of Romans, Latins, and Italian Greeks defeated the Etruscans and drove them out of Latium for good. Throughout the fifth century B.C., the powerful Etruscan city of Veii, only twelve miles north of the Tiber River, raided Roman territory. After a hard struggle and a long siege, the Romans took it in 392 B.C., more than doubling the size of Rome. Roman policy toward defeated enemies used both the carrot and the stick. When they made friendly alliances with some, they gained new soldiers for their army. When they treated others more harshly by annexing their land, they achieved a similar end, for service in the Roman army was based on property, and the distribution to poor Romans of conquered land made soldiers of previously useless men. It also gave the poor a stake in Rome and reduced the pressure against its aristocratic regime. The long siege of Veii kept soldiers from their farms during the campaign. From that time on the Romans paid their soldiers, thus giving their army greater flexibility and a more professional quality.

Roman Expansion in Italy

Fall of Veii; Etruscans defeated	392 B.C.
Gauls burn Rome	387 B.C.
Latin League defeated	338 B.C.
Battle of Sentinum; Samnites and allies defeated	295 B.C.
Pyrrhus driven from Italy	275 B.C.
Rome rules Italy south of the Po River	265 B.C.

Gallic Invasion of Italy and Roman Reaction

At the beginning of the fourth century B.C. the Romans were the chief power in central Italy, but a disaster struck. In 387 B.C. the Gauls, barbaric Celtic tribes from across the Alps, defeated the Roman army and captured, looted, and burned Rome. The Gauls sought plunder, not conquest, so they extorted a ransom from the Romans and returned to their homes in the north. Rome's power appeared to have been wiped out. When the Gauls left, some of Rome's allies and old enemies tried to take advantage of its weakness, but by about 350 B.C. the Romans had recovered their leadership of central Italy and were more dominant than ever. Their success in turning back new Gallic raids added still more to their power and prestige. As the Romans tightened their grip on Latium, the Latins became resentful. In 340 B.C. they demanded independence from Rome or full equality, and when the Romans refused, they launched a war of independence that lasted until 338. The victorious Romans dissolved the Latin League, and their treatment of the defeated opponents provided a model for the settlement of Italy.

Roman Policy Toward the Conquered

The Romans did not destroy any of the Latin cities or their people, nor did they treat them all alike. Some in the vicinity of Rome received full Roman citizenship; others farther away gained municipal status, which gave them the private rights of intermarriage and commerce with Romans but not the public rights of voting and holding office in Rome. They retained the rights of local self-government and could obtain full Roman citizenship if they moved to Rome. They followed Rome in foreign policy and provided soldiers to serve in the Roman legions.

Still other states became allies of Rome on the basis of treaties, which differed from city to city. Some were given the private rights of intermarriage and commerce with Romans and some were not; the allied states were always forbidden to exercise these rights with one another. Some, but not all, were allowed local autonomy. Land was taken from some but not from others, nor was the percentage always the same. All the allies supplied troops to the army, in which they fought in auxiliary battalions under Roman officers, but they did not pay taxes to Rome.

On some of the conquered land the Romans placed colonies, permanent settlements of veteran soldiers in the territory of recently defeated enemies. The colonists retained their Roman citizenship and enjoyed home rule, and in return for the land they had been given, they served as a kind of permanent garrison to deter or suppress rebellion. These colonies were usually connected to Rome by a network of military roads built as straight as possible and so durable that some are used even today. They guaranteed that a Roman army could swiftly reinforce an embattled colony or put down an uprising in any weather.

The Roman settlement of Latium reveals even more clearly than before the principles by which Rome was able to conquer and dominate Italy for many centuries. The excellent army and the diplomatic skill that allowed Rome to separate its enemies help to explain its conquests. The reputation for harsh punish-

The Via Latina was part of the network of military roads that tied all Italy to Rome. These roads enabled Roman legions to move swiftly to enforce their control of Italy. The Via Latina dates from the fourth century B.C. [*Fototeca Unione*]

Livy Describes Rome's Treatment of the Italians

Livy (59 B.C.–A.D. 17) wrote a history of Rome from its origins until his own time. The following passage describes the different kinds of treatment Rome gave to the defeated Latin cities after their revolt in the years 340–338 B.C.

The principal members of the senate applauded the consul's statement on the business on the whole; but said that, as the states were differently circumstanced, their plan might be readily adjusted and determined according to the desert of each, if they should put the question regarding each state specifically. The question was therefore so put regarding each separately and a decree passed. To the people of Lanuvium the right of citizenship was granted, and the exercise of their religious rights was restored to them with this provision, that the temple and grove of Juno Sospita should be common between the Lanuvian burghers and the Roman people. The peoples of Aricia, Nomentum, and Pedum were admitted into the number of citizens on the same terms as the Lanuvians. To the Tusculans the rights of citizenship which they already possessed were continued; no public penalty was imposed and the crime of rebellion was visited on its few instigators. On the people of Velitrae, Roman citizens of long standing, measures of great severity were inflicted because they had so often rebelled; their walls were razed, and their senate deported and ordered to dwell on the other side of the Tiber; any individual who should be caught on the hither side of the river should be fined one thousand asses, and the person who had apprehended him should not discharge his prisoner from confinement until the money was paid down. Into the lands of the senators colonists were sent; by their addition Velitrae recovered its former populous appearance.

Livy, *History of Rome,* Vol. 1, trans. by D. Spillan et al. (New York: American Book Company, n.d.), p. 561.

ment of rebels and the sure promise that such punishment would be delivered, made unmistakably clear by the presence of colonies and military roads, help to account for the slowness to revolt. But the positive side, represented by Rome's organization of the defeated states, is at least as important. The Romans did not regard the status given each newly conquered city as permanent. They held out to loyal allies the prospect of improving their status, even of achieving the ultimate prize, full Roman citizenship. In so doing, the Romans gave their allies a stake in Rome's future and success and a sense of being colleagues, though subordinate ones, rather than subjects. The result, in general, was that most of Rome's allies remained loyal even when put to the severest test.

Defeat of the Samnites

The next great challenge to Roman arms came in a series of wars with a tough mountain people of the southern Appenines, the Samnites. Some of Rome's allies rebelled, and soon the Etruscans and Gauls joined in the war against Rome. But most of the allies remained loyal. In 295 B.C., at Sentinum, the Romans defeated an Italian coalition, and by 280 they were masters of central Italy. Their power extended from the Po valley south to Apulia and Lucania.

The victory over the Samnites brought the Romans into direct contact with the Greek cities of southern Italy. Roman intervention in a quarrel between Greek cities brought them face to face with Pyrrhus, king of Epirus. Pyrrhus, probably the best general of his time, commanded a well-disciplined and experienced mercenary army, which he hired out for profit, and a new weapon: twenty war elephants. He defeated the Romans twice but suffered many casualties. When one of his officers rejoiced at the victory, Pyrrhus told him, "If we win one more battle against the Romans we shall be completely ruined." This "Pyrrhic" victory led him to withdraw to Sicily in 275 B.C. The Greek cities that had hired him were

Pyrrhus, king of Epirus (295–272 B.C.), *in what is today Albania. Pyrrhus was one of the greatest generals of his time, but his victories against the Romans were too costly to be sustained.* [*Alinari/Art Resource*]

forced to join the Roman confederation. By 265 B.C. Rome ruled all Italy as far north as the Po River, an area of 47,200 square miles. The year after the defeat of Pyrrhus, Ptolemy Philadelphus, king of Egypt, sent a message of congratulation to establish friendly relations with Rome. This act recognized Rome's new status as a power in the Hellenistic world.

Rome and Carthage

Rome's acquisition of coastal territory and her expansion to the toe of the Italian boot brought her face to face with the great naval power of the western Mediterranean, Carthage (see Map 4.2). Late in the ninth century B.C. the Phoenician city of Tyre had planted a colony on the coast of northern Africa near modern Tunis, calling it the New City, or Carthage. In the sixth century B.C. the conquest of Phoenicia by the Assyrians and the Persians made Carthage independent and free to exploit its very advantageous situation. The city was located on a defensible site and commanded an excellent harbor that encouraged commerce. The coastal plain grew abundant grain, fruits, and vegetables. An inland plain allowed sheep herding. The Phoenician settlers conquered the native inhabitants and used them to work the land. Beginning in the sixth century B.C. the Carthaginians expanded their domain to include the coast of northern Africa west beyond the Straits of Gibraltar and eastward into Libya. Overseas they came to control the southern part of Spain, Sardinia, Corsica, Malta, the Balearic Islands, and western Sicily. The people of these territories, though originally allies, were all reduced to subjection like the natives of the Carthaginian home territory, and they all served in the Carthaginian army or navy and paid tribute. Carthage also profited greatly from the mines of Spain and from an absolute monopoly of trade imposed on the western Mediterranean.

Early relations between Rome and Carthage had been few but not unfriendly. Because Rome was neither a commercial nor a naval state and Carthage had no designs on central Italy, there was no reason for conflict. But an attack by Hiero, tyrant of Syracuse, on the Sicilian city of Messana just across from Italy caused trouble. Messana was held by a group of Italian mercenary soldiers who called themselves *Mamertines,* the sons of the war god Mars. Some years earlier they had seized the city, killed the men, taken the women, and launched a career of piracy, extortion, and attacks on their neighbors. When Hiero defeated the Mamertines, some of them called on the Cathaginians to help save their city. Carthage agreed and sent a garrison, for the Carthaginians wanted to prevent Syracuse from dominating the straits. One Mamertine faction, however, fearing that Carthage might take undue advantage of the opportunity, asked Rome for help.

In 264 B.C. the request came to the Senate, where it was debated at length, and rightly so, for the issue was momentous. The Punic garrison (the Romans called the Carthaginians *Phoenicians;* in Latin the word is *Poeni* or *Puni,* hence the adjective *Punic*) was in place at Messana. The Romans knew that intervention would not be against Syracuse but against the mighty empire of Carthage, a powerful state that was getting too close to Italy. Unless Rome intervened, Carthage would gain control of all Sicily and the straits. The assembly voted to protect the Mamertines, sent an army to Messana, and expelled the Punic garrison. The First Punic War was on.

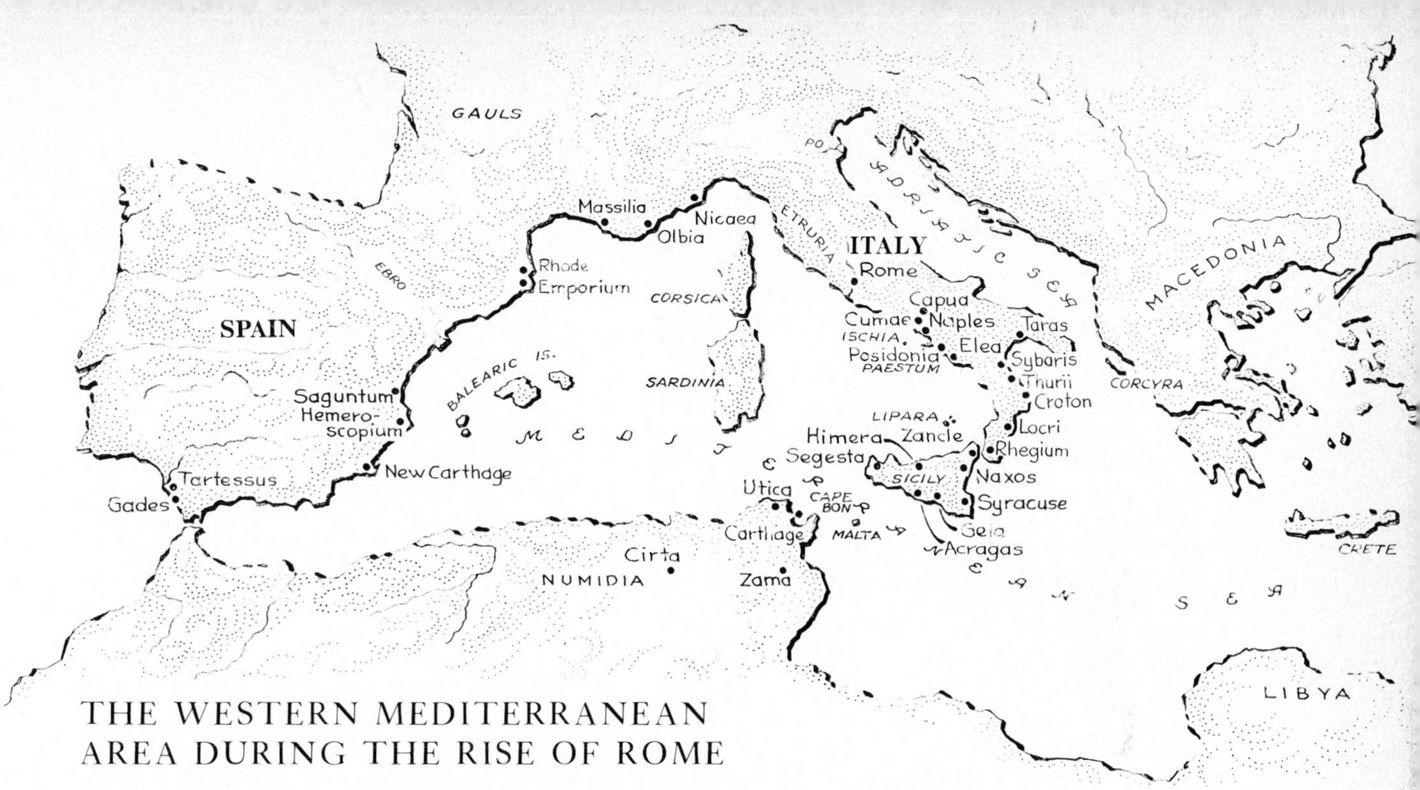

MAP 4-2 *This map covers the theater of the conflicts between the growing Roman dominions and those of Carthage in the third century* B.C. *The Carthaginian empire stretched westward from the city (in modern Tunisia) along the North African coast and into southern Spain.*

The First Punic War (264–241 B.C.)

The war in Sicily soon settled into a stalemate. At last the Romans built a fleet to cut off supplies to the besieged Carthaginian cities at the western end of Sicily. When Carthage sent its own fleet to raise the siege, the Romans destroyed it. In 241 B.C. Carthage signed a treaty giving up Sicily and the islands between Italy and Sicily and agreed to pay a war indemnity in ten annual installments, to keep its ships out of Italian waters, and not to recruit mercenaries in Italy. Neither side was to attack the allies of the other. Rome had earned Sicily, and Carthage could well afford the indemnity. The peace reflected reality without undue harshness. It left Carthage most of its empire and its self-respect and created no obvious grounds for future conflict. If the treaty had been carried out in good faith, it might have brought lasting peace.

The treaty did not bring peace to Carthage, even for the moment. A rebellion broke out among the Carthaginian mercenaries, newly recruited from Sicily and demanding their pay. In 238 B.C., while Carthage was still in danger, Rome seized Sardinia and Corsica and demanded that Carthage pay an additional indemnity. This was a harsh and cynical action by the Romans; even the historian Polybius, a great champion of Rome, could find no justification for it. The Romans were moved, no doubt, by the fear of giving Carthage a base so near Italy, but their action was unwise. It undid the calming effects of the peace of 241

The Punic Wars

First Punic War	264–241 B.C.
Rome seizes Sardinia and Corsica	238 B.C.
Hannibal takes command of Punic army in Spain	221 B.C.
Second Punic War	218–202 B.C.
Battle of Cannae	216 B.C.
Scipio takes New Carthage	209 B.C.
Battle of Zama	202 B.C.
Third Punic War	149–146 B.C.
Destruction of Carthage	146 B.C.

B.C. and angered the Carthaginians without preventing them from recovering their strength to seek vengeance in the future.

The Roman conquest of territory overseas presented a new problem. Instead of following the policy they had pursued in Italy, the Romans made Sicily a province and Sardinia and Corsica another. It became common to extend the term of the governors of these provinces beyond a year. The governors were unchecked by colleagues and exercised full *imperium*. New magistracies, in effect, were thus created free of the limits put on the power of officials in Rome. The new populations were neither Roman citizens nor allies; they were subjects who did not serve in the army but paid tribute instead. The old practice of extending citizenship and, with it, loyalty to Rome stopped at the borders of Italy. Rome collected the new taxes by "farming" them out at auction to the highest bidder. At first, the tax collectors were natives from the same province, later Roman allies, and finally Roman citizens below senatorial rank who became powerful and wealthy by squeezing the provincials hard. These innovations were the basis for Rome's imperial organization in the future; in time they strained the constitution and traditions of Rome to such a degree as to threaten the existence of the republic.

After the First Punic War, campaigns against the Gauls and across the Adriatic distracted Rome. Meanwhile Hamilcar Barca was leading Carthage on the road to recovery. Hamilcar sought to compensate for losses elsewhere by building a Punic empire in Spain. As governor of Spain from 237 B.C. until his death in 229 B.C., he improved the ports and their commerce, exploited the mines, gained control of the hinterland, won over many of the conquered tribes, and built a strong and disciplined army.

Hamilcar's successor, his son-in-law Hasdrubal, pursued the same policies. His success alarmed the Romans, and they imposed a treaty in which he promised not to take an army north across the Ebro River in Spain, although Punic expansion in Spain was well south of that river at the time of the treaty. Even though the agreement preserved the appearance of Rome's giving orders to an inferior, the treaty gave equal benefits to both sides: if the Carthaginians agreed to accept the limit of the Ebro on their expansion in Spain, the Romans would not interfere with that expansion.

The Second Punic War (218–202 B.C.)

On Hasdrubal's assassination in 221 B.C. the army chose as his successor Hannibal, son of Hamilcar Barca, still a young man of twenty-five. He quickly consolidated and extended the Punic Empire in Spain. A few years before his accession Rome had received an offer from the people of the Spanish town of Saguntum, about one hundred miles south of the Ebro, to become the friends of Rome. The Romans accepted, thereby accepting the responsibilities of friendship with a foreign state. The Roman association with Saguntum may not have violated the letter of the Ebro treaty, but it certainly was contrary to its spirit. At first, Hannibal was careful to avoid interfering with the friends of Rome, but the Saguntines, confident of Rome's protection, began to interfere with some of the Spanish tribes allied with Hannibal.

Finally, the Romans sent an embassy to Hannibal warning him to let Saguntum alone and repeating the injunction not to cross the Ebro. The Romans probably expected Hannibal to yield as his predecessors had, but they misjudged their man. Hannibal ignored Rome's warning, besieged Saguntum, and took the town.

On hearing of Saguntum's fall, the Romans sent an ultimatum to Carthage demanding the surrender of Hannibal. Carthage refused, and Rome declared war in 218 B.C. Rome's policy between the wars had been the worst possible combination of approaches. Rome had insulted and injured Carthage by the annexation of Sardinia in 238 B.C. and had repeatedly provoked and insulted Carthage by interventions in Spain. But Roman policy took no measures to prevent the construction of a powerful and dangerous Punic Empire or even to build defenses against a Punic attack from Spain. Hannibal saw to it that the Romans paid the price for their blunders. By September of 218 B.C. he was across the Alps. His army was weary, bedraggled, and greatly reduced, but he was in Italy and among the friendly Gauls.

Hannibal defeated the Romans at the Ticinus River and crushed the joint consular armies at the Trebia River. In 217 B.C. he outmaneuvered and trapped another army at Lake Trasimene. Hannibal's first victory brought him reinforcements of fifty thousand Gauls, and his second confirmed that his superior generalship could defeat the Roman army. The key to success, however, would be defection by Rome's allies. Hannibal released Italian prisoners without harm or ransom and moved his army south of Rome to encourage rebellion. But the allies remained firm, perhaps because Hannibal was accompanied by the hated Gauls, perhaps because they were not convinced yet of Rome's ultimate defeat, and perhaps even out of loyalty to Rome.

Sobered by their defeats, the Romans elected Quintus Fabius Maximus dictator. He understood that Hannibal could not be beaten by the usual tactics and that the Roman army, decimated and demoralized, needed time to recover. His strategy was to avoid battle while following and harassing Hannibal's army. When the Roman army had recovered and Fabius could fight Hannibal on favorable ground, only then would the Romans fight.

In 216 B.C. Hannibal marched to Cannae in Apulia to tempt the Romans into another open fight. The Romans could not allow him to ravage the country freely, so they sent off an army of some eighty thousand men to meet him. Almost the entire Roman army was killed or captured. It was the worst defeat in Roman history; Rome's prestige was shattered, and most of her allies in southern Italy as well as Syracuse in Sicily now went over to Hannibal. In 215 B.C. Philip V, king of Macedon, made an alliance with Hannibal and launched a war to recover his influence on the Adriatic. For more than a decade no Roman army would dare face Hannibal in the open field, and he was free to roam over all Italy and do as he pleased.

Hannibal had neither the numbers nor the supplies to besiege such walled cities as Rome and the major allies, nor did he have the equipment to take them by assault. To win the war in Spain, the Romans appointed Publius Cornelius Scipio (237–183 B.C.), later called Africanus, to the command in Spain with proconsular *imperium*. This was such a breach of tradition as to be almost unconstitutional, for

The Origins of the Hannibalic War

The Second Punic War was often called the Hannibalic War after the brilliant Carthaginian general who launched it. The Roman historian Livy wrote some two centuries after the event, and his account of its origin presents what had become an orthodox Roman view.

I may be permitted to premise at this division of my work, what most historians have professed at the beginning of their whole undertaking; that I am about to relate the most memorable of all wars that were ever waged: the war which the Carthaginians, under the conduct of Hannibal, maintained with the Roman people. For never did any states and nations more efficient in their resources engage in contest; nor had they themselves at any other period so great a degree of power and energy. They brought into action too no arts of war unknown to each other, but those which had been tried in the first Punic war; and so various was the fortune of the conflict, and so doubtful the victory, that they who conquered were more exposed to danger. The hatred with which they fought also was almost greater than their resources; the Romans being indignant that the conquered aggressively took up arms against their victors; the Carthaginians, because they considered that in their subjection it had been lorded over them with haughtiness and avarice. There is besides a story, that Hannibal, when about nine years old, while he boyishly coaxed his father Hamilcar that he might be taken to Spain, (at the time when the African war was completed, and he was employed in sacrificing previously to transporting his army thither,) was conducted to the altar; and, having laid his hand on the offerings, was bound by an oath to prove himself, as soon as he could, an enemy to the Roman people. The loss of Sicily and Sardinia grieved the high spirit of Hamilcar: for he deemed that Sicily had been given up through a premature despair of their affairs; and that Sardinia, during the disturbances in Africa, had been treacherously taken by the Romans, while, in addition, the payment of a tribute had been imposed.

Livy, 21. 1–18, trans. by D. Spiller and C. Edmonds.

A war elephant, such as Hannibal brought over the Alps into Italy. Fighting elephants were the heavy tanks of ancient warfare. [*Ronald Sheridan's Photo Library*]

(*Below*) *Scipio Africanus, who conquered Spain and decisively defeated Hannibal at Zama in* 202 B.C. [*Alinari/ Art Resource*]

Scipio was not yet twenty-five and had held no high office. But he was a general almost as talented as Hannibal. In 209 B.C. he captured New Carthage, the main Punic base in Spain. His skillful and tactful treatment of the native Iberians won them away from the enemy and over to his own army. Within a few years young Scipio had conquered all Spain and had deprived Hannibal of hope of help from that region.

In 204 B.C. Scipio landed in Africa, defeated the Carthaginians, and forced them to accept a peace whose main clause was the withdrawal of Hannibal and his army from Italy. Hannibal had won every battle but lost the war, for he had not counted on the determination of Rome and the loyalty of her allies. Hannibal's return inspired Carthage to break the peace and to risk all in battle. In 202 B.C. Scipio and Hannibal faced each other at the battle of Zama. The generalship of Scipio and the desertion of Hannibal's mercenaries gave the victory to Rome. The new peace terms reduced Carthage to the status of a dependent ally to Rome. The Second Punic War ended the Carthaginian command of the western Mediterranean and Carthage's term as a great power. Rome ruled the seas and the entire Mediterranean coast from Italy westward.

The Republic's Conquest of the Hellenistic World

The East

By the middle of the third century B.C. the eastern Mediterranean had reached a condition of stability. It was based on a balance of power among the three great kingdoms, and even lesser states had an established place. That equilibrium was threatened by the activities of two aggressive monarchs, Philip V of Macedon (221–179 B.C.) and Antiochus III of the Seleucid kingdom (223–187 B.C.). Philip and Antiochus moved swiftly, the latter against Syria and Palestine, the former against cities in the Aegean, in the Hellespontine region, and on the coast of Asia Minor.

The threat that a more powerful Macedon might pose to Rome's friends and, perhaps, even to Italy was enough to persuade the Romans to intervene.

In 200 B.C. the Romans sent an ultimatum to Philip ordering him not to attack any Greek city and to pay reparations to Pergamum. These orders were meant to provoke, not avoid, war, and Philip refused to obey. Two years later the Romans sent out a talented young general, Flamininus, who demanded that Philip withdraw from Greece entirely. In 197 B.C., with Greek support, he defeated Philip in the hills of Cynoscephalae in Thessaly, bringing an end to the Second Macedonian War (the first had been fought while the Romans were still occupied with Carthage, from 215 to 205 B.C.). The Greek cities freed from Philip were made autonomous, and in 196 B.C. Flamininus proclaimed the freedom of the Greeks.

Soon after the Romans withdrew from Greece, they came into conflict with Antiochus, who was expanding his power in Asia and on the European side of the Hellespont. On the pretext of freeing the Greeks from Roman domination, he landed an army on the Greek mainland. The Romans routed Antiochus at Thermopylae and quickly drove him from Greece, and in 189 B.C. they crushed his army at Magnesia in Asia Minor. The peace of Apamia in the next year deprived Antiochus of his elephants and his navy and imposed a huge indemnity on him. Once again, the Romans took no territory for themselves and left a number of Greek cities in Asia free. They continued their policy of regarding Greece, and now Asia Minor, as a kind of protectorate in which they could intervene or not as they chose.

In 179 B.C. Perseus succeeded Philip V as king of Macedon. He tried to gain popularity in Greece by favoring the democratic and revolutionary forces in the cities. The Romans, troubled by this threat to stability, launched the Third Macedonian War (172–168 B.C.), and in 168 Aemilius Paullus defeated Perseus at Pydna. The peace imposed by the Romans reveals a change in policy and a growing harshness. It divided Macedon into four separate republics, whose citizens were forbidden to intermarry or even to do business across the new national boundaries.

The new policy reflected a change in Rome from the previous relatively gentle one to the stern and businesslike approach favored by the conservative censor Cato. The new harshness was applied to allies and bystanders as well as to defeated opponents. Leaders of anti-Roman factions in the Greek cities were punished severely.

When Aemilius Paullus returned from his victory, he celebrated a triumph that lasted three days, during which the spoils of war, royal prisoners, and great wealth were paraded through the streets of Rome behind the proud general. The public treasury benefited to such a degree that the direct property tax on Roman citizens was abolished. Part of the booty went to the general and part to his soldiers. New motives were thereby introduced into Roman foreign policy, or, perhaps, old motives were given new prominence. Foreign campaigns could bring profit to the state, rewards to the army, and wealth, fame, honor, and political power to the general.

Roman Engagement Overseas

First Macedonian War	215–205 B.C.
Second Macedonian War	200–197 B.C.
Proclamation of Greek freedom by Flamininus at Corinth	196 B.C.
Battle of Magnesia; Antiochus defeated in Asia Minor	189 B.C.
Third Macedonian War	172–168 B.C.
Battle of Pydna	168 B.C.
Roman wars in Spain	154–133 B.C.
Numantia taken	134 B.C.

The West

Harsh as the Romans had become toward the Greeks, they were even worse in their treatment of the people of the Iberian Peninsula, whom they considered barbarians. They committed dreadful atrocities, lied, cheated, and broke treaties in their effort to exploit and pacify the natives, who fought back fiercely in guerrilla style. From 154 to 133 B.C. the fighting waxed, and it became hard to recruit Roman soldiers to fight in the increasingly ugly war. At last, in 134, Scipio Aemilianus took the key city of Numantia by siege, burned it to the ground, and put an end to the war in Spain.

Roman treatment of Carthage was no better.

Although Carthage lived up to its treaty with Rome faithfully and posed no threat, some Romans refused to abandon their hatred and fear of the traditional enemy. Cato is said to have ended all his speeches in the Senate with the same sentence: "Ceterum censeo delendam esse Carthaginem" ("Besides, I think that Carthage must be destroyed"). At last the

Plutarch Describes a Roman Triumph

In 168 B.C. L. Aemilius Paullus defeated King Perseus in the battle of Pydna, bringing an end to the Third Macedonian War. For his great achievement the Senate granted Paullus the right to celebrate a triumph, the great honorific procession granted only for extraordinary victories and eagerly sought by all Roman generals. Plutarch described the details of Paullus's triumph.

The people erected scaffolds in the forum, in the circuses, as they call their buildings for horse-races, and in all other parts of the city where they could best behold the show. The spectators were clad in white garments; all the temples were open, and full of garlands and perfumes; the ways were cleared and kept open by numerous officers, who drove back all who crowded into or ran across the main avenue. This triumph lasted three days. On the first, which was scarcely long enough for the sight, were to be seen the statues, pictures, and colossal images which were taken from the enemy, drawn upon two hundred and fifty chariots. On the second was carried in a great many wagons the finest and richest armour of the Macedonians, both of brass and steel, all newly polished and glittering; the pieces of which were piled up and arranged purposely with the greatest art, so as to seem to be tumbled in heaps carelessly and by chance: . . .

. . . .

On the third day, early in the morning, first came the trumpeters, who did not sound as they were wont in a procession or solemn entry, but such a charge as the Romans use when they encourage the soldiers to fight. Next followed young men wearing frocks with ornamented borders, who led to the sacrifice a hundred and twenty stalled oxen, with their horns gilded, and their heads adorned with ribbons and garlands; and with these were boys that carried basins for libation, of silver and gold.

. . . .

After his children and their attendants came Perseus himself, clad all in black, and wearing the boots of his country, and looking like one altogether stunned and deprived of reason, through the greatness of his misfortunes. Next followed a great company of his friends and familiars, whose countenances were disfigured with grief, and who let the spectators see, by their tears and their continual looking upon Perseus, that it was his fortune they so much lamented, and that they were regardless of their own.

. . . .

. . . After these were carried four hundred crowns, all made of gold, sent from the cities by their respective deputations to Æmilius, in honour of his victory. Then he himself came, seated on a chariot magnificently adorned (a man well worthy to be looked at, even without these ensigns of power), dressed in a robe of purple, interwoven with gold, and holding a laurel branch in his right hand. All the army, in like manner, with boughs of laurel in their hands, divided into their bands and companies, followed the chariot of their commander; some singing verses, according to the usual custom, mingled with raillery; others, songs of triumph and the praise of Æmilius's deeds; who, indeed, was admired and accounted happy by all men, and unenvied by every one that was good; except so far as it seems the province of some god to lessen that happiness which is too great and inordinate, and so to mingle the affairs of human life that no one should be entirely free and exempt from calamities; but, as we read in Homer, that those should think themselves truly blessed whom fortune has given an equal share of good and evil.

Plutarch, "Aemilius Paullus," in *Lives of the Noble Grecians and Romans*, trans. by John Dryden, rev. by A. H. Clough (New York: Random House, n.d.), pp. 340–341.

Romans took advantage of a technical breach of the peace to destroy Carthage. In 146 B.C. Scipio Aemilianus took the city, plowed up its land, and put salt in the furrows as a symbol of the permanent abandonment of the site. The Romans incorporated it as the province of Africa, one of six Roman provinces, including Sicily, Sardinia–Corsica, Macedonia, Hither Spain, and Further Spain.

Civilization in the Early Roman Republic

Among the most important changes wrought by Roman expansion overseas were those in the Roman style of life and thought brought about by close and continued association with the Greeks of the Hellenistic world. Attitudes toward the Greeks themselves ranged from admiration for their culture and history to contempt for their constant squabbling, their commercial practices, and their weakness. Conservatives such as Cato might speak contemptuously of the Greeks as "Greeklings" *(Graeculi)*, but even he learned Greek and absorbed Greek culture. Before long the education of the Roman upper classes was bilingual. In addition to the Twelve Tables young Roman nobles studied Greek rhetoric, literature, and sometimes philosophy. These studies even had an effect on education and the Latin language. As early as the third century B.C. Livius Andronicus, a liberated Greek slave, translated the *Odyssey* into Latin. It became a primer for young Romans and put Latin on the road to becoming a literary language.

Religion

Roman religion was influenced by the Greeks almost from the beginning; the Romans identified their own gods with Greek equivalents and incorporated Greek mythology into their own. For the most part, however, Roman religious practice remained simple and Italian, until the third century B.C. brought important new influences from the east. In 205 the Senate approved the public worship of Cybele, the Great Mother goddess from Phrygia. Hers was a fertility cult accompanied by ecstatic, frenzied, and sensual rites that shocked and outraged conservative Romans to such a degree that they soon banned the cult to Romans. Similarly, the Senate banned the worship of

The temple of Vesta, at Rome, first century B.C. *Vesta was the Roman goddess of the hearth. Her cult included an eternal flame, which was tended by the famous Vestal Virgins.* [*Art Resource*]

Dionysus, or Bacchus, in 186 B.C. In the second century B.C. interest in Babylonian astrology also grew, and the Senate's attempt in 139 to expel the "Chaldaeans," as the astrologers were called, did not prevent the continued influence of their superstition.

Education

Human society depends on the passing on from generation to generation of the knowledge, skills, and values needed for life in any particular community. A system of education, whether formal or informal, is essential to each culture and reveals its character even as it tries to stamp that character on its children. The education provided in the early centuries of the Roman Republic reflected the limited, conservative, and practical nature of that community of plain farmers and soldiers. Education was entirely the responsibility of the family, the father teaching his own son at home. It is not clear whether in these early times girls received any education, though they certainly did later on. The boys learned to read, write, and calculate, and they learned the skills of farming. They memorized the laws of the Twelve Tables, Rome's earliest code of law; learned how to perform the usual religious rites; heard stories of the great deeds of early Roman history and particularly those of their ancestors; and engaged in the physical training appropriate for potential soldiers. This course of study was practical, vocational, and moral. It aimed at making the boys moral, pious, patriotic, law-abiding, and respectful of tradition.

In the third century B.C. the Romans came into contact with the Greeks of southern Italy, and this contact produced momentous changes in Roman education. Greek teachers came to Rome and introduced the study of language, literature, and philosophy, as well as the idea of a liberal education, or what the Romans called *humanitas,* the root of our concept of the humanities. The aim of education changed from the practical, vocational goals of earlier times to an emphasis on broad intellectual training, critical thinking, an interest in ideas, and the development of a well-rounded person.

The first need was to learn Greek, for Rome did not yet have a literature of its own. For this purpose schools were established where the teacher, called a *grammaticus,* taught his students the Greek language and its literature, especially the poets and particularly Homer. Hereafter educated Romans were expected to be bilingual. After the completion of this elementary education, Roman boys of the upper classes studied rhetoric, the art of speaking and writing well, with Greeks who were expert in those arts. For the Greeks rhetoric was a subject of less importance than philosophy, but the more practical Romans took to it avidly, for it was of great use in legal disputes and was becoming ever more valuable in political life. Some Romans, however, were powerfully attracted to Greek literature and philosophy. So important and powerful a Roman aristocrat as Scipio Aemilianus, the man who finally defeated and destroyed Carthage, surrounded himself and his friends with such Greek thinkers as the historian Polybius and the philosopher Panaetius. Other Romans, equally outstanding, such as Cato the Elder, were more conservative and opposed the new learning on

Cato Educates His Son

Marcus Porcius Cato (234–149 B.C.) was a remarkable Roman who rose from humble origins to the highest offices in the state. He stood as the firmest defender of the old Roman traditions at a time when Hellenic ideas were strongly influential. In the following passage Plutarch tells how Cato attended to his son's education.

. . . After the birth of his son, no business could be so urgent, unless it had a public character, as to prevent him from being present when his wife bathed and swaddled the babe. For the mother nursed it herself, and often gave suck also to the infants of her slaves, that so they might come to cherish a brotherly affection for her son. As soon as the boy showed signs of understanding, his father took him under his own charge and taught him to read, although he had an accomplished slave, Chilo by name, who was a school-teacher, and taught many boys. Still, Cato thought it not right, as he tells us himself, that his son should be scolded by a slave, or have his ears tweaked when he was slow to learn, still less that he should be indebted to his slave for such a priceless thing as education. He was therefore himself not only the boy's reading-teacher, but his tutor in law, and his athletic trainer, and he taught his son not merely to hurl the javelin and fight in armour and ride the horse, but also to box, to endure heat and cold, and to swim lustily through the eddies and billows of the Tiber. His History of Rome, as he tells us himself, he wrote out with his own hand and in large characters, that his son might have in his own home an aid to acquaintance with his country's ancient traditions.

Plutarch, *Cato Major,* 20, trans. by Bernadotte Perrin (London and New York: Loeb Classical Library, William Heinemann, 1914).

the grounds that it would weaken Roman moral fiber; they were able on more than one occasion to pass laws expelling philosophers and teachers of rhetoric. But these attempts to go back to older ways failed. The new education suited the needs of the Romans of the second century B.C., who found themselves changing from a rural to an urban society, and who were being thrust into the sophisticated world of Hellenistic Greeks.

By the last century of the Roman Republic, the new Hellenized education had become dominant. Latin literature had come into being along with Latin translations of Greek poets, and these formed part of the course of study, but Roman gentlemen were expected to be bilingual, and Greek language and literature were still central to the curriculum. Many schools were established, and the number of educated people grew, extending beyond the senatorial class to the equestrians and outside Rome to the cities of Italy. Though the evidence is limited, we can be sure that girls of the upper classes were educated similarly to boys, at least through the earlier stages. They were probably taught by tutors at home rather than going to school, as was the increasing fashion among boys in the late republic. Young women did not study with philosophers and rhetoricians, for they were usually married by the age the men were pursuing their higher education. Still, some women found ways to continue their education. Some became prose writers and others poets. By the first century A.D. there were apparently enough learned women to provoke the complaints of a crotchety and conservative satirist:

Portrait bust of a Roman noblewoman from the first century B.C. *Roman women had a respectable position and were responsible for managing their households.* [*M. B. Cookson*]

Still more exasperating is the woman who begs as soon as she sits down to dinner, to discourse on poets and poetry, comparing Virgil with Homer; professors, critics, lawyers, auctioneers—even another woman—can't get a word in. She rattles on at such a rate that you'd think that all the pots and pans in the kitchen were crashing to the floor or that every bell in town was clanging. All by herself she makes as much noise as some primitive tribe chasing away an eclipse. She should learn the philosopher's lesson: "moderation is necessary even for intellectuals." And, if she still wants to appear educated and eloquent, let her dress as a man, sacrifice to men's gods and bathe in the men's baths. Wives shouldn't try to be public speakers; they shouldn't use rhetorical devices; they shouldn't read all the classics—there should be some things women don't understand. I myself cannot understand a woman who can quote the rules of grammar and never make a mistake and cites obscure, long-forgotten poets—as if men cared about such things. If she has to correct somebody let her correct her girl friends and leave her husband alone.[2]

In the late republic, Roman education, though still entirely private, became more formal and organized. From the ages of seven to twelve, boys went to elementary school accompanied by a Greek slave called a *paedagogus* (whence our term *pedagogue*) who looked after his physical well-being and his manners, and who improved his ability in Greek conversa-

[2]Juvenal, *Satires* 6.434–456, trans. by Roger Killian, Richard Lynch, Robert J. Rowland, and John Sims, cited by Sarah B. Pomeroy in *Goddesses, Whores, Wives, and Slaves* (New York: Schocken Books, 1975), p. 172.

The temple of Fortuna Virilis in Rome, late second century B.C. *The Romans modified Greek architecture with local Italian traditions. The Ionic order here is Greek, but the temple stands on a high podium in the Etruscan manner. Moreover, only the six columns at the front of the temple are free standing in the Greek style. The others are built into the walls, a favorite Roman practice.* [*Chauffourier, Rome/Art Resource*]

tion. At school the boy learned to read and write, using a wax tablet and a stylus, and to do simple arithmetic with the aid of an abacus and pebbles *(calculi)*. Discipline was harsh and corporal punishment frequent. From twelve to sixteen, boys went to a higher school, where the *grammaticus* undertook to provide a liberal education, using Greek and Latin literature as his subject matter. In addition, he taught dialectic, arithmetic, geometry, astronomy, and music. Sometimes he included the elements of rhetoric, especially for those boys who would not go on to a higher education.

At sixteen, some boys went on to advanced study in rhetoric. The instructors were usually Greek, and they trained their charges by study of models of fine speech of the past and by having them write, memorize, and declaim speeches suitable for different occasions. Sometimes the serious student attached himself to some famous public speaker and followed him about to learn what he could. Sometimes a rich and ambitious Roman would support a Greek philosopher in his own home so that his son could converse with him and acquire the learning and polish thought necessary for the fully cultured gentleman. Some, like the great orator Cicero, undertook what we might call postgraduate study by traveling abroad to study with great teachers of rhetoric and philosophy in the Greek world. One consequence of this whole style of education was to broaden the Romans' understanding through the careful study of a foreign language and culture and to make them a part of the older and wider culture of the Hellenistic world, a world that they had come to dominate and needed to understand.

Roman Imperialism

Rome's expansion in Italy and overseas was accomplished without a grand general plan.

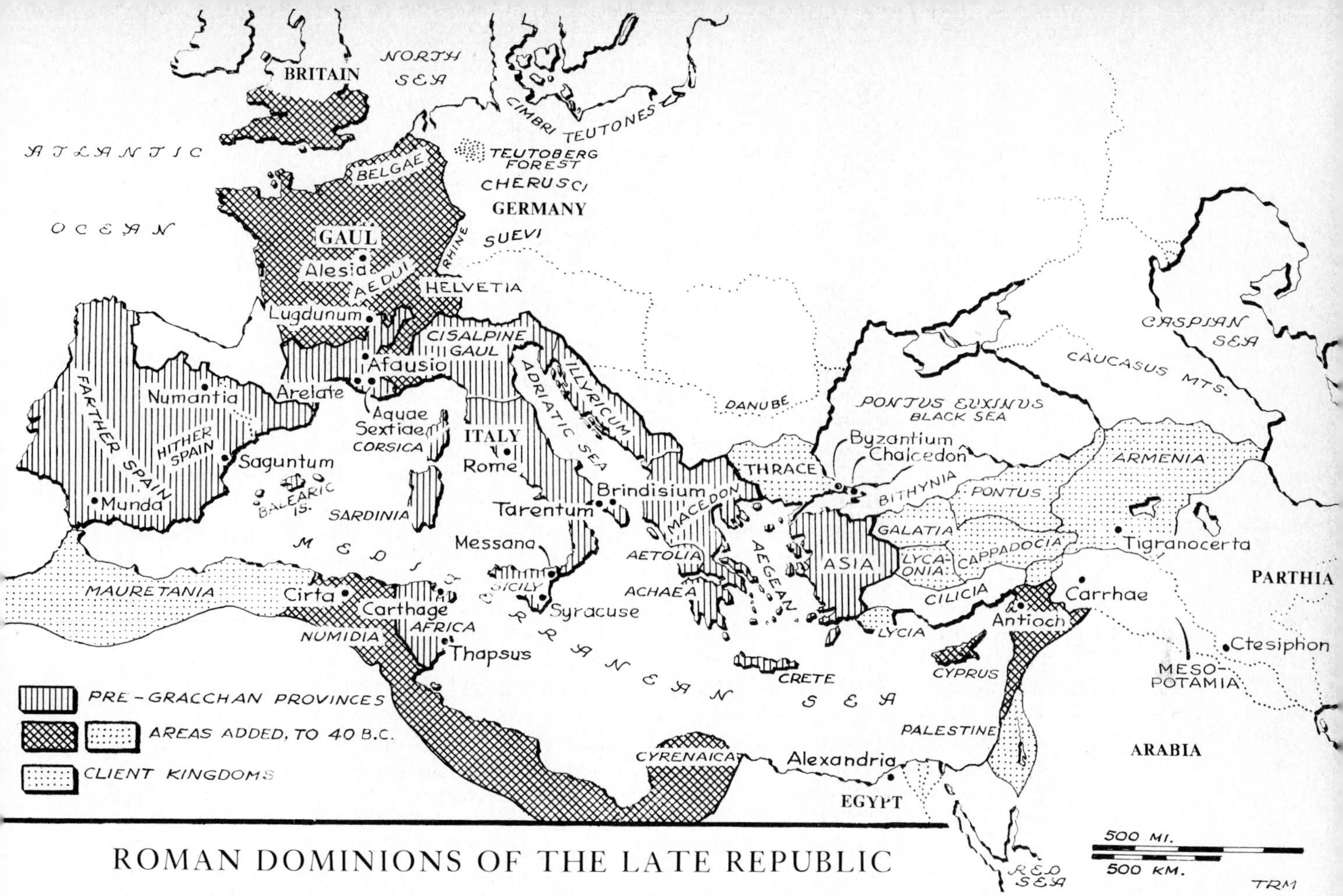

MAP 4-3 *The Roman Republic's conquest of Mediterranean lands—and beyond—until the death of Julius Caesar is shown here. Areas conquered before Tiberius Gracchus (ca.* 133 B.C.*) are distinguished from later ones and from client areas owing allegiance to Rome.*

The new territories were acquired as a result of wars that the Romans believed were either defensive or preventive. Their foreign policy was aimed at providing security for Rome on Rome's terms, but these terms were often unacceptable to other nations and led to continued conflict. Whether intended or not, Rome's expansion brought the Romans an empire and, with it, power, wealth, and responsibilities. The republican constitution that had served Rome well during its years as a city-state and that had been well adapted to the mastery of Italy would be severely tested by the need to govern an empire beyond the seas. Roman society and the Roman character had maintained their integrity through the period of expansion in Italy. But these would be tested by the temptations and strains presented by the wealth and the complicated problems presented by an overseas empire.

The Aftermath of Conquest

War and expansion changed the economic, social, and political life of Italy. Before the Punic wars most Italians owned their own farms, which provided most of the family's needs. Some families owned larger holdings, but their lands chiefly grew grain, and they used the labor of clients, tenants, and hired workers rather than slaves. Fourteen years of fighting in the Second Punic War did terrible damage to much Italian farmland. Many veterans returning from the wars found it impossible or unprofitable to go back to their farms. Some moved to Rome, where they could find work as occasional laborers, but most stayed in the country to work as tenant farmers or hired hands. No longer landowners, they were no longer eligible for the army. Often the land they abandoned was gathered into large parcels by the wealthy. They converted these large units, later called *latifundia,* into large plantations for growing cash crops—grain, olives, and grapes for wine—or into cattle ranches.

The upper classes had plenty of capital to stock and operate these estates because of profits from the war and from exploiting the provinces. Land was cheap, and slaves conquered in war provided cheap labor. By fair means and foul, large landholders obtained large quantities of public land and forced small farmers from it. These changes separated the people of Rome and Italy more sharply into rich and poor, landed and landless, privileged and deprived. The result was political, social, and ultimately constitutional conflict that threatened the existence of the republic.

The Gracchi

By the middle of the second century B.C. the problems caused by Rome's rapid expansion troubled perceptive Roman nobles. The fall in status of peasant farmers made it harder to recruit soldiers and came to present a political threat as well. The patron's traditional control over his clients was weakened by their flight from their land. Even those former landowners who worked on the land of their patrons as tenants or hired hands were less reliable. The introduction of the secret ballot in the 130s made them even more independent.

In 133 B.C. Tiberius Gracchus tried to solve these problems. He became tribune for 133 B.C. on a program of land reform; some of the most powerful members of the Roman aristocracy helped him draft the bill. They meant it to be a moderate attempt at solving Rome's problems. The bill's target was public land that had been acquired and held illegally, some of it for many years. The bill allowed holders of this land to retain as many as 300 acres in clear title as private property, but the state would reclaim anything over that. The recovered land would be redistributed in small lots to the poor, who would pay a small rent to the state and could not sell what they had received.

The bill aroused great hostility. Many senators held vast estates and would be hurt by its passage. Others thought it would be a bad precedent to allow any interference with property rights, even ones so dubious as those pertaining to illegally held public land. Still others feared the political gains that Tiberius and his associates would make if the beneficiaries of their law were properly grateful to its drafters.

When Tiberius put the bill before the tribal assembly, one of the tribunes, M. Octavius, interposed his veto. Tiberius went to the Senate to discuss his proposal, but the senators continued their opposition. Tiberius now had to choose between dropping the matter and undertaking a revolutionary course. Unwilling to give up, he put his bill before the tribal assembly again. Again Octavius vetoed, so Tiberius, strongly supported by the people, had Octavius removed from office, violating the constitution. The assembly's removal of a magistrate implied a fundamental shift of power from the Senate to the people. If the assembly could pass laws opposed by the Senate and vetoed by a tribune, if they could remove magistrates, then Rome would become a democracy like Athens instead of a traditional oligarchy. At this point many of Tiberius' powerful senatorial allies deserted him.

Tiberius proposed a second bill, harsher than the first and more appealing to the people, for he had given up hope of conciliating the Senate. This bill, which passed the assembly, provided for a commission to carry it out. When King Attalus of Pergamum died and left his kingdom to Rome, Tiberius proposed to use the Pergamene revenue to finance the commission. This proposal challenged the Senate's control both of finances and of foreign affairs. Hereafter there could be no compromise: either Tiberius or the Roman constitution must go under.

Tiberius understood the danger that he would face if he stepped down from the tribunate, so he announced his candidacy for a second successive term, another blow at tradition. His opponents feared that he might go on to hold office indefinitely, to dominate Rome in what appeared to them a demagogic tyranny. They concentrated their fire on the constitutional issue, the deposition of the tribune. They appear to have had some success, for many of Tiberius' supporters did not come out to vote. At the elections a riot broke out, and a mob of senators and their clients killed Tiberius and some three hundred of his followers and threw their bodies into the Tiber River. The Senate had put down the threat to its rule, but at the price of the first internal bloodshed in Roman political history.

The tribunate of Tiberius Gracchus brought a permanent change to Roman politics. Heretofore Roman political struggles had generally been struggles for honor and reputation between great families or coalitions of such families. Fundamental issues were rarely at stake. The revolutionary proposals of Tiberius, however, and the senatorial resort to bloodshed created a new situation. Tiberius' use of the tribunate to challenge senatorial rule encouraged imitation in spite of his failure. From then on, Romans could pursue a political career that was not based solely on influence within the aristocracy; pressure from the people might be an effective substitute. In the last century of the republic such politicians were called *populares,* whereas those who supported the traditional role of the Senate were called *optimates* ("the best men").

These groups were not political parties with formal programs and party discipline, but they were more than merely vehicles for the political ambitions of unorthodox politicians. Fundamental questions such as land reform, the treatment of the Italian allies, the power of the assemblies versus the power of the Senate, and other problems divided the Roman people, from the time of the Gracchi brothers to the fall of the republic. Some popular leaders, of course, were cynical self-seekers who used the issues only for their own ambitions. Some few may have been sincere advocates of a principled position. Most, no doubt, were a mixture of the two, like most politicians in most times.

The tribunate of Gaius Gracchus (brother of Tiberius) was much more dangerous than that of Tiberius because all the tribunes of 123 B.C. were his supporters, so there could be no veto, and a recent law permitted the reelection of tribunes. Gaius developed a program of such

The Murder of Tiberius Gracchus

In 133 B.C. the attempt of the tribune Tiberius Gracchus to introduce a limited redistribution of the land provoked violent resistance. As Plutarch told the story, Tiberius' enemies interpreted an innocent gesture by him as a request to be made king.

This news created general confusion in the senators, and Nasica at once called upon the consul to punish this tyrant, and defend the government. The consul mildly replied, that he would not be the first to do any violence; and as he would not suffer any freeman to be put to death, before sentence had lawfully passed upon him, so neither would he allow any measure to be carried into effect, if by persuasion or compulsion on the part of Tiberius the people had been induced to pass an unlawful vote. But Nasica, rising from his seat, "Since the consul," said he, "regards not the safety of the commonwealth, let everyone who will defend the laws, follow me." He then, casting the skirt of his gown over his head, hastened to the capitol; those who bore him company, wrapped their gowns also about their arms, and forced their way after him. And as they were persons of the greatest authority in the city, the common people did not venture to obstruct their passing, but were rather so eager to clear the way for them, that they tumbled over one another in haste. The attendants they brought with them had furnished themselves with clubs and staves from their houses, and they themselves picked up the feet and other fragments of stools and chairs, which were broken by the hasty flight of the common people. Thus armed, they made towards Tiberius, knocking down those whom they found in front of him, and those were soon wholly dispersed and many of them slain. Tiberius tried to save himself by flight. As he was running, he was stopped by one who caught hold of him by the gown; but he threw it off, and fled in his under-garment only. And stumbling over those who before had been knocked down, as he was endeavouring to get up again, Publius Satureius, a tribune, one of his colleagues, was observed to give him the first fatal stroke, by hitting him upon the head with the foot of a stool. The second blow was claimed, as though it had been a deed to be proud of, by Lucius Rufus. And of the rest there fell above three hundred killed by clubs and staves only, none by an iron weapon.

This, we are told, was the first sedition amongst the Romans, since the abrogation of kingly government, that ended in the effusion of blood.

Plutarch, *Tiberius Gracchus,* trans. by John Dryden.

breadth as to appeal to a variety of groups. First, he revived the agrarian commission, which had been allowed to lapse. Because there was not enough good public land left to meet the demand, he proposed to establish new colonies: two in Italy and one on the old site of Carthage. Among other popular acts, he put through a law stabilizing the price of grain in Rome, which involved building granaries to guarantee an adequate supply.

Gaius broke new ground in appealing to the equestrian order in his struggle against the Senate. The equestrians (so called because they served in the Roman cavalry) were neither peasants nor senators. A highly visible minority of them were businessmen who supplied goods and services to the Roman state and collected its taxes. Almost continuous warfare and the need for tax collection in the provinces had made many of them rich. Most of the time these wealthy men had the same outlook as the Senate; generally they used their profits to purchase land and to try to reach senatorial rank themselves. Still they had a special interest in Roman expansion and in the exploitation of the provinces; toward the latter part of the second century B.C., they came to have a clear sense of group interest and to exert political influence.

In 129 B.C. Pergamum became the new province of Asia. Gaius put through a law turning over to the equestrian order the privilege of collecting its revenue. He also barred senators from serving as jurors on the courts that tried provincial governors charged with extortion. The combination was a wonderful gift for wealthy equestrian businessmen, who were now free to squeeze profits out of the rich province of Asia without much fear of interference from the governors. The results for Roman provincial administration were bad, but the immediate political consequences for Gaius were excellent. The equestrians were now given reality as a class, as a political unit that might be set against the Senate, and they might be formed into a coalition to serve Gaius' purposes.

Gaius easily won reelection as tribune for 122 B.C. He aimed at giving citizenship to the Italians, both to solve the problem that their dissatisfaction presented and to add them to his political coalition. But the common people did not want to share the advantages of Roman citizenship, and the Senate seized on this proposal as a way of driving a wedge between Gaius and his supporters.

The Romans did not reelect Gaius for 121 B.C., and he stood naked before his enemies. A hostile consul provoked an incident that led to violence. The Senate invented an extreme decree ordering the consuls to see to it that no harm came to the republic; in effect, this decree established martial law. Gaius was hunted down and killed, and a senatorial court condemned and put to death without trial some three thousand of his followers.

Marius and Sulla

For the moment the senatorial oligarchy had fought off the challenge to its traditional position. Before long it faced more serious dangers arising from troubles abroad. The first grew out of a dispute over the succession to the throne of Numidia, a client kingdom of Rome's near Carthage. The victory of Jugurtha, who became king of Numidia, and his massacre of Roman and Italian businessmen in Numidia gained Roman attention. Although the Senate was reluctant to become involved, pressure from the equestrians and the people forced the declaration of what became known as the Jugurthine War in 111 B.C.

As the war dragged on, the people, sometimes with good reason, suspected the Senate of taking bribes from Jugurtha. They elected C. Marius (157–86 B.C.) to the consulship for 107, and the assembly, usurping the role of the Senate, assigned him to the province of Numidia. This action was significant in several ways: Marius was a *novus homo,* a "new man," that is, the first in the history of his family to reach the consulship. Although a wealthy equestrian, he had been born in the town of Arpinum and was outside the closed circle of the old Roman aristocracy. His earlier career had won him a reputation as an outstanding soldier and something of a political maverick.

Marius quickly defeated Jugurtha, but Jugurtha escaped and guerrilla warfare continued. Finally Marius' subordinate, L. Cornelius Sulla (138–78 B.C.), trapped Jugurtha and brought the war to an end. Marius celebrated the victory, but Sulla, an ambitious but impoverished descendant of an old Roman family, resented being cheated of the credit he thought he deserved. Soon rumors circulated crediting Sulla with the victory and diminishing Marius' role. Thus were the seeds planted for a personal rivalry and a mutual hostility that would last until Marius' death.

While the Romans were fighting Jugurtha, a far greater danger threatened Rome from the north. In 105 B.C. two barbaric tribes, the Cimbri and the Teutones, had come down the Rhone valley and crushed a Roman army at Arausio (Orange). To meet the danger, the Romans elected Marius to his second consulship when these tribes threatened again. From 104 he served five consecutive terms until 100 B.C., when the crisis was over.

While the barbarians were occupied elsewhere, Marius used the time to make important changes in the army. He began using volunteers for the army, mostly the dispossessed farmers and rural proletarians whose problems had not been solved by the Gracchi. They enlisted for a long term of service and looked on the army not as an unwelcome duty but as an opportunity and a career. They became semiprofessional clients of their general and sought guaranteed food, clothing, shelter, and booty from victories. They came to expect a piece of land as a form of mustering-out pay or veteran's bonus when they retired. Volunteers were most likely to enlist with a man who was a capable soldier and influential enough to obtain what he needed for them. They looked to him rather than to the state for their rewards. He, on the other hand, had to obtain these favors from the Senate if he was to maintain his power and reputation. Marius' innovation created both the opportunity and the necessity for military leaders to gain enough power to challenge civilian authority. The promise of rewards won these leaders the personal loyalty of their troops, and that loyalty allowed them to frighten the Senate into granting their demands.

The War Against the Italian Allies (90–88 B.C.)

For a decade Rome avoided serious troubles, but in that time the Senate took no action to deal with Italian discontent. The Italians were excluded from the land bill for Marius' veterans, and their discontent was serious enough to cause the Senate to expel all Italians from

Sallust Describes the New Model Army of Marius

Sallust (86–ca. 34 B.C.) wrote a number of historical monographs. In the one describing Rome's war against Jugurtha, king of Numidia in North Africa, he told the story of the important changes in army recruitment introduced by Marius. With the aid of the new troops Marius was able to win the war against Jugurtha in the years 107–105 B.C.

Marius, who as I said before, had been made consul with great eagerness on the part of the populace, began, though he had always been hostile to the patricians, to inveigh against them, after the people gave him the province of Numidia, with great frequency and violence. . . . He also enlisted all the bravest men from Latium, most of whom were known to him by actual service, some few only by report, and induced, by earnest solicitation, even discharged veterans to accompany him. Nor did the senate, though adverse to him, dare to refuse him anything; the additions to the legions they had voted even with eagerness, because military service was thought to be unpopular with the multitude, and Marius seemed likely to lose either the means of warfare, or the favour of the people. But such expectations were entertained in vain, so ardent was the desire of going with Marius that had seized on almost all. Every one cherished the fancy that he should return home laden with spoil, crowned with victory, or attended with some similar good fortune. Marius himself, too, had excited them in no small degree by a speech. . . .

. . . .

He himself, in the mean time, proceeded to enlist soldiers, not after the ancient method, or from the classes, but taking all that were willing to join him, and the greater part from the lowest ranks.

Sallust; *Jugurtha,* trans. by J. S. Watson (London: Bohn Classical Library, 1852), pp. 171, 172, 181.

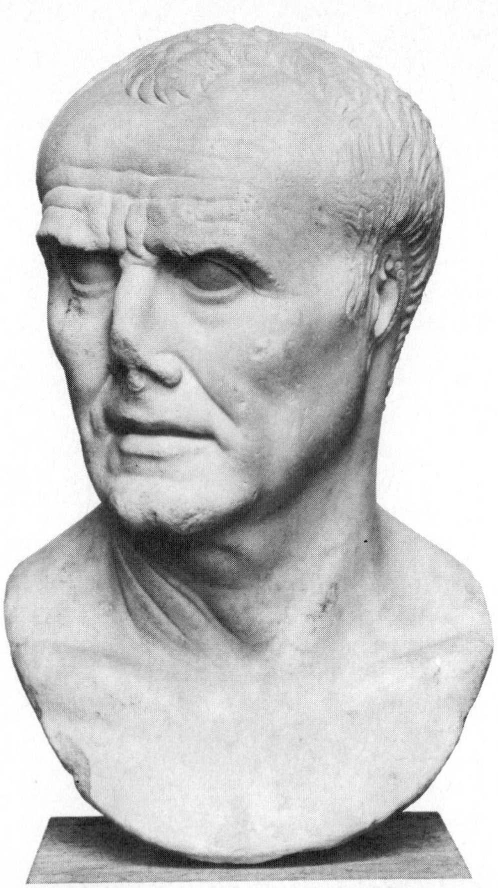

Marius (157–86 B.C.), *top, and Sulla* (138–78 B.C.). *Their bloody struggle for power marked the beginning of the end of the Roman Republic.* [*Hartwig Koppermann*]

Rome in 95 B.C. Four years later the tribune M. Livius Drusus put forward a bill to enfranchise the Italians. Drusus seems to have been a sincere aristocratic reformer, but he was assassinated in 90 B.C. In frustration the Italians revolted and established a separate confederation with its own capital and its own coinage.

Employing the traditional device of divide and conquer, the Romans immediately offered citizenship to those cities that remained loyal and soon made the same offer to the rebels if they laid down their arms. Even then, hard fighting was needed to put down the uprising, but by 88 B.C. the war against the allies was over. All the Italians became Roman citizens with the protections that citizenship offered, but they retained local self-government and a dedication to their own municipalities that made Italy flourish. The passage of time blurred the distinction between Romans and Italians and forged them into a single nation.

Sulla and His Dictatorship

During the war against the allies Sulla had performed well, and he was elected consul for 88 B.C. and was given command of the war against Mithridates, who was leading a major rebellion in Asia. At this point the seventy-year-old Marius emerged from obscurity and sought the command for himself. With popular and equestrian support, he got the assembly to transfer the command to him. Sulla, defending the rights of the Senate and his own interests, marched his army against Rome. This was the first time a Roman general had used his army against fellow citizens. Marius and his friends fled, and Sulla regained the command. No sooner had he left again for Asia than Marius joined with the consul Cinna and reconquered Rome by force. He outlawed Sulla and launched a bloody massacre of the senatorial opposition. Marius died soon after his election to a seventh consulship, for 86 B.C. Cinna now was the chief man at Rome. Supported by Marius' men, he held the consulship from 87 to 84 B.C. His future depended on Sulla's fortunes in the east.

By 85 B.C. Sulla had driven Mithridates from Greece and had crossed over to Asia Minor.

Appian Describes Sulla's Proscriptions of His Opponents

In 83 B.C. Sulla triumphed over the friends of Marius in a civil war and became dictator. In the following selection Appian describes Sulla's treatment of his defeated opponents.

Sulla recounted Sulpicius' and Marius' insulting treatment of himself and without saying anything definite—he was unwilling to speak yet about such a move as he contemplated—wanted them [his soldiers] to be on the alert for action. They understood what he meant and, fearing they would miss the campaign, themselves made Sulla's desires explicit and urged him to take courage and lead them against Rome. He was delighted and forthwith ordered his six legions to march. . . .

. . . .

So the political struggle progressed from strife and faction to murder, and from murder to regular wars and now for the first time an army of citizens invaded their native city as if it were hostile territory. Henceforth political conflicts continued to be settled by armies, and there were constant assaults on Rome and sieges and military operations. Nothing induced any sense of shame in the authors of violence, neither the laws nor the constitution nor patriotism. Then a vote was passed that Sulpicius, who was still tribune, and Marius, who had been six times consul, and Marius' son, Publius Cethegus, Junius Brutus, Gnaeus and Quintus Granius, Publius Albinovinus and Marcus Laetorius, and about a dozen others who had fled from Rome, were enemies of the republic, having caused sedition and made war on the consuls and promised freedom to slaves to incite them to revolt. Any person was authorized to kill them without penalty or produce them before the consuls, and their property was confiscated.

Appian, *Civil Wars,* trans. by Horace White (London and New York: William Heinemann and The Macmillan Company, 1913), pp. 175–177.

Eager to regain control of Rome, he negotiated a compromise peace. In 83 B.C. he returned to Italy and fought a civil war that lasted for more than a year. Sulla won and drove the followers of Marius from Italy. He now held all power and had himself appointed dictator, not in the traditional sense, but for the express purpose of reconstituting the state.

Sulla's first step was to wipe out the opposition. The names of those proscribed were posted in public. As outlaws they could be killed by anyone, and the killer received a reward. Sulla proscribed not only political opponents but his personal enemies and men whose only crime was having wealth and property. With the proceeds from the confiscations, Sulla rewarded his veterans, perhaps as many as 100,000 men, and thereby built a solid base of support.

Sulla had enough power and influence to make himself the permanent ruler of Rome, but he was traditional enough to want a restoration of senatorial government, reformed in such a way as to prevent the misfortunes of the past. To deal with the decimation of the Senate caused by the proscriptions and the civil war, he enrolled 300 new members, many of them from the equestrian order and the upper classes of the Italian cities. The office of tribune, used by the Gracchi to attack senatorial rule, was made into a political dead-end.

Sulla's most valuable reforms improved the quality of the courts and the entire legal system. He created new courts to deal with specified crimes, to bring the total number of courts to eight. As both judge and jurors were senators, these courts, too, enhanced senatorial power. These actions were the most permanent of Sulla's reforms, laying the foundation for Roman criminal law.

Sulla retired to a life of ease and luxury in 79 B.C. He could not, however, undo the effect of his own example, of a general using the loyalty of his own troops to take power and to massacre his opponents, as well as innocent men. These actions proved to be more significant than his constitutional arrangements.

Fall of the Republic

Pompey, Crassus, Caesar, and Cicero

Within a year of Sulla's death his constitution came under assault. To deal with an armed threat to its powers, the Senate violated the very procedures meant to defend them. It gave the command of the army to Pompey (106–48 B.C.), who was only twenty-eight and had never been elected to a magistracy. Then, when Sertorius, a Marian general, resisted senatorial control, the Senate appointed Pompey proconsul in Spain in 77 B.C., once again violating the constitution by ignoring Sulla's rigid rules for office holding, which had been meant to guarantee experienced, loyal, and safe commanders. In 71 B.C. Pompey returned to Rome with new glory, having put down the rebellion of Sertorius. In 73 B.C. the Senate made another extraordinary appointment to put down a great slave rebellion led by the gladiator Spartacus. Marcus Licinius Crassus, a rich and ambitious senator, received powers that gave him command of almost all Italy and, together

Plutarch Describes How Crassus Became a Millionaire

Marcus Licinius Crassus (ca. 112–53 B.C.) was a fine general, a powerful politician, and the richest man in Rome. There is no doubt that his wealth contributed greatly to his power. In the following selection Plutarch describes how Crassus acquired his riches.

Now the Romans say that the many virtues of Crassus were obscured by his sole vice of avarice, and it seems that the one vice which became stronger than all the others in him dimmed the rest. The chief proofs of his avarice were the way in which he acquired his property and the size of it. For at first he was not worth more than 300 talents; then, during his consulship, he dedicated the tenth part of his property to Hercules, feasted the people, and gave to every citizen enough to live on for three months; still, when he made an inventory of his property before his Parthian expedition, he found it to have a value of 7,100 talents.

Most of this, if one must tell the scandalous truth, he gathered by fire and war, making the public calamities his greatest source of revenue. For when Sulla seized Rome and sold the property of those put to death by him, regarding and calling it booty, and wishing to make as many influential men as he could partners in the crime, Crassus refused neither to accept nor buy such property. Moreover, observing how natural and familiar at Rome were the burning and collapse of buildings, because of their massiveness and their closeness to one another, he bought slaves who were builders and architects. Then, when he had more than 500 of these, he would buy houses that were on fire and those adjoining the ones on fire. The owners would let them go for small sums, because of their fear and uncertainty, so that the greatest part of Rome came into his hands. But though he had so many artisans, he never built any house but the one he lived in, and used to say that those that were addicted to building would undo themselves without the help of other enemies. And though he had many silver mines, and very valuable land with laborers on it, yet one might consider all this as nothing compared with the value of his slaves, such a great number and variety did he possess—readers, amanuenses, silversmiths, stewards and table-servants. He himself directed their training, and took part in teaching them himself, accounting it, in a word, the chief duty of a master to care for his slaves as the living tools of household management.

Plutarch, *Life of Crassus,* trans. by N. Lewis and M. Reinhold, in *Roman Civilization,* Vol. 1 (New York: Columbia University Press, 1955), pp. 458–459.

Pompey the Great (106–48 B.C.) [*Alinari/Art Resource*]

with the newly returned Pompey, crushed the rebellion in 71 B.C. Extraordinary commands of this sort proved to be the ruin of the republic.

Crassus and Pompey were ambitious men whom the Senate feared. Both demanded special honors and election to the consulship for the year 70 B.C. Pompey was legally ineligible because he had never gone through the strict course of offices prescribed in Sulla's constitution, and Crassus needed Pompey's help. They joined forces, though they disliked and were jealous of one another. They gained popular support by promising to restore the full powers of the tribunes, which Sulla had curtailed, and they gained equestrian backing by promising to restore equestrians to the extortion court juries. They both won election and repealed most of Sulla's constitution, opening the way for further attacks on senatorial control and for collaboration between ambitious generals and demagogic tribunes.

In 67 B.C. a special law gave Pompey *imperium* for three years over the entire Mediterranean and fifty miles in from the coast, as well as the power to raise great quantities of troops and money to rid the area of pirates. The assembly passed the law over senatorial opposition, and in three months Pompey cleared the seas of piracy. Meanwhile a new war had broken out with Mithridates, and in 66 B.C. the assembly transferred the command to Pompey, giving him unprecedented powers. He held *imperium* over all Asia, with the right to make war and peace at will, and his *imperium* was superior to that of any proconsul in the field.

Once again Pompey justified his appointment. He defeated Mithridates and drove him to suicide. By 62 B.C. he had extended Rome's frontier to the Euphrates River and had organized the territories of Asia so well that his arrangements remained the basis of Roman rule well into the imperial period. When he returned to Rome in 62 B.C., he had more power, prestige, and popular support than any Roman in history. The Senate and his personal enemies had reason to fear that he might emulate Sulla and establish his own rule.

Rome had not been quiet in Pompey's absence. Crassus was the foremost among those who had reason to fear Pompey's return. Although rich and influential, he did not have

The Fall of the Roman Republic

Tribunate of Tiberius Gracchus	133 B.C.
Tribunate of Gaius Gracchus	123–122 B.C.
Jugurthine War	111–105 B.C.
Consecutive consulships of Marius	104–100 B.C.
War against the Italian allies	90–88 B.C.
Sulla's march on Rome	88 B.C.
Sulla assumes dictatorship	82 B.C.
Crassus crushes rebellion of Spartacus	71 B.C.
Pompey defeats Sertorius in Spain	71 B.C.
Consulship of Crassus and Pompey	70 B.C.
Formation of First Triumvirate	60 B.C.
Caesar in Gaul	58–50 B.C.
Crassus killed in Battle of Carrhae	53 B.C.
Caesar crosses Rubicon; civil war begins	49 B.C.
Pompey defeated at Pharsalus; killed in Egypt	48 B.C.
Caesar's dictatorship	46–44 B.C.
End of civil war	45 B.C.
Formation of Second Triumvirate	43 B.C.
Triumvirs defeat Brutus and Cassius at Philippi	42 B.C.
Octavian and Agrippa defeat Anthony at Actium	31 B.C.

the confidence of the Senate, a firm political base of his own, or the kind of military glory needed to rival Pompey. During the 60s, therefore, he allied himself with various popular leaders. The ablest of these men was Gaius Julius Caesar (100–44 B.C.), a descendant of an old patrician family that claimed descent from the kings and even from the goddess Venus, but one that was politically obscure. In spite of this noble lineage, Caesar was connected to the popular party through his aunt, who was the wife of Marius, and through his own wife, Cornelia, the daughter of Cinna. Caesar was an ambitious and determined young politician whose daring and whose rhetorical skill made him a valuable ally in winning the discontented of every class to the cause of the *populares*. Though Crassus was very much the senior partner, each needed the other to achieve what both wanted: significant military commands whereby they might build a reputation, a political following, and a military force to compete with Pompey's.

The chief opposition to Crassus' candidates for the consulship for 63 B.C. came from Cicero (106–43 B.C.), a "new man" from Marius' home town of Arpinum. He had made a spectacular name as the leading lawyer in Rome. Cicero, though he came from outside the senatorial aristocracy, was no *popularis*. His program was to preserve the republic against demagogues and ambitious generals by making the government more liberal. He wanted to unite the stable elements of the state—the Senate and the equestrians—in a harmony of the orders. This program did not appeal to the senatorial oligarchy, but the Senate preferred him to Catiline, a dangerous and popular politician thought to be linked with Crassus. Cicero and Antonius were elected consuls for 63 B.C., Catiline running third.

Cicero soon learned of a plot hatched by

Plutarch Tells of the Luxury Practiced by Rome's Most Famous Epicure

The wealth produced by Rome's conquests introduced considerable luxury into the lives of the upper classes. Lucius Licinius Lucullus (ca. 117–56 B.C.) was a general who served with considerable success in Asia Minor. In 63 B.C. he retired to private life and devoted himself to the art of elegant living.

And, indeed, Lucullus' life, like the Old Comedy, presents us at the beginning with political acts and military commands, and at the end with drinking bouts and banquets, and what were practically orgies, and torch races, and all manner of frivolity. For I count as frivolity his sumptuous buildings, porticoes, and baths, still more his paintings and statues, and all his enthusiasm for these arts, which he collected at vast expense, lavishly pouring out on them the vast and splendid wealth which he acquired in his campaigns. Even now, with all the advance of luxury, the Lucullan gardens are counted the most costly of the imperial gardens. When Tubero the Stoic saw Lucullus' works on the seashore and near Naples, where he suspended hills over vast tunnels, encircling his residences with moats of sea water and with streams for breeding fish, and built villas into the sea, he called him Xerxes in a toga. . . .

Lucullus' daily dinners were ostentatiously extravagant—not only their purple coverlets, beakers adorned with precious stones, choruses, and dramatic recitations, but also their display of all sorts of meats and daintily prepared dishes—making him an object of envy to the vulgar. . . . Once when he dined alone, he became angry because only one modest course had been prepared, and called the slave in charge. When the latter said that he did not think that there would be need of anything expensive since there were no guests, Lucullus said, "What, do you not know that today Lucullus dines with Lucullus?"

Plutarch, *Life of Lucullus*, trans. by N. Lewis and M. Reinhold, in *Roman Civilization*, Vol. 1 (New York: Columbia University Press, 1955), pp. 459–460.

Catiline. Catiline had run in the previous election on a platform of cancellation of debts, which appealed to discontented elements in general but especially to the heavily indebted nobles and their many clients. Made desperate by defeat, Catiline planned to stir up rebellions around Italy, to cause confusion in the city, and to take it by force. Quick action by Cicero defeated Catiline.

Formation of the First Triumvirate

Toward the end of 62 B.C. Pompey landed at Brundisium and, to general surprise, disbanded his army, celebrated a great triumph, and returned to private life. He had delayed his return in the hope of finding Italy in such a state as to justify his keeping the army and dominating the scene. Cicero's quick suppression of Catiline prevented his plan. Pompey, therefore, had either to act illegally or to lay down his arms. Because he had not thought of monarchy or revolution but merely wanted to be recognized and treated as the greatest Roman, he chose the latter course. He had achieved amazing things for Rome and simply wanted the Senate to approve his excellent arrangements in the east and to make land allotments to his veterans. His demands were far from unreasonable, and a prudent Senate would have granted them and would have tried to employ his power in defense of the constitution. But the Senate was jealous and fearful of overmighty individuals and refused his requests. In this way Pompey was driven to an alliance with his natural enemies, Crassus and Caesar, because all three found the Senate standing in the way of what they wanted.

In 60 B.C. Caesar returned to Rome from his governorship of Spain. He wanted the privilege of celebrating a triumph, the great victory procession that the Senate granted certain generals to honor especially great achievements, and of running for consul, but the law did not allow him to do both, requiring him to stay outside the city with his army but demanding that he canvass for votes personally within the city. He asked for a special dispensation, but the Senate refused. Caesar then performed a political miracle: he reconciled Crassus with Pompey and gained the support of both for his own ambitions. So was born the First Triumvirate, an informal agreement among three Roman politicians, each seeking his private goals, that further undermined the future of the republic.

Julius Caesar and His Government of Rome

Though he was forced to forgo his triumph, Caesar's efforts were rewarded with election to the consulship for 59 B.C. His colleague was M. Calpernius Bibulus, the son-in-law of Cato and a conservative hostile to Caesar and the other *populares.* Caesar did not hesitate to override his colleague. The triumvirs' program was quickly enacted. Caesar got the extraordinary command that would give him a chance to earn the glory and power with which to rival Pompey: the governorship of Illyricum and Gaul for five years. A land bill settled Pompey's veterans comfortably, and his eastern settlement was ratified. Crassus, much of whose influence came from his position as champion of the equestrians, won for them a great windfall by having the government renegotiate a tax contract in their favor. To guarantee themselves against any reversal of these actions, the triumvirs continued their informal but effective collaboration, arranging for the election of friendly consuls and the departure of potential opponents.

Caesar was now free to seek the military suc-

A triumph of Roman engineering, the Pont du Gard in southern France. The Romans were able to supply enormous quantities of fresh water to their cities. This aqueduct, built in the first century A.D., brought water to the city of Nimes. [*Michael Holford*]

Caesar Tells What Persuaded Him to Cross the Rubicon

Julius Caesar competed with Pompey for the leading position in the Roman state. Complicated maneuvers failed to produce a compromise. In the following selection Caesar gives his side of the story of the beginning of the Roman civil war. Note that Caesar writes about himself in the third person.

These things being made known to Caesar, he harangued his soldiers; he reminded them ''of the wrongs done to him at all times by his enemies, and complained that Pompey had been alienated from him and led astray by them through envy and a malicious opposition to his glory, though he had always favored and promoted Pompey's honor and dignity. He complained that an innovation had been introduced into the republic, that the intercession of the tribunes, which had been restored a few years before by Sulla, was branded as a crime, and suppressed by force of arms; that Sulla, who had stripped the tribunes of every other power, had, nevertheless, left the privilege of intercession unrestrained; that Pompey, who pretended to restore what they had lost, had taken away the privileges which they formerly had; that whenever the senate decreed, 'that the magistrates should take care that the republic sustained no injury' (by which words and decree the Roman people were obliged to repair to arms), it was only when pernicious laws were proposed; when the tribunes attempted violent measures; when the people seceded, and possessed themselves of the temples and eminences of the city; (and these instances of former times, he showed them were expiated by the fate of Saturninus and the Gracchi): that nothing of this kind was attempted now, nor even thought of: that no law was promulgated, no intrigue with the people going forward, no secession made; he exhorted them to defend from the malice of his enemies the reputation and honor of that general under whose command they had for nine years most successfully supported the state; fought many successful battles, and subdued all Gaul and Germany.'' The soldiers of the thirteenth legion, which was present (for in the beginning of the disturbances he had called it out, his other legions not having yet arrived), all cry out that they are ready to defend their general, and the tribunes of the commons, from all injuries.

Having made himself acquainted with the disposition of his soldiers, Caesar set off with that legion to Ariminum, and there met the tribunes, who had fled to him for protection.

Julius Caesar, *Commentaries,* trans. by W. A. McDevitte and W. S. Bosh (New York: Harper and Brothers, 1887), pp. 249–250.

cess he craved. His province included Cisalpine Gaul in the Po valley, by now occupied by many Italian settlers as well as Gauls, and Narbonese Gaul beyond the Alps, modern Provence.

Relying first on the excellent quality of his army and the experience of his officers, then on his own growing military ability, Caesar made great progress. By 56 B.C. he had conquered most of Gaul, but he had not yet consolidated his victories firmly. He therefore sought an extension of his command, but quarrels between Crassus and Pompey so weakened the Triumvirate that the Senate was prepared to order Caesar's recall. To prevent the dissolution of his base of power, Caesar persuaded Crassus and Pompey to meet with him at Luca in northern Italy to renew the coalition. They agreed that Caesar would get another five-year command in Gaul, and Crassus and Pompey would be consuls again in 55 B.C. After that they would each receive an army and a five-year command. Caesar was free to return to Gaul and finish the job. The capture of Alesia in 50 B.C. marked the end of the serious Gallic resistance and of Gallic liberty. For Caesar it brought the wealth, fame, and military power he wanted. He commanded thirteen loyal legions, a match for his enemies as well as for his allies.

By the time Caesar was ready to return to Rome, the Triumvirate had dissolved and a crisis was at hand. At Carrhae, in 53 B.C., Crassus died trying to conquer the Parthians, successors to the Persian Empire. His death broke one link between Pompey and Caesar. The death of Caesar's daughter Julia, who had been Pompey's wife, dissolved another. As Caesar's star rose, Pompey became jealous and fearful. He did not leave Rome but governed his province through a subordinate. In the late 50s political rioting at Rome caused the Senate to appoint Pompey sole consul. This grant of unprecedented power and responsibility brought Pompey closer to the senatorial aristocracy in mutual fear of and hostility to Caesar. The Senate wanted to bring Caesar back to Rome as a private citizen after his proconsular command expired. He would then be open to attack for past illegalities. Caesar tried to avoid the trap by asking permission to stand for the consulship in absentia.

Early in January of 49 B.C. the more extreme faction in the Senate had its way and ordered Pompey to defend the state and Caesar to lay down his command by a specified day. For

Suetonius Describes Caesar's Dictatorship

Suetonius (ca. A.D. 69–ca. 140) wrote a series of biographies of the emperors from Julius Caesar to Domitian. In the following selection he describes some of Caesar's actions during his dictatorship in the years 46–44 B.C.

His other words and actions, however, so far outweigh all his good qualities, that it is thought he abused his power, and was justly cut off. For he not only obtained excessive honours, such as the consulship every year, the dictatorship for life, and the censorship, but also the title of emperor, and the surname of Father of His Country, besides having his statue amongst the kings, and a lofty couch in the theatre. He even suffered some honours to be decreed to him, which were unbefitting the most exalted of mankind; such as a gilded chair of state in the senate-house and on his tribunal, a consecrated chariot, and banners in the Circensian procession, temples, altars, statues among the gods, a bed of state in the temples, a priest, and a college of priests dedicated to himself, like those of Pan; and that one of the months should be called by his name. There were, indeed, no honours which he did not either assume himself, or grant to others, at his will and pleasure. In his third and fourth consulship, he used only the title of the office, being content with the power of dictator, which was conferred upon him with the consulship; and in both years he substituted other consuls in his room, during the last three months; so that in the intervals he held no assemblies of the people, for the election of magistrates, excepting only tribunes and ediles of the people; and appointed officers, under the name of præfects, instead of the prætors, to administer the affairs of the city during his absence. The office of consul having become vacant, by the sudden death of one of the consuls the day before the calends of January [the 1st Jan.], he conferred it on a person who requested it of him, for a few hours. Assuming the same licence, and regardless of the customs of his country, he appointed magistrates to hold their offices for terms of years. He granted the insignia of the consular dignity to ten persons of prætorian rank. He admitted into the senate some men who had been made free of the city, and even natives of Gaul, who were semi-barbarians. He likewise appointed to the management of the mint, and the public revenue of the state, some servants of his own household; and entrusted the command of three legions, which he left at Alexandria, to an old catamite of his, the son of his freed-man Rufinus.

He was guilty of the same extravagance in the language he publicly used, as Titus Ampius informs us; according to whom he said, "The republic is nothing but a name, without substance or reality. Sulla was an ignorant fellow to abdicate the dictatorship. Men ought to consider what is becoming when they talk with me, and look upon what I say as a law."

Suetonius, *The Lives of the Twelve Caesars,* trans. by Alexander Thompson, rev. by T. Forster (London: George Bell and Sons, 1903) pp. 45–47.

Caesar this meant exile or death, so he ordered his legions to cross the Rubicon River, the boundary of his province. This action was the first act of the civil war. In 45 B.C. he defeated the last of the enemy forces under Pompey's sons at Munda in Spain. The war was over, and Caesar, in Shakespeare's words, bestrode "the narrow world like a Colossus."

From the beginning of the civil war until his death in 44 B.C., Caesar spent less than a year and a half in Rome, and many of his actions were attempts to deal with immediate problems between campaigns. His innovations generally sought to make rational and orderly what was traditional and chaotic. An excellent example is Caesar's reform of the calendar. By 46 B.C. it was eighty days ahead of the proper season because the official year was lunar, containing only 355 days. Using the best scientific advice, Caesar instituted a new calendar, which, with minor changes by Pope Gregory XIII in the sixteenth century, is the one in use today. Another general tendency of his reforms in the political area was the elevation of the role of Italians and even provincials at the expense of the old Roman families, most of whom were his political enemies. He raised the number of senators to 900 and filled the Senate's depleted ranks with Italians and even Gauls. He was free with grants of Roman citizenship, giving the franchise to Cisalpine Gaul as a whole and to many individuals of various regions.

Caesar made few changes in the government of Rome. The Senate continued to play its role, in theory, but its increased size, its packing with supporters of Caesar, and his own monopoly of military power made the whole thing a sham. He treated the Senate as his creature and sometimes with disdain. His legal position rested on a number of powers. In 46 B.C. he was appointed dictator for ten years and in the next year for life. He also held the consulship, the immunity of a tribune (although, being a patrician, he had never been a tribune), the chief priesthood of the state, and a new position, prefect of morals, which gave him the censorial power. Usurping the elective power of the assemblies, he even named the magistrates for the next few years, because he expected to be away in the east.

The enemies of Caesar were quick to seize on every pretext to accuse Caesar of aiming at monarchy. A senatorial conspiracy gathered strength under the leadership of Gaius Cassius Longinus and Marcus Junius Brutus and included some sixty senators in all. On March 15, 44 B.C., Caesar entered the Senate, characteristically without a bodyguard, and was stabbed to death. The assassins regarded themselves as heroic tyrannicides and did not have a clear plan of action after the tyrant was dead. No doubt they simply expected the republic to be restored in the old way, but things had gone too far for that. There followed instead thirteen years of more civil war, at the end of which the republic received its final burial.

The Second Triumvirate and the Emergence of Octavian

Caesar had had legions of followers, and he had a capable successor in Mark Antony. But the dictator had named his eighteen-year-old grandnephew, Gaius Octavius (63 B.C.–A.D. 14), as his heir and had left him three quarters of his vast wealth. To everyone's surprise, the sickly and inexperienced young man come to Rome to claim his legacy, gathered an army, won the support of many of Caesar's veterans, and became a figure of importance—the future Augustus.

At first, the Senate tried to use Octavius against Antony, but when the conservatives rejected his request for the consulship, Octavius broke with them. Following Sulla's grim precedent, he took his army and marched on Rome. There he finally assumed his adopted name, C. Julius Caesar Octavianus. Modern historians refer to him at this stage in his career as Octavian, although he insisted on being called Caesar. In August of 43 B.C. he became consul and declared the assassins of Caesar outlaws. As Brutus and Cassius had an army of their own, Octavian sought help on the Caesarean side. He made a pact with Mark Antony and M. Aemilius Lepidus, a Caesarean governor of the western provinces. They took control of Rome and had themselves appointed "Triumvirs to put the republic in order," with great powers. This was the Second Triumvirate, and unlike the first, it was legally empowered to rule almost dictatorially.

The need to pay their troops, their own greed, and the passion that always emerges in civil wars led the triumvirs to start a wave of proscriptions that outdid even those of Sulla. In 42 B.C. the triumviral army defeated Brutus and Cassius at Philippi in Macedonia, and the last hope of republican restoration died with the tyrannicides. Each of the triumvirs received a command. The junior partner, Lepidus, was given Africa, Antony took the rich and inviting east, and Octavian got the west and the many troubles that went with it. He had to fight a war against Sextus, the son of Pompey, who held Sicily. He also had to settle 100,000 veterans in Italy, confiscating much property and making many enemies. Helped by his friend Agrippa, he defeated Sextus Pompey in 36 B.C. Among his close associates was Maecenas, who served him as adviser and diplomatic agent. Maecenas helped manage the delicate relations with Antony and Lepidus, but perhaps equally important was his role as a patron of the arts. Among his clients were Vergil and Horace, both of whom did important work for Octavian, painting him as a restorer of traditional Roman values, as a man of ancient Roman lineage and of traditional Roman virtues, and as the culmination of Roman destiny. More and more he was identified with Italy and the west as well as with order, justice, and virtue.

Meanwhile Antony was in the east, chiefly at Alexandria with Cleopatra, the queen of Egypt. In 36 B.C. he attacked Parthia, with disastrous results. Octavian had promised to send troops to support Antony's Parthian campaign but never sent them. Antony was forced to depend on the east for support, and to some considerable degree this meant Cleopatra. Octavian clearly understood the advantage of representing himself as the champion of the west, Italy, and Rome, while representing Antony as the man of the east, the dupe of Cleopatra, her tool in establishing Alexandria as the center of an empire and herself as its ruler. Such propaganda made it easier for Caesareans to abandon their veteran leader in favor of the young heir of Caesar. It did not help Antony's cause that he agreed to a public festival at Alexandria in 34 B.C., where he and Cleopatra sat on golden thrones. She was proclaimed "Queen of Kings," her son by Julius Caesar was named "King of Kings," and parts of the Roman Empire were doled out to her various children.

By 32 B.C. all pretense of cooperation came to an end. Octavian and Antony each tried to put the best face on what was essentially a struggle for power. Lepidus had been put aside some years earlier. Antony sought senatorial support and promised to restore the republican constitution. Octavian seized and published what was alleged to be the will of Antony, revealing his gifts of provinces to the children of Cleopatra, thereby causing the conflict in terms of east against west, Rome against Alexandria.

Profile of Brutus, one of Caesar's assassins, on a silver coin. The reverse shows a cap of liberty between two daggers and reads "Ides of March." [*H. Roger Viollet*]

MAP 4-4

THE TRANSITION FROM

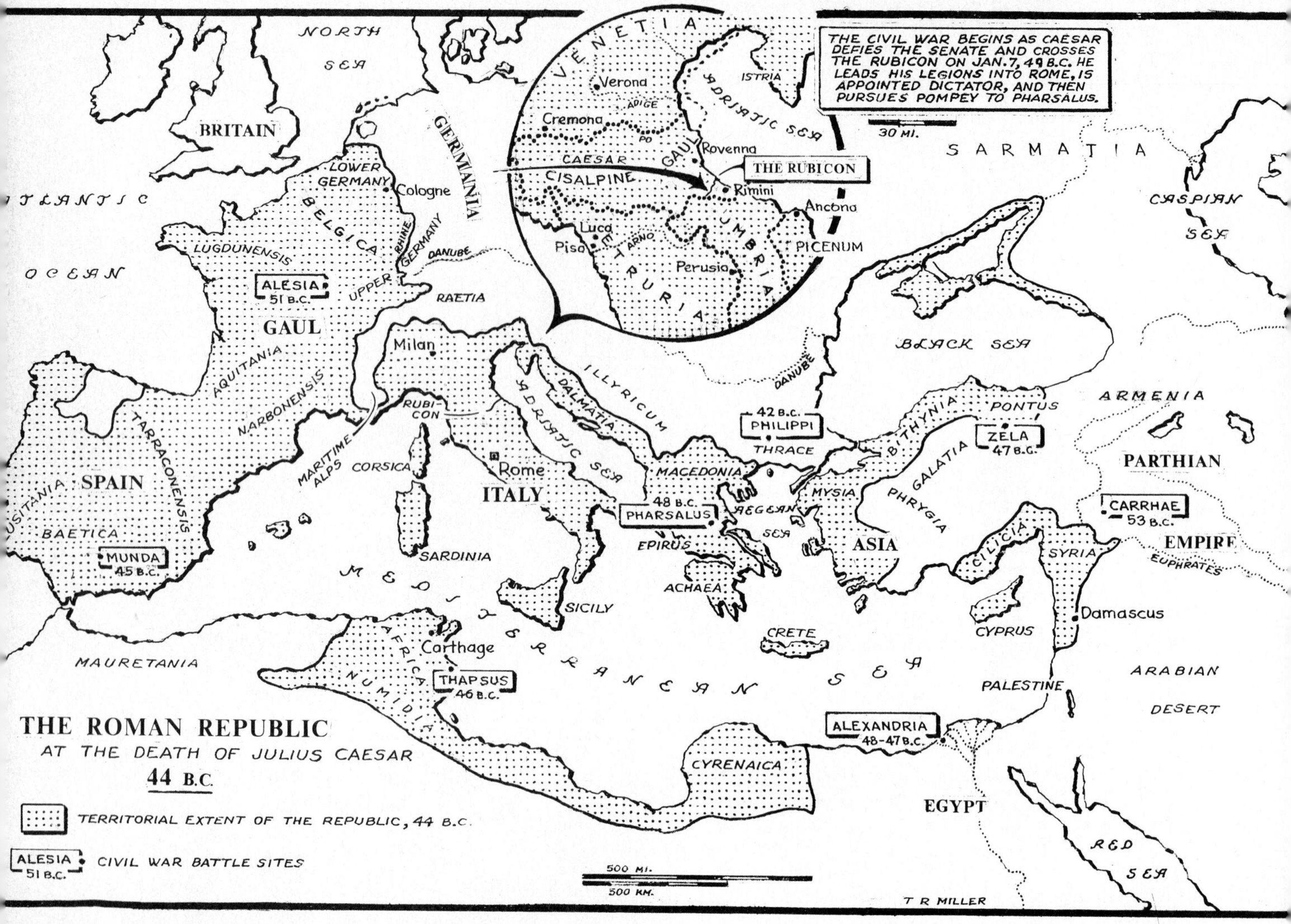

By the time of Julius Caesar's dictatorship, Rome had grown from a small city-state in central Italy to the head of a vast Mediterranean Empire. The conquest of this territory posed many problems for the Republic that it could not ultimately solve. Commands in the provinces came to be sources of profit and prestige for the Roman nobility, and politics in the late Republic often consisted of quarrels over desired provincial assignments. At last, a quarrel between Julius Caesar and Pompey, on behalf of the Senate, led to a civil war that destroyed the Republic. This map shows the extent of the territory controlled by republican Rome at the time of Caesar's death. The insert indicates Caesar's route as he returned from his province, Gaul, to challenge Pompey and the Senate in January, 49 B.C. By crossing the Rubicon River, the border of his province, Caesar violated the law forbidding a proconsul from bringing his army into Italy and made the difficult and irrevocable choice for civil war rather than risk condemnation by a hostile Senate.

The reign of Augustus (31 B.C.–A.D. 14) produced a transition from an imperial aristocratic republic dominated by a narrow class of nobles to an autocratic empire. Augustus cloaked himself with republican titles and powers and ostensibly shared the government with the Senate, but he himself controlled the army on which all real power rested. This map shows the extent of the Roman Empire at the death of Augustus and how it had grown in the course of his reign. His most important gain came at the very beginning of his rule, when the victory over Cleopatra gave him Egypt, which he treated as a private possession and which provided him with vast wealth independent of senatorial control. By the end of his life he was the unquestioned ruler of Rome, secure enough to pass the Empire on to his chosen successor, Tiberius. Thereafter the cloak of republicanism was soon shed and the monarchical nature of imperial rule was entirely clear.

REPUBLIC TO EMPIRE

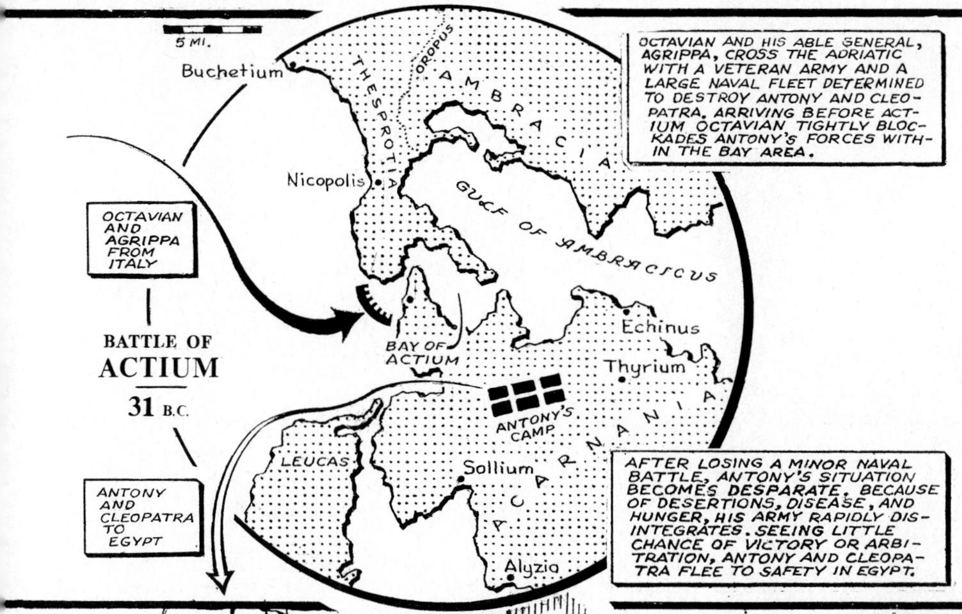
5 MI.
Buchetium
THESPROTIA
OROPUS
AMBRACIA
OCTAVIAN AND HIS ABLE GENERAL, AGRIPPA, CROSS THE ADRIATIC WITH A VETERAN ARMY AND A LARGE NAVAL FLEET DETERMINED TO DESTROY ANTONY AND CLEOPATRA. ARRIVING BEFORE ACTIUM OCTAVIAN TIGHTLY BLOCKADES ANTONY'S FORCES WITHIN THE BAY AREA.
Nicopolis
GULF OF AMBRACICUS
OCTAVIAN AND AGRIPPA FROM ITALY
BATTLE OF ACTIUM 31 B.C.
BAY OF ACTIUM
Echinus
Thyrium
ANTONY'S CAMP
ACARNANIA
LEUCAS
Sollium
Alyzia
ANTONY AND CLEOPATRA TO EGYPT
AFTER LOSING A MINOR NAVAL BATTLE, ANTONY'S SITUATION BECOMES DESPARATE. BECAUSE OF DESERTIONS, DISEASE, AND HUNGER, HIS ARMY RAPIDLY DISINTEGRATES. SEEING LITTLE CHANCE OF VICTORY OR ARBITRATION, ANTONY AND CLEOPATRA FLEE TO SAFETY IN EGYPT.

After Caesar's death his experienced lieutenant Mark Antony and his young heir Octavian (later called Augustus) pursued and defeated his killers Brutus and Cassius at Philippi in Macedonia in 42 B.C. The victors were soon at odds, and the civil war resumed. This map shows the site of the Battle of Actium that brought an end to civil war and victory for Octavian in 31 B.C. The battle was in the area of the Ambracian Gulf in northwestern Greece. The architect of victory was Agrippa, Octavian's able assistant and close friend.

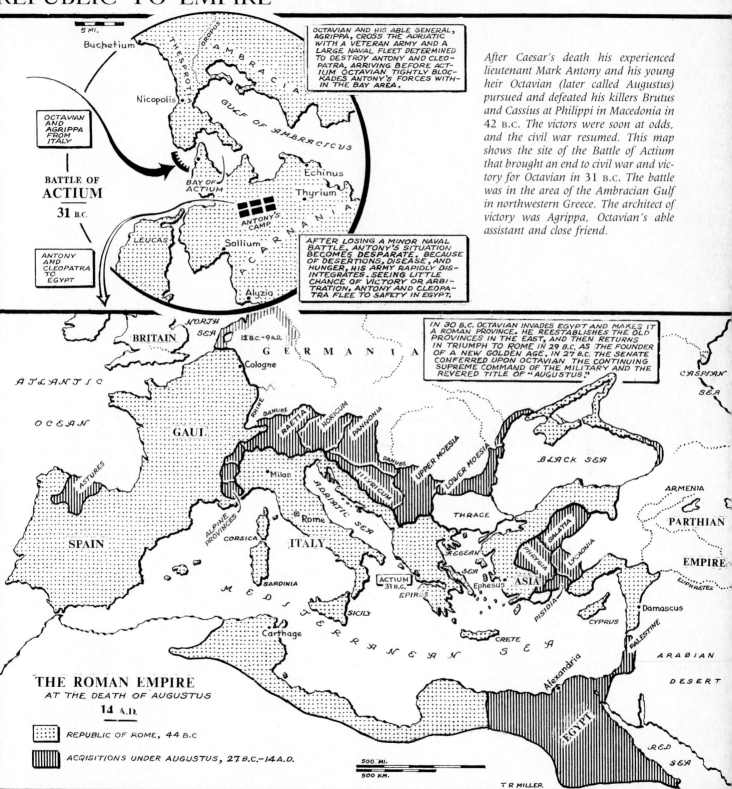

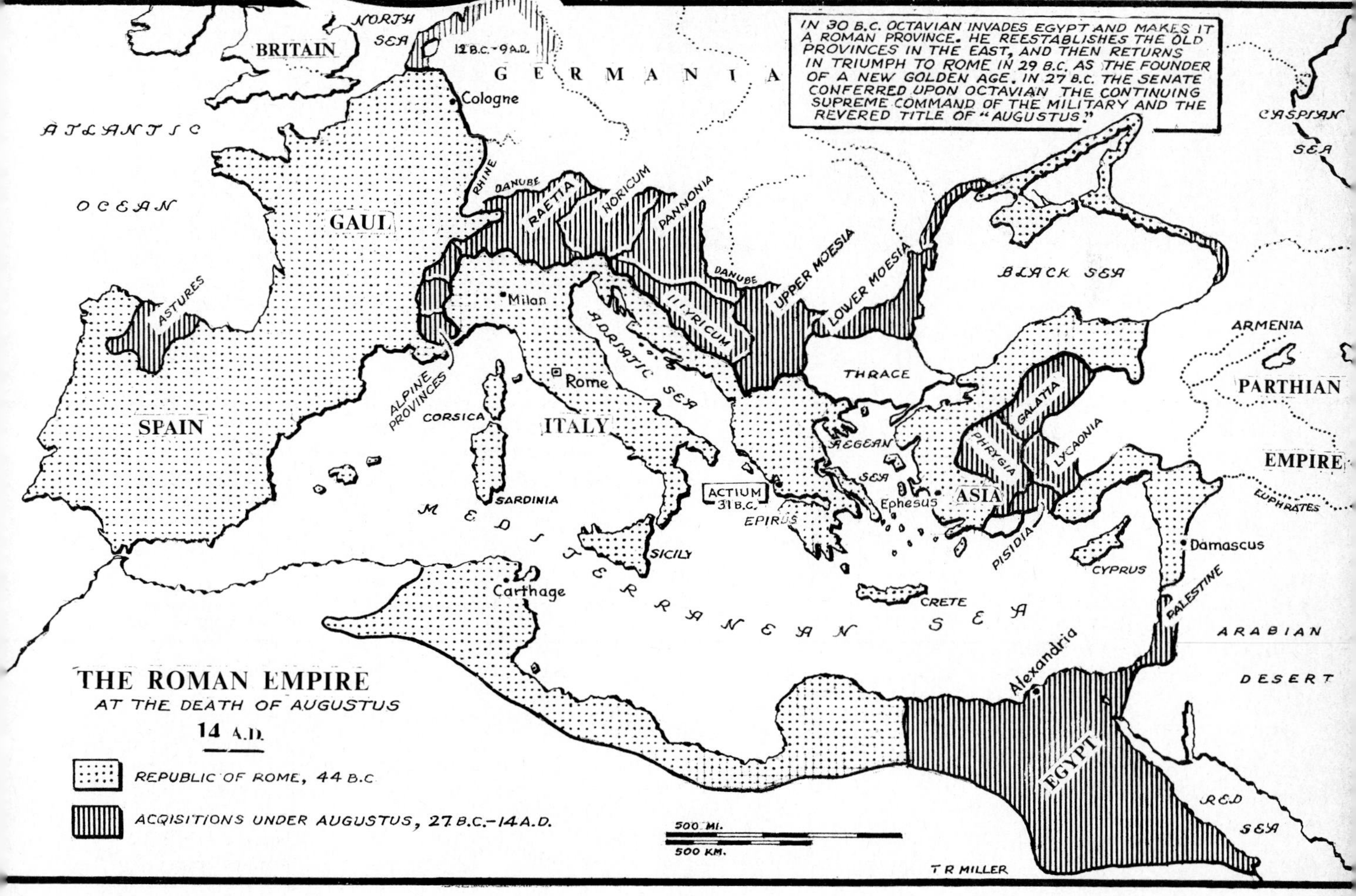
IN 30 B.C. OCTAVIAN INVADES EGYPT AND MAKES IT A ROMAN PROVINCE. HE REESTABLISHES THE OLD PROVINCES IN THE EAST, AND THEN RETURNS IN TRIUMPH TO ROME IN 29 B.C. AS THE FOUNDER OF A NEW GOLDEN AGE. IN 27 B.C. THE SENATE CONFERRED UPON OCTAVIAN THE CONTINUING SUPREME COMMAND OF THE MILITARY AND THE REVERED TITLE OF "AUGUSTUS."
NORTH SEA
BRITAIN
12 B.C.–9 A.D.
GERMANIA
Cologne
CASPIAN SEA
ATLANTIC OCEAN
RHINE
DANUBE
RAETIA
NORICUM
PANNONIA
GAUL
DANUBE
UPPER MOESIA
LOWER MOESIA
BLACK SEA
ASTURES
Milan
ILLYRICUM
ADRIATIC SEA
ARMENIA
THRACE
Rome
ALPINE PROVINCES
CORSICA
PARTHIAN EMPIRE
SPAIN
ITALY
GALATIA
AEGEAN SEA
PHRYGIA
LYCAONIA
ACTIUM 31 B.C.
EPIRUS
Ephesus
ASIA
SARDINIA
EUPHRATES
MEDITERRANEAN SEA
PISIDIA
Damascus
SICILY
CYPRUS
Carthage
CRETE
PALESTINE
ARABIAN DESERT
Alexandria
THE ROMAN EMPIRE AT THE DEATH OF AUGUSTUS 14 A.D.
EGYPT
REPUBLIC OF ROME, 44 B.C
ACQISITIONS UNDER AUGUSTUS, 27 B.C.–14 A.D.
RED SEA
500 MI.
500 KM.
T R MILLER

Roman bust of Cleopatra, the last Ptolemaic ruler of Egypt. Her ambition to create a great Hellenistic empire in the East was shattered at the battle of Actium in 31 B.C. [*Courtesy of the Trustees of the British Museum*]

In 31 B.C. the matter was settled at Actium in western Greece. Agrippa, Octavian's best general, cut off the enemy by land and sea, forcing and winning a naval battle. Antony and Cleopatra escaped to Egypt, but Octavian pursued them to Alexandria, where both committed suicide. The civil wars were over, and at the age of thirty-two Octavian was absolute master of the Mediterranean world. His power was enormous, but so too was the task before him. He had to restore peace, prosperity, and confidence, and all of these required the establishment of a constitution that would reflect the new realities without offending unduly the traditional republican prejudices that still had so firm a grip on Rome and Italy.

Suggested Readings

F. E. Adcock, *The Roman Art of War Under the Republic* (1940).

E. Badian, *Foreign Clientelae* (1958). A brilliant study of the Roman idea of a client–patron relationship extended to foreign affairs.

E. Badian, *Roman Imperialism in the Late Republic*, 2nd ed. (1968).

A. H. Bernstein, *Tiberius Sempronius Gracchus: Tradition and Apostasy* (1978). A new interpretation of Tiberius' place in Roman politics.

R. Bloch, *Origins of Rome* (1960). A good account of the most generally accepted point of view.

P. A. Brunt, *Social Conflicts in the Roman Republic* (1971).

B. Caven, *The Punic Wars* (1980).

T. Cornell and J. Matthews, *Atlas of the Roman World* (1982). Much more than the title indicates, this book presents a comprehensive view of the Roman world in its physical and cultural setting.

D. C. Earl, *The Moral and Political Tradition of Rome* (1967).

R. M. Errington, *The Dawn of Empire: Rome's Rise to Power* (1972). An account of Rome's conquest of the Mediterranean.

M. Gelzer, *Caesar: Politician and Statesman*, trans. by P. Needham (1968). The best biography of Caesar.

E. Gjerstad, *Legends and Facts of Early Roman History* (1962). An unorthodox but interesting account of early Rome.

E. S. Gruen, *The Last Generation of the Roman Republic* (1973). An interesting but controversial interpretation of the fall of the republic.

W. V. Harris, *War and Imperialism in Republican Rome*, 327–70 B.C. (1975). An analysis of Roman attitudes and intentions concerning imperial expansion and war.

L. P. Homo, *Primitive Italy and the Beginning of Roman Imperialism* (1967). A study of early Roman relations with the peoples of Italy.

F. B. Marsh, *A History of the Roman World from* 146 *to* 30 B.C., 3rd ed., rev. by H. H. Scullard (1963). An excellent narrative account.

C. Nicolet, *The World of the Citizen in Republican Rome* (1980).

M. Pallottino, *The Etruscans*, 6th ed. (1974). Makes especially good use of archaeological evidence.

E. T. Salmon, *Roman Colonization Under the Republic* (1970).

H. H. Scullard, *A History of the Roman World* 753–146 B.C., 4th ed. (1980). An unusually fine narrative history with useful critical notes.

H. H. Scullard, *From the Gracchi to Nero*, 5th ed. (1982). A work of the same character and quality.

A. N. Sherwin-White, *Roman Citizenship* (1939). A useful study of the Roman franchise and its extension to other peoples.

R. E. Smith, *Cicero the Statesman* (1966). A sound biography.

D. Stockton, *Cicero: A Political Biography* (1971). A readable and interesting study.

D. Stockton, *The Gracchi* (1979). An interesting analytical narrative.

L. R. Taylor, *Party Policies in the Age of Caesar* (1949). A fascinating analysis of Roman political practices.

B. H. Warmington, *Carthage* (1960). A good survey.

G. Williams, *The Nature of Roman Poetry* (1970). An unusually graceful and perceptive literary study.

Marcus Aurelius (A.D. 161–180), *one of the five ''good emperors,'' under whose rule the Roman Empire reached its peak stability and prosperity. This bronze is the only Roman equestrian statue that has survived. It stands in Rome's Piazza del Campidaglio on a marble base designed during the Renaissance by Michelangelo.*

5

The Roman Empire

The Augustan Principate

IF THE PROBLEMS FACING OCTAVIAN after the Battle of Actium were great, so too were his resources for addressing them. He was the master of a vast military force, the only one in the Roman world, and he had loyal and capable assistants. Of enormous importance was the great, seemingly inexhaustible treasury of Egypt, which Octavian treated as his personal property. Perhaps his most valuable asset, however, was the great eagerness of the people of Italy for an end to civil war and a return to peace, order, and prosperity. In exchange for these most of them were prepared to accept a considerable abandonment of republican practices and to give significant power to an able ruler. Even the resistance of the old Roman families was greatly reduced, for a remarkable number of their members had perished in the civil wars from 49 to 31 B.C. Yet the memory of Julius Caesar's fate was still clear in Octavian's mind, and its lesson was that it was dangerous to flaunt unprecedented powers and to disregard all republican traditions.

Octavian's constitutional solution proved to be successful and lasting, subtle and effective. It was not created at a single stroke but developed gradually as Octavian tried new devices to fit his perception of changing conditions. Behind all the republican trappings and the apparent sharing of authority with the Senate, the government of Octavian, like that of his successors, was a monarchy. All real power, both civil and military, lay with the ruler, whether he was called by the unofficial title of "first citizen" (*princeps*), like Octavian, the founder of the regime, or "emperor" (*imperator*), like those who followed. During the civil war Octavian's powers came from his triumviral status, whose dubious legality and unrepublican character were an embarrassment. From 31 B.C. on, he held the consulship each year, but this circumstance was not strictly legal or very satisfactory either. On January 13, 27 B.C., he put forward a new plan in dramatic style, coming before the Senate to give up all his powers and provinces. In what was surely a rehearsed response, the Senate begged him to reconsider, and at last he agreed to accept the provinces of Spain, Gaul, and Syria with proconsular power for military command and to retain the consulship in Rome. The other provinces would be governed by the Senate as before. Because his were the border provinces and contained twenty of the twenty-six legions, his true power was undiminished, but the Senate responded with almost hysterical gratitude, voting him many honors. Among them was the semireligious title "Augustus," which carried implications of veneration, majesty, and holiness. From this time on, historians speak of Rome's first emperor as Augustus and of his regime as the Principate. This would have pleased him, for it helps conceal the novel, unrepublican nature of the regime and the naked power on which it rested.

Emperor Augustus (27 B.C.–A.D. 14). *This statue, now in the Vatican, stood in the villa of Augustus's wife Livia. The figures on the elaborate breastplate are all of symbolic significance. At the top, for example, Dawn in her chariot brings in a new day under the protective mantle of the sky god; in the center Tiberius, Augustus's future successor, accepts the return of captured Roman army standards from a barbarian prince; and at the bottom, Mother Earth offers a horn of plenty.* [*Copyright by Leonard von Matt*]

In 23 B.C. Augustus resigned his consulship and held that office only rarely thereafter. Instead he was voted two powers that were to be the base of his rule thenceforth, the proconsular *imperium maius* and the tribunician power. The former made his proconsular power greater than that of any other proconsul and permitted him to exercise it even within the city of Rome. The latter gave him the right to conduct public business in the assemblies and the Senate, the power of the veto, the tribunician sacrosanctity, and a connection with the popular tradition. Thereafter there were minor changes in Augustus' position, but his powers were chiefly those conferred by the settlement of 23 B.C..

Administration

Augustus made important changes in the government of Rome, Italy, and the provinces. Most of these had the effect of reducing inefficiency and corruption, eliminating the danger to peace and order from ambitious individuals, and reducing the distinction between Romans and Italians, senators and equestrians. The assemblies lost their significance as a working part of the constitution, and the Senate took on most of the functions of the assemblies. Augustus purged the old Senate of undesirable members and fixed its number at 600. He recruited its members from wealthy men of good character, who entered after serving as lesser magistrates. Augustus controlled the elections and saw to it that promising young men, whatever their origin, served the state as administrators and provincial governors. In this way equestrians and Italians who had no connection with the Roman aristocracy entered the Senate in great numbers. For all his power Augustus was careful always to treat the Senate with respect and honor.

Among his many other talents Augustus had a genius for practical administration. He divided Rome into regions and wards with elected local officials. He gave the city, with its rickety wooden tenements, its first public fire department and rudimentary police force. Grain distribution to the poor was carefully controlled and limited, and organizations were created for providing an adequate water supply. The Augustan period was one of great prosperity, based on the wealth Augustus had brought in by the conquest of Egypt, on the great increase in commerce and industry made possible by general peace and a vast program of public works, and on a strong return to successful small farming on the part of Augustus' resettled veterans.

The union of political and military power in the hands of the *princeps* made it possible for him to install rational, efficient, and stable government in the provinces for the first time. The emperor, in effect, chose the governors, removed the incompetent or rapacious, and allowed the effective ones to keep their provinces for longer periods of time. At the same time he provided for much greater local autonomy, giving considerable responsibility to the upper classes in the provincial cities and towns and to the tribal leaders in less civilized areas.

The Army and Defense

The main external problem facing Augustus—and one that haunted all his successors—was the northern frontier. Rome needed to pacify the regions to the north and the northeast of Italy and to find defensible frontiers against the recurring waves of barbarians. Augustus' plan was to push forward into central Europe to create the shortest possible defensive line. The eastern part of the plan succeeded, and the campaign in the west started well. In A.D. 9, however, a revolt broke out led by the German tribal leader Herrmann, or Arminius, as the Romans called him. He ambushed and destroyed three Roman legions under the general Varus as they marched through the Teutoburg Forest. The aged Augustus abandoned the campaign, leaving a problem of border defense that caused great trouble for his successors.

Under Augustus, the armed forces achieved true professional status. Enlistment, chiefly by Italians, was for twenty years, but the pay was relatively good and there were occasional bonuses and the promise of a pension on retirement in the form of money or a plot of land. Together with the auxiliaries from the provinces, these forces formed a frontier army of about 300,000 men. In normal times this number was barely enough to hold the line. The Roman army permanently based in the provinces played a vital role in bringing Roman culture to the natives. The soldiers spread their language and customs, often marrying local women and settling down in the area of their service. They attracted merchants, who often became the nuclei of new towns and cities that became centers of Roman civilization. As time

The Secret of Rome's Military Success: Training

Vegetius was a Roman military writer of the fourth and fifth centuries A.D. His military handbook had great influence on European armies from the Renaissance on. In the following passage, he emphasizes the crucial role of training in the achievements of the Roman army.

In every battle victory is granted not by mere numbers and innate courage but by skill and training. For we see that the Roman people owed the conquest of the world to no other cause than military training, discipline in their camps, and practice in warfare. What chance would the small number of Romans have had against the multitude of Gauls? How could they have ventured, with their small stature, against the tall Germans? It is clear that the Spaniards excelled our men not only in numbers but also in physical strength. We have always been inferior to the Africans in the use of deception and in wealth. And no one doubts that we were surpassed by the Greeks in skills and intelligence. But against all these we prevailed by skillful selection of recruits, by teaching, as I have said, the principles of war, by hardening them in daily exercise, by acquainting them beforehand through field maneuvers with everything that can happen in the line of march and in battles, and by severe punishment for indolence. For knowledge of military science nourishes boldness in combat. No one fears to do what he is confident he has learned well. . . .

Vegetius, *Military Science,* trans. by N. Lewis and M. Reinhold, in *Roman Civilization,* Vol. 2 (New York: Columbia University Press, 1955), p. 497.

Roman soldiers building a fort on the Danube. Along the Rhine and Danube frontier, the Roman army built many forts, which often became the nuclei of new cities. (*Art Resource*)

passed, the provincials on the frontiers became Roman citizens and helped strengthen Rome's defenses against the barbarians outside.

Religion and Morality

A century of political strife and civil war had undermined many of the foundations of traditional Roman society. Augustus thought it desirable to try to repair the damage, and he undertook a program aimed at preserving and restoring the traditional values of the family and religion in Rome and Italy. He introduced laws curbing adultery and divorce and encouraging early marriage and the procreation of legitimate children. He set an example of austere behavior in his own household and even banished his daughter, Julia, whose immoral behavior had become public knowledge. He worked at restoring the dignity of formal Roman religion, building many temples, reviving old cults, and reorganizing and invigorating the priestly colleges, and he banned the worship of newly introduced foreign gods. Augustus himself occupied some of the traditional priesthoods, and writers whom he patronized, such as Vergil, pointed out his family's legendary connection with Venus. During his lifetime he did not accept divine honors, though he was deified after his death, and as with Julius Caesar, a state cult was dedicated to his worship.

Civilization of the Ciceronian and Augustan Ages

The high point of Roman culture came in the last century of the republic and during the principate of Augustus. Both periods reflected the dominant influence of Greek culture, especially in its Hellenistic mode. The education of Romans of the upper classes was in Greek rhetoric, philosophy, and literature, which also served as the models for Roman writers and artists. Yet in spirit and sometimes in form, the art and writing of both periods show uniquely Roman qualities, though each in different ways.

The Late Republic

CICERO. The towering literary figure of the late republic was Cicero. He is most famous for his orations delivered in the law courts and in the Senate. Together with a considerable body of his private letters, these orations provide us with a clearer and fuller insight into his mind than into that of any other figure in antiquity. We see the political life of his period largely through his eyes. He also wrote treatises on rhetoric, ethics, and politics that put Greek philosophical ideas into Latin terminology and at the same time changed them to suit Roman conditions and values. Cicero's own views combined the teachings of the Academy, the Stoa, and other Greek schools to provide support for his moderate and conservative practicality. He believed in a world governed by divine and natural law that human reason could perceive and human institutions reflect. He looked to law, custom, and tradition to produce both stability and liberty. His literary

The Emperor Augustus Writes His Testament

Emperor Augustus wrote a record of his achievements to be read, engraved, and placed outside his mausoleum after his death. The following selections are from that document.

13. The temple of Janus Quirinus, which our ancestors desired to be closed whenever peace with victory was secured by sea and by land throughout the entire empire of the Roman people, and which before I was born is recorded to have been closed only twice since the founding of the city, was during my principate three times ordered by the senate to be closed.

. . . .

34. In my sixth and seventh consulships, after I had put an end to the civil wars, having attained supreme power by universal consent, I transferred the state from my own power to the control of the Roman senate and people. For this service of mine I received the title of Augustus by decree of the senate, and the doorposts of my house were publicly decked with laurels, the civic crown was affixed over my doorway, and a golden shield was set up in the Julian senate house, which, as the inscription on this shield testifies, the Roman senate and people gave me in recognition of my valor, clemency, justice, and devotion. After that time I excelled all in authority, but I possessed no more power than the others who were my colleagues in each magistracy.

35. When I held my thirteenth consulship, the senate, the equestrian order, and the entire Roman people gave me the title of "father of the country" and decreed that this title should be inscribed in the vestibule of my house, in the Julian senate house, and in the Augustan Forum on the pedestal of the chariot which was set up in my honor by decree of the senate. At the time I wrote this document I was in my seventy-sixth year.

Augustus, *Res Gestae,* trans. by N. Lewis and M. Reinhold, in *Roman Civilization,* Vol. 2 (New York: Columbia University Press, 1955), pp. 13, 19.

Cicero (106–43 B.C.) *was the most important writer of the late Republic.* [*EPA*]

style, as well as his values and ideas, was an important legacy for the Middle Ages and, reinterpreted, for the Renaissance.

HISTORY. The last century of the republic produced some historical writing, much of which is lost to us. Sallust (86–35 B.C.) wrote a history of the years 78–67 B.C., but only a few fragments remain to remind us of his reputation as the greatest of republican historians. His surviving work consists of two pamphlets on the Jugurthine War and on the Catilinarian conspiracy of 63 B.C. They reveal his Caesarean and antisenatorial prejudices and the stylistic influence of Thucydides.

Julius Caesar wrote important treatises on the Gallic and civil wars. They are not fully rounded historical accounts but chiefly military narratives written from Caesar's point of view and with propagandist intent. Their objective manner (Caesar always referred to himself in the third person) and their direct, simple, and vigorous style make them persuasive even today, and they must have been most effective with their immediate audience.

LAW. The period from the Gracchi to the fall of the republic was important in the development of Roman law. Before that time Roman law was essentially national and had developed chiefly by means of juridical decisions, case by case, but contact with foreign peoples and the influence of Greek ideas forced a change. From the last century of the republic on, the edicts of the praetors, which interpreted and even changed and added to existing law, had increasing importance in developing the Roman legal code. Quite early the edicts of the magistrates who dealt with foreigners developed the idea of the *jus gentium,* or law of peoples, as opposed to that arising strictly from the experience of the Romans. In the first century B.C. the influence of Greek thought made the idea of *jus gentium* identical with that of the *jus naturale,* or natural law, taught by the Stoics. It was this view of a world ruled by divine reason that Cicero enshrined in his treatise on the laws, *De Legibus.*

POETRY. The time of Cicero was also the period of two of Rome's greatest poets, Lucretius and Catullus, each representing a different aspect of Rome's poetic tradition. The Hellenistic poets and literary theorists saw two functions for the poet, as entertainer and as teacher. They thought the best poet combined both roles, and the Romans adopted the same view. When Naevius and Ennius wrote epics on Roman history, they combined historical and moral instruction with pleasure. Lucretius (ca. 99–ca. 55 B.C.) pursued a similar path in his epic poem *De Rerum Natura (On the Nature of the World).* In it he set forth the scientific and philosophical ideas of Epicurus and Democritus with the zeal of a missionary trying to save society from fear and superstition. He knew that his doctrine might be bitter medicine to the reader: "That is why I have tried to administer it to you in the dulcet strain of poesy, coated with the sweet honey of the Muses."[1]

Catullus (ca. 84–ca. 54 B.C.) was a poet of a thoroughly different kind. He wrote poems that were personal, even autobiographical. In imitation of the Alexandrians he wrote short poems filled with learned allusions to mythology, but he far surpassed his models in intensity of feeling. He wrote of the joys and pains of love, he hurled invective at important contemporaries like Julius Caesar, and he amused himself in witty poetic exchanges with others. He offered no moral lessons and was not interested in Rome's glorious history and in contemporary politics. In a sense he is an example of the proud, independent, pleasure-seeking nobleman who characterized part of the aristocracy at the end of the republic.

The Age of Augustus

The spirit of the Augustan Age, the Golden Age of Roman literature, was quite different, reflecting the new conditions of society. The old aristocratic order, with its system of independent nobles following their own particular interests, was gone. So was the world of poets of the lower orders, receiving patronage from any of a number of individual aristocrats. Augustus replaced the complexity of republican patronage with a simple scheme in which all patronage flowed from the *princeps,* usually through his chief cultural adviser, Maecenas. The major poets of this time, Vergil and Horace, had lost their property during the civil wars. The patronage of the *princeps* allowed them the leisure and the security to write poetry and at the same time made them dependent on him and limited their freedom of expression. They wrote on subjects that were useful for his policies and that glorified him and his family, but they were not mere propagandists. It seems evident that for the most part they were persuaded of the virtues of Augustus and his reign and sang its praises with some degree of sincerity. Because they were poets of genius, they were also able to maintain a measure of independence in their work.

VERGIL. Vergil (70–19 B.C.) was the most important of the Augustan poets. His first important works, the *Eclogues* or *Bucolics,* are pastoral idylls in a somewhat artificial mode. The subject of the *Georgics,* however, was suggested to Vergil by Maecenas. The model here was the early Greek poet Hesiod's *Works and Days,* but the mood and purpose of Vergil's poem are far different. It is, to be sure, a didactic account of the agricultural life, but it is also a paean to the beauties of nature and a hymn to the cults, traditions, and greatness of Italy. All this, of course, served the purpose of glorifying Augus-

[1]I, Lucretius, *De Rerum Natura,* lines 931ff.

tus' resettlement of the veterans of the civil wars on Italian farms and his elevation of Italy to special status in the empire. Vergil's greatest work is the *Aeneid*, a long national epic that succeeded in placing the history of Rome in the great tradition of the Greeks and the Trojan War. Its hero, the Trojan warrior Aeneas, personifies the ideal Roman qualities of duty, responsibility, serious purpose, and patriotism. As the Romans' equivalent of Homer, Vergil glorified not the personal honor and excellence of the Greek epic heroes but the civic greatness represented by Augustus and the peace and prosperity that he and the Julian family had given to imperial Rome.

HORACE. Horace (65–8 B.C.) was the son of a freed man and fought on the republican side until its defeat at Philippi. He was won over to the Augustan cause by the patronage of Maecenas and by the attractions of the Augustan reforms. His *Satires* are genial and humorous. His great skills as a lyric poet are best revealed in his *Odes*, which are ingenious in their adaptation of Greek meters to the requirements of Latin verse. Two of the *Odes* are directly in praise of Augustus, and many of them glorify the new Augustan order, the imperial family, and the empire.

OVID. The darker side of Augustan influence on the arts is revealed by the career of Ovid (43 B.C.–A.D. 18). He wrote light and entertaining love elegies that reveal the sophistication and the loose sexual code of a notorious sector of the Roman aristocracy. Their values and way of life were contrary to the seriousness and family-centered life Augustus was trying to foster. Ovid's *Ars Amatoria*, a poetic textbook on the art of seduction, angered Augustus and was partly responsible for the poet's exile in A.D. 8 to Tomi on the Black Sea. Ovid tried to recover favor, especially with his *Fasti*, a poetic treatment of Roman religious festivals, but to no avail. His most popular work is the *Metamorphoses*, a kind of mythological epic that turns Greek myths into charming stories in a graceful and lively style. Ovid's fame did not fade with his exile and death, but his fate was an effective warning to later poets.

HISTORY. The achievements of Augustus and his emphasis on tradition and on the continuity of his regime with the glorious history of Rome encouraged both historical and antiquarian prose works. A number of Augustan writers wrote scholarly treatises on history and geography in Greek. By far the most important and influential prose writer of the time, how-

Vergil on the Destiny of Rome

Vergil (70–19 B.C.) was the leading poet of the Augustan Age. His great epic, the *Aeneid*, is full of praise for Augustus, his family, his ancestors, and the settlement of the Roman world he achieved. The *Aeneid* was written in the last decade of Vergil's life.

Now fix your sight, and stand intent, to see
Your Roman race, and Julian progeny.
There mighty Caesar waits his vital hour,
Impatient for the world, and grasps his promised power.
But next behold the youth of form divine—
Caesar himself, exalted in his line—
Augustus, promised oft, and long foretold,
Sent to the realm that Saturn ruled of old;
Born to restore a better age of gold.
Africa and India shall his power obey;
He shall extend his propagated sway
Beyond the solar year, without the starry way. . . .

. . . .
Let others better mould the running mass
Of metals, and inform the breathing brass,
And soften into flesh, a marble face;
Plead better at the bar; describe the skies,
And when the stars descend, and when they rise.
But Rome! 'tis thine alone, with awful sway,
To rule mankind, and make the world obey,
Disposing peace and war, thy own majestic way:
To tame the proud, the fettered slave to free;—
These are imperial arts, and worthy thee.

John Dryden, *The Works of Vergil* (New York: American Book Exchange, 1881), pp. 262–265.

The Gemma Augustea. This carved onyx from the first century glorifies the Emperor Augustus, who is shown on the upper left crowned with the laurels of victory and triumph. His wife Livia sitting beside him is arrayed as the goddess Roma. On the right, her son, the future emperor Tiberius, is portrayed descending from a triumphal chariot. Below the imperial family, Roman soldiers display prisoners of war and erect emblems of victory. [*Kunsthistorisches Museum, Vienna*]

ever, was Livy (59 B.C.–A.D. 17), an Italian from Padua. His *History of Rome* was written in Latin and treated the period from the legendary origins of Rome until 9 B.C. Only a fourth of his work is extant; of the rest we have only pitifully brief summaries. He based his history on earlier accounts, chiefly the Roman annalists, and made no effort at original research. His great achievement was in telling the story of Rome in a continuous and impressive narrative. Its purpose was moral, setting up historical models as examples of good and bad behavior, and, above all, patriotic. He glorified Rome's greatness and connected it with Rome's past, just as Augustus tried to do.

ARCHITECTURE AND SCULPTURE. The visual arts revealed the same tendencies as other aspects of Roman life under Augustus. Augustus was the great patron of the visual arts as he was of literature. He embarked on a building program that beautified Rome, glorified his reign, and contributed to the general prosperity and his own popularity. He filled the Campus Martius with beautiful new buildings, theaters, baths, and basilicas; the Roman Forum was rebuilt; and Augustus built a forum of his own. At its heart was the temple of Mars the Avenger to commemorate Augustus' victory and the greatness of his ancestors. On Rome's Palatine hill he built a splendid temple to his patron god, Apollo. This was one of the many temples he constructed in pursuit of his religious policy.

Most of the building was influenced by the Greek classical style, which aimed at serenity and the ideal type. The same features were visible in the portrait sculpture of Augustus and his family. The greatest monument of the age is the Altar of Peace *(Ara Pacis)* dedicated in 9 B.C. Set originally in an open space in the Campus Martius, its walls still carry a relief. Part of it shows a procession in which Augustus and his family appear to move forward, followed in order by the magistrates, the Senate, and the people of Rome. There is no better symbol of the new order.

Life in Imperial Rome: The Apartment House

The civilization of the Roman Empire depended on the vitality of its cities, of which no more than three or four had a population of more than 75,000, the typical city having about 20,000 inhabitants. The population of Rome, however, was certainly greater than 500,000, and some scholars think it was more than a million. People coming to it for the first time found it overwhelming and were either thrilled or horrified by its size, bustle, and noise. The rich lived in elegant homes called *domus*, single-storied houses with plenty of space, an open central courtyard, and several rooms designed for specific and different purposes, such as dining, sitting, or sleeping, in privacy and relative quiet. Though only a small portion of Rome's population lived in them, these houses took up as much as a third of the city's space. Public space for temples, markets, baths, gymnasiums, theaters, forums, and governmental buildings took up another quarter of Rome's territory.

This left less than half of Rome's area to house the mass of its inhabitants. Inevitably, as the population grew, it was squeezed into mul-

Juvenal on Life in Rome

The satirical poet Juvenal lived and worked in Rome in the late first and early second centuries A.D. His poems present a vivid picture of the material and cultural world of the Romans of his time. In the following passages, he tells of the discomforts and dangers of life in the city, both indoors and out.

Who, in Praeneste's cool, or the wooded Volsinian uplands,
Who, on Tivoli's heights, or a small town like Gabii, say,
Fears the collapse of his house? But Rome is supported on pipestems,
Matchsticks; it's cheaper, so, for the landlord to shore up his ruins,
Patch up the old cracked walls, and notify all the tenants
They can sleep secure, though the beams are in ruins above them.
No, the place to live is out there, where no cry of Fire!
Sounds the alarm of the night, with a neighbor yelling for water,
Moving his chattels and goods, and the whole third story is smoking.
This you'll never know: for if the ground floor is scared first,
You are the last to burn, up there where the eaves of the attic
Keep off the rain, and the doves are brooding over their nest eggs.
. . . .
Look at other things, the various dangers of nighttime.
How high it is to the cornice that breaks, and a chunk beats my brains out,
Or some slob heaves a jar, broken or cracked, from a window.
Bang! It comes down with a crash and proves its weight on the sidewalk.
You are a thoughtless fool, unmindful of sudden disaster,
If you don't make your will before you go out to have dinner.
There are as many deaths in the night as there are open windows
Where you pass by; if you're wise, you will pray, in your wretched devotions,
People may be content with no more than emptying slop jars.

Juvenal, *Satires*, trans. by Rolfe Humphries (Bloomington: Indiana University Press, 1958), pp. 40, 43.

tiple dwellings that grew increasingly tall. Most Romans during the imperial period lived in apartment buildings called *insulae* ("islands") that rose to a height of five or six stories and sometimes even more. The most famous of them, the Insula of Febiala, seems to have "towered above the Rome of the Antonines like a skyscraper."[2] These buildings were divided into separate apartments (*cenicula*) of undifferentiated rooms, the same plan on each floor. The apartments were cramped and uncomfortable. They had neither central heating nor an open fireplace; heat and fire for cooking came from small, portable stoves or braziers. The apartments were hot in summer, cold in winter, and stuffy and smoky when the stoves were lit. There was no plumbing, so tenants needed to go into the streets to wells or fountains for water and to public baths and latrines, or to less well-regulated places, to perform some natural functions. The higher up one lived, the more difficult these trips, so chamber pots and commodes were kept in the rooms. These receptacles were emptied into vats on the staircase landings or in the alleys outside, or on occasion, the contents, and even the containers, were tossed out the window. Roman satirists complained of the discomforts and dangers of walking the streets beneath such windows, and Roman law tried to find ways to assign responsibility for the injuries done to dignity and person.

In spite of these difficulties, the attractions of the city and the shortage of space caused rents to rise, making life in these buildings expensive

[2]J. Carcopino, *Daily Life in Ancient Rome* (New Haven, Conn.: 1940), p. 26.

Ruins of apartment houses in Ostia, the port of Rome. Built of brick and concrete, such tenements were originally several stories high. [*Art Resource*]

as well as uncomfortable. It was also dangerous. The houses were lightly built of concrete and brick, far too high for the limited area of their foundations, so they often collapsed. Laws limiting the height of buildings were not always obeyed and did not, in any case, always prevent disaster. The satirist Juvenal did not exaggerate much when he wrote, "We inhabit a city held up chiefly by slats, for that is how the landlord patches up the cracks in the old wall, telling the tenants to sleep peacefully under the ruin that hangs over their heads." Even more serious was the threat of fire. The floors were supported by wooden beams, and the rooms were lit by torches, candles, and oil lamps and heated by braziers. Fires broke out easily and, without running water, were not easily put out; once started, they usually led to disaster.

When we consider the character of these apartments and compare them with the attractive public places in the city, we can easily understand why the people of Rome spent most of their time out of doors.

Peace and Prosperity: Imperial Rome A.D. 14–180

The central problem for Augustus' successors was the position of the ruler and his relationship to the ruled. Augustus tried to cloak the monarchical nature of his government, but his successors soon abandoned all pretense. The ruler came to be called *imperator*—from which comes our word *emperor*—as well as *Caesar*. The latter title signified connection with the imperial house, and the former indicated the military power on which everything was based. Because Augustus was ostensibly only the "first citizen" of a restored republic and his powers were theoretically voted him by the Senate and the people, he could not legally name his successor. In fact, he plainly designated his heirs by favors lavished on them and by giving them a share in the imperial power and responsibility. Tiberius (emperor A.D. 14–37),[3] his immediate successor, was at first embarrassed by the ambiguity of his new role, but soon the monarchical and hereditary nature of the regime became patent. Gaius (Caligula, A.D. 37–41), Claudius (A.D. 41–54), and Nero (A.D. 54–68) were all descended from either Augustus or his wife, Livia, and all were elevated because of that fact. In A.D. 41 the naked military basis of imperial rule was revealed when the Praetorian Guard dragged the lame, stammering, and frightened Claudius from behind a curtain and made him emperor. In A.D. 68 the frontier legions learned what the historian Tacitus called "the secret of Empire . . . that an emperor could be made elsewhere than at Rome." Nero's incompetence and unpopularity, and especially his inability to control his armies, led to a serious rebellion in Gaul in A.D. 68. The year 69 saw four different emperors assume power in quick succession as different Roman armies took turns placing their commanders on the throne.

Vespasian (A.D. 69–79) emerged victorious from the chaos, and his sons, Titus (A.D. 79–

[3]Dates for emperors give the years of each reign.

Nero (A.D. 54–68) *was the last descendant of Augustus's family to become emperor. His incompetent rule ended in rebellion and civil war.* [*Alinari/SCALA*]

Rulers of the Early Empire

Augustus	27 B.C.–A.D. 14
	The Julio-Claudian Dynasty
Tiberius	A.D. 14–37
Gaius (Caligula)	A.D. 37–41
Claudius	A.D. 41–54
Nero	A.D. 54–68
Year of the Four Emperors	A.D. 69
	The Flavian Dynasty
Vespasian	A.D. 69–79
Titus	A.D. 79–81
Domitian	A.D. 81–96
	The "Good Emperors"
Nerva	A.D. 96–98
Trajan	A.D. 98–117
Hadrian	A.D. 117–138
Antoninus Pius	A.D. 138–161
Marcus Aurelius	A.D. 161–180

81) and Domitian (A.D. 81–96), carried forward his line, the Flavian dynasty. Vespasian was the first emperor who did not come from the old Roman nobility. He was a tough soldier who came from the Italian middle class. A good administrator and a hard-headed realist of rough wit, he resisted all attempts by flatterers to find noble ancestors for him. On his deathbed he is said to have ridiculed the practice of deifying emperors by saying, "Alas, I think I am becoming a god."

The assassination of Domitian put an end to the Flavian dynasty. Because Domitian had no close relative who had been designated as successor, the Senate put Nerva (A.D. 96–98) on the throne to avoid chaos. He was the first of the five "good emperors," who included Trajan (A.D. 98–117), Hadrian (A.D. 117–138), Antoninus Pius (A.D. 138–161), and Marcus Aurelius (A.D. 161–180). Until Marcus Aurelius none of these emperors had sons, so they each followed the example set by Nerva of adopting an able senator and establishing him as successor. This rare solution to the problem of monarchical succession was, therefore, only a historical accident. The result, nonetheless, was almost a century of peaceful succession and competent rule, which ended when Marcus Aurelius allowed his incompetent son, Commodus (A.D. 180–192), to succeed him, with unfortunate results.

The genius of the Augustan settlement lay in its capacity to enlist the active cooperation of the upper classes and their effective organ, the Senate. The election of magistrates was taken from the assemblies and given to the Senate; it became the major center for legislation; and it exercised important judicial functions. This semblance of power persuaded some contemporaries and even some modern scholars that Augustus had established a "dyarchy," a system of joint rule by *princeps* and Senate. This was never true, and the hollowness of the senatorial role became more apparent as time passed. Some emperors, like Vespasian, took pains to maintain, increase, and display the prestige and dignity of the Senate; others, like Caligula, Nero, and Domitian, degraded the Senate and paraded their own despotic power, but from the first its powers were illusory. Magisterial elections were, in fact, controlled by the emperors, and the Senate's legislative function quickly degenerated into mere assent to what was put before it by the emperor or his representatives. The true function of the Senate was to be a legislative and administrative extension of the emperor's rule.

There was, of course, some real opposition

WALL OF ANTONINUS
WALL OF HADRIAN
NORTH SEA
HIBERNIA
BRITAIN
ATLANTIC OCEAN
RHINE
SEINE
LOIRE
Cologne
GERMANIA (INF.)
GERMANIA
ELBE
ODER
VISTULA
DNIEPER
SARMA
DNIESTER
PRUTH
DANUBE
LUGDUNENSIS
GERMANIA (SUP.)
GAUL
RAETIA
NOR-ICUM
AQUITANIA
(SUP.) PANNONIA (INF.)
DACIA
TARRACONENSIS
CISALPINE GAUL
NARBONENSIS
PO
DUERO
EBRO
RHÔNE
DALMATIA
LUSITANIA
SPAIN
CORSICA
ITALY
(SUP.) MOESIA (INF.)
BLAC
Rome
THRACE
Byzantium
BAETICA
BALEARIC IS.
Apollonia
MACEDONIA
BITHY
SARDINIA
MEDITERRANEAN SEA
ILLYRIA
GREECE
ASIA
PISIDIA
MAURETANIA
Carthage
SICILY
ACHAEA
LYCIA
CRETE
AFRICA
NUMIDIA
CYRENAICA
LIBYA
EGY
14 A.D.— DEATH OF AUGUSTUS
14-98 A.D.— ACQUISITIONS, AUGUSTUS TO TRAJAN
98-117 A.D.— ACQUISITIONS DURING THE REIGN OF TRAJAN
T R MILLER

PROVINCES OF THE ROMAN EMPIRE TO A.D. 117

to the imperial rule. It sometimes took the form of plots against the life of the emperor. Plots and the suspicion of plots led to repression, the use of spies and paid informers, book burning, and executions. The opposition consisted chiefly of senators who looked back to republican liberty for their class and who found justification in the Greek and Roman traditions of tyrannicide as well as in the precepts of Stoicism. Plots and repression were most common under Nero and Domitian. From Nerva to Marcus Aurelius, however, the emperors, without yielding any power, again learned to enlist the cooperation of the upper class by courteous and modest deportment.

The Administration of the Empire

The provinces flourished economically and generally accepted Roman rule easily (see Map 5.1). In the eastern provinces the emperor was worshiped as a god, and even in Italy most emperors were deified after their death as long as the imperial cult established by Augustus continued. Imperial policy was for the most part a happy combination of an attempt to unify the empire and its various peoples with a respect for local customs and differences. Roman citizenship was spread ever more widely, and by A.D. 212 almost every inhabitant of the empire was a citizen. Latin became the language of the western provinces, and although the east remained essentially Greek in language and culture, even it adopted many aspects of Roman life. The spread of *Romanitas*, or Roman-ness, was more than nominal, for senators and even emperors began to be drawn from provincial families.

The army played an important role in the spread of Roman culture and the spiritual unification of the empire. The legionaries married

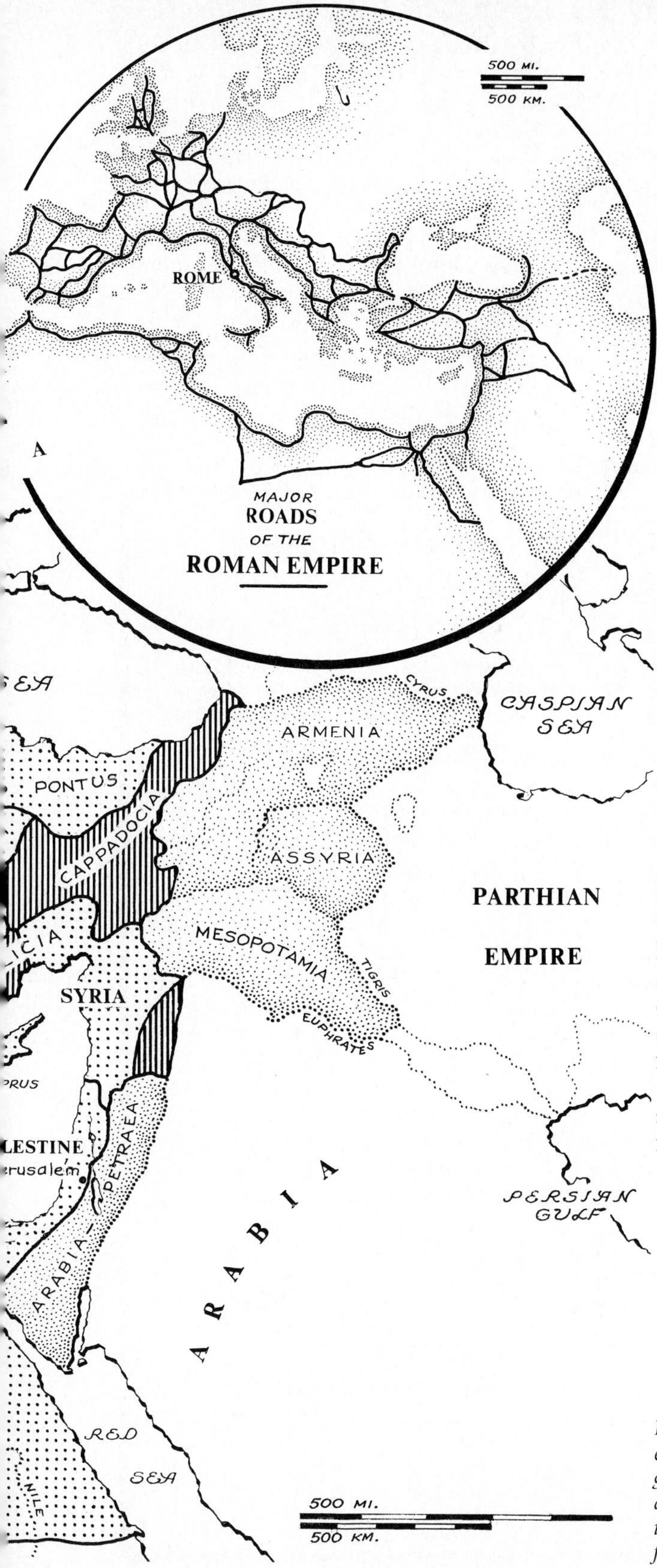

MAPS 5-1, 5-2 *The growth of the Empire to its greatest extent is here shown in three states—at the death of Augustus in* A.D. 14, *at the death of Nerva in* 98, *and at the death of Trajan in* 117. *The division into provinces is also indicated. The inset outlines the main roads that tied the far-flung empire together.*

local women and frequently settled in the province of their service when their term was over.

From an administrative and cultural standpoint the empire was a collection of cities and towns and had little to do with the countryside. Roman policy during the Principate was to raise urban centers to the status of Roman municipalities with the rights and privileges attached to them. A typical municipal charter left much responsibility in the hands of local councils and magistrates elected from the local aristocracy. Moreover, the holding of a magistracy, and later a seat on the council, carried Roman citizenship with it. Therefore the Romans enlisted the upper classes of the provinces in their own government, spread Roman law and culture, and won the loyalty of the influential people.

There were exceptions to this picture of success. The Jews found their religion incompatible with Roman demands and experienced savage repression of their rebellions in A.D. 66–70, 115–117, and 132–135. In Egypt the

Daily Life in a Roman Provincial Town: Graffiti from Pompeii

On the walls of the houses of Pompeii, buried and preserved by the eruption of Mount Vesuvius in A.D. 79, are many scribblings that give us an idea of what the life of ordinary people was like.

I

Twenty pairs of gladiators of Decimus Lucretius Satrius Valens, lifetime flamen *of Nero son of Caesar Augustus, and ten pairs of gladiators of Decimus Lucretius Valens, his son, will fight at Pompeii on April 8, 9, 10, 11, 12. There will be a full card of wild beast combats, and awnings [for the spectators]. Aemilius Celer [painted this sign], all alone in the moonlight.*

II

Market days: Saturday in Pompeii, Sunday in Nuceria, Monday in Atella, Tuesday in Nola, Wednesday in Cumae, Thursday in Puteoli, Friday in Rome.

III

Pleasure says: "You can get a drink here for an as *[a few cents], a better drink for two, Falernian for four."*

IV

A copper pot is missing from this shop. 65 sesterces reward if anybody brings it back, 20 sesterces if he reveals the thief so we can get our property back.

V

The weaver Successus loves the inkeeper's slave girl, Iris by name. She doesn't care for him, but he begs her to take pity on him. Written by his rival. So long.

[Answer by the rival:] Just because you're bursting with envy, don't pick on a handsomer man, a lady-killer and a gallant.

[Answer by the first writer:] There's nothing more to say or write. You love Iris, who doesn't care for you.

VI

Take your lewd looks and flirting eyes off another man's wife, and show some decency on your face!

VII

Anybody in love, come here. I want to break Venus' ribs with a club and cripple the goddess' loins. If she can pierce my tender breast, why can't I break her head with a club?

VIII

I write at Love's dictation and Cupid's instruction;

But damn it! I don't want to be a god without you.

IX

[A prostitute's sign:] I am yours for 2 asses *cash.*

N. Lewis and M. Reinhold, *Roman Civilization*, Vol. 2 (New York: Columbia University Press, 1955), pp. 359–360.

The ruins of Pompeii, an Italian provincial town on the Bay of Naples that was buried by volcanic ash from Mount Vesuvius in A.D. 79. *Like many provincial centers during the early empire, Pompeii was a pleasant, prosperous town with elegant public buildings and comfortable houses.* [*Fotocielo*]

Romans exploited the peasants ruthlessly and did not pursue a policy of urbanization.

As the efficiency of the bureaucracy grew, so did the number and scope of its functions and therefore its size. The emperors came to take a broader view of their responsibilities for the welfare of their subjects than before. Nerva conceived and Trajan introduced the *alimenta*, a program of public assistance on behalf of the children of indigent parents. More and more the emperors intervened when municipalities got into difficulties, usually financial, sending imperial troubleshooters to deal with problems. The importance and autonomy of the municipalities shrank as the central administration took a greater part in local affairs. The provincial aristocracy came to regard public service in their own cities as a burden rather than an opportunity; the price paid for the increased efficiency offered by centralized control was the loss of the vitality of the cities throughout the empire.

Augustus' successors, for the most part, accepted his conservative and defensive foreign policy. Trajan was the first emperor to take the offensive in a sustained way. Between A.D. 101 and 106 he crossed the Danube and, after hard fighting, established the new province of Dacia between the Danube and the Carpathian Mountains. He was tempted, no doubt, by its important gold mines, but he probably was also pursuing a new general strategy: to defend the empire more aggressively by driving wedges into the territory of

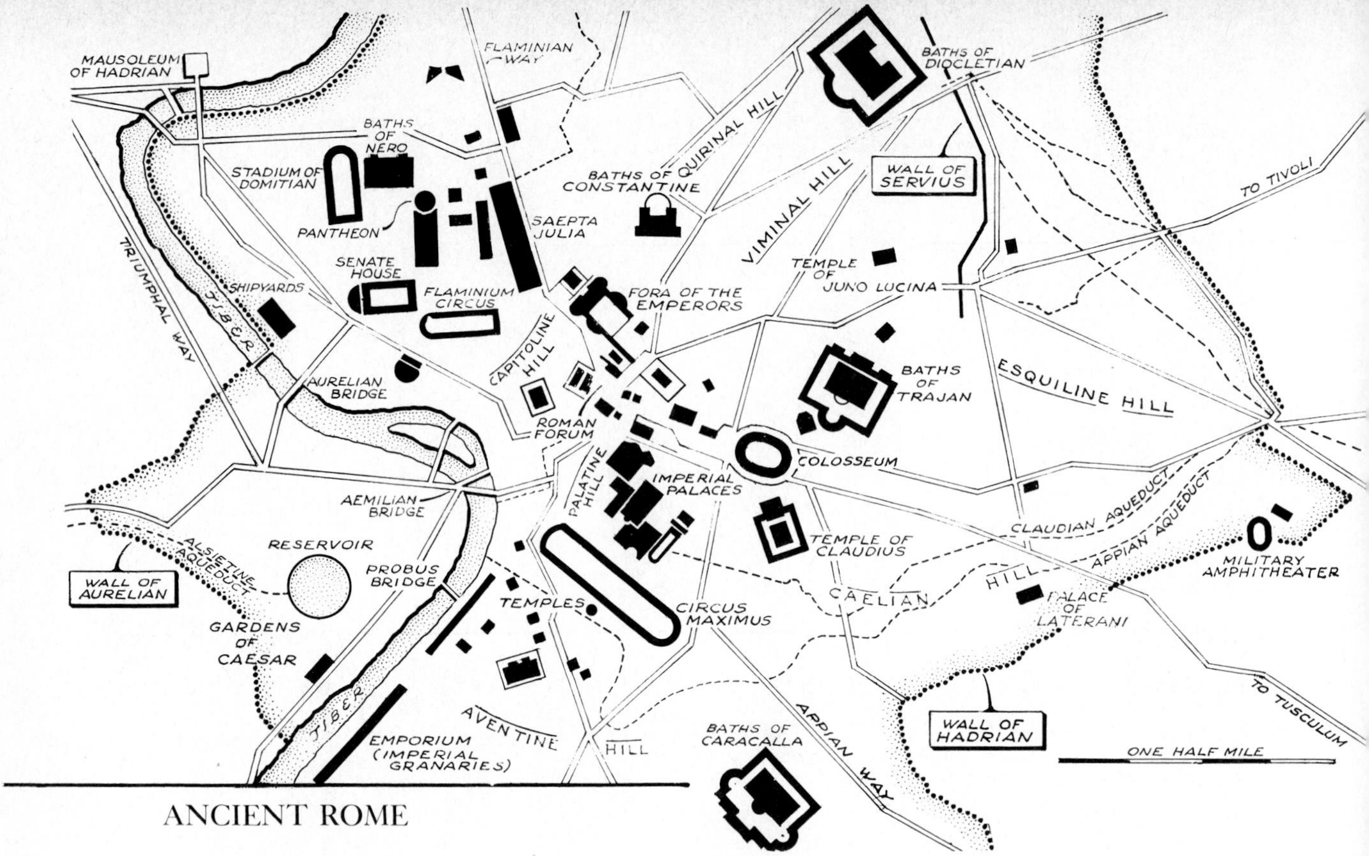

ANCIENT ROME

The Philanthropy of Herodes Atticus

The second century was a time of prosperity in the Roman Empire, when wealthy men often engaged in great philanthropic gestures to demonstrate their magnanimity and dedication to civic improvement. In the following passage, we read of the deeds of Herodes Atticus, an Athenian who reached the highest offices of the Roman Empire.

No man used his wealth to better purpose. . . . The sources of his wealth were many and derived from several families, but the greatest were the fortunes that came from his father [Atticus] and his mother. . . . This Atticus [the father] was also distinguished for his lordly spirit. As an instance, at a time when his son Herodes was overseer of the free cities of Asia, he observed that Troy was ill supplied with baths and that the inhabitants drew muddy water from their wells and had to dig cisterns to catch rain water. Accordingly, he wrote to the Emperor Hadrian to ask him not to allow an ancient city, conveniently near the sea, to perish from lack of water, but to bestow 3,000,000 drachmas upon them for a water supply, since he had already bestowed on mere villages many times that sum. The emperor approved of his advice in the letter as being in accordance with his own disposition and appointed Herodes himself to take charge of the water project. But when the outlay had reached the sum of 7,000,000 drachmas and the officials who governed Asia kept writing to the emperor that it was a scandal that the tribute of five hundred cities should be spent on the fountain of one city, the emperor expressed his disapproval of this to Atticus; whereupon Atticus replied in the most lordly fashion in the world, ''Do not, O Emperor, allow yourself to be irritated over such trifles. The amount spent in excess of 3,000,000 I am presenting to my son, and my son will present it to the city.''

Philostratus, *Lives of the Sophists,* trans. by N. Lewis and M. Reinhold, *Roman Civilization,* Vol. 2 (New York: Columbia University Press, 1955), p. 350.

MAP 5-3 *This is a sketch of the city of Rome during the late Empire. It indicates the seven hills on and around which the city was built, as well as the major walls, bridges, and other public sites and buildings. The Forum is between the Capitoline and Palatine hills.*

threatening barbarians. The same strategy dictated the invasion of the Parthian Empire in the east (A.D. 113–117). Trajan's early success was astonishing, and he established three new provinces in Armenia, Assyria, and Mesopotamia, but his lines were overextended. Rebellions sprang up, and the campaign crumbled. Trajan was forced to retreat and died before getting back to Rome.

Hadrian returned to the traditional policy, keeping Dacia but abandoning the eastern provinces. Hadrian's reign marked an important shift in Rome's frontier policy. Heretofore, even under the successors of Augustus, Rome had been on the offensive against the barbarians. Although the Romans rarely gained new territory, they launched frequent attacks to chastise and pacify troublesome tribes. Hadrian hardened the Roman defenses, building a stone wall in the south of Scotland and a wooden one across the Rhine–Danube triangle. The Roman defense became rigid, and

Tacitus Gives a Provincial View of the Imperial Peace

Tacitus (A.D. 55–ca. 115) was a Roman senator. He is most famous as historian of Rome for the period A.D. 14–68, but the following selection comes from a eulogy for his father-in-law, Agricola. It gives an insight into the Roman Empire viewed critically.

The Britons, . . . convinced at length that a common danger must be averted by union, had, by embassies and treaties, summoned forth the whole strength of all their states. More than 30,000 armed men were now to be seen, and still there were pressing in all the youth of the country, with all whose old age was yet hale and vigorous, men renowned in war and bearing each decorations of his own. Meanwhile, among the many leaders, one superior to the rest in valour and in birth, Galgacus by name, is said to have thus harangued the multitude gathered around him and clamouring for battle:—

"Whenever I consider the origin of this war and the necessities of our position, I have a sure confidence that this day, and this union of yours, will be the beginning of freedom to the whole of Britain. To all of us slavery is a thing unknown; there are no lands beyond us, and even the sea is not safe, menaced as we are by a Roman fleet. And thus in war and battle, in which the brave find glory, even the coward will find safety. Former contests, in which, with varying fortune, the Romans were resisted, still left in us a last hope of succour, inasmuch as being the most renowned nation of Britain, dwelling in the very heart of the country and out of sight of the shores of the conquered, we could keep even our eyes unpolluted by the contagion of slavery. To us who dwell on the uttermost confines of the earth and of freedom, this remote sanctuary of Britain's glory has up to this time been a defence. Now, however, the furthest limits of Britain are thrown open, and the unknown always passes for the marvellous. But there are no tribes beyond us, nothing indeed but waves and rocks, and the yet more terrible Romans, from whose oppression escape is vainly sought by obedience and submission. Robbers of the world, having by their universal plunder exhausted the land, they rifle the deep. If the enemy be rich, they are rapacious; if he be poor, they lust for dominion; neither the east nor the west has been able to satisfy them. Alone among men they covet with equal eagerness poverty and riches. To robbery, slaughter, plunder, they give the lying name of empire; they make a solitude and call it peace."

Tacitus, *Agricola*, in *Complete Works of Tacitus*, trans. by A. J. Church and W. Brodribb (New York: Random House, 1942), pp. 694–695.

Spoils from the temple in Jerusalem carried in triumphal procession by Roman troops. This relief from Titus's arch of victory in the Roman Forum celebrates his capture of Jerusalem after a two-year seige. The Jews found it difficult to reconcile their religion with Roman rule and frequently rebelled. [*Art Resource*]

initiative passed to the barbarians. Marcus Aurelius was compelled to spend most of his reign resisting dangerous attacks in the east and on the Danube frontier, and these attacks put enormous pressure on the human and financial resources of the empire.

This pressure took its toll only late in this period, which, in general, experienced considerable economic prosperity and growth. Internal peace and efficient administration benefited agriculture as well as trade and industry; farming and trade developed together as political conditions made it easier to sell farm products at a distance. This latter element encouraged the earlier tendency toward specialization of crops and the growth of large holdings. Small farms continued to exist, but the large estate, managed by an absentee owner and growing cash crops, became the dominant form of agriculture. At first, these estates were worked chiefly by slaves, but in the first century this began to change. The end of wars of conquest made slaves less available and more expensive, for ancient societies never succeeded in breeding slaves. The tenant farmer, or *colonus*, became the mainstay of agricultural labor. Typically these sharecroppers paid rent in labor or in kind, though sometimes they made cash payments. Eventually their movement was restricted, and they were tied to the land they worked, much as were the manorial serfs of the Middle Ages. But the system was economically efficient and contributed to the general prosperity, whatever its social cost.

The Younger Pliny Describes the Growth of Tenant Farming

The reign of the Emperor Trajan (A.D. 98–117) has usually been considered near the peak of the Roman Empire's prosperity. The Younger Pliny (ca. A.D. 61–114), however, one of Trajan's associates, described conditions that showed that the growth of economic and social problems characteristic of the late empire had already begun in his own time. In the following letter to a friend, Pliny made it clear that tenant farming was characteristic of Roman agriculture and that tenants were not faring well.

Gaius Plinius to his dear Paulinus, greeting. . . . I am detained by the necessity of leasing my estates so as to set them in order for several years. In which connection I am obliged to adopt new arrangements. For in the last five-year period, despite large reductions [of rent], the arrears mounted. Hence several tenants no longer have any concern to reduce a debt which they despair of being able to pay off; they even seize and consume whatever is produced, acting like people who think they no longer have to be thrifty since it is not their own property. The growing evils, therefore, have to be faced and relieved. There is one method of remedying them—to least not for a rent in money but on shares, and then to place some of my men to superintend the work and guard the produce. . . . It is true that this requires great integrity, keen eyes, and many hands. However, I must try the experiment and, as in a chronic disease, try and see what help a change may bring.

Pliny, *Letters,* in N. Lewis and M. Reinhold, *Roman Civilization,* Vol. 2 (New York: Columbia University Press, 1955), p. 177.

The Culture of the Early Empire

LITERATURE. In Latin literature the years between the death of Augustus and the time of Marcus Aurelius are known as the Silver Age, and as the name implies, work of high quality was produced although probably not of so high a quality as in the Augustan era. In contrast to the hopeful, positive optimists of the Augustans, the writers of the Silver Age were gloomy, negative, and pessimistic. In the works of the former period, praise of the emperor, his achievements, and the world abounds; in the latter, criticism and satire lurk everywhere.

Some of the most important writers of the Silver Age came from the Stoic opposition and reflected its hostility to the growing power and personal excesses of the emperors.

The writers of the second century A.D. appear to have turned away from contemporary affairs and even recent history. Historical writing was about remote periods so that there was less danger of irritating imperial sensibilities. Scholarship was encouraged, but we hear little of poetry, especially any dealing with dangerous subjects.

In the third century A.D. romances written in Greek became popular and provide further evidence of the tendency of writers of the time to seek and provide escape from contemporary realities.

ARCHITECTURE. The prosperity and relative stability of the first two centuries of imperial Rome allowed for the full development of the Roman contribution to architecture. To the fundamental styles of buildings developed by the Greeks, the Romans added little; the great public bath and a new, free-standing kind of amphitheater were the main innovations.

The main contribution of the Romans lay in the great size of the structures they could build and in the advances in engineering that made these large structures possible. While keeping the basic post-and-lintel construction used by the Greeks, the Romans added to it the principle of the semicircular arch, borrowed from the Etruscans. They also made good use of concrete, a building material first used by the Hellenistic Greeks and fully developed by the Romans. The new principle, sometimes combined with the new material, allowed progress

Interior of the Pantheon, Rome. Built by the emperor Hadrian ca. A.D. 126, *it is a great concrete drum with a cupola. Its design has inspired architects for centuries, including the dome of St. Peter's in Rome and Frank Lloyd Wright's Guggenheim Museum in New York. [Robert Frerck]*

over the old style. The arch combined with the post and lintel produced the great Colosseum built by the Flavian emperors. When used internally in the form of vaults and domes, the arch permitted great buildings like the baths, of which the most famous and best preserved are those of the later emperors Caracalla and Diocletian.

One of Rome's most famous buildings, the Pantheon, begun by Augustus' friend Agrippa and rebuilt by Hadrian, is a good example of the combination of all these elements. Its portico of Corinthian columns is of Greek origin, but its rotunda of brick-faced concrete with its domed ceiling and relieving arches is thoroughly Roman. The new engineering also made possible the construction of more mundane but more useful structures like bridges and aqueducts.

Society. Seen from the harsh perspective of human history, the first two centuries of the Roman Empire deserve their reputation of a "golden age," but by the second century A.D., troubles had arisen, troubles that foreshadowed the difficult times ahead. The literary efforts of the time reveal a flight from the present and from reality and the public realm to the past, to romance, to private pursuits. Some of the same aspects may be seen in the more prosaic world of everyday life, especially in the decline of vitality in local government.

In the first century A.D. members of the upper classes vied with one another for election to municipal office and for the honor of doing service to their communities. By the second century A.D. much of their zeal had disappeared, and it became necessary for the emperors to intervene to correct abuses in local affairs

This sandstone relief from a Roman tomb in the Rhineland illustrates the comfortable life of the provincial upper classes in the first two centuries A.D. *It shows a wealthy lady seated in a wicker chair. Her four slave girls attend her: one does her hair, while another holds up a mirror. The other two hold a perfume flask and a small pitcher.*

The Roman Baths: Two Views

Public baths played an important part in the lives of the Romans of the imperial period. The finest architects built them, beautifully and expensively, for the citizens not only of Rome, but of most of the major cities in the empire. The baths served as vast community centers for social life and recreation. The first selection was written by Lucian, a writer of the second century A.D., who described the magnificence of the baths. The second selection presents a more jaundiced view of the people who used them. It was written by Lucius Annaeus Seneca (ca. 4 B.C.–A.D. 65), who was Nero's tutor and a leading Roman representative of the Stoic school of philosophy.

The building suits the magnitude of the site, accords well with the accepted idea of such an establishment, and shows regard for the principles of lighting. The entrance is high, with a flight of broad steps of which the tread is greater than the pitch, to make them easy to ascend. On entering, one is received into a public hall of good size, with ample accommodations for servants and attendants. On the left are the lounging rooms, also of just the right sort for a bath, attractive, brightly lighted retreats. Then, besides them, a hall, larger than need be for the purposes of a bath, but necessary for the reception of richer persons. Next, capacious locker rooms to undress in, on each side, with a very high and brilliantly lighted hall between them, in which are three swimming pools of cold water; it is finished in Laconian marble, and has two statues of white marble in the ancient style, one of Hygeia, the other of Aesculapius.

On leaving this hall, you come into another which is slightly warmed instead of meeting you at once with fierce heat; it is oblong, and has an apse on each side. Next to it, on the right, is a very bright hall, nicely fitted up for massage, which has on each side an entrance decorated with Phrygian marble, and receives those who come in from the exercising floor. Then near this is another hall, the most beautiful in the world, in which one can stand or sit with comfort, linger without danger, and stroll about with profit. It also is refulgent with Phrygian marble clear to the roof. Next comes the hot corridor, faced with Numidian marble. The hall beyond it is very beautiful, full of abundant light and aglow with color like that of purple hangings. It contains three hot tubs.

When you have bathed, you need not go back through the same rooms, but can go directly to the cold room through a slightly warmed chamber. Everywhere there is copious illumination and full indoor daylight. . . . Why should I go on to tell you of the exercising floor and of the cloak rooms? . . . Moreover, it is beautiful with all other marks of thoughtfulness—with two toilets, many exits, and two devices for telling time, a water clock that makes a bellowing sound and a sundial.

Lucian, *Hippias, or the Bath,* in N. Lewis and M. Reinhold, *Roman Civilization,* Vol. 2 (New York: Columbia University Press, 1955), pp. 227–228.

I live over a bathing establishment. Picture to yourself now the assortment of voices, the sound of which is enough to sicken one. When the stronger fellows are exercising and swinging heavy leaden weights in their hands, when they are working hard or pretending to be working hard, I hear their groans; and whenever they release their pent-up breath, I hear their hissing and jarring breathing. When I have to do with a lazy fellow who is content with a cheap rubdown, I hear the slap of the hand pummeling his shoulders, changing its sound according as the hand is laid on flat or curved. If now a professional ball player comes along and begins to keep score, I am done for. Add to this the arrest of a brawler or a thief, and the fellow who always likes to hear his own voice in the bath, and those who jump into the pool with a mighty splash as they strike the water. In addition to those whose voices are, if nothing else, natural, imagine the hair plucker keeping up a constant chatter in his thin and strident voice, to attract more attention, and never silent except when he is plucking armpits and making the customer yell instead of yelling himself. It disgusts me to enumerate the varied cries of the sausage dealer and confectioner and of all the peddlers of the cook shops, hawking their wares, each with his own peculiar intonation.

Seneca, *Moral Epistles,* in N. Lewis and M. Reinhold, *Roman Civilization,* Vol. 2 (New York: Columbia University Press, 1955), p. 228.

A gladitorial show. This mosaic was found in Leptis Magna, a prosperous Roman city in North Africa, modern Libya. On the top we see the orchestra that played during the show. In the middle armed men duel with each other. At the bottom men hunt wild beasts, while leopards savage condemned criminals tied to stakes. [*Roger Wood*]

and even to force unwilling members of the ruling classes to accept public office. The reluctance to serve was caused largely by the imperial practice of holding magistrates and councilmen personally and collectively responsible for the revenues due. There were even some instances of magistrates' fleeing to avoid their office, a practice that became widespread in later centuries.

All of these difficulties reflected the presence of more basic problems. The prosperity brought by the end of civil war and the influx of wealth from the east, especially Egypt, could not sustain itself beyond the first half of the second century A.D. There also appears to have been a decline in population for reasons that remain mysterious. The cost of government kept rising as the emperors were required to maintain a costly standing army, to keep the people in Rome happy with "bread and circuses," to pay for an increasingly numerous bureaucracy, and, especially in the reign of Marcus Aurelius, to wage expensive wars to defend the frontiers against dangerous and determined barbarian enemies. The ever-increasing need for money compelled the emperors to raise taxes, to press hard on their subjects, and to bring on inflation by debasing the coinage. These were the elements that were to bring on the desperate crises that ultimately destroyed the empire, but under the able emperors, from Trajan to Marcus Aurelius, the Romans met the challenge successfully.

The Rise of Christianity

The story of how Christianity emerged, spread, survived, and ultimately conquered the Roman Empire is one of the most remarkable in history. Its origin among poor people from an unimportant and remote province of the empire gave little promise of what was to come. Christianity faced the hostility of the established religious institutions of its native Judaea and had to compete not only against the official cults of Rome and the highly sophisticated philosophies of the educated classes but even against other "mystery" religions like the cults of Mithra, Isis and Osiris, and many others. In

Seneca Describes Gladiatorial Shows at Rome

Roman society was never gentle, but by imperial times the public had become addicted to brutal public displays of violence in the form of combats involving gladiators. At first, gladiators were enslaved prisoners of war or condemned criminals, but later free men entered the combats, driven by poverty. They were all trained in schools by professional trainers. The following selection by Seneca gives an unfriendly account of the shows and of the spectators who watched them.

I chanced to stop in at a midday show, expecting fun, wit, and some relaxation, when men's eyes take respite from the slaughter of their fellow men. It was just the reverse. The preceding combats were merciful by comparison; now all trifling is put aside and it is pure murder. The men have no protective covering. Their entire bodies are exposed to the blows, and no blow is ever struck in vain. . . . In the morning men are thrown to the lions and the bears, at noon they are thrown to their spectators. The spectators call for the slayer to be thrown to those who in turn will slay him, and they detain the victor for another butchering. The outcome for the combatants is death; the fight is waged with sword and fire. This goes on while the arena is free. "But one of them was a highway robber, he killed a man!" Because he killed he deserved to suffer this punishment, granted. . . . "Kill him! Lash him! Burn him! Why does he meet the sword so timidly? Why doesn't he kill boldly? Why doesn't he die game? Whip him to meet his wounds! Let them trade blow for blow, chests bare and within reach!" And when the show stops for intermission, "Let's have men killed meanwhile! Let's not have nothing going on!"

Seneca, *Moral Epistles,* in N. Lewis and M. Reinhold, *Roman Civilization,* Vol. 2 (New York: Columbia University Press, 1955), p. 230.

addition to all this, the Christians faced the opposition of the imperial government and even formal persecution, yet Christianity achieved toleration and finally exclusive command as the official religion of the empire.

Jesus of Nazareth

An attempt to understand this amazing outcome must begin with Jesus of Nazareth, though there are many problems in arriving at a clear picture of his life and teachings. Apart from the question of sectarian prejudices that might affect the historian's judgment, the sources present special difficulties. The most important evidence is in the Gospel accounts. All of them were written well after the death of Jesus; the earliest, by Mark, is dated about A.D. 70, and the latest, by John, about A.D. 100. They are not, moreover, attempts at simply describing the life of Jesus with historical accuracy; they are statements of faith by true believers. The authors of the Gospels believed that Jesus was the son of God and that he had come into the world to redeem humanity and to bring immortality to those who believed in him and followed his way; to the Gospel writers, Jesus' resurrection was striking proof of his teachings. At the same time, the Gospels regard Jesus as a figure in history, and they recount events in his life as well as his sayings. To distinguish historical fact from myth and religious doctrine is not easy, but there is agreement on some of the basic points.

Mark Describes the Resurrection of Jesus

Belief that Jesus rose from the dead after his Crucifixion (about A.D. 30) was and is central to traditional Christian doctrine. The record of the Resurrection in the Gospel of Mark, written a generation later (toward A.D. 70), is the earliest we have. The significance to most Christian groups revolves about the assurance given them that death and the grave are not final and that, instead, salvation for a future life is possible. The appeal of these views was to be nearly universal in the West during the Middle Ages. The church was commonly thought to be the means of implementing the promise of salvation; hence the enormous importance of the church's sacramental system, its rules, and its clergy.

And when evening had come, since it was the day of Preparation, that is, the day before the sabbath, Joseph of Arimathea, a respected member of the council, who was also himself looking for the kingdom of God, took courage and went to Pilate, and asked for the body of Jesus. And Pilate wondered if he were already dead; and summoning the centurion, he asked him whether he was already dead. And when he learned from the centurion that he was dead, he granted the body to Joseph. And he bought a linen shroud, and taking him down, wrapped him in the linen shroud, and laid him in a tomb which had been hewn out of the rock; and he rolled a stone against the door of the tomb. Mary Magdalene and Mary the mother of Jesus saw where he was laid.

And when the sabbath was past, Mary Magdalene, and Mary the mother of James, and Salome, bought spices, so that they might go and anoint him. And very early on the first day of the week they went to the tomb when the sun had risen. And they were saying to one another, "Who will roll away the stone for us from the door of the tomb?" And looking up, they saw that the stone was rolled back; for it was very large. And entering the tomb, they saw a young man sitting on the right side, dressed in a white robe; and they were amazed. And he said to them, "Do not be amazed; you seek Jesus of Nazareth, who was crucified. He has risen, he is not here, see the place where they laid him. But go, tell his disciples and Peter that he is going before you to Galilee; there you will see him, as he told you." And they went out and fled from the tomb; for trembling and astonishment had come upon them; and they said nothing to any one, for they were afraid.

Gospel of Mark 15:42–47; 16:1–8, *Revised Standard Version of the Bible* (New York: Thomas Nelson and Sons, 1946, 1952).

Early Christian art showing Christ arrested by soldiers on the night before his crucifixion. Note that Christ is portrayed clean-shaven and dressed in the toga of a Roman aristocrat. [*Hirmir Fotoarchiv*]

There is no reason to doubt that Jesus was born in the province of Judaea in the time of Augustus and that he was a most effective teacher in the tradition of the prophets. This tradition promised the coming of a Messiah (in Greek, *christos*—so *Jesus Christ* means "Jesus the Messiah"), the redeemer who would make Israel triumph over its enemies and establish the kingdom of God on earth. In fact, Jesus seems to have insisted that the Messiah would not establish an earthly kingdom but would bring an end to the world as human beings knew it at the Day of Judgment. On that day God would reward the righteous with immortality and happiness in heaven and condemn the wicked to eternal suffering in hell. Until that day, which his followers believed would come very soon, Jesus taught the faithful to abandon sin and worldly concerns; to follow him and his way; to follow the moral code described in the Sermon on the Mount, which preached love, charity, and humility; and to believe in him and his divine mission.

Jesus had success and won a considerable following, especially among the poor. This success caused great suspicion among the upper classes. His novel message and his criticism of the current religious practices connected with the temple at Jerusalem and its priests provoked the hostility of the religious establishment. A misunderstanding of the movement made it easy to convince the Roman governor that Jesus and his followers might be dangerous revolutionaries. He was put to death in Jerusalem by the cruel and degrading device of crucifixion, probably in A.D. 30. His followers believed that he was resurrected on the third day after his death, and that belief became a critical element in the religion that they propagated throughout the Roman Empire and beyond.

Although the new belief spread quickly to the Jewish communities of Syria and Asia Minor, there is reason to believe that it might have had only a short life as a despised Jewish heresy were it not for the conversion and career of Saint Paul.

Paul of Tarsus

Paul was born Saul, a citizen of the Cilician city of Tarsus in Asia Minor. Even though he had been trained in Hellenistic culture and was a Roman citizen, he was a zealous member of the Jewish sect known as the Pharisees, the group that was most strict in its insistence on adherence to the Jewish law. He took a vigorous part in the persecution of the early Christians until his own conversion outside Damascus about A.D. 35. The great problem facing the early Christians was their relationship to Judaism. If the new faith was a version of Judaism, then it must adhere to the Jewish law and seek converts only among Jews. James, called the brother of Jesus, was a conservative who held to that view, whereas the Hellenist Jews tended to see it as a new and universal religion. To force all converts to adhere to Jewish law would have been fatal to the growth of the new sect, for its many technicalities and dietary prohibitions were strange to gentiles, and the necessity of circumcision—a frightening, painful, and dangerous operation for adults—would have been a tremendous deterrent to conversion. Paul, converted and with his new name, supported the position of the Hellenists and soon won many converts among the gentiles. After some conflict within the sect, Paul won out, and the "apostle to the gentiles" deserves recognition as a crucial contributor to the success of Christianity.

Paul believed it important that the followers of Jesus be evangelists (messengers), to spread the gospel ("good news") of God's gracious gift, for he taught that Jesus would soon return for the Day of Judgment, and it was important that all who would should believe in him and accept his way. Faith in Jesus as the Christ was necessary but not sufficient for salvation, nor could good deeds alone achieve it. That final blessing of salvation was a gift of God's grace that would be granted to some but not to all.

Organization

Paul and the other apostles did their work well, and the new religion spread throughout the Roman Empire and even beyond its borders. It had its greatest success in the cities and for the most part among the poor and uneducated. The rites of the early communities appear to have been simple and few. Baptism by water removed original sin and permitted participation in the community and its activities. The central ritual was a common meal called the *agape* ("love feast"), followed by the ceremony of the *eucharist* ("thanksgiving"), a celebration of the Lord's Supper in which unleavened bread was eaten and unfermented wine was drunk. There were also prayers, hymns, and readings from the Gospels.

Not all the early Christians were poor, and it became customary for the rich to provide for the poor at the common meals. The sense of common love fostered in these ways focused the community's attention on the needs of the weak, the sick, the unfortunate, and the unprotected. This concern gave the early Christian communities a warmth and a human appeal that stood in marked contrast to the coldness and impersonality of the pagan cults. No less attractive were the promise of salvation, the importance to God of each individual human soul, and the spiritual equality of all in the new faith. As Paul put it, "There is neither Jew nor Greek, there is neither slave nor free, there is neither male nor female; for you are all one in Christ Jesus."[4]

The future of Christianity depended on its communities' finding an organization that would preserve unity within the group and help protect it against enemies outside. At first, the churches had little formal organization. Soon, it appears, affairs were placed in the hands of boards of *presbyters* ("elders") and *deacons* ("those who serve"). By the second century A.D., as their numbers grew, the Christians of each city tended to accept the authority and leadership of bishops (*episkopoi*, or "overseers"), who were elected by the congregation to lead them in worship and to supervise funds. As time passed, the bishops extended their authority over the Christian communities in outlying towns and the countryside. The power and almost monarchical authority of the bishops was soon enhanced by the doctrine of Apostolic Succession, which asserted that the

[4]Galatians 3:28. *Revised Standard Version of the Bible.*

powers that Jesus had given his original disciples were passed on from bishop to bishop by ordination.

The bishops kept in touch with one another, maintained communications between different Christian communities, and prevented doctrinal and sectarian splintering, which would have destroyed Christian unity. They maintained internal discipline and dealt with the civil authorities. After a time they began the practice of coming together in councils to settle difficult questions, to establish orthodox opinion, and even to expel as heretics those who would not accept it. It seems unlikely that Christianity could have survived the travails of its early years without such strong internal organization and government.

A Roman painting on glass of Saints Peter and Paul. [Metropolitan Museum of Art, Rogers Fund, 1916]

The Persecution of Christians

The new faith soon incurred the distrust of the pagan world and of the imperial government. At first Christians were thought of as a Jewish sect and were therefore protected by

Nero's Persecution of Christians

In the year A.D. 64 a terrible fire broke out in the city of Rome. The people blamed the Emperor Nero, and to divert suspicion from himself, he launched the first official prosecutions of Christians by the Roman government.

. . . All human efforts, all the lavish gifts of the emperor, and the propitiations of the gods, did not banish the sinister belief that the conflagration was the result of an order. Consequently, to get rid of the report, Nero fastened the guilt and inflicted the most exquisite tortures on a class hated for their abominations, called Christians by the populace. Christus, from whom the name had its origin, suffered the extreme penalty during the reign of Tiberius at the hands of one of our procurators, Pontius Pilatus, and a most mischievous superstition, thus checked for the moment, again broke out not only in Judaea, the first source of the evil, but even in Rome, where all things hideous and shameful from every part of the world find their centre and become popular. Accordingly, an arrest was first made of all who pleaded guilty; then, upon their information, an immense multitude was convicted, not so much of the crime of firing the city, as of hatred against mankind. Mockery of every sort was added to their deaths. Covered with the skins of beasts, they were torn by dogs and perished, or were nailed to crosses, or were doomed to the flames and burnt, to serve as a nightly illumination, when daylight had expired.

Nero offered his gardens for the spectacle, and was exhibiting a show in the circus, while he mingled with the people in the dress of a charioteer or stood aloft on a car. Hence, even for criminals who deserved extreme and exemplary punishment, there arose a feeling of compassion; for it was not, as it seemed, for the public good, but to glut one man's cruelty, that they were being destroyed.

Tacitus, *Annals*, 15. 44, trans. by A. J. Church and W. J. Brodribb.

Roman law. It soon became clear, however, that they were something quite different. They seemed both mysterious and dangerous. They denied the existence of the pagan gods and so were accused of atheism. Their refusal to worship the emperor was judged to be treason. Because they kept mostly to themselves, took no part in civic affairs, engaged in secret rites, and had an organized network of local associations, they were misunderstood and suspected. The love feasts were erroneously reported to be scenes of sexual scandal, and the alarming doctrine of the actual presence of Jesus' body in the eucharist was distorted into an accusation of cannibalism. The privacy and secrecy of Christian life and worship ran counter to a traditional Roman dislike of any private association, especially any of a religious nature, and the Christians thus earned the reputation of being "haters of humanity." Claudius expelled them from the city of Rome, and Nero tried to make them scapegoats for the great fire that struck the city in A.D. 64. By the end of the first century "the name alone"—that is, simple membership in the Christian community—was a crime.

But for the most part the Roman government did not take the initiative in attacking Christians in the first two centuries. When one of the emperor Trajan's governors sought instructions for dealing with the Christians, Trajan urged moderation: Christians were not to be sought out, anonymous accusations were to be disregarded, and anyone denounced could be acquitted merely by abjuring Christ and sacrificing to the emperor. Unfortunately no true Christian could meet the conditions, so there were some martyrdoms.

Most persecutions in this period, however, were instituted not by the government but by mob action. Though they lived quiet, inoffensive lives, some Christians must have seemed

Pliny and Trajan Discuss the Christians in the Empire

Pliny the Younger was the governor of the province of Bithynia in Asia Minor about A.D. 112. The following exchange between him and the Emperor Trajan is important evidence of imperial policy toward the Christians at the time.

TO THE EMPEROR TRAJAN

Having never been present at any trials of the Christians, I am unacquainted with the method and limits to be observed either in examining or punishing them.

. . . .

In the meanwhile, the method I have observed towards those who have been denounced to me as Christians is this: I interrogated them whether they were Christians; if they confessed it, I repeated the question twice again, adding the threat of capital punishment; if they still persevered, I ordered them to be executed. For whatever the nature of their creed might be, I could at least feel no doubt that contumacy and inflexible obstinacy deserved chastisement. There were others also possessed with the same infatuation, but being citizens of Rome, I directed them to be carried thither. . . .

TRAJAN TO PLINY

The method you have pursued, my dear Pliny, in sifting the cases of those denounced to you as Christians is extremely proper. It is not possible to lay down any general rule which can be applied as the fixed standard in all cases of this nature. No search should be made for these people, when they are denounced and found guilty they must be punished; with the restriction, however, that when the party denies himself to be a Christian, and shall give proof that he is not (that is, by adoring our Gods) he shall be pardoned on the ground of repentance, even though he may have formerly incurred suspicion. Informations without the accuser's name subscribed must not be admitted in evidence against anyone, as it is introducing a very dangerous precedent, and by no means agreeable to the spirit of the age.

Pliny the Younger, *Letters*, trans. by W. Melmoth, rev. by W. M. Hutchinson (London: William Heinemann, Ltd; Cambridge, Mass.: Harvard University Press, 1935), pp. 401, 403, 407.

unbearably smug and self-righteous. Unlike the tolerant, easygoing pagans, who were generally willing to accept the new gods of foreign people and add them to the pantheon, the Christians denied the reality of the pagan gods. They proclaimed the unique rightness of their own way and looked forward to their own salvation and the damnation of nonbelievers. It is not surprising, therefore, that pagans disliked these strange and unsocial people, tended to blame misfortunes on them, and, in extreme cases, turned to violence. But even this adversity had its uses. It weeded out the weaklings among the Christians, brought greater unity to those who remained faithful, and provided the church with martyrs around whom legends could grow that would inspire still greater devotion and dedication.

The Emergence of Catholicism

Division within the Christian church may have been an even greater threat to its existence than persecution from outside. The great majority of Christians never accepted complex, intellectualized opinions but held to what even then were traditional, simple, conservative beliefs. This body of majority opinion and the church that enshrined it came to be called *Catholic*, which means "universal." Its doctrines were deemed orthodox, whereas those holding contrary opinions were heretics.

The need to combat heretics, however, compelled the orthodox to formulate their own views more clearly and firmly. By the end of the second century A.D., an orthodox canon had been shaped that included the Old Testament, the Gospels, and the Epistles of Paul, among other writings. The process was not completed for at least two more centuries, but a vitally important start had been made. The orthodox declared the church itself to be the depository of Christian teaching and the bishops to be its receivers. They also drew up creeds, brief statements of faith to which true Christians should adhere. In the first century all that was required of one to be a Christian was to be baptized, to partake of the eucharist, and to call Jesus the Lord. By the end of the second century an orthodox Christian—that is, a member of the Catholic Church—was required to accept its creed, its canon of holy writings, and the authority of the bishops. The loose structure of the apostolic church had given way to an organized body with recognized leaders able to define its faith and to exclude those who did not accept it. Whatever the shortcomings of this development, there can be little doubt that it provided the clarity, unity, and discipline needed for survival.

Rome As a Center of the Early Church

During this same period the church in the city of Rome came to have special prominence. As the center of communications and the capital of the empire, Rome had natural advantages. After the Roman destruction of Jerusalem in 135 A.D., no other city had any convincing claim to primacy in the church. Besides having the largest single congregation of Christians, Rome also benefited from the tradition that both Jesus' apostles Peter and Paul were martyred there. Peter, moreover,

The Catacomb of the Jordani in Rome. The early Christians built miles of tunnels, called catacombs, in Rome. They were used as underground cemeteries and as refuges from persecution. [*Leonard von Matt.*]

was thought to be the first bishop of Rome, and the Gospel of Matthew (16:18) reported Jesus' statement to Peter: "Thou art Peter [in Greek, *Petros*] and upon this rock [in Greek, *petra*] I will build my church." Eastern Christians might later point out that Peter had been leader of the Christian community at Antioch before he went to Rome, but in the second century the church at Antioch, along with the other Christian churches of Asia Minor, was fading in influence, and by 200 A.D. Rome was the most important center of Christianity. Because of the city's early influence and because of the Petrine doctrine derived from the Gospel of Matthew, later bishops of Rome claimed supremacy in the Catholic Church, but as the era of the "good emperors" came to a close, this controversy was far in the future.

The Crisis of the Third Century

Dio Cassius, a historian of the third century A.D., wrote of the Roman Empire after the death of Marcus Aurelius as a decline from "a kingdom of gold into one of iron and rust," and though we have seen that the gold contained more than a little impurity, there is no reason to quarrel with Dio's assessment of his own time. Commodus (A.D. 180–192), the son of Marcus Aurelius, proved the wisdom of the "good emperors" in selecting their successors for their talents rather than for family ties, for Commodus was incompetent and autocratic. He reduced the respect in which the imperial office was held, and his assassination brought the return of civil war. Even an excellent emperor, however, would have had a difficult time as Rome's troubles, internal as well as external, grew.

Barbarian Invasions

The pressure on Rome's frontiers, already serious in the time of Marcus Aurelius, reached massive proportions in the third century. In the east the frontiers were threatened by a new power arising in the old Persian Empire. In the third century B.C. the Parthians had succeeded in making the Iranians independent of the Hellenistic kings and had established an empire of their own on the old foundations of the Persian Empire. Several Roman attempts to conquer them had failed, but as late as A.D. 198 the Romans were able to reach and destroy the Parthian capital and bring at least northern Mesopotamia under their rule. In A.D. 224, however, a new Iranian dynasty, the Sassanians, seized control from the Parthians and brought new vitality to Persia. They soon recovered Mesopotamia and made raids deep into Roman provinces. In A.D. 260 they humiliated the Romans by actually taking the Emperor Valerian prisoner; he died in captivity.

On the western and northern frontiers the pressure came not from a well-organized rival empire but from an ever-increasing number of German tribes. Though they had been in contact with the Romans at least since the second century B.C., they had not been much affected by civilization. The men did no agricultural work, confining their activities to hunting, drinking, and fighting. They were organized on a family basis by clans, hundreds, and tribes led by chiefs, usually from a royal family, elected by the assembly of fighting men. The king was surrounded by a collection of warriors, whom the Romans called his *comitatus*. These tough barbarians were always eager for plunder and were much attracted by the civilized delights they knew existed beyond the frontier of the Rhine and the Danube rivers.

The most aggressive of the Germans in the third century A.D. were the Goths. Centuries earlier they had wandered from their ancestral home near the Baltic Sea into the area of southern Russia. In the 220s and 230s A.D. they began to put pressure on the Danube frontier, and by about A.D. 250 they were able to penetrate into the empire and overrun the Balkan provinces. The need to meet this threat and the one posed by the Persian Sassanids in the east made the Romans weaken their western frontiers, and other Germanic peoples—the Franks and the Alemanni—broke through in those regions. There was a considerable danger that Rome would be unable to meet this challenge.

Rome's perils were caused, no doubt, by the unprecedentedly numerous and simultaneous attacks against her, but Rome's internal weakness encouraged these attacks. The Roman army was not what it had been in its best days. By the second century A.D. it was made up mostly of romanized provincials. The pressure on the frontiers and epidemics of plague in the time of Marcus Aurelius forced the emperor to resort to the conscription of slaves, gladiators, barbarians, and brigands. Even more important, the Romans failed to respond to the new conditions of constant pressure on all the frontiers. A strong, mobile reserve that could meet a threat in one place without causing a weakness elsewhere might have helped, but no such unit was created.

Septimius Severus (emperor A.D. 193–211) and his successors played a crucial role in the transformation of the character of the Roman army. Septimius was a military usurper who owed everything to the support of his soldiers. He meant to establish a family dynasty, in contrast to the policy of the "good emperors" of the second century, and he was prepared to make Rome into an undisguised military monarchy. Septimius drew recruits for the army increasingly from peasants of the less civilized provinces, and the result was a barbarization of Rome's military forces.

Reigns of Selected Late Empire Rulers (All dates are A.D.)

Commodus	180–192
Septimius Severus	193–211
Alexander Severus	222–235
Decius	249–251
Valerian	253–260
Gallienus	253–268
Claudius II Gothicus	268–270
Aurelian	270–275
Diocletian	284–305
Constantine	306–337
Constantine sole emperor	324–337
Constantius II	337–361
Julian the Apostate	361–363
Valentinian	364–375
Valens	364–378
Theodosius	379–395

Economic Difficulties

These changes were a response to the great financial needs caused by the barbarian attacks. Inflation had forced Commodus to raise the soldiers' pay, but the Severan emperors had to double it to keep up with prices, which increased the imperial budget by as much as 25 per cent. The emperors resorted to inventing new taxes, debasing the coinage, and even to selling the palace furniture, to raise money. Even then it was hard to recruit troops, and the new style of military life introduced by Septimius—with its laxer discipline, more pleasant duties, and greater opportunity for advancement, not only in the army but in Roman society—was needed to attract men into the army. The policy proved effective for a short time but could not prevent the chaos of the late third century.

The same forces that caused problems for the army did great damage to society at large. The shortage of workers reduced agricultural pro-

Roman tax collectors. The economic, military, and social problems of the third century forced the emperors to increase the burden of taxation, which fell with increasing severity on the middle and upper classes of the provinces. [*Trier Museum*]

duction. As external threats distracted the emperors, they were less able to preserve domestic peace. Piracy, brigandage, and the neglect of roads and harbors all hampered trade. So, too, did the debasement of the coinage and the inflation in general. Imperial exactions and confiscations of the property of the rich removed badly needed capital from productive use. More and more the government was required to demand services that had been given gladly in the past. Because the empire lived hand-to-mouth, with no significant reserve fund and no system of credit financing, the emperors were led to compel the people to provide food, supplies, money, and labor. The upper classes in the cities were made to serve as administrators without pay and to meet deficits in revenue out of their own pockets. Sometimes these demands caused provincial rebellions, as in Egypt and Gaul. More typically they caused peasants and even town administrators to flee to escape their burdens. The result of all these difficulties was to weaken Rome's economic strength when it was most needed.

The Social Order

The new conditions caused important changes in the social order. The Senate and the traditional ruling class were decimated by direct attacks from hostile emperors and by economic losses. Their ranks were filled by men coming up through the army. The whole state began to take on an increasingly military appearance. Distinctions among the classes by dress had been traditional since the republic, but in the third and fourth centuries A.D. they developed to the point where the people's everyday clothing was a kind of uniform that precisely revealed their status. Titles were assigned to ranks in society as to ranks in the army, although they were more grandiloquent. The most important distinction was the one formally established by Septimius Severus, which drew a sharp line between the *honestiores* (senators, equestrians, the municipal aristocracy, and the soldiers) and the lower classes, or *humiliores*. Septimius gave the *honestiores* a privileged position before the law. They were given lighter punishments, could not be tortured, and alone had the right of appeal to the emperor.

As time passed, it became more difficult to move from the lower order to the higher, another example of the growing rigidity of the late Roman Empire. Peasants were tied to their lands, artisans to their crafts, soldiers to the army, merchants and shipowners to the needs of the state, and citizens of the municipal upper class to the collection and payment of increasingly burdensome taxes. Freedom and private initiative gave way before the needs of the state and its ever-expanding control of its citizens.

Civil Disorder

Commodus was killed on the last day of A.D. 192, and the succeeding year was like the year 69: three emperors ruled in swift succession, Septimius Severus emerging, as we have seen, to establish firm rule and a dynasty. The death of Alexander Severus, the last of the dynasty, in A.D. 235 brought on a half century of internal anarchy and foreign invasion.

The empire seemed on the point of collapse, but the two conspirators who overthrew and then succeeded Gallienus were able soldiers. Claudius II Gothicus (A.D. 268–270) and Aurelian (A.D. 270–275) drove back the barbarians and stamped out internal disorder. The soldiers who followed Aurelian on the throne were good fighters and made significant changes in Rome's system of defense. They built heavy walls around Rome, Athens, and other cities that could resist barbarian attack. They drew back their best troops from the frontiers, relying chiefly on a newly organized heavy cavalry and a mobile army near the emperor's own residence. Hereafter the army was composed largely of mercenaries who came from among the least civilized provincials and even from among the Germans. The officers gave personal loyalty to the emperor rather than to the empire. These officers became a foreign, hereditary caste of aristocrats that increasingly supplied high administrators and even emperors. In effect, the Roman people hired an army of mercenaries, only technically Roman, to protect them.

The Fourth Century and Imperial Reorganization

The period from Diocletian (A.D. 284–305) to Constantine (A.D. 306–337) was one of reconstruction and reorganization after a time of civil war and turmoil. Diocletian was from Illyria (now Yugoslavia), a man of undistinguished birth who rose to the throne through the ranks of the army. He knew that he was not a great general and that the job of defending and governing the entire empire was too great for one man. He therefore decreed the introduction of the tetrarchy, the rule of the empire by four men with power divided on a territorial basis (see Map 5.4). Diocletian allotted the provinces of Thrace, Asia, and Egypt to himself. His co-emperor, Maximian, shared with him the title of Augustus and governed Italy, Africa, and Spain. In addition, two men were given the subordinate title of Caesar:

MAP 5-4 *Diocletian divided the sprawling empire into four prefectures for more effective government and defense. The inset map shows their boundaries, and the larger map gives some details of regions and provinces. The major division between East and West was along the broken line running south between Pannonia and Moesia.*

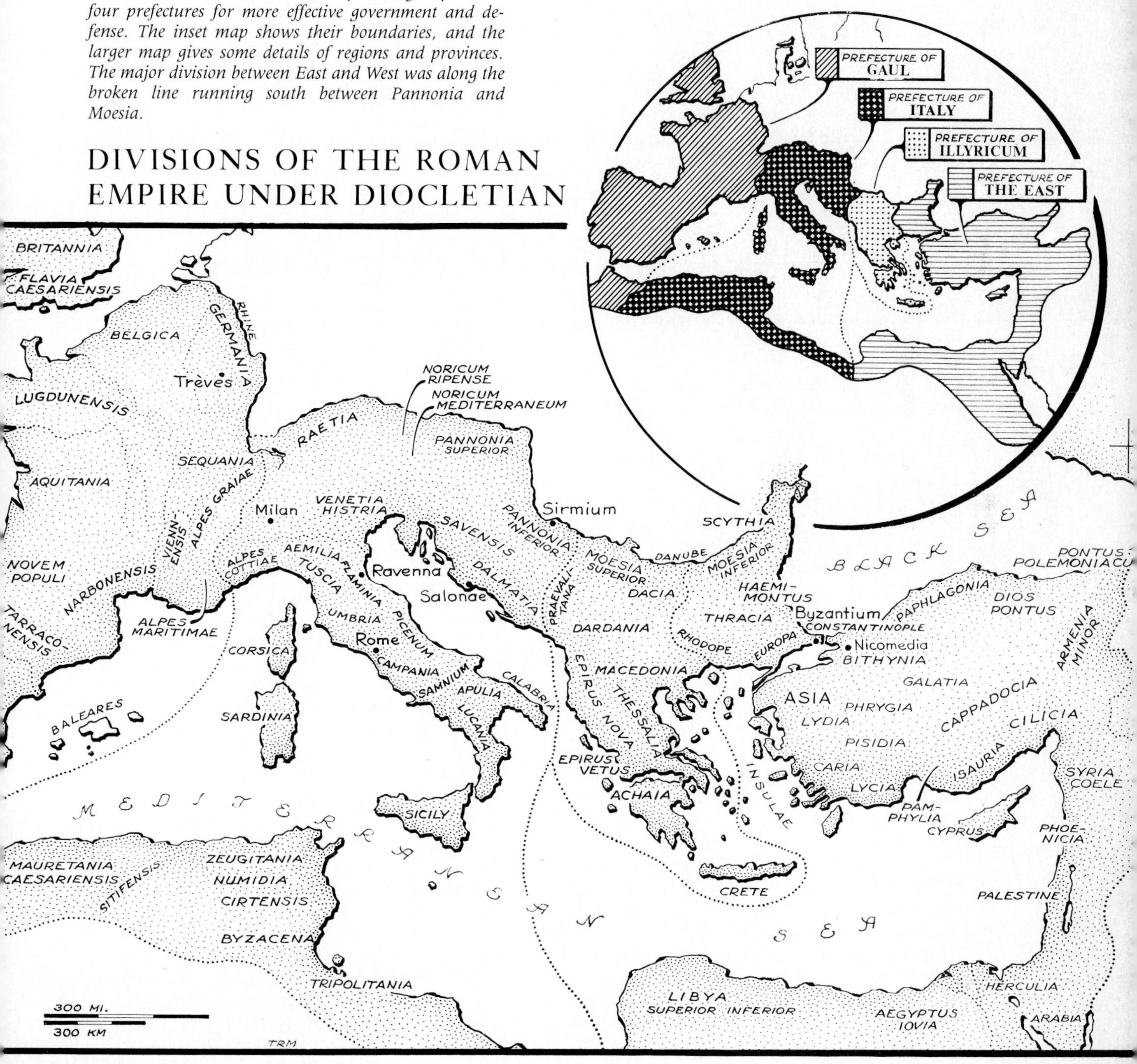

The Tetrarchs. This porphyry sculpture on the corner of the church of San Marco in Venice depicts Emperor Diocletian (234–305) *and his three imperial colleagues. They are in battle dress and clasp one another to express solidarity. This fourth-century sculpture was part of the booty brought back by the Venetians from their capture of Constantinople during the Fourth Crusade about nine hundred years later.* [*AHM*]

Galerius, who was in charge of the Danube frontier and the Balkans, and Constantius, who governed Britain and Gaul. This arrangement not only provided a good solution to the military problem but also provided for a peaceful succession. Diocletian was recognized as the senior Augustus, but each tetrarch was supreme in his own sphere. The Caesars were recognized as successors to each half of the empire, and their loyalty was enhanced by marriages to daughters of the Augusti. It was a return, in a way, to the happy precedent of the "good emperors," who chose their successors from the ranks of the ablest men, and it seemed to promise orderly and peaceful transitions instead of assassinations, chaos, and civil war.

Each man established his residence and capital at a place convenient for frontier defense, and none chose Rome. The effective capital of Italy became the northern city of Milan. Diocletian beautified Rome by constructing his monumental baths, but he visited the city only once and made his own capital at Nicomedia in Bithynia. This was another step in the long leveling process that had reduced the eminence of Rome and Italy, and it was also evidence of the growing importance of the east.

In 305 Diocletian retired and compelled his co-emperor to do the same. But his plan for a smooth succession failed completely. In 310 there were five Augusti and no Caesars. Out of this chaos Constantine, son of Constantius, produced order. In 324 he defeated his last opponent and made himself sole emperor, uniting the empire once again; he reigned until 337. For the most part Constantine carried forward the policies of Diocletian. The one exception was his support of Christianity, which Diocletian had tried to suppress.

The development of the imperial office toward autocracy was carried to the extreme by Diocletian and Constantine. The emperor ruled by decree, consulting only a few high officials, whom he himself appointed. The Senate had no role whatever, and its dignity was further diminished by the elimination of all distinction between senator and equestrian.

The emperor was a remote figure surrounded by carefully chosen high officials. He lived in a great palace and was almost unapproachable. Those admitted to his presence had to prostrate themselves before him and kiss the hem of his robe, which was purple and had golden threads going through it. The emperor was addressed as *dominus* ("lord"), and his right to rule was not derived from the Roman people but from God. All this remoteness and ceremony had a double purpose: to enhance the dignity of the emperor and to safeguard him against assassination.

Constantine erected the new city of Constantinople on the site of ancient Byzantium on the Bosporus, which leads to both the Aegean and Black seas, and made it the new capital of the empire. Its strategic location was excellent for protecting the eastern and Danubian fron-

Diocletian Attempts to Control Prices and Wages

Rome's troubles in the third century A.D. caused serious economic problems. Debased currency and vast government expenditures produced a runaway inflation. In an attempt to control it, Diocletian took the unprecedented step of issuing a decree that put ceilings on prices and wages throughout the empire in the year 301. In spite of the most drastic penalties prescribed by the decree, it was widely evaded. After a time its failure was acknowledged, and the decree was at last revoked.

. . . Who does not know that wherever the common safety requires our armies to be sent, the profiteers insolently and covertly attack the public welfare, not only in villages and towns, but on every road? They charge extortionate prices for merchandise, not just fourfold or eightfold, but on such a scale that human speech cannot find words to characterize their profit and their practices. Indeed, sometimes in a single retail sale a soldier is stripped of his donative and pay. Moreover, the contributions of the whole world for the support of the armies fall as profits into the hands of these plunderers, and our soldiers appear to bestow with their own hands the rewards of their military service and their veterans' bonuses upon the profiteers. The result is that the pillagers of the state itself seize day by day more than they know how to hold.

Aroused justly and rightfully by all the facts set forth above, and in response to the needs of mankind itself, which appears to be praying for release, we have decided that maximum prices of articles for sale must be established. We have not set down fixed prices, for we do not deem it just to do this, since many provinces occasionally enjoy the good fortune of welcome low prices and the privilege, as it were, of prosperity. Thus, when the pressure of high prices appears anywhere—may the gods avert such a calamity!—avarice . . . will be checked by the limits fixed in our statute and by the restraining curbs of the law.

It is our pleasure, therefore, that the prices listed in the subjoined schedule be held in observance in the whole of our Empire. And every person shall take note that the liberty to exceed them at will has been ended, but that the blessing of low prices has in no way been impaired in those places where supplies actually abound. . . . Moreover, this universal edict will serve as a necessary check upon buyers and sellers whose practice it is to visit ports and other provinces. For when they too know that in the pinch of scarcity there is no possibility of exceeding the prices fixed for commodities, they will take into account in their calculations at the time of sale the localities, the transportation costs, and all other factors. In this way they will make apparent the justice of our decision that those who transport merchandise may not sell at higher prices anywhere.

It is agreed that even in the time of our ancestors it was the practice in passing laws to restrain offenses by prescribing a penalty. For rarely is a situation beneficial to humanity accepted spontaneously; experience teaches that fear is the most effective regulator and guide for the performance of duty. Therefore it is our pleasure that anyone who resists the measures of this statute shall be subject to a capital penalty for daring to do so. And let no one consider the statute harsh, since there is at hand a ready protection from danger in the observance of moderation. . . . We therefore exhort the loyalty of all, so that a regulation instituted for the public good may be observed with willing obedience and due scruple, especially as it is seen that by a statute of this kind provision has been made, not for single municipalities and peoples and provinces but for the whole world. . . .

"Diocletian's Edict on Maximum Prices," from the *Corpus Inscriptionum Latinarum,* Vol. 3, in N. Lewis and M. Reinhold, *Roman Civilization,* Vol. 2 (New York: Columbia University Press, 1955), pp. 465–466.

tiers, and, surrounded on three sides by water, it was easily defended. This location also made it easier to carry forward the policies of fostering autocracy and Christianity. Rome was full of tradition, the center of senatorial and even republican memories and of pagan worship. Constantinople was free from both, and its dedication in A.D. 330 marked the beginning of a new era. Until its fall to the Turks in 1453, it served as the bastion of civilization, the preserver of classical culture, a bulwark against barbarian attack, and the greatest city in Christendom.

The autocratic rule of the emperors was carried out by a civilian bureaucracy, which was carefully separated from the military service to reduce the chances of rebellion by anyone combining the two kinds of power. Below the emperor's court the most important officials were the praetorian prefects, each of whom administered one of the four major areas into which the empire was divided: Gaul, Italy, Illyricum, and the Orient. The four prefectures were subdivided into twelve territorial units called *dioceses*, each under a vicar who was subordinate to the prefect. The dioceses were further divided into almost a hundred provinces, each under a provincial governor.

The operation of the entire system was supervised by a vast system of spies and secret police, without whom the increasingly rigid totalitarian organization could not be trusted to perform. In spite of these efforts, the system was filled with corruption and inefficiency.

The cost of maintaining a 400,000-man army as well as the vast civilian bureaucracy, the expensive imperial court, and the imperial taste for splendid buildings put a great strain on an already weak economy. Diocletian's attempts at establishing a uniform and reliable currency failed and merely led to increased inflation. To deal with it, he resorted to price control with his Edict of Maximum Prices in 301. For each product and each kind of labor, a maximum price was set, and violations were punishable by death. The edict failed despite the harshness of its provisions.

Peasants unable to pay their taxes and officials unable to collect them tried to escape, and Diocletian resorted to stern regimentation to keep all in their places and at the service of the government. The terror of the third century had turned many peasants into *coloni*, tenant farmers who fled for protection to the *villa* ("country estate") of a large and powerful landowner. They were tied to the land, as were their descendants, as the caste system hardened.

Division of the Empire

The peace and unity established by Constantine did not last long. His death was followed by a struggle for succession that was won by Constantius II (337–361), whose death, in turn, left the empire to his young cousin Julian (361–363), called by the Christians "the Apostate" because of his attempt to stamp out Christianity and restore paganism. Julian undertook a campaign against Persia with the aim of putting a Roman on the throne of the Sassanids and ending the Persian menace once and for all. He penetrated deep into Persia but was killed in battle. His death put an end to the expedition and to the pagan revival.

The Germans in the west took advantage of the eastern campaign to attack along the Rhine River and the upper Danube River, but even greater trouble was brewing along the middle and upper Danube (see Map 5.5). That territory was occupied by the eastern Goths, the Ostrogoths. They were being pushed hard by their western cousins, the Visigoths, who in turn had been driven from their home in the Ukraine by the fierce Huns, a nomadic people from central Asia. The Emperor Valentinian (364–375) saw that he could not defend the empire alone and appointed his brother Valens (364–378) as co-ruler. Valentinian made his own headquarters at Milan and spent the rest of his life fighting successfully against the Franks and the Alemanni in the west. Valens was given control of the east. The empire was once again divided in two. The two emperors maintained their own courts, and the two halves of the empire became increasingly separate and different. Latin was the language of the west and Greek of the east.

In 376 the hard-pressed Visigoths asked and received permission to enter the empire to escape the Huns. Contrary to the bargain, the Goths kept their weapons and began to plunder the Balkan provinces. Valens attacked the Goths and died, along with most of his army, at Adrianople in Thrace in 378. Theodosius (379–395), an able and experienced general, was named co-ruler in the east. By a combination of military and diplomatic skills Theodosius pacified the Goths, giving them land and a high degree of autonomy and enrolling many of them in his army. He made important military reforms, putting greater emphasis on the cav-

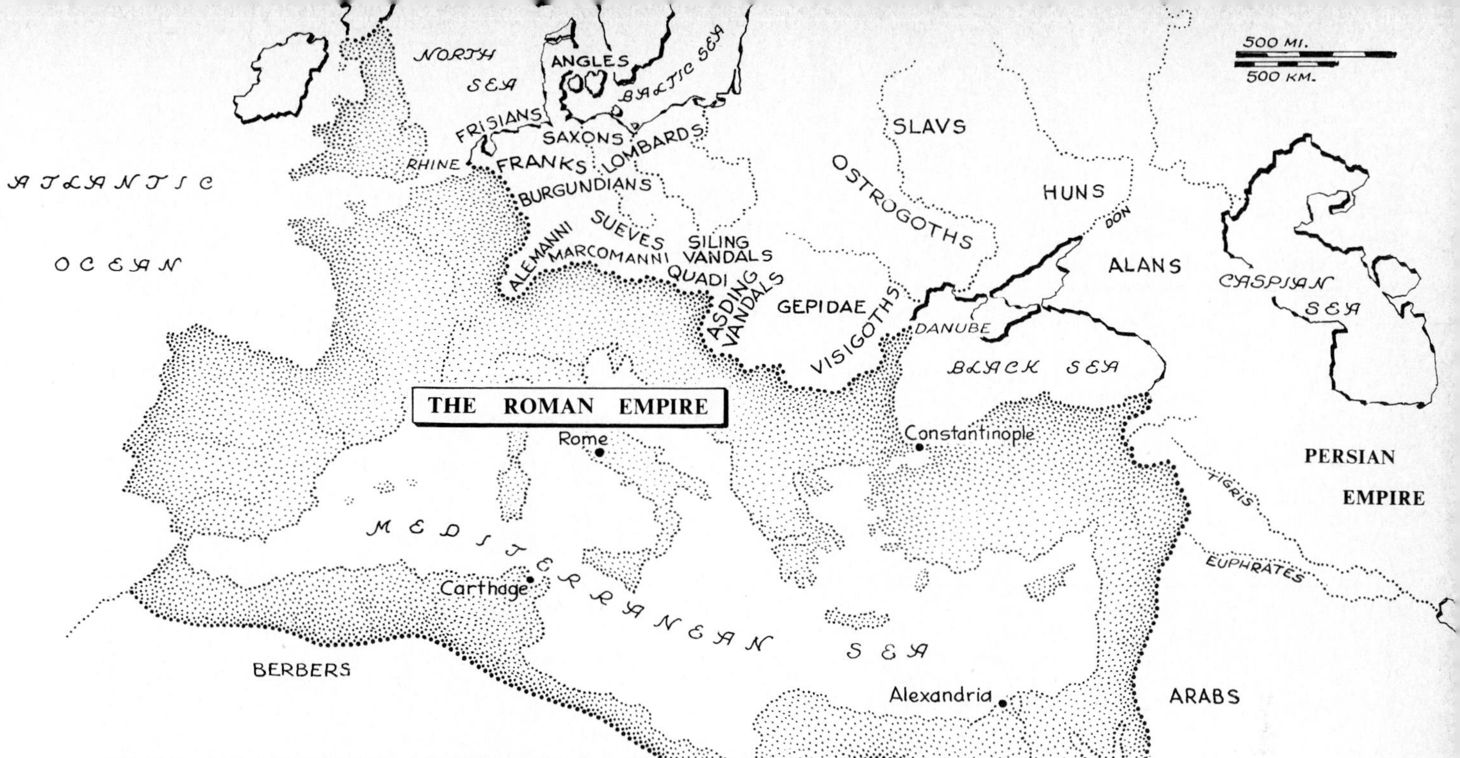

THE EMPIRE'S NEIGHBORS

MAP 5-5 *In the fourth century the Roman Empire was nearly surrounded by ever more threatening neighbors. The map shows who these so-called barbarians were and where they lived before their armed contact with the Romans.*

alry. Theodosius tried to unify the empire again, but his death in 395 left it divided and weak.

For the future the two parts of the empire went their separate and different ways. The west became increasingly rural as barbarian invasions continued and grew in intensity. The *villa*, a fortified country estate, became the basic unit of life. There, *coloni* gave their services to the local magnate in return for economic assistance and protection from both barbarians and imperial officials. Many cities shrank to no more than tiny walled fortresses ruled by military commanders and bishops. The upper classes moved to the country and asserted ever greater independence of imperial authority. The failure of the central authority to maintain the roads and the constant danger from robber bands sharply curtailed trade and communications, forcing greater self-reliance and a more primitive style of life. The new world emerging in the west by the fifth century and after was increasingly made up of isolated units of rural aristocrats and their dependent laborers. The only institution providing a high

Theodosius the Great (379–395), shown here at the chariot races in Constantinople. Theodosius was virtually the last emperor to control both the eastern and western halves of the empire. [Hirmer Verlag, Munich]

degree of unity was the Christian Church. The pattern for the early Middle Ages in the west was already formed.

In the east the situation was quite different. Constantinople became the center of a vital and flourishing culture that we call *Byzantine* and that lasted until the fifteenth century. Because of its defensible location, the skill of its emperors, and the firmness and strength of its base in Asia Minor, it was able to deflect and repulse barbarian attacks. A strong navy allowed commerce to flourish in the eastern Mediterranean and, in good times, far beyond. Cities continued to prosper and the emperors

The Empire Tries to Control Corruption in the Governmental Bureaucracy

As the role of the government in the lives of the people grew, so did the size of its bureaucracy. Our documents indicate that a significant amount of financial corruption existed among government officials, and its amount seems to have grown at least as fast as the size of the bureaucracy itself. In 438 the Emperor Theodosius II (A.D. 408–450) published his important code of Roman law, which included the following provisions aimed at suppressing corruption.

The rapacious hands of the functionaries shall immediately stop, they shall stop, I say; for, if after due warning they do not stop, they shall be cut off with the sword. The curtain of the judge['s chamber] shall not be venal; entrance shall not be purchased; his private chamber shall not be notorious for its bids; the very sight of the governor shall not be at a price. The ears of the judge shall be open equally to the poorest as well as to the rich. The introduction of persons inside shall be free from depredation by the one who is called the office head; the assistants of the said office heads shall employ no extortion on litigants; the intolerable onslaught of the centurions and other officials who demand small and large sums shall be crushed; and the unsated greed of those who deliver records to litigants shall be restrained. The ever-watchful diligence of the governor shall see that nothing is taken from a litigant by the aforesaid classes of men. And if they imagine they had to demand something in connection with civil cases, armed punishment will be at hand to cut off the heads and necks of the scoundrels, for all persons who have suffered extortion will be given an opportunity to provide information for an investigation by the governors. And if they dissemble, we open to all persons the right of complaint thereon before the comites *of the provinces—or before the Praetorian prefects, if they are closer at hand—so that we may be informed by their referrals and may produce punishments for such villainy.*

Theodosian Code I. xxxii. I; A.D. 333

Through the fault of the procurators of the privy purse, of dyeworks, and of weaving establishments, our private substance is being diminished, the products manufactured in the weaving establishments are being ruined, and in the dyeworks the fraudulent admixture of impure dye produces blemishes. Such procurators shall abstain from the patronage whereby they obtain the aforementioned administrative positions, or, if they contravene this order, they shall be removed from the number of Roman citizens and beheaded.

Theodosian Code X. iv. I; A.D. 313 or 326

If any person is harassed by an agent or procurator of our privy purse, he shall not hesitate to lodge a complaint concerning his chicanery and depredations. When such a charge is proved, we sanction that such person as dares to contrive anything against a provincial shall be publicly burned, since graver punishment should be fixed against those who are under our jurisdiction and ought to observe our mandates.

Theodosian Code, in N. Lewis and M. Reinhold, *Roman Civilization,* Vol. 2 (New York: Columbia University Press, 1955), pp. 484–485.

Ammianus Marcellinus Describes the People Called Huns

Ammianus Marcellinus was born about A.D. 330 in Syria, where Greek was the language of his well-to-do family. After a military career and considerable travel, he lived in Rome and wrote an encyclopedic Latin history of the empire, covering the years 96–378 and giving a special emphasis to the difficulties of the fourth century. Here he describes the Huns, one of the barbarous peoples pressing on the frontiers.

The people called Huns, barely mentioned in ancient records, live beyond the sea of Azof, on the border of the Frozen Ocean, and are a race savage beyond all parallel. At the very moment of birth the cheeks of their infant children are deeply marked by an iron, in order that the hair, instead of growing at the proper season on their faces, may be hindered by the scars; accordingly the Huns grow up without beards, and without any beauty. They all have closely knit and strong limbs and plump necks; they are of great size, and low legged, so that you might fancy them two-legged beasts or the stout figures which are hewn out in a rude manner with an ax on the posts at the end of bridges.

They are certainly in the shape of men, however uncouth, and are so hardy that they neither require fire nor well-flavored food, but live on the roots of such herbs as they get in the fields, or on the half-raw flesh of any animal, which they merely warm rapidly by placing it between their own thighs and the backs of their horses.

They never shelter themselves under roofed houses, but avoid them, as people ordinarily avoid sepulchers as things not fit for common use. Nor is there even to be found among them a cabin thatched with reeds; but they wander about, roaming over the mountains and the woods, and accustom themselves to bear frost and hunger and thirst from their very cradles. . . .

There is not a person in the whole nation who cannot remain on his horse day and night. On horseback they buy and sell, they take their meat and drink, and there they recline on the narrow neck of their steed, and yield to sleep so deep as to indulge in every variety of dream.

And when any deliberation is to take place on any weighty matter, they all hold their common council on horseback. They are not under kingly authority, but are contented with the irregular government of their chiefs, and under their lead they force their way through all obstacles. . . .

Ammianus Marcellinus, *Res Gestae,* trans. by C. D. Yonge (London: George Bell and Son, 1862), pp. 312–314.

made their will good over the nobles in the countryside. The civilization of the Byzantine Empire was a unique combination of classical culture, the Christian religion, Roman law, and eastern artistic influences. While the west was being overrun by barbarians, the Roman Empire, in altered form, persisted in the east. While Rome shrank to an insignificant ecclesiastical town, Constantinople flourished as the seat of empire, the "New Rome," and the Byzantines called themselves "Romans." When we contemplate the decline and fall of the Roman Empire in the fourth and fifth centuries, we are speaking only of the west. A form of classical culture persisted in the Byzantine east for a thousand years more.

The Triumph of Christianity

Religious Currents in the Empire

The rise of Christianity to dominance in the empire was closely connected with the political and cultural experience of the third and fourth centuries. Political chaos and decentralization had religious and cultural consequences. In some of the provinces, native languages replaced Latin and Greek, sometimes even for official purposes, and the classical tradition that had been the basis of imperial life became the exclusive possession of a small, educated aristocracy. In religion the public cults had grown up in an urban environment and were largely political in character. As the importance of the cities diminished, so did the significance of their gods. People might still take comfort in the worship of the friendly, intimate deities of family, field, hearth, storehouse, and craft, but these were too petty to serve their needs in a confused and frightening world. The only universal worship was of the emperor, but he was far off, and obeisance to his cult was more a political than a religious act.

In the troubled times of the fourth and fifth centuries people sought powerful, personal deities who would bring them safety and prosperity in this world and immortality in the next. Paganism was open and tolerant, and it was by no means unusual for people to worship new deities alongside the old and even to intertwine elements of several to form a new amalgam by the device called *syncretism*.

Manichaeism was an especially potent rival of Christianity. Named for its founder, Mani, a Persian who lived in the third century A.D., it contained aspects of various religious traditions, including Zoroastrianism from Persia and both Judaism and Christianity. The Manichaeans pictured a world in which light and darkness, good and evil, were constantly at war. Good was spiritual and evil was material; because human beings were made of matter, their bodies were a prison of evil and darkness, but they also contained an element of light and good. The "Father of Goodness" had sent Mani, among other prophets, to free humanity and gain its salvation. To achieve salvation, humans must want to reach the realm of light and to abandon all physical desires. Manichaeans led an ascetic life and practiced a simple worship guided by a well-organized

Marble relief depicting the sacrifice of a bull. Animal sacrifice was an integral part of the official Roman cults and continued until all pagan ritual was banned by the emperor Theodosius in A.D. 394. [*Vatican Museum*]

church. The movement reached its greatest strength in the fourth and fifth centuries, and some of its central ideas persisted into the Middle Ages.

Obviously Christianity had something in common with these cults and answered many of the same needs felt by their devotees. There can be no doubt that Christianity's success owed something to the same causes as accounted for the popularity of these other cults, and they are often spoken of as its rivals. None of them, however, attained Christianity's universality, and none appears to have given the early Christians and their leaders as much competition as the ancient philosophies or the state religion.

Imperial Persecution

By the third century Christianity had taken firm hold in the eastern provinces and in Italy, though it had not made much headway in the west. Christian apologists pointed out that the Christians were good citizens who differed from others only in not worshipping the public gods. Until the middle of the third century the emperors tacitly accepted this view, without granting official toleration. As times became bad and the Christians became more numerous and visible, that policy changed. Popular opinion blamed disasters, natural and military, on the Christians. About 250 the Emperor Decius (249–251) invoked the aid of the gods in his war against the Goths and required that all citizens worship the state gods publicly. True Christians could not obey, and Decius instituted a major persecution. Many Christians, even some bishops, yielded to threats and torture, but others held out and were killed. Valerian (253–260) resumed the persecutions, partly in order to confiscate the wealth of rich Christians. His successors, however, found other matters more pressing, and the persecution lapsed until the end of the century.

By the time of Diocletian the number of Christians had grown still greater and included some high state officials. At the same time hostility to the Christians grew on every level. Diocletian was not generous toward unorthodox intellectual or religious movements, and his own effort to bolster imperial power with the aura of divinity boded ill for the church, yet he did not attack the Christians for almost twenty years. In 303, however, he launched the most serious persecution inflicted on the Christians in the Roman Empire. He issued a series of

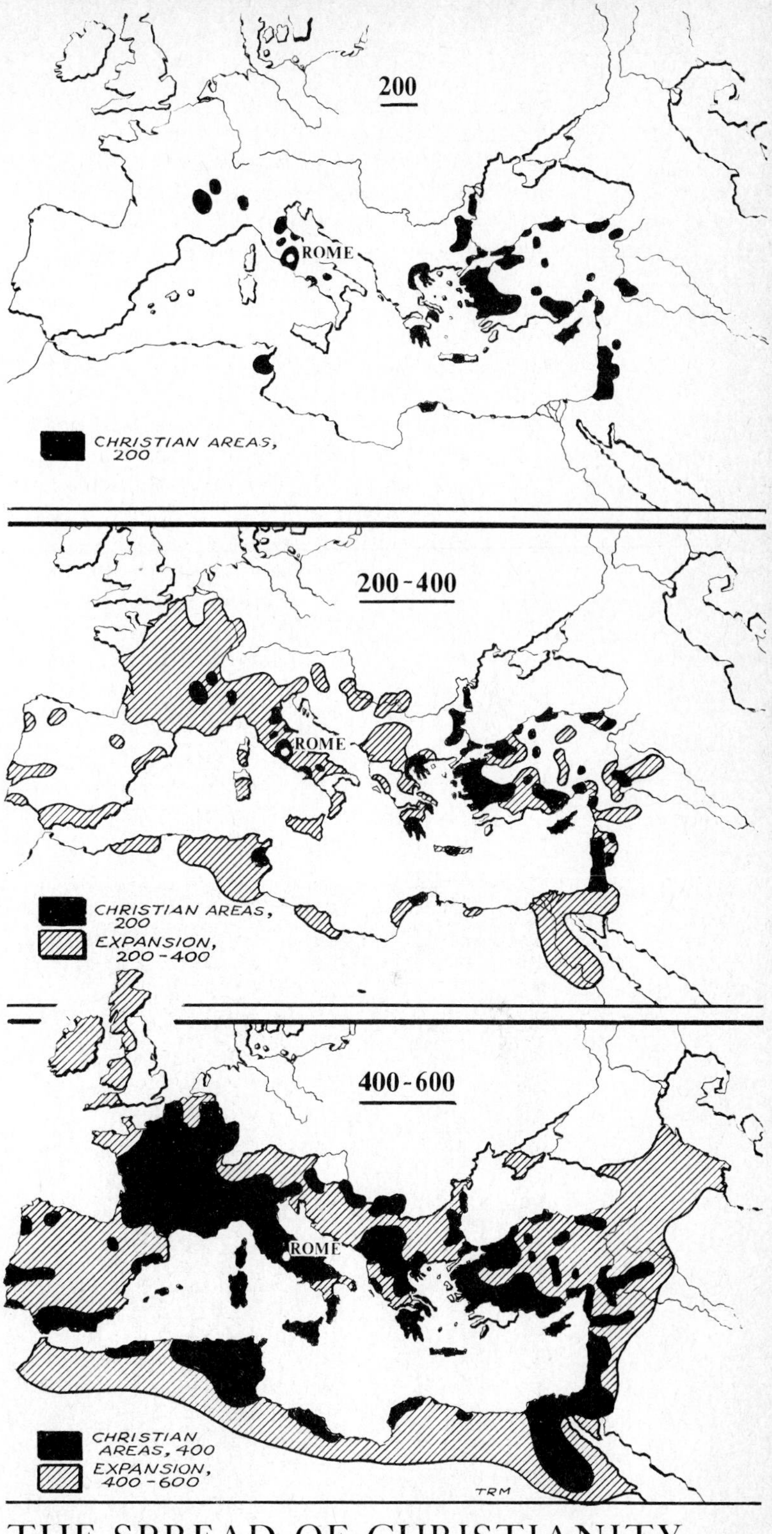

THE SPREAD OF CHRISTIANITY

MAP 5-6 *Christianity grew swiftly in the third, fourth, fifth, and sixth centuries—especially after the conversion of the emperors in the fourth century. By 600, on the eve of the birth of Mohammed's new Moslem religion, Christianity was dominant throughout the Mediterranean world and most of Western Europe.*

edicts confiscating church property and destroying churches and their sacred books; he deprived upper-class Christians of public office and judicial rights, imprisoned clergy, enslaved Christians of the lower classes, and placed heavy fines on anyone refusing to sacrifice to the public gods. A final decree required public sacrifices and libations. The decrees were harsh, and there were many Christian martyrs, but enforcement was by no means uniform. The edict against the upper classes was the one most easily and widely enforced, but the persecution horrified many pagans, and the plight and the demeanor of the martyrs often aroused pity and sympathy. For these reasons, as well as the incapacity of any large ancient state to carry out a program of terror with the thoroughness of modern totalitarian governments, the Christians and their church survived to enjoy what they must have considered a miraculous change of fortune. In 311 Galerius, who had been one of the most vigorous persecutors, was influenced, perhaps by his Christian wife, to issue an edict of toleration permitting Christian worship.

The victory of Constantine and his emergence as sole ruler of the empire changed the condition of Christianity from a precariously tolerated sect to the religion favored by the emperor and put it on the path to becoming the official and only legal religion in the empire.

Emergence of Christianity As the State Religion

The sons of Constantine continued to favor the new religion, but the succession of Julian the Apostate posed a new threat. He was a devotee of traditional classical pagan culture and, as a believer in Neoplatonism, an opponent of Christianity. Neoplatonism was a religious philosophy, or a philosophical religion, whose connection with Platonic teachings was dis-

The Neoplatonist philosopher Plotimus instructing his followers, from a third-century sarcophagus. [*German Archaeological Institute, Rome*]

tant. Its chief formulator was Plotinus (A.D. 205–270), who attempted to combine classical and rational philosophical speculation with the mystical spirit of his time. Plotinus' successors were bitter critics of Christianity, and Julian was influenced by their views. Though he refrained from persecution, he tried to undo the work of Constantine by withdrawing the privileges of the church, removing Christians from high offices, and attempting to introduce a new form of pagan worship. His reign, however, was short, and his work did not last.

In 394 Theodosius forbade the celebration of pagan cults and abolished the pagan religious calendar. At the death of Theodosius, Christianity was the official religion of the Roman Empire.

The establishment of Christianity as the state religion did not put an end to the troubles of the Christians and their church; instead it created new ones and complicated some that were old. The favored position of the church attracted converts for the wrong reasons and diluted the moral excellence and spiritual fervor of its adherents. The problem of the relationship between church and state arose, presenting the possibility that religion would become subordinate to the state, as it had been in the classical world and in earlier civilizations. In the east that is what happened to a considerable degree. In the west the weakness of the emperors prevented such a development and permitted church leaders to exercise remarkable independence. In 390 Ambrose, bishop of Milan, excommunicated Emperor Theodosius for a massacre he had carried out, and the emperor did humble penance. This act provided an important precedent for future assertions of the church's autonomy and authority, but it did not put an end to secular interference and influence in the church by any means.

Arianism and the Council of Nicaea

Internal divisions proved to be even more troubling as new heresies emerged. Because they threatened the unity of an empire that was now Christian, they took on a political character and inevitably involved the emperor and the powers of the state. Before long the world could view Christians persecuting other Christians with a zeal at least as great as had

The Council at Nicaea Creates the Test of Religious Orthodoxy

In A.D. 325 Emperor Constantine called a general council of leading Christians at Nicaea in Asia Minor in an attempt to end the quarreling over the question of the Trinity. The Nicene Creed was the result. Adherence to it became a test of orthodoxy, and those rejecting it were declared heretics.

We believe in one God, the Father Almighty, maker of all things visible and invisible; and in one Lord Jesus Christ, the Son of God, the only-begotten of his Father, of the substance of the Father, God of God, Light of Light; very God of very God, begotten not made, being of one substance with the Father, By whom all things were made, both which be in heaven and in earth. Who for us men and for our salvation came down [from heaven] and was incarnate and was made man. He suffered and the third day he rose again, and ascended into heaven. And he shall come again to judge both the quick and the dead. And [we believe] in the Holy Ghost. And whosoever shall say that there was time when the Son of God was not, or that before he was begotten he was not, or that he was made of things that were not, or that he is of a different substance or essence [from the Father] or that he is a creature, or subject to change or conversion—all that so say, the Catholic and Apostolic Church anathematizes them.

"The Nicene Creed," from *The Seven Ecumenical Councils,* Vol. 14, trans. by A. C. McGiffort and E. C. Richardson (New York: Library of the Nicene and Post-Nicene Fathers, 2nd Series, 1900), p. 3.

been displayed against them by the most fanatical pagans.

Among the many controversial views that arose, the most important and the most threatening was Arianism, founded by a priest named Arius of Alexandria (ca. 280–336) in the fourth century. The issue creating difficulty was the relation of God the Father and God the Son. Arius argued that Jesus was a created being, unlike God the Father. He was, therefore, not made of the substance of God and was not eternal. "The Son has a beginning," he said, "but God is without beginning." For Arius, Jesus was neither fully man nor fully God but something in between. Arius' view did away with the mysterious concept of the Trinity, the difficult doctrine that God is three persons (the Father, the Son, and the Holy Spirit) and at the same time one in substance and essence. The Arian concept had the advantage of appearing to be simple, rational, and philosophically acceptable, but to its ablest opponent, Athanasius, it had serious shortcomings. Athanasius (ca. 293–373), later bishop of Alexandria, saw the Arian view as an impediment to any acceptable theory of salvation, to him the most important religious question. He adhered to the old Greek idea of salvation as involving the change of sinful mortality into divine immortality through the gift of "life." Only if Jesus were both fully human and fully God could the transformation of humanity to divinity have taken place in him and be transmitted by him to his disciples. "Christ was made man," he said, "that we might be made divine."

To deal with the growing controversy, Constantine called a council of Christian bishops at Nicaea, not far from Constantinople, in 325. For the emperor the question was essentially political, but for the disputants salvation was at stake. At Nicaea the view expounded by Athanasius won out, became orthodox, and was embodied in the Nicene Creed. But Arianism persisted and spread. Some later emperors were either Arians or sympathetic to that view. Some of the most successful missionaries to the barbarians were Arians, with the result that many of the German tribes that overran the empire were Arians. The Christian emperors hoped to bring unity to their increasingly decentralized realms by imposing the single religion, and over time it did prove to be a unifying force, but it also introduced new divisions where none had existed before.

Arts and Letters in the Late Empire

The art and literature of the late empire reflect the confluence of pagan and Christian ideas and traditions as well as the conflict between them. Much of the literature is of a polemical nature and much of the art is propaganda. At the same time, the great social changes that began to accelerate in the third century had parallel effects.

The salvation of the empire from the chaos of the third century was accomplished by a military revolution based on and led by provincials whose origins were in the lower classes. They brought with them the fresh winds of cultural change, which blew out not only the dust of classical culture but much of its substance as well. Yet the new ruling class was not interested in leveling; it wanted instead to establish itself as a new aristocracy. It thought of itself as effecting a great restoration rather than a revolution and sought to restore classical culture and absorb it. The confusion and uncertainty of the times were tempered in part, of course, by the comfort of Christianity, but the new ruling class sought order and stability—ethical, literary, and artistic—in the classical tradition as well.

The Preservation of Classical Culture

One of the main needs and accomplishments of this period was the preservation of classical culture and the discovery of ways to make it available and useful to the newly arrived ruling class. The great classical authors were reproduced in many copies, and their works were transferred from perishable and inconvenient papyrus rolls to sturdier codices, bound volumes that were as easy to use as modern books. Scholars also digested long works like Livy's *History of Rome* into shorter versions and wrote learned commentaries and compiled grammars. Original works by pagan writers of the late empire were neither numerous nor especially distinguished.

Christian Writers

Of Christian writings, on the other hand, the late empire saw a great outpouring. There were many examples of Christian apologetics in poetry as well as in prose, and there were sermons, hymns, and biblical commentaries. Christianity could also boast important scholars, Jerome (348–420), thoroughly trained in both the east and the west in classical Latin literature and rhetoric, produced a revised version of the Bible in Latin, commonly called the Vulgate, which became the Bible used by the Catholic church. Probably the most important eastern scholar was Eusebius of Caesarea (ca. 260–ca. 340). He wrote apologetics; an idealized biography of Constantine; and a valuable attempt to reconstruct the chronology of important events in the past. His most important contribution, however, was his *Ecclesiastical History,* an attempt to set forth the Christian view of history. He saw all of history as the working out of God's will. All of history, therefore, had a purpose and a direction, and Constantine's victory and the subsequent unity of empire and church were its culmination.

Augustine of Hippo. The closeness and also the complexity of the relationship between classical pagan culture and that of the

Late Roman art was a transition between classical and medieval, pagan and Christian. These reliefs from the arch of Constantine, which was built in A.D. 313, *reveal the conflicting influences at work at the time. The circular medallion on the right depicts an emperor offering incense to Jupiter. The emperor is Hadrian, for whom the panel had originally been carved 200 years earlier. Although Constantine already sympathized with Christianity when the arch was built, he nonetheless incorporated this pagan religious scene in its structure.* [*EPA*]

Christianity of the late empire are nowhere better displayed than in the career and writings of Augustine (354–430), bishop of Hippo in north Africa. He was born at Carthage and was trained as a teacher of rhetoric. His father was a pagan, but his mother was a Christian and hers was ultimately the stronger influence. He passed through a number of intellectual way stations, skepticism and Neoplatonism among others, before his conversion to Christianity. His training and skill in pagan rhetoric and philosophy made him peerless among his contemporaries as a defender of Christianity and as a theologian. His greatest works are his *Confessions*, an autobiography describing the road to his conversion, and *The City of God*. The latter was a response to the pagan charge that Rome's sack by the Goths in 410 was caused by the abandonment of the old gods and the advent of Christianity. The optimistic view held by some Christians that God's will worked its way in history and was easily comprehensible needed further support in the face of this disaster. Augustine sought to separate the fate of Christianity from that of the Roman Empire. He contrasted the secular world, the City of Man, with the spiritual, the City of God. The former was selfish, the latter unselfish; the former evil, the latter good. Augustine argued that history was moving forward, in the spiritual sense, to the Day of Judgment but that there was no reason to expect improvement before then in the secular sphere. The fall of Rome was neither surprising nor important, for all states, even a Christian Rome, were part of the City of Man and therefore corrupt and mortal. Only the City of God was immortal, and it, consisting of all the saints on earth and in heaven, was untouched by earthly calamities.

Though the *Confessions* and *The City of God* are Augustine's most famous works, they emphasize only a part of his thought. His treatises *On the Trinity* and *On Christian Education* reveal the great skill with which he supported Christian belief with the learning, logic, and philosophy of the pagan classics. Augustine believed that faith is essential and primary, a thoroughly Christian view, but that it is not a substitute for reason, the foundation of classical thought. Instead, faith is the starting point for and liberator of human reason, which continues to be the means by which people can understand what is revealed by faith. His writings constantly reveal the presence of both Christian faith and pagan reason, as well as the tension between them, a legacy he left to the Middle Ages.

Problem of the Decline and Fall of the Empire in the West

Whether important to Augustine or not, the massive barbarian invasions of the fifth century put an end to effective imperial government in the west. For centuries people have speculated about the causes of the collapse of the ancient world. Every kind of reason has been put forward, and some suggestions seem to have nothing to do with reason at all. Soil exhaustion, plague, climatic change, and even poisoning caused by lead water pipes have been suggested as reasons for Rome's decline in population, vigor, and the capacity to defend itself. Some blame the institution of slavery and the failure to make advances in science and technology that they believe resulted from it. Others blame excessive government interference in the economic life of the empire, others the destruction of the urban middle class, the carrier of classical culture.

Perhaps a plausible explanation can be found that is more simple and obvious. It might begin with the observation that the growth of so mighty an empire as Rome's was by no means inevitable. Rome's greatness had come from conquests that provided the Romans with the means to expand still further, until there were not enough Romans to conquer and govern any more peoples and territory. When pressure from outsiders grew, the Romans lacked the resources to advance and defeat the enemy as in the past. The tenacity and success of their resistance for so long were remarkable. Without new conquests to provide the immense wealth needed for the defense and maintenance of internal prosperity, the Romans finally yielded to unprecedented onslaughts by fierce and numerous attackers.

To blame the ancients and the institution of slavery for the failure to produce an industrial and economic revolution like that of the later Western world, one capable of producing wealth without taking it from another, is to stand the problem on its head. No one yet has a satisfactory explanation for those revolutions, so it is improper to blame any institution or society for not achieving what has been achieved only once in human history, in what are still mysterious circumstances. Perhaps we would do well to think of the problem as Gibbon did:

The decline of Rome was the natural and inevitable effect of immoderate greatness. Prosperity ripened the principle of decay; the cause of the destruction multiplied with the extent of conquest; and, as soon as time or accident had removed the artificial supports, the stupendous fabric yielded to the pressure of its own weight. The story of the ruin is simple and obvious; and instead of inquiring why the Roman Empire was destroyed, we should rather be surprised that it had subsisted so long.[5]

[5]Edward Gibbon, *Decline and Fall of the Roman Empire,* 2nd ed., Vol. 4, ed. by J. B. Bury (London, 1909), pp. 173–174.

Suggested Readings

J. P. V. D. Balsdon, *Roman Women* (1962).

P. Brown, *Augustine of Hippo* (1967). A splendid biography.

P. Brown, *The World of Late Antiquity,* A.D. 150–750 (1971). A brilliant and readable essay.

J. Burckhardt, *The Age of Constantine the Great* (1956). A classic work by the Swiss cultural historian.

J. Carcopino, *Daily Life in Ancient Rome,* trans. by E. O. Lorimer (1940).

C. M. Cochrane, *Christianity and Classical Culture* (1957). A study of intellectual change in the late empire.

S. Dill, *Roman Society in the Last Century of the Western Empire* (1958).

E. R. Dodds, *Pagan and Christian in an Age of Anxiety* (1965). An original and perceptive study.

E. Gibbon, *The History of the Decline and Fall of the Roman Empire,* 7 vols., ed. by J. B. Bury, 2nd ed. (1909–1914). One of the masterworks of the English language.

T. Rice Holmes, *Architect of the Roman Empire,* 2 vols. (1928–1931). An account of Augustus' career in detail.

A. H. M. Jones, *The Later Roman Empire,* 3 vols. (1964). A comprehensive study of the period.

D. Kagan (Ed.), *The End of the Roman Empire: Decline or Transformation?,* 2nd. ed. (1978). A collection of essays discussing the problem of the decline and fall of the Roman Empire.

M. L. W. Laistner, *The Greater Roman Historians* (1963). Essays on the major Roman historical writers.

J. Lebreton and J. Zeiller, *History of the Primitive Church,* 3 vols. (1962). From the Catholic viewpoint.

H. Lietzmann, *History of the Early Church,* 2 vols. (1961). From the Protestant viewpoint.

F. Lot, *The End of the Ancient World and the Beginnings of the Middle Ages* (1961). A study that emphasizes gradual transition rather than abrupt change.

E. N. Luttwak, *The Grand Strategy of the Roman Empire* (1976). An original and fascinating analysis by a keen student of modern strategy.

R. MacMullen, *Enemies of the Roman Order* (1966). An original and revealing examination of opposition to the emperors.

R. MacMullen, *Paganism in the Roman Empire* (1981).

F. B. Marsh, *The Founding of the Roman Empire* (1959).

F. G. B. Millar, *The Roman Empire and Its Neighbors* (1968).

F. G. B. Millar, *The Emperor in the Roman World,* 31 B.C.–A.D. 337 (1977).

A. Momigliano (Ed.), *The Conflict Between Paganism and Christianity* (1963). A valuable collection of essays.

H. M. D. Parker, *A History of the Roman World from* A.D. 138 *to* 337 (1969). A good survey.

M. I. Rostovtzeff, *Social and Economic History of the Roman Empire,* 2nd. ed. (1957). A masterpiece whose main thesis has been much disputed.

E. T. Salmon, *A History of the Roman World,* 30 B.C. *to* A.D. 138 (1968). A good survey.

C. G. Starr, *Civilization and the Caesars* (1965). A study of Roman culture in the Augustan period.

R. Syme, *The Roman Revolution* (1960). A brilliant study of Augustus, his supporters, and their rise to power.

L. R. Taylor, *The Divinity of the Roman Empire* (1931). A study of the imperial cult.

The Middle Ages, 476–1300

During the eight centuries between the fall of Rome and the beginning of the Renaissance, the major institutions of western European civilization acquired a definite shape. The many formative outside influences that had come upon the West from the Eastern or Byzantine Empire, the invading Germanic tribes, and the Muslim world during the early Middle Ages were folded into a distinctive civilization.

The Roman Catholic church emerged from the chaos of the Roman Empire's collapse as a major custodian of Western culture. Firmly based in the cities, yet centered in Rome, its broad network of loyal clergy made it the only Western institution capable of extending its influence over many diverse regions.

During the reign of the Carolingian rulers, who came to power in the seventh century, a modest revival of Western imperial pretensions occurred, assisted by the church. Particularly during the long reign of Charlemagne, Christian bishops and clergy became important allies in the organization of the Carolingian Empire, both in the countryside and in the towns.

New developments in farming increased the productivity of the rural manors, where 95 per cent of the population lived. By Charlemagne's time a better harness for oxen and ploughs that could cut deeply into the soil and furrow it improved yields. Rotation of crops among three fields kept land fertile and productive. These new techniques aided both population growth and cultural development.

Thanks to soaring mercantile activity in the twelfth and thirteenth centuries, towns and urban culture grew very rapidly. A new merchant class emerged in the towns and took its place alongside the nobility and the clergy. From the towns, the rulers increasingly drew lay servants and administrators, who formed a loyal bureaucracy and braintrust that made it possible for the rulers to challenge the nobility and the church successfully. This alliance between rulers and towns was an important factor in the rise of Europe's new secular monarchies and the creation of Europe's major nation-states.

Emperors and kings clashed repeatedly with popes during the twelfth and thirteenth centuries, when the Roman Catholic church was still a formidable political power. At the end of the Investiture Controversy in the twelfth century, a clear distinction was drawn between the spheres of ecclesiastical and secular authority. After 1300, monarchs progressively limited the church's influence over their political and economic affairs, restricting the church to an important but less threatening spiritual and cultural sphere of influence.

The Crusades to the Holy Land attested to the church's continuing popularity in the high Middle Ages, even though these ventures had acquired a mercenary character by the thirteenth century. In an increasingly materialistic age, the rise of the Dominican and Franciscan friars signaled a new spiritual revival among the clergy that also attracted large numbers of pious laity. Under the banner of apostolic poverty church reformers rallied until the Reformation.

This sixth-century ivory panel depicts the Byzantine emperor as the Champion of the Faith. For six centuries, from about 500 to 1100, Byzantium was the center of Christian civilization. [*Giraudon, Art Resource*]

6

The Early Middle Ages (476–1000): The Birth of Europe

THE EARLY MIDDLE AGES mark the birth of Europe. This was the period in which a distinctive western European culture began to emerge. In geography, government, religion, and language, western Europe became a land distinct from both the eastern or Byzantine world and the Arab or Muslim world. It was a period of recovery from the collapse of Roman civilization, a time of forced experimentation with new ideas and institutions. Western European culture, as we know it today, was born of a unique, inventive mix of surviving Graeco-Roman, new Germanic, and evolving Christian traditions.

The early Middle Ages have been called, and not with complete fairness, a "dark age." This is because they lost touch with classical, especially Greek, learning and science. In this period there were fierce invasions from the north and the east by peoples that the Romans somewhat arrogantly called barbarians, and to the south the Mediterranean was transformed by Arab dominance into an inhospitable "Muslim lake." Although western trade with the east was by no means completely cut off, western people became more isolated than they had been before. A Europe thus surrounded and assailed from north, east, and south understandably became somewhat insular and even stagnant. On the other hand, being forced to manage by itself, western Europe also learned to develop its native resources. The early Middle Ages were not without a modest renaissance of antiquity during the reign of Charlemagne. And the peculiar social and political forms of this period—manorialism and feudalism—proved to be not only successful ways to cope with unprecedented chaos on local levels but also a fertile seedbed for the growth of distinctive Western institutions.

On the Eve of the Frankish Ascendancy

Germanic and Arab Invasions

As we have already seen, by the late third century the Roman Empire had become too large for a single sovereign to govern. For this reason the Emperor Diocletian (284–305) permitted the evolution of a dual empire by establishing an eastern and a western half, each with its own emperor and, eventually, imperial bureaucracy. The Emperor Constantine the Great (306–337) briefly reunited the empire by conquest and was sole emperor of the east and the west after 324. (The empire was redivided by his sons and subsequent successors.) In 330 Constantine created the city of Constantinople as the new administrative center of the empire and the imperial residence. Constantinople gradually became a "new Rome," replacing the old, whose internal political quarrels and geographical distance from new military fronts in Syria and along the Danube River made it less appealing. Rome and the western empire were actually on the wane in the late third and fourth centuries, well before the barbarian invasions in the west began. In 286 Milan had already replaced Rome as the imperial residence; in 402 the seat of western government was moved still again, to Ravenna. When the barbarian invasions began in the late fourth century, the west was in political disarray, and the imperial power and prestige had shifted decisively to Constantinople and the east.

German Tribes and the West. The German tribes did not burst on the west all of a sudden. They were at first a token and benign presence. Before the great invasions from the north and the east, there had been a period of peaceful commingling of the Germanic and the Roman cultures. The Romans "imported" barbarians as domestics and soldiers before they came as conquerors. Barbarian soldiers rose to positions of high leadership and fame in Roman legions. In the late fourth century, however, this peaceful coexistence came to an end because of a great influx of Visigoths (west Goths) into the empire. They were stampeded there in 376 by the emergence of a new, violent people, the Huns, who migrated from the area of modern Mongolia. The Visigoths were a Christianized Germanic tribe who won from the eastern emperor Valens rights of settlement and material assistance within the empire in exchange for their defense of the frontier as *foederati*, special allies of the emperor. When in place of promised assistance the Visigoths received harsh treatment from their new allies, they rebelled, handily defeating Roman armies under Valens at the battle of Adrianople in 378.

After Adrianople the Romans passively permitted settlement after settlement of barbarians within the very heart of western Europe. Why was there so little resistance to the German tribes? The invaders found a badly overextended western empire physically weakened by decades of famine, pestilence, and overtaxation, and politically divided by ambitious military commanders. In the second half of the fourth century its will to resist had simply been sapped. The Roman Empire did not fall simply because of unprecedented moral decay and materialism, but because of a combination of political mismanagement, disease, and sheer poverty.

The late fourth and early fifth centuries saw the invasion of still other tribes: the Vandals, the Burgundians, and the Franks. In 410 Visigoths revolted under Alaric (ca. 370–410) and sacked the "eternal city" of Rome. From 451 to 453 Italy suffered the invasions of Attila the Hun (d. 453), who was known to contemporaries as the "scourge of God." In 455 the Vandals overran Rome.

By the mid-fifth century, power in western Europe had passed decisively from the hands of the Roman emperors to those of barbarian chieftains. In 476, the traditional date for the fall of the Roman Empire, the barbarian Odoacer (ca. 434–493) deposed and replaced the western emperor Romulus Augustulus and ruled as "king of the Romans." The eastern

Coin of Alaric the Visigoth (ca 370–410).

Salvian the Priest Compares the Romans and the Barbarians

Salvian, a Christian priest writing around 440, found the barbarians morally superior to the Romans—indeed, truer to Roman virtues than the Romans themselves, whose failings are all the more serious because they, unlike the barbarians, had knowledge of Christianity.

In what respects can our customs be preferred to those of the Goths and Vandals, or even compared with them? And first, to speak of affection and mutual charity, . . . almost all barbarians, at least those who are of one race and kin, love each other, while the Romans persecute each other. . . . The many are oppressed by the few, who regard public exactions as their own peculiar right, who carry on private traffic under the guise of collecting the taxes. . . . So the poor are despoiled, the widows sigh, the orphans are oppressed, until many of them, born of families not obscure, and liberally educated, flee to our enemies that they may no longer suffer the oppression of public persecution. They doubtless seek Roman humanity among the barbarians, because they cannot bear barbarian inhumanity among the Romans. And although they differ from the people to whom they flee in manner and in language; although they are unlike as regards the fetid odor of the barbarians' bodies and garments, yet they would rather endure a foreign civilization among the barbarians than cruel injustice among the Romans.

It is urged that if we Romans are wicked and corrupt, that the barbarians commit the same sins. . . . There is, however, this difference, that if the barbarians commit the same crimes as we, yet we sin more grieviously. . . . All the barbarians . . . are pagans or heretics. The Saxon race is cruel, the Franks are faithless . . . the Huns are unchaste,—in short there is vice in the life of all the barbarian peoples. But are their offenses as serious as [those of Christians]? Is the unchastity of the Hun so criminal as ours? Is the faithlessness of the Frank so blameworthy as ours?

Of God's Government, in James Harvey Robinson, *Readings in European History,* Vol. 1 (Boston: Athenaeum, 1904), pp. 28–30.

emperor, Zeno (emperor 474–491), recognized Odoacer's authority in the west, and Odoacer ceded to Zeno authority as sole emperor, being content to serve as his western viceroy. In a subsequent coup in 493 manipulated by Zeno, Theodoric (ca. 454–526), king of the Ostrogoths (east Goths), defeated Odoacer and thereafter ruled Italy with full acceptance by the Roman people and the Christian Church.

By the end of the fifth century the western empire was thoroughly overrun by barbarians. The Ostrogoths settled in Italy, the Franks in northern Gaul, the Burgundians in Provence, the Visigoths in southern Gaul and Spain, the Vandals in Africa and the Mediterranean, and the Angles and Saxons in England (see Map 6.1). Barbarians were now the western masters—but masters who were also willing to learn from the people they had conquered.

Western Europe was not transformed into a savage land. The military victories of the barbarians did not result in a great cultural defeat of the Roman Empire. The barbarians were militarily superior, but the Romans retained their cultural strength. Apart from Britain and northern Gaul, Roman language, law, and government continued to exist side by side with the new Germanic institutions. In Italy under Theodoric, Roman law gradually replaced tribal custom. Only the Vandals and the Anglo-Saxons refused to profess at least titular obedience to the emperor in Constantinople.

Behind this accommodation of cultures was the fact that the Visigoths, the Ostrogoths, and the Vandals entered the west as Christianized people. They professed, however, a religious creed that was considered heretical in the west. They were Arian Christians, that is, Christians who believed that Jesus Christ was not of one

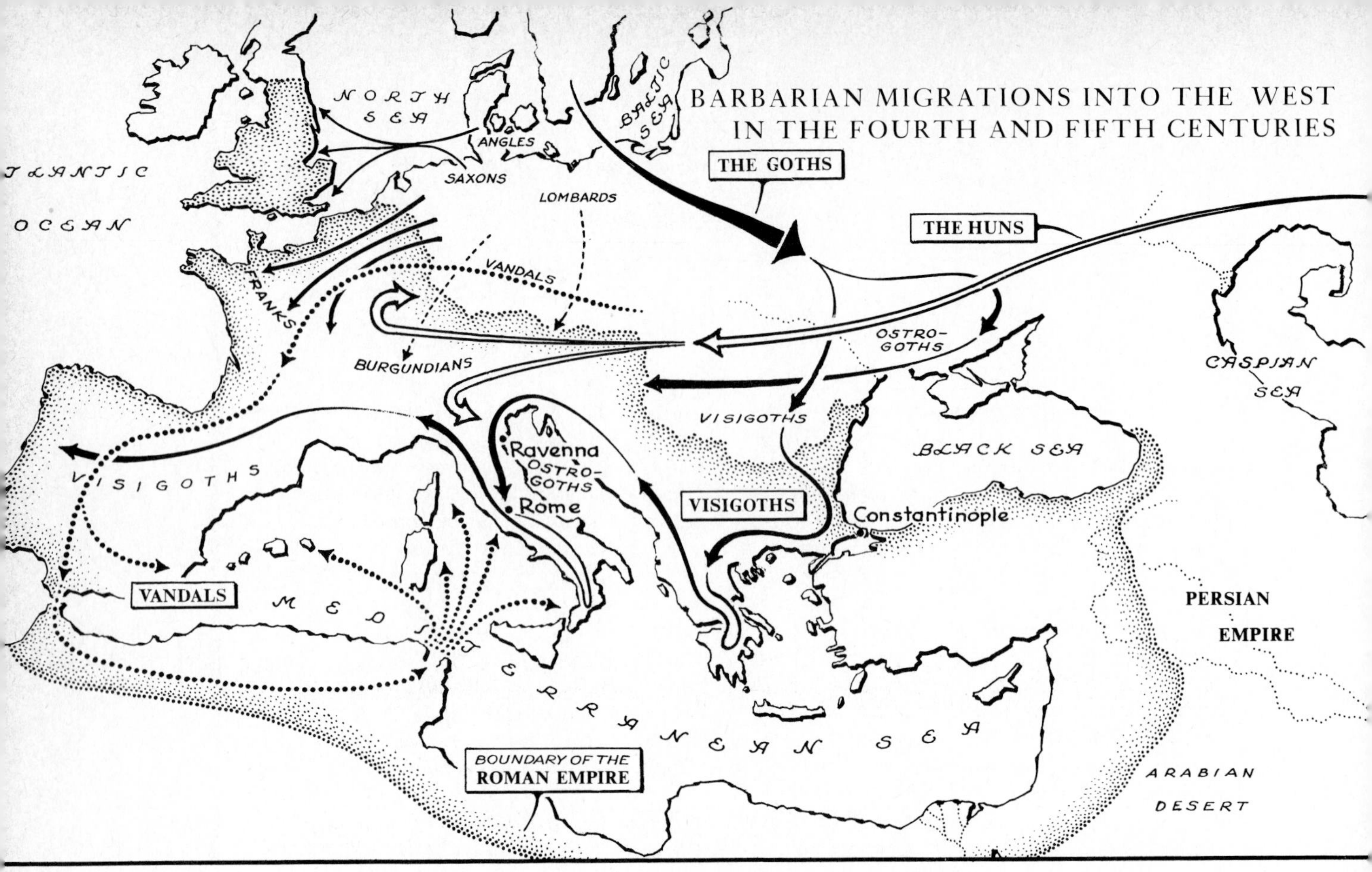

MAP 6-1 *The forceful intrusion of Germanic and non-Germanic barbarians into the Empire from the last quarter of the fourth century through the fifth century made for a constantly changing pattern of movement and relations. However, the map shows the major routes taken by the usually unwelcome newcomers and the areas most deeply affected by main groups.*

identical substance with God the Father—a point of view that had been condemned in 325 by the Council of Nicaea (see Chapter 5). Later, around 500, the Franks, under their strong king, Clovis, converted to the orthodox or "Catholic" form of Christianity supported by the bishops of Rome, and they helped conquer and convert the Goths and other barbarians in western Europe.

All things considered, rapprochement and a gradual interpenetration of two strong cultures—a creative tension—marked the period of the Germanic migrations. The stronger culture was the Roman, and it became dominant in a later fusion. Despite western military defeat, it can still be said that the Goths and the Franks became far more romanized than the Romans were germanized. Latin language, Nicene Christianity, and eventually Roman law and government were to triumph in the west during the Middle Ages.

The Byzantine Empire

As western Europe succumbed to the Germanic invasions, imperial power shifted to the Byzantine Empire, that is, the eastern part of the Roman Empire established in 330. Constantinople, created in 324 as the "new Rome," became the sole capital of the empire and remained such until the revival of the western empire in the eighth century by Charlemagne.

There are three distinct periods in the history of the Byzantine Empire: from the creation of Constantinople in 324 to the rise of Islam to dominance in the mid-seventh century; from 650 to the conquest of Asia Minor by the Turks in the 1070s *or*, as some prefer, to the fall of Constantinople to the western Crusaders in 1204; and finally, from 1070 or 1204 to the defeat of Constantinople by the Turks in 1453. Between 324 and 1453 the empire passed from an early period of expansion and splendor, to a time of contraction and splintering, to final catastrophic defeat.

In terms of territory, political power, and culture, the first period (324–650) was far and away the greatest. By the end of Justinian's reign (527–565), the Byzantines had spread an urban civilization around virtually the entire Mediterranean. In it they imaginatively integrated Christianity and Graeco-Roman culture. The empire at this time comprised a population in excess of 30 million. After the sixth century, the Arabs and the western Germanic tribes became the ascendant powers. They alternately invaded and conquered portions of the Byzantine Empire, shrinking it to Asia Minor and the Aegean islands. In the late sixth century migrating Slavs "barbarized" the Balkan peninsula. By the early seventh century Persians and Arabs had successively overrun Syria, Palestine, Egypt, and North Africa and had penetrated into Asia Minor.

A strong central government existed in Constantinople until the eleventh century. Much of its success was due to a large and growing voluntary army, in excess of a half million men by the end of the fourth century, by far the largest contingent of imperial servants. Although many of these soldiers lived in special camps, a substantial number were billeted in the cities.

MAP 6-2

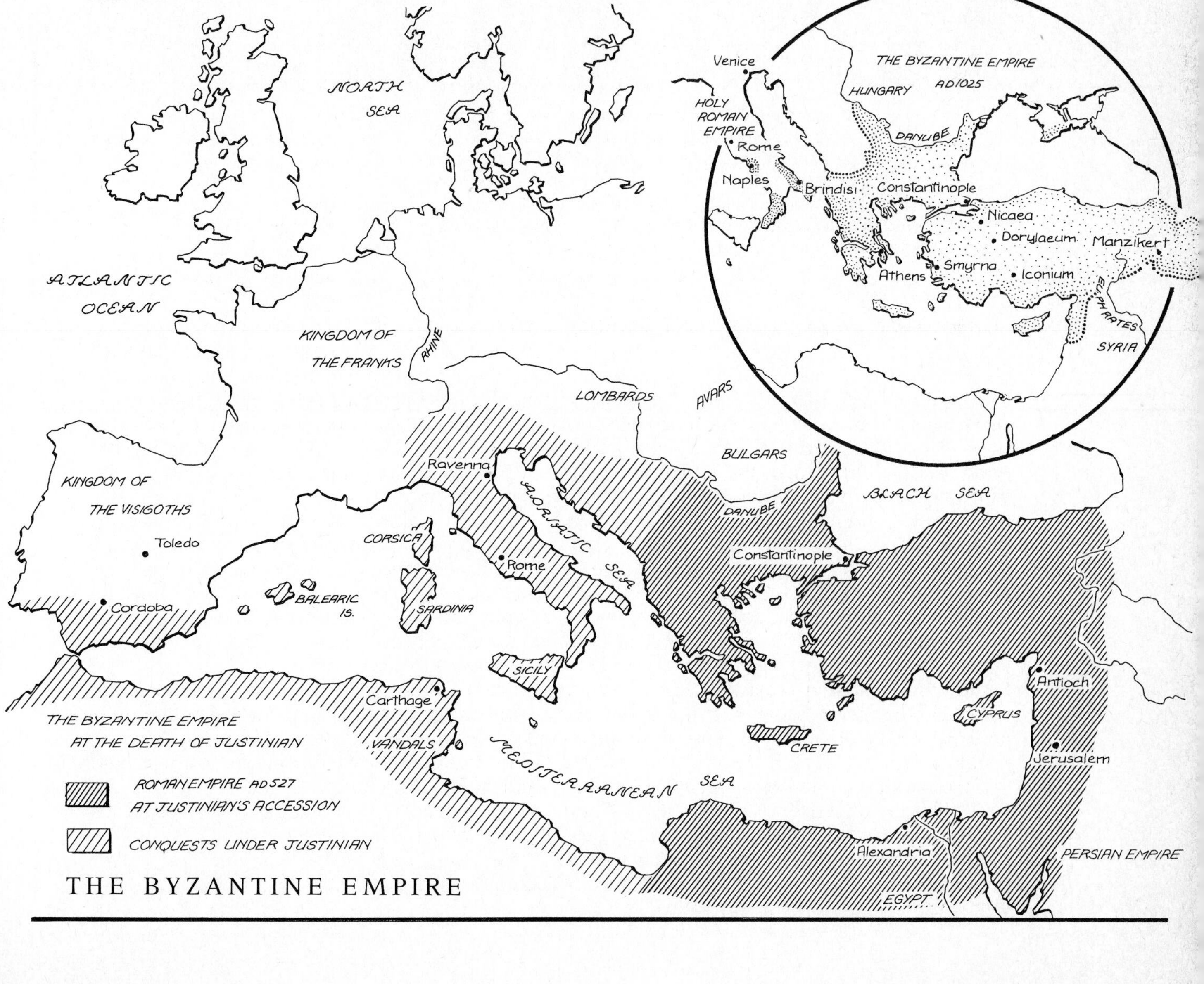

THE BYZANTINE EMPIRE

One of the most influential achievements of Byzantine art was the great church of Hagia Sophia (Holy Wisdom) built by the emperor Justinian between 532 and 537. Its great dome, 107 feet in diameter, and rich decoration of marbles and mosaics dazzled visitors to Constantinople for centuries. This mosaic from the south door of the Church shows two emperors, Justinian on the left and Constantine on the right, adoring the Virgin and Christ Child. Justinian holds his Church of Hagia Sophia, Constantine his city of Constantinople. [*Hirmer Fotoarchiv*]

In its heyday the empire *was* its cities. During Justinian's reign more than fifteen hundred cities existed. The largest, with perhaps 350,000 inhabitants, was Constantinople, the cultural crossroads of the Asian and European civilizations. The large provincial cities had populations of 50,000. Between the fourth and fifth centuries councils composed of local wealthy landowners, numbering around two hundred, governed the cities. Known as *decurions*, they made up the intellectual and economic elite of the empire. Heavily taxed, they were not always the emperor's most docile or loyal imperial servants. By the sixth century special governors and bishops, appointed from the landholding classes, replaced the decurion councils. They were better instruments of the emperor's will and helped to centralized imperial power.

A fifth-century statistical record gives us some sense of the size and splendor of Constantinople at its peak. According to the record, there were 5 imperial and 9 princely palaces; 8 public and 153 private baths; 4 public fora; 5 granaries; 2 theaters; a hippodrome; 322 streets; 4,388 substantial houses; 52 porticoes; 20 public and 120 private bakers; and 14 churches.[1] The most popular entertainments were the theater, frequently denounced by the clergy for nudity and immorality, and the races at the hippodrome. Numerous public taverns and baths existed, and evidence suggests laxity in sexual morality.

Since the fifth century the patriarch of Constantinople had crowned emperors in Constantinople. This practice reflected the close ties between the state and Christianity. In 380 Trinitarian Christianity was proclaimed the official religion of the eastern empire. All other religions and sects were denounced as "demented and insane."[2] Between the fourth and sixth centuries the patriarchs of Constantinople, Alexandria, Antioch, and Jerusalem acquired enormous wealth in the form of land and gold. The church, in turn, acted as the state's welfare agency, drawing on its generous

[1]Cyril Mango, *Byzantium: The Empire of New Rome* (New York: Charles Scribners Sons, 1980), p. 76.
[2]*Ibid.*, p. 88.

endowments from pious rich donors to aid the poor and needy. The prestige and comfort of the clergy swelled the clerical ranks.

Imperial policy was always to centralize and conform: "one God, one empire, one religion." To this end Justinian collated and revised Roman law, creating his famous Code in 533, the foundation of most subsequent European law. Religion also served imperial centralization. Orthodox Christianity was not, however, the only religion in the empire with a significant following. Nor did the rulers view religion as merely a political tool. At one time or another the Christian heresies of Arianism, Monophysitism, and Iconoclasm also received imperial support, and apparently because of genuine belief. Persecution and absorption into popular Christianity curtailed many pagan practices. The Jews, who lived in large numbers within the empire, had legal protection under Roman law as long as they did not proselytize among Christians, build new synagogues, or attempt to enter sensitive public offices or professions. Justinian, the emperor most intent on conformity, adopted a policy of Jewish conversion. The later emperors Heraclius (d. 641) and Leo III (717–740) ordered all Jews baptized and granted tax breaks to those who voluntarily complied. None of these efforts converted the Jews, however. Persecuted in the fifth century for proselytizing, Jews joined political revolts against the emperor in the sixth century.

Among the numerous Christian heresies, the most threatening to the empire was Monophysitism. The Monophysites taught that Jesus had only one nature, a composite divine-human nature, a point of doctrine fanatically held. The majority and orthodox view was that Jesus was of two separate natures, fully human and fully divine. The Monophysites gained a powerful ally in the person of the Empress Theodora, who disagreed on this sensitive point of Christological doctrine with her husband, Justinian, who remained strictly orthodox. Neither persecution nor compromise could break the Monophysites. In the sixth century they became a separate church, strong in the eastern provinces of the empire. Their persecution was costly to the empire in the seventh century, when Persians and Arabs laid siege to the eastern frontiers. Bitter about their treatment by the imperial government, the Monophysites apparently did little to resist.

As is clear from this discussion, the Byzantine world view was strongly biblical and theological. For the many who accepted official religion, Christian ascetic values and eschatological beliefs made the afterlife far more important than the present. Such a point of view tended to encourage political subservience and clearly aided political order as long as the emperor was perceived as holding the "true" religion.

The great mosque at Qairawan in modern Tunisia, eighth–ninth centuries. By the eighth century Islamic armies had conquered an empire that stretched from Spain to Persia. [Roger Wood]

Islam and Its Effects on East and West

A new drama began to unfold at this time, and it was to prove decisive for western Europe's future. In the south an enemy far more dangerous than the German tribes was on the march: the faith of Islam. During the lifetime of the prophet Muhammad (570–632) and thereafter, invading Arab armies absorbed the attention and resources of the emperors in

Constantinople, who found themselves in a life-and-death struggle.

In the early Middle Ages the Arabs were both open and cautious. During the ninth and tenth centuries they borrowed and integrated elements of Persian and Greek culture into their own. They also tolerated Jews and other religious minorities within their midst. However, they were also keen to protect the purity and integrity of Arab religion, language, and law from foreign corruption. With the passage of time—and increased conflict with the West—this protective instinct grew stronger. In the end, Arab culture did not creatively penetrate the West as did Germanic culture.

Muhammad had been raised an orphan by a family of modest means. He became a successful businessman, helped to this end by marriage to a wealthy widow in Mecca. When he was about forty, he had a religious experience in which he was called by God to preach against immorality and idolatry. His religion, Islam, means "submission to the will of Allah," and Muslims (Arabic for "true believers") are people who obey the will of Allah as revealed to Muhammad. This will is contained in the Koran (*Qur'an*, literally, "reciting" of God's will), a series of revelations received by Muhammad over a period of time and compiled by his successor. The Koran recognizes Jesus Christ as a prophet sent by God, but not one so great as Muhammad, and not God's coequal son as the Christians believe. Muhammad is the last in a line of God's prophets going back to Noah and Abraham, in this sense, "the Prophet."

Islam is uncompromisingly monotheistic. Among the things required of the faithful are prayer five times each day, generous almsgiving, fasting during the daylight hours for one month each year, and a pilgrimage to the holy city of Mecca, in what is now Saudi Arabia, at least once during one's lifetime. Muslims also permit polygamy (each man may have up to four wives) and forbid the eating of pork and the drinking of alcoholic beverages. Unlike Christianity, Islam makes no rigid distinction between the clergy and the laity. Another striking difference from Christianity, especially Western Christianity, is the complete unity of religion and politics.

Muhammad preached his message unsuccessfully for several years in what he considered "pagan" Mecca before fleeing the city in 622 for the neighboring and more receptive city of Medina. There many of his followers also migrated, making Medina the center of his movement. This flight, know to Muslims as the *Hegira*, became a key event in the history of Islam—the beginning of the new religion's political organization and geographical expansion and the starting point for its calendar. Muhammad and his followers were severely persecuted before becoming strong enough to fight back and win. Once established, Muhammad, supported by a great army of followers and able to impose his will, absolutely opposed any accommodation with pagans, and he converted fellow Arabs by holy war. He also turned sharply against Jews and Christians, having initially spoken well of them, because of their rejection of his message and authority. Mecca, a city of long association with Arab pagan rites, capitulated and became the center of Muslim activity and government. By its ability to define a common Arab culture and its willingness to impose it by force, Islam became a spiritual force capable of uniting the Arab tribes in a true Arab empire.

By the middle of the eighth century, Muslims had conquered the southern and eastern Mediterranean coastline (territories mostly still held by Islamic states today) and occupied parts of Spain, which they controlled or strongly influenced until the fifteenth century. In addition, their armies had pushed north and east through Mesopotamia and Persia and beyond (see Map 6.3). These conquests would not have been so rapid and thorough had the contemporary Byzantine and Persian empires not been exhausted by a long period of war. The Muslims struck at the conclusion of the successful campaign of Byzantine Emperor Heraclius (d. 641) against the Persian King Chosroes II. Most of the population in the conquered area was Semitic and more easily fired by hatred of the Byzantine Greek army of occupation than it was inspired to unity by a common Christian tradition. The Christian community was itself badly divided. The Egyptian (also known as *Coptic*) and Syrian churches were Monophysitic. Heraclius' efforts to impose Greek "orthodox" beliefs on these churches only increased the enmity between Greek and Semitic Christians, many of whom leaned toward Monophysitism. Many Egyptian and Syrian Christians may have looked on the Arabs as deliverers from the Byzantine conquerors.

Muslims tolerated conquered Christians, whether orthodox or Monophysite, provided they paid taxes, kept their distance, and made

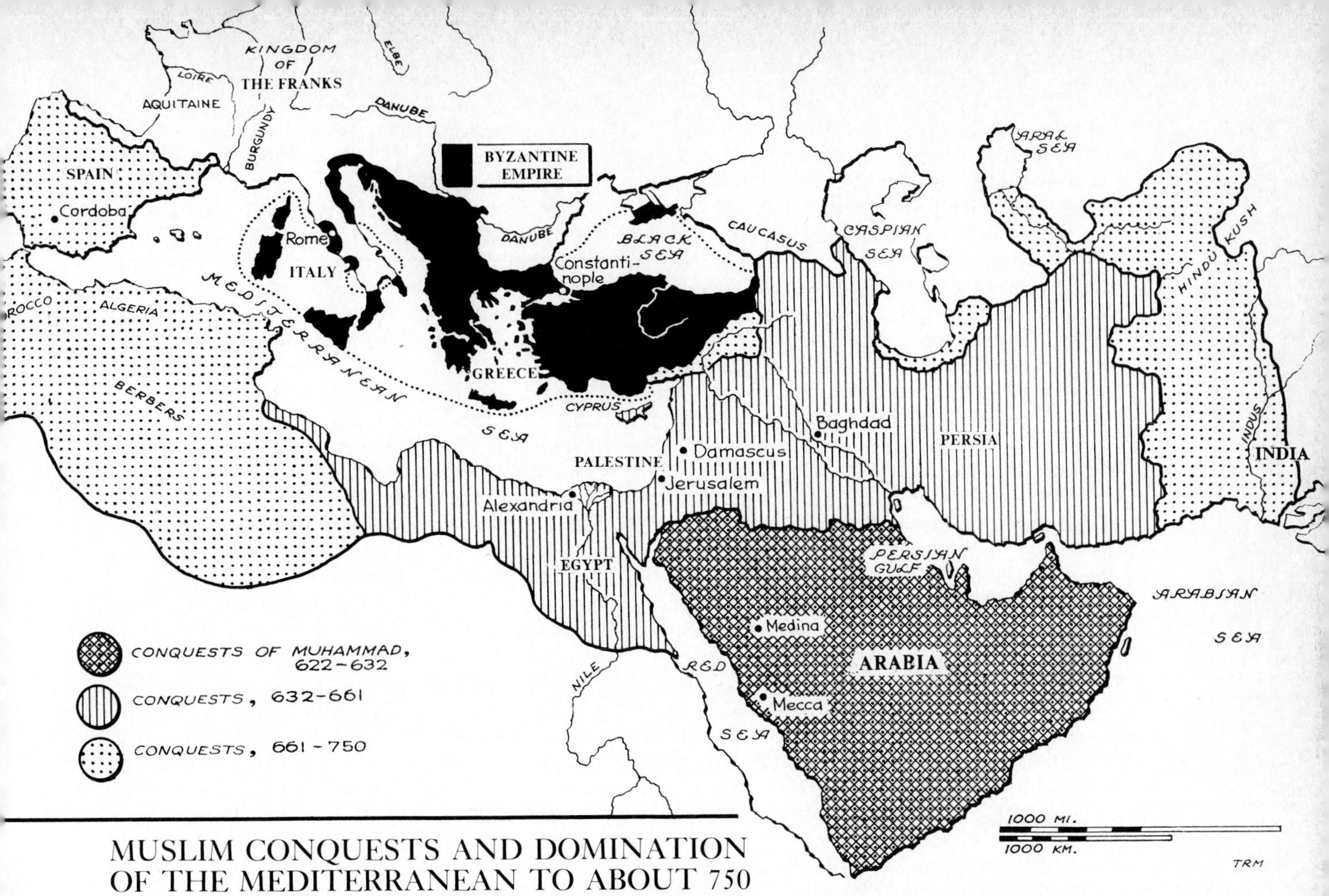

MUSLIM CONQUESTS AND DOMINATION OF THE MEDITERRANEAN TO ABOUT 750

MAP 6-3 *The rapid spread of Islam (both religion and military-political power) is shown here. From the West's viewpoint, the important fact was that in the* 125 *years after Muhammad's rise Muslims came to dominate Spain and all areas south and east of the Mediterranean.*

no efforts to proselytize Muslim communities. Anxious to maintain the purity of their religion and culture, the Arabs forbade mixed marriages. Special taxes on conquered peoples encouraged them to convert to Islam. After the middle of the eighth century, by which time the seat of Islam had been moved from Arabia to Damascus in Syria and from there to the brand-new city of Baghdad in Mesopotamia, the huge Muslim empire tended to break into separate states. These states often had their own caliphs (or rulers), each claiming to be the true successor of Muhammad.

Assaulted on both their eastern and their western frontiers and everywhere challenged in the Mediterranean, the Europeans developed a lasting fear and suspicion of the Muslims. In the east, during the reign of the Byzantine Leo III (717–740), the Arabs were stopped after a year's siege of Constantinople (717–718). Leo and his successors in the Isaurian dynasty of Byzantine rulers created a successful defensive organization against the Arabs. It was so effective that it permitted the rulers of the following Macedonian dynasty (867–1057) to expand militarily and commercially into Muslim lands. Byzantine armies were also assisted by Muslim disunity. In 1071 the Seljuk Turks from central Asia, by way of Persia and Mesopotamia, overran Armenia at the eastern end of the empire in the first of a series of confrontations that would finally end with the fall of Constantinople in 1453 to the Seljuks' relatives, the Ottoman Turks. In 1096 the first Crusaders from western Europe arrived in Constantinople in the first of a series of moves to the east that ended with the capture of Constantinople in 1204 and the establishment of a half century of Latin or western rule over Byzantium.

As for the west's own dangers, the ruler of the Franks, Charles Martel, defeated a raiding party of Arabs on the western frontier of Europe at Poitiers (today in central France) in 732, a victory that ended any possible Arab effort to expand into western Europe by way of Spain. From the end of the seventh century to the middle of the eleventh century, the Mediterranean still remained something of a Muslim lake; although the trade of the western empire with the Orient was not cut off during these centuries, it was significantly decreased and was carried on in keen awareness of Muslim dominance.

When trade wanes, cities decline, and with them those centers for the exchange of goods and ideas that enable a society to look and live beyond itself. The Arab invasions and domination of the Mediterranean during a crucial part of the early Middle Ages created the essential conditions for the birth of western Europe as a distinctive cultural entity. Arab belligerency forced western Europeans to fall back on their own distinctive resources and to develop their peculiar Germanic and Graeco-Roman heritage into a unique culture. The Arabs accomplished this by diverting the attention and energies of the eastern empire at a time of Frankish and Lombard ascendancy (thereby preventing Byzantine expansion into the west) and by greatly reducing western navigation of the Mediterranean (thereby closing off much eastern trade and cultural influence).

As western shipping was reduced in the Mediterranean, coastal urban centers declined. Populations that would otherwise have been engaged in trade-related work in the cities moved in great numbers into interior regions, there to work the farms of the great landholders. The latter needed their labor and welcomed the new emigrants, who were even more in need of the employment and protection that the landholders could provide. Ninety per cent of the population was peasants. There were free peasants, who owned their own land, and peasants who became "serfs" by surrendering their land to a more powerful landholder in exchange for assistance in time of dire need, like prolonged crop failure or foreign invasion. Basically serfdom was a status of servitude to an economically and politically stronger man, who provided land and dwelling in exchange for labor and goods. As the demand for agricultural products diminished in the great urban centers and as traffic between town and country was reduced, the farming belts became regionally insular and self-contained. Production and travel adjusted to local needs, and there was little incentive for bold experimentation and exploration. The domains of the great landholders became the basic social and political units of society, and

One of the reasons the Byzantines were able to repulse the Arab attack on Constantinople in 717–718 was a secret weapon: Greek fire, a highly inflammable mixture of petroleum, sulphur, and pitch that would burn even on water. In this fourteenth-century manuscript, the Byzantine navy is spraying Greek fire from a copper tube onto an enemy vessel. [Mas]

local barter economies sprang up within them. In these developments were sown the seeds of what would later come to be known as manorial and feudal society, the former an ordering of peasant society in which land and labor were divided among lords, peasants, and serfs for the profit and protection of all, the latter an ordering of aristocratic society in which a special class of warrior knights emerged as guarantors of order.

One institution remained firmly entrenched within the cities during the Arab invasions: the Christian Church. The church had long modeled its own structure on that of the imperial Roman administration. Like the latter, it was a centralized, hierarchical government with strategically placed "viceroys" (bishops) in European cities who looked for spiritual direction to their leader, the bishop of Rome. As the western empire crumbled and populations emigrated to the countryside after the barbarian and Arab invasions, local bishops and cathedral chapters filled the vacuum of authority left by the removal of Roman governors. The local cathedral became the center of urban life and the local bishop the highest authority for those who remained in the cities—just as in Rome, on a larger and more fateful scale, the pope took control of the city as the western emperors gradually departed and died out. Left to its own devices, western Europe soon discovered that the Christian Church was a rich repository of Roman administrative skills and classical culture.

The Developing Roman Church

The Christian Church had been graced with special privileges, great lands, and wealth by Emperor Constantine and his successors. In the first half of the fourth century, Christians gained legal standing and a favored status within the empire. In 391 Emperor Theodosius I (ca. 379–395), after whose death the empire would again be divided into eastern and western parts, raised Christianity to the official religion of the empire. Both Theodosius and his predecessors acted as much for political effect as out of religious conviction; in 313 Christians composed about one fifth of the population of the empire and were unquestionably the strongest of the competing religions. Mithraism, the religion popular among army officers and restricted to males, was its main rival.

Challenged to become a major political force, the church survived the period of Germanic and Arab invasions as a somewhat spiritually weakened and compromised institution; yet it was still a most potent civilizing and unifying force. It had a religious message of providential purpose and individual worth that could give solace and meaning to life at its worst. After the fall of Rome, this message was eloquently defined by Augustine (354–430) in his *City of God,* a favorite book of the Frankish king Charlemagne nearly four hundred years later. The western church also had a ritual of baptism and a creedal confession that united people beyond the traditional barriers of social class, education, and sex. After the Germanic and Arab invasions the church alone possessed an effective hierarchical administration, scattered throughout the old empire, staffed by the best-educated minds in Europe, and centered in emperorless Rome. The church also enjoyed the services of growing numbers of monks, who were not only loyal to its mission but also objects of great popular respect. Monastic culture proved again and again to be the peculiar strength of the church during the Middle Ages.

MONASTIC CULTURE. Monks were originally hermits, individuals who withdrew from society to pursue a more perfect way of life. They were inspired by the Christian ideal of a life of complete self-denial in imitation of Christ, who had denied himself even unto death. The popularity of monasticism began to grow as Roman persecution of Christians waned in the mid-third century. As the Romans stopped feeding Christians to the lions—indeed, as Christianity became the favored religion of the empire—monasticism replaced martyrdom as the most perfect way to imitate Christ and to confess one's faith. Embracing the biblical "counsels of perfection" (chastity, poverty, and obedience), the monastic life became the purest form of religious practice in the Middle Ages. Christians came to view monastic life as the superior Christian life, beyond the baptism and creedal confession that identified ordinary believers. This view evolved during the Middle Ages into a belief in the general superiority of the clergy and the mission of the church over the laity and the state—a belief that served the papacy in later confrontations with secular rulers.

Anthony of Egypt (ca. 251–356), the father of hermit monasticism, was inspired by Jesus' command to the rich young ruler: "If you will be perfect, sell all that you have, give it to the

A monastic scriptorium, *or study. In the center, St. Gregory the Great is receiving the divine word from a dove that has perched on his shoulder. Below St. Gregory three monks are shown writing. Note the inkwell held by the middle monk. [Kunsthistorisches Museum, Vienna]*

poor, and follow me'' (Matthew 19:21). Anthony went into the desert to pray and work, setting an example followed by hundreds in Egypt, Syria, and Palestine in the fourth and fifth centuries. This hermit monasticism was soon joined by the development of communal monasticism. In southern Egypt in the first quarter of the fourth century, Pachomius (ca. 286–346) organized monks into a highly regimented common life. Hundreds shared a life together that was ordered and disciplined by a strict penal code and assigned manual labor. Such monastic communities grew to contain a thousand or more inhabitants, little ''cities of God,'' separated from the collapsing Roman and the nominal Christian world. Basil the Great (329–379) popularized communal monasticism throughout the east, providing a rule that lessened the asceticism of Pachomius and directed monks beyond their enclaves of perfection into such social services as caring for orphans, widows, and the infirm in surrounding communities.

Athanasius (ca. 293–373) and Martin of Tours (ca. 315–ca. 399) introduced monasticism into the west, where the teaching of John Cassian (ca. 360–435) and Jerome (ca. 340–420) helped shape its basic values and practices. The great organizer of western monasticism was Benedict of Nursia (ca. 480–547). In 529 Benedict founded the mother monastery of the Benedictines at Monte Cassino in Italy, the foundation on which all western monasticism has been built. Benedict also wrote a sophisticated *Rule for Monasteries,* a comprehensive plan for every activity of the monks, even detailing how they were to sleep. The monastery was hierarchically organized and directed by an abbot, whose command was beyond question. Periods of devotion (about four hours each day were set aside for the ''work of God,'' that is, regular prayers and liturgical activities) and study alternated with manual labor—a program that permitted not a moment's idleness and carefully promoted the religious, intellectual, and physical well-being of the cloistered. Each Benedictine monastery remained autonomous until the later Middle Ages, when the Benedictines became a unified order of the church.

THE DOCTRINE OF PAPAL PRIMACY. Constantine and his successors, especially the eastern emperors, ruled religious life with an

The Benedictine Order Sets Its Requirements for Entrance

The religious life had great appeal in a time of political and social uncertainty. Entrance into a monastery was not, however, escapism. Much was demanded of the new monk, both during and after his probationary period, which is here described. Benedict's contribution was to prescribe a balanced blend of religious, physical, and intellectual activities within a well-structured community.

When anyone is newly come for the reformation of his life, let him not be granted an easy entrance; but, as the Apostle says, "Test the spirits to see whether they are from God." If the newcomer, therefore, perseveres in his knocking, and if it is seen after four or five days that he bears patiently the harsh treatment offered him and the difficulty of admission, and that he persists in his petition, then let entrance be granted him, and let him stay in the guest house for a few days.

After that let him live in the novitiate, where the novices study, eat, and sleep. A senior shall be assigned to them who is skilled in winning souls, to watch over them with the utmost care. Let him examine whether the novice is truly seeking God, and whether he is zealous for the Work of God, for obedience and for humiliations. Let the novice be told all the hard and rugged ways by which the journey to God is made.

If he promises stability and perseverance, then at the end of two months let this Rule be read through to him, and let him be addressed thus: "Here is the law under which you wish to fight. If you can observe it, enter; if you cannot, you are free to depart." If he still stands firm, let him be taken to the above-mentioned novitiate and again tested in all patience. And after the lapse of six months let the Rule be read to him, that he may know on what he is entering. And if he still remains firm, after four months let the same Rule be read to him again.

Then, having deliberated with himself, if he promises to keep it in its entirety and to observe everything that is commanded him, let him be received into the community. But let him understand that, according to the law of the rule, from that day forward he may not leave the monastery nor withdraw his neck from under the yoke of the Rule which he was free to refuse or to accept during that prolonged deliberation.

St. Benedict's Rule for Monasteries, trans. by Leonard J. Doyle (Collegeville, Minn.: Liturgical Press, 1948), Chap. 58, p. 79–80.

iron hand and consistently looked on the church as little more than a department of the state. Such political assumption of spiritual power involved the emperor directly in the church's affairs, even to the point of playing the theologian and imposing conciliar solutions on its doctrinal quarrels. State control of religion was the original Church–State relation in the west. The bishops of Rome never accepted such intervention and opposed it in every way they could. In the fifth and sixth centuries, taking advantage of imperial weakness and distraction, they developed for their own defense the weaponry of the doctrine of "papal primacy." This teaching raised the Roman pontiff to an unassailable supremacy within the church when it came to defining church doctrine; it also put him in a position to make important secular claims. The doctrine was destined to occasion repeated conflicts between church and state, pope and emperor, throughout the Middle Ages.

The notion of papal primacy was first conceived as a papal response to the decline of imperial Rome in favor of Milan and Ravenna and to the concurrent competitive claims of the patriarchs of the eastern church. The latter looked on the bishop of Rome as a peer, not as a superior, after imperial power was transferred to Constantinople. In 381 the ecumenical Council of Constantinople declared the bishop of Constantinople to be of first rank after the bishop of Rome "because Constantinople is the new Rome." In 451 the ecumenical Council of Chalcedon recognized Constantinople as having the same religious primacy in the east as Rome had traditionally possessed in the west. By the mid-sixth century the bishop of Constantinople regularly described himself in correspondence as a "universal" patriarch.

Roman pontiffs, understandably jealous of such claims and resentful of the ecclesiastical interference of eastern emperors, launched a counteroffensive. Pope Damasus I (366–384)[3] took the first of several major steps in the rise of the Roman church when he declared a Roman "apostolic" primacy. Pointing to Jesus' words to Peter in the Gospel of Matthew (16:18), the pope claimed to be in direct succession from Peter as the unique "rock" on which the Christian Church was built. Pope Leo I (440–461) took still another fateful step by assuming the title *pontifex maximus*—"supreme priest"—and he further proclaimed himself to be endowed with a "plentitude of power." During Leo's reign an imperial decree had already recognized his exclusive jurisdiction over the western church in 455. At the end of the fifth century Pope Gelasius I (492–496) proclaimed the authority of the clergy to be "more weighty" than the power of kings.

[3]Papal dates give the years of each reign.

The western church was favored by events as well as ideology. It was the chief beneficiary of imperial adversity in the face of Germanic and Arab invasions. Islam may even be said to have "saved" the western church from eastern domination, and the emergent Lombards and Franks provided it with new political allies. The success of Arab armies ended eastern episcopal competition with Rome as the area of bishopric after bishopric fell to the Muslims in the east. The power of the exarch of Ravenna, who was the Byzantine emperor's regent in the west, was eclipsed by invading Lombards, who, thanks to Frankish prodding, became Nicene Christians loyal to Rome in the late seventh century. In an unprecedented act Pope Gregory I, "the Great" (590–604), negotiated an independent peace treaty with the Lombards that completely ignored the emperor and the imperial government in Ravenna, who were at the time too weak to offer resistance.

Augustine of Hippo Describes His Conversion to Christianity

Augustine of Hippo (354–430) frankly confessed his utter sinfulness and domination by lust until Christianity gave him the will to resist.

Who am I, and what am I? Is there any evil that is not found in my acts, or if not in my acts, in my words, or if not in my words, in my will? But you, O Lord, are good and merciful, and your right hand has had regard for the depth of my death, and from the very bottom of my heart it has emptied out an abyss of corruption. This was the sum of it: not to will what I willed and to will what you willed.

But throughout these long years where was my free will? Out of what deep and hidden pit was it called forth in a single moment, wherein to bend my neck to your mild yoke and my shoulders to your light burden, O Christ Jesus, "my helper and my redeemer"? How sweet did it suddenly become to me to be free of the sweets of folly: things that I once feared to lose it was now joy to put away. You cast them forth from me, you the true and highest sweetness, you cast them forth, and in their stead you entered in, sweeter than every pleasure, but not to flesh and blood, brighter than every light, but deeper within me than any secret retreat, higher than every honor, but not to those who exalt themselves. Now was my mind free from the gnawing cares of favor-seeking, of striving for gain, of wallowing in the mire, and of scratching lust's itchy sore. I spoke like a child to you, my light, my wealth, my salvation, my Lord God.

The Confessions of St. Augustine, trans. by John K. Ryan (New York: Doubleday, 1960), pp. 205–206.

The Division of Christendom. The division of Christendom into eastern and western churches has its roots in the early Middle Ages. From the start there was the difference in language (Greek in the east, Latin in the west) and culture. Compared with their western counterparts, eastern Christians seemed to attribute less importance to life in this world. They were more concerned about questions affecting their eternal destiny. This concern made them more receptive than the western Christian to Oriental mysticism and theological ideas. It was, after all, a combination of Greek, Roman, and Oriental elements that formed Byzantine culture. The strong mystical orientation to the next world may also have caused the eastern church to submit more passively than western popes could ever do to royal intervention in church affairs.

As in the west, eastern church organization closely followed that of the secular state. A patriarch ruled over metropolitans and archbishops in the cities and provinces, and they, in turn, ruled over bishops, who stood as authorities over the local clergy. With the exception of the patriarch Michael Cerularius, who tried unsuccessfully to free the church from its traditional tight state control, the patriarchs were normally carefully regulated by the emperor.

Contrary to the evolving western tradition of universal clerical celibacy, which western monastic culture encouraged, the eastern church permitted the marriage of secular priests, while strictly forbidding bishops to marry. The eastern church also used leavened bread in the Eucharist, contrary to the western custom of using unleavened bread. Also unliked by the west was the tendency of the eastern church to compromise doctrinally with the politically powerful Arian and Monophysite Christians. In the background were also conflicting political claims over jurisdiction over the newly converted areas in the north Balkans.

Beyond these issues the major factors in the religious break between east and west revolved around questions of doctrinal authority. The eastern church put more stress on the authority of the Bible and of the ecumenical councils of the church than on the counsel and decrees of the bishop of Rome. The councils and Holy Scripture were the ultimate authorities in the definition of Christian doctrine. The claims of Roman popes to a special primacy of authority

Pope Gelasius I Declares the "Weightiness" of Priestly Authority

Some see this famous letter of Pope Gelasius to Emperor Anastasius I in 494 as an extreme statement of papal supremacy. Others believe it is a balanced, moderate statement that recognizes the independence of both temporal and spiritual power and seeks their close cooperation, not the domination of church over state.

There are two powers, august Emperor, by which this world is chiefly ruled, namely, the sacred authority of the priests and the royal power. Of these, that of the priests is the more weighty, since they have to render an account for even the kings of men in the divine judgment. You are also aware, dear son [emperor], that while you are permitted honorably to rule over humankind, yet in things divine you bow your head humbly before the leaders of the clergy and await from their hands the means of your salvation. In the reception and proper disposition of the heavenly mysteries you recognize that you should be subordinate rather than superior to the religious order, and that in these matters you depend on their judgment rather than wish to force them to follow your will. [And] if the ministers of religion, recognizing the supremacy granted you from heaven in matters affecting the public order, obey your laws, lest otherwise they obstruct the course of secular affairs . . . , with what readiness should you not yield them obedience to whom is assigned the dispensing of the sacred mysteries of religion?

James Harvey Robinson (Ed.), *Readings in European History,* Vol. 1 (Boston: Athenaeum, 1904), pp. 72–73.

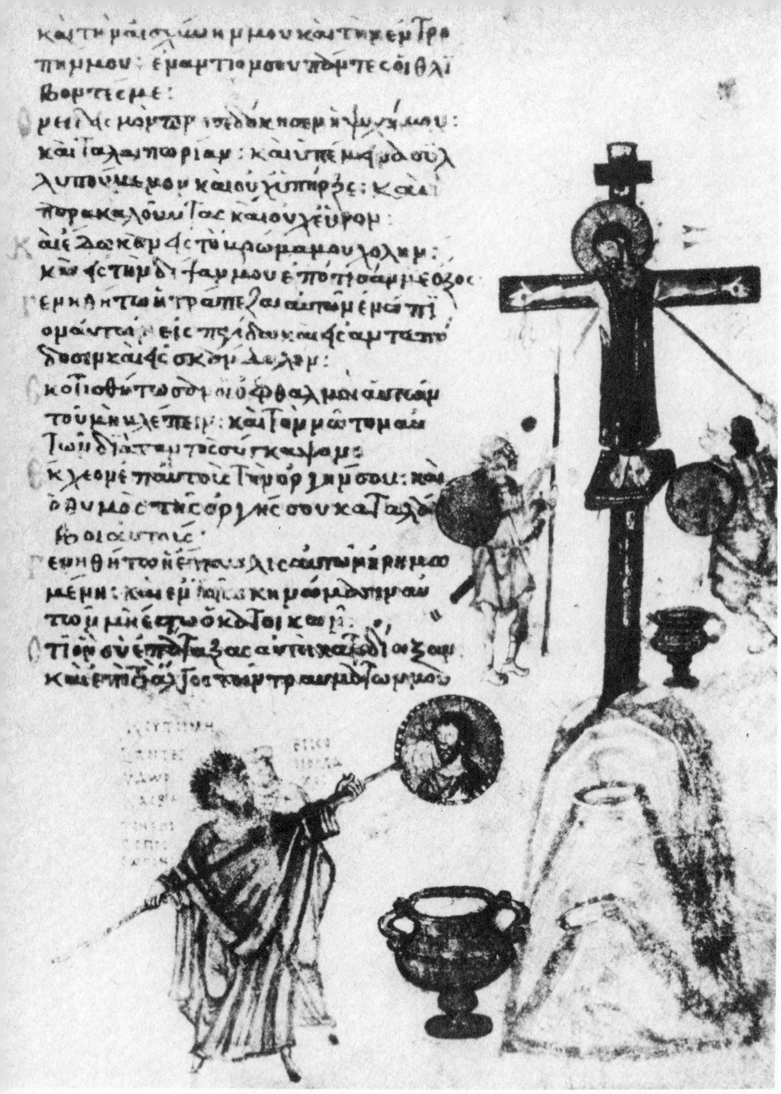

This ninth-century Byzantine manuscript shows an iconoclast whiting out an image of Christ. The iconoclast controversy was an important stage in dividing Christendom into separate Latin and Greek branches. [*Public Library, Moscow*]

on the basis of the apostle Peter's commission from Jesus in Matthew 16:18 ("Thou art Peter, and upon this rock I will build my church") were completely unacceptable to the east, where the independence and autonomy of national churches held sway. As Steven Runciman summarized, "The Byzantine ideal was a series of autocephalous state churches, linked by intercommunion and the faith of seven councils."[4] This basic issue of authority in matters of faith lay behind the mutual excommunication of Pope Nicholas I and Patriarch Photius in the ninth century and that of Pope Leo IX and Patriarch Michael Cerularius in 1054.

A second major issue in the separation of the two churches was the western addition of the *filioque* clause to the Nicene–Constantinopolitan Creed—an anti-Arian move that made the Holy Spirit proceed "also from the Son" (*filioque*) as well as from the Father. This addition made clear the western belief that Christ was "fully substantial with God the Father" and not a lesser being.

The final and most direct issue in the religious division of Christendom was the iconoclastic controversy of the first half of the eighth century. After 725 the eastern emperor, Leo III (717–740), attempted to force western popes to abolish the use of images in their churches. This stand met fierce official and popular resistance in the west, where images were greatly cherished. Emperor Leo punished the disobedient west by confiscating papal lands in Sicily and Calabria (in southern Italy) and placing them under the jurisdiction of the subservient patriarch of Constantinople. Because these territories provided essential papal revenues, the western church could not but view the emperor's action as a declaration of war. Later the empress Irene (mother of Constantine VI) made peace with the Roman church on this issue and restored the use of images at the sixth ecumenical council in Nicea in 787.

Leo's direct challenge of the pope came almost simultaneously with still another aggressive act against the western church: attacks by the heretofore docile Lombards of northern Italy. Assailed by both the emperor and the Lombards, the pope in Rome seemed surely doomed. But there has not been a more resilient and enterprising institution in Western history than the Roman papacy. Since the pontificate of Gregory the Great, Roman popes had eyed the Franks of northern Gaul as Europe's ascendant power and their surest protector. Imperial and Lombard aggression against the Roman pope in the first half of the eighth century provided the occasion for the most fruitful political alliance of the Middle Ages. In 754 Pope Stephen II (752–757) enlisted Pepin III and his Franks as defenders of the church against the Lombards and as a western counterweight to the eastern emperor. This marriage of religion and politics created a new western church and empire; it also determined much of the course of Western history into our times.

[4]*Byzantine Civilization* (London: A. and C. Black, 1933), p. 128.

The Kingdom of the Franks

Merovingians and Carolingians: From Clovis to Charlemagne

A warrior chieftain, Clovis (466?–511), a convert to Christianity around 496, made the Franks and their first ruling family, the Merovingians, a significant force in western Europe. Clovis and his successors subdued the pagan Burgundians and the Arian Visigoths and established within ancient Gaul the kingdom of the Franks. The Franks were a broad belt of people scattered throughout modern Belgium, the Netherlands, and western Germany, whose loyalties remained strictly tribal and local. The Merovingians attempted to govern this sprawling kingdom by pacts with landed nobility and by the creation of the royal office of count. The most persistent problem of medieval political history was the competing claims of the "one" and the "many"—on the one hand, the king, who struggled for a centralized government and transregional loyalty, and on the other, powerful local magnates, who strove to preserve their regional autonomy and traditions. The Merovingian counts were men without possessions to whom the king gave great lands in the expectation that they would be, as the landed aristocrats often were not, loyal officers of the kingdom. But like local aristocrats the Merovingian counts also let their immediate self-interests gain the upper hand. Once established in office for a period of time, they too became territorial rulers in their own right, with the result that the Frankish kingdom progressively fragmented into independent regions and tiny principalities. This centrifugal tendency was further assisted by the Frankish custom of dividing the kingdom equally among the king's legitimate male heirs.

Clovis Converts to Christianity

One of the attractions of Christianity in the late ancient and early medieval world was its belief in a God providentially active in history who assisted those loyal to Him against their enemies. In the following account of Clovis's conversion, provided by the Christian Church historian Gregory of Tours, the Frankish king is said to have turned Christian because he believed that the Christian God had given him a military victory over a rival German tribe, the Alemanni.

Clovis took to wife Clotilde, daughter of the king of the Burgundians and a Christian. The queen unceasingly urged the king to acknowledge the true God, and forsake idols. But he could not in any wise be brought to believe until a war broke out with the Alemanni. . . . The two armies were in battle and there was great slaughter. Clovis' army was near to utter destruction. He saw the danger . . . and raised his eyes to heaven, saying: Jesus Christ, whom Clotilde declares to be the son of the living God, who it is said givest aid to the oppressed and victory to those who put their hope in thee, I beseech thy . . . aid. If thou shalt grant me victory over these enemies . . . I will believe in thee and be baptized in thy name. For I have called upon my gods, but . . . they are far removed from my aid. So I believe that they have no power, for they do not succor those who serve them. Now I call upon thee, and I long to believe in thee. . . . When he had said these things, the Alemanni turned their backs and began to flee. When they saw that their king was killed, they submitted to the sway of Clovis, saying . . . Now we are thine.

After Clovis had forbidden further war and praised his soldiers, he told the queen how he had won the victory by calling on the name of Christ. Then the queen sent for the blessed Remigius, bishop of the city of Rheims, praying him to bring the gospel of salvation to the king. The priest, little by little and secretly, led him to believe in the true God . . . and to forsake idols, which could not help him nor anybody else.

James Harvey Robinson (Ed.), *Readings in European History,* Vol. 1 (Boston: Athenaeum, 1904), pp. 52–54.

Rather than purchasing allegiance and unity within the kingdom, the Merovingian largess simply occasioned the rise of competing magnates and petty tyrants, who became laws unto themselves within their regions. By the seventh century the Frankish king existed more in title than in effective executive power. Real power came to be concentrated in the office of the *mayor of the palace,* who was the spokesman at the king's court for the great landowners of the three regions into which the Frankish kingdom was divided: Neustria, Austrasia, and Burgundy. Through this office the Carolingian dynasty rose to power.

The Carolingians controlled the office of the mayor of the palace from the ascent to that post of Pepin I of Austrasia (d. 639) until 751, at which time the Carolingians, with the enterprising connivance of the pope, simply expropriated the Frankish crown. Pepin II (d. 714) ruled in fact if not in title over the Frankish kingdom. His illegitimate son, Charles Martel ("the Hammer," d. 741), created a great cavalry by bestowing lands known as *benefices* or *fiefs* on powerful noblemen, who, in return, agreed to be ready to serve as the king's army. It was such an army that checked the Arab probings on the western front at Poitiers in 732—an important battle that helped to secure the borders of western Europe.

Carolingian cavalry, from a ninth-century Swiss manuscript. [*Mansell Collection*]

The fiefs so generously bestowed by Charles Martel to create his army came in large part from landed property that he usurped from the church. His alliance with the landed aristocracy in this grand manner permitted the Carolingians to have some measure of political success where the Merovingians had failed. The Carolingians created counts almost entirely out of the landed nobility from which the Carolingians themselves had risen. The Merovingians, in contrast, had tried to compete directly with these great aristocrats by raising landless men to power. By playing to strength rather than challenging it, the Carolingians strengthened themselves, at least for the short term. Because the church was by this time completely dependent of the protection of the Franks against the eastern emperor and the Lombards, it gave little thought at this time to the fact that its savior had been created in part with lands to which it held claim. Later the Franks partially compensated the church for these lands.

The Frankish Church. The church came to play a large and initially quite voluntary role in the Frankish government. By Carolingian times monasteries were a dominant force. Their intellectual achievements made them respected repositories of culture. Their religious teaching and example imposed order on surrounding populations. Their relics and rituals made them magical shrines to which pilgrims came in great numbers. And, thanks to their many gifts and internal discipline and industry, many had become very profitable farms and landed estates, their abbots rich and powerful magnates. Already in Merovingian times the higher clergy were employed in tandem with counts as royal agents. It was the policy of the Carolingians, perfected by Charles Martel and his successor, Pepin III ("the Short," d. 768), to use the church to pacify conquered neighboring tribes—Frisians, Thüringians, Bavarians, and especially the Franks' archenemies, the Saxons. Conversion to Nicene Christianity became an integral part of the successful annexation of conquered lands and people: the cavalry broke their bodies, while the clergy won their hearts and minds. The Anglo-Saxon missionary Saint Boniface (born Wynfrith; 680?–754) was the most important of the German clergy who served Carolingian kings in this way. Christian bishops in missionary districts and elsewhere became lords, appointed by and subject to the king—an ominous integration of secular and religious policy in which lay the seeds of the later Investiture Controversy of the eleventh and twelfth centuries.

The church served more than Carolingian territorial expansion. Pope Zacharias (741–752) also sanctioned Pepin the Short's termination of the vestigial Merovingian dynasty and supported the Carolingian accession to outright kingship of the Franks. With the pope's public blessing, Pepin was proclaimed king by the nobility in council in 751, while the last of the Merovingians, the puppet king Childeric III, was hustled off to a monastery and dynastic oblivion. According to legend, Saint Boniface first anointed Pepin, thereby investing Frankish rule from the very start with a certain sacral character.

Zacharias's successor, Pope Stephen II (752–757), did not let Pepin forget the favor of his predecessor. Driven from Rome in 753 by the Lombards, Pope Stephen appealed directly to Pepin to cast out the invaders and to guarantee papal claims to central Italy, which was dominated at this time by the eastern emperor. In 754 the Franks and the church formed an alliance against the Lombards and the eastern emperor. Carolingian kings became the protectors of the Catholic Church and thereby "kings by the grace of God." Pepin gained the title *patricius Romanorum,* "patrician of the Romans," a title first borne by the ruling families of Rome and heretofore applied to the representative of the eastern emperor. In 755 the Franks defeated the Lombards and gave the pope the lands surrounding Rome, an event that created what came to be known as the *Papal States.* The lands earlier appropriated by Charles Martel and parceled out to the Frankish nobility were never returned to the church, despite the appearance in this period of a most enterprising fraudulent document designed to win their return, the *Donation of Constantine* (written between 750 and 800), which, however, was never universally accepted in the west. This imperial parchment alleged that the Emperor Constantine had personally conveyed to the church his palace and "all provinces and districts of the city of Rome and Italy and of the regions of the West" as permanent possessions. It was believed by many to be a genuine document until definitely exposed as a forgery in the fifteenth century by the Humanist Lorenzo Valla.

The papacy had looked to the Franks for an ally strong enough to protect it from the eastern emperors. It is an irony of history that the church found in the Carolingian dynasty a western imperial government that drew almost as slight a boundary between State and Church, secular and religious policy, as did eastern emperors. Although eminently preferable to eastern domination, Carolingian patronage of the church proved in its own way to be no less dominating.

Major Political and Religious Developments of the Early Middle Ages

Emperor Constatine issues the Edict of Milan	313
Council of Nicaea defines Christian doctrine	325
Rome invaded by Visigoths under Alaric	410
St. Augustine writes *The City of God*	413–426
Council of Chalcedon further defined Christian doctrine	451
Europe invaded by the Huns under Attila	451–453
Barbarian Odoacer deposes western emperor and rules as king of the Romans	476
Theodoric establishes kingdom of Ostrogoths in Italy	488
Saint Benedict founds monastery at Monte Cassino	529
Justinian codifies Roman law	533
Muhammad's flight from Mecca (*Hegira*)	622
Charles Martel defeats Arabs at Poitiers	732
Pope Stephen II and Pepin III ally	754

The Reign of Charlemagne (768–814)

Charlemagne continued the role of his father, Pepin the Short, as papal protector in Italy and his policy of territorial conquest in the north. After King Desiderius and the Lombards of northern Italy were decisively defeated in 774, Charlemagne took upon himself the title "King of the Lombards" in Pavia. He widened the frontiers of his kingdom further by

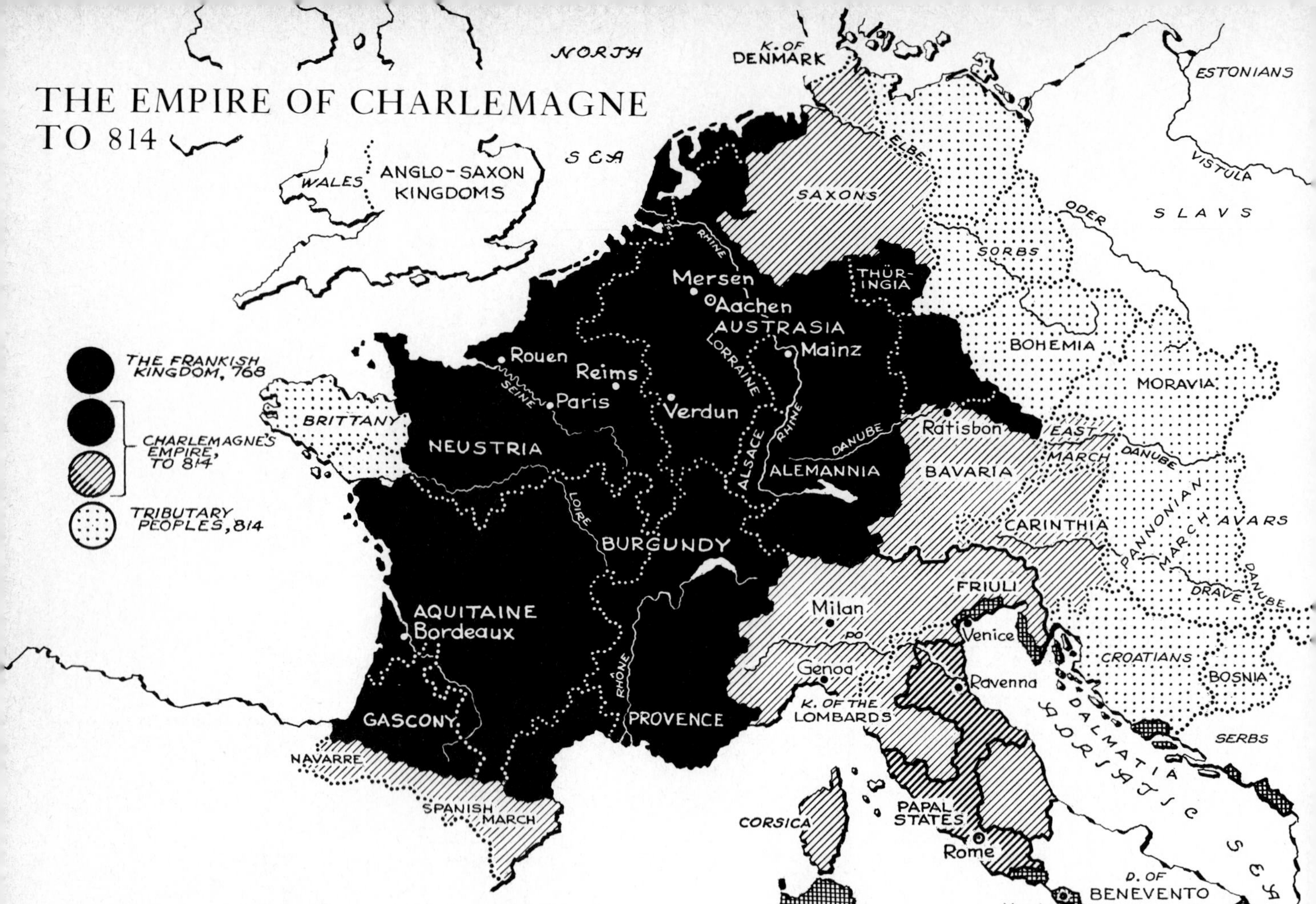

MAP 6-4 *Building on the successes of his predecessors, Charlemagne greatly increased the Frankish domains. Such traditional enemies as the Saxons and the Lombards fell under his sway.*

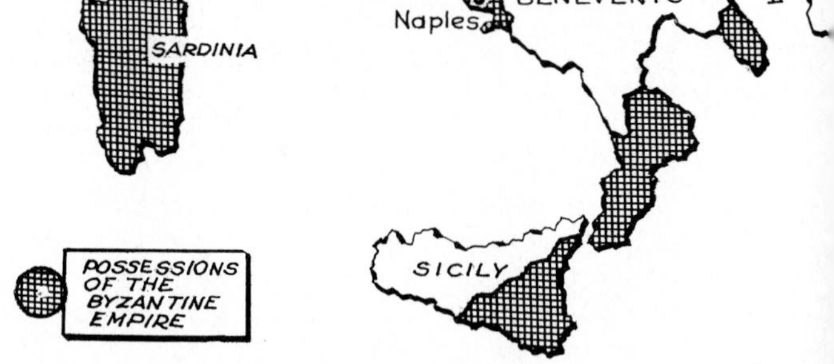

subjugating surrounding pagan tribes, foremost among whom were the Saxons, whom the Franks brutally Christianized and dispersed in small groups throughout Frankish lands. The Avars (a tribe related to the Huns) were practically annihilated, so that the Danubian plains were brought into the Frankish orbit. The Arabs were chased beyond the Pyrenees. By the time of his death on January 28, 814, Charlemagne's kingdom embraced modern France, Belgium, Holland, Switzerland, almost the whole of western Germany, much of Italy, a portion of Spain, and the island of Corsica—an area approximately equal to that of the modern Common Market (see Map 6.4).

THE NEW EMPIRE. Encouraged by his ambitious advisers, Charlemagne came to harbor imperial designs; he desired to be not only king of the Germans but a universal emperor as well. He had his sacred palace city, Aachen (in French, Aix-la-Chapelle), constructed in conscious imitation of the courts of the ancient Roman and of the contemporary eastern emperors. Although permitted its distinctiveness, the church was looked after by Charlemagne with a paternalism almost as great as that of any eastern emperor. He used the church, above all, to promote social stability and hierarchical order throughout the kingdom—as an aid in the creation of a great Frankish Christian empire. Frankish Christians were ceremoniously baptized, professed the Nicene Creed (with the *filioque* clause), and learned in church to revere Charlemagne.

In the 790s the formation of a peculiar Carolingian Christendom was made clear by the royal issuance of the so-called *Libri Carolini.* In these documents Charlemagne attacked the second ecumenical Council of Nicaea, which had met in 787 to construct a new, approving, eastern position on the use of images in churches—actually a friendly gesture toward the west. The height of Charlemagne's imperial pretension was reached, however, on Christmas Day, 800, when Pope Leo II (795–816) crowned Charlemagne emperor. Only a short time before, Charlemagne had restored to power this contested pope, whom the Roman aristocracy had briefly imprisoned in 799 before his escape to Charlemagne. This fateful coronation was in part an effort by the pope to enhance the church's stature and to gain a certain leverage over this king who seemed to dominate everything in his path. It was no papal *coup d'etat,* however; Charlemagne's control over the church was as strong after as before the event. If the coronation benefited the church, as it certainly did, it also served Charlemagne's purposes. Before Christmas Day, 800, Charlemagne was a minor western potentate in the eyes of eastern emperors. After the coronation, eastern emperors reluctantly recognized his new imperial dignity, and Charlemagne even found it necessary to disclaim ambitions to rule as emperor over the east. Here began what would come to be known as the Holy Roman Empire, a revival, based in Germany, of the old Roman Empire in the west.

The New Emperor. Charlemagne stood a majestic six feet three and one-half inches tall—a fact secured when his tomb was opened and exact measurements were taken in 1861. He was nomadic, ever ready for a hunt. Informal and gregarious, he insisted on the presence of friends even when he bathed and was widely known for his practical jokes, lusty good humor, and warm hospitality. Aachen was a festive palace city to which people and gifts came from all over the world. In 802

Emperor and pope: This ninth-century mosaic from the Cathedral of St. John Lateran in Rome depicts St. Peter giving spiritual authority to Pope Leo III and temporal power to the emperor Charlemagne. [*Vatican Library*]

Charlemagne even received from the caliph of Baghdad, Harun-al-Rashid, a white elephant, the transport of which across the Alps was as great a wonder as the creature itself.

Charlemagne had five official wives, possessed many mistresses and concubines, and sired numerous children. This connubial variety created special problems. His oldest son by his first marriage, Pepin, jealous of the attention shown by his father to the sons of his second wife and fearing the loss of paternal favor, joined with noble enemies in a conspiracy against his father. He ended his life in confinement in a monastery after the plot was exposed.

Problems of Government. Charlemagne governed his kingdom through counts, of whom there were perhaps as many as 250. They were strategically located within the administrative districts into which the kingdom was divided. In Carolingian practice the count tended to be a local magnate, one who already possessed the armed might and the self-interest to enforce the will of a generous king. He had three main duties: to maintain a local army loyal to the king, to collect tribute and dues, and to administer justice throughout his district. This last responsibility he undertook through a district law court known as the *mallus*. The *mallus* assessed *wergeld*, or the compensation to be paid to an injured party in a feud, the most popular way of settling grievances and ending hostilities. In

The False Donation of Constantine

Among the ways in which Roman ecclesiasts fought to free the western church from political domination was to assert its own sovereign territorial and political rights. One of the most ambitious of such assertions was the so-called *Donation of Constantine* (eighth century), a fraudulent document claiming papal succession to much of the old Roman Empire.

The Emperor Caesar Flavius Constantinus in Christ Jesus . . . to the most Holy and blessed Father of fathers, Silvester, Bishop of the Roman city and Pope; and to all his successors, the pontiffs, who shall sit in the chair of blessed Peter to the end of time. . . . Grace, peace, love, joy, long-suffering, mercy . . . be with you all. . . . For we wish you to know . . . that we have forsaken the worship of idols . . . and have come to the pure Christian faith. . . .

To the holy apostles, my lords the most blessed Peter and Paul, and through them also to blessed Silvester, our father, supreme pontiff and universal pope of the city of Rome, and to the pontiffs, his successors, who to the end of the world shall sit in the seat of blessed Peter, we grant and by this present we convey our imperial Lateran palace, which is superior to and excels all palaces in the whole world; and further the diadem, which is the crown of our head; and the miter; as also the super-humeral, that is, the stole which usually surrounds our imperial neck; and the purple cloak and the scarlet tunic and all the imperial robes. . .

And we decree that those most reverend men, the clergy of various orders serving the same most holy Roman Church, shall have that eminence, distinction, power and precedence, with which our illustrious senate is gloriously adorned; that is, they shall be made patricians and consuls. And we ordain that they shall also be adorned with other imperial dignities. Also we decree that the clergy of the sacred Roman Church shall be adorned as are the imperial officers. . . .

We convey to the oft-mentioned and most blessed Silvester, universal pope, both our palace, as preferment, and likewise all provinces, palaces and districts of the city of Rome and Italy and of the regions of the West; and, bequeathing them to the power and sway of him and the pontiffs, his successors, we do determine and decree that the same be placed at his disposal, and do lawfully grant it as a permanent possession to the holy Roman Church.

Henry Bettenson (Ed.)., *Documents of the Christian Church* (New York: Oxford University Press, 1961), pp. 137–141.

Charlemagne as law-giver, from a tenth-century French manuscript. [*Bibliotheque Nationale, Paris*]

very difficult cases where guilt or innocence was unclear, recourse was often had to judicial duels or to such "divine" judgments as the length of time it took a defendant's hand to heal after immersion in boiling water. In the ordeal by water, another divine test when human judgment was stymied, a defendant was thrown with his hands and feet bound into a river or pond that was first blessed by a priest; if he floated, he was pronounced guilty, because the pure water had obviously rejected him; if, however, the water received him and he sank, then he was deemed innocent.

As in Merovingian times, many counts used their official position and new judicial powers to their own advantage, becoming little despots within their districts. As the strong were made stronger, they became more independent. They looked on the land grants with which they were paid as hereditary possessions rather than generous royal donations—a development that began to fragment Charlemagne's kingdom. Charlemagne tried to oversee his overseers and improve local justice by creating special royal envoys known as *missi dominici.* These were lay and clerical agents (counts and archbishops and bishops) who made annual visits to districts other than their own. But their impact was only marginal. Permanent provincial governors, bearing the title of prefect, duke, or margrave, were created in what was still another attempt to supervise the counts and organize the outlying regions of the kingdom. But as these governors became established in their areas, they proved no less corruptible than the others. Charlemagne never solved the problem of a loyal bureaucracy. Ecclesiastical agents proved no better than secu-

The Duties of the Missi Dominici

Although they did not succeed in rendering universal justice, Charlemagne's special royal agents, the *missi dominici,* were an effort to implement Charlemagne's idea of what government should ideally do to gain respect and retain allegiance. The following is a general description of the *missi* and their duties from a capitulary (or Frankish legal ordinance) of 802.

The most serene and most Christian lord emperor Charles has chosen from his nobles the wisest and most prudent men, archbishops and some of the other bishops also, together with venerable abbots and pious laymen, and has sent them throughout his whole kingdom; through them he would have all persons live strictly in accordance with the law. Moreover, where anything which is not right and just has been enacted in the law, he has ordered them to inquire into this most diligently and to inform him of it; he desires, God granting, to reform it. . . . Let the missi *themselves make a diligent investigation whenever any man claims that an injustice has been done to him by any one, just as they desire to deserve the grace of omnipotent God and to keep their fidelity pledged to him, so that in all cases, everywhere, they shall, in accordance with the will and fear of God, administer the law fully and justly in the case of the holy churches of God and of the poor, of wards and widows, and of the whole people. And if there shall be anything . . . that they, together with the provincial counts, are not able of themselves to correct and to do justice concerning it, they shall, without any reservations, refer this, together with their reports, to the judgment of the emperor. The straight path of justice shall not be impeded by any one on account of flattery or gifts, or on account of any relationship, or from fear of the powerful.*

James Harvey Robinson (Ed.), *Readings in European History,* Vol. 1 (Boston: Athenaeum, 1904), pp. 139–140.

lar ones in this regard. Landowning bishops had not only the same responsibilities but also the same secular lifestyles and aspirations as the royal counts. Save for their attendance to the liturgy and to church prayers, they were largely indistinguishable from the lay nobility. Capitularies or royal decrees discouraged the more outrageous behavior of the clergy. But Charlemagne also sensed, rightly as the Gregorian reform of the eleventh century would prove, a danger to royal government in the emergence of a distinctive and reform-minded class of ecclesiastical landowners. Charlemagne purposefully treated his bishops as he treated his counts, that is, as vassals who served at the king's pleasure.

To be a Christian in this period was more a matter of ritual and doctrine, being baptized and reciting the Creed, than a prescribed ethical behavior and social service. For both the clergy and the laity it was a time when more primitive social goals were being contested. A legislative achievement of Charlemagne's reign, for example, was to give a free vassal the right to break his oath of loyalty to his lord if the lord tried to kill him, to reduce him to an unfree serf, to withhold promised protection in time of need, or to seduce his wife.

Alcuin and the Carolingian Renaissance. Charlemagne accumulated a great deal of wealth in the form of loot and land from conquered tribes. He used a substantial part of this booty to attract Europe's best scholars to Aachen, where they developed court culture and education. By making scholarship materially as well as intellectually rewarding, Charlemagne attracted such scholars as Theodulf of Orleans, Angilbert, his own biographer Einhard, and the renowned Anglo-Saxon master Alcuin of York (735–804), who, at almost fifty, became director of the king's palace school in 782. Alcuin brought classical and Christian learning to Aachen and was handsomely rewarded for his efforts with several monastic estates, including that of Saint Martin of Tours, the wealthiest in the kingdom.

Although Charlemagne also appreciated learning for its own sake, this grand palace school was not created simply for love of antiquity. Charlemagne intended it to upgrade the administrative skills of the clerics and officials who staffed the royal bureaucracy. By preparing the sons of the nobility to run the religious and secular offices of the realm, court scholarship served kingdom building. The school provided basic instruction in the seven liberal arts, with special concentration on grammar, logic, and mathematics, that is, training in reading, writing, speaking, and sound reasoning—the basic tools of bureaucracy. A clearer style of handwriting—the Carolingian minuscule—and accurate Latin appeared in the official documents. Lay literacy increased. Through personal correspondence and visitations Alcuin created a genuine, if limited, community of scholars and clerics at court and did much to infuse the highest administrative levels with a sense of comradeship and common purpose.

A modest renaissance or rebirth of antiquity occurred in the palace school as scholars col-

Einhard Describes His Admired Emperor, Charlemagne

We are fortunate to have an eye-witness account of Charlemagne by a court scholar, Einhard. Here are his remarks on the king's features, habits, and aspirations.

Charles was large and robust, of commanding stature and excellent proportions. . . . He took constant exercise in riding and hunting, which was natural for a Frank, since scarcely any nation can be found to equal them in these pursuits. He also delighted in the natural warm baths, frequently exercising himself by swimming, in which he was very skillful, no one being able to outstrip him. It was on account of the warm baths at Aix-la-Chapelle that he built his palace there and lived there constantly during the last years of his life and until his death. . . .

He wore the dress of his native country, that is, the Frankish. . . . He thoroughly disliked the dress of foreigners, however fine; and he never put it on except at Rome. . . .

In his eating and drinking he was temperate; more particularly so in his drinking, for he had the greatest abhorrence of drunkenness in anybody, but more especially in himself and his companions. . . . While he was dining he listened to music or reading. History and the deeds of men of old were most often read. He derived much pleasure from the works of St. Augustine, especially from his book called The City of God.

He was ready and fluent in speaking, and able to express himself with great clearness. He did not confine himself to his native tongue, but took pains to learn foreign languages, acquiring such knowledge of Latin that he could make an address in that language as well as in his own. Greek he could better understand than speak. Indeed, he was so polished in speech that he might have passed for a learned man.

He was an ardent admirer of the liberal arts, and greatly revered their professors, whom he promoted to high honors. In order to learn grammar, he attended the lectures of the aged Peter of Pisa, a deacon; and for other branches of knowledge he chose as his preceptor Alcuin, also a deacon,—a Saxon by race, from Britain, the most learned man of the day, with whom the king spent much time in learning rhetoric and logic, and more especially astronomy. He learned the art of determining the dates upon which the movable festivals of the Church fall, and with deep thought and skill most carefully calculated the courses of the planets.

Charles also tried to learn to write, and used to keep his tablets and writing book under the pillow of his couch, that when he had leisure he might practice his hand in forming letters; but he made little progress in this task, too long deferred and begun too late in life.

Life of Charlemagne, in James Harvey Robinson (Ed.), *Readings in European History,* Vol. 1 (Boston: Athenaeum, 1904), pp. 126–128.

Einhard, the chronicler of Charlemagne's reign. Einhard was among the many European scholars whom Charlemagne attracted to his court at Aachen. [*Bibliotheque Nationale, Paris*]

lected and preserved ancient manuscripts for a more curious posterity. Alcuin worked on a correct text of the Bible and made editions of the works of Gregory the Great and the monastic *Rule* of Saint Benedict. These scholarly activities aimed at concrete reforms and served official efforts to bring uniformity to church law and liturgy, to educate the clergy, and to improve moral life within the monasteries.

THE MANOR. The agrarian economy of the Middle Ages was organized and controlled through village farms known as *manors*. Here peasants labored as farmers in subordination to a lord, that is, a more powerful landowner who gave them land and tenements in exchange for their services and a portion of their crops. That part of the land farmed by the peasants for the lord was the *demesne*, on average about one quarter to one third of the arable land, and all crops grown there were harvested for the lord. The peasants were treated differently according to their personal status and the size of their tenement, all in strict accordance with custom; indeed, a social hierarchy existed among the peasantry. When a *freeman*, that is, a peasant with his own modest allodial or hereditary property (property free from the claims of a feudal overlord) became a serf by surrendering this property to a greater landowner in exchange for his protection and assistance, the freeman received it back from the lord with a clear definition of economic and legal rights that protected the freeman's self-interest. Although the land was no longer his property, he had full possession and use of it, and the number of services and amount of goods to be supplied the lord were often carefully spelled out. On the other hand, peasants who entered the service of a lord without any real property to bargain with (perhaps some farm implements and a few animals) ended up as *unfree* serfs and were much more vulnerable to the lord's demands, often spending up to three days a week working the lord's fields. Truly impoverished peasants who lived and worked on the manor as serfs had the lowest status and were the least protected. Weak serfs often fled to a monastery rather than continue their servitude, and therefore this avenue of escape was eventually closed by law.

By the time of Charlemagne the moldboard plow and the three-field system of land cultivation were coming into use, developments that improved agricultural productivity. Unlike the older "scratch" plow, which crisscrossed the field with only slight penetration, the moldboard cut deep into the soil and turned it so that it formed a ridge, providing a natural drainage system to the field as well as permitting the deep planting of seeds. Unlike the earlier two-field system of crop rotation, which simply alternated fallow with planted fields each year, the three-field system increased the amount of cultivated land by leaving only one third fallow in a given year. It also better adjusted crops to seasons. In winter one field was planted with winter crops of wheat or rye; in the summer a second field was planted with summer crops of oats, barley, and lentils; and the third field was left fallow, to be planted in its turn with winter and summer crops.

Serfs were subject to so-called dues in kind: firewood for cutting the lord's wood, sheep for grazing their sheep on the lord's land, and the like. In this way the lord, by furnishing shacks and small plots of land from his vast domain, created an army of servants who provided him with everything from eggs to boots.

The discontent of the serfs is witnessed by the high number of recorded escapes. An astrological calendar from the period even marks the days most favorable for escaping. Escaped serfs roamed the land as beggars and vagabonds, searching for new and better masters.

Religion and the Clergy. The lower clergy lived among and were drawn from the peasant class. They fared hardly better than peasants in Carolingian times. As owners of the churches on their lands, the lords had the right to raise chosen serfs to the post of parish priest, placing them in charge of the churches on the lords' estates. Although church law directed the lord to set a serf free before he entered the clergy, lords were reluctant to do this and risk thereby a possible later challenge to their jurisdiction over the ecclesiastical property with which the serf, as priest, was invested. Lords rather preferred a "serf priest," one who not only said the Mass on Sundays and holidays but who also continued to serve his lord during the week, waiting on the lord's table and tending his steeds. Like Charlemagne with his bishops, Frankish lords cultivated a docile parish clergy.

The ordinary people looked to religion for

In this eleventh-century manuscript, peasants harvest grain, trim vines, and plow fields behind yoked oxen.

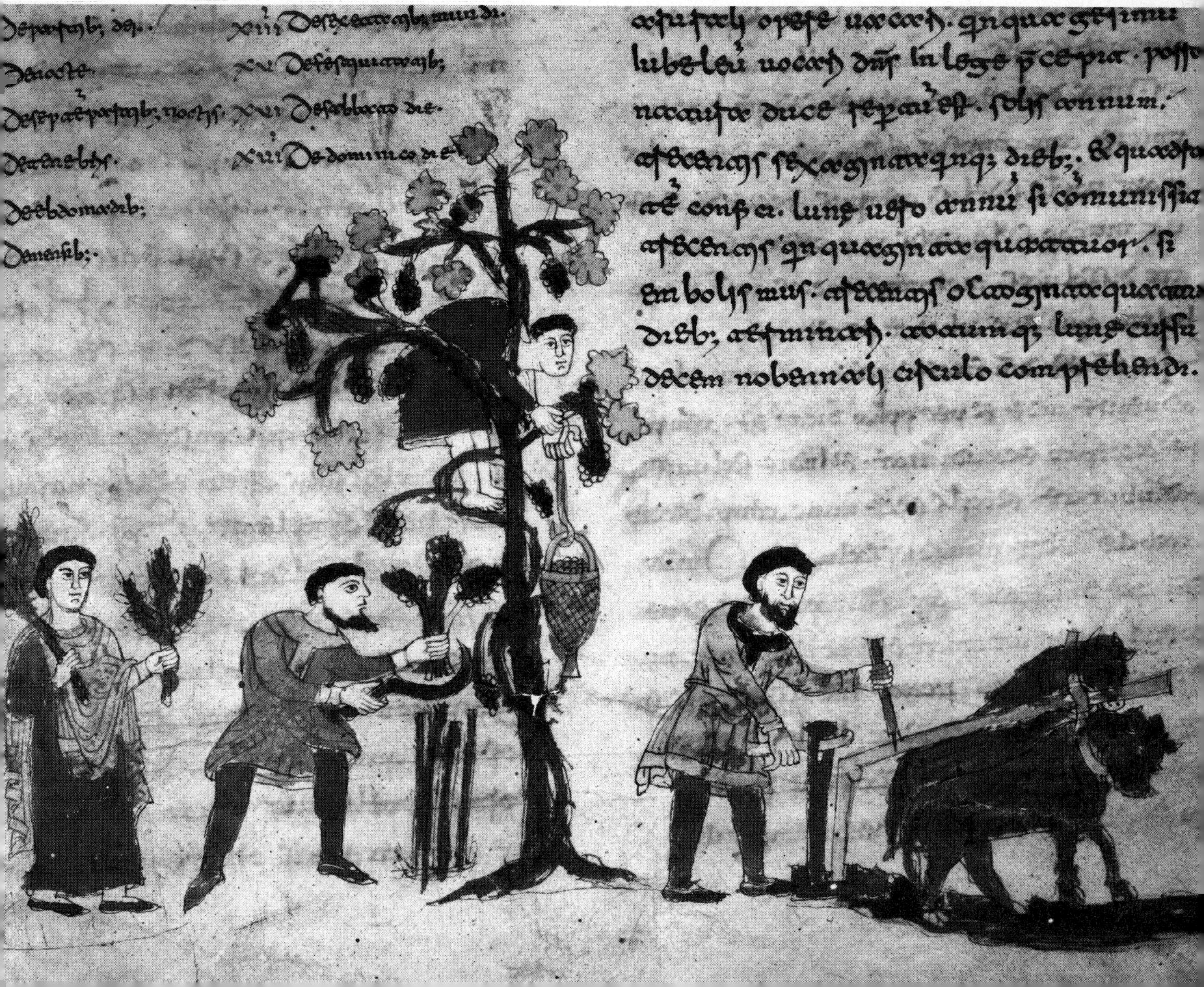

comfort and consolation. They considered baptism and confession of the Creed a surety of future salvation. They baptized their children, attended mass, tried to learn the Lord's Prayer, and received extreme unction from the priest as death approached. This was all probably done with more awe and simple faith than understanding. Religious instruction in the meaning of Christian doctrine and practice remained at a bare minimum, and local priests on the manors were no better educated than their congregations. People understandably became particularly attached in this period to the more tangible veneration of relics and saints. Religious devotion to saints has been compared to secular subjection to powerful lords; both the saint and the lord were protectors whose honor the serfs were bound to defend and whose favor and help in time of need they hoped to receive. Veneration of saints also had strong points of contact with old tribal customs, from which the commoners were hardly detached, as Charlemagne's enforcement of laws against witchcraft, sorcery, and the ritual sacrifice of animals by monks makes all too clear. But religion also has an intrinsic appeal and special meaning to those who, like the masses of medieval men and women, find themselves burdened, fearful, and with little hope of material betterment this side of eternity. Charlemagne shared many of the religious beliefs of his ordinary subjects. He collected and venerated relics, made pilgrimages to Rome, frequented the church of Saint Mary in Aachen several times a day, and directed in his last will and testament that all but a fraction of his great treasure be spent to endow masses and prayers for his departed soul.

Breakup of the Carolingian Kingdom

In the last years of his life an ailing Charlemagne knew that his empire was ungovernable. The seeds of dissolution lay in regionalism, that is, the determination of each region, no matter how small, to look first—and often only—to its own self-interest. Despite his considerable skill and resolution, Charlemagne's realm became too fragmented among powerful regional magnates. Although they were his vassals, these same men were also landholders and lords in their own right. They knew that their sovereignty lessened as Charlemagne's increased and accordingly became reluctant royal servants. In feudal society a direct relationship existed between physical proximity to authority and loyalty to authority. Local people obeyed local lords more readily than they obeyed a glorious but distant king. Charlemagne had been forced to recognize and even to enhance the power of regional magnates in order to win needed financial and military support. But as in the Merovingian kingdom, so also in the Carolingian, the tail came increasingly to wag the dog. Charlemagne's major attempt to enforce subordination to royal dictates and a transregional discipline—through the institution of the *missi dominici*—proved ultimately unsuccessful.

Louis the Pious. Carolingian kings did not give up easily. Charlemagne's only surviving son and successor was Louis the Pious (814–840), so-called because of his close alliance with the church and his promotion of puritanical reforms. Before his death Charlemagne secured the imperial succession for Louis by raising him to "co-emperor" in a grand public ceremony. After Charlemagne's death Louis no longer referred to himself as "king of the Franks." He bore instead the single title of *emperor*. The assumption of this title reflected not only Carolingian pretense to an imperial dynasty, but also Louis's determination to unify his kingdom and raise its people above mere regional and tribal loyalties. Unfortunately Louis's own fertility joined with Salic law and Frankish custom to prevent the attainment of this high goal.

Louis had three sons by his first wife. According to Salic, or Germanic, law, a ruler partitioned his kingdom equally among his surviving sons. (Salic law forbade women to inherit the throne.) Louis, who saw himself as an emperor and no mere German king, recognized that a tripartite kingdom would hardly be an empire and acted early in his reign, in the year 817, to break this legal tradition. This he did by making his eldest son, Lothar (d. 855), co-regent and sole imperial heir. To Lothar's brothers he gave important but much lesser appanages, or assigned hereditary lands; Pepin (d. 838) became king of Aquitaine, and Louis "the German" (d. 876) became king of Bavaria, over the eastern Franks.

In 823 Louis's second wife, Judith of Bavaria, bore him still a fourth son, Charles, later called "the Bald" (d. 877). Mindful of Frankish law and custom and determined that her son should receive more than just a nominal inheritance, the queen incited the brothers Pepin and Louis to war against Lothar, who fled for refuge to the pope. More important, Judith was instrumental in persuading Louis to reverse his earlier decision and divide the kingdom equally among his four living sons. As their stepmother and the young Charles rose in their father's favor, the three brothers feared still further reversals, so they decided to act against their father. Supported by the pope, they joined forces and defeated their father in a battle near Colmar (833).

As the bestower of crowns on emperors, the pope had an important stake in the preservation of the revived western empire and the imperial title, both of which Louis's belated agreement to an equal partition of his kingdom threatened to undo. The pope condemned Louis and restored Lothar to his original inheritance. But Lothar's regained imperial dignity only stirred anew the resentments of his brothers, including his stepbrother, Charles, who resumed their war against him.

The tenth-century crown of the Holy Roman Emperor reveals the close alliance between Church and throne. Not only is the crown surmounted by a cross, but it includes panels depicting the great kings of the Bible, David and Solomon. [Kunsthistorisches Museum, Vienna]

The Treaty of Verdun and Its Aftermath. Peace finally came to the heirs of Louis the Pious in 843 in the Treaty of Verdun. But this agreement also brought about the disaster that Louis had originally feared: the great Carolingian empire was partitioned according to Frankish law into three equal parts, Pepin having died in 838. Lothar received a middle section, which came to be known as Lotharingia and embraced roughly modern Holland, Belgium, Switzerland, Alsace-Lorraine, and Italy. Charles the Bald received the western part of the kingdom, or roughly modern France. And Louis the German came into the eastern part, or roughly modern Germany (see Maps 6.5, 6.6). Although Lothar retained the imperial title, the universal empire of Charlemagne and Louis the Pious ceased to exist after

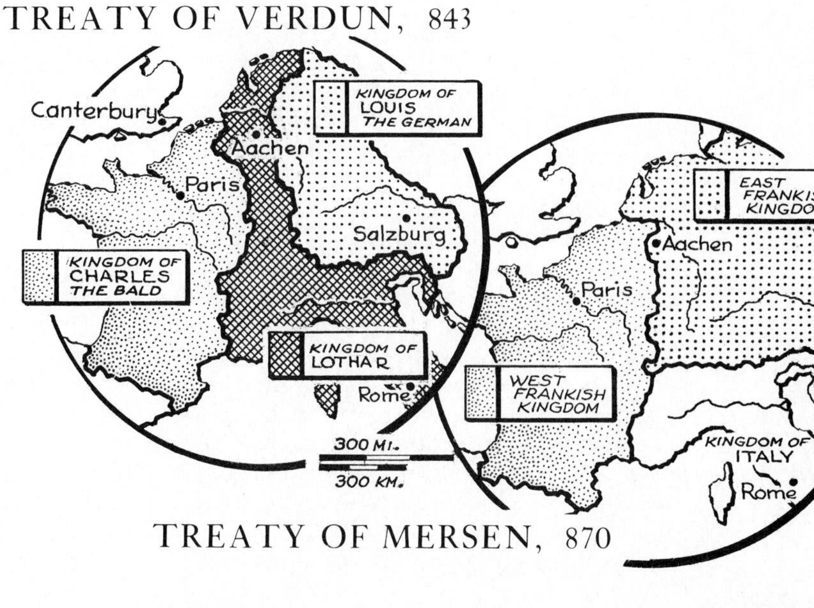

MAPS 6-5,6-6 *The Treaty of Verdun divided the kingdom of Louis the Pious among his three feuding children: Charles the Bald, Lothar, and Louis the German. After Lothar' death in* 855 *the middle kingdom was so weakened by division among his three sons that Charles the Bald and Louis the German divided it between themselves in the Treaty of Mersen in* 870.

The Carolingian Dynasty (751–987)

Pepin III "the Short" becomes King of the Franks	751
Franks drive Lombards out of central Italy; creation of Papal States	755
Charlemagne rules as King of the Franks	768–814
Charlemagne defeats Lombards in northern Italy	774
Donation of Constantine protests Frankish domination of church	750–800
Pope Leo III crowns Charlemagne	800
Louis the Pious succeeds Charlemagne as "emperor"	814–840
Treaty of Verdun partitions the Carolingian Empire	843
Treaty of Mersen further divides Carolingian Empire	870
New invasions of Vikings, Muslims, and Magyars	875–950
Ottonian dynasty succeeds Carolingian in Germany	962
Capetian dynasty succeeds Carolingian in France	987

Verdun. Not until the sixteenth century, with the election in 1519 of Charles I of Spain as the Holy Roman Emperor Charles V, would the western world again see a kingdom so vast as Charlemagne's.

The Treaty of Verdun proved to be only the beginning of Carolingian fragmentation. When Lothar died in 855, his middle kingdom was divided equally among his three surviving sons, the eldest of whom, Louis II, retained Italy and the imperial title. This partition of the partition left the middle, or imperial, kingdom much smaller and weaker than those of Louis the German and Charles the Bald. In fact, it sealed the dissolution of the great empire of Charlemagne. Henceforth western Europe saw an eastern and a western Frankish kingdom—roughly Germany versus France—at war over the fractionalized middle kingdom, a contest that has continued into modern times.

In Italy the demise of the Carolingian emperors enhanced for the moment the power of the popes, who had long been adept at filling vacuums. The popes were now strong enough to excommunicate and override the wishes of weak emperors. Pope Nicholas I (858–867) excommunicated Lothar II for divorcing his wife in a major church crackdown on the serial polygamy of the Germans. After the death of the childless emperor Louis II (875), Pope John VIII (872–882) installed Charles the Bald as emperor against the express last wishes of Louis II.

When Charles the Bald died in 877, both the papal and the imperial thrones suffered defeat. Each became a pawn in the hands of powerful Italian and German magnates, respectively. Neither pope nor emperor knew dignity and power again until a new western imperial dynasty—the Ottonians—attained dominance during the reign of Otto I (962–973). It is especially at this juncture in European history—the last quarter of the ninth and the first half of the tenth century—that one may speak with some justification of a "dark age." Simultaneously with the internal political breakdown of the empire and the papacy came new barbarian attacks, set off probably by overpopulation and famine in northern Europe. The late ninth and the tenth centuries saw successive waves of Normans (North-men), better known as Vikings, from Scandinavia; Magyars, or Hungarians, the great horsemen from the eastern plains; and Muslims from the south (see Map 6.7). In the 880s the Vikings penetrated to the imperial residence of Aachen and to Paris. Moving rapidly in ships and raiding coastal towns, they were almost impossible to defend against and kept western Europe on edge. The Franks built fortified towns and castles in strategic locations, which served as refuges. When they could, they bought off the invaders with outright grants of land (for example, Normandy) and payments of silver. In this period local populations became more dependent than ever before on local strongmen for life, limb, and livelihood. This brute fact of life provided the essential precondition for the maturation of feudal society.

Feudal Society

A chronic absence of effective central government and the constant threat of famine and war characterized the Middle Ages. *Feudal society* is a term used to describe the adjustment to this state of affairs as the weaker sought protection from the stronger. The term refers to the social, political, and economic system that emerged from repeated experience showing that only those who could guarantee immedi-

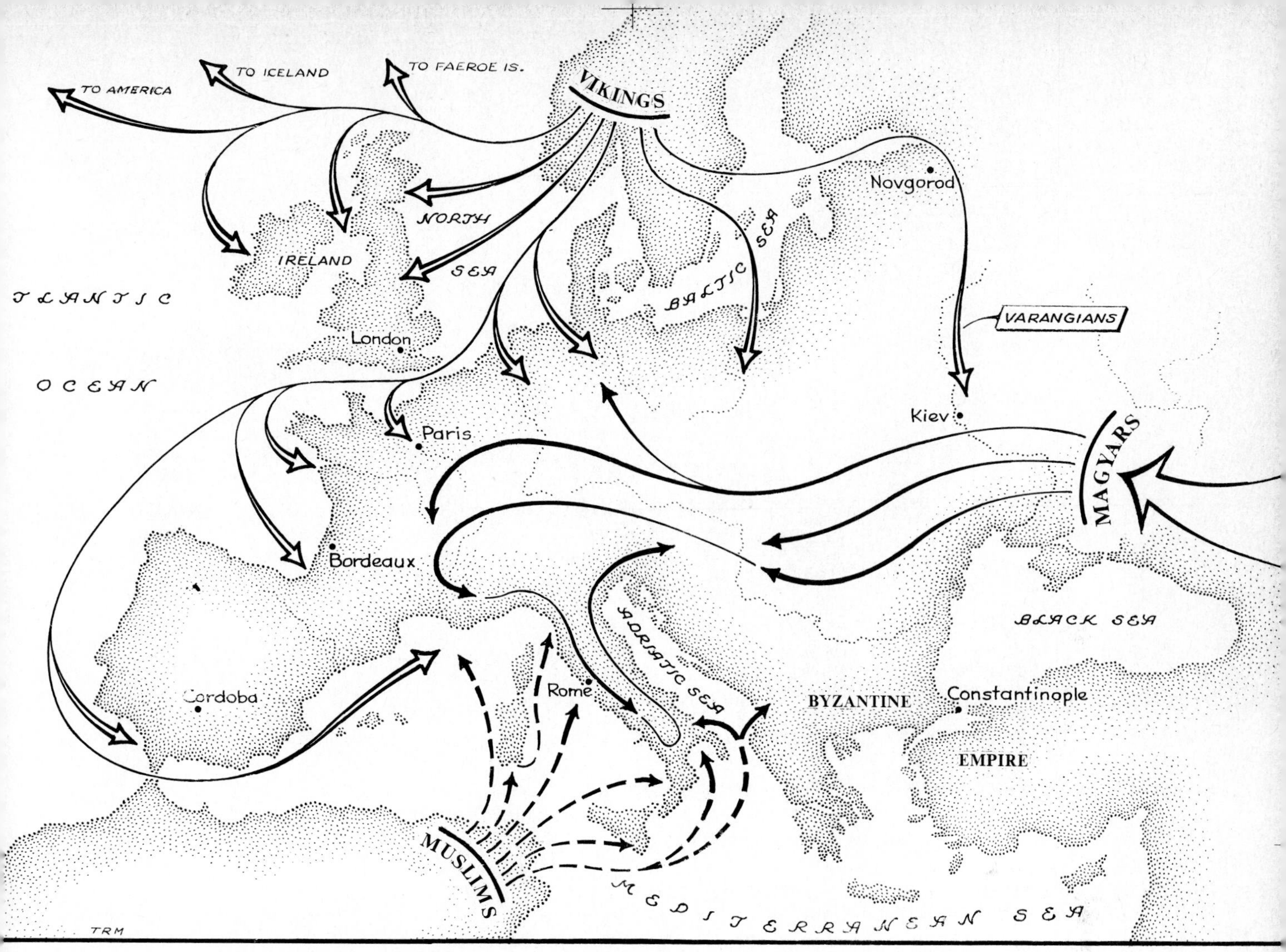

VIKING, MUSLIM, AND MAGYAR INVASIONS TO THE ELEVENTH CENTURY

MAP 6-7 *Western Europe was sorely beset by new waves of outsiders from the ninth to the eleventh century. From north, east, and south a stream of invading Vikings, Magyars, and Muslims brought the West at times to near collapse and of course gravely affected institutions within Europe.*

ate protection from rapine and starvation were true lords and masters. In a feudal society what people need most is the firm assurance that others can be depended on in time of dire need. Powerful individuals (princes or local lords) were recognized as personal superiors by lesser men who pledged themselves to them, promising faithful service. This network of relationships based on mutual loyalty enabled lords to acquire armies and to rule over territory without necessarily owning land or having a royal title to legitimate their rule. Large warrior groups of vassals sprang up, and they developed into a prominent professional military class with its own code of knightly conduct. The extensive military organization was an adaptation to the absence of strong central government and a rural, noncommercial economy.

Origins

The main features of feudal government can be found in the divisions and conflicts of Merovingian society. In the sixth and seventh centuries there evolved the custom of individual freemen placing themselves under the protection of more powerful freemen. In this way the

A Viking longship. Huge and menacing, these ships struck terror into the coastal populations of Western Europe in the ninth and tenth centuries. [*Giraudon*]

latter built up armies and became local magnates, and the former solved the problem of simple survival. Freemen who so entrusted themselves to others were known as *ingenui in obsequio* ("freemen in a contractual relation of dependence"). Those who so gave themselves to the king were called *antrustiones*. All men of this type came to be described collectively as *vassi* ("those who serve"), from which evolved the term *vassalage*, meaning the placement of oneself in the personal service of another who promises protection in return.

Landed nobility, like kings, tried to acquire as many such vassals as they could, because military strength in the early Middle Ages lay in numbers. As it proved impossible to maintain these growing armies within the lord's own household, as was the original custom, or to support them by special monetary payments, the practice evolved of simply granting them land as a "tenement." Such land came to be known as a *benefice*, or a *fief*, and vassals were expected to dwell on it and maintain their horses and other accouterments of war in good order. Originally vassals, therefore, were little more than gangs-in-waiting.

Vassalage and the Fief

Vassalage involved "fealty" to the lord. To swear fealty was to promise to refrain from any action that might in any way threaten the lord's well-being and to perform personal services for him on his request. Chief among the expected services was military duty as a mounted knight. This could involve a variety of activities: a short or long military expedition, escort duty, standing castle guard, and/or the placement of one's own fortress at the lord's disposal, if the vassal was of such stature as to have one. Continuous bargaining and bickering occurred over the terms of service. Limitations were placed on the number of days a lord could require services from a vassal. In France in the eleventh century about forty days of service a year were considered sufficient. It

harm of the others, should a direct conflict among them arise.

The problem of loyalty was reflected not only in the literature of the period, with its praise of the virtues of honor and fidelity, but also in the ceremonial development of the very act of "commendation" by which a freeman became a vassal. In the mid-eighth century an "oath of fealty" highlighted the ceremony. A vassal reinforced his promise of fidelity to the lord by swearing a special oath with his hand on a sacred relic or the Bible. In the tenth and eleventh centuries paying homage to the lord involved not only the swearing of such an oath but also the placement of the vassal's hands between the lord's and the sealing of the ceremony with a kiss.

As the centuries passed, personal loyalty and service became quite secondary to the acquisition of property. The fief overshadowed fealty; the benefice became more important than vassalage; freemen proved themselves prepared to swear allegiance to the highest bidder—developments that signaled the waning of feudal society.

Suggested Readings

MARC BLOCH, *Feudal Society,* Vols. 1 and 2, trans. by L. A. Manyon (1971). A classic on the topic and as an example of historical study.

PETER BROWN, *Augustine of Hippo: A Biography* (1967). Late antiquity seen through the biography of its greatest Christian thinker.

HENRY CHADWICK, *The Early Church* (1967). Among the best treatments of early Christianity.

R. H. C. DAVIS, *A History of Medieval Europe: From Constantine to St. Louis* (1972). Unsurpassed in clarity.

K. F. DREW (ED.), *The Barbarian Invasions: Catalyst of a New Order* (1970). Collection of essays that focuses the issues.

HEINRICH FICHTENAU, *The Carolingian Empire: The Age of Charlemagne,* trans. by Peter Munz (1964). Strongest on political history of the era.

F. L. GANSHOF, *Feudalism,* trans. by Philip Grierson (1964). The most profound brief analysis of the subject.

A. F. HAVIGHURST (ED.), *The Pirenne Thesis: Analysis, Criticism, and Revision* (1958). Excerpts from the scholarly debate over the extent of Western trade in the East during the early Middle Ages.

DAVID KNOWLES, *Christian Monasticism* (1969). Sweeping survey with helpful photographs.

M. L. W. LAISTNER, *Thought and Letters in Western Europe, 500 to 900* (1957). Among the best surveys of early medieval intellectual history.

JEAN LECLERCQ, *The Love of Learning and the Desire for God: A Study of Monastic Culture,* trans. by Catherine Misrahi (1962). Lucid, delightful, absorbing account of the ideals of monks.

J. LECLERCQ, F. VANDENBROUCKE, AND L. BOUYER, *The Spirituality of the Middle Ages* (1968). Perhaps the best survey of medieval Christianity, East and West, to the eve of the Protestant Reformation.

CYRIL MANGO, *Byzantium: The Empire of New Rome* (1980).

PETER MUNZ, *The Age of Charlemagne* (1971). Penetrating social history of the period.

HENRI PIRENNE, *A History of Europe, I: From the End of the Roman World in the West to the Beginnings of the Western States,* trans. by Bernhard Maill (1958). Comprehensive survey, with now-controversial views on the demise of Western trade and cities in the early Middle Ages.

STEVEN RUNCIMAN, *Byzantine Civilization* (1970). Succinct, comprehensive account by a master.

PETER SAWYER, *The Age of the Vikings* (1962). The best account.

R. W. SOUTHERN, *The Making of the Middle Ages* (1973). Originally published in 1953, but still a fresh account by an imaginative historian.

CARL STEPHENSON, *Medieval Feudalism* (1969). Excellent short summary and introduction.

A. A. VASILIEV, *History of the Byzantine Empire 324–1453* (1952). The most comprehensive treatment in English.

LYNN WHITE, JR., *Medieval Technology and Social Change* (1962). Often fascinating account of the way primitive technology changed life.

A professor lecturing at the University of Paris. The University of Paris, which received a royal charter in 1200, was the most famous university in northern Europe. Its faculties of arts, theology, canon law, and medicine attracted students from all over Europe. [Giraudon/Art Resource]

7

The High Middle Ages (1000–1300): Revival of Empire, Church, and Towns

THE HIGH MIDDLE AGES marked a period of political expansion and consolidation and of intellectual flowering and synthesis. The noted medievalist Joseph Strayer called it the age that saw "the full development of all the potentialities of medieval civilization."[1] Some even argue that as far as the development of Western institutions is concerned, this was a more creative period than the later Italian Renaissance and the German Reformation.

The high Middle Ages saw the borders of western Europe largely secured against foreign invaders. Although there was intermittent Muslim aggression well into the sixteenth century, fear of assault from without diminished. A striking change occurred in the late eleventh century and the twelfth century. Western Europe, which had for so long been the prey of foreign powers, became through the Crusades and foreign trade the feared hunter within both the Eastern and the Arab worlds.

During the high Middle Ages "national" monarchies emerged in France, England, and Germany. Parliaments and popular assemblies representing the interests of the nobility, the clergy, and the townspeople also appeared at this time to secure local rights and customs against the claims of the developing nation-states. The foundations of modern representative institutions can be found in this period.

The high Middle Ages saw a revolution in agriculture that increased both food supplies and populations. This period witnessed a great revival of trade and commerce, the rise of towns, and the emergence of a "new-rich" merchant class, the ancestors of modern capitalists. Urban culture and education flourished through the recovery of the writings of the ancient Greek philosophers, which was made possible by the revival of Eastern trade and by way of Spanish contacts with Muslim intellectuals. Unlike the dabbling in antiquity during Carolingian times, the twelfth century enjoyed a true renaissance of classical learning.

The high Middle Ages were also the time when the Latin or Western church established itself as an authority independent of monarchical secular government, thereby sowing the seeds of the distinctive Western separation of Church and State. This occurred during the Investiture Struggle of the late eleventh century and the twelfth century. In this confrontation between popes and emperors a reformed

[1] *Western History in the Middle Ages—A Short History* (New York: Appleton-Century-Crofts, 1955), pp. 9, 127.

papacy overcame its long subservience to the Carolingian and Ottonian kings. The papacy won out, however, by becoming itself a monarchy among the world's emerging monarchies, thereby preparing the way for still more dangerous confrontations between popes and emperors in the later Middle Ages. Some religious reformers would later see in the Gregorian papacy of the high Middle Ages the fall of the church from its spiritual mission as well as its declaration of independence from secular power.

The Emperor Otto II (913–983). *The four tribute-bearing maidens symbolize his dominion over all of Western Europe.* [*Giraudon/Art Resource*]

Otto I and the Revival of the Empire

The fortunes of both the old empire and the papacy began to revive after the dark period of the late ninth century and the early tenth century when the Saxon Henry I ("the Fowler," d. 936), the strongest of the German dukes, became the first non-Frankish king of Germany in 918. Henry rebuilt royal power by forcibly consolidating the duchies of Swabia, Bavaria, Saxony, Franconia, and Lotharingia. He secured imperial borders by checking the invasions of the Hungarians and the Danes. Although greatly reduced in size by comparison with Charlemagne's empire, Henry's German kingdom still placed his son and successor Otto I (936–973) in a strong territorial position.

The very able Otto maneuvered his own kin into positions of power in Bavaria, Swabia, and Franconia. He refused to treat each duchy as an independent hereditary dukedom, as was the trend among the nobility. He dealt with each as a subordinate member of a unified kingdom. In a truly imperial gesture in 951, Otto invaded Italy and proclaimed himself its king. In 955 he won his most magnificent victory when he defeated the Hungarians at Lechfeld, a feat comparable to Charles Martel's earlier victory over the Saracens at Poitiers in 732. The victory at Lechfeld secured German borders against new barbarian attack, further unified the German duchies, and earned Otto the well-deserved title "the Great."

As part of a careful rebuilding program, Otto, following the example of his predecessors, enlisted the church. Bishops and abbots, men who possessed a sense of universal empire yet did not marry and found competitive dynasties, were made royal princes and agents of the king. Because these clergy, as royal bureaucrats, received great land holdings and immunity from local counts and dukes, they also found such vassalage to the king very attractive. The medieval church did not become a great territorial power reluctantly. It appreciated the blessings of receiving, while teaching the blessedness of giving.

In 961 Otto, who had long aspired to the imperial crown, responded to a call for help from Pope John XII (955–964), who was at this time being bullied by an Italian enemy of the German king, Berengar of Friuli. In recompense for this rescue Pope John crowned Otto emperor on February 2, 962. At this time Otto also recognized the existence of the Papal States and proclaimed himself their special protector. The church was now more than ever under royal control. Its bishops and abbots were Otto's appointees and bureaucrats, and the pope reigned in Rome only by the power of the emperor's sword. Pope John belatedly recognized the royal web in which the church had become entangled. As a countermeasure he joined Italian opposition to the new emperor. This turnabout brought Otto's swift revenge. An ecclesiastical synod over which Otto personally presided deposed Pope John and proclaimed that henceforth no pope could take office without first swearing an oath of allegiance to the emperor. Under Otto I popes ruled at the emperor's pleasure.

Otto had shifted the royal focus from Germany to Italy. His successors—Otto II (973–983), Otto III (983–1002), and Henry II (1002–1024)—became so preoccupied with running the affairs of Italy that their German base began to disintegrate, sacrificed to imperial dreams. They might have learned a lesson from the contemporary Capetian kings, the successor dynasty to the Carolingians in France, who wisely mended local fences and concentrated their limited resources on securing a tight grip on their immediate royal domain, which was never neglected for the sake of foreign adventure. The Ottonians, in contrast, reached far beyond their grasp when they tried to subdue Italy. As the briefly revived empire began to crumble in the first quarter of the eleventh century, the church, long unhappy with Carolingian and Ottonian domination, prepared to declare its independence and exact its own vengeance.

The Reviving Catholic Church

The Cluny Reform Movement

During the late ninth and early tenth centuries the clergy had become tools of kings and magnates, and the papacy a toy of Italian nobles. The Ottonians made bishops their servile princes, and popes also served at their pleasure. A new day dawned for the church, however, thanks not only to the failing fortunes of the overextended empire but also to a new force for reform within the church itself. In a great monastery in Cluny in east-central France, a reform movement appeared that, by progressively winning the support of secular lords and German kings for monastic reform, gradually placed the church in a position to challenge political power over it at both episcopal and papal levels.

The reformers of Cluny were aided by widespread popular respect for the church. Most people admired clerics and monks. The church was medieval society's most democratic institution. In the Middle Ages any man could theoretically rise to the position of pope, and all were candidates for the church's grace and salvation. The church promised a better life to come to the great mass of ordinary people, who found the present one brutish and without hope. Since the fall of the Roman Empire popular support for the church had been especially inspired by the example of the monks. Monasteries provided an important alternative style of life for the religiously earnest in an age when most people had very few options. The tenth and eleventh centuries saw an unprecedented boom in their construction. Monks remained the least secularized and most spiritual of the church's clergy. Their cultural achievements were widely admired, their relics and rituals were considered magical, and their high religious ideals and sacrifices were imitated by the laity.

Cluny, the main source of the reform movement, was founded in 910 by William the Pious, duke of Aquitaine. It was a Benedictine monastery devoted to the strictest observance of Saint Benedict's *Rule for Monasteries,* with a special emphasis on liturgical purity. Although they were loosely organized and their demands not always consistent, the Cluny reformers were intent on maintaining a spiritual church. They absolutely rejected the subservience of the clergy, especially that of the German bishops, to royal authority. They taught that the pope in Rome was sole ruler over all the clergy. The Cluny reformers further resented the transgression of ascetic piety by "secular" parish clergy, who maintained concubines in a relationship akin to marriage. (Later a distinction would be formalized between the secular clergy who lived and ministered in the world *[saeculum]* and the regular clergy, monks and nuns withdrawn from the world and living according to a special rule *[regula].*)

The Cluny reformers resolved to free the clergy from both kings and "wives," to create an independent and chaste clergy. The church alone was to be the clergy's lord and spouse. The distinctive Western separation of Church

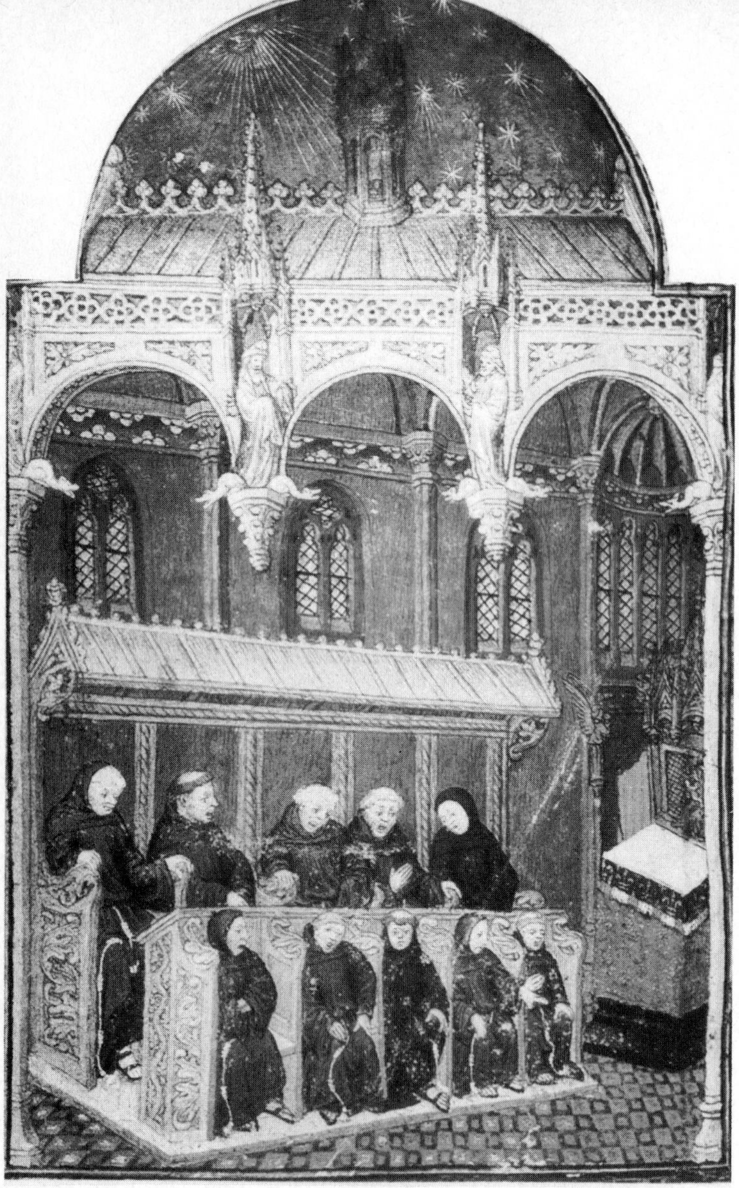

Benedictine monks at choir. The reform movement that began at the Benedictine monastery at Cluny in northern France in the tenth century spread throughout the Church and was ultimately responsible for the reassertion of papal authority. [*Trustees of the British Museum*]

and State and the celibacy of the Catholic clergy, both of which continue today, had their definitive origins in the Cluny reform movement.

Cluny rapidly became a center from which reformers were dispatched to monasteries throughout France and Italy. Under its aggressive abbots, especially Saint Odo (926–946), it grew to embrace almost fifteen hundred dependent cloisters, each devoted to monastic and church reform. In the last half of the eleventh century the Cluny reformers reached the summit when their reform program was embraced by the papacy itself.

In the late ninth and early tenth centuries the influence of this religious reform movement was demonstrated by the proclamation of the "Peace of God," a cooperative venture between the clergy and the higher nobility. This was a series of church decrees that attempted to lessen the endemic warfare of medieval society by threatening excommunication for all who, at any time, harmed such vulnerable groups as women, peasants, merchants, and clergy. The Peace of God was subsequently reinforced by proclamations of the "Truce of God," a church order that all men must abstain from every form of violence and warfare during a certain part of each week (eventually from Wednesday night to Monday morning) and in all holy seasons.

Popes devoted to reforms like those urged by Cluny came to power during the reign of Emperor Henry III (1039–1056). Pope Leo IX (1049–1054) promoted regional synods in opposition to simony (that is, the selling of spiritual things, such as church offices) and clerical concubinage. He also placed Cluniacs in key administrative posts in Rome. During the turbulent minority of Henry III's successor, Henry IV (1056–1106), reform popes began to assert themselves more openly. Pope Stephen IX (1057–1058) reigned without imperial ratification, contrary to the earlier declaration of Otto I. Pope Nicholas II (1059–1061) took the unprecedented step of establishing a College of Cardinals in 1059, and henceforth this body alone elected the pope. Only thirteen years earlier Henry III had deposed three schismatic popes, each a pawn of a Roman noble faction, and had installed a German bishop of his own choosing who ruled as Pope Clement II (1046–1047).

Such highhanded practices ended after 1059. With the creation of the College of Cardinals the popes declared their full independence of both local Italian and distant royal interference, although rulers continued to have considerable indirect influence on the election of popes. Pope Nicholas II also embraced Cluny's strictures against simony and clerical concubinage and even struck his own political alliances with the Normans in Sicily and with France and Tuscany. His successor, Pope Alexander II (1061–1073), was elected solely by the College of Cardinals, albeit not without a struggle.

The Peace and the Truce of God

The following proclamation of the Peace and the Truce of God occurred at the Council of Toulouse in the mid-eleventh century. It was designed to protect the property of the church and the persons of the clergy from the bullying of secular powers. In the "ordeal of cold water," mentioned at the conclusion, innocence or guilt was determined by whether a person sank (innocent) or floated (guilty) when thrown into a pool of blessed water—the belief being that blessed water would reject the guilty by divine intervention.

This Peace has been confirmed by the bishops, by the abbots, by the counts and viscounts and the other God-fearing nobles in this bishopric to the effect that in the future . . . no man may commit an act of violence in a church. . . . Furthermore, it is forbidden that any one attack the clergy, who do not bear arms, or the monks and religious persons, or do them any wrong; likewise it is forbidden to despoil or pillage the communities of canons, monks, and religious persons, the ecclesiastical lands . . . under the protection of the Church, or the clergy, who do not bear arms; and if any one shall do such a thing, let him pay a double composition [i.e., fine in compensation]. [Further] let no one burn or destroy the dwellings of the peasants and the clergy, the dove-cotes, and the granaries. Let no man dare to kill, to beat, or to wound a peasant or serf, or the wife of either, or to seize them and carry them off, except for misdemeanors which they have committed. . . . Let any one who has broken the peace, and has not paid his fines within a fortnight, make amends to him whom he has injured by paying a double amount. . . . The bishops . . . have [also] solemnly confirmed the Truce of God, which has been enjoined upon all Christians, from the setting of the sun of the fourth day of the week, that is to say, Wednesday, until the rising of the sun on Monday, the second day. . . . If any one during the Truce shall violate it, let him pay a double composition and subsequently undergo the ordeal of cold water.

James Harvey Robinson (Ed.), *Readings in European History,* Vol. 1 (Boston: Anthenaeum, 1904), pp. 230–231.

The Investiture Struggle: Gregory VII and Henry IV

It was Alexander's successor, Pope Gregory VII (1073–1085), a fierce advocate of Cluny's reforms who had entered the papal bureaucracy a quarter century earlier during the pontificate of Leo IX, who put the church's declaration of independence to the test. Cluniacs had repeatedly inveighed against simony. A case had been built up by Cardinal Humbert against the lay investiture of clergy as the supreme form of this evil practice. In 1075 Pope Gregory embraced these arguments and condemned under penalty of excommunication the lay investiture of clergy at any level. He had primarily in mind the emperor's well-established custom of installing bishops by presenting them with the ring and staff that symbolized episcopal office. After Gregory's ruling, bishops, no more than popes, were to enter their offices appearing to be the appointees of emperors. As popes were elected by the College of Cardinals and were not raised up by kings or nobles, so bishops would henceforth be installed in their offices by high ecclesiastical authority as empowered by the pope and none other.

Gregory's prohibition was a jolt to royal authority. Since the days of Otto I emperors had routinely passed out bishoprics to favored clergy. Bishops, who received royal estates, were the emperors' appointees and servants of the state. Henry IV's Carolingian and Ottonian predecessors had carefully nurtured the theocratic character of the empire in both concept and administrative bureaucracy. The church and religion were integral parts of government. Now Henry found himself ordered to secularize the empire by drawing a distinct line between the spheres of temporal and spiritual—royal and ecclesiastical—authority and jurisdiction.

Pope Gregory VII Asserts the Power of the Pope

Church reformers of the high Middle Ages vigorously asserted the power of the pope within the church and his rights against emperors and all others who might encroach on the papal sphere of jurisdiction. Here is a statement of the basic principles of the Gregorian reformers, known as the *Dictatus Papae* ("The Sayings of the Pope"), which is attributed to Pope Gregory VII (1073–1085).

That the Roman Church was founded by God alone.
That the Roman Pontiff alone is rightly to be called universal.
That the Pope may depose the absent.
That for him alone it is lawful to enact new laws according to the needs of the time, to assemble together new congregations, to make an abbey of a canonry; and . . . to divide a rich bishopric and unite the poor ones.
That he alone may use the imperial insignia.
That the Pope is the only one whose feet are to be kissed by all princes.
That his name alone is to be recited in churches.
That his title is unique in the world.
That he may depose emperors.
That he may transfer bishops, if necessary, from one See to another.
That no synod may be called a general one without his order.
That no chapter or book may be regarded as canonical without his authority.
That no sentence of his may be retracted by any one; and that he, alone of all, can retract it.
That he himself may be judged by no one.
That the Roman Church has never erred, nor ever, by the witness of Scripture, shall err to all eternity.
That the Pope may absolve subjects of unjust men from their fealty.

Church and State Through the Centuries: A Collection of Historic Documents, trans. and ed. by S. Z. Ehler and John B. Morrall (New York: Biblo and Tannen, 1967), pp. 43–44.

But if his key administrators were no longer to be his own carefully chosen and sworn servants, then was not his kingdom in jeopardy? Henry considered Gregory's action a direct challenge to his authority. The territorial princes, on the other hand, ever tending away from the center and eager to see the emperor weakened, were quick to see the advantages of Gregory's ruling: if the emperor did not have a bishop's ear, then a territorial prince might. In the hope of gaining an advantage over both the emperor and the clergy in their territory, the princes fully supported Gregory's edict.

The lines of battle were quickly drawn. Henry assembled his loyal German bishops at Worms in January 1076 and had them proclaim their independence from Gregory. Gregory promptly responded with the church's heavy artillery: he excommunicated Henry and absolved all Henry's subjects from loyalty to him. The German princes were delighted by this turn of events, and Henry found himself facing a general revolt led by the duchy of Saxony. He had no recourse but to come to terms with Gregory. In a famous scene Henry prostrated himself outside Gregory's castle retreat at Canossa on January 25, 1077. There he reportedly stood barefoot in the snow off and on for three days before the pope absolved his royal penitent. Papal power had, at this moment, reached its pinnacle. But heights are also for descending, and Gregory's grandeur, as he must surely have known when he pardoned Henry and restored him to power, was very soon to fade.

Henry regrouped his forces, regained much of his power within the empire, and soon acted as if the humiliation at Canossa had never occurred. In March 1080 Gregory excommunicated Henry once again, but this time such action was ineffectual. (Historically, repeated excommunications of the same individual have proved to have diminishing returns.) In 1084 Henry, absolutely dominant, installed his own antipope, Clement III, and forced Gregory into exile, where he died the following year. It

Pope Gregory VII Describes in a Letter Henry IV's Penance at Canossa

Had Henry IV not succeeded in having the papal ban revoked, his powerful vassals in the empire were prepared to remove him from office. Both sides were aware of the high stakes; hence Henry's extreme penance to win absolution and the pope's long delay in granting it. Because it was against the church's own rule to refuse absolution to a sincere penitent, Henry had an advantage in the confrontation at Canossa. As Gregory himself pointed out, in the selection below, the longer forgiveness was withheld from the king, the more people suspected the pope of betraying his spiritual office.

Gregory . . . to all archbishops, bishops, dukes, counts, and other princes of the realm. . . .

Inasmuch as for love of justice you assumed common cause and danger with us in the struggle [with Henry] . . . we have taken care to inform you . . . how the king, humbled to penance, obtained the pardon of absolution. . . .

Before entering Italy, he sent to us suppliant legates, offering in all things to render satisfaction. . . . And he renewed his promise that, besides amending his ways of living, he would observe all obedience, if only he might deserve to obtain from us the favor of absolution and the apostolic benediction. When, after long postponing a decision, we . . . severely [took] him to task . . . he came at length of his own accord, with a few followers, showing nothing of hostility or boldness, to the town of Canossa where we were tarrying. And there, having laid aside all the belongings of royalty, wretchedly with bare feet and clad in wool, he continued for three days to stand before the gate of the castle. Nor did he desist from imploring with many tears the aid and consolation of the apostolic mercy until he had moved all . . . present . . . to such pity and depth of compassion that, interceding for him with many prayers and tears, all wondered at the unaccustomed hardness of our heart, while some actually cried out that we were exercising, not the dignity of apostolic severity, but the cruelty . . . of a tyrannical madness.

Finally, won by the persistence of his suit . . . we loosed the chain of anathema and . . . received him into the favor of communion and into the lap of the Holy Mother Church.

Frederic A. Ogg (Ed.), *A Source Book of Mediaeval History* (New York: American Book Company, 1908), pp. 275–276.

appeared as if the old practice of kings' controlling popes had been restored, and with a vengeance. Clement, however, was never recognized within the church, and the Gregorian party, which retained wide popular support, regained power during the pontificates of Victor III (1086–1087) and Urban II (1088–1099).

The settlement of the investiture controversy came in 1122 with the Concordat of Worms. Emperor Henry V (1106–1125), having early abandoned his predecessors' practice of nominating popes and raising up antipopes, formally renounced his power to invest bishops with ring and staff. In exchange Pope Calixtus II (1119–1124) recognized the emperor's right to be present and to invest bishops with fiefs before or after their investment with ring and staff by the church. The old Church–State "back scratching" in this way continued, but now on very different terms. The clergy received their offices and attendant religious powers solely from ecclesiastical authority and no longer from kings and emperors. Rulers continued to bestow lands and worldly goods on high clergy in the hope of influencing them; the Concordat of Worms made the clergy more independent but not necessarily less worldly.

The Gregorian party won the independence of the clergy at the price of encouraging the divisiveness of the feudal forces within the empire. The pope made himself strong by making imperial authority weak. In the end those who profited most from the investiture con-

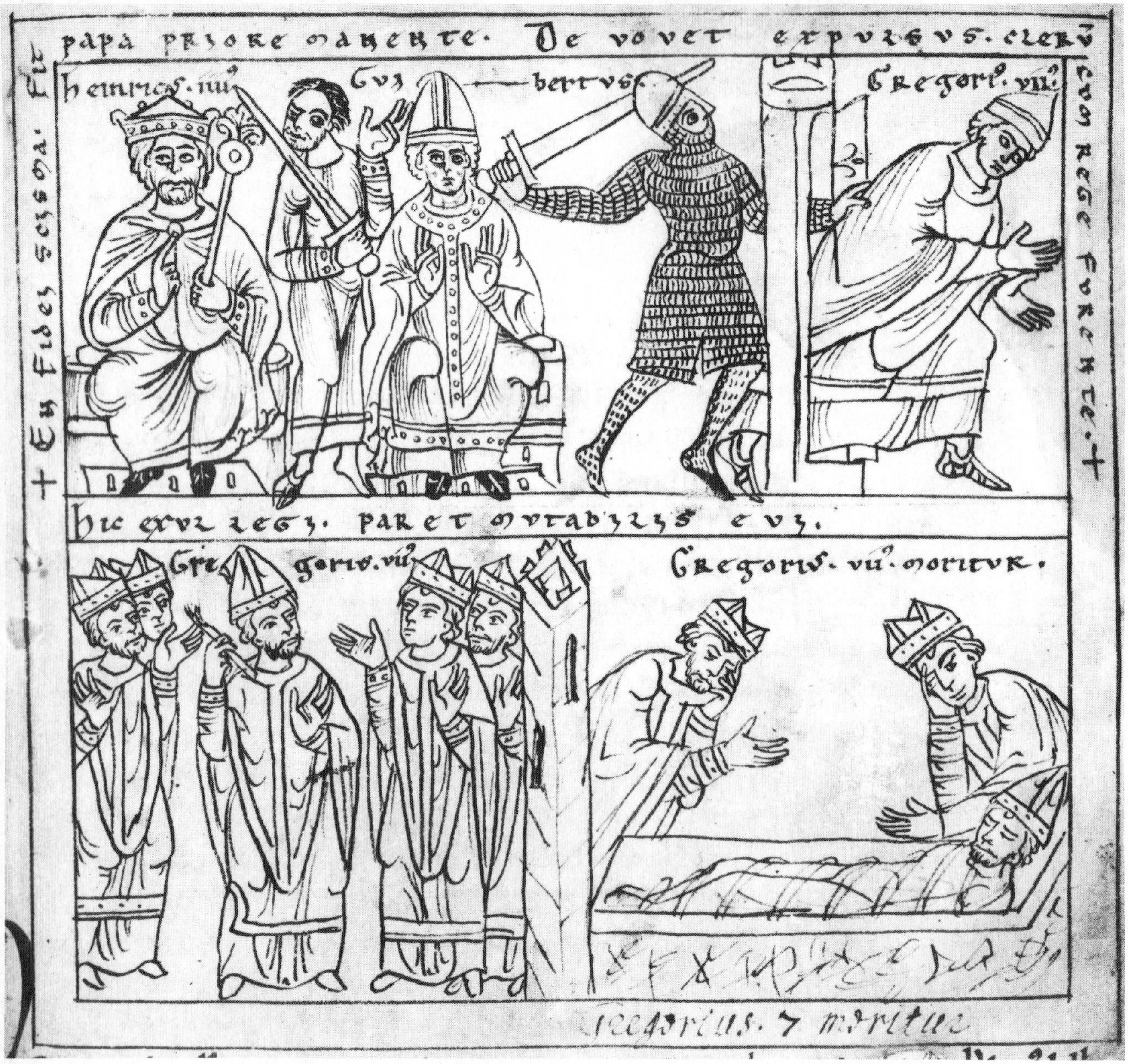

A twelfth-century German manuscript illustrating the struggle between Emperor Henry IV and Pope Gregory VII. In the top panel, Henry installs his puppet pope Clement III, and drives Gregory from Rome. Below, Gregory dies in exile. As can be seen, the sympathies of the artist, a monk, were with Gregory, not Henry. [*University of Jena*]

troversy were the local princes in Germany.

The new Gregorian fence between temporal and spiritual power did not prevent kings and popes from remaining good neighbors if each was willing. However, succeeding centuries demonstrated that royal and papal aspirations were too competitive for peaceful coexistence. The most bitter clash between Church and State was still to come. It would occur during the late thirteenth century and early fourteenth century in the confrontation between Pope Boniface VIII and King Philip IV of France.

Calixtus II and Henry V End the Investiture Controversy

The Concordat of Worms between Pope Calixtus II (1119–1124) and Emperor Henry V (1106–1125) on September 23, 1122, ended the investiture controversy. Calixtus acknowledged the emperor's right to be present as a judge and to bestow temporal rights and revenues (as distinct from ecclesiastical) on the candidate, and Henry acknowledged the exclusive right of the pope to invest clergy in their religious offices and further promised to restore previously usurped church possessions.

PRIVILEGE OF THE POPE:

I, Bishop Calixtus, servant of the servants of God, concede to you beloved son Henry—by the grace of God August Emperor of the Romans—that the election of those bishops and abbots in the German kingdom who belong to the kingdom [i.e., those in Germany, Italy, and Burgundy] shall take place in your presence without simony and without any violence; so that if any discord occurs between the parties concerned, you may—with the counsel or judgment of the metropolitan and the co-provincials—give your assent and assistance to the party which appears to have the better case. The candidate elected may receive the "regalia" [i.e., the temporal rights and revenues connected with the benefice] from you through the sceptre and he shall perform his lawful duties to you for them. But he who is elected in the other parts of the Empire shall, within six months, receive the "regalia" from you through the sceptre and shall perform his lawful duties for them, saving all things which are known as pertaining to the Church. If you complain to me in any of these matters and ask for help, I will furnish you the aid, if such is the duty of any office. I grant true peace to you and to all those who are or have been of your party during this discord.

PRIVILEGE OF THE EMPEROR:

In the name of Holy and Indivisible Trinity. I, Henry, by the grace of God August Emperor of the Romans, for the love of God and of the Holy Roman Church and of the lord Pope Calixtus and for the healing of my soul, do surrender to God, to the Holy Apostles of God, Peter and Paul, and to the Holy Roman Church all investiture through ring and staff; and do agree that in all churches throughout my kingdom and empire there shall be canonical elections and free consecration. I restore to the same Roman Church all the possessions and temporalities ("regalia") which have been abstracted until the present day either in the lifetime of my father or in my own and which I hold; and I will faithfully aid in the restoration of those which I do not hold. The possessions also of all other churches and princes and of every one else, either cleric or layman, which had been lost in that war, I will restore, so far as I hold them, according to the counsel of the princes or according to justice; and I will faithfully aid in the restoration of those that I do not hold. And I grant a true peace to the lord Pope Calixtus and to the Holy Roman Church and to all who are or have been on its side. In matters where the Holy Roman Church would seek assistance I will faithfully grant it; and in those where she shall complain to me, I will duly grant justice to her.

Church and State Through the Centuries: A Collection of Historic Documents, trans. and ed. by S. Z. Ehler and John B. Morrall (New York: Biblo and Tannen, 1967), pp. 48–49.

The First Crusades

If an index of popular piety and support for the pope in the high Middle Ages is needed, the Crusades amply provide it. What the Cluny reform was to the clergy, the First Crusade to the Holy Land, proclaimed by Pope Urban II at the Council of Clermont in France in 1095, was to the laity: an outlet for the heightened religious zeal of what was Europe's most religious century before the Protestant Reformation. Actually there had been an earlier Crusade of

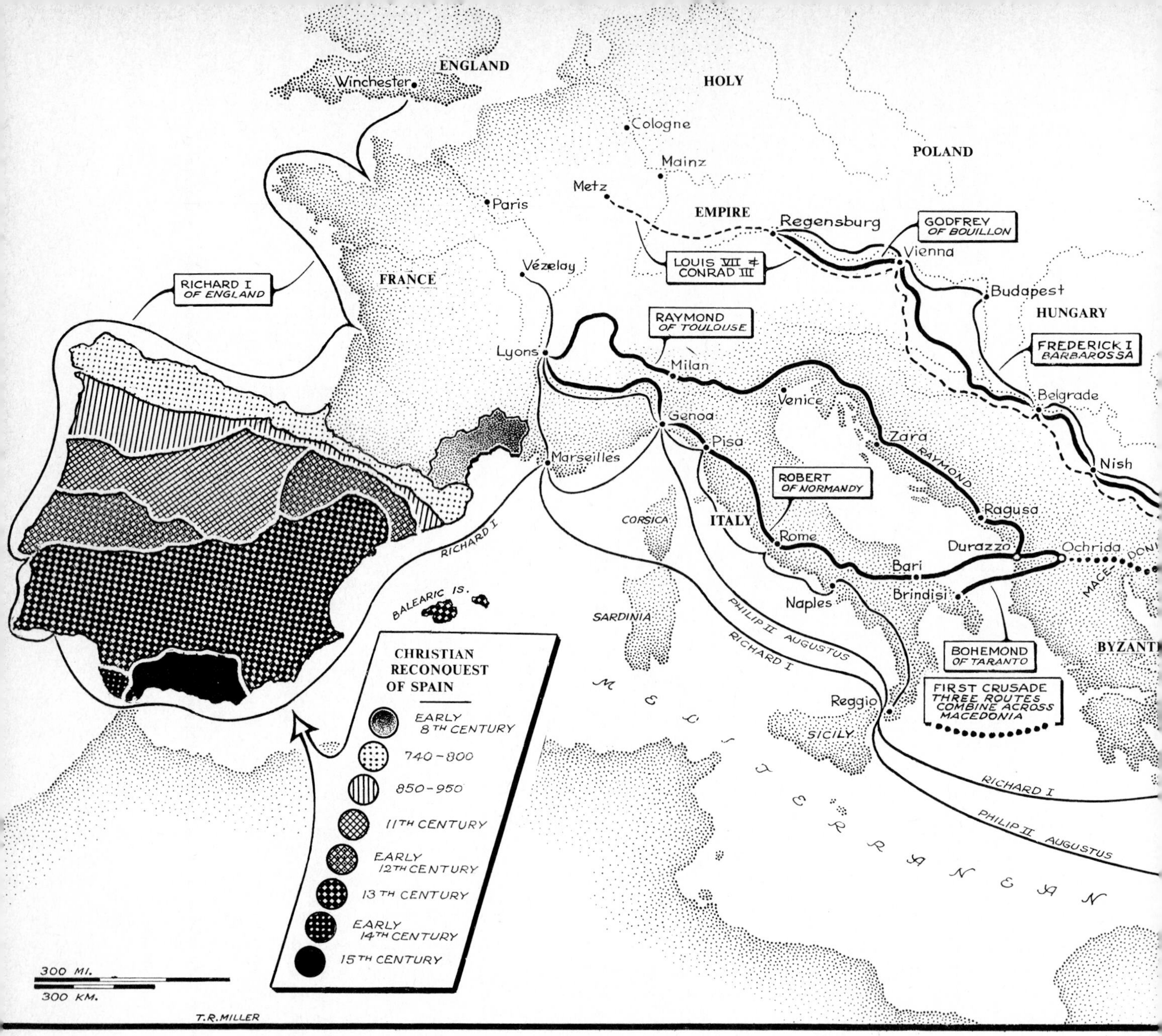

French knights, who, inspired by Pope Alexander II, attacked Muslims in Spain in 1064. Unlike the later Crusades, which were undertaken for patently mercenary as well as religious motives, the early Crusades were to a very high degree inspired by genuine religious piety and were carefully orchestrated by the revived papacy. Participants in the First Crusade to the Holy Land were promised a plenary indulgence should they die in battle, that is, a complete remission of any outstanding temporal punishment for unrepented mortal sins and hence release from suffering for them in purgatory. But this spiritual reward was only part of the crusading impulse. Other factors were the widespread popular respect for the reformed papacy and the existence of a nobility newly strengthened by the breakdown of imperial power and eager for military adventure. These elements combined to make the First Crusade a rousing success.

The Eastern emperor welcomed any aid against advancing Muslim armies. The Western Crusaders did not, however, assemble for the purpose of defending Europe's borders against aggression. They freely took the offensive to

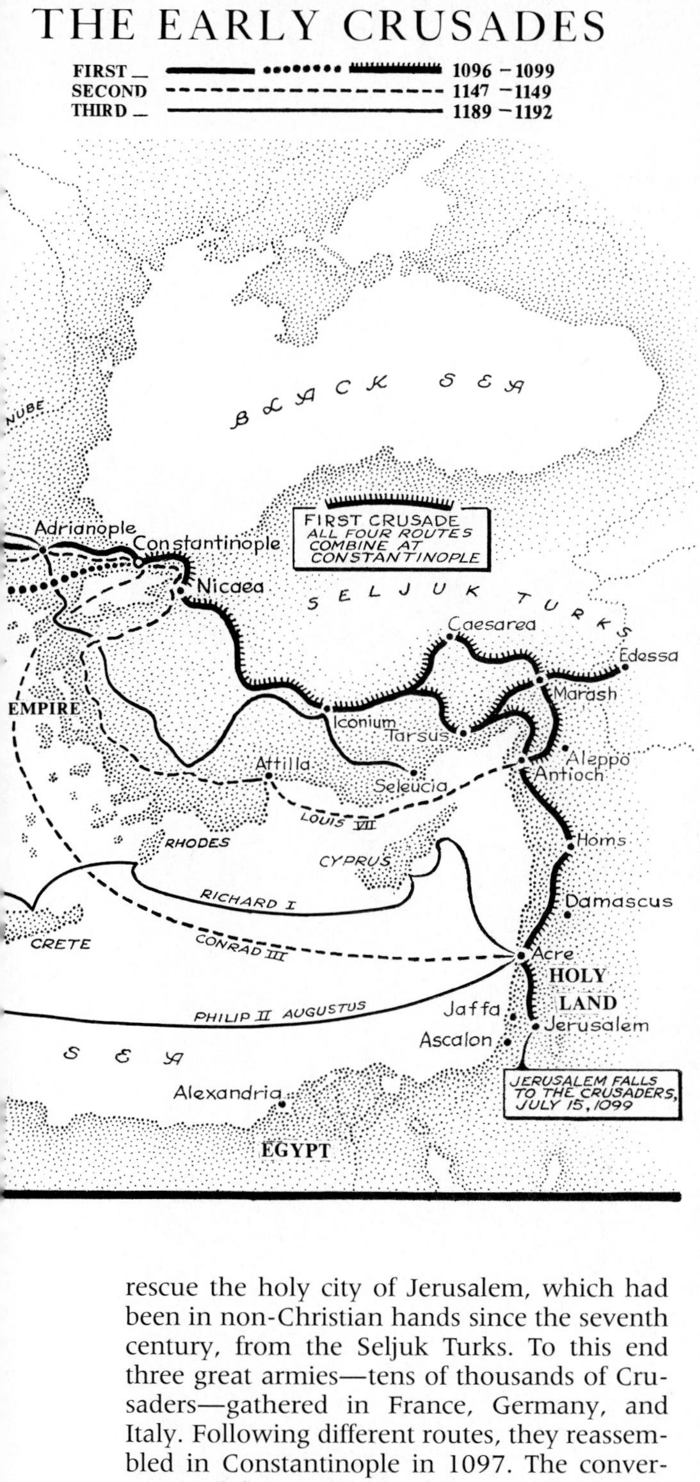

MAP 7-1 *Routes and several leaders of the crusades during the first century of the movement. Indicated names of the great nobles of the First Crusade do not exhaust the list. The even showier array of monarchs of the Second and Third still left the crusades, on balance, ineffective in achieving their ostensible goals.*

rescue the holy city of Jerusalem, which had been in non-Christian hands since the seventh century, from the Seljuk Turks. To this end three great armies—tens of thousands of Crusaders—gathered in France, Germany, and Italy. Following different routes, they reassembled in Constantinople in 1097. The convergence of these spirited soldiers on the Eastern capital was a cultural shock that only deepened Eastern antipathy toward the West. The weakened Eastern emperor, Alexis I, suspected their true motives, and the common people, who were forced to give them room and board, hardly considered them Christian brothers in a common cause. Nonetheless these fanatical Crusaders accomplished what no Eastern army had ever been able to do. They soundly defeated one Seljuk army after another in a steady advance toward Jerusalem, which fell to them on July 15, 1099.

The victorious Crusaders divided the conquered territory into the feudal states of Jerusalem, Edessa, and Antioch, which they allegedly held as fiefs from the pope. Godfrey of Bouillon, leader of the French-German army (and after him his brother Baldwin), ruled over the kingdom of Jerusalem. However, the Crusaders remained only small islands within a great sea of Muslims, who looked on the Western invaders as hardly more than savages. The conquerors built defensive fortifications and received assistance from the new religious-military orders of the Knights Hospitalers (founded in 1113) and the Knights Templars (founded ca. 1119). The Templars were orders of crack soldiers who took religious vows and dedicated themselves to protect pilgrims to the Holy Land against the infidel. But native persistence finally broke the Crusaders around mid-century, and the forty-odd-year Latin presence in the East began to crumble. Edessa fell to Muslim armies in 1144. A Second Crusade, preached by the eminent Bernard of Clairvaux (1091–1153), Christendom's most powerful monastic leader, attempted a rescue, but it met with dismal failure. In October 1187 Jerusalem itself was reconquered by Saladin (1138–1193), king of Egypt and Syria, and, save for a brief interlude in the thirteenth century, it remained thereafter in Islamic hands until modern times.

A Third Crusade in the twelfth century (1189–1192) attempted yet another rescue, enlisting as its leaders the most powerful Western rulers: Emperor Frederick Barbarossa; Richard the Lion-Hearted, king of England; and Philip Augustus, king of France. But the Third Crusade proved a tragicomic commentary on the passing of the original crusading spirit. Frederick Barbarossa accidentally drowned in the Saleph River while en route to the Holy Land. Richard the Lion-Hearted and Philip Augustus reached the outskirts of Jerusalem, but their intense personal rivalry shattered the Crusaders' unity and chances of victory. Philip Augustus returned to France and made war on English continental territories, and Richard fell captive to the Emperor Henry VI as he was returning to England. (Henry VI suspected Richard of plotting against him with Henry's mortal enemy, Henry the Lion, the duke of Saxony, who happened also to be Richard's brother-in-law.) The English were forced to pay a handsome ransom for their adventurous king's release. Popular resentment of taxes for this ransom became part of the background to the revolt against the English monarchy that led to the royal recognition of Magna Carta in 1215.

The long-term achievement of the first three Crusades had little to do with their original

A thirteenth-century depiction of Godfrey of Bouillon leading his knights on the First Crusade. [Bibliotheque Nationale/Art Resource]

Pope Eugenius III Promotes the Second Crusade

Full absolution and remission of all sins were just a part of the many benefits promised by the church to those who went on Crusades to the Holy Land. Here are the inducements offered by Pope Eugenius III (1145–1153) in 1146.

In virtue of the authority vested by God in us, we . . . have promised and granted to those who from a spirit of devotion have resolved to enter upon and accomplish this holy and necessary undertaking, that full remission of sins which our predecessor, Pope Urban, granted. We have also commanded that their wives and children, their property and possessions, shall be under the protection of the holy Church. . . . Moreover we ordain, by our apostolic authority, that until their return or death is fully proven, no lawsuit shall be instituted hereafter in regard to any property of which they were in peaceful possession when they took the cross.

Those who with pure hearts enter upon this sacred journey, and who are in debt, shall pay no interest. And if they, or others for them, are bound by oath or promise to pay interest, we free them by our apostolic authority. And after they have sought aid of their relatives, or of the lords of whom they hold their fiefs, if the latter are unable or unwilling to advance them money, we allow them freely to mortgage their lands and other possessions to churches, ecclesiastics, or other Christians, and their lords shall have no redress.

Following the example of our predecessor, and through the authority of omnipotent God and St. Peter, prince of the apostles, which is vested in us by God, we grant absolution and remission of sins, so that those who devoutly undertake and accomplish this holy journey, or who die by the way, shall obtain absolution for all their sins which they confess with humble and contrite heart, and shall receive from him who grants to each his due reward the prize of eternal life.

James Harvey Robinson (Ed.), *Readings in European History,* Vol. 1 (Boston: Anthenaeum, 1904), pp. 337–338.

purpose. Politically and religiously they were a failure, and the Holy Land reverted as firmly as ever to Muslim hands. These Crusades were more important for the way they stimulated Western trade with the East. The merchants of Venice, Pisa, and Genoa followed the Crusaders' cross to lucrative new markets. The need to resupply the new Christian settlements in the Near East not only reopened old trade routes that had long been closed by Arab domination of the Mediterranean but also established new ones. It is a commentary on both the degeneration of the original intent of the Crusades and their true historical importance that the Fourth Crusade became an enterprising commercial venture manipulated by the Venetians.

Trade and the Growth of Towns (1100–1300)

During the centuries following the collapse of the Roman Empire, western Europe became a closed and predominantly agricultural society, with small international commerce and even less urban culture. The great seaports of Italy were the exceptions. Venice, Pisa, and Genoa continued to trade actively with Constantinople and throughout the eastern Mediterranean, including Palestine, Syria, and Egypt, during the Middle Ages. The Venetians, Europe's most sober businessmen, jealously guarded their Eastern trade, attacking Western Christian competitors as quickly as Muslim predators. The latter were largely subdued by the success of the First Crusade, which proved a trade bonanza for Italian cities as the Mediterranean was opened to greater Western shipping. Venice, Pisa, and Genoa maintained major trading posts throughout the Mediterranean by the twelfth century. (See Map 7.2)

The Fourth Crusade

In an unintended chain reaction, Crusades created trade, which in turn gave rise to new towns and industry, which in turn brought about major social upheavals. The enterprising way in which the Venetians turned the Fourth Crusade to their own advantage reveals the interdependence of religion and business in the later Crusades. In 1202 Crusaders, some thirty thousand strong, arrived in Venice to set sail for Egypt. When they were unable to pay the price of transport, the Venetians negotiated as an alternative to payment the conquest of a rival Christian port city on the Adriatic: Zara.

Two views of Italian merchants at work: bargaining with customers (above) and recording the price of grain (below). [*Art Resource*]

To the shock of Pope Innocent III, the Crusaders obligingly subdued Zara. This proved to be only the beginning of the Crusaders' digression from their original goal. They further conquered Constantinople itself in support of disputed imperial claims made by the dethroned Greek prince Alexis. In July 1203 Constantinople fell, and by April 1204 it was completely in Western hands. Venice acquired thereby new lands and maritime rights that assured its domination of the eastern Mediterranean. During the decades of its occupation, Constantinople was the center for Western trade throughout the Near East.

The New Merchant Class

The Western commercial revival attendant on these events repopulated the old Roman urban centers and gave birth to new industries. Trade put both money and ideas into circulation. New riches, or the prospect of them, improved living conditions, raised hopes, and increased populations. In the twelfth century western Europe became a "boomtown." Among the most interesting creations were the traders themselves, who formed a new, distinctive social class. These prosperous merchants did not, as might first be suspected, spring from the landed nobility, although Venetian and Genoese traders began with the advantages of wealth. A goodly number of traders, however, were, to the contrary, poor, landless adventurers who had absolutely nothing to lose and everything to gain by the risks of foreign trade. For mutual protection they traveled together in great armed caravans, buying their products as cheaply as possible at the source and selling them as dearly as possible in Western marketplaces. They have been called the first Western capitalists, men inspired by profit and devoted to little more than amassing fortunes. But their very greed and daring laid the foundations for Western urban life as we have come to know it today.

Although in power, wealth, and privilege the great merchants were destined to join and eventually eclipse the landed aristocracy, they were initially misfits in traditional medieval society. They were freemen, often possessed of great wealth, yet they neither owned land nor tilled the soil. They did not value land and farming but were men of liquid wealth constantly on the move. Aristocrats and clergy looked down on them as degenerates, and the commoners viewed them with suspicion. They

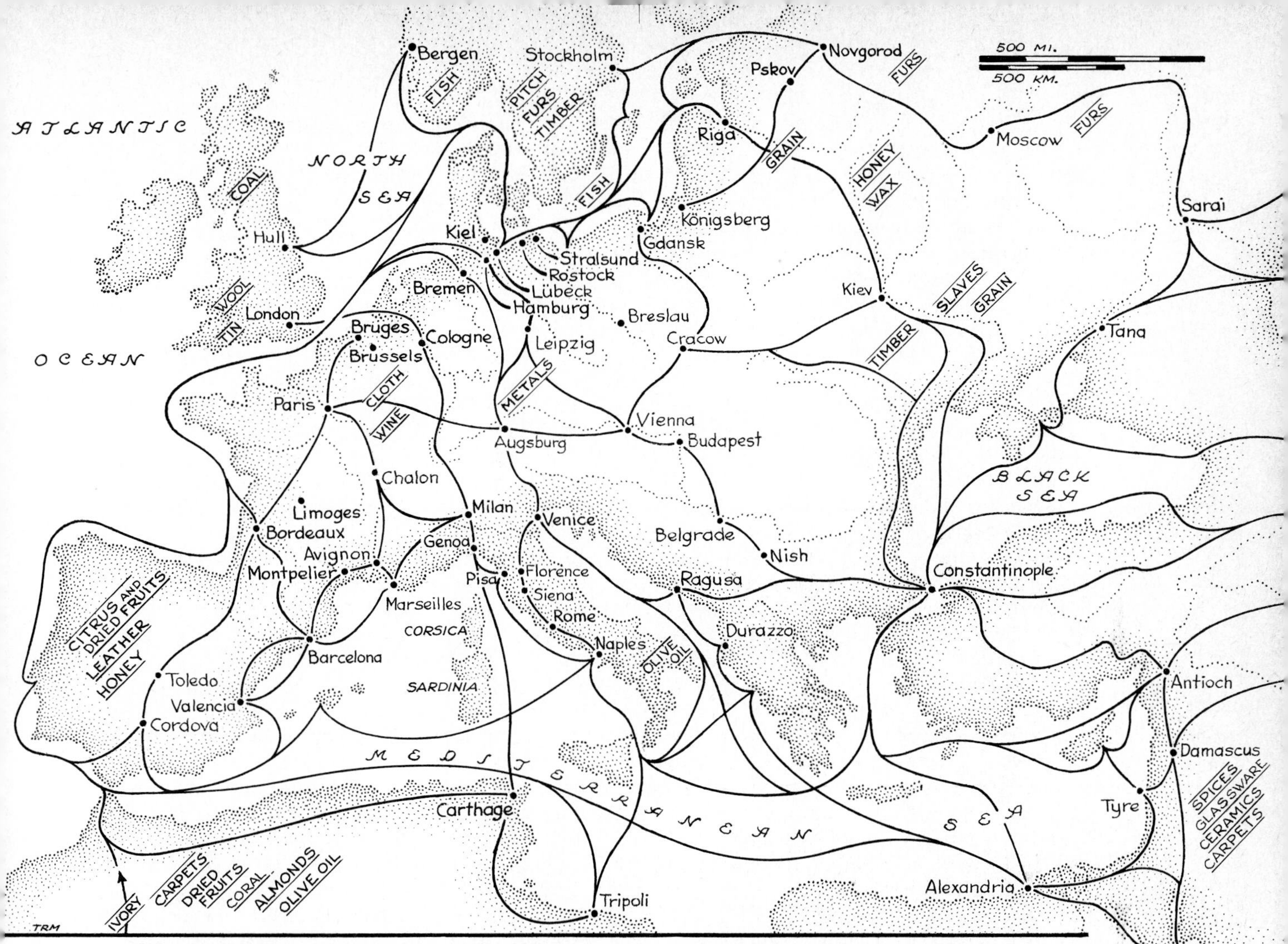

SOME MEDIEVAL TRADE ROUTES AND REGIONAL PRODUCTS

MAP 7-2 *Medieval trade in the West was not of the same intensity nor of the same geographical breadth in different periods. The map shows some of the channels that came to be used in interregional commerce. Labels tell part of what was carried in that commerce.*

were intruders within medieval society, a new breed who did not fit into the neat hierarchy of clergy, nobility, and serfs.

Merchants fanned out from the great Flemish and Italian trading centers: Bruges, Ghent, Venice, Pisa, Genoa, Florence. Wherever they settled in large numbers, they lobbied for the degree of freedom necessary for successful commerce, opposing tolls, tariffs, and other petty restrictions that discouraged the flow of trade. This activity brought them initially into conflict with the norms of static agricultural society. But as they demonstrated the many advantages of vigorous trade, the merchants progressively won their case. They not only remodeled city government to favor their new industries and the free flow of trade but also imparted to cities an aura of importance unknown during previous centuries. By the late Middle Ages cities commonly saw themselves as miniature states, even self-contained Christendoms. "God has become a citizen of Bern," wrote a Bernese chronicler in the fourteenth century, "and who can fight against God?"

As they grew and became prosperous, medieval cities also became very jealous of their good fortune. They took every measure to protect skilled industries, to expand trade, and to prevent competition from the surrounding countryside. Government remained in the hands of the rich and the few—patricians, *grandi*, the "old rich"—although wealthy merchants, aspiring to the noble style of life, increasingly found their way into the inner circles of government, as money proved early that it could talk. By the thirteenth century city councils, operating on the basis of aristocratic constitutions and composed of patricians and wealthy merchants—the old rich *and* the new rich—internally controlled city life. These oligarchies were increasingly confronted by small artisans, who demanded improved living conditions and a role in making policy. Skilled artisans formed the far greater part of the new burgher class and organized to express their will through powerful corporations or craft guilds. These were exclusive organizations for the various skilled trades; they set standards, certified craftsmen, and in every way worked to enhance the economic well-being and political influence of their members (see Chapter 8, "Townspeople"). The high and late Middle Ages also saw a deepening conflict between craft masters, who were determined to keep their numbers at an absolute minimum, and journeymen, who found themselves frozen at the lower levels of their trade. The self-protectiveness and internal conflicts of medieval cities did not, however, prevent them from forming larger trade associations, such as the famous German Hanseatic League, or Hansa, which kept Baltic trade a German monopoly well into the fifteenth century.

Changes in Society

The rise of a merchant class was an important crack in the old social order. New-rich merchants, a class originally sprung from ordinary, landless people, broke into the aristocracy, and in doing so, they drew behind them the leadership of the new artisan class created by the urban industries that had grown up in the wake of the growth of trade. In the late Middle Ages the "middle classes" firmly established themselves and have been enlarging their numbers ever since.

Although from one perspective medieval towns were overly self-protective and "egoistic," they also became a force for innovation and change far beyond their walls. This fact is all the more remarkable when it is remembered that towns at this time contained hardly more than 5 per cent of the population. Townspeople became a major force in the breakup of feudal society, aiding both kings and the peasantry at the expense of the landed nobility. Generally speaking, towns and kings

Two Romanesque churches: ABOVE, *the Abbey of Germigny des Pres in northern France;* BELOW, *the interior of the Chapel of St. Michael in the Loire Valley. The architecture of the early Middle Ages is known as* Romanesque *because it was closely related to the style of the late Roman Empire. It is characterized by thick stone walls and rounded arches to support the roof. The few windows were often very small, often mere slits. This gives Romanesque buildings a fortresslike appearance.*

tended to ally themselves against the great feudal lords. A notable exception may be seen in England, where the towns joined the barons against the oppressive monarchy of King John (1199–1216) and became a part of the parliamentary opposition. Townspeople generally, however, found their autonomy better preserved by having one distant master rather than several nearer and factious overlords. Kings, in turn, courted the liquid wealth and the administrative skills of the town dwellers, who began to replace the clergy and the nobility in the royal bureaucracy. Urban money made it possible for kings to hire mercenary armies and thereby decrease their dependence on the noble cavalry—an important step in the consolidation of territories divided for centuries by feudal allegiances and customs.

From the burgher ranks kings drew the skilled lawyers who began the long process of replacing feudal custom with centralized Roman law, and towns also often had powerful militias that could be enlisted in royal service. Kings, in return, gave towns political recognition and guaranteed their constitutions against territorial magnates. This was more easily done in the stronger coastal towns than in interior areas, where urban life remained less vigorous and territorial power was on the rise. In France, towns became integrated into the royal government. In Germany and Austria, by contrast, towns fell under ever tighter control by territorial princes. In Italy towns uniquely grew to absorb their surrounding territory, becoming city-states.

Towns also aided the peasantry, to the detriment of the landed nobility. A popular maxim of the time in German cities was *"Stadtluft macht frei"*—"City air makes one free." Cities passed legislation making serfs who spent a year and a day within their walls free men. New urban industries provided lucky peasants vocations alternative to farming. The new money economy made it possible for serfs or their urban patrons to buy their freedom from

feudal services and rents as the latter became translatable into direct money payments. A serf or his patron could simply buy up the "contract." The growth of a free peasantry became especially evident in the thirteenth century.

All of this worked against the landed nobility. As urban trade and industries put more money into circulation, its value decreased (inflation). The great landowners, whose wealth was static, found themselves confronted, on the one hand, by serfs who longed to flee to the city and, on the other, by rising prices. They were losing their cheap labor supply and facing diminished productivity; at the same time they had to pay more for their accustomed style of life. The nobility were not disciplined people, and many fell prey to money-wise urban merchants, who beat them out of their landed wealth.

The new urban economy worked, then, to free both kings and peasants from dependence on feudal lords, although this was a long and complex process. As royal authority became centralized and kings were able to hire mercenary soldiers, the noble cavalry became militarily obsolescent, at most a minor part of the king's armed forces. And as towns and urban industries grew, attracting serfs from the farms, the nobility gradually lost its once all-powerful economic base. The long-term consequence was a strengthening of monarchy.

Medieval Universities and Scholasticism

Thanks to Spanish Muslim scholars, the logical works of Aristotle, the writings of Euclid and Ptolemy, the basic works of Greek physicians and Arab mathematicians, and the larger texts of Roman law became available to Western scholars in the early twelfth century. Muslim scholars preserved these works, translated portions of the Greek ones into Latin, and wrote extensive, thought-provoking commentaries on ancient texts. This renaissance of ancient knowledge, in turn, provided the occasion for the rise of universities.

Bologna and Paris

The first important Western university was in Bologna. It received its formal grant of rights and privileges from the emperor Frederick Barbarossa in 1158. University members, like clergy, were granted royal immunity from local jurisdiction and were viewed by local townspeople as a group apart. In Bologna we find the first formal organizations of students and professors and the first degree programs—the institutional foundations of the modern university. The "university" was at first simply a program of study that gave the student a license to teach others. Originally the term *university* meant no more than a group or corporation of individuals who were united by common self-interest and for mutual protection. As the local townspeople viewed both masters and students as foreigners without civil rights, such a union was necessary. It followed the model of a medieval trade guild. Bolognese students formed such a bloc in order to guarantee fair rents and prices from the townspeople and regular and high-quality teaching from their professors. Price gouging by townspeople was met with the threat to move the university to another town—a threat that could easily be carried out because the university at this time was not a great, fixed physical plant. Professors who failed to meet student expectations were boycotted. The mobility of the first universities gave them a unique independence.

Professors also formed protective associations and established procedures and standards for certification to teach within their ranks. The first academic degree was a certificate *(licentia docendi)* given by the professors' guild, which granted graduates in the liberal arts program or in the higher professional sciences of medicine, theology, and law "the right to teach anywhere" *(ius ubique docendi).*

Bologna was distinguished as the center for the revival of Roman law. From the seventh to the eleventh centuries only the most rudimentary manuals of Roman law had survived and circulated. With the growth of trade and towns in the late eleventh century, Western scholars came into contact with the larger and more important parts of the Roman *Corpus Juris Civilis* of Justinian. The study and dissemination of this new material was directed by Irnerius (fl. early twelfth century). He and his students made authoritative commentaries or glosses on individual laws following their broad knowledge of the *Corpus Juris.* Around 1140 a monk named Gratian, also resident in Bologna, created the standard legal text in church or canon law, the *Concordance of Discordant Canons,* known more commonly as Gratian's *Decretum.*

As Bologna proved the model for southern

The University of Bologna in central Italy was distinguished as the center for the revival of Roman law. This carving from the tomb of a professor of law shows students attending one of his lectures. [*SCALA/Art Resource*]

European universities and the study of law, Paris became the model for northern Europe and the study of theology. Oxford, Cambridge, and, much later, Heidelberg were among Paris's imitators. All these universities required a foundation in the liberal arts for further study in the higher sciences of medicine, theology, and law. The arts program consisted of the *trivium* (grammar, rhetoric, and logic) and the *quadrivium* (arithmetic, geometry, astronomy, and music).

Before the emergence of the universities, the liberal arts had been taught in the cathedral and monastery schools, that is, schools attached to cathedrals or monasteries for the purpose of training clergy. The most famous of the cathedral schools were those of Rheims and Chartres. Chartres won fame under the direction of such distinguished teachers as Saint Ivo and Saint Bernard of Chartres (not to be confused with Saint Bernard of Clairvaux), and Gerbert, who later became Pope Sylvester II (999–1003), guided Rheims to greatness in the last quarter of the tenth century. Gerbert was filled with enthusiasm for knowledge and promoted both logical and rhetorical studies. He did much to raise the study of logic to preeminence within the liberal arts, despite his personal belief in the greater relevance of rhetoric to the promotion of Christianity.

The University of Paris grew institutionally out of the cathedral school of Notre Dame, receiving its charter in 1200 from King Philip Augustus and Pope Innocent III. Papal sanction and regulations, among them the right of the faculty to strike, were issued in 1231 in the bull *Parens scientiarum* and gave the university freedom from local church control. At this time the University of Paris consisted of independent faculties of arts, canon law, medicine, and theology, with the masters of arts, who were grouped together in four national factions (French, Norman, English-German, and Picard), the dominant faculty.

At Paris the college system originated. At first, colleges were no more than hospices providing room and board for poor students. But the educational life of the university rapidly expanded into these fixed buildings and began to thrive on their sure endowments. In Paris the most famous college was the Sorbonne, founded around 1257 by Robert de Sorbon, chaplain to the king, for the purpose of educating advanced theological students. In Oxford and Cambridge the colleges became the basic unit of student life, indistinguishable from the university. By the fifteenth and sixteenth centuries colleges had tied the universities to physical plants and fixed foundations, restricting their previous autonomy and freedom of movement.

The Curriculum

Before the renaissance of the twelfth century the education available within the cathedral and monastic schools was quite limited. Students learned grammar, rhetoric, and elementary geometry and astronomy. They used the Latin grammars of Donatus and Priscian and studied Saint Augustine's *On Christian Doctrine,* Cassiodorus's *On Divine and Secular Learning,* and the various writings of Boethius (d. 524). Boethius was important for instruction in arithmetic and music and especially for the transmission of the small body of Aristotle's logical works known before the twelfth century. After the textual finds of the early twelfth century, Western scholars had the whole of Aristotle's logic, the astronomy of Ptolemy, the writings of Euclid, and many Latin classics. By the mid-thirteenth century the ethical, physical, and metaphysical writings of Aristotle were in circulation in the West.

Logic and dialectic rapidly triumphed in importance over the other arts. They were tools designed to discipline knowledge and thought. Even before the twelfth century, cathedral schools had directed students to Boethius's translation and commentary on Porphyry's *Introduction to Aristotle* and to his translation and commentaries on Aristotle's *Categories* and *On Interpretation.* In the high Middle Ages the learning process was very basic. The student wrote commentaries on authoritative texts, especially those of Aristotle. His teachers did not encourage him to strive independently for undiscovered truth. He was taught rather to organize and harmonize the accepted truths of tradition. The basic assumption was that truth already existed; it was not something to be discovered but something at hand, requiring systematic organization and elucidation. Such conviction made logic and dialectic supreme within the liberal arts.

The Scholastic program of study, based on logic and dialectic, reigned supreme in all the faculties—in law and medicine as well as in philosophy and theology. Scholasticism was a peculiar method of study. The student read the traditional authorities in his field, formed short summaries of their teaching, disputed it by elaborating arguments pro and con, and then drew his own modest conclusions. The twelfth century saw the rise of the "summa," a summary of all that was known about a topic, and works whose purpose was to conciliate traditional authorities. In canon law there was Gratian's *Concordance of Discordant Canons.* In theology Peter Lombard's *Four Books of Sentences,* published around 1150, embraced traditional opinion on God, the creation, Christ, and the sacraments. It also enumerated the seven sacraments, which became traditional in the high Middle Ages (baptism, confirmation, penance, the Eucharist, extreme unction, holy orders, and marriage). Lombard's work evolved from Peter Abelard's *Sic et Non,* a juxtaposition of seemingly contradictory statements on the same subject by revered authorities. Lombard's *Sentences* became the standard theological textbook until the Protestant Reformation in the sixteenth century. In biblical studies the *Glossa Ordinaria* of Anselm of Laon (ca. 1120) and his disciples was the authoritative summary. In the thirteenth century came Saint Thomas Aquinas's magnificent *Summa Theologica,* an ambitious summary of the whole of theological knowledge from the Creation to the Last Day, which many consider the greatest theological work ever written.

Scholasticism had harsh critics even in the twelfth century. Such prominent men as John of Salisbury (ca. 1120–1180) and Saint Bernard of Clairvaux (1090–1153) rejected the dialectic of the logicians, which they found to be heartless and presumptuous. The later Humanist criticism of Scholastic learning as

The seven liberal arts of the medieval university curriculum: rhetoric, geometry, astronomy, music, natural and moral philosophy, and theology. At their feet sit the great teachers of antiquity: Cicero, Euclid, Ptolemey, Aristotle, Seneca, and Augustine. [*Art Resource*]

"useless" can be heard in their complaints. Although grammar and eloquence were eclipsed by dialectic and logic in medieval universities, professional rhetoricians, known as *dictatores,* retained their places within the universities and continued to give practical instruction in the composition of letters and official documents. These professional rhetoricians were the forerunners of the later Humanists, and their skills as secretaries were much in private demand in the high Middle Ages. The ability to persuade others by clear argument and eloquent prose and speech was the essence of successful government. A famous allegorical poem appeared in commentary on the domination of logic and dialectic within the universities. It was known as *The Battle of the Seven Arts* (1250). In the poem, which argues the rhetorician's position, vain logic is seen driving noble grammar into exile, where the latter patiently waits in confident expectation that a more enlightened age will demand its return.

Philosophy and Theology: Friends or Foes?

Scholastic thinkers in medieval universities quarreled over two basic problems: (1) the proper relation of philosophy, which was virtually identical with the writings of Aristotle, and theology (or of rational and revealed knowledge), and, to a lesser extent, (2) the status of so-called universal concepts.

The first problem arose from the fact that in Christian eyes there were manifestly heretical tenets in the corpus of Aristotle's writings, especially as his teaching was elaborated by the Muslim commentators. For example, Aristotle's belief in the eternality of the world called into question the Judeo-Christian teaching about the world's creation according to the

Bishop Stephen Complains About the New Scholastic Learning

Scholasticism involved an intellectual, learned approach to religion and its doctrines rather than simple, uncritical piety. Many saw in it a threat to the study of the Bible and the Church Fathers, as doctrines that should simply be believed and revered were rationally dissected for their logical meaning by allegedly presumptuous and none-too-well-trained youths. Here is a particularly graphic description of the threat, replete with classical allusion, as perceived by Stephen, Bishop of Tournai, in a letter to the pope written between 1192 and 1203.

The studies of sacred letters among us are fallen into the workshop of confusion, while both disciples applaud novelties alone and masters watch out for glory rather than learning. They everywhere compose new and recent summulae *[little summaries] and commentaries, by which they attract, detain, and deceive their hearers, as if the works of the holy fathers were not still sufficient, who, we read, expounded Holy Scripture in the same spirit in which we believe the apostles and prophets composed it. They prepare strange and exotic courses for their banquet, when at the nuptials of the son of the king of Taurus his own flesh and blood are killed and all prepared, and the wedding guests have only to take and eat what is set before them. Contrary to the sacred canons there is public disputation over the incomprehensible deity; concerning the incarnation of the Word, verbose flesh and blood irreverently litigate. The indivisible Trinity is cut up and wrangled over . . . so that now there are as many errors as doctors, as many scandals as classrooms, as many blasphemies as squares. . . . Faculties called liberal having lost their pristine liberty are sunk in such servitude that adolescents with long hair impudently usurp their professorships, and beardless youths sit in the seat of their seniors, and those who don't yet know how to be disciples strive to be named masters. And they write their* summulae *moistened with drool and dribble but unseasoned with the salt of philosophers. Omitting the rules of the arts and discarding the authentic books of the artificers, they seize the flies of empty words in their sophisms like the claws of spiders. Philosophy cries out that her garments are torn and disordered and, modestly concealing her nudity by a few specific tatters, neither is consulted nor consoles as of old. All these things, father, call for the hand of apostolic correction. . . .*

Lynn Thorndike, *University Records and Life in the Middle Ages* (New York: Octagon Books, 1971), pp. 22–24.

book of Genesis. Aristotelian teaching that intellect was one seemed to deny all individuality, Christian teaching about individual responsibility, and the personal immortality of the soul.

When theologians began to adopt the logic and the metaphysics of Aristotle, some critics saw a mortal threat to biblical and traditional authority. Berengar of Tours (d. 1088) applied logic to the sacrament of the Eucharist and came to question the church's teaching on transubstantiation. Peter Abelard (1079–1142) subjected the Trinity to logical examination. The curiosity of these new logicians shocked conservatives such as Lanfranc (d. 1089), the reformer of the Abbey of Bec, and especially the powerful Saint Bernard. The latter questioned whether the liberal arts course, dominated by Aristotelian logic, had become more a foe than an ally of theological study. A century of suspicion and criticism of Aristotle's influence on theological study culminated when the bishop of Paris condemned 219 philosophical propositions in 1277. This massive condemnation was directed against devotees of Aristotle, many of whom followed the Muslim authority Averroës (1126–1198), but it also caught in its net a few teachings of such orthodox Western theologians as Thomas Aquinas (d. 1274), who had tried to reconcile Aristotle with traditional Christian teaching.

After this condemnation philosophy never again had such importance within theology. William of Ockham (d. 1349), who represented conservative opinion in this controversy and may be seen as a watershed in the development of Scholasticism, strictly limited the ability of reason, assisted by logic and dialectic, to fathom the nature and decisions of God independently of divine revelation. Ockham taught that one must abandon all such efforts to penetrate the divine mind in essential theological matters and must be content with the Bible's teaching.

The Problem of Universals: Aquinas and Ockham

The classic Scholastic problem concerned the question whether or not universal concepts really exist apart from the human mind. Do words that signify a multitude of individual things, such as *man, dog,* and *chair,* refer to realities that have extramental existence? The question, perhaps strange at first to modern people, involved a very basic discussion of how one truly knows anything. Because individual physical things—a man, a dog, a chair—are perishable, philosophical realists, who closely followed the views of Plato, believed that they could not be known by an immaterial and immortal soul. They reasoned that like can know and be known only by like. What is immaterial and immortal can know directly only immaterial and immortal things. Hence, these realists argued, there must be a transcendent world of being in which perfect, imperishable, immaterial models of individual things exist. It is because the human mind is privy to such a world that it can know immediately the world of physical things. These models, existing in a transcendent world of being, are the "universals," and according to the realists, they exist apart from the human mind. They are the original models of the individual things of the world, the ultimate principles of being and intelligibility. It is because individual things participate in universals that they both exist and can be known.

The moderate realists, who followed Aristotle more than Plato on this question, agreed that universals were really distinct from individual things. But they argued that such uni-

Thomas Aquinas Defines the Nature of Christian Theology

Although its premises and data came from divine revelation rather than from empirical observation, theology was considered a "science" in its own right in the Middle Ages, indeed, the "queen" of the sciences. Here Thomas Aquinas (ca. 1225–1274) defines Christian theology and explains its use of human reasoning to elucidate the truths of faith.

The premises of Christian theology are revealed truths, accepted on the word of the teacher who reveals them. Consequently its typical method is the appeal to authority. This does not impair its scientific dignity, for though to cite human authority is the poorest form of argument, the appeal to divine authority is the highest and most cogent.

Nevertheless, Christian theology also avails itself of human reasoning to illustrate the truths of faith, not to prove them. Grace does not scrap nature, but improves it; reason subserves faith, and natural love runs through charity. Theology invokes great thinkers on matters where they are received authorities. . . . Theology treats them as sources of external evidence for its arguments. Its proper and indispensable court of appeal is to the authority of the canonical Scriptures. The writings of the Fathers of the Church are also proper sources, yet their authority is not final. Faith rests on divine revelation made through the prophets and apostles and set down in the canonical Scriptures, not on revelations, if there by any, made to other holy teachers.

From the *Summa Theologica,* Ia, i. 8, ad 2, in Thomas Gilby (Ed. and Trans.), *St. Thomas Aquinas: Theological Texts* (New York: Oxford University Press, 1955), pp. 22–23.

William of Ockham on Universals

William of Ockham (ca. 1300–1349) rejected any hint of the extramental existence of human concepts. Universals were only contents of the mind and verbal conventions.

We have to say that every universal is one singular thing. Therefore nothing is universal except by signification, that is, by being a sign of several things. . . . It must, however, be understood that there are two sorts of universal. There is one sort which is naturally universal; it is a sign naturally predicable of many things, in much the same way as smoke naturally signifies fire, or a groan the pain of a sick man, or laughter an inner joy. Such a universal is nothing other than a content of the mind; and therefore no substance outside the mind and no accident outside the mind is such a universal. . . . The other sort of universal is so by convention. In this way, an uttered word, which is really a single quality, is universal; for it is a conventional sign meant to signify many things. Therefore, just as the word is said to be common, so it can be said to be universal. But it is not so by nature, only by convention.

William of Ockham, *Summa Totius Logicae,* Ic, xiv, in *Ockham: Philosophical Writings,* ed. and trans. by Philotheus Boehner (New York: Nelson, 1962), pp. 33–34.

versals existed only *within* individual things as intrinsic qualities that gave them form and intelligibility. According to this point of view, championed by Thomas Aquinas, one came to know individual things by isolating and "abstracting" their intrinsic universal features. The universal, which is within individual things, is "extracted" from them by intellection and is lodged in the mind as a so-called intelligible species. It is by way of such abstracted universals in the mind that one knows the surrounding world.

Later the nominalists took the most radical position on the question of universals. They looked on universal concepts as simply "names" or "terms" created by the mind and existing only within the mind. William of Ockham was the most famous exponent of this point of view. As a general principle he believed that the simpler explanation was always the more convincing explanation. This was his famous "razor": "What can be explained by assuming fewer terms is vainly explained by assuming more." A special "world of being" and "intelligible species" were neither necessary nor helpful assumptions. Ockham felt that such speculations led only to greater confusion and skepticism. He taught that individual things were known directly and without mediation and that simple "intuitive knowledge" provided the foundation for the mind's formation of the universal concepts it used to aid its recall and verbal communication. Universals were extrapolations from ordinary sensory experience and reflection, "conventions," naturally formed by the mind as essential aids to knowledge, but *really* existing only in the mind and in words.

Suggested Readings

JOHN W. BALDWIN, *The Scholastic Culture of the Middle Ages:* 1000–1300 (1971). Best brief synthesis available.

M. W. BALDWIN (Ed.), *History of the Crusades,* I: *The First Hundred Years.* (1955). Basic historical narrative.

GEOFFREY BARRACLOUGH, *The Medieval Papacy* (1968). Brief, comprehensive survey, with pictures.

F. C. COPLESTON, *Aquinas* (1965). Best introduction to Aquinas's philosophy.

FREDERICK COPLESTON, *A History of Philosophy,* III/1: *Ockham to the Speculative Mystics* (1963). The best introduction to Ockham and his movement.

ETIENNE GILSON, *Heloise and Abelard* (1968). Analysis and defense of medieval scholarly values.

CHARLES H. HASKINS, *The Renaissance of the Twelfth Century* (1927). Still the standard account.

CHARLES H. HASKINS, *The Rise of Universities* (1972). A short, minor classic.

GORDON LEFF, *Paris and Oxford Universities in the Thirteenth and Fourteenth Centuries: An Instutitional and Intellectual History* (1968). Very good on Scholastic debates.

EMILE MÂLE, *The Gothic Image: Religious Art in France in the Thirteenth Century* (1913). A classic.

HANS EBERHARD MAYER, *The Crusades*, trans. by John Gilligham (1972). Extremely detailed, and best one-volume account.

ERWIN PANOFSKY, *Gothic Architecture and Scholasticism* (1951). A controversial classic.

HENRI PIRENNE, *Medieval Cities: Their Origins and the Revival of Trade*, trans. by Frank D. Halsey (1970). A minor classic.

HASTINGS RASHDALL, *The Universities of Europe in the Middle Ages*, Vols. 1–3 (1936). Dated but still standard comprehensive work.

FRITZ RÖRIG, *The Medieval Town*, trans. by D. J. A. Matthew (1971). Excellent on northern Europe.

BRIAN TIERNEY, *The Crisis of Church and State 1050–1300* (1964). Very useful collection of primary sources on key Church–State conflicts.

S. WILLIAMS (Ed.), *The Gregorian Epoch: Reformation, Revolution, Reaction* (1964). Variety of scholarly opinion on the significance of Pope Gregory's reign presented in debate form.

R. L. WOLFF AND H. W. HAZARD (Eds.), *History of the Crusades*, II: *The Later Crusades* 1189–1311 (1962).

Vassals paying homage to their lord. The word "vassal" means "one who serves." The ceremony of homage symbolized the vassal's dependence on his lord and the lord's tie to his vassal. [*Art Resource*]

8

The High Middle Ages: Society and Politics

The Order of Life

FOUR BASIC SOCIAL GROUPS were distinguished in the Middle Ages: those who fought (the landed nobility), those who prayed (the clergy), those who labored (the peasantry), and, after the revival of towns in the eleventh century, those who traded and manufactured (the townspeople). It would be false to view each of these groups as closed and homogeneous. Throughout medieval society, like tended to be attracted to like regardless of social grouping. Barons, archbishops, rich farmers, and successful merchants had far more in common with each other than they did with the middle and lower strata of their various professions.

Nobles

As a distinctive social group all noblemen did not begin simply as great men with large hereditary lands. Many rose from the ranks of feudal vassals or warrior knights. The successful vassal attained a special social and legal status based on his landed wealth (accumulated fiefs), his exercise of authority over others, and his distinctive social customs—all of which set him apart from others in medieval society. By the late Middle Ages there had evolved a distinguishable higher and lower nobility living in both town and country. The higher were the great landowners and territorial magnates; the lower were petty landlords, descendants from minor knights, new-rich merchants who could buy country estates, and wealthy farmers patiently risen from ancestral serfdom.

It was a special mark of the nobility that they lived on the labor of others. Basically lords of manors, the nobility of the early and high Middle Ages neither tilled the soil like the peasantry nor engaged in the commerce of merchants—activities considered beneath their dignity. The nobleman resided in a country mansion or, if he were particularly wealthy, a castle. He was drawn to the countryside as much by personal preference as by the fact that his fiefs were usually rural manors. Arms were his profession; the nobleman's sole occupation and reason for living was waging war. His fief provided the means to acquire the expensive military equipment that his rank required, and he maintained his enviable position as he had gained it, by fighting for his chief.

The nobility accordingly celebrated the physical strength, courage, and constant activity of warfare. Warring gave them both new

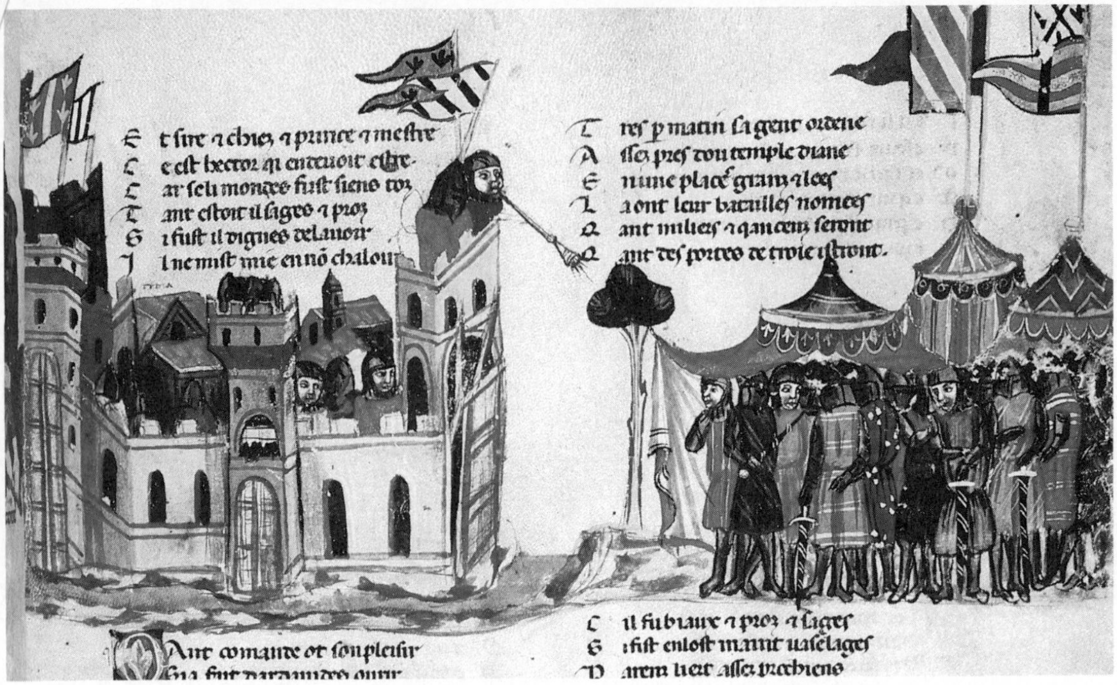

The siege of a city, from a twelfth-century French manuscript. The medieval nobility existed to wage war. Arms were the nobleman's profession, and warfare his means of acquiring riches and glory. (*Art Resource*)

riches and an opportunity to gain honor and glory. Knights were paid a share in the plunder of victory, and in time of war everything became fair game. Special war wagons, designed for the collection and transport of booty, followed them into battle. Periods of peace were greeted with great sadness, as they meant economic stagnation and boredom. Whereas the peasants and the townspeople counted peace the condition of their occupational success, the nobility despised it as unnatural to their profession. They looked down on the peasantry as cowards who ran and hid in time of war. Urban merchants, who amassed wealth by business methods strange to feudal society, were held in equal contempt, which increased as the affluence and political power of the townspeople grew. The nobility possessed as strong a sense of superiority over these "unwarlike" people as the clergy did over the general run of laity.

The nobleman nurtured his sense of distinctiveness within medieval society by the chivalric ritual of dubbing to knighthood, a ceremonial entrance into the noble class that became almost a religious sacrament. The ceremony was preceded by a bath of purification, confession, communion, and a prayer vigil. Thereafter the priest blessed the knight's standard, lance, and sword. As prayers were chanted, the priest girded the knight with his sword and presented him his shield, enlisting him as much in the defense of the church as in the service of his lord. Dubbing raised the nobleman to a state as sacred in his sphere as clerical ordination made the priest in his. This comparison is quite legitimate. The clergy and the nobility were medieval society's privileged estates. The appointment of noblemen to high ecclesiastical office and their eager participation in the church's Crusades had strong ideological and social underpinnings as well as economic and political motives.

In peacetime the nobility had two favorite amusements: hunting and tournaments. Because of the threat to towns and villages posed by wild animals, the great hunts actually aided the physical security of the ordinary people, while occupying the restless noblemen. However, where they could, noblemen progressively monopolized the rights to game, forbidding the common man from hunting in the "lord's" forests. This practice built resentment among common people to the level of revolt. Free game, fishing, and access to wood were basic demands in the petitions of grievance and the revolts of the peasantry throughout the high and later Middle Ages.

The pastime of tournaments also sowed seeds of social disruption, but more within the ranks of the nobility itself. Tournaments were designed not only to keep men fit for war, but also to provide the excitement of war without the useless maiming and killing of prized vassals. But as regions competed fiercely with one another for victory and glory, even mock battles with blunted weapons proved to be deadly. Tournaments tended to get out of hand, ending with bloodshed and animosity among the combatants. Remnants survive today in the intense regional rivalry of European soccer. The church came to oppose tournaments as occasions of pagan revelry and senseless violence. Kings and princes also turned against them as sources of division within their realms. Henry II of England proscribed them in the twelfth century. They did not end in France until the mid-sixteenth century, after Henry II of France received a mortal shaft through his visor during a tournament celebrating his daughter's marriage.

From the repeated assemblies in the courts of barons and kings, set codes of social conduct or "courtesy" developed in noble circles. With the French leading the way, mannered behavior and court etiquette became almost as important as battlefield expertise. Knights became literate gentlemen, and lyric poets sang and moralized at court. The cultivation of a code of behavior and a special literature to eulogize it was not unrelated to problems within the social life of the nobility. Noblemen were notorious philanderers; their illegitimate children mingled openly with their legitimate offspring in their houses. The advent of courtesy was in part an effort to reform this situation. Although the poetry of courtly love was sprinkled with frank eroticism and the beloved in these epics were married women pursued by those to whom they were not married, the love recommended by the poet was usually love at a distance, unconsummated by sexual intercourse. It was love without touching, a kind of sex without physical sex, and only as such was it considered ennobling. Court poets depicted those who did carnally consummate their illicit love as reaping at least as much suffering as joy from it.

In the twelfth century, knighthood was legally restricted to men of high birth. This circumscription of noble ranks came in reaction to the growing wealth, political power, and successful social climbing of the emergent urban patriciate. Kings remained free, however, to raise up knights at will and did not shrink from increasing royal revenues by selling noble titles to wealthy merchants. But the law was building fences—fortunately not without gates—between town and countryside in the high Middle Ages.

For their part, the merchants supported the passage of statutes prohibiting the nobility, who maintained houses and family businesses in the towns, from disrupting the merchants' carefully created monopolies by engaging in long-distance trade. Such jockeying to protect self-interests brought lawyers into a prominence that they have never lost in Western society.

Noblewomen watching a tournament. These mock battles were designed to provide the excitement of war without its mayhem. However, they tended to get out of hand, resulting in bloodshed and even death. [*University of Heidelberg*]

No medieval social group was absolutely uniform—not the nobility, the clergy, the townspeople, not even the peasantry. Not only was the nobility a class apart, it also had strong social divisions within its own ranks. Noblemen formed a broad social spectrum—from minor vassals without subordinate vassals to mighty barons, the principal vassals of a king or prince, who had many vassals of their own. Dignity and status within the nobility were directly related to the exercise of authority over others; a chief with many vassals obviously far excelled the small country nobleman who served another and was lord over none but himself.

Even among the domestic servants of the nobility, a broad social hierarchy developed in accordance with assigned manorial duties. Although they were peasants in the eyes of the law, the chief stewards charged to oversee the operation of the lord's manor and entrusted with the care and education of the noble children became powerful "lords" within their "domains." Some freemen found the status of the steward enviable enough to surrender their own freedom and become domestic servants in the hope of attaining it. In time the social superiority of the higher ranks of domestic servants won legal recognition as medieval law adjusted to acknowledge the privileges of wealth and power at whatever level they appeared.

In the late Middle Ages several factors forced the landed nobility into a steep economic and political decline from which it never recovered. These were the great population losses of the fourteenth century brought on by the great plague; the changes in military tactics occasioned by the use of infantry and heavy artillery during the Hundred Years' War; and the alliance of the wealthy towns with the king. Generally one can speak of a waning of the landed nobility after the fourteenth century. Thereafter the effective possession of land and wealth counted far more than parentage and family tree as qualification for entrance into the highest social class.

Clergy

Unlike the nobility and the peasantry, the clergy was an open estate. Although clerical ranks reflected the social classes from which the clergy came and a definite clerical hierarchy formed, one was still a cleric by religious training and ordination, not by the circumstances of birth or military prowess. There were two basic types of clerical vocation: the regular and the secular clergy. The former were the orders of monks, who lived according to a special ascetic rule *(regula)* in cloisters separated from the world. They were the spiritual elite among the clergy, and theirs was not a way of life lightly entered. Canon law required that one be at least twenty-one years of age before making a final profession of the monastic vows of poverty, chastity, and obedience. Their personal sacrifices and high religious ideals made the monks much respected in high medieval society. This popularity was a major factor in the success of the Cluny reform movement and of the Crusades of the eleventh and twelfth centuries. The Crusades became a way for the layman to participate in the admired life of asceticism and prayer. They were holy pilgrimages providing the opportunity to imitate the suffering of Jesus even unto death, just as the monks imitated his suffering and death by their retreat from the world and their severe self-denial.

Although many monks (and also nuns, who increasingly embraced the vows of poverty, obedience, and chastity without a clerical rank) secluded themselves altogether, the regular clergy were never completely cut off from the secular world. They maintained frequent contact with the laity through such charitable activities as feeding the destitute and tending the sick, through liberal arts instruction in monastic schools, through special pastoral commissions from the pope, and as supplemental preachers and confessors in parish churches during Lent and other peak religious seasons. It became the special mark of the Dominican and Franciscan friars to live a common life according to a special rule, and still to be active in worldly ministry. Some monks, because of their learning and rhetorical skills, even rose to prominence as secretaries and private confessors to kings and queens.

The secular clergy were those who lived and worked directly among the laity in the world *(saeculum)*. They formed a vast hierarchy. There were the high prelates—the wealthy cardinals, archbishops, and bishops, who were drawn almost exclusively from the nobility—the urban priests, the cathedral canons, and the court clerks; and, finally, the great mass of poor parish priests, who were neither financially nor intellectually very far above the common people they served (the basic educational requirement was an ability to say the Mass.) Until the Gregorian reform in the eleventh century began to reverse the trend, parish priests lived with women in a relationship akin to marriage, and their concubines and children were accepted within the communities they served. Because of their relative poverty, it was not unusual for priests to "moonlight" as teachers, artisans, or farmers, a practice also accepted and even admired by their parishioners.

One of the results of the Gregorian reform was the creation of new religious orders aspiring to live a life of poverty and self-sacrifice in imitation of Christ and the first apostles. The more important were the Canons Regular (founded 1050–1100), the Carthusians (founded 1084), the Cistercians (founded 1098), and the Praemonstratensians (founded 1121). Carthusians, Cistercians, and Praemonstratensians were extremely puritanical in their quest to recapture the purer religious life of the early church. The Cistercians were known as the white monks and the Praemonstratensians as the white order; both wore all-white attire—symbolic of apostolic purity. The Carthusians devoted themselves to long periods of silence and even self-flagellation in their quest for perfect conformity with Christ. The Canons Regular were independent groups of secular clergy and also earnest laity, who, in addition to services to souls in the world, also adopted the Rule of Saint Augustine, a monastic guide dating from around the year 500, and practiced the virtues of regular clerics. As there were monks who renounced exclusive withdrawal from the world, so were there priests who renounced exclusive involvement in it. By merging the life of the cloister with traditional clerical duties, the Canons Regular foreshadowed the mendicant friars of the thirteenth century, the Dominicans and the Franciscans, who combined the ascetic ideals of the cloister with a very active ministry in the world.

The monasteries and nunneries of the established orders recruited candidates from among the wealthiest social groups. Crowding in the convents and the absence of patronage were factors in the thirteenth-century growth of lay satellite convents known as *beguinages,* which housed large numbers of religiously earnest unmarried women from the upper and middle social strata. The city of Cologne established 100 such houses between 1250 and 1350, each containing eight to twelve women. A number of these convents, in Cologne and elsewhere, became heterodox in religious doctrine and practice, falling prey to heresy. Among the responsibilities of the new religious orders of Dominicans and Franciscans was the "regularization" of such convents.

Nuns at table. Communities of nuns became extremely numerous during the later Middle Ages. [*Alinari*]

There was a far greater proportion of clergy within medieval than within modern society. It has been estimated that 1.5 per cent of fourteenth-century Europe was in clerical garb.

The clergy were concentrated in urban areas, especially in towns with universities and cathedrals, where in addition to their studies they found work in a wide variety of religious services. In late-fourteenth-century England there was one cleric for every seventy laypeople, and in counties with a cathedral or a university the proportion rose to one cleric for every fifty laypeople.[1] In large university towns the clergy could exceed 10 per cent of the population. One of the most popular reforms of the Protestant Reformation in the sixteenth century, a uniquely urban movement, was a sharp reduction of the proportion of clergy in society. An early Protestant pamphleteer, Eberlin von Günzburg, for example, reflected a pervasive lay sentiment when he proposed that there be but one cleric for every three hundred laity.

Despite the moonlighting of poorer parish priests, the clergy as a whole, like the nobility, lived on the labor of others. Their income came from the regular collection of tithes and church taxes according to an elaborate system that evolved in the high and later Middle Ages. The church was, of course, a major landowner and regularly collected rents and fees. Monastic communities and high prelates amassed truly great fortunes; there was a popular saying that the granaries were always full in the monasteries. The immense secular power attached to high clerical posts can be seen in the intensity of the investiture struggle, when the loss of the right to present chosen clergy with the ring and staff of episcopal office seemed a direct threat to the emperor's control of his realm precisely because the bishops had become royal agents and were endowed to that purpose with royal lands that the emperor could ill afford to have slip from his control.

During the greater part of the Middle Ages the clergy were the "first estate," and theology was the queen of the sciences. How did the clergy come into such prominence? It was basically popular reverence for the clergy's role as mediator between God and humanity that made this superiority possible. The priest brought the very Son of God down to earth when he celebrated the sacrament of the Eucharist; his absolution released penitents from punishment for mortal sin. It was considered improper for mere laypeople to sit in judgment on such a priest. Theologians elaborated the distinction between the clergy and the laity very much to the clergy's benefit. The belief in the superior status of the clergy underlay the evolution of clerical privileges and immunities in both person and property. As holy persons, the clergy could not be taxed by secular rulers without special permission from the proper ecclesiastical authorities. Clerical crimes were under the jurisdiction of special ecclesiastical courts, not the secular courts. Because churches and monasteries were deemed holy places, they, too, were free from secular taxation and legal jurisdiction. Hunted criminals, lay and clerical, regularly sought asylum within them, disrupting the normal processes of law and order. Ecclesiastical authorities were quick to threaten excommunication and interdict (the suspension of the church's sacraments, including Christian burial), which medieval towns feared almost as much as they did criminals, when this privilege of asylum was violated by city officials.

In the late Middle Ages townspeople came increasingly to resent the special immunities of the clergy. They complained that it was not proper for the clergy to have greater privileges yet far fewer responsibilities than all others who lived within the town walls. An early sixteenth-century lampoon reflected what had by then become a widespread sentiment:

> Priests, monks,and nuns
> Are but a burden to the earth.
> They have decided
> That they will not become citizens.
> That's why they're so greedy—
> They stand firm against our city
> And will swear no allegiance to it.
> And we hear their fine excuses:
> "It would cause us much toil and trouble
> Should we pledge our troth as burghers."[2]

Although the separation of Church and State and the distinction between the clergy and the laity have persisted into modern times, after the fifteenth century the clergy ceased to be the superior class they had been for so much of the Middle Ages. In both Protestant and Catholic lands governments progressively subjected them to the basic responsibilities of citizenship.

Peasants

The largest and lowest social group in medieval society was the one on whose labor the

[1] Denys Hay, *Europe in the Fourteenth and Fifteenth Centuries* (New York: Holt, Rinehart, 1966), pp. 58–59.

[2] Cited by S. Ozment, *The Reformation in the Cities* (New Haven, Conn.: Yale University Press, 1975), p. 36.

This aerial view of the fields surrounding a village in Leicestershire, England, where the medieval division of land has been preserved, reveals the relatively small plots farmed by medieval peasants. [*Aerofilms, Ltd.*]

welfare of all the others depended: the agrarian peasantry. They lived on and worked the manors of the nobility, the primitive cells of rural social life, and all were to one degree or another dependent on their lords and considered their property. The manor was originally a plot of land within a village, ranging from twelve to seventy-five acres in size, assigned to a certain member by a settled tribe or clan. This member and his family became lords of the land, and those who came to dwell there formed a smaller, self-sufficient community within a larger village community. In the early Middle Ages such a manor consisted of the dwellings of the lord and his family, the cottages of the peasant workers, agricultural sheds, and fields. The landowner or lord of the manor required a certain amount of produce (grain, eggs, and the like) and a certain number of services from the peasant families that came to dwell on and farm his land. The tenants were free to divide the labor as they wished, and what goods remained after the lord's levies were met were their own. A powerful lord might own many such manors, and kings later based their military and tax assessments on the number of manors owned by a vassal landlord.

There were both servile and free manors. The tenants of the latter had originally been freemen known as *coloni,* original inhabitants and petty landowners who swapped their small possessions for a guarantee of security from a more powerful lord, who came in this way to possess their land. Unlike the pure serfdom of the servile manors, whose tenants had no original claim to a part of the land, the tenancy obligations on free manors tended to be limited and their rights more carefully defined. Tenants of servile manors were by comparison far more vulnerable to the whims of their landlords. These two types of manor tended, however, to merge; the most common situation was the manor on which tenants of greater and lesser degrees of servitude dwelt together, their services to the lord defined by their personal status and local custom. In many regions free, self-governing peasant communities existed without any overlords and tenancy obligations.

Marc Bloch, the modern authority on manorial society, has vividly depicted the duties of tenancy:

> On certain days the tenant brings the lord's steward perhaps a few small silver coins or, more often, sheaves of grain harvested on his fields, chickens from his farmyard, cakes of wax from his beehives or from the swarms of the neighboring forest. At other times he works on the arable or the meadows of the demesne [the lord's plot of land in the manoral fields, between one third and one half of that available]. Or else we find him carting casks of wine or sacks of grain on behalf of the master to distant residences. His is the labour which repairs the walls or moats of the castle. If the master has guests the peasant strips his own bed to provide the necessary extra bed-clothes. When the hunting season comes round he feeds the pack. If war breaks out he does duty as a footsoldier or orderly, under the leadership of the reeve of the village.[3]

The lord also had the right to subject his tenants to exactions known as *banalities.* He could, for example, force them to breed their cows with his bull, and to pay for the privilege, as well as to grind their corn in his mill, bake their bread in his oven, make their wine in his wine press, buy their beer from his brewery, and even surrender to him the tongues or other choice parts of all animals slaughtered on his lands. He had the right to levy small taxes at will.

Exploited as the serfs may appear to have been from a modern point of view, their status was far from chattel slavery. It was to the lord's advantage to keep his serfs healthy and happy; his welfare, like theirs, depended on a successful harvest. Serfs had their own dwellings and modest strips of land and lived by the produce of their own labor and organization. They were permitted to market for their own profit what surpluses might remain after the harvest. They were free to choose their spouses within the local village, although the lord's permission was required if a wife or husband was sought from another village. And serfs were able to pass their property (their dwellings and field strips) and worldly goods on to their children.

Peasants lived in mud huts with thatched roofs and, with the exception of the higher domestic servants, seldom ventured beyond their own villages. The local priest often was their window on the world, and church festivals were their major communal entertainment. Their religiosity was based in large part on the fact that the church was the only show in town, although their religious beliefs were by no means unambiguously Christian. Despite the social distinctions between free and servile serfs—and, within these groups, between those who owned ploughs and oxen and those who possessed only hoes—the common dependence on the soil forced close cooperation. As the ratio of seed to grain yield was consistently poor—about two bushels of seed were required to produce six to ten bushels of grain in good times—there was rarely an abundance of bread and ale, the staple peasant foods. There was no corn or potatoes in Europe until the sixteenth century. Pork was the major source of protein and every peasant household had its pigs. At slaughter time a family might also receive a little tough beef. But basically everyone depended on the grain crops. When they failed or fell short, the peasantry simply went hungry unless the lord had surplus stores that he was willing to share.

Two basic changes occurred in the evolution of the manor from the early to the later Middle Ages. The first was the fragmentation of the manor and the rise to dominance of the single-family unit. As the lords parceled out their land to new tenants, their own plots became pro-

[3] *Feudal Society,* trans. by L. A. Manyon (Chicago: University of Chicago Press 1968), p. 250.

A panorama of medieval society: above, soldiers, scholars, and merchants; below, peasants shown with two of the new tools which were developed between 1000 *and* 1200 A.D.: *the large scythes with handgrips (left) made it much easier to harvest grain. The heavy plough (right) cut deeper into the soil, reducing ploughing time by half.* [*Bibliothèque Nationale, Paris*]

A peasant sowing his field. About two bushels of seed were required to produce six to ten bushels of grain. Since medieval peasants depended on grain for most of their food, this poor yield meant that there was rarely abundant bread. [*Trustees of the British Museum*]

gressively smaller. The increase in tenants and the decrease in the lord's fields brought about a corresponding reduction in the labor services exacted from the tenants. In France, by the reign of Louis IX (1226–1270), only a few days a year were required, whereas in the time of Charlemagne peasants had worked the lord's fields several days a week. By the twelfth century the manor was hopelessly fragmented. As the single-family unit replaced the clan as the basic nuclear group, assessments of goods and services fell on individual fields and house-

A woodcut showing wild animals damaging peasant crops. One of the greatest problems for peasants was how to protect their crops from stags and deer. Forbidden by law from hunting them, the peasants built fences and used clubs to drive the animals away. [*Deutsche Fotothek, Dresden*]

Slaughter time on a medieval manor. Pork was the main source of protein for the peasantry and every household kept pigs. (*Art Resource*)

holds, no longer on manors as a whole. Family farms replaced manorial units. The peasants' carefully nurtured communal life made possible a family's retention of its land and dwelling after the death of the head of the household. In this way land and property remained in the possession of a single family from generation to generation.

The second change in the evolution of the manor was the translation of feudal dues into money payments, a change made possible by the revival of trade and the rise of the towns. This development, which was completed by the thirteenth century, permitted serfs to hold their land as rent-paying tenants and to overcome their servile status. Although tenants thereby gained greater freedom, they were not necessarily better off materially. Whereas servile workers had been able to count on the benevolent assistance of their landlords in hard times, rent-paying workers were left, by and large, to their own devices; their independence caused some landlords to treat them with indifference and even resentment.

Lands and properties that had been occupied by generations of peasants and were recognized as their own were always under the threat of the lord's claim to a prior right of inheritance and even outright usurpation. As their demesnes declined, the lords were increasingly tempted to encroach on such traditionally common lands. The peasantry fiercely resisted such efforts, instinctively clinging to the little they had. In many regions they successfully organized to win a role in the choice of petty rural officials. By the mid-fourteenth century a declining nobility in England and France, faced with the ravages of the great plague and the Hundred Years' War, attempted to turn back the historical clock by increasing taxes on the peasantry and passing laws to restrict their migration into the cities. The peasantry responded with armed revolts in the countryside. These revolts were rural equivalents of the organization of late medieval cities in sworn communes to protect their self-interests against territorial rulers. The revolts of the agrarian peasantry, like those of the urban proletariat, were brutally crushed. They stand out at the end of the Middle Ages as violent testimony to the breakup of medieval society. As growing national sentiment would break its political unity and heretical movements would end its nominal religious oneness, the revolts of the peasantry revealed the absence of medieval social unity.

Townspeople

In the eleventh century, towns and cities held only about 5 per cent of western Europe's population. Nonetheless one could find there the whole of medieval society: nobles visiting their townhouses, peasants living or working within the walls, resident monks and priests, university scholars, great merchants and poor journeymen, pilgrims en route to shrines, and beggars passing through. By modern comparison the great majority of medieval towns were merely small villages. Of some three thousand late medieval German towns, for example, twenty-eight hundred had populations under 1,000 and only fifteen had in excess of 10,000 inhabitants. Only London, Paris, and the great merchant capitals of Italy—Florence, Venice, and Naples—approached 100,000 by the fifteenth century.

The term *bourgeois* first appeared in the eleventh century to describe a new addition to the three traditional social ranks of knight (noble), cleric, and serf. The term initially designated the merchant groups, which formed new communities or "bourgs" as bases of operation in or around the old Roman towns that were governed by the landed nobility. These men, whose business was long-distance trade and commerce, were at first highly suspect within traditional medieval society. Clerics condemned the profits they gained from lending money as immoral usury, and noblemen viewed their fluid wealth and mobility as politically disruptive. The merchants, in turn, resented the laws and customs of feudal society that gave the nobility and the clergy special privileges. Town life was often disrupted because regional laws permitted the nobility and the clergy to live beyond the rules that governed the activities of everyone else.

Merchants especially wanted an end to the arbitrary tolls and tariffs imposed by regional magnates over the surrounding countryside. Such regulations hampered and could even bring to a standstill the flow of commerce on which both merchants and craftsmen in the growing urban export industries depended. The townspeople needed simple, uniform laws and a government sympathetic to their business interests; they wanted a government in which merchants and craftsmen had a major voice. That need created internal and external struggles with the old landed nobility. This basic conflict led towns in the high and late Middle Ages to form their own independent

The Rue du Matelas, a street in Rouen, Normandy, which was preserved intact from the Middle Ages to World War II. Note the narrowness of the street and the open sewer running down its center. The houses were built of rough cast stone, mud, and timber. [*Roger-Viollet*]

A medieval money lender. The Church condemned the profits merchants gained from lending money as usury. (Art Resource)

communes and to ally themselves with kings against the nobility—developments that bespoke the dissolution of feudal society.

Manorial society actually helped to create its urban challenger. Nobles longed for finished goods and the luxuries that came from faraway places. They urged their serfs to become skilled craftsmen. In return for a fixed rent and proper subservience, they granted charters conveying rights and privileges to those who would create towns on their land. By the eleventh century skilled serfs were beginning to pay their feudal dues in manufactured goods. Many serfs took their new skills to the growing urban centers, where they found greater freedom, as well as profits that could catapult an industrious craftsman into higher social ranks. As the migration of serfs to the towns accelerated, the lords offered them greater freedom and more favorable terms of tenure to keep them on the land. The twelfth and thirteenth centuries saw a mass "freeing" of serfs in the sense of a formal contractual fixing of rights and required services—a privilege heretofore known only by freemen. But serfs simply could not be kept down on the farm after they had seen the opportunities of town life. Rural society not only gave the towns their craftsmen and day laborers, but the first merchants themselves appear to have been wandering, enterprising serfs.

Despite unified resistance to external domination, the medieval town was not an internally harmonious social unit. It was a collection of many selfish, competitive communities. Only families of long standing and those who owned property had the full rights of citizenship and a say in the town's government. Workers in the same trade lived together on streets that bore their name, apparently doing so as much to monitor one another's business practices as to dwell among peers. Sumptuary laws regulated not only the dress but even the architecture of the residences of the various social groups. Merchant guilds appeared in the eleventh century and were followed in the twelfth by the craft guilds (organizations of drapers, haberdashers, furriers, hosiers, goldsmiths, and so on). These organizations existed solely to advance the business interests of their members and to advance their personal well-being. They won favorable government policies and served as collection agencies for the unpaid accounts of individual members. The guilds also formed distinctive religious confraternities, close-knit associations that ministered to the needs of member families in both life and death.

The merchants and the stronger craft guilds quickly won a role in town government. "New-rich" patricians married into the old nobility and aped their social customs. Sharing the power of government in the city councils, the craft guilds used their position in the most selfish way to limit their membership, to regulate their own wages favorably, and to establish exacting standards of workmanship so that their products could not be copied by others (trademarks first appeared in the twelfth century). So rigid and exclusive did the dominant

A medieval apothecary weighing out his herbs. Apothecaries, like other merchants and craftsmen, were organized in their own guild. (*Art Resource*)

guilds become that they stifled their own creativity and inflamed the journeymen who were excluded from joining their ranks. In the fourteenth century unrepresented artisans and craftsmen, a true urban proletariat prevented by law from either forming their own guilds or entering the existing guilds, revolted in a number of places: Florence, Paris, and the cities of Flanders. Their main opponents were the merchant and craft guilds, which had themselves risen to prominence by opposing the antiquated laws and privileges of the old nobility.

A medieval shoemaker. Guilds of shoemakers date back to Ancient Rome. In the Middle Ages most people wore homemade clogs or wooden shoes. Leather shoes made to order by skilled craftsmen could be quite costly and elaborate in style and were mostly for the upper classes. [*Vincent Virga Archives*]

Medieval Women

The image and the reality of medieval women are two very different things. The image, both for contemporaries and for us today, was strongly influenced by male Christian clergy, whose ideal was the celibate life of chastity, poverty, and obedience. Drawing on classical medical, philosophical, and legal traditions that predated Christianity, as well as on ancient biblical theology, Christian theologians depicted women as physically, mentally, and morally weaker than men. On the basis of such assumptions medieval church and society sanctioned the coercive treatment of women, including corrective wife-beating. Christian clergy generally considered marriage a debased state by comparison with the religious life, and in their writings they praised virgins and celibate widows over wives. Women, as the Bible clearly taught, were the "weaker vessel." In marriage their role was to be subject and obedient to their husbands, who, as the stronger, had a duty to protect and discipline them.

This image of the medieval woman suggests that she had two basic options in life: to become either a subjugated housewife or a confined nun. In reality, the vast majority of medieval women were neither.

Both within and outside Christianity this image of women—not yet to speak of the reality of their lives—was contradicted. In chivalric romances and courtly love literature of the twelfth and thirteenth centuries, as in the contemporaneous cult of the Virgin Mary, women were presented as objects of service and devotion to be praised and admired, even put on pedestals and treated as superior to men. If the church shared traditional misogynist sentiments, it also condemned them, as in the case of the *Romance of the Rose* (late thirteenth century) and other popular "bawdy" literature. The learned churchman Peter Lombard (1100–1169) sanctioned an image of women that was often invoked in didactic Christian literature. Why, he asked, was Eve created from Adam's rib and not instead taken from his head or his feet? The answer was clear. God took Eve from Adam's side because he wanted woman neither to rule over nor to be enslaved by man, but to stand squarely at his side, as his companion and partner in mutual aid and trust. By so insisting on the spiritual equality of men and women and their shared responsibility to one another within marriage, the church also helped to raise the dignity of women.

A lady and her knight. The literature of chivalry and courtly love presented aristocratic women as objects of service and devotion, to be put on a pedastal by men. [University of Heidelberg]

Women also had basic rights under secular law that prevented them from being treated as mere chattel. All the major Germanic law codes recognized the economic freedom of women, that is, their right to inherit, administer, dispose of, and confer on their children family property and wealth. They could press charges in court against men for bodily injury and rape. Depending on the country in question, punishments for rape ranged from fines, flogging, and banishment to blinding, castration, and death.

The nunnery was an option for only a very small number of unmarried women from the uppermost classes. Entrance required a dowry *(dos)* and could be almost as expensive as a wedding, although usually it was less. Within the nunnery, a woman could rise to a position of leadership as abbess or mother superior and could exercise an organizational and administrative authority denied her in much of secular

The vast majority of medieval women were working peasants and townswomen. This fourteenth-century English manuscript shows women at their daily tasks: carrying jugs of fresh milk from the sheep pen, feeding chickens, and, most importantly, spinning and carding wool. [*Trustees of the British Museum*]

Townswomen at work in a medieval market. Although they practised virtually every ''blue-collar'' trade, medieval women were especially active in the food industry. (*Art Resource*)

life. However, the nunneries of the established religious orders were also under male supervision, so that even abbesses had finally to answer to higher male authority.

Nunneries also provided women an escape from the debilitating effects of multiple pregnancies. When, in the ninth century, under the influence of Christianity, the Carolingians made monogamous marriage their official policy (heretofore they had practiced polygyny and concubinage and had permitted divorce), it was both a boon and a burden to women. On the one hand, the selection of a wife now became a very special event. Wives gained greater dignity and legal security. On the other hand, a woman's labor as household manager and the bearer of children greatly increased. The aristocratic wife not only ran a large household but was also the agent of her husband during his absence. In addition to these responsibilities, one wife now had sole responsibility for the propagation of heirs. Such demands clearly took their toll. The mortality rates of Frankish women increased and their longevity decreased after the ninth century. The Carolingian wife also became the sole object of her husband's wrath and displeasure. Under such conditions the cloister could serve as a welcome refuge to women. However, the number of women in cloisters was never very great. In late medieval England, for example, there are estimated to have been no more than thirty-five hundred.

The vast majority of medieval women were neither aristocratic housewives nor nuns, but working women. Every evidence suggests that they were respected and loved by their husbands, perhaps because they worked shoulder by shoulder and hour by hour with them. Between the ages of ten and fifteen, girls were apprenticed in a trade much as were boys, and they learned to be skilled workers. If they married, they either continued their particular trade, operating their bakeshops or dress shops next to their husbands' business, or they became assistants and partners in the shops of their husbands. Women appeared in virtually every "blue-collar" trade, from butchers to goldsmiths, although they were especially active in the food and clothing industries.

Women belonged to guilds, just like men, and they became craftmasters. In the later Middle Ages, townswomen increasingly had the opportunity to go to school and to gain vernacular literacy.

It is also true that women did not have as wide a range of vocations as men. They were excluded from the learned professions of scholarship, medicine, and law. They often found their freedom of movement within a profession more carefully regulated than a man's. Usually women performed the same work as men for a wage 25 per cent lower. And, as is still true today, they filled the ranks of domestic servants in disproportionate numbers. Still, women were as prominent and as creative a part of workaday medieval society as men.

Medieval Children

Historians have found much evidence to suggest that medieval parents remained emotionally distant from their children, showing them little interest and affection. Evidence of low parental regard for children comes from a variety of sources. First, the art and sculpture of the Middle Ages rarely portray children as distinct from adults; pictorially, children and adults look alike. Then, there was high infant and child mortality, which could only have made emotional investment in children risky. How could a medieval parent, knowing that a child had a 30–50 per cent chance of dying before age five, dare become too emotionally attached? Also, during the Middle Ages, children directly assumed adult responsibilities. The children of peasants became laborers in the fields alongside their parents as soon as they could physically manage the work. Urban artisans and burghers sent their children out of their homes to apprentice in various crafts and trades between the ages of eight and twelve. In many, perhaps most, instances a child was placed in the home of a known relative or friend, but often he or she ended up with a mere acquaintance, even a complete stranger. That children were expected to grow up fast in the Middle Ages is also suggested by the canonical ages for marriage: twelve for girls and fourteen for boys.

Infanticide is an even more striking indication of low esteem for children. The ancient Romans exposed unwanted children at birth. In this way they regulated family size, and the surviving children appear to have been given both attention and affection. The Germanic tribes of medieval Europe, by contrast, had large families but tended to neglect their children. Infanticide appears to have been directed primarily against girls. Early medieval penance books and church synods condemned the practice outright and also forbade parents to sleep with infants and small children, as this became an occasion and an excuse (alleged accidental suffocation) for killing them.

Also, among the German tribes one paid a much lower *wergild*, or fine, for injury to a child than for injury to an adult. The *wergild* for injuring a child was only one fifth that for injuring an adult. That paid for injury to a female child under fifteen was one half that for injury to a male child—a strong indication that female children were the least esteemed members of German tribal society. Mothers appear also to have nursed boys longer than they did girls, which favored boys' health and survival. However, a woman's *wergild* increased a full eightfold between infancy and her childbearing years, at which time she had obviously become highly prized.[4]

Despite such varied evidence of parental neglect of children, there is another side to the story. Since the early Middle Ages, physicians and theologians, at least, have clearly understood childhood to be a distinct and special stage of life. Isidore of Seville (560–636), the metropolitan of Seville and a leading intellectual authority throughout the Middle Ages, carefully distinguished six ages of life, the first four of which were infancy (between one and seven years of age), childhood (seven to fourteen), adolescence, and youth. According to the medical authorities, infancy proper extended from birth to anywhere between six months and two years (depending on the authority) and covered the period of speechlessness and suckling. The period thereafter, until age seven, was considered a higher level of infancy, marked by the beginning of a child's ability to speak and his or her weaning. At age seven, when a child could think and act decisively and speak clearly, childhood proper began. After this point, a child could be reasoned with, could profit from regular discipline, and could begin to train for a lifelong vocation. At seven a child was ready for schooling, private tutoring, or an apprenticeship in a chosen craft or trade. Until physical

[4]David Herlihy, "Medieval Children," in *Essays on Medieval Civilization*, ed. by B. K. Lackner and K. R. Phelp (University of Texas Press, 1978), pp. 109–131.

growth was completed, however—and that could extend to twenty-one years of age—a child or youth was legally under the guardianship of parents or a surrogate authority.

There is evidence that high infant and child mortality, rather than distancing parents from children, actually made them look on them as all the more precious. The medical authorities of the Middle Ages—Hippocrates, Galen, and Soranus of Ephesus—dealt at length with postnatal care and childhood diseases. Both in learned and popular medicine, sensible as well as fanciful cures can be found for the leading killers of children (diarrhea, worms, pneumonia, and fever). When infants and children died, medieval parents grieved as pitiably as modern parents do. In the art and literature of the Middle Ages, we find mothers baptizing dead infants and children or carrying them to pilgrim shrines in the hope of reviving them. There are also examples of mental illness and suicide brought on by the death of a child.[5]

We also find a variety of children's toys, even devices like walkers and potty chairs, clear evidence of special attention being paid to children. The medieval authorities on child rearing

[5]Klaus Arnold, *Kind und Gesellschaft im Mittelalter und Renaissance* (Paderborn, 1980), pp. 31, 37.

Parents bathing a child. High child mortality may have made medieval parents consider those children who survived even more precious. [*Trustees of the British Museum*]

Children watching a puppet show. [*Trustees of the British Museum*]

widely condemned child abuse and urged moderation in the disciplining of children. In church art and drama, parents were urged to love their children as Mary loved Jesus. By the high Middle Ages, if not earlier, children were widely viewed as special creatures with their own needs and possessed of their own rights.

England and France: Hastings (1066) to Bouvines (1214)

William the Conqueror

The most important change in English political life was occasioned in 1066 by the death of the childless Anglo-Saxon ruler Edward the Confessor, so-named because of his reputation for piety. Edward's mother was a Norman princess, and this fact gave the duke of Normandy a hereditary claim to the English throne. Before his death Edward, who was not a strong ruler, acknowledged this claim and even directed that his throne be given to William of Normandy (d. 1087). But the Anglo-Saxon assembly, which customarily bestowed the royal power, had a mind of its own and vetoed Edward's last wishes. It chose instead Harold Godwinsson. This defiant action brought the swift conquest of England by the powerful Normans. William's forces defeated Harold's army at Hastings on October 14, 1066. Within weeks of the invasion William was crowned king of England in Westminster Abbey, both by right of heredity and by right of conquest.

Thereafter all of England became William's domain. Every landholder, whether large or small, was henceforth his vassal, holding land legally as a fief from the king. William organized his new English nation shrewdly. On the one hand, he established a strong monarchy whose power was not fragmented by independent territorial princes. On the other hand, he took care not to destroy Anglo-Saxon democratic traditions, which had been nurtured by Alfred the Great (871–899), who, although a strong and willful king, still cherished the advice of his councilors in the making of laws, and had been respected by Canute (1016–1035), the Dane who restored order and brought unity to England after the civil wars

*William the Conqueror, on horseback, leads his Norman troops against the English at the Battle of Hastings (*October 14, 1066*). From the Bayeux Tapestry, about* 1073–1083. [*Musée de l'Évêché, Bayeux, France. Avec autorisation spéciale de la ville de Bayeux. Giraudon*]

How William the Conqueror Won the Battle of Hastings

This account of the Battle of Hastings appears in the *Chronicle* of the kings of England, written by a Benedictine monk, William of Malmesbury, the son of a Norman father and an English mother. Although William wrote over a half century after the Battle of Hastings, his chronicle is our fullest account of these events.

The courageous leaders mutually prepared for battle, each according to his national custom. The English passed the night without sleep, in drinking and singing, and in the morning proceeded without delay against the enemy. All on foot, armed with battle-axes, and covering themselves in front by joining their shields, they formed an impenetrable body. . . . King Harold himself, on foot, stood with his brothers near the standard in order that, so long as all shared equal danger, none could think of retreating. . . .

The Normans passed the whole night in confessing their sins, and received the communion of the Lord's body in the morning. Their infantry, with bows and arrows, formed the vanguard, while their cavalry, divided into wings, was placed in the rear. The duke [of Normandy], with serene countenance, declaring aloud that God would favor his . . . side, called for his arms. . . . Then starting the song of Roland, in order that . . . the example of that [early French war] hero might stimulate the soldiers, and calling on God for assistance, the battle commenced on both sides . . . neither side yielding ground during the greater part of the day.

Observing this, William gave a signal to his troops, that, pretending flight, they should withdraw from the field. By means of this device the solid phalanx of the English opened for the purpose of cutting down the fleeing enemy and thus brought upon itself swift destruction; for the Normans, facing about, attacked them, thus disordered, and compelled them to fly. . . . [The English were not] without their own revenge, for, by frequently making a stand, they slaughtered their pursuers in heaps. . . . [Such] alternating victory, first by one side and then by the other, continued as long as Harold lived to check the retreat; but when he fell, his brain pierced by an arrow, the flight of the English ceased not until night.

Frederic Austin Ogg (Ed.), *A Source Book of Mediaeval History: Documents Illustrative of European Life and Institutions from the German Invasions to the Renaissance* (New York: American Book Co., 1908), pp. 235–237.

that had engulfed the land during the reign of the incompetent Ethelred II (978–1016). The Norman king thoroughly subjected his noble vassals to the crown, yet he also consulted with them regularly about decisions of "state." The result was a unique blending of the "one" and the "many," a balance between monarchical and parliamentary elements that has ever since characterized English government.

For the purposes of administration and taxation William commissioned a county-by-county survey of his new realm, a detailed accounting known as the *Domesday Book* (1080–1086). The title of the book reflects the thoroughness of the survey: just as none would escape the doomsday judgment of God, so none was overlooked by William's assessors.

Henry II

William's son, Henry I (ruled 1100–1135), died without a male heir, throwing England into virtual anarchy until Henry II (1154–1189), son of the duke of Anjou and Matilda, daughter of Henry I, mounted the throne as head of the new Plantagenet dynasty. Under Henry II the English monarchy began to drift toward an oppressive rule. Henry brought to the throne greatly expanded French holdings, partly by inheritance from his father (Burgundy and Anjou) and partly by his marriage to Eleanor of Aquitaine (1122?–1204), a union that created the so-called Angevin or English-French empire. Eleanor married Henry while he was still the count of Anjou and not yet king of England. The marriage occurred only eight weeks after the annulment of Eleanor's fifteen-year marriage to the ascetic French king Louis VII in March 1152. Although the annulment was granted on grounds of consanguinity (blood relationship), the true reason for the dissolution of the marriage was Louis's suspicion of infidelity (according to rumor, Eleanor had been intimate with her cousin). The annulment was very costly to Louis, who lost Aquitaine together with his wife. Eleanor bore Henry eight children, five of them sons, among them the future kings Richard the Lion-Hearted and John. Not only did England, under Henry, come to control most of the coast of France, but Henry also conquered a part of Ireland and made the king of Scotland his vassal.

The French king, Louis VII, who had lost both his wife and considerable French land to Henry, saw a mortal threat to France in this English expansion. He responded by adopting what came to be a permanent French policy of containment and expulsion of the English from their continental holdings in France—a policy that was not finally successful until the mid-fifteenth century, when English power on the Continent collapsed at the conclusion of the Hundred Years' War.

The effigy of Eleanor of Aquitaine, who had been queen of France as well as queen of England, is on her tomb at Fontevrault Abbey in France. [*The Granger Collection*]

Eleanor of Aquitaine and Court Culture

Eleanor of Aquitaine helped shape court culture and literature in France and England. After marrying Henry, she settled in Angers, the chief town of Anjou, where she sponsored troubadours and poets at her lively court. There the troubadour Bernart de Ventadorn composed in Eleanor's honor many of the most popular love songs of high medieval aristocratic society. Eleanor spent the years 1154–1170 as Henry's queen in England. She separated from him in 1170, partly because of his public philandering and cruel treatment, taking revenge by joining Louis VII in stirring Henry's three sons, who were unhappy with the terms of their inheritance, to rebellion against their father in 1173. During the last years of his life (1179–1189), Henry placed Eleanor under mild house arrest to prevent any further such mischief.

After her separation from Henry in 1170 Eleanor lived in Poitiers with her daughter Marie, the countess of Champagne, and the two made the court of Poitiers a famous center for the literature of courtly love. This literary genre, with its thinly veiled eroticism, has been viewed as an attack on medieval ascetic values. Be that as it may, it was certainly a commentary on contemporary problems within the domestic life of the aristocracy. The code of chivalry that guided the relations between lords and their vassals looked on the seduction of the wife of one's lord as the most heinous of offenses. In some areas such adultery was punished by castration and/or execution. The troubadours hardly promoted such promiscuity at court. They rather presented in a frank and entertaining way stories that satirized or depicted in tragic irony illicit carnal love, while glorifying the ennobling power of friendly or "courteous" love. The most famous courtly literature was Chrétien de Troyes's stories of King Arthur and the Knights of the Round Table, which contained the tragic story of Sir Lancelot's secret and illicit love for Arthur's wife, Guinevere.

Popular Rebellion and Magna Carta

As Henry II acquired new lands abroad, he became more autocratic at home, subjecting his vassals more than ever to the royal yoke.

He forced his will on the clergy in the Constitutions of Clarendon (1164), measures that placed limitations on judicial appeals to Rome, subjected the clergy to the civil courts, and gave the king control over the election of bishops. The result was strong political resistance from both the nobility and the clergy. The archbishop of Canterbury, Thomas à Becket (1118?–1170), once Henry's compliant chancellor, broke openly with the king and fled to Louis VII. Becket's subsequent assassination in 1170 and his canonization by Pope Alexander III in 1172 forced the king to retreat from his heavy-handed tactics, as popular resentment grew. (Two hundred years later Geoffrey Chaucer, writing in an age made cynical by the Black Death and the Hundred Years' War, had the pilgrims of his *Canterbury Tales* journey to the shrine of Thomas à Becket.)

English resistance to the king became outright rebellion under Henry's successors, the brothers Richard the Lion-Hearted (1189–1199) and John (1199–1216). Their burdensome taxation in support of unnecessary foreign Crusades and a failing war with France left the English people little alternative. Richard had to be ransomed at a high price from the Holy Roman Emperor Henry VI, who had taken him prisoner during his return from the ill-fated Third Crusade. In 1209 Pope Innocent III excommunicated King John and placed England under interdict. This humiliating experience saw the king of England declare his country a fief of the pope. But it was the defeat

Henry II of England with Archibishop Thomas à Becket of Canterbury. Becket's murder by courtiers of the king brought the wrath of the Church on Henry, who was forced to abandon his autocratic attempt to control the English Church. [*Trustees of the British Museum*]

The English Nobility Imposes Restraints on King John

The gradual building of a sound English constitutional system in the Middle Ages was in danger of going awry if a monarch overstepped the fine line dividing necessary strength from outright despotism. The danger became acute under the rule of King John. The English nobility, therefore, forced the king's recognition of Magna Carta (1215), which reaffirmed the traditional rights and personal liberties of free men against royal authority. The document has remained enshrined in English law.

A free man shall not be fined for a small offense, except in proportion to the gravity of the offense; and for a great offense he shall be fined in proportion to the magnitude of the offense, saving his freehold; and a merchant in the same way, saving his merchandise; and the villein shall be fined in the same way, saving his wainage, if he shall be at our [i.e., the king's] mercy; and none of the above fines shall be imposed except by the oaths of honest men of the neighborhood. . . .

No constable or other bailiff of ours [i.e., the king's] shall take anyone's grain or other chattels without immediately paying for them in money, unless he is able to obtain a postponement at the good will of the seller.

No constable shall require any knight to give money in place of his ward of a castle [i.e., standing guard] if he is willing to furnish that ward in his own person, or through another honest man if he himself is not able to do it for a reasonable cause; and if we shall lead or send him into the army he shall be free from ward in proportion to the amount of time which he has been in the army through us.

No sheriff or bailiff of ours [i.e., the king's], or any one else, shall take horses or wagons of any free man, for carrying purposes, except on the permission of that free man.

Neither we nor our bailiffs will take the wood of another man for castles, or for anything else which we are doing, except by the permission of him to whom the wood belongs. . . .

No free man shall be taken, or imprisoned, or dispossessed, or outlawed, or banished, or in any way injured, nor will we go upon him, nor send upon him, except by the legal judgment of his peers, or by the law of the land.

To no one will we sell, to no one will we deny or delay, right or justice.

James Harvey Robinson (Ed.), *Readings in European History,* Vol. 1 (Boston: Atheneaum, 1904), pp. 236–237.

of the English by the French at Bouvines in 1214 that proved the last straw. With the full support of the clergy and the townspeople, the English barons revolted against John. The popular rebellion ended with the king's grudging recognition of Magna Carta ("Great Charter") in 1215.

This monumental document was a victory of feudal over monarchical power in the sense that it secured the rights of the many—the nobility, the clergy, and the townspeople—over the autocratic king; it restored the internal balance of power that had been the English political experience since the Norman Conquest. The English people, at least the privileged English people, thereby preserved their right to be represented at the highest levels of government, especially in matters of taxation. The monarchy remained intact, however, and its legitimate powers and rights were duly recognized and preserved. This outcome contrasted with the experience on the Continent, where victorious nobility tended to humiliate kings and emperors and undo all efforts at centralization.

With a peculiar political genius the English consistently refused to tolerate either the absorption of the power of the monarchy by the nobility or the abridgment of the rights of the nobility by the monarchy. Although King John continued to resist the Great Charter in every way he could, his son Henry III formally ratified it, and it has ever since remained a cornerstone of English law.

Although Gothic architecture was adopted throughout medieval Europe (Gothic cathedrals were built in cities from Compostella in northern Spain to Cracow in Poland), it originated in France and enjoyed immense popularity there. Gothic was, in fact, often known in the Middle Ages as the ''French style.'' Among the earliest examples of French Gothic architecture was the abbey church of Saint Denis near Paris, built by Abbot Suger between 1137–1144. *This photograph shows the ribbed vaulting and pointed arches in the interior of the church.* [*Jean Roubier*]

Beginning in the mid-twelfth century, the Gothic style evolved from romanesque architecture. Gothic at first meant ''barbaric'' and was applied to the new style by its critics. Its most distinctive visible features are its ribbed, criss-crossing vaulting, its pointed arches rather than rounded ones, and its frequent exterior buttresses. The result gives an essential impression of vertical lines. The vaulting and the extensive addition of ''flying'' buttresses made possible more height than the Romanesque style and sought. Because walls, therefore, did not have to carry all of a structure's weight, wide expanses of windows were possible—hence the extensive use of stained glass and the characteristic color that often floods Gothic cathedrals. Use of the windows to show stories from the Bible, saints' lives, and local events was similar to earlier use of mosaics.

This diagram show the typical vaulting, arches, and buttresses of a Gothic building. [World Architecture, *Trewin Copplestone, General Editor (London: Hamlyn,* 1963), *p. 216.)*

Two further examples of French Gothic: (left) Reims, where the kings of France were crowned, and (opposite) Chartres, one of the supreme masterpieces of medieval architecture. (Jean Roubier, Scala/Art Resource; Manley Photo/Shostal)

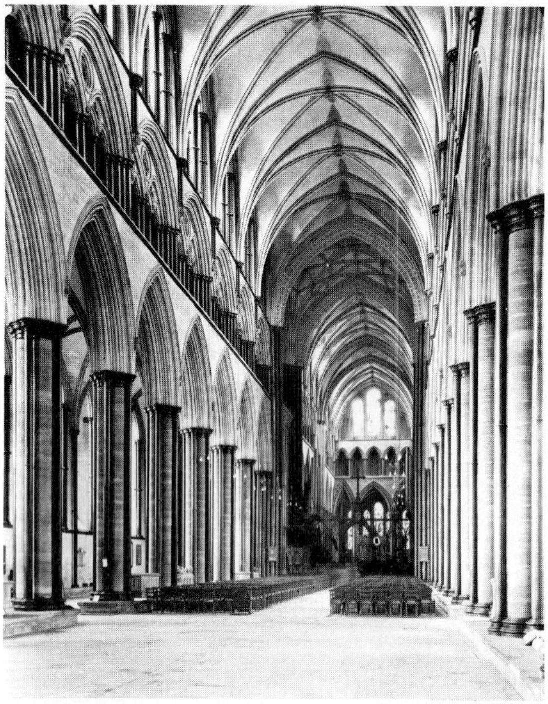

The interior of Salisbury cathedral, showing the vaulting and the pointed arches. [*The National Monuments Record, London*]

ABOVE: *The ability of Gothic architecture to achieve a light, airy effect and, as it were, to lift the viewer heavenward, is illustrated by the whole of Milan cathedral, of which this illustration shows only one detail. Begun in 1386, the cathedral was not completed until the nineteenth century. This is the main spire, built in 1750, as seen from the roof.* [*AHM*]

LEFT: *The cathedral at Amiens, France, is another splendid example of the thirteenth-century flowering of Gothic architecture.* [*Aerofilms Limited*]

Salisbury cathedral, built 1220–1265, an example of English Gothic. Note the flying buttresses, which permit greater height, and the soaring towers and spire. [*British Tourist Authority, New York*]

Philip II Augustus

During the century and a half between the Norman Conquest (1066) and Magna Carta (1215), a strong monarchy was never in question in England. The English struggle in the high Middle Ages was to secure the rights of the many, not the authority of the king. The French faced the reverse problem in this period. Powerful feudal princes dominated France for two centuries, from the beginning of the Capetian dynasty (987) until the reign of Philip II Augustus (1180–1223). During this period the Capetian kings wisely concentrated their limited resources on securing the royal domain, their uncontested territory round about Paris known as the Île-de-France. They did not rashly challenge the more powerful nobility. Aggressively exercising their feudal rights in this area, they secured absolute obedience and a solid base of power. By the time of Philip II, Paris had become the center of French government and culture, and the Capetian dynasty had become a secure hereditary monarchy. Thereafter the kings of France were in a position to impose their will on the French nobles, who were always in law, if not in political fact, the king's sworn vassals.

The Norman conquest of England helped stir France to unity and make it possible for the Capetian kings to establish a truly national monarchy. The duke of Normandy, who after 1066 was master of the whole of England, was also among the vassals of the French king in Paris. Capetian kings understandably watched with alarm as the power of their Norman vassal grew. Other powerful vassals of the king also watched with alarm. King Louis VI (1108–1137) entered an alliance with Flanders, which had traditionally been a Norman enemy. King Louis VII (1137–1180), assisted by a brilliant minister, Suger, the abbot of St. Denis and famous for his patronage of Gothic architecture, found allies in the great northern French cities and used their wealth to build a royal army. Philip II Augustus, Louis VII's successor, inherited financial resources and an administrative bureaucracy, which in his capable hands resisted the divisive French nobility and clergy and pressed the contest with the English king.

Philip Augustus faced, at the same time, an internal and an international struggle, and he was successful in both. His armies occupied all the English territories on the French coast, with the exception of Aquitaine. As the showdown with the English neared on the Continent, however, the Holy Roman Emperor Otto IV (1198–1215) entered the fray on the side of the English, and the French found themselves assailed from both east and west. But when the international armies finally clashed at Bouvines on July 27, 1214, in what became the first great European battle in history, the French won handily over the English and the Germans. This victory unified France around the monarchy and thereby laid the foundation for French ascendancy in the later Middle Ages. Philip Augustus also gained control of the lucrative urban industries of Flanders. The defeat so weakened Otto IV that he fell from power in Germany.

The Pontificate of Innocent III (1198–1215)

The New Papal Monarchy

Pope Innocent III, a papal monarch in the Gregorian tradition of papal independence from secular domination, proclaimed and practiced as none before him the doctrine of the plenitude of papal power. In a famous statement he likened the relationship of the pope to the emperor—or the Church to the State—to that of the sun to the moon. As the moon received its light from the sun, so the emperor received his brilliance (that is, his crown) from the hand of the pope—an allusion to the famous precedent set on Christmas Day, 800, when Pope Leo III crowned Charlemagne. Although this pretentious theory greatly exceeded Innocent's ability to practice it, he and his successors did not hesitate to act on their ambitions. When Philip II tried unlawfully to annul his marriage, Innocent placed France under interdict, suspending all church services save baptism and the last rites. And the same punishment befell England with even greater force when King John refused to accept Innocent's nominee to the archbishopric of Canterbury.

Innocent made the papacy a great secular power, with financial resources and a bureaucracy equal to those of contemporary monarchs. It was during his reign that the papacy transformed itself into that efficient ecclesiocommercial complex attacked by reformers throughout the later Middle Ages. Innocent consolidated and expanded ecclesiastical taxes on the laity, the chief of which at this time was

Pope Innocent III (1198–1215). *Innocent made the papacy a great power, with financial resources and a bureaucracy equal to those of secular monarchies.* [*SCALA/Art Resource*]

Peter's pence, long a levy on all but the poorest English houses, which became a lump-sum payment by the English crown in the twelfth century. He imposed an income tax of 2.5 per cent on the clergy. Annates (the payment of a portion or all of the first year's income received by the holder of a new benefice) and fees for the pallium (the symbol of episcopal office) became especially popular revenue-gathering devices employed by the pope. Innocent also reserved to the pope the absolution of many sins and religious crimes, forcing those desirous of pardons or exemptions to bargain directly with Rome. It was a measure of the degree to which the papacy had embraced the new money economy that Lombard merchants and bankers were employed by Rome to collect the growing papal revenues.

Crusades in France and the East

Innocent's predilection for power politics also expressed itself in his use of the Crusade, the traditional weapon of the church against Islam, to suppress internal dissent and heresy. The latter had grown under the influence of religious reform movements attempting, often naively, to disassociate the church from the growing materialism of the age and to keep it pure of political purpose. In 1209 he launched a Crusade against the Albigensians, or Cathars ("pure ones"), advocates of an ascetic, dualist religion who were concentrated in the area of Albi in Languedoc in southern France, but who also had adherents among the laity in Italy and Spain. The Albigensians opposed Christian teaching on several points. They denied the Old Testament and its God of wrath, as well as the Christian belief in God's incarnation in Jesus Christ, and many rejected human procreation either by extreme sexual asceticism or by the use of contraceptives (sponges and acidic ointments) and even abortion—this in the belief that to continue corporeal bodies was to prolong the imprisonment of one's immortal soul. They sought instead a pure and simple religious life, following the model of the apostles of Jesus in the New Testament. It was in opposition to such sects, who even challenged the propagation of the human species, that the church developed its social teachings on contraception and abortion.

The Crusades against the heretics were carried out by powerful noblemen from northern France. These great magnates, led by Simon de Montfort, were as much attracted by the great wealth of the area of Languedoc, among the richest regions of Europe at the time, as they were moved by Christian conscience to stamp out heresy. A succession of massacres occurred, ending with a Crusade led by King Louis VIII of France in 1225–1226, which completely destroyed the Albigensians as a political entity. Pope Gregory IX (1227–1241) introduced the Inquisition into the region to complete the work of the Crusaders. This institution, a formal tribunal for the detection and punishment of heresy, had been in use by the church since the mid-twelfth century as a way for bishops to maintain diocesan discipline. During Innocent's pontificate it became centralized in the papacy, and papal legates were dispatched to chosen regions to conduct the interrogations and subsequent trials and executions.

It was also during Innocent's pontificate that the Fourth Crusade to the Holy Land was launched (1202). Its stunning capture of Constantinople established Latin control of the Eastern Empire until 1261, when the Eastern emperor Michael Paleologus, assisted by the Genoese, who envied Venetian prosperity in the East, finally recaptured the city. Innocent was initially embarrassed by the fall of Constantinople to the Crusaders. But the papacy soon adjusted to this unforeseen turn of events and shared in the spoils. The Eastern base gave the Western church a unique opportunity. A confidant of Innocent's, Tommaso Morosini, became patriarch of Constantinople and launched a mission to win the Greeks and the Slavs back to the Roman church. The almost fifty-year occupation of Constantinople did nothing to heal the political and religious divisions between East and West. To the contrary, it only intensified Eastern resentment of the West.

The Fourth Lateran Council

Under Innocent's direction the Fourth Lateran Council met in 1215 to establish hierarchical church discipline from pope to parish. This council was a landmark in ecclesiastical legislation. It gave the controversial theory of transubstantiation full dogmatic sanction, and the Catholic Church has ever since taught that the bread and wine of the Lord's Supper become the true body and blood of Christ on consecration by the priest. The council also made annual confession and Easter communion mandatory for every adult Christian. This latter legislation formalized the sacrament of pen-

Saint Francis of Assisi Sets Out His Religious Ideals

Saint Francis of Assisi (1182–1226) was the founder of the Franciscan Order of friars. Here are some of his religious principles as stated in the definitive Rule of the Order, approved by the pope in 1223; the rule especially stresses the ideal of living in poverty.

This is the rule and way of living of the Minorite brothers, namely, to observe the holy Gospel of our Lord Jesus Christ, living in obedience, without personal possessions, and in chastity. Brother Francis promises obedience and reverence to our lord Pope Honorius, and to his successors who canonically enter upon their office, and to the Roman Church. And the other brothers shall be bound to obey Brother Francis and his successors.

I firmly command all the brothers by no means to receive coin or money, of themselves or through an intervening person. But for the needs of the sick and for clothing the other brothers, the ministers alone and the guardians shall provide through spiritual friends, as it may seem to them that necessity demands, according to time, place, and the coldness of the temperature. This one thing being always borne in mind, that, as has been said, they receive neither coin nor money.

Those brothers to whom God has given the ability to labor shall do so faithfully and devoutly, but in such manner that idleness, the enemy of the soul, being averted, they may not extinguish the spirit of holy prayer and devotion, to which other temporal things should be subservient. As a reward, moreover, for their labor, they may receive for themselves and their brothers the necessities of life, but not coin or money; and this humbly, as becomes the servants of God and the followers of most holy poverty.

The brothers shall appropriate nothing to themselves, neither a house, nor a place, nor anything; but as pilgrims and strangers in this world, in poverty and humility serving God, they shall confidently go seeking for alms. Nor need they be ashamed, for the Lord made Himself poor for us in this world.

A Source Book of Mediaeval History, ed. by Frederic Austin Ogg (New York: Cooper Square Publishers, 1972), pp. 375–376.

ance as the church's key instrument of religious education and discipline in the later Middle Ages.

Franciscans and Dominicans

No action of Pope Innocent affected religious life more than his official sanction of the mendicant orders of the Franciscans and the Dominicans. Lay interest in religious devotion, especially among urban women, was particularly intense at the turn of the twelfth century. In addition to the heretical Albigensians, there were movements of Waldensians, Beguines, and Beghards, each of which stressed biblical simplicity in religion and aspired to a life of poverty in imitation of Christ. They were especially vocal in Italy and France. The heterodox teachings and critical frame of mind within these movements caused the pope deep concern that lay piety would turn against the church in militant fashion. The Franciscan and Dominican orders were a response to heterodox piety as well as an answer to lay criticism of the worldliness of the papal monarchy. Unlike other regular clergy, the friars went out into the world to preach the church's mission and to combat heresy, begging or working to support themselves.

The Franciscan Order was founded by Saint Francis of Assisi (1182–1226), the son of a rich Italian cloth merchant, who became disaffected with wealth and urged his followers to practice extreme poverty. Pope Innocent recognized the order in 1210 and its official rule was approved in 1223. The Dominican Order, the Order of Preachers, was founded by Saint Dominic (1170–1221), a well-educated Spanish cleric, and was sanctioned in 1216. Both orders received special privileges from the pope and were solely under his jurisdiction. This special relationship with Rome gave the friars an independence from local clerical authority that caused them to be resented by some secular clergy.

Pope Gregory IX (1227–1241) canonized Saint Francis only two years after his death. That was both a fitting honor for Francis and a stroke of genius on the part of the pope. By bringing the age's most popular religious figure, one who had even miraculously received the stigmata (bleeding wounds like those of the crucified Jesus), so emphatically within the confines of the church, he enhanced papal authority over lay piety.

Two years after the canonization Gregory

New religious orders were founded throughout the Middle Ages. Unlike the clergy of other orders, however, Franciscans (in dark robes) and Dominicans (in white) did not live in cloister, but went out into the world to combat heresy. [*Bibliotheque Nationale*]

canceled Saint Francis's own *Testament,* which had admonished a life of strictest poverty. The pope set it aside as an authoritative rule for Franciscans both because he found it to be an impractical guide for the order and because the nonconventual life of nomadic poverty urged by Francis on his followers conflicted with papal plans to enlist the order as an arm of church policy. A majority of Franciscans themselves, under the leadership of moderates like Saint Bonaventure, general of the order between 1257 and 1274, also came to doubt the wisdom of extreme asceticism. During the thirteenth century the order progressively complied with papal wishes. In the fourteenth century the Spiritual Franciscans, extreme followers of Saint Francis who considered him almost a new Messiah, were condemned, and absolute poverty was declared a fictitious ideal that not even Christ endorsed.

The Dominicans, a less factious order, combated doctrinal error through visitations and preaching. They conformed convents of Beguines to the church's teaching, led the church's campaign against heretics in southern France, and staffed the offices of the Inquisition after its centralization by Pope Gregory IX in 1223. Their leading theologian, Thomas Aquinas, was canonized in 1322, and his teaching has remained the most definitive statement of Catholic belief.

The Dominicans and the Franciscans strengthened the church among the laity. Through the institution of so-called Third Orders they provided ordinary men and women the opportunity to affiliate with the monastic life and pursue the high religious ideals of poverty, obedience, and chastity, while still remaining laymen and laywomen. Laity who joined such orders were known as *tertiaries.* Such organizations helped keep lay piety orthodox and within the church during a period of heightened religiosity.

The Hohenstaufen Empire (1152–1272)

During the twelfth and thirteenth centuries stable governments developed in both England and France. In England Magna Carta balanced the rights of the nobility against the authority of the kings, and in France the reign of Philip II Augustus secured the authority of the king over the competitive claims of the nobility. The experience within the Holy Roman Empire, which embraced Germany, Burgundy, and northern Italy by the mid-thirteenth century, was a very different story. There, primarily because of the efforts of the Hohenstaufen dynasty to extend imperial power into southern Italy, disunity and blood feuding remained the order of the day for two centuries and left as a legacy the fragmentation of Germany until modern times.

Frederick I Barbarossa

The investiture struggle had earlier weakened imperial authority. After the Concordat of Worms the German princes held the dominant lay influence over episcopal appointments and within the rich ecclesiastical territories.

A new day seemed to dawn for imperial power, however, with the accession to the throne of Frederick I Barbarossa (1152–1190), the first of the Hohenstaufens, the successor dynasty within the empire to the Franks and the Ottonians. The Hohenstaufens not only reestablished imperial authority but also initiated a new phase in the contest between popes and emperors, one that was to prove even more deadly than the investiture struggle had been. Never have kings and popes despised and persecuted one another more than during the Hohenstaufen dynasty.

As Frederick I surveyed his empire, he saw powerful feudal princes in Germany and Lombardy and a pope in Rome who believed that the emperor was his creature. There existed, however, widespread disaffection with the incessant feudal strife of the princes and the turmoil caused by the theocratic pretensions of the papacy. Popular opinion was on the emperor's side. Thus Frederick had a foundation on which to rebuild imperial authority, and he was shrewd enough to take advantage of it. He championed Roman law, which was at the time enjoying a revival in Bologna under Irnerius. Roman law served Frederick on both his fronts: on the one hand, it enhanced centralized authority against the nobility; on the other, it stressed the secular foundation of imperial power against Roman election, and especially against the tradition of papal coronation of the emperor.

Switzerland became Frederick's base of operation. From there he attempted to hold the empire together by involking feudal bonds. He was relatively successful in Germany, thanks largely to the fall from power in 1180 and the exile to England of his strongest German rival,

The Emperor Fredrick I Barbarossa (1152–1190) *submitting to Pope Alexander III* (1159–1181) *in* 1177. [*Art Resource*]

Henry the Lion (d. 1195), the duke of Saxony. Although realistically acknowledging the power of the German duchies, Frederick never missed the opportunity to apprise each duchy of its prescribed duties as a fief of the king. If Frederick was not everywhere ruler in fact, he was clearly so in law, and no one was permitted to forget it. The same tactic had been successfully employed by the Capetian kings of France when they faced superior noble forces.

Italy proved to be the great obstacle to imperial plans. In 1155 Frederick restored Pope Adrian IV (1154–1159) to power in Rome after a religious revolutionary, Arnold of Brescia (d. 1155), had gained control of the city. For his efforts Frederick won a coveted papal coronation—and strictly on his terms, not on those of the pope. The door to Italy thereby opened. Having won recognition of his rights of jurisdiction in Burgundy in 1157, Frederick attempted to secure the same recognition in Italy. Resistance to him became fiercest in Lombardy. The Milanese balked at the implementation of these rights, which had been defined by the imperial Diet of Roncaglia, and refused to recognize Frederick's representatives within the city.

As this challenge to royal authority was occurring, one of Europe's most skilled lawyers, Cardinal Roland, was elected Pope Alexander III (1159–1181). While a cardinal he had negotiated an alliance between the papacy and the Norman kingdom of Sicily in a clever effort to strengthen the papacy against imperial influence. Perceiving him to be a very capable foe, Frederick had opposed his election as pope and had even backed a schismatic pope against him in a futile effort to undo Alexander's election. Frederick now found himself at war with the pope, Milan, and Sicily. In 1167 the combined forces of the north Italian communes drove him back into Germany. The final blow to imperial plans in Italy came a decade later, in 1176, when Italian forces soundly defeated Frederick at Legnano. In the final Peace of Constance in 1183 Frederick recognized the claims of the Lombard cities to full rights of self-rule.

Henry VI and the Sicilian Connection

Frederick's reign ended with stalemate in Germany and defeat in Italy. At his death in 1190 he was not a ruler of the stature of the kings of England and France. After the Peace of Constance in 1183 he seems himself to have conceded as much, as he accepted the reality of the empire's indefinite division among the feudal princes of Germany. An opportunity both to solve his problem with Sicily, still a papal ally, and to form a new territorial base of power for future emperors opened when the

Norman ruler of the kingdom of Sicily, William II (1166–1189), sought an alliance with Frederick that would free him to pursue a scheme to conquer Constantinople. The alliance was sealed in 1186 by a most fateful marriage between Frederick's son, the future Henry VI (1190–1197), and Constance, heiress to the kingdom of Sicily. This alliance proved, however, to be only another well-laid political plan that went astray. The Sicilian connection became a fatal distraction for Hohenstaufen kings, leading them repeatedly to sacrifice their traditional territorial base in northern Europe to that temptress, imperialism. Equally ominous, this union of the empire with Sicily left Rome encircled, thereby ensuring the undying hostility of a papacy already thoroughly distrustful of the emperor. The marriage alliance with Sicily proved to be the first step in what soon became a fight to the death between pope and emperor.

When Henry VI came to rule in 1190, he faced a multitude of enemies: a hostile papacy, still smarting from the refusal of his father to recognize territorial claims within the Papal States; supremely independent German princes, led by the archbishop of Cologne; and an England whose adventurous king, Richard the Lion-Hearted, was encouraged to plot against Henry by the exiled duke of Saxony, Henry the Lion.

Into this divided kingdom a son, the future Frederick II, was born in 1194. To stabilize his monarchy, Henry campaigned vigorously for the recognition of the principle of hereditary succession; he wanted birth alone to secure the imperial throne uncontestably. He won a large number of German princes to this point of view by granting them full hereditary rights to their fiefs—an appropriate exchange. But the encircled papacy was not disposed to secure Hohenstaufen power by supporting a hereditary right to the imperial throne. The pope wanted, rather, to return to the period before 1152, when imperial power had been diffused among many princes. He accordingly joined dissident German princes against Henry.

Otto IV and the Welf Interregnum

Henry died in September 1197 and chaos proved his immediate heir. Between English intervention in its politics and the pope's deliberate efforts to sabotage the Hohenstaufen dynasty, Germany was thrown into anarchy and civil war. England gave financial support to anti-Hohenstaufen factions, and its candidate for the imperial throne, Otto of Brunswick of the rival Welf dynasty, the son of Henry the Lion, bested Philip of Swabia, Henry VI's brother. Otto was crowned Otto IV by his supporters in Aachen in 1198 and later won general recognition in Germany. With England supporting Otto, the French rushed in on the side of the fallen Hohenstaufen—the beginning of periodic French fishing in troubled German waters. Meanwhile Henry VI's four-year-old son, Frederick, was safely tucked away as a ward of Pope Innocent III (1198–1215), a shrewd pope determined to break imperial power and restore papal power in Italy and willing to play one German dynasty against the other to do so.

Hohenstaufen support remained alive in Germany, however, and Otto reigned over a very divided kingdom. In October 1209 Pope Innocent crowned him emperor, a recognition that enhanced his authority. But the pope quickly moved from benefactor to mortal enemy when, after his coronation, Otto proceeded to reconquer Sicily and once again to pursue an imperial policy that left Rome encircled. Within four months of his papal coronation Otto received a papal excommunication.

Frederick II

Pope Innocent, casting about for a counterweight to the treacherous Otto, joined the French, who had remained loyal to the Hohenstaufens against the English-Welf alliance. His new ally, Philip Augustus, impressed on Innocent the fact that a solution to their problems with Otto IV lay near at hand in Innocent's ward, Frederick of Sicily. Frederick, the son of the late Hohenstaufen Emperor Henry VI, was now of age and, unlike Otto, had an immediate hereditary claim to the imperial throne. In December 1212 the young Frederick, with papal, French, and German support, was crowned king of the Romans in Mainz. Within a year and a half Philip Augustus ended the Welf interregnum of Otto IV on the battlefield of Bouvines. Philip sent Frederick II Otto's fallen imperial banner from the battlefield, a bold gesture that suggests the extent to which Frederick's ascent to the throne was intended to be that of a French-papal puppet. In 1215 Frederick repeated his earlier crowning, this time in the imperial city of Aachen.

If Frederick had been intended by Innocent

A marble head of Emperor Frederick II (1215–1250), *whose preoccupation with Italy and Sicily led to the collapse of imperial power in Germany.* [*German Archaeological Institute, Rome*]

to be a puppet king, he soon disappointed any such hopes. His reign was an absolute disaster for Germany and may be credited with securing German fragmentation until modern times. Frederick was Sicilian and dreaded travel beyond the Alps. Only nine of his thirty-eight years as emperor were spent in Germany, and six of those were before 1218. Although Frederick continued to pursue royal policies in Germany through his representatives, he seemed to desire only one thing from the German princes, the imperial title for himself and his sons, and he was willing to give them what they wanted to secure it. His eager compliance with their demands laid the foundation for six centuries of German division. In 1220 he recognized the jurisdictional claims of the ecclesiastical princes of Germany, and in 1232 he extended the same recognition to the secular princes. The German princes had become too powerful to be denied. Thereafter they were undisputed lords over their territories. Frederick's concessions were tantamount to an abdication of imperial responsibility in Germany. They have been characterized as a German equivalent to Magna Carta in the sense that they secured the rights of the German nobility. Unlike Magna Carta, however, they did so without at the same time securing the rights of monarchy. Magna Carta placed the king and the nobility (parliament) in England in a creative tension; the reign of Frederick II simply made the German nobility petty kings.

GERMANY AND ITALY IN THE MIDDLE AGES

MAP 8-1 *Medieval Germany and Italy were divided lands. The Holy Roman Empire (Germany) embraced hundreds of independent territories that the emperor ruled only in name. The papacy controlled the Rome area and tried to enforce its will on Romagna. Under the Hohenstaufens (mid-12th to mid-13th century), internal German divisions and papal conflict reached new heights; German rulers sought to extend their power to southern Italy and Sicily.*

Frederick's relations with the pope were equally disastrous. He was excommunicated no fewer than four times, the first in 1227 for refusing to undertake a Crusade at the pope's request. The papacy came to view Frederick as the Anti-Christ, the biblical beast of the Apocalypse whose persecution of the faithful signaled the end of the world. The basis of the conflict lay once again in an imperial policy that encircled Rome. Although Frederick abandoned Germany, he was determined to control Lombardy. His efforts to establish a dominant Lombardy–Sicily axis in Italy brought his excommunication in 1238, an action that Frederick fiercely resisted as unwarranted papal interference in his secular rights as emperor.

The pope finally won the long struggle that ensued, although his victory proved in time to be a Pyrrhic one. In the contest with Frederick II, Pope Innocent IV (1243–1254) launched the church into European politics on a massive scale, and this wholesale secularization of the papacy made the church highly vulnerable to the criticism of religious reformers and royal apologists. Innocent organized and led the German princes against Frederick, who—thanks to Frederick's grand concessions to them—had become a superior force and were in full control of Germany by the 1240s. German and Italian resistance kept Frederick completely on the defensive throughout his last years.

When Frederick died in 1250, the German monarchy died with him. The princes established an informal electoral college in 1257, which thereafter reigned supreme (it was formally recognized by the emperor in 1356). The "king of the Romans" became their puppet, this time with firmly attached strings; he was elected and did not rule by hereditary right. Between 1250 and 1272 the Hohenstaufen dynasty slowly faded into oblivion. It finally died altogether after the dual defeat of Frederick's illegitimate son Manfred in 1266

Frederick II Denounces the Pope

When Frederick II learned that he had once again been excommunicated by the pope, this time at the council of Lyons in 1245, he raged at the presumption of popes to depose kings—an ominous condemnation of the temporal power of popes that would be heard again and again in the later Middle Ages. The following report of Frederick's reaction comes from the *Greater Chronicle* of Matthew of Paris.

When the Emperor Frederick was made fully aware of all these proceedings [his excommunication at Lyons] he could not contain himself, but burst into a violent rage, and, darting a scowling look on those who sat around him, he thundered forth: "The Pope in his synod has disgraced me by depriving me of my crown. Whence arises such great audacity? Whence proceeds such rash presumption? Where are my chests which contain my treasures?" And on their being brought and unlocked before him, by his order, he said, "See if my crowns are lost now"; then finding one, he placed it on his head and, being thus crowned, he stood up, and, with threatening eyes and a dreadful voice, unrestrainable from passion, he said aloud, "I have not yet lost my crown, nor will I be deprived of it by any attacks of the Pope or the council, without a bloody struggle. Does his vulgar pride raise him to such heights as to enable him to hurl from the imperial dignity me, the chief prince of the world, than whom none is greater—yea, I who am without an equal . . . ? In some things I was bound to obey, at least to respect, him [the pope]; but now I am released from all ties of affection and veneration, and also from the obligation of any kind of peace with him." From that time forth, therefore, Frederick, in order to injure the Pope more effectually . . . did all kinds of harm to his Holiness, to his money, as well as to his friends and relatives.

Frederic Austin Ogg (Ed.), *A Source Book of Mediaeval History: Documents Illustrative of European Life and Institutions from the German Invasions to the Renaissance* (New York: American Book Co., 1908), pp. 408–409.

and his grandson Conradino in 1268 by Charles of Anjou, the adventurous brother of the sainted French King Louis IX.

The Hohenstaufen legacy was to make permanent the divisions within the empire. Independent princes now controlled Germany. Italy fell to local magnates. The connection between Germany and Sicily, established by Frederick I, was permanently broken. And the papal monarchy emerged as one of Europe's most formidable powers, soon to enter its most costly conflict with the French and the English.

Medieval Russia

Early in the ninth century missionaries from Byzantium had converted Russia to the Christianity of the Eastern Orthodox Church. This development meant that Russia would remain culturally separated from the Latin Christianity of western Europe. Between the late ninth century and the mid-thirteenth century the city of Kiev was the center of Russian political life. Although the city enjoyed fairly extensive trade relations with its neighbors, it failed to develop a political system that provided effective resistance to foreign domination. The external threat to Kievan Russia came from the east when the Mongols moved across the vast Eurasian plains and into Russia as Genghis Khan built his empire. By 1240 the Mongols had conquered most of Russia and had turned its various cities and their surrounding countryside into dependent principalities from which tribute could be exacted. The portion of the Mongol Empire to which Russia thus stood in the relationship of a vassal was called the *Golden Horde*. It included the steppe, in what is now south Russia, with its largely nomadic population. This vassal relationship encouraged an Eastern orientation on the part of the Russians for over two centuries, although the connection of the Russian church to the Byzantine Empire remained important. During this period there was no single central political authority in Russia. The land was divided into numerous appanages, or feudal principalities, each of which was militarily weak and subject in one degree or another to the Golden Horde.

The rise of Moscow as a relatively strong power eventually brought the appanage age of Russian history to an end. In the fourteenth century, under Grand Prince Ivan I, the city began to cooperate with its Mongol—or as the Russians called them, Tatar—overlords in the collection of tribute. Ivan kept much of this tribute for himself and was soon called Ivan Kalita, or John of the Moneybag. When Mongol authority began to weaken, the princes of Moscow, who had become increasingly wealthy, filled the political power vacuum in the territory near the city. The princes extended their authority and that of the city by purchasing some territory, colonizing other areas, and conquering new lands. This slow extension of the appanage, or principality, of Moscow is usually known as *gathering the Russian land*.

In 1380 Grand Prince Dmitry of Moscow defeated the Mongols in battle. The result was not militarily decisive, but Moscow had demonstrated that the Mongol armies were not invincible. Conflict with the Mongols continued for another century before they were driven out. During these years the princes of Moscow asserted their right to be regarded as the successors of the earlier Kievan rulers, and they also made Moscow the religious center of Russia.

France in the Thirteenth Century: The Reign of Louis IX

If Innocent III realized the fondest ambitions of medieval popes, Louis IX (1226–1270), the grandson of Philip Augustus, embodied the medieval view of the perfect ruler. His reign was a striking contrast to that of his contemporary, Frederick II of Germany. Coming to power in the wake of the French victory at Bouvines (1214), Louis inherited a unified and secure kingdom. Although he was also endowed with a moral character that far excelled that of his royal and papal contemporaries, he was also at times prey to naiveté. Not beset by the problems of sheer survival, and a reformer at heart, Louis found himself free to concentrate on what medieval people believed to be the business of civilization.

Magnanimity in politics is not always a sign of strength, and Louis could be very magnanimous. Although in a position to drive the English from their French possessions during negotiations for the Treaty of Paris (1259), he refused to take such advantage. Had he done so and ruthlessly confiscated English territories on the French coast, he might have lessened, if not averted altogether, the conflict of the Hun-

King Louis IX (1226–1270) *giving justice. Louis, who was canonized in* 1297, *was the medieval ideal of a perfect ruler.* [*Giraudon/Art Resource*]

dred Years' War. Instead he surrendered to Henry III disputed territory on the borders of Gascony and confirmed Henry's possession of the duchy of Aquitaine. Although he occasionally chastised popes for their crude ambitions, Louis remained neutral during the long struggle between Frederick II and the papacy, and his neutrality redounded very much to the pope's advantage. Louis also remained neutral when his brother, Charles of Anjou, intervened in Italy and Sicily against the Hohenstaufens. Urged on by the Welfs and the pope, Charles was crowned king of Sicily in Rome, and his subsequent defeat of the grandsons of Frederick II ended the Hohenstaufen dynasty. For their assistance, both by action and by inaction, the Capetian kings of the thirteenth century became the objects of many papal favors.

Louis's greatest achievements lay at home. The efficient French bureaucracy, which his predecessors had used to exploit their subjects, became under Louis an instrument of order and fair play in local government. He sent forth royal commissioners *(enquêteurs),* reminiscent of Charlemagne's far less successful *missi dominici,* to monitor the royal officials responsible for local governmental administration (especially the *baillis* and *prévôts,* whose offices had been created by his predecessor, Philip Augustus) and to ensure that justice would truly be meted out to all. These royal ambassadors were received as genuine tribunes of the people. Louis further abolished private wars and serfdom within his royal domain, gave his subjects the judicial right of appeal from local to higher courts, and made the tax system, by medieval standards, more equitable. The French people came to associate their king with justice, and national feeling, the glue of nationhood, grew very strong during his reign.

Respected by the kings of Europe, Louis became an arbiter among the world's powers, having far greater moral authority than the pope. During his reign French society and culture became an example to all of Europe, a pattern that would continue into the modern period. Northern France became the showcase of monastic reform, chivalry, and Gothic art and architecture. Louis's reign also coincided with the golden age of Scholasticism, which saw the convergence of Europe's greatest thinkers on Paris, among them Saint Thomas Aquinas and Saint Bonaventure.

Louis's perfection remained, however, that of a medieval king. Like his father, Louis VIII (1223–1226), who had led the second Albigensian Crusade, Louis was something of a religious fanatic. He sponsored the French Inquisition. He led two French Crusades against the Arabs, which were inspired by the purest religious motives but proved to be personal disasters. During the first (1248–1254), Louis was captured and had to be ransomed out of Egypt. He died of a fever during the second in 1270. It was especially for this selfless, but also quite useless, service on behalf of the church that Louis later received the rare church honor of sainthood.

Suggested Readings

Philippe Ariès, *Centuries of Childhood: A Social History of Family Life* (1962). Pioneer effort on the subject.

Geoffrey Barraclough, *The Origins of Modern Germany* (1963). Penetrating political narrative.

Marc Bloch, *French Rural Society,* trans. by J. Sondheimer (1966). A classic by a great modern historian.

Andreas Capellanus, *The Art of Courtly Love,* trans. by J. J. Parry (1941). Documents from the court of Marie de Champagne.

M. Clagett, G. Post, and R. Reynolds (Eds.), *Twelfth-Century Europe and the Foundations of Modern Society* (1966). Demanding but stimulating collection of essays.

R. H. C. Davis, *A History of Medieval Europe: From Constantine to St. Louis* (1972), Part 2.

Georges Duby, *Rural Economy and Country Life in the Medieval West* (1968). Slice-of-life analysis.

Georges Duby, *The Three Orders: Feudal Society Imagined,* trans. by Arthur Goldhammer (1981). Large, comprehensive, authoritative.

Robert Fawtier, *The Capetian Kings of France: Monarchy and Nation* 987–1328, trans. by L. Butler and R. J. Adam (1972). Detailed, standard account.

E. H. Kantorowicz, *The King's Two Bodies* (1957). Controversial analysis of political concepts in the high Middle Ages.

R. S. Loomis (Ed.), *The Development of Arthurian Romance* (1963). Basic study.

Robert S. Lopez and I. W. Raymond (Eds.), *Medieval Trade in the Mediterranean World* (1955). Illuminating collection of sources, concentrated on southern Europe.

P. Mandonnet, *St. Dominic and His Work* (1944). For the origins of the Dominican Order.

Lloyd de Mause, (Ed.), *The History of Childhood* (1974).

John Moorman, *A History of the Franciscan Order* (1968). The best survey.

John B. Morrall, *Political Thought in Medieval Times* (1962). Readable and illuminating account.

John T. Noonan, *Contraception: A History of Its Treatment by the Catholic Theologians and Canonists* (1967). Fascinating account of medieval theological attitudes toward sexuality and sex-related problems.

Charles Petit-Dutaillis, *The Feudal Monarchy in France and England from the Tenth to the Thirteenth Century,* trans. by E. D. Hunt (1964). Political narrative.

J. M. Powell, *Innocent III: Vicar of Christ or Lord of the World* (1963). Excerpts from the scholarly debate over Innocent's reign.

Eileen Power, *Medieval Women* (1975). Seminal essays.

F. W. Powicke, *The Thirteenth Century* (1962). Outstanding treatment of English political history.

Shulamith Shahar, *The Fourth Estate: A History of Women in the Middle Ages* (1983). Best survey.

R. W. Southern, *Medieval Humanism and Other Studies* (1970). Provocative and far-ranging essays on topics in intellectual history of high Middle Ages.

W. L. Wakefield and A. P. Evans (Eds.), *Heresies of the High Middle Ages* (1969). A major document collection.

Suzanne Wemple, *Women in Frankish Society: Marriage and the Cloister* 500–900 (1981). What marriage and the cloister meant to medieval women.

Europe in Transition, 1300–1750

Between the early fourteenth and the mid-eighteenth centuries, Europe underwent far-reaching changes. These were years both of remarkable cultural and political construction and of massive physical suffering brought on by disease and war.

The era began with one of the greatest disasters in European history: a bubonic plague, known as the *Black Death,* that had killed an estimated two fifths of the population by the mid-fourteenth century. That event had been preceded by a century of sharp conflicts between the pope and the secular rulers. A hundred years of warfare between England and France followed the great demographic crisis. The emergence of strong, ruthless monarchies accompanied the decline in papal power during the later Middle Ages. Commanding greater economic and military resources, the new rulers steadily gained control over the church in their lands. By the fourteenth century, the nation-states of Europe were warring with one another, not with the armies of the pope.

Also in the fourteenth century the great cultural resurgence of Europe known as the *Renaissance* began. This was a rebirth of education and culture closely associated with the discovery of new Greek and Latin writings and with the rapid growth of colleges and universities throughout western Europe.

Interest in the past was not the only way in which Europeans extended their minds in directions previously uncharted. In the late fifteenth century voyages began to America, around Africa, and across the Indian Ocean to Asia. These voyages of discovery introduced Europeans to exotic cultures and non-Western values. Science was still another frontier. Beginning with Copernicus and culminating in Sir Isaac Newton, a new view of the universe emerged. The voyages of discovery and the scientific revolution gave Europeans both new confidence in the power of the human mind and a new perspective on their society.

In the sixteenth century a major religious revolt divided Europe spiritually and led to a restructuring of Christendom. The Protestant Reformation began in 1517 when an obscure German professor named Martin Luther challenged the religious teaching and authority of the papacy. Within a quarter century Europe was permanently divided between a growing variety of Protestant churches and the Roman Catholic church. For a century and a half the new religious differences also fueled political conflict. Religious warfare devastated France in the second half of the sixteenth century and wreaked havoc on Germany in the first half of the seventeenth.

By the middle of the seventeenth century most religious warfare had ended. The religious turmoil had strengthened the hand of the secular state. For many rulers and their subjects, political stability now became a higher value than religious allegiance. By the early eighteenth century, Europe's rulers, with the notable exception of the English monarchs, were imitating the French king, Louis XIV. Through efficient tax collectors, loyal administrators, and a powerful standing army, Louis subjected France to his will, making it the model of the absolute state. By the second half of the seventeenth century the balance of power had shifted away from Spain to the strong monarchies of France, Austria, and Prussia and to the parliamentary monarchy of Great Britain. Also, for the first time, Russia emerged as a major European power.

With the end of religious conflict, energies were turned toward economic expansion. New, more efficient farming methods appeared, and nations took the first steps toward industrialization. In the New World, the colonies grew and were consolidated. By the eighteenth century competition over trade had replaced religion as the cause of war. The demand for political independence, most notably by the English colonies in America, now replaced the earlier demands for religious independence. A new age had dawned, one still believing in the power of God, but increasingly fascinated by human power.

The School of Athens *by Raphael* (1483–1520). *Painted in* 1510–1511 *for the Vatican Palace in Rome, this fresco is one of the most significant examples of the impact of the ancient world on the Renaissance. The model for the figure of Plato* (*center with upraised arm*) *was Leonardo da Vinci; for the figure in the foreground with his head on his arm, Michelangelo.* [*Art Resource*]

9

The Late Middle Ages and the Renaissance: Decline and Renewal (1300–1527)

THE LATE MIDDLE AGES and the Renaissance marked a time of unprecedented calamity and of bold new beginnings. There was the Hundred Years' War between England and France (1337–1453), an exercise in seemingly willful self-destruction, which was made even more terrible in its later stages by the invention of gunpowder and heavy artillery. There was almost universal bubonic plague, known to contemporaries as the Black Death. Between 1348 and 1350 the plague killed as much as one third of the population in many regions and transformed many pious Christians into believers in the omnipotence of death. There was a schism within the church that lasted thirty-seven years (1378–1415) and saw, by 1409, the election of no fewer than three competing popes and colleges of cardinals. And there was the onslaught of the Turks, who in 1453 marched seemingly invincibly through Constantinople and toward the West. As their political and religious institutions buckled, as disease, bandits, and wolves ravaged their cities in the wake of war, and as Muslim armies gathered at their borders, Europeans beheld what seemed to be the imminent total collapse of Western civilization.

But if the late Middle Ages saw unprecedented chaos, it also witnessed a rebirth that would continue into the seventeenth century. Two modern Dutch scholars have employed the same word (*Herfsttij*, "harvesttide") with different connotations to describe the period, one interpreting the word as a "waning" or "decline" (Johan Huizinga), the other as a true "harvest" (Heiko Oberman). If something was dying away, some ripe fruit and seed grain were also being gathered in. The late Middle Ages were a creative breaking up.

It was in this period that such scholars as Marsilius of Padua, William of Ockham, and Lorenzo Valla produced lasting criticisms of medieval assumptions about the nature of God, humankind, and society. It was a period in which kings worked through parliaments and clergy through councils to place lasting limits on the pope's temporal power. The principle that a sovereign (in this case, the pope) is accountable to the body of which he or she is head was established. The arguments used by conciliarists (advocates of the judicial superiority of a church council over a pope) to establish papal accountability to the body of the faithful provided an example for the secular sphere, as sovereigns, who also had an independent tradition of ruler accountability in Roman law, were reminded of their responsibility to the body politic.

The late Middle Ages also saw an unprecedented scholarly renaissance, as Italian Humanists made a full recovery of classical knowledge and languages and set in motion educational reforms and cultural changes that would spread throughout Europe in the fifteenth and sixteenth centuries. In the process the Italian Humanists invented, for all practical purposes, critical historical scholarship and exploited a new fifteenth-century invention, the "divine art" of printing with movable type. It was in this period that the vernacular, the local language, began to take its place alongside Latin, the international language, as a widely used literary and political language. The independent nation-states of Europe progressively superseded the universal church as the community of highest allegiance, as patriotism and incipient nationalism became a major force. Nations henceforth "transcended" themselves not by journeys to Rome but by competitive voyages to the Far East and the Americas, as the age of global exploration opened.

A time of both waning and harvest, constriction (in the form of nationalism) and expansion (in the sense of world exploration), the late Middle Ages saw medieval culture grudgingly give way to the age of Renaissance and Reformation.

Political and Social Breakdown

The Hundred Years' War and the Rise of National Sentiment

CAUSES OF THE WAR. From May 1337 to October 1453 England and France periodically engaged in what was for both a futile and devastating war. The conflict was initiated by the English king Edward III (1327–1377), who held a strong claim to the French throne as the grandson of Philip the Fair (1285–1314). When Charles IV (1322–1328), the last of Philip the Fair's surviving sons, died, Edward, who was only fifteen at the time, asserted his right to Capetian succession. The French barons, however, were not willing to place an English king on the French throne. They chose instead the first cousin of Charles IV, Philip VI of Valois (1328–1350), the first of a new French dynasty that was to rule into the sixteenth century.

But there was much more to the Hundred Years' War than just a defense of Edward's prestige. In the background were other equally important factors that help to explain both Edward's success in gaining popular and parliamentary support after the war started and the determination of the English and the French people to endure the war to its bitter end. For one thing, the English king held Gascony, Anjou, Guyenne, and other French territories as fiefs from the French king. Thus he was, in law, a vassal of the French king—a circumstance that stretched back to the Norman Conquest. In May 1329 Edward journeyed to Amiens and, most perfunctorily, swore fealty to Philip VI. As Philip's vassal Edward was, theoretically if not in fact, committed to support policies detrimental to England, if his French lord so commanded. If such vassalage was intolerable to Edward, the English possession of French lands was even more repugnant to the French, especially inasmuch as the English presence remained a permanent threat to the royal policy of centralization.

Still another factor that fueled the conflict was French support of the Bruces of Scotland, strong opponents of the English overlordship of Scotland who had won a victory over the English in 1314. The French and the English were also at this time quarreling over Flanders, a French fief, yet also a country whose towns were completely dependent for their livelihood on imported English wool. Edward III and his successors manipulated this situation to English advantage throughout the conflict; by controlling the export of wool to Flanders, England influenced Flanders' foreign policy. Finally, there were decades of prejudice and animosity between the French and the English people, who constantly confronted one another on the high seas and in port towns. Taken together, these various factors made the Hundred Years' War a struggle to the death for national control and identity.

FRENCH WEAKNESS. Throughout the conflict France was the stronger on paper; it had three times the population of England, was far the wealthier, and fought on its own soil. Yet, for the greater part of the conflict, until after 1415, the major battles ended in often stunning English victories. France was not as strong as it appeared. It was, first of all, internally disunited by social conflict and the absence of a centralized system of taxation to fund the war. French kings raised funds by

Edward III paying homage to his feudal lord Philip VI of France. In law, the king of England was a vassal of the king of France. [Snark/EPA]

depreciating the currency, taxing the clergy, and borrowing heavily from Italian bankers—self-defeating practices that created a financial crisis by mid-century. As a tool to provide him money, the king raised up a representative council of townsmen and noblemen that came to be known in subsequent years as the *Estates General.* It convened in 1355, and although it levied taxes at the king's request, its members also used the king's plight to enhance their own regional rights and privileges. Just how successful they were is indicated by the creation in this period of the Burgundian state, a powerful new territory that became a thorn in the sides of French kings throughout the fifteenth century. France, unlike England, was still struggling in the fourteenth century to make the transition from a fragmented feudal society to a centralized "modern" state.

Beyond this struggle, there was the clear fact of English military superiority, due to the greater discipline of its infantry and the rapid-fire and long-range capability of that ingeniously simple weapon, the English longbow, which could shoot six arrows a minute with a force sufficient to pierce an inch of wood or the armor of a knight at two hundred yards. The longbow scattered the French cavalry and crossbowmen in one engagement after the other. Only in the later stages of the war, with the introduction of heavy artillery, did the French alter their military tactics to advantage.

Finally, French weakness was related in no small degree to the comparative mediocrity of royal leadership during the Hundred Years' War. English kings were far the shrewder. Historians have found it to be a telling commentary on the leadership ability of French kings in this period that the most memorable military leader on the French side in the popular imagination is Joan of Arc.

Progress of the War

The war had three major stages of development, each ending with a seemingly decisive victory by one or the other side: (1) during the reign of Edward III (d. 1377); (2) from Edward's death to the Treaty of Troyes (1420); and (3) from the appearance of Joan of Arc (1429) to the English retreat.

THE CONFLICT DURING THE REIGN OF EDWARD III. Edward prepared for the first

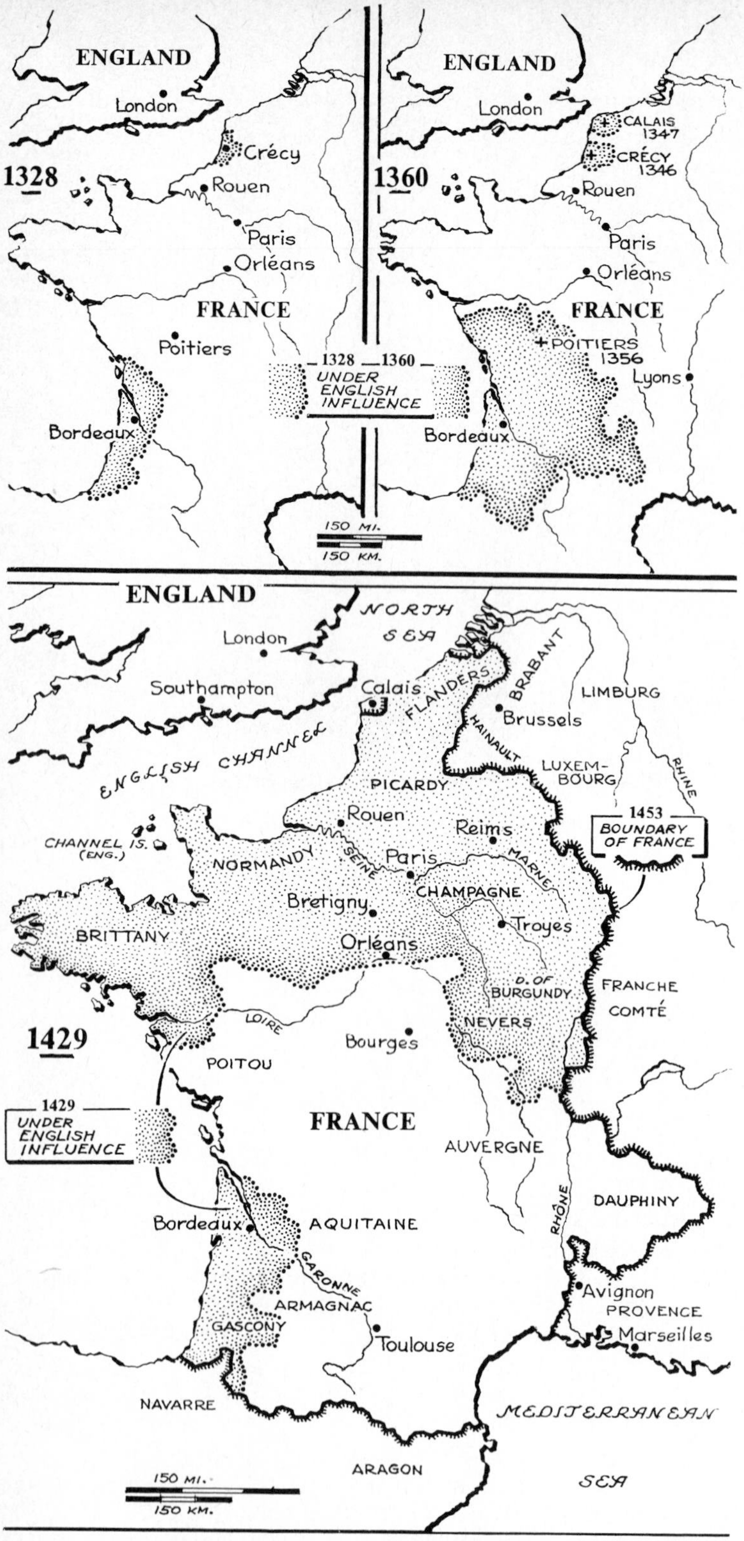

THE HUNDRED YEARS' WAR

MAP 9–1 *The Hundred Years' War went on intermittently from the late* 1330s *until* 1453. *These maps show the remarkable English territorial gains up to the sudden and decisive turning of the tide of battle in favor of the French by the forces of Joan of Arc in* 1429.

stage of the war by securing allies in the Netherlands and a personal pledge of support from the emperor Louis IV of Bavaria (1314–1347). By slapping an embargo on English wool to Flanders, Edward sparked urban rebellions by merchants and the trade guilds. Inspired by a rich merchant, Jacob van Artevelde, the Flemish cities, led by Ghent, revolted against the French. Having at first taken as neutral a stand as possible in the conflict, these cities, whose economies faced total collapse without imported English wool, signed a half-hearted alliance with England in January 1340, acknowledging Edward as king of France.

Edward defeated the French fleet in the first great battle of the war in the Bay of Sluys on June 23, 1340. But his subsequent effort to invade France by way of Flanders failed, largely because his allies proved undependable. As a stalemate developed, a truce was struck and was more or less observed until 1346. In that year Edward attacked Normandy and won a series of easy victories that were capped by that at Crécy in August. This was quickly followed by the seizure of Calais, which the English held thereafter for over two hundred years. Both sides employed scorched-earth tactics and completely devastated the areas of conflict.

Exhaustion and the onset of the Black Death forced a second truce in late 1347, and the war entered a lull until 1355. On September 19, 1356, the English won their greatest victory, near Poitiers, routing the noble cavalry and even taking the French king, John II the Good (1350–1364), captive back to England. After Poitiers there was a complete breakdown of political order in France. Disbanded soldiers from both sides became professional bandits, roaming the land, pillaging areas untouched by the war, and bringing disaster almost as great as the war itself.

Power in France lay with the privileged classes, who expressed their will through the representative assembly of the Estates General. Convened in 1355 by the faltering king so that revenues might be provided to continue the war, the Estates General, led by powerful merchants of Paris under Étienne Marcel, had demanded and received rights similar to those granted the English privileged classes in Magna Carta. The English Parliament, too, had grown out of councils convened by kings (John, 1199–1216, and Henry III, 1216–1272), which were widely representative of the English upper classes and were designed to provide the king an opportunity to discuss (and thereby to persuade those attending to adopt) the king's views on laws and taxes. During the reign of Edward I (1272–1307) these "parliaments" or "parleyings" with the king became a fixed political institution. Unlike the English Parliament, which represented the interests of a comparatively unified English nobility, the French Estates General was a many-tongued lobby, a forum for the diverse interests of the new-rich urban commercial and industrial classes, the territorial princes, and the clergy. Such a diverse body was no instrument for effective government.

The war also occasioned internal political policies that alienated and embittered the peasants. To secure their rights, the privileged classes bullied the French peasantry, who were forced to pay ever-increasing taxes and to repair without compensation the war-damaged properties of the nobility. The pressure became more than the peasantry could bear. Burdened by the Estates General, terrified by the Black Death, and emboldened by the cowardly retreat of the French cavalry at Poitiers, the peasantry exploded in several regions in a series of bloody uprisings known as the *Jacquerie*. The revolt was, however, put down by the nobility, who matched "Jacques Bonhomme," as the peasant revolutionary was popularly known, atrocity for atrocity.

On May 9, 1360, another milestone of the war was reached when England forced the Peace of Bretigny on the French. This agreement declared Edward's vassalage to the king of France ended and affirmed his sovereignty over English territories in France (including Gascony, Guyenne, Poitou, and Calais). France also pledged to pay a ransom of three million gold crowns to win King John the Good's release. In return, Edward renounced his claim to the French throne.

Such a partition of French territorial control was completely unrealistic, and sober observers on both sides knew it could not long continue. France became strong enough to strike back in the late 1360s, during the reign of John the Good's successor, Charles V (1364–1380). In 1369 Flanders came into the French fold when Charles's brother, Philip the Bold, who held the duchy of Burgundy as his appanage (landed inheritance), married the daughter of the count of Flanders. Backed by the Estates General and blessed with a brilliant military commander in Bertrand du Guesclin, the French launched a successful counteroffensive.

Edward I (1271–1307) *presiding over parliament. It was during Edward's reign that parliament became a fixed political institution.* [*Royal Library, Windsor Castle, by gracious permission of HM the Queen*]

By the time of Edward's death in 1377, the English had been beaten back to coastal enclaves and the territory of Bordeaux.

French Defeat and the Treaty of Troyes. After Edward's death the English war effort lessened considerably, partly because of domestic problems within England. During the reign of Richard II (1377–1399), England had its own version of the *Jacquerie*. To counter the economic strain of the war with France and the ravages of the Black Death, Parliament had reduced the wages of peasants and artisans, imposed new tolls and taxes, and reasserted old domainal rights in an effort to keep the peasants bound to the land. Both the urban proletariat and the agrarian peasantry greatly resented these measures, which the king's uncle and regent, John of Gaunt, the duke of Lancaster, enforced. In June 1381 a great revolt of the unprivileged classes exploded under the leadership of John Ball, a secular priest, and Wat Tyler, a journeyman. As in France, the revolt was short-lived, brutally crushed within the year. But it left the country divided for decades.

In 1396 France and England signed still another truce, this time backed up by the marriage of Richard II to the daughter of the French king, Charles VI (1380–1422). This truce lasted through the reign of Richard's successor, Henry IV of Lancaster (1399–1413). His successor, Henry V (1413–1422), reheated the war with France by taking advantage of the internal French turmoil created by the rise to power of the duchy of Burgundy. Charles VI had gone mad in the second half of his reign, and control of the French government had devolved on his brother, the duke of Orléans. Orléans struggled manfully but in vain to contain the aggressive duke of Burgundy, John the Fearless (1404–1419). Indeed, the latter succeeded in having Orléans assassinated in 1407. Thereafter civil war enveloped France; the count of Armagnac took up the royal banner, while John the Fearless found allies in the French cities.

With France so internally divided, Henry V struck hard in Normandy. John the Fearless and the Burgundians foolishly watched from the sidelines while Henry's army routed the numerically stronger but tactically less shrewd Armagnacs at Agincourt on October 25, 1415. In the years thereafter the Burgundians closed ranks behind the royal forces as they belatedly recognized that a divided France would remain an easy prey to the English. But this inchoate French unity, which promised to bring eventual victory, shattered in September 1419. In a belated reprisal for the assassination of the duke of Orléans twelve years earlier, soldiers of Charles VI stabbed John the Fearless to death only hours after the two men had quarreled. This shocking turn of events stampeded John's son, Philip the Good (1419–1467). He determined to avenge his father's death at any price, even if it meant giving the English control of France. The result was a Burgundian alliance with England.

With Burgundian support behind the English, France became Henry V's for the taking—at least in the short run. The Treaty of Troyes in 1420 disinherited the legitimate heir to the French throne, the dauphin (a title used by the king's oldest son), the future Charles VII, and made Henry V successor to the mad Charles VI. When Henry V and Charles VI died within months of one another in 1422, the infant Henry VI of England was proclaimed in Paris to be king of both France and England under the regency of the duke of Bedford. The dream of Edward III, the pretext for continuing the great war, was now, for the moment, realized: in 1422 an English king was the proclaimed ruler of France.

The dauphin went into retreat in Bourges, where, on the death of his father, he became Charles VII to most of the French, who ignored the Treaty of Troyes. Although some years were to pass before he was powerful enough to take his crown in fact, the French people would not deny the throne to a legitimate successor, regardless of the terms dictated by the Treaty of Troyes. National sentiment, spurred to unprecedented heights by Joan of Arc, soon brought the French people together as never before in a victorious coalition.

Joan of Arc and the War's Conclusion. Joan of Arc (1412–1431), a peasant from Domrémy, presented herself to Charles VII in March 1429. When she declared that the King of Heaven had called her to deliver besieged Orléans from the English, Charles was understandably skeptical. But the dauphin and his advisers, in retreat from what seemed to be a completely hopeless war, were desperate men, willing to try anything to reverse French fortunes on the battlefield. Certainly the deliverance of Orléans, a city strategic to the control of the territory south of the Loire, would be a godsend. Charles's desperation overcame his skepticism, and he gave Joan his leave.

Circumstances worked perfectly to Joan's advantage. The English force was already exhausted by its six-month siege of Orléans and actually at the point of withdrawal when Joan arrived with fresh French troops. After the English were repulsed at Orléans, there followed a succession of French victories that were popularly attributed to Joan. Joan truly deserved much of the credit; not, however, because she was a military genius. She gave the French people and armies something military experts could not: a unique inspiration and an almost mystical confidence in themselves as a nation. Within a few months of the liberation of Orléans, Charles VII received his crown in Rheims and ended the nine-year "disinheritance" prescribed by the Treaty of Troyes.

Charles forgot his liberator as quickly as he had embraced her. Joan was captured by the Burgundians in May 1430, and although he was in a position to secure her release, the French king did little to help her. She was turned over to the Inquisition in English-held Rouen. The Burgundians and the English wanted Joan publicly discredited, believing this would also discredit her patron, Charles VII, and might demoralize French resistance. The skilled inquisitors broke the courageous "Maid of Orléans" in ten weeks of merciless interrogation, and she was executed as a relapsed heretic on May 30, 1431. Charles reopened Joan's trial at a later date, and she was finally declared innocent of all the charges against her on July 7, 1456, twenty-five years after her execution. In 1920 the church declared her a saint.

Joan of Arc (1412–1421). *This painting in the National Archives in Paris is believed to be a contemporary portrait.* [*Giraudon*]

Joan of Arc Refuses to Recant Her Beliefs

Joan of Arc, threatened with torture, refused to recant her beliefs and instead defended the instructions she had received from the voices that spoke to her. Here is a part of her self-defense from the contemporary trial record.

On Wednesday, May 9th of the same year [1431], *Joan was brought into the great tower of the castle of Rouen before us the said judges and in the presence of the reverend father, lord abbot of St. Cormeille de Compiegne, of masters Jean de Châtillon and Guillaume Erart, doctors of sacred theology, of André Marguerie and Nicolas de Venderes, archdeacons of the church of Rouen, of William Haiton, bachelor of theology, Aubert Morel, licentiate in canon law; Nicolas Loiseleur, canon of the cathedral of Rouen, and master Jean Massieu.*

And Joan was required and admonished to speak the truth on many different points contained in her trial which she had denied or to which she had given false replies, whereas we possessed certain information, proofs, and vehement presumptions upon them. Many of the points were read and explained to her, and she was told that if she did not confess them truthfully she would be put to the torture, the instruments of which were shown to her all ready in the tower. There were also present by our instruction men ready to put her to the torture in order to restore her to the way and knowledge of truth, and by this means to procure the salvation of her body and soul which by her lying inventions she exposed to such grave perils.

To which the said Joan answered in this manner: "Truly if you were to tear me limb from limb and separate my soul from my body, I would not tell you anything more: and if I did say anything, I should afterwards declare that you had compelled me to say it by force." Then she said that on Holy Cross Day last she received comfort from St. Gabriel; she firmly believes it was St. Gabriel. She knew by her voices whether she should submit to the Church, since the clergy were pressing her hard to submit. Her voices told her that if she desired Our Lord to aid her she must wait upon Him in all her doings. She said that Our Lord has always been the master of her doings, and the Enemy never had power over them. She asked her voices if she would be burned and they answered that she must wait upon God, and He would aid her.

The Trial of Jeanne D'Arc, trans. by W. P. Barrett (New York: Gotham House, 1932), pp. 303–304.

The Hundred Years' War (1337–1443)

English victory at Bay of Sluys	1340
English victory at Crécy and seizure of Calais	1346
Black Death strikes	1347
English victory at Poitiers	1356
Jacquerie disrupts France	1358
Peace of Bretigny recognizes English holdings in France	1360
English peasants revolt	1381
English victory at Agincourt	1415
Treaty of Troyes proclaims Henry VI ruler of both England and France	1422
Joan of Arc leads French to victory at Orléans	1429
Joan of Arc executed as a heretic	1431
War ends; English retain only coastal town of Calais	1453

Charles VII and Philip the Good made peace in 1435, and a unified France, now at peace with Burgundy, progressively forced the English back. By 1453, the date of the war's end, the English held only the coastal enclave of Calais.

During the Hundred Years' War there were sixty-eight years of at least nominal peace and forty-four of hot war. The political and social consequences were lasting. Although the war devastated France, it also awakened the giant of French nationalism and hastened the transition in France from a feudal monarchy to a centralized state. Burgundy became a major European political power. The seesawing allegiance of the Netherlands throughout the conflict encouraged the English to develop their own clothing industry and foreign markets. In both France and England the on-again, off-again war devastated the peasantry, who were forced to bear its burden in taxes and services. After the *Jacquerie* of 1358 France did not see another significant peasant uprising until the French Revolution in the eighteenth century.

The Black Death

Preconditions and Causes. In the late Middle Ages nine tenths of the population were still farmers. The three-field system, in use in most areas since well before the fourteenth century, had increased the amount of arable land and thereby the food supply. The growth of cities and trade had also stimulated agricultural science and productivity. But as the food supply grew, so also did the population. It is estimated that Europe's population doubled between the years 1000 and 1300. By 1300 the balance between food supply and population was decisively tipped in favor of the latter. There were now more people than food to feed them or jobs to employ them, and the average European faced the probability of extreme hunger at least once during his or her expected thirty-five-year life span.

Famines followed the population explosion in the first half of the fourteenth century. Between 1315 and 1317 crop failures produced the greatest famine of the Middle Ages. Great suffering was inflicted on densely populated urban areas like the industrial towns of the Netherlands. Decades of overpopulation, economic depression, famine, and bad health progressively weakened Europe's population and made it highly vulnerable to a virulent bubonic plague that struck with full force in 1348. This Black Death, so called by contemporaries because of the way it discolored the body, followed the trade routes from Asia into Europe. Appearing in Sicily in late 1347, it entered Europe through the port cities of Venice, Genoa, and Pisa in 1348, and from there it swept rapidly through Spain and southern France and into northern Europe. Areas that lay outside the major trade routes, like Bohemia, appear to have remained virtually unaffected. By the end of the fourteenth century it is estimated that western Europe as a whole had lost as much as two fifths of its population, and a full recovery was not made until the sixteenth century. (See Map 9.2.)

Popular Remedies. In the Black Death people confronted a catastrophe against which they had neither understanding nor defense. Never have Western people stood so helpless against the inexplicable and the uncontrollable. Contemporary physicians did not know that the disease was transmitted by rat- or human-transported fleas, and hence the most rudimentary prophylaxis was lacking. Popular wisdom held that a corruption in the atmosphere caused the disease. Some blamed poisonous fumes released by earthquakes, and many adopted aromatic amulets as a remedy. According to the contemporary observations of Boccaccio, who recorded the varied reactions to the plague in the *Decameron* (1353), some sought a remedy in moderation and a temperate life; others gave themselves over entirely to

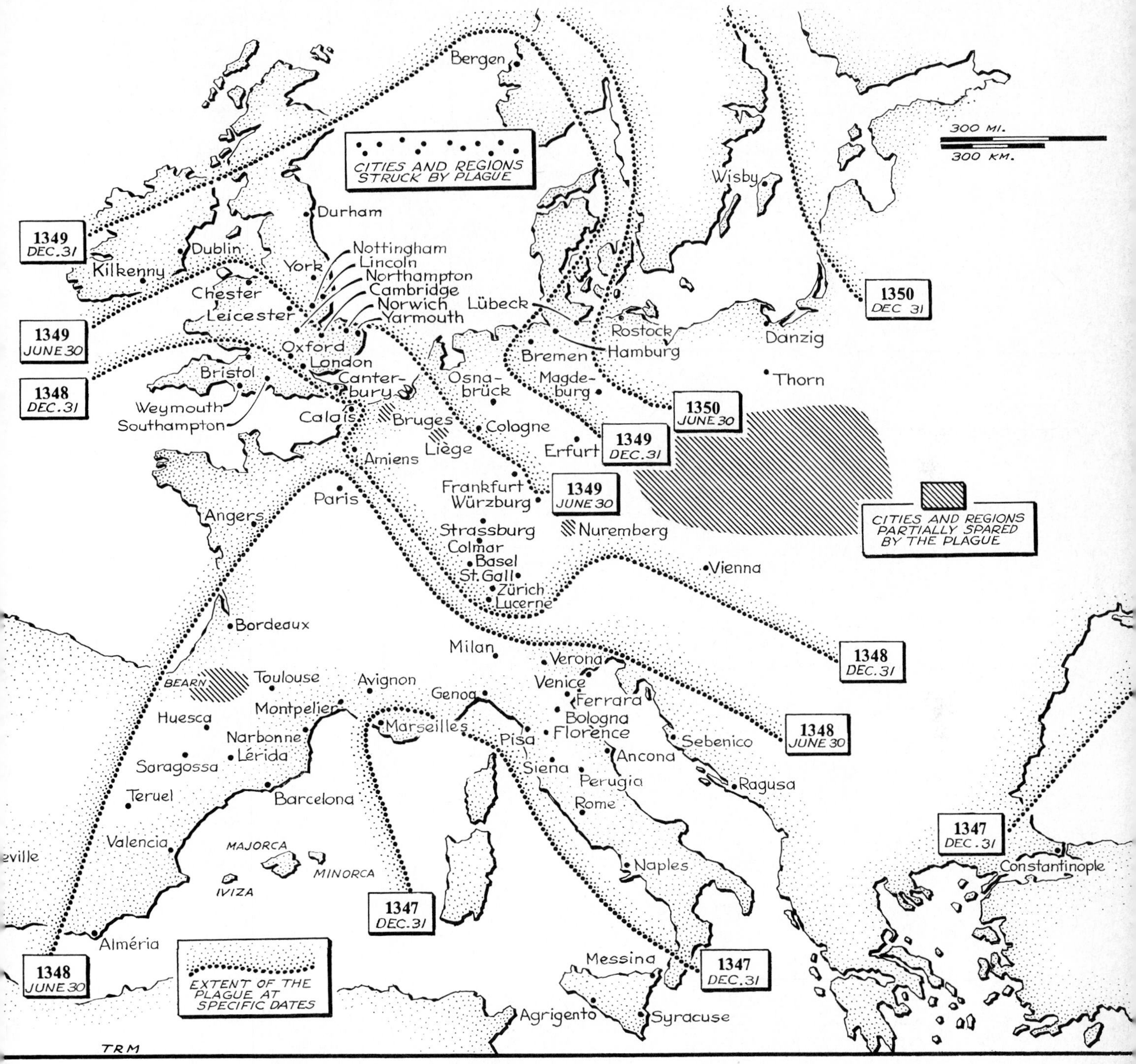

SPREAD OF THE BLACK DEATH

MAP 9–2 *Apparently introduced by sea-borne rats from Black Sea areas where plague-infested rodents have long been known, the Black Death brought huge human, social, and economic consequences. One of the lower estimates of Europeans dying is 25,000,000. The map charts its spread in the mid-fourteenth century. Generally following trade routes, the plague reached Scandinavia by* 1350, *and some believe it then went on to Iceland and even Greenland. Areas off the main trade routes were largely spared.*

their passions (sexual promiscuity among the stricken apparently ran high); and still others, "the most sound, perhaps, in judgment," chose flight and seclusion as the best medicine.

Among the most extreme social reactions were processions of flagellants. These were religious fanatics who beat their bodies in ritual penance until they bled, believing that such action would bring divine intervention. The Jews, who were hated by many because of centuries of Christian propaganda against them and because they had become society's moneylenders, a disreputable and resented profession but one of the few that Jews were allowed to practice, became scapegoats. Pogroms occurred in several cities, sometimes incited by the advent of flagellants. The terror created by the flagellants, whose dirty bodies may have actually served to transport the disease, became so socially disruptive and threatening even to established authority that the church finally outlawed such processions.

SOCIAL AND ECONOMIC CONSEQUENCES. Among the social and economic consequences of the plague were a shrunken labor supply and the devaluation of the estates of the nobility. Villages vanished in the wake of the plague. As the number of farm laborers decreased, their wages increased and those of

Boccaccio Describes the Ravages of the Black Death in Florence

The Black Death provided an excuse to the poet, Humanist, and storyteller Giovanni Boccaccio (1313–1375) to assemble his great collection of tales, the *Decameron.* Ten congenial men and women flee Florence to escape the plague and to while away the time telling stories. In one of the stories, Boccaccio embedded a fine clinical description of plague symptoms as seen in Florence in 1348 and of the powerlessness of physicians and the lack of remedies.

In Florence, despite all that human wisdom and forethought could devise to avert it, even as the cleansing of the city from many impurities by officials appointed for the purpose, the refusal of entrance to all sick folk, and the adoption of many precautions for the preservation of health; despite also humble supplications addressed to God, and often repeated both in public procession and otherwise, by the devout; towards the beginning of the spring of the said year [1348] *the doleful effects of the pestilence began to be horribly apparent by symptoms that shewed as if miraculous.*

Not such were these symptoms as in the East, where an issue of blood from the nose was a manifest sign of inevitable death; but in men and women alike it first betrayed itself by the emergence of certain tumours in the groin or the armpits, some of which grew as large as a common apple, others as an egg, some more, some less, which the common folk called gavoccioli. *From the two said parts of the body this deadly* gavocciolo *soon began to propagate and spread itself in all directions indifferently; after which the form of the malady began to change, black spots or livid making their appearance in many cases on the arm or the thigh or elsewhere, now few and large, now minute and numerous. And as the* gavocciolo *had been and still was an infallible token of approaching death, such also were these spots on whomsoever they shewed themselves. Which maladies seemed to set entirely at naught both the art of the physician and the virtues of physic; indeed, whether it was that the disorder was of a nature to defy such treatment, or that the physicians were at fault . . . and, being in ignorance of its source, failed to apply the proper remedies; in either case, not merely were those that recovered few, but almost all died within three days of the appearance of the said symptoms, sooner or later, and in most cases without any fever or other attendant malady.*

The Decameron of Giovanni Boccaccio, trans. by J. M. Rigg (New York: Dutton, 1930), p. 5.

skilled artisans soared. Many serfs now chose to commute their labor services by money payments, to abandon the farm altogether, and to pursue more interesting and rewarding jobs in skilled craft industries in the cities, an important new vocational option opened by the Black Death. Agricultural prices fell because of lowered demand, and the price of luxury and manufactured goods—the work of skilled artisans—rose. The noble landholders suffered the greatest decline in power from this new state of affairs. They were forced to pay more for finished products and for farm labor, and they received a smaller return on their agricultural produce. Everywhere their rents were in steady decline after the plague.

To recoup their losses, some landowners converted arable land to sheep pasture, substituting more profitable wool production for labor-intensive grain crops. Others abandoned the effort to farm their land and simply leased it to the highest bidder. Most ominously, legislation was sought to force peasants to stay on their farms and to freeze their wages at low levels, that is, to close off immediately the new economic opportunities opened for the peasantry by the demographic crisis. In France the direct tax on the peasantry, the *taille*, was increased, and opposition to it was prominent among the grievances behind the *Jacquerie*. A Statute of Laborers was passed by the English Parliament in 1351 that limited wages to preplague levels and restricted the ability of peasants to leave the land of their traditional masters. Opposition to such legislation was also a prominent factor in the English Peasants' Revolt of 1381.

Although the plague hit urban populations especially hard, the cities and their skilled industries came, in time, to prosper from it. Cities had always been careful to protect their interests; as they grew, they passed legislation to regulate competition from rural areas and to control immigration. After the plague their laws were progressively extended over the surrounding lands of nobles and feudal landlords, many of whom were peacefully integrated into urban life on terms very favorable to the cities.

The basic unit of urban industry was the master and his apprentices (usually one or two). Their numbers were purposely kept low and jealously guarded. As the craft of the skilled artisan was passed from master to apprentice only very slowly, the first wave of plague created a short supply of skilled labor almost overnight. But this short supply also

More than one European in three died of the Black Death. In some localities so many people died that the traditional rites of death were abandoned in favor of hurried mass burials in communal pits. [*Vincent Virga Archives*]

raised the prices of available manufactured and luxury items to new heights. Ironically the omnipresence of death whetted the appetite for the things that only skilled urban industries could produce. Expensive cloths and jewelry, furs from the north, and silks from the south were in great demand in the second half of the fourteenth century. Faced with life at its worst, people insisted on having the very best. The townspeople profited coming and going: as wealth poured into the cities and per capita income rose, the cost to urban dwellers of agricultural products from the countryside, which were now less in demand, actually declined.

The church also profited from the plague as gifts and bequests multiplied. Although the church, as a great landholder, also suffered losses, it had offsetting revenues from the vastly increased demand for religious services for the dead and the dying.

New Conflicts and Opportunities. By increasing the importance of skilled artisans, the plague contributed to new conflicts within the cities. The economic and political power of local artisans and trade guilds grew steadily in the late Middle Ages along with the demand for their goods and services. The merchant and patrician classes found it increasingly difficult to maintain their traditional dominance and grudgingly gave guild masters a voice in city government. As the guilds won political power, they encouraged restrictive legislation to protect local industries. These restrictions, in turn, brought confrontations between master artisans, who wanted to keep their numbers low and expand their industries at a snail's pace, and the many journeymen, who were eager to rise to the rank of master. To the long-existing conflict between the guilds and the urban patriciate was now added a conflict within the guilds themselves.

Another indirect effect of the great plague was to assist monarchies in the development of centralized states. The plague caused the landed nobility to lose much of their economic power in the same period that the military superiority of paid professional armies over the traditional noble cavalry was being demonstrated by the Hundred Years' War. The plague also killed large numbers of clergy—perhaps one third of the German clergy fell victim to it as they heroically ministered to the sick and dying. This reduction in clerical ranks occurred in the same century in which the residence of the pope in Avignon (1309–1377) and the Schism (1378–1415) were undermining much of the church's popular support. After 1350 the two traditional "containers" of monarchy—the landed nobility and the church—were on the defensive, and to no small degree as a consequence of the plague. Kings took full advantage of the new situation, as they drew on growing national sentiment to centralize their governments and economies.

Ecclesiastical Breakdown and Revival: The Late Medieval Church

The Thirteenth-Century Papacy

At first glance the popes may appear to have been in a very favorable position in the latter half of the thirteenth century. Frederick II had been vanquished and imperial pressure on Rome had been removed. The French king, Louis IX, was an enthusiastic supporter of the church, as his two disastrous Crusades, which won him sainthood, testify. Although it lasted only seven years, a reunion of the Eastern church with Rome was proclaimed by the Council of Lyons in 1274, as the Western church took advantage of the Emperor Michael Palaeologus's request for aid against the Turks. Despite these positive events, the church was not really in as favorable a position as it appeared.

As early as the reign of Pope Innocent III (1198–1216), when papal power reached its height, there were ominous developments. Innocent had elaborated the doctrine of papal plenitude of power and on that authority had declared saints, disposed of benefices, and created a centralized papal monarchy with a clearly political mission. Innocent's transformation of the papacy into a great secular power had the consequence of weakening the church religiously as he sought to strengthen it politically. Thereafter the church as a papal monarchy and the church as the "body of the faithful" came increasingly to be differentiated; it was against the "papal church" and in the name of the "true Christian church" that both reformers and heretics raised their voices in protest until the Protestant Reformation.

What Innocent began, his successors perfected. Under Urban IV (1261–1264) the papacy established its own law court, the Rota Romana, which tightened and centralized the church's legal proceedings. The latter half of the thirteenth century saw an elaboration of the system of clerical taxation; what had begun in the twelfth century as an emergency measure to raise funds for the Crusades became a fixed institution. In the same period, papal power to determine appointments to many major and minor church offices—the so-called reservation of benefices—was greatly broadened. The thirteenth-century papacy became a powerful political institution governed by its own law and courts, serviced by an efficient international bureaucracy, and preoccupied with secular goals.

Papal centralization of the church tended to undermine both diocesan authority and popular support. Rome's interests, not local needs, came to control church appointments, policies, and discipline. Discontented lower clergy appealed to the higher authority of Rome against the disciplinary measures of local bishops. In the second half of the thirteenth century bishops and abbots protested such undercutting of their power. To its critics the church in Rome seemed hardly more than a legalized, fiscalized, bureaucratic institution. As early as the late twelfth century, heretical movements of Cathars and Waldensians had appealed to the biblical ideal of simplicity and separation from the world as opposed to a perceived materialism in official religion against which reformers loyal to the church, such as St. Francis of Assisi, would also protest.

The church of the thirteenth century was

being undermined by more than internal religious disunity. The demise of imperial power meant that the papacy in Rome was no longer the leader of antiimperial (Guelf, or propapal) sentiment in Italy. Instead of being the center of Italian resistance to the emperor, popes now found themselves on the defensive against their old allies. That was the ironic price paid by the papacy to vanquish the Hohenstaufens.

Rulers with a stake in Italian politics now directed the intrigue formerly aimed at the emperor toward dominating the college of cardinals. Charles of Anjou, king of Sicily, for example, managed to create a French-Sicilian faction within the college. Such efforts to control the decisions of the college led Pope Gregory X (1271–1276) to establish the so-called conclave of cardinals. This was the practice of sequestering the cardinals immediately on the death of the pope so that extraneous political influence on the election of new popes might be kept to a minimum. But the conclave proved to be of little avail, so politicized had the college of cardinals become.

In 1294 such a college, in frustration after a deadlock of over two years, chose a saintly but inept Calabrian hermit as Pope Celestine V. Celestine abdicated under suspicious circumstances after only a few weeks in office and also died under suspicious circumstances (his successor's critics later argued that he had been murdered to ensure the unity of the papal office). His tragicomic reign shocked a majority of the college into unified affirmative action. He was quickly replaced by his very opposite, Pope Boniface VIII (1294–1303), a nobleman and a skilled politician, whose pontificate, however, saw the beginning of the end of papal pretensions to great power status.

Boniface VIII and Philip the Fair

Boniface came to rule when England and France were maturing as nation-states. In England a long tradition of consultation between the king and powerful members of English society evolved into formal "parliaments" during the reigns of Henry III (1216–1272) and Edward I (1272–1307), and these Parliaments

Pope Boniface VIII (1294–1303) *who opposed the taxation of clergy by the kings of France and England and issued one of the strongest declarations of papal authority, the bull* Unam Sanctam. *The statue is in the Museo Civico, Bologna, Italy.* [*Alinari/SCALA*]

helped to create a unified kingdom. The reign of the French king Philip IV the Fair (1285–1314) saw France become an efficient, centralized monarchy. Philip was no Saint Louis, but a ruthless politician intent on ending England's continental holdings, controlling wealthy Flanders, and establishing French hegemony within the Holy Roman Empire. Boniface had the further misfortune of bringing to the papal throne memories of the way earlier popes had brought kings and emperors to their knees. Very painfully he was to discover that the papal monarchy of the early thirteenth century was no match for the new political powers of the late thirteenth century.

France and England were on the brink of all-out war when Boniface became pope (1294). Only Edward I's preoccupation with rebellion in Scotland, which the French encouraged, prevented a full-scale English invasion of France around the turn of the century—a turn of events that would have started the Hundred Years' War a half century earlier. As both countries mobilized for war, they used the pretext of preparing for a Crusade to tax the clergy heavily. In 1215 Pope Innocent III had decreed that the clergy were to pay no taxes to rulers without prior papal consent. Viewing English and French taxation of the clergy as an assault on traditional clerical rights, Boniface took a strong stand against it. On February 5, 1296, he issued a bull, *Clericis Laicos,* which forbade lay taxation of the clergy without prior papal approval and took back all previous papal dispensations in this regard.

In England Edward I retaliated by denying the clergy the right to be heard in royal court, in effect removing from them the protection of the king. But it was Philip the Fair who struck back with a vengeance. In August 1296 he forbade the exportation of money from France to Rome, thereby denying the papacy revenues without which it could not operate. Boniface had no choice but to come quickly to terms with Philip. He conceded Philip the right to tax the French clergy "during an emergency," and, not coincidentally, he canonized Louis IX in the same year.

Boniface was at this time also under siege by powerful Italian enemies, whom Philip did not fail to patronize. A noble family (the Colonnas), rivals of Boniface's family (the Gaetani) and radical followers of Saint Francis of Assisi (the Spiritual Franciscans), were at this time seeking to invalidate Boniface's election as pope on the grounds that Celestine V had resigned the office under coercion. Charges of heresy, simony, and even the murder of Celestine, who had died shortly after his abdication, were hurled against Boniface.

In the year 1300 Boniface's fortunes appeared to revive. Tens of thousands of pilgrims flocked to Rome in that year for the Jubilee celebration. In a Jubilee year all Catholics who visited Rome and there fulfilled certain conditions received a special indulgence, or remission of their sins. Heady with this display of popular religiosity, Boniface reinserted himself into international politics. He championed Scottish resistance to England, for which he received a firm rebuke from an outraged Edward I and from Parliament.

But once again a confrontation with the king of France proved the more costly. Philip, seemingly spoiling for another fight with the pope, arrested Boniface's Parisian legate, Bernard Saisset, the bishop of Pamiers and also a powerful secular lord, whose independence Philip had opposed. Saisset was accused of heresy and treason and was tried and convicted in the king's court. Thereafter Philip demanded that Boniface recognize the process against Saisset, something that Boniface could do only if he was prepared to surrender his jurisdiction over the French episcopate. This challenge could not be sidestepped, and Boniface acted swiftly to champion Saisset as a defender of clerical political independence within France. He demanded Saisset's unconditional release, revoked all previous agreements with Philip in the matter of clerical taxation, and ordered the French bishops to convene in Rome within a year. A bull, *Ausculta Fili* ("Listen, My Son"), was sent to Philip in December 1301, pointedly informing him that "God has set popes over kings and kingdoms."

Unam Sanctam (1302). Philip unleashed a ruthless antipapal campaign. Two royal apologists, Pierre Dubois and John of Paris, refuted papal claims to the right to intervene in temporal matters. Increasingly placed on the defensive, Boniface made a last-ditch stand against state control of national churches when on November 18, 1302, he issued the bull *Unam Sanctam.* This famous statement of papal power declared that temporal authority was "subject" to the spiritual power of the church. On its face a bold assertion, *Unam Sanctam* was in truth the desperate act of a besieged papacy.

After *Unam Sanctam* the French and the

Boniface VIII Reasserts the Church's Claim to Temporal Power

Defied by the French and the English, Pope Boniface VIII (1294–1303) boldly reasserted the temporal power of the church in the bull *Unam Sanctam* (November 1302). This document claimed that both spiritual and temporal power on earth were under the pope's jurisdiction, because, in the hierarchy of the universe, spiritual power both preceded and sat in judgment on temporal power.

We are taught by the words of the Gospel that in this church and in her power there are two swords, a spiritual one and a temporal one. . . . Certainly anyone who denies that the temporal sword is in the power of Peter has not paid heed to the words of the Lord when he said, ''Put up thy sword into its sheath'' (Matthew 26:52). Both then are in the power of the church, the material sword and the spiritual. But the one is exercised for the church, the other by the church, the one by the hand of the priest, the other by the hand of kings and soldiers, though at the will and suffrance of the authority subject to the spiritual power. . . . For, according to the blessed Dionysius, it is the law of divinity for the lowest to be led to the highest through intermediaries. In the order of the universe all things are not kept in order in the same fashion and immediately but the lowest are ordered by the intermediate and inferiors by superiors. But that the spiritual power excels any earthly one in dignity and nobility we ought the more openly to confess in proportion as spiritual things excel temporal ones. Moreover we clearly perceive this from the giving of tithes, from benediction and sanctification, from the acceptance of this power and from the very government of things. For, the truth bearing witness, the spiritual power has to institute the earthly power and to judge it if it has not been good. So it is verified the prophecy of Jeremiah (1:10) concerning the church and the power of the church, ''Lo, I have set thee this day over the nations and over kingdoms.''

Brian Tierney, *The Crisis of Church and State* 1050–1300 (Englewood Cliffs, N.J.: Prentice-Hall, 1964), pp. 188–189.

Colonnas moved against Boniface with force. Guillaume de Nogaret, Philip's chief minister, denounced Boniface to the French clergy as a common heretic and criminal. An army, led by Nogaret and Sciarra Colonna, surprised the pope in mid-August 1303 at his retreat in Anagni. Boniface was badly beaten up and almost executed before an aroused populace liberated and returned him safely to Rome. But the ordeal proved too much for the pope, who died a few months later, in October 1303.

Boniface's immediate successor, Benedict XI (1303–1304), excommunicated Nogaret for his deed, but there was to be no lasting papal retaliation. Benedict's successor, Clement V (1305–1314), was forced into French subservience. A former archbishop of Bordeaux, Clement declared that *Unam Sanctam* should not be understood as in any way diminishing French royal authority. He released Nogaret from excommunication and pliantly condemned the Knights Templars, whose treasure Philip thereafter forcibly expropriated. Clement established the papal court at Avignon, on the southeastern border of France, in 1309. The imperial city of Avignon, situated on land that belonged to the pope, maintained its independence from the king. In 1311 Clement made the city his permanent residence, both to escape a Rome ridden with strife after the confrontation between Boniface and Philip, and also to escape pressure from Philip. There the papacy was to remain until 1377.

After Boniface's humiliation popes never again so seriously threatened kings and emperors, despite continuing papal excommunications and political intrigue. In the future the relation between Church and State would tilt toward state control of religion within particular monarchies and the subordination of ecclesiastical authority to larger secular political purposes.

Palace of the popes in Avignon, France. In 1311 Clement V made the city his permanent residence, and the popes remained there until 1377.

Petrarch Describes the Papal Residence at Avignon

Petrarch, the father of Humanism, lived in Avignon and personally observed the papacy there over a long period of time. In this letter written between 1340 and 1353, he described with deep, pious outrage the ostentation and greed of the Avignon popes.

I am now living in [Avignon], in the Babylon of the West. . . . Here reign the successors of the poor fishermen of Galilee [who] have strangely forgotten their origin. I am astounded, as I recall their predecessors, to see these men loaded with gold and clad in purple, boasting of the spoils of princes and nations; to see luxurious palaces and heights crowned with fortifications, instead of a boat turned downwards for [their] shelter. We no longer find the simple nets which were once used to gain a frugal living from the lake of Galilee. . . . One is stupefied nowadays to hear the lying tongues, and to see worthless parchments turned by a leaden seal [i.e., official bulls of the pope] into nets which are used, in Christ's name, but by the arts of Belial [i.e., the devil], to catch hordes of unwary Christians. These fish, too, are dressed and laid on the burning coals of anxiety before they fill the insatiable maw of their captors.

Instead of holy solitude we find a criminal host and crowds . . . ; instead of sobriety, licentious banquets . . . ; instead of pious pilgrimages . . . foul sloth; instead of the bare feet of the apostles . . . horses decked in gold. . . . In short, we seem to be among the kings of the Persians or Parthians, before whom we must fall down and worship, and who cannot be approached except presents be offered.

James Harvey Robinson (Ed.), *Readings in European History,* Vol. 1 (Boston: Athenaeum, 1904), pp. 502–530.

The Avignon Papacy (1309–1377)

The Avignon papacy was in appearance, although not always in actual fact, under strong French influence. During Clement V's pontificate the French came to dominate the college of cardinals. Clement also expanded papal taxes, especially the practice of collecting annates, the first year's revenue of a church office or benefice bestowed by the pope—a practice that contributed much to the Avignon papacy's reputation as being materialistic and politically motivated.

POPE JOHN XXII. Pope John XXII (1316–1334), the most powerful Avignon pope, tried to restore papal independence and return to Italy. This goal led him into war with the Visconti, the most powerful ruling family of Milan, and a costly contest with Emperor Louis IV, whose election as emperor in 1314 John had challenged in favor of the rival Habsburg candidate. The result was a minor replay of the confrontation between Philip the Fair and Boniface VIII. When John obstinately and without legal justification refused to recognize Louis's election, the emperor retaliated by declaring John deposed and setting in his place an antipope. As Philip the Fair had also done, Louis enlisted the support of the Spiritual Franciscans, whose views on absolute poverty John had condemned as heretical. Two outstanding pamphleteers wrote lasting tracts for the royal cause: William of Ockham, whom John excommunicated in 1328, and Marsilius of Padua (ca. 1290–1342/43), whose teaching John declared heretical in 1327.

MARSILIUS OF PADUA. In his *Defender of Peace* (1324), Marsilius of Padua stressed the independent origins and autonomy of secular government. Clergy were subjected to the strictest apostolic ideals and confined to purely spiritual functions, and all power of coercive judgment was denied the pope. Marsilius argued that spiritual crimes must await an eter-

Marsilius of Padua Denies Coercive Power to the Clergy

According to Marsilius, the Bible gave the pope no right to pronounce and execute sentences on any person. The clergy held a strictly moral and spiritual rule, their judgments to be executed only in the afterlife, not in the present one. Here, on earth, they should be obedient to secular authority. Marsilius argued this point by appealing to the example of Jesus.

We now wish . . . to adduce the truths of the holy Scripture . . . which explicitly command or counsel that neither the Roman bishop called pope, nor any other bishop or priest, or deacon, has or ought to have any rulership or coercive judgment or jurisdiction over any priest or non-priest, ruler, community, group, or individual of whatever condition. . . . Christ himself came into the world not to dominate men, nor to judge them [coercively] . . . not to wield temporal rule, but rather to be subject as regards the . . . present life; and moreover, he wanted to and did exclude himself, his apostles and disciples, and their successors, the bishops or priests, from all coercive authority or worldly rule, both by his example and by his word of counsel or command. . . . When he was brought before Pontius Pilate . . . and accused of having called himself king of the Jews, and [Pilate] asked him whether he had said this . . . [his] reply included these words . . . "My kingdom is not of this world," that is, I have not come to reign by temporal rule or dominion, in the way . . . worldly kings reign. . . . This, then, is the kingdom concerning which he came to teach and order, a kingdom which consists in the acts whereby the eternal kingdom is attained, that is, the acts of faith and the other theological virtues; not however, by coercing anyone thereto.

Marsilius of Padua: The Defender of Peace: The Defensor Pacis, trans. by Alan Gewirth (New York: Harper, 1967), pp. 113–116.

nal punishment. Transgressions of divine law, over which the pope had jurisdiction, were to be punished in the next life, not in the present one, unless the secular ruler declared a divine law also a secular law. This assertion was a direct challenge of the power of the pope to excommunicate rulers and place countries under interdict. The *Defender of Peace* depicted the pope as a subordinate member of a society over which the emperor ruled supreme and in which temporal peace was the highest good.

John XXII made the papacy a sophisticated international agency and adroitly adjusted it to the growing European money economy. The more the Curia (or papal court) mastered the latter, however, the more vulnerable it became to criticism. Under John's successor, Benedict XII (1334–1342), the papacy became entrenched in Avignon. Seemingly forgetting Rome altogether, Benedict began construction of the great Palace of the Popes and attempted to reform both papal government and the religious life. His high-living French successor, Clement VI (1342–1352), placed papal policy in lockstep with the French. In this period the cardinals became barely more than lobbyists for policies favorable to their secular patrons.

National Opposition to the Avignon Papacy. As Avignon's fiscal tentacles probed new areas, monarchies took strong action to protect their interests. The latter half of the fourteenth century saw legislation restricting papal jurisdiction and taxation in France, England, and Germany. In England, where the Avignon papacy was identified with the French enemy after the outbreak of the Hundred Years' War, statutes of *provisors* and *praemunire,* which restricted payments and appeals to Rome, were several times passed by Parliament between 1351 and 1393. In France ecclesiastical appointments and taxation were regulated by the so-called Gallican liberties. These national rights over religion had long been exercised in fact and were legally acknowledged by the church in the Pragmatic Sanction of Bourges in 1438. This agreement recognized the right of the French church to elect its own clergy without papal interference, prohibited the payment of annates to Rome, and limited the right of appeals from French courts to the Curia in Rome. In German and Swiss cities in the fourteenth and fifteenth centuries, local governments also took the initiative to limit and even to overturn traditional clerical privileges and immunities.

John Wycliffe and John Huss. The popular lay religious movements that most successfully assailed the late medieval church were the Lollards in England and the Hussites in Bohemia. Both John Wycliffe (d. 1384) and John Huss (d. 1415) would have disclaimed the extremists who revolted in their name, yet Wycliffe's writings gave at least a theoretical justification to the demands of the Lollards and Huss's writings to the programs of both moderate and extreme Hussites.

Wycliffe's work initially served the anticlerical policies of the English government. An Oxford theologian and a philosopher of high standing, Wycliffe became within England what William of Ockham and Marsilius of Padua had been at the Bavarian court of Emperor Louis IV: a major intellectual spokesman for the rights of royalty against the secular pretensions of popes. After 1350 English kings greatly reduced the power of the Avignon papacy to make ecclesiastical appointments and collect taxes within England, a position that Wycliffe strongly supported. His views on clerical poverty followed original Franciscan ideals and, more by accident than by design, gave justification to government restriction and even confiscation of church properties within England. Wycliffe argued that the clergy "ought to be content with food and clothing." He also maintained that personal merit, not rank and office, was the only basis of religious authority—a dangerous teaching because it raised allegedly pious laypeople above allegedly corrupt ecclesiasts, regardless of the latter's official stature. There was a threat in such teaching to secular as well as to ecclesiastical dominion and jurisdiction. At his posthumous condemnation by the pope, Wycliffe was accused of the ancient heresy of Donatism—the teaching that the efficacy of the church's sacraments did not lie in their sheer performance but also depended on the moral character of the clergy who administered them. Wycliffe also anticipated certain Protestant criticisms of the medieval church by challenging papal infallibility, the sale of indulgences, and the dogma of transubstantiation.

English advocates of Wycliffe's teaching were called *Lollards*. Like the Waldensians, they preached in the vernacular, disseminated translations of Holy Scripture, and championed clerical poverty. At first, they came from every social class, being especially prominent among the groups that had something tangible to gain from the confiscation of clerical properties (the nobility and the gentry) or that had suffered most under the current church system (the lower clergy and the poor people). After the English Peasants' Revolt of 1381, an uprising filled with egalitarian notions that could find support in Wycliffe's teaching, Lollardy was officially viewed as subversive. Opposed by an alliance of church and crown, it became a capital offense in England by 1401.

Heresy was not so easily harnessed in Bohemia, where it coalesced with a strong national movement. The University of Prague, founded in 1348, became the center for both Czech nationalism and a native religious reform movement. The latter began within the bounds of orthodoxy and was led by local intellectuals and preachers, the most famous of whom was John Huss, the rector of the university after 1403. The reformers supported vernacular translations of the Bible and were critical of traditional ceremonies and allegedly superstitious practices, particularly those relating to the sacrament of the Eucharist. They advocated lay communion with cup as well as bread (traditionally only the priest received communion with both cup and bread, the laity with bread only, a sign of the clergy's spiritual superiority over the laity), taught that bread and wine remained bread and wine after priestly consecration, and questioned the validity of sacraments performed by priests in mortal sin. Wycliffe's teaching appears to have influenced the movement very early. Regular traffic between England and Bohemia had existed for decades, ever since the marriage in 1381 of Anne of Bohemia to King Richard II. Czech students studied at Oxford, and many returned with copies of Wycliffe's writings.

Huss became the leader of the pro-Wycliffe faction at the University of Prague, and in 1410 his activities brought about his excommunication and the placement of Prague under papal interdict. In 1414 Huss won an audience with the newly assembled Council of Constance. He journeyed to the council eagerly, armed with a safe-conduct pass from Emperor Sigismund, and naively believing that he would convince his strongest critics of the truth of his teaching. Within weeks of his arrival in early November 1414, he was formally accused of heresy and imprisoned. He died at the stake on July 6, 1415, and was followed there less than a year later by his colleague Jerome of Prague. The reaction in Bohemia to the execution of these national heroes was fierce revolt as militant Hussites, the Taborites, set out to transform Bohemia by force into a religious and social paradise under the military leadership of John Ziska. After a decade of belligerent protest, the Hussites won significant religious reforms and control over the Bohemian church from the Council of Basel.

A German portrayal of the burning of John Huss for heresy. His ashes were dumped into the Rhine to prevent their becoming relics. [*Vincent Virga Archives*]

The Great Schism (1378–1417) *and the Conciliar Movement to* 1449

Urban VI and Clement VII. Pope Gregory XI (1370–1378) reestablished the papacy in Rome in January 1377, ending what had come to be known as the "Babylonian Captivity" of the church in Avignon, the reference being to the biblical bondage of the Israelites. The return to Rome proved to be shortlived, however. On Gregory's death on March 27, 1378, the cardinals, in Rome, elected an Italian archbishop as Pope Urban VI (1378–1389), who immediately proclaimed his intention to reform the Curia. This announcement came as an unexpected challenge to the cardinals, most of whom were French, and made them amenable to royal pressures to return the papacy to Avignon. The French king, Charles V, not wanting to surrender the benefits of a papacy located within the sphere of French influence, lent his support to a schism. Five months after Urban's election, on September 20, 1378, thirteen cardinals, all but one of whom was French, formed their own conclave and elected a cousin of the French king as Pope Clement VII (1378–1397). They insisted, probably with some truth, that they had voted for Urban in fear of their lives, surrounded by a Roman mob that demanded the election of an Italian pope. Be that as it may, thereafter the papacy became a "two-headed thing" and a scandal to Christendom. Allegiance to the two papal courts divided along political lines: England and its allies (the Holy Roman Empire, Hungary, Bohemia, and Poland) acknowledged Urban VI, whereas France and its orbit (Naples, Scotland, Castile, and Aragon) supported Clement VII. Only the Roman line of popes, however, came to be recognized as official in subsequent church history.

Two approaches were initially taken to end the schism. One tried to win the mutual cession of both popes, thereby clearing the way for a new election of a single pope. The other sought to secure the resignation of the one in favor of the other. Both proved completely fruitless, however. Each pope considered himself fully legitimate, and too much was at stake for a magnanimous concession on the part of either. There was one way left: the forced deposition of both popes by a special council of the church.

Conciliar Theory of Church Government. Legally a church council could be convened only by a pope, and the competing popes were not inclined to summon a council for their own deposition. Also, the deposition of a legitimate pope against his will by a council of the church was as serious a matter as the forced dethronement of a legally recognized hereditary monarch by a representative body.

The correctness of a conciliar deposition of a pope was debated a full thirty years before any direct action was taken. Conciliar theorists, chief among whom were the masters of the University of Paris, Conrad of Gelnhausen, Henry of Langenstein, Jean Gerson, and Pierre d'Ailly, challenged the popes' identification of the church's welfare with their own and developed arguments in favor of a more representative government of the church; their goal was a church in which a representative council could effectively regulate the actions of the pope. Conciliarists defined the church as the whole body of the faithful, a body of which the elected head, the pope, was only one part, and a part whose sole purpose was to maintain the unity and well-being of the body as a whole—something that the schismatic popes were far from doing. The conciliarists further argued that a council of the church, as a Holy Spirit–inspired spokesman for a majority of the faithful, acted with greater authority than the pope alone. In the eyes of the pope(s) such a concept of the church threatened both its political and its religious unity.

The Council of Pisa (1409–1410). On the basis of such arguments, cardinals representing both sides convened a council on their own authority in Pisa in 1409. There they deposed both the Roman and the Avignon popes and elected in their stead a new pope, Alexander V. To the council's consternation neither pope accepted its action, and after 1409 Christendom confronted the spectacle of three contending popes. Although the vast majority of Latin Christendom did at this time accept Alexander and his Pisan successor John XXIII (1410–1415), the popes of Rome and Avignon refused to step down.

The Council of Constance (1414–1417). This intolerable situation ended when the emperor Sigismund prevailed on John XXIII to summon a "legal" council of the church in Constance in 1414, a council also recognized by the Roman pope Gregory XII. Gregory, however, soon resigned his office, raising grave doubts forevermore about whether the council was truly convened with Rome's blessing and hence valid. In a famous declaration entitled *Haec Sancta,* the council fathers asserted their supremacy and proceeded to conduct the business of the church. In November 1417 the council successfully accomplished its main business when it elected a new pope, Martin V (1417–1431), after the

The Chronicler Calls the Roll at the Council of Constance

The Council of Constance, in session for three years (1414–1417), not only drew many clergy and political representatives into its proceedings but also required a great variety of supporting personnel. Here is an inventory from the contemporary chronicle by Ulrich Richental.

Pope John XXIII came with 600 *men.*
Pope Martin, who was elected pope at Constance, came with 30 *men.*
5 *patriarchs, with* 118 *men.*
33 *cardinals, with* 3,056 *men.*
47 *archbishops, with* 4,700 *men.*
145 *bishops, with* 6,000 *men.*
93 *suffragan bishops, with* 360 *men.*
Some 500 *spiritual lords, with* 4,000 *men.*
24 *auditors and secretaries, with* 300 *men.*
37 *scholars from the universities of all nations, with* 2,000 *men.*
217 *doctors of theology from the five nations, who walked in the processions, with* 2,600 *men.*
361 *doctors of both laws, with* 1,260 *men.*
171 *doctors of medicine, with* 1,600 *men.*
1,400 *masters of arts and licentiates, with* 3,000 *men.*
5,300 *simple priests and scholars, some by threes, some by twos, some alone.*
The apothecaries who lived in huts, with 300 *men. (*16 *of them were masters.)*
72 *goldsmiths, who lived in huts.*
Over 1,400 *merchants, shopkeepers, furriers, smiths, shoemakers, innkeepers, and handworkers, who lived in huts and rented houses and huts, with their servants.*
24 *rightful heralds of the King, with their squires.*
1,700 *trumpeters, fifers, fiddlers, and players of all kinds.*
Over 700 *harlots in brothels came, who hired their own houses, and some who lay in stables and wherever they could, beside the private ones whom I could not count.*
In the train of the Pope were 24 *secretaries with* 200 *men,* 16 *doorkeepers,* 12 *beadles who carried silver rods,* 60 *other beadles for the cardinals, auditors and auditors of the camera, and many old women who washed and mended the clothes of the Roman lords in private and public.*
132 *abbots, all named, with* 2,000 *men.*
155 *priors, all recorded with their names, with* 1,600 *men.*
Our lord King, two queens, and 5 *princely ladies.*
39 *dukes,* 32 *princely lords and counts,* 141 *counts,* 71 *barons, more than* 1,500 *knights, more than* 20,000 *noble squires.*
Embassies from 83 *kings of Asia, Africa, and Europe, with full powers; envoys from other lords without number, for they rode in and out every day. There were easily* 5,000.
472 *envoys from imperial cities.*
352 *envoys from baronial cities.*
72,460 *persons.*

Richental's *Chronicle of the Council, Constance,* in *The Council of Constance,* ed., by J. H. Mundy and K. M. Woodey, trans. by Louise R. Roomis (New York: Columbia University Press, 1961), pp. 189–190.

three contending popes had either resigned (Gregory XIII) or were deposed (Benedict XIII and John XXIII). The council made provisions for regular meetings of church councils, scheduling a general council of the church for purposes of reform within five, then seven, and thereafter every ten years. Constance has remained, however, an illegitimate church council in official eyes; nor are the schismatic popes of Avignon and Pisa recognized as legitimate (for this reason, another pope could take the name John XXIII in 1958).

The Council of Basel (1431–1449). Conciliar government of the church both peaked and declined during the Council of Basel. In 1432 the council invited the Hussites to send a delegation to Basel to make peace.

The Council of Constance Declares Conciliar Supremacy

The decree *Haec Sancta* (April 1415) asserted the supremacy of councils over popes in time of emergency in the church. This was the legal basis on which the Council of Constance proceeded to remove the contending popes from power and end the schism by electing a new pope, Martin V (1417–1431).

This holy Council of Constance . . . declares, first that it is lawfully assembled in the Holy Spirit, that it constitutes a General Council, representing the Catholic Church, and that therefore it has its authority immediately from Christ; and that all men, of every rank and condition, including the pope himself, are bound to obey it in matters concerning the Faith, the abolition of the schism, and the reformation of the Church of God in its head and its members. Secondly, it declares that anyone, of any rank and condition, who shall contumaciously refuse to obey the orders, decrees, statutes or instructions, made or to be made by this holy Council, or by any other lawfully assembled general council . . . shall, unless he comes to a right frame of mind, be subjected to fitting penance and punished appropriately: and, if need be, recourse shall be had to the other sanctions of the law.

From *Documents of the Christian Church,* ed. by Henry Bettenson (New York: Oxford University Press, 1961), pp. 192–193.

The Hussites presented a doctrinal statement known as the *Four Articles of Prague,* which served as a basis for the negotiations. This document contained requests for (1) giving the laity the Eucharist with cup as well as bread (hence their name *Utraquists,* from the Latin word meaning "both," and *Calixtines,* from the Latin word for "cup"); (2) free, itinerant preaching; (3) the exclusion of the clergy from holding secular offices and possessing property; and (4) just punishment of clergy who have committed mortal sins. In November 1433 an agreement was reached between the emperor, the council, and the Hussites. The Bohemian church received jurisdictional rights similar to those already secured by France and England. Three of the four Prague articles were conceded: communion with cup, free preaching by ordained clergy, and like punishment of clergy and laity for mortal sins. The church firmly retained the right to possess and dispose of property.

THE COUNCIL OF FERRARA–FLORENCE (1438–1439). The termination of the Hussite wars and the reform legislation curtailing the papal power of appointment and taxation were the high points of the Council of Basel. Heady with success, the Basel council seemed to its critics to assert its powers beyond the original intention of the decrees of Constance and in doing so undermined much internal and external support. Original supporters of the council, prominent among them the philosopher Nicholas of Cusa, turned their backs on the council when Pope Eugenius IV (1431–1447) ordered it to transfer to Ferrara in 1437. The pope had a golden opportunity to upstage the Council of Basel by negotiating a reunion with the Eastern church, which was bargaining for Western aid against new Turkish advances. A majority of Basel's members refused to transfer to Ferrara, and their defiance made Basel a schismatic council. Those in Basel watched while the reunion of the Eastern and Western churches was proclaimed in Florence, where the council of Ferrara had transferred because of plague, in 1439. This agreement, although short-lived, restored papal prestige and signaled the demise of the conciliar movement.

The notion of conciliar superiority suffered a mortal blow with the collapse of the Council of Basel in 1449. A decade later the papal bull *Execrabilis* (1460) condemned appeals to councils as "erroneous and abominable" and "completely null and void."

Although many who had worked for reform

now despaired of ever attaining it, the conciliar movement was not a total failure. It planted deep within the conscience of all Western peoples the conviction that the leader of an institution must be responsive to its members and that the head exists to lead and serve, not to bring disaster on, the body.

A second consequence of the conciliar movement was the devolving of religious responsibility on the laity. In the absence of papal leadership, secular control of national or territorial churches increased. Kings asserted power over the church in England and France. Magistrates and city councils reformed and regulated religious life in German, Swiss, and Italian cities. This development was not reversed by the powerful "restoration" popes of the high Renaissance. On the contrary, as the papacy became a limited territorial regime, national control of the church simply ran apace. Perceived as just one among several Italian states, the Papal States could be opposed as much on the grounds of "national" policy as for religious reasons.

Revival of Monarchy: Nation Building in the Fifteenth Century

After 1450 there was a progressive shift from divided feudal to unified national monarchies as "sovereign" rulers emerged. This is not to say that the dynastic and chivalric ideals of feudal monarchy did not continue. Territorial princes did not pass from the scene, and representative bodies persisted and in some areas even grew in influence. But in the late fifteenth and early sixteenth centuries the old problem of the one and the many was decided clearly in favor of the interests of monarchy.

The feudal monarchy of the high Middle Ages was characterized by the division of the basic powers of government between the king and his semiautonomous vassals. The nobility and the towns acted with varying degrees of unity and success through such evolving representative assemblies as the English Parliament, the French Estates General, and the Spanish Cortes to thwart the centralization of royal power. Because of the Hundred Years' War and the schism in the church, the nobility and the clergy were in decline in the late Middle Ages. The increasingly important towns began to ally with the king. Loyal, business-wise townspeople, not the nobility and the clergy, staffed the royal offices and became the king's lawyers, bookkeepers, military tacticians, and foreign diplomats. It was this new alliance between king and town that finally broke the bonds of feudal society and made possible the rise of sovereign states.

In a sovereign state the power of taxation, war making, and law enforcement is no longer the local right of semiautonomous vassals but is concentrated in the monarch and is exercised by his or her chosen agents. Taxes, wars, and laws become national rather than merely regional matters. Only as monarchs were able to act independently of the nobility and the representative assemblies could they overcome the decentralization that had been the basic obstacle to nation building. Ferdinand and Isabella rarely called the Cortes into session. The French Estates General did not meet at all from 1484 to 1560. Henry VII (1485–1509) of England managed to raise revenues without going begging to Parliament after Parliament voted him customs revenues for life in 1485. Monarchs were also assisted by brilliant theorists, from Marsilius of Padua in the fourteenth century to Machiavelli and Jean Bodin in the sixteenth, who eloquently argued the sovereign rights of monarchy.

The many were, of course, never totally subjugated to the one, and still today the cry of "states' rights" is very distinct. But in the last half of the fifteenth century, rulers increasingly demonstrated that the law was their creature. Civil servants whose vision was no longer merely local or regional filled royal offices. In Castile they were the *corregidores,* in England the justices of the peace, in France bailiffs operating through well-drilled lieutenants. These royal ministers and agents were not immune to becoming closely attached to the localities they administered in the ruler's name. And regions were able to secure congenial royal appointments. Throughout England local magnates served as representatives of the Tudors. Nonetheless these new executives were truly *royal* executives, bureaucrats whose outlook was "national" and whose loyalty was to the "state."

Monarchies also began to create standing national armies in the fifteenth century. As the noble cavalry receded and the infantry and the artillery became the backbone of the armies, mercenary soldiers were recruited from Switzerland and Germany to form the major part of the "king's army." Professional soldiers who fought for pay and booty proved far more efficient than feudal vassals who fought simply for honor's sake. Monarchs who failed to meet their payrolls, however, faced a new danger of mutiny and banditry on the part of alien troops.

The more expensive warfare of the fifteenth and sixteenth centuries increased the need to develop new national sources of royal income. The expansion of royal revenues was especially hampered by the stubborn belief among the highest classes that they were immune from government taxation. The nobility guarded their properties and traditional rights and despised taxation as an insult and a humiliation. Royal revenues accordingly grew at the expense of those least able to resist, and least able to pay. The monarchs had several options. As feudal lords they could collect rents from their royal domain. They could also levy national taxes on basic food and clothing, such as the *gabelle* or salt tax in France and the *alcabala* or 10 per cent sales tax on commercial transactions in Spain. The rulers could also levy direct taxes on the peasantry. This they did through agreeable representative assemblies of the privileged classes in which the peasantry did not sit. The *taille*, which the French kings independently determined from year to year after the Estates General was suspended in 1484, was such a tax. Sale of public offices and issuance of high-interest government bonds appeared in the fifteenth century as innovative fund-raising devices. But rulers did not levy taxes on the powerful nobility. They turned to rich nobles, as they did to the great bankers of Italy and Germany, for loans, bargaining with the privileged classes, who in many instances remained as much the kings' creditors and competitors as their subjects.

France

Charles VII (1422–1461) was a king made great by those who served him. His ministers created a professional army, which—thanks initially to the inspiration of Joan of Arc—drove the English out of France. And largely because of the enterprise of an independent merchant banker named Jacques Coeur, the French also developed a strong economy, diplomatic corps, and national administration during Charles VII's reign. These were the sturdy tools with which Charles's successor, the ruthless Louis XI (1461–1483), made France a great power.

There were two cornerstones of French nation-building in the fifteenth century. The first was the collapse of the English empire in France following the Hundred Years' War. The second was the defeat of Charles the Bold and the duchy of Burgundy. Perhaps Europe's strongest political power in the mid-fifteenth century, Burgundy aspired to dwarf both France and the Holy Roman Empire as the leader of a dominant middle kingdom. It might have succeeded in doing so had not the continental powers joined together in opposition. When Charles the Bold died in defeat in a battle at Nancy in 1477, the dream of Burgundian empire died with him. Louis XI and Habsburg Emperor Maximilian I divided the conquered Burgundian lands between them, with the treaty-wise Habsburgs getting the better part. The dissolution of Burgundy ended its constant intrigue against the French king and left Louis XI free to secure the monarchy. The newly acquired Burgundian lands and his own Angevin inheritance permitted the king to end his reign with a kingdom almost twice the size of that with which he had started. Louis successfully harnessed the nobility, expanded the trade and industry so carefully nurtured by Jacques Coeur, created a national postal system, and even established a lucrative silk industry at Lyons (later transferred to Tours).

A strong nation is a two-edged sword. It was because Louis's successors inherited such a secure and efficient government that France was able to pursue Italian conquests in the 1490s and to fight a long series of losing wars with the Habsburgs in the first half of the sixteenth century. By the mid-sixteenth century France was again a defeated nation and almost as divided internally as during the Hundred Years' War.

Spain

Spain, too, became a strong country in the late fifteenth century. Both Castile and Aragon had been poorly ruled and divided kingdoms in the mid-fifteenth century. The union of Isabella of Castile (1474–1504) and Ferdinand of Aragon (1479–1516) changed that situation. The two future sovereigns married in 1469, despite strong protests from neighboring Portugal and France, both of which foresaw the formidable European power such a union would create. Castile was by far the richer and more populous of the two, having an estimated five million inhabitants to Aragon's population of under one million. Castile was also distinguished by its lucrative sheep-farming industry, which was run by a government-backed organization called the *Mesta*, another example of developing centralized economic planning. Although the two kingdoms were dynastically united by the marriage of Ferdinand and Isabella in 1469, they remained constitutionally separated, as each retained its respective government agencies—separate laws, armies, coinage, and taxation—and cultural traditions.

Ferdinand and Isabella could do together what neither was able to accomplish alone: subdue their realms, secure their borders, and venture abroad militarily. Between 1482 and 1492 they conquered the Moors in Granada. Naples became a Spanish possession in 1504. By 1512 Ferdinand had secured his northern borders by conquering the kingdom of Navarre. Internally Ferdinand and Isabella won the allegiance of the Hermandad, a powerful league of cities and towns, which served them against stubborn landowners. Townspeople allied themselves with the crown and progressively replaced the nobility within the royal administration. The crown also extended its authority over the wealthy chivalric orders, a further circumscription of the power of the nobility.

Spain had long been remarkable among European lands as a place where three religions—Islam, Judaism, and Christianity—coexisted with a certain degree of toleration. This toleration was to end dramatically under Ferdinand and Isabella, who made Spain the prime example of state-controlled religion. Ferdinand and Isabella exercised almost total control over the Spanish church as they placed religion in the service of national unity. They appointed the higher clergy and the officers of the Inquisition. The Inquisition, run by Tomás de Torquemada (d. 1498), Isabella's confessor, was a key national agency established in 1479 to monitor the activity of converted Jews *(conversos)* and Muslims *(Moriscos)* in Spain. In 1492 the Jews were exiled and their properties were confiscated. In 1502 nonconverting Moors in Granada were driven into exile by Cardinal Francisco Jiménez de Cisneros (1437–1517), the great spiritual reformer and educator. Spanish spiritual life remained largely uniform and successfully controlled—a major reason for Spain's remaining a loyal Catholic country throughout the sixteenth century and providing a base of operation for the European Counter-Reformation.

Ferdinand (1479–1516) *and Isabella* (1474–1504), *from the royal chapel in the Cathedral of Granada. Their marriage in* 1469, *which joined the kingdoms of Aragon and Castile, made Spain a united nation.* [*Robert Frerck*]

Despite a certain internal narrowness, Ferdinand and Isabella were rulers with wide horizons. They contracted anti-French marriage alliances that came to determine a large part of European history in the sixteenth century. In 1496 their eldest daughter, Joanna, later known as "the Mad," married Archduke Philip, the son of Emperor Maximilian I. The fruit of this union, Charles I of Spain, the first ruler over a united Spain, came by his inheritance and election as emperor in 1519 to rule over a European kingdom almost equal in size to that of Charlemagne. A second daughter, Catherine of Aragon, wed Arthur, the son of the English King Henry VII, and after Arthur's premature death, she married his brother, the future King Henry VIII. The failure of this latter marriage became the key factor in the emergence of the Anglican church and the English Reformation.

The new Spanish power was also revealed in Ferdinand and Isabella's promotion of overseas exploration. Their patronage of the Genoese adventurer Christopher Columbus (1451–1506), who discovered the islands of the Caribbean while sailing west in search of a shorter route to the spice markets of the Far East, led to the creation of the Spanish empire in Mexico and Peru, whose gold and silver mines helped to make Spain Europe's dominant power in the sixteenth century.

England

The last half of the fifteenth century was a period of especially difficult political trial for the English. Following the Hundred Years' War, a defeated England was subjected to internal warfare between two rival branches of the royal family, the House of York and the House of Lancaster. This conflict, known to us today as the War of the Roses (as York's symbol, according to legend, was a white rose, and Lancaster's a red rose), kept England in turmoil from 1455 to 1485.

The Lancastrian monarchy of Henry VI (1422–1461) was consistently challenged by the duke of York and his supporters in the prosperous southern towns. In 1461 Edward IV (1461–1483), son of the duke of York, successfully seized power and instituted a strong-arm rule that lasted over twenty years, being only briefly interrupted in 1470–1471 by Henry VI's short-lived restoration. Edward, assisted by loyal and able ministers, effectively bent Parliament to his will. His brother and successor was Richard III (1483–1485). During the reign of the Tudors a tradition arose that painted Richard III as an unprincipled villain who murdered Edward's sons in the Tower of London to secure the throne. The best-known version of this characterization—unjust according to some—is found in Shakespeare's *Richard III.* Be that as it may, Richard's reign saw the growth of support for the exiled Lancastrian Henry Tudor. Henry returned to England to defeat Richard on Bosworth Field in August 1485.

Henry Tudor ruled as Henry VII (1485–1509), the first of the new Tudor dynasty that would dominate England throughout the sixteenth century. In order to bring the rival royal families together and to make the hereditary claim of his offspring to the throne uncontestable, Henry married Edward IV's daughter, Elizabeth of York. He succeeded in disciplining the English nobility through a special instrument of the royal will known as the *Court of Star Chamber.* Created in 1487 with the sanction of Parliament, this court enabled the king to act quickly and decisively against his opponents. Henry shrewdly construed legal precedents to the advantage of the crown, using English law to further his own ends. He managed to confiscate noble lands and fortunes with such success that he governed without dependence on Parliament for royal funds, always a cornerstone of strong monarchy. In these ways Henry began to shape a monarchy that would develop into one of early modern Europe's most exemplary governments during the reign of his granddaughter, Elizabeth I.

The Holy Roman Empire

Germany and Italy were the striking exceptions to the steady development of centralized nation-states in the last half of the fifteenth century. Unlike England, France, and Spain, the empire saw the many thoroughly repulse the one. In Germany territorial rulers and cities resisted every effort at national consolidation and unity. As in Carolingian times rulers continued to partition their kingdoms, however small, among their sons, and by the late fifteenth century Germany was hopelessly divided into some three hundred autonomous political entities.

The princes and the cities did work together to create the machinery of law and order, if not of union, within the divided empire. An agreement reached between the emperor and the major German territorial rulers in 1356, known as the *Golden Bull,* established a seven-member electoral college consisting of the archbishops of Mainz, Trier, and Cologne; the duke of Saxony; the margrave of Brandenburg; the count Palatine; and the king of Bohemia. This group also functioned as an administrative body. They elected the emperor and, in cooperation with him, provided what transregional unity and administration existed. The figure of the emperor gave the empire a single ruler in law, if not in actual fact. As the conditions of his rule and the extent of his powers over his subjects, especially the seven electors, were renegotiated with every imperial election, the rights of the many (the princes) were always balanced against the power of the one (the emperor). In the fifteenth century an effort was made to control incessant feuding by the creation of an imperial diet (*Reichstag*). This was a national assembly of the seven electors, the nonelectoral princes, and the sixty-five imperial free cities. The cities were the weakest of the three bodies represented in the diet. During such an assembly in Worms in 1495, the members won from the emperor, Maximilian I (1493–1519), concessions that had been suc-

Emperor Maximilian (1493–1519) *and his family, painted in* 1515 *by Bernard Strigel. Note the prominent Habsburg chin of the middle child.* [*Kunsthistoriches Museum, Vienna*]

cessfully resisted by his predecessor, Frederick III (1440–1493). Led by Berthold of Henneberg, the archbishop of Mainz, the Diet of Worms secured an imperial ban on private warfare, a court of justice (the *Reichskammergericht*) to enforce internal peace, and an imperial Council of Regency (the *Reichsregiment*) to coordinate imperial and internal German policy. The latter was very grudgingly conceded by the emperor because it gave the princes a share in executive power.

Although important, these reforms were still a poor substitute for true national unity. In the sixteenth and seventeenth centuries the territorial princes became virtually sovereign rulers in their various domains. Such disunity aided religious dissent and conflict. It was in the cities and territories of still-feudal, fractionalized, backward Germany that the Protestant Reformation broke out in the sixteenth century.

The Renaissance in Italy (1375–1527)

In his famous study, *Civilization of the Renaissance in Italy* (1860), Jacob Burckhardt described the Renaissance as the prototype of the modern world. He believed that it was in fourteenth- and fifteenth-century Italy, through the revival of ancient learning, that new secular and scientific values first began to supplant traditional religious beliefs. This was the period in which people began to adopt a rational, objective, and statistical approach to reality and to rediscover the importance of the individual and his or her artistic creativity. The result, in Burckhardt's words, was a release of the "full, whole nature of man."

Other scholars have found Burckhardt's description far too modernizing an interpretation of the Renaissance and have accused him of overlooking the continuity between the Middle Ages and the Renaissance. His critics especially stress the still strongly Christian character of Humanism and the fact that earlier "renaissances," especially that of the twelfth century, also revived the ancient classics, professed interest in Latin language and Greek science, and appreciated the worth and creativity of individuals.

Despite the exaggeration and bias of Burckhardt's portrayal of the Renaissance, most scholars agree that the Renaissance was a time of transition from the medieval to the modern world. Medieval Europe, especially before the twelfth century, had been a fragmented feudal society with an agriculturally based economy, and its thought and culture were largely dominated by the church. Renaissance Europe, especially after the fourteenth century, was characterized by growing national consciousness and political centralization, an urban economy based on organized commerce and capitalism, and ever greater lay and secular control of thought and culture, including religion.

It was especially in Italy between the late fourteenth and the early sixteenth centuries, from roughly 1375 to 1527, the year of the infamous sack of Rome by imperial soldiers, that the distinctive features and achievements of the Renaissance, which also deeply influenced northern Europe (see Chapter 10), are most strikingly revealed.

The Italian City-State: Social Conflict and Despotism

Renaissance society was no simple cultural transformation. It first took distinctive shape within the cities of late medieval Italy. Italy had always had a cultural advantage over the rest of Europe because its geography made it the natural gateway between East and West. Venice, Genoa, and Pisa traded uninterruptedly with the Near East throughout the Middle Ages and maintained vibrant urban societies.

When commerce revived on a large scale in the eleventh century, Italian merchants quickly mastered the business skills of organization, bookkeeping, scouting new markets, and securing monopolies. During the thirteenth and fourteenth centuries trade-rich cities expanded to become powerful city-states, dominating the political and economic life of the surrounding countryside. By the fifteenth century the great Italian cities had become the bankers of much of Europe.

The growth of Italian cities and urban culture was assisted by the endemic warfare between the emperor and the pope and the Guelf (propapal) and Ghibelline (proimperial) factions that this warfare had created. Either of these might have successfully challenged the cities had they permitted the other to concentrate on it. They chose instead to weaken one another and thus strengthened the merchant oligarchies of the cities. Unlike in northern Europe, where the cities tended to be dominated by kings and territorial princes, the great Italian cities were left free to expand into states. They became independent states, absorbing the surrounding countryside and assimilating the area's nobility in a unique urban meld of old and new rich. There were five such major, competitive states in Italy; the duchy of Milan; the republics of Florence and Venice; the Papal States; and the kingdom of Naples (see Map 9.3).

Social strife and competition for political power were so intense within the cities that,

An Italian bank in the late fourteenth century. By 1400, the great Italian cities had become the bankers of much of Europe. [*Mansell Collection*]

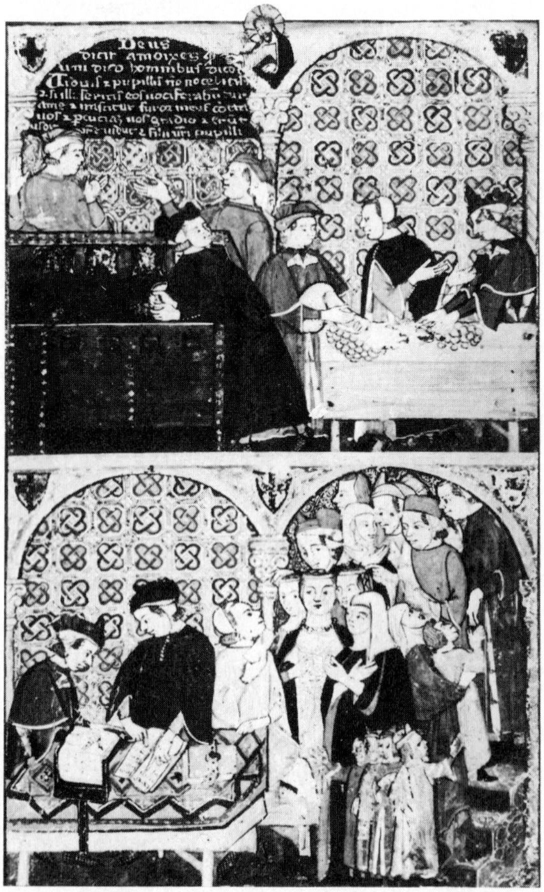

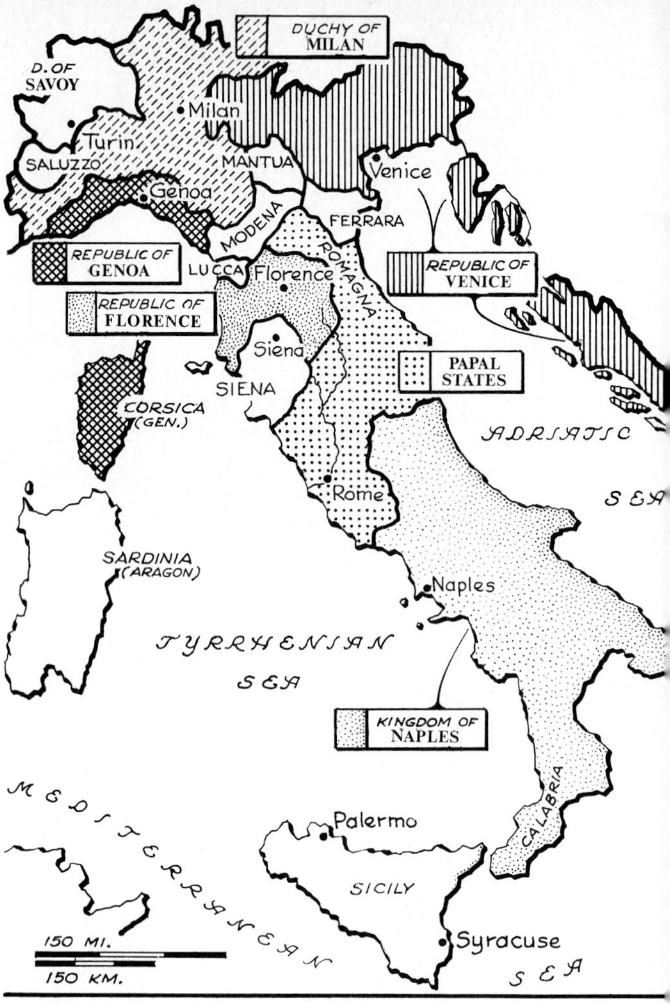

RENAISSANCE ITALY

MAP 9–3 *The city-states of Renaissance Italy were self-contained principalities whose internal strife was monitored by their despots and whose external aggression was long successfully controlled by treaty.*

for sheer survival's sake, most evolved into despotisms by the fifteenth century. Venice was the notable exception to this rule. It was ruled by a successful merchant oligarchy with power located in a patrician senate of 300 members and a ruthless judicial body, the Council of Ten, that anticipated and suppressed rival groups. Elsewhere the new social classes and divisions within society produced by rapid urban growth fueled chronic, near-anarchic conflict.

Florence was the most striking example. There were four distinguishable social groups within the city. The first was the old rich, or *grandi*, the nobles and merchants who traditionally ruled the city. The second group was the emergent new-rich merchant class, capitalists and bankers known as the *popolo grosso*, or "fat people." They began to challenge the old rich for political power in the late thirteenth and early fourteenth centuries. Then there were the middle-burgher ranks of guild-masters, shopowners, and professionals, those smaller businessmen who, in Florence as elsewhere, tended to take the side of the new rich against the conservative policies of the old rich. Finally, there was the *popolo minuto*, the little people, the lower middle classes. In 1457 one third of the population of Florence, about thirty thousand people, were officially listed as paupers.

Florentine women at work. Needlework, spinning, and weaving took up much of a woman's time, and contributed to the elegance of dress for which both male and female Florentines were famed. [*Alinari*]

These social divisions produced conflict at every level of society, to which was added the ever-present fear of foreign intrigue. In 1378 feuding between the old and the new rich combined with the social pressures of the Black Death, which cut the city's population almost in half, and with the collapse of the banking houses of Bardi and Peruzzi, to ignite a great revolt by the poor. It was known as the

The Duomo, or Cathedral of Florence. One of the masterpieces of Renaissance architecture, it was begun in 1296 *and completed in* 1461. *The famous campanile, or bell tower, which stands to one side of the front of the Cathedral, was begun by Giotto in* 1334. [*EPA*]

Ciompi Revolt and established a chaotic four-year reign of power by the lower Florentine classes. True stability did not return to Florence until the ascent to power in 1434 of Cosimo de' Medici (1389–1464).

Cosimo de' Medici, the wealthiest Florentine and an astute statesman, controlled the city internally from behind the scenes, skillfully manipulating the constitution and influencing elections. Florence was governed by a council of six (later eight) members known as the *Signoria*. These men were chosen from the most powerful guilds—those representing the major clothing industries (cloth, wool, fur, and silk) and such other groups as bankers, judges, and doctors. Through his informal, cordial relations with the electoral committee, Cosimo was able to keep councillors loyal to him in the *Signoria*. As head of the Office of Public Debt, he was able to favor congenial factions. His grandson Lorenzo the Magnificent (1449–1492) ruled Florence in almost totalitarian fashion during the last quarter of the fifteenth century, having been made cautious by the assassination of his brother in 1478 by a rival Florentine family, the Pazzi, who plotted with the pope against Medici rule.

Despotism was less subtle elsewhere. In order to prevent internal social conflict and foreign intrigue from paralyzing their cities, the dominant groups cooperated to install a hired strongman, known as a *podestà*, for the purpose of maintaining law and order. He was given executive, military, and judicial authority, and his mandate was direct and simple: to permit, by whatever means required, the normal flow of business activity without which not the old rich, the new rich, or the poor of a city could long survive. Because these despots could not depend on the divided populace, they operated through mercenary armies, which they obtained through military brokers known as *condottieri*. It was a hazardous job. Despots were not only subject to dismissal by the oligarchies that hired them, but they were also popular objects of assassination attempts. However, the spoils of success were very great. In Milan it was as despots that the Visconti family came to power in 1278 and the Sforza family in 1450, both ruling without constitutional restraints or serious political competition. The latter produced one of Machiavelli's heroes, Ludovico il Moro.

Political turbulence and warfare gave birth to diplomacy, by which the various city-states were able to stay abreast of foreign military developments and, if shrewd enough, to gain power and advantage short of actually going to war. Most city-states established resident embassies in the fifteenth century, and their ambassadors not only represented them in ceremonies and as negotiators but also became their watchful eyes and ears at rival courts.

A terra cotta bust of Lorenzo de' Medici by the sculptor Andrea del Verrocchio (ca. 1435–1488). [*National Gallery of Art, Washington; Samuel H. Kress Collection*]

Whether within the comparatively tranquil republic of Venice, the strong-arm democracy of Florence, or the undisguised despotism of Milan, the disciplined Italian city proved a most congenial climate for an unprecedented flowering of thought and culture. Italian Renaissance culture was promoted as vigorously by despots as by republicans and by secularized popes as enthusiastically as by the more spiritually minded. Such widespread support resulted from the fact that the main requirement for patronage of the arts and letters was the one thing that Italian cities of the high Renaissance had in abundance: great wealth.

Humanism

There are several schools of thought on the essence of Humanism. Those who follow the nineteenth-century historian Jacob Burckhardt, who saw the Italian Renaissance as the birth of modernity, view it as an unchristian philosophy that stressed the dignity of humankind and championed individualism and secular values.Others argue that Humanists were

The Striding God from Artemisium. This bronze statue dated about 460 B.C. was found in the sea near Artemisium, at the northern tip of the large Greek island of Euboea. Exactly whom the statue represents is not known. Some have thought him to be Poseidon holding a trident; others believe that he is Zeus hurling a thunderbolt. In either case he is a brilliant representative of the early classical period of Greek sculpture and is now located in the Greek National Archaeological Museum in Athens. [Art Resource]

The Athenian Acropolis. The Acropolis in Athens was both a religious and a civic center. In the second half of the fifth century B.C., *Pericles and his successors crowned it with three major temples and a grand entrance building. This picture taken from the northwest shows the reconstructed remains of all the major buildings. The Parthenon, in the upper center, dominates the picture as it does the Acropolis and the city of Athens. In front of it is the entrance building called the Propylaea. At the extreme right is the small temple to Nike (Victory). On the extreme left is the Erechtheum with its famous porch of columns in the shape of young women.* [*Art Resource*]

OPPOSITE: *The Roman Forum. Originally a marketplace, the Roman Forum was the civic center of Rome from its earliest days. It contained many public buildings and temples which were frequently altered and improved or torn down and replaced. Most of the buildings in this picture are from the Imperial period.* [*Art Resource*]

C-3

Rehearsal of a Satyr Play Depicted in a Roman Mosaic. The satyr play was a Greek art form that originally accompanied a trilogy of tragedies. It was a comic piece in which a chorus confronted the god Dionysus. It became popular among the Romans in its own right, and wealthy Romans often presented a satyr play as part of the entertainment at elaborate banquets. This mosaic from the Villa of Cicero at Pompeii shows actors and musicians preparing for a performance. [*Art Resource*]

A Street in Herculaneum. Herculaneum was a provincial town just east of Naples. It lay along the lower slopes of Mt. Vesuvius and was destroyed along with Pompeii in the terrible and famous eruption of A.D. 79. *Since both towns were well preserved by the covering lava, excavations have given us a good idea of the appearance and daily life of Roman Italy.* [*Art Resource*]

Ships in the Harbor of Puteoli. This painting of ships moored in the port of Puteoli, a Campanian city on the Bay of Naples, comes from Herculaneum. It now hangs at the National Museum in Naples. [*Art Resource*]

The Colosseum at Rome. The Romans called this building the Flavian Amphitheatre because it was built by three successive emperors of the Flavian family—begun by Vespasian (r. 69–79), *dedicated in* A.D. 80 *by his son Titus* (r. 79–81), *and finished by his younger son Domitian* (r. 81–96). *How it acquired its present name is uncertain; it may come from its great size or from its proximity to a colossal statue of the Emperor Nero. Said to have been built by prisoners from the Jewish War* (A.D. 66–70), *it held 50,000 spectators for the animal hunts, gladiatorial combats, mock sea battles, and other spectacles held in it.* [*Art Resource*]

A reconstruction of imperial Rome. At its peak in the third century A.D., *Rome may well have had more than one million inhabitants, far more than any other city of the ancient world. The large open space in the center beyond the Tiber River is the Circus Maximus, a race course for chariots, which could hold as many as 250,000 spectators. The Coliseum is beyond it. The buildings between the two arenas make up the Roman forum.* [*Art Resource*]

''Good Government'' in Siena. Ambrogio Lorenzetti was an Italian painter who worked in Siena during the fourteenth century. His most famous works are the frescoes of the Hall of Peace (Sala della Pace) of the Public Palace in Siena painted in 1338–1339. They present two allegories, ''Good Government'' and ''Bad Government,'' and four compositions showing the effects of each on city and country. This section shows the results of good government in both city and country: amid general prosperity, merchants and travelers come and go peacefully, while maidens dance unmolested in the city streets (lower left corner). [Art Resource]*

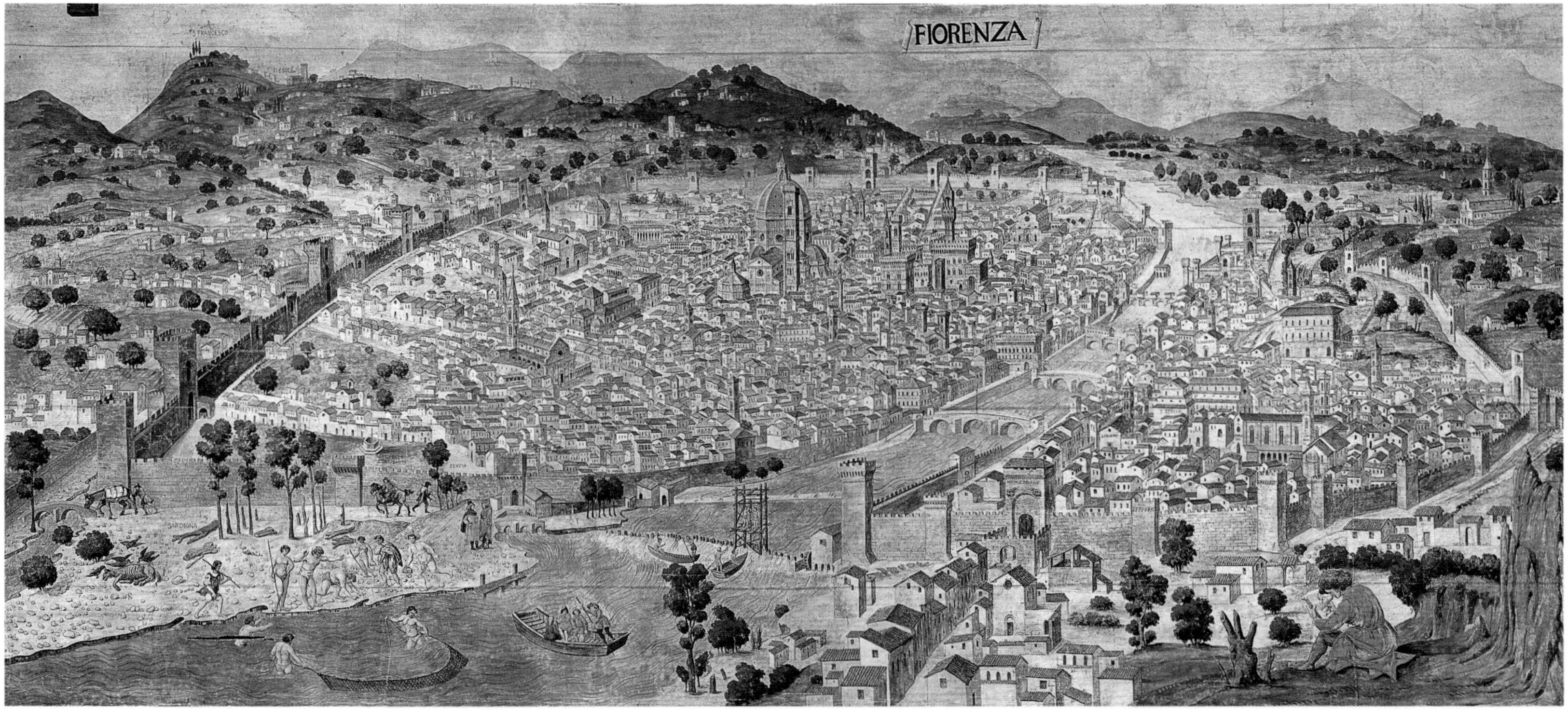

A fourteenth-century depiction of Florence, the center of Renaissance civilization in Italy. The cathedral and major public buildings are shown in the center of the city of the left bank of the Arno River. [*Art Resource*]

The Baptistry, Dome of the Cathedral, and Bell Tower at Florence. Perhaps the peak of medieval architecture is represented by this complex of buildings that make up the cathedral group at Florence. The Cathedral with its great dome by Filippo Brunelleschi comes chiefly from the fourteenth century; the Bell Tower (Campanile) was built in the mid-fourteenth century by Giotto, and the Baptistry still earlier, in the eleventh century, though some details were added in the fifteenth century. [*Art Resource*]

The Gates of Paradise, by Ghiberti. These doors, now located on the east side of the Baptistry at Florence, were designed and executed by Lorenzo Ghiberti (1378–1455), one of the early Florentine humanists. In 1401 he won a competition for the commission of a second pair of doors on the Baptistry. After finishing these in 1424 he agreed to make still a third pair, the "Gates of Paradise," ten panels containing some thirty-seven scenes from the Old Testament. The two sets of doors occupied him for about half a century. The two panels shown in close up here depict the stories of Noah (upper) and Esau (lower). [Art Resource]

The Street of the Wool and Silk Merchants in Bologna. This miniature from an illuminated manuscript dated to 1470 *shows the street of the wool and silk merchants in Bologna. Like most cities of the Italian Renaissance, Bologna was heavily engaged in the commerce and manufacture of textiles.* [*Art Resource*]

A Visit from the Doctor. These scenes of a physician attending a patient comes from the mid-fifteenth century. It is an illustration on a manuscript of the great Canon of Medicine *by Avicenna (980–1047), a Muslim physician and philosopher. His* Canon, *a summary of Arabic and ancient Greek medical knowledge, was translated into Latin in the twelfth century and became the chief European medical book. The manuscript is in the University Library in Bologna. [Art Resource]*

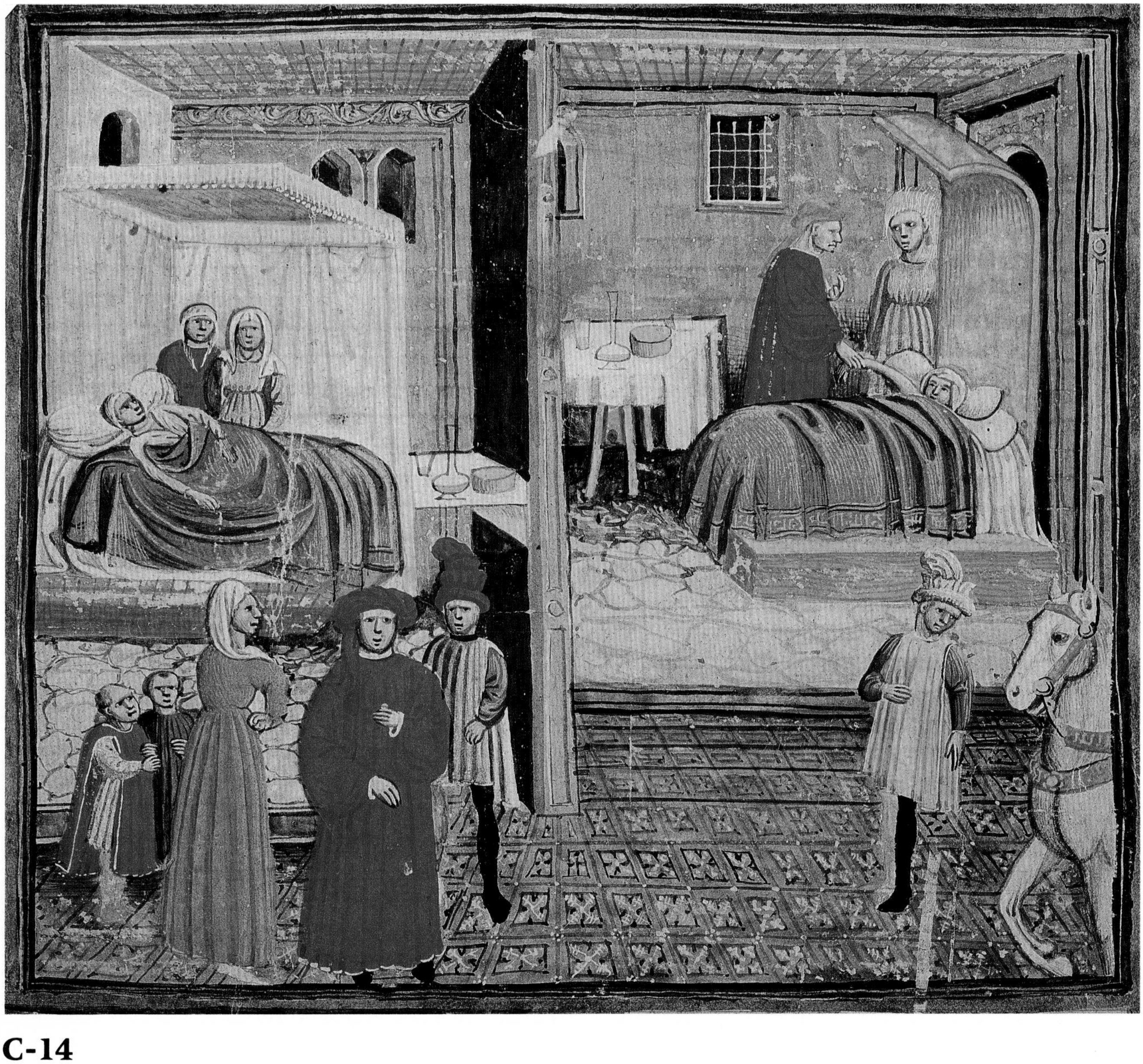

A Renaissance Pharmacy. This depiction of a pharmacy comes from the same illustrated manuscript of Avicenna's Canon of Medicine *made in the fifteenth century. Pharmacists, like other professionals in the Middle Ages and Renaissance, belonged to a guild. The assistants shown on the right mixing medicine were apprentices, living as well as working with the master-pharmacist.* [*Art Resource*]

The main altar of St. Peter's, Rome. The elaborate bronze baldachino or canopy over the altar was designed by Gian Lorenzo Bernini (1598–1680) *to be the focal point of the basilica's vast interior space.* [*Art Resource*]

the very champions of authentic Catholic Christianity, who opposed the pagan teaching of Aristotle and the ineloquent Scholasticism that his writings nurtured. Still others see Humanism as a form of scholarship consciously designed to promote a sense of civic responsibility and political liberty. One of the most authoritative modern commentators, Paul O. Kristeller, has accused all these views of dealing more with the secondary effects than with the essence of Humanism. Humanism, he believes, was no particular philosophy or value system but simply an educational program concentrated on rhetoric and sound scholarship for their own sake.

There is truth in each of these definitions. Humanism was the scholarly study of the Latin and Greek classics and the ancient Church Fathers both for their own sake and in the hope of a rebirth of ancient norms and values. Humanists were advocates of the *studia humanitatis,* a liberal arts program of study that embraced grammar, rhetoric, poetry, history, politics, and moral philosophy. Not only were these subjects considered a joy in themselves, they were also seen as celebrating the dignity of humankind and preparing people for a life of virtuous action. The Florentine Leonardo Bruni (1374–1444) first gave the name *humanitas* ("humanity") to the learning that resulted from such scholarly pursuits. Bruni was a student of Manuel Chrysoloras, a Byzantine scholar who opened the world of Greek scholarship to a generation of young Italian Humanists when he taught at Florence between 1397 and 1403.

The first Humanists were orators and poets. They wrote original literature, in both the classical and the vernacular languages, inspired by and modeled on the newly discovered works of the ancients, and they taught rhetoric within the universities. When Humanists were not employed as teachers of rhetoric, their talents were sought as secretaries, speech writers, and diplomats in princely and papal courts.

The study of classical and Christian antiquity

Petrarch's Letter to Posterity

In old age Petrarch wrote a highly personal letter to posterity in which he summarized the lessons he had learned during his lifetime. The letter also summarizes the original values of Renaissance Humanists: their suspicion of purely materialistic pleasure, the importance they attached to friendship, and their utter devotion to and love of antiquity.

I have always possessed extreme contempt for wealth; not that riches are not desirable in themselves, but because I hate the anxiety and care which are invariably associated with them . . . I have, on the contrary, led a happier existence with plain living and ordinary fare. . . .

The pleasure of dining with one's friends is so great that nothing has ever given me more delight than their unexpected arrival, nor have I ever willingly sat down to table without a companion. . . .

The greatest kings of this age have loved and courted me. . . . I have fled, however, from many . . . to whom I was greatly attached; and such was my innate longing for liberty that I studiously avoided those whose very name seemed incompatible with the freedom I loved.

I possess a well-balanced rather than a keen intellect—one prone to all kinds of good and wholesome study, but especially to moral philosophy and the art of poetry. The latter I neglected as time went on, and took delight in sacred literature. . . . Among the many subjects that interested me, I dwelt especially upon antiquity, for our own age has always repelled me, so that, had it not been for the love of those dear to me, I should have preferred to have been born in any other period than our own. In order to forget my own time, I have constantly striven to place myself in spirit in other ages, and consequently I delighted in history. . . .

If only I have lived well, it matters little to me how I have talked. Mere elegance of language can produce at best but an empty fame.

Frederic A. Ogg (Ed.), *A Source Book of Mediaeval History* (New York: American Book Company, 1908), pp. 470–473.

Petrarch (1304–1374) *is considered to be the father of humanism.* [*Roger-Viollet*]

existed before the Italian Renaissance. There were recoveries of ancient civilization during the Carolingian renaissance of the ninth century, within the cathedral school of Chartres in the twelfth century, during the great Aristotelian revival in Paris in the thirteenth century, and among the Augustinians in the early fourteenth century. However, these precedents only partially compare with the grand achievements of the Italian Renaissance of the late Middle Ages. The latter was far more secular and lay-dominated, possessed much broader interests, was blessed with far more recovered manuscripts, and was endowed with far superior technical skills than had been the case in the earlier "rebirths" of antiquity. Unlike their Scholastic rivals, Humanists were less bound to recent tradition; their method was not to summarize and compare the views of recognized authorities on a text or question, but to go directly to the original source itself and draw their own conclusions. Avidly searching out manuscript collections, Italian Humanists made the full sources of Greek and Latin antiquity available to scholars during the fourteenth and fifteenth centuries. Mastery of Latin and Greek was the surgeon's tool of the Humanist. There is a kernel of truth—but only a kernel—in the arrogant boast of the Humanists that the period between themselves and classical civilization was a "dark middle age."

PETRARCH, DANTE, AND BOCCACCIO. Francesco Petrarch (1304–1374) was the father of Humanism. He left the legal profession to pursue his love of letters and poetry. Although most of his life was spent in and around Avignon, he became caught up in Cola di Rienzo's popular revolt and two-year reign (1347–1349) in Rome as "tribune" of the Roman people. He also served the Visconti family in Milan in his later years. Petrarch celebrated ancient Rome in his *Letters to the Ancient Dead,* fancied personal letters to Cicero, Livy, Vergil, and Horace. He also wrote a Latin epic poem (*Africa,* a poetic historical tribute to the Roman general Scipio Africanus) and a set of biographies of famous Romans (*Lives of Illustrious Men*). His critical textual studies, elitism, and contempt for the allegedly useless learning of the Scholastics were features that many later Humanists also shared. Petrarch's most famous contemporary work was a collection of highly introspective love sonnets to a certain Laura, a married woman whom he romantically admired from a safe distance. Classical and Christian values coexist, not always harmoniously, in his work, and this uneasy coexistence is

Dante Aligheri (1265–1321). *This drawing is considered the most authentic likeness of the poet. Dante's* Divine Comedy *was one of the first works to appear in Italian. Its style so influenced subsequent writers that Dante has been called the creator of modern literary Italian.* [*National Library, Florence*]

true, too, of many later Humanists. Medieval Christian values can be seen in Petrarch's imagined dialogues with Saint Augustine and in tracts written to defend the personal immortality of the soul against the Aristotelians. Petrarch was, however, far more secular in orientation than his famous near contemporary Dante Alighieri (1265–1321), whose *Vita Nuova* and *Divine Comedy* form with Petrarch's sonnets the cornerstones of Italian vernacular literature. Petrarch's student and friend Giovanni Boccaccio (1313–1375), author of the *Decameron,* one hundred bawdy tales told by three men and seven women in a country retreat from the plague that ravaged Florence in 1348, was also a pioneer of Humanist studies. An avid collector of manuscripts, Boccaccio also assembled an encyclopedia of Greek and Roman mythology.

EDUCATIONAL REFORMS AND GOALS. The goal of Humanist studies was to be wise and to speak eloquently, both to know what is good and to practice virtue. Learning was not to remain abstract and unpracticed. "It is better to will the good than to know the truth," Petrarch had taught, and this became a motto of many later Humanists. Pietro Paolo Vergerio (1349–1420) left a classic summary of the Humanist concept of a liberal education:

> We call those studies liberal which are worthy of a free man; those studies by which we attain and practice virtue and wisdom; that education which calls forth, trains, and develops those highest gifts of body and mind which ennoble men and which are rightly judged to rank next in dignity to virtue only, for to a vulgar temper, gain and pleasure are the one aim of existence, to a lofty nature, moral worth and fame.[1]

The ideal of a useful education and well-rounded people inspired far-reaching reforms in traditional education. Quintilian's *Education of the Orator,* the full text of which was discovered by Poggio Bracciolini (d. 1459) in 1416, became the basic classical guide for the Humanist revision of the traditional curriculum. The most influential Renaissance tract on education, Vergerio's *On the Morals That Befit a Free Man,* was written directly from classical models. Vittorino da Feltre (d. 1446) was a teacher who not only directed his students to a highly disciplined reading of Pliny, Ptolemy, Terence, Plautus, Livy, and Plutarch but also combined vigorous physical exercise and games with intellectual pursuits. Another educator, Guarino da Verona (d. 1460), rector of the new University of Ferrara and a student of the Greek scholar Manuel Chrysoloras, streamlined the study of classical languages and gave it systematic form. Baldassare Castiglione's (1478–1529) famous *Book of the Courtier,* written for the cultured nobility at the court of Urbino, also embodied the highest ideals of Italian Humanism. It stressed the importance of integrating knowledge of language and history with athletic, military, and musical skills, as well as good manners and moral character.

Humanists were not bashful scholars. They delighted in going directly to primary sources. They refused to be slaves of tradition, satisfied, as they felt their Scholastic rivals to be, with the commentaries of the accepted masters. Such an attitude not only made Humanists innovative educators but also kept them constantly in search of new sources of information. Poggio Bracciolini and Francesco Filelfo (d. 1481) assembled magnificent manuscript collections.

THE FLORENTINE ACADEMY AND THE REVIVAL OF PLATONISM. Of all the important recoveries of the past made during the Italian Renaissance, none stands out more than the revival of Greek studies, especially the works of Plato, in fifteenth-century Florence. Many factors combined to bring this revival about. An important foundation was laid in 1397 when the city invited Manuel Chrysoloras to come from Constantinople and promote Greek learning. A half century later (1439), the ecumenical Council of Ferrara–Florence, having convened to negotiate the reunion of the Eastern and Western churches, opened the door for many Greek scholars and manuscripts to enter the West. After the fall of Constantinople to the Turks in 1453, Greek scholars fled to Florence for refuge. This was the background against which the Florentine Platonic Academy evolved under the patronage of Cosimo de' Medici and the supervision of Marsilio Ficino (1433–1499) and Pico della Mirandola (1463–1494).

Although the thinkers of the Renaissance were interested in every variety of ancient wisdom, they seemed to be especially attracted to the Platonic tradition and to those Church Fathers who tried to synthesize Platonic philoso-

[1]Cited by De Lamar Jensen, *Renaissance Europe: Age of Recovery and Reconciliation* (Lexington, Mass.: D. C. Health, 1981), p. 111.

phy and Christian teaching. The Florentine Academy, a small villa designed for comfortable discussion, became both a cultic and a scholarly center for the revival of Plato and the Neoplatonists: Plotinus, Proclus, Porphyry, and Dionysius the Areopagite. There Ficino edited and saw to the publication of the complete works of Plato.

The appeal of Platonism lay in its flattering view of human nature. Platonism distinguished between an eternal sphere of being and the perishable world in which humans actually lived. Human reason was believed to belong to the former, indeed, to have preexisted in this pristine world and to continue to commune with it, as the present knowledge of mathematical and moral truth bore witness. Strong Platonic influence can be seen in Pico's *Oration on the Dignity of Man*, perhaps the most famous Renaissance statement on the nature of humankind. Pico wrote the *Oration* as an introduction to a pretentious collection of nine hundred theses, which were published in Rome in December 1486 and were intended to serve as the basis for a public debate on all of life's important topics. The *Oration* drew on Platonic teaching to depict man as the one creature in the world who possessed the freedom to be whatever he or she chose, able at will to rise to the height of angels or to descend to the level of pigs.

Critical Work of the Humanists: Lorenzo Valla. Because they were guided by a scholarly ideal of philological accuracy and historical truthfulness, the Humanists could become critics of tradition even when that was not their intention. Dispassionate critical scholarship shook long-standing foundations, not the least of which were those of the medieval church.

The work of Lorenzo Valla (1406–1457),

Pico della Mirandola States the Renaissance Image of Man

One of the most eloquent descriptions of the Renaissance image of humankind comes from the Italian Humanist Pico della Mirandola (1463–1494). In his famed *Oration on the Dignity of Man* (ca. 1486), Pico described humans as free to become whatever they choose.

The best of artisans [God] ordained that that creature (man) to whom He had been able to give nothing proper to himself should have joint possession of whatever had been peculiar to each of the different kinds of being. He therefore took man as a creature of indeterminate nature and, assigning him a place in the middle of the world, addressed him thus: "Neither a fixed abode nor a form that is thine alone nor any function peculiar to thyself have we given thee, Adam, to the end that according to thy longing and according to thy judgment thou mayest have and possess what abode, what form, and what functions thou thyself shalt desire. The nature of all other beings is limited and constrained within the bounds of laws prescribed by Us. Thou, constrained by no limits, in accordance with thine own free will, in whose hand We have placed thee, shall ordain for thyself the limits of thy nature. We have set thee at the world's center that thou mayest from thence more easily observe whatever is in the world. We have made thee neither of heaven nor of earth, neither mortal nor immortal, so that with freedom of choice and with honor, as though the maker and molder of thyself, thou mayest fashion thyself in whatever shape thou shalt prefer. Thou shalt have the power to degenerate into the lower forms of life, which are brutish. Thou shalt have the power, out of thy soul's judgment, to be reborn into the higher forms, which are divine." O supreme generosity of God the Father, O highest and most marvelous felicity of man! To him it is granted to have whatever he chooses, to be whatever he wills.

Giovanni Pico della Mirandola, *Oration on the Dignity of Man*, in *The Renaissance Philosophy of Man*, ed. by E. Cassirer et al. (Chicago: Phoenix Books, 1961), pp. 224–225.

author of the standard Renaissance text on Latin philology, the *Elegances of the Latin Language* (1444), reveals the explosive character of the new learning. Although a good Catholic, Valla became a hero to later Protestants. His popularity among Protestants stemmed from his defense of predestination against the advocates of free will, and especially from his exposé of the Donation of Constantine, a fraudulent document written in the eighth century alleging that the Emperor Constantine had given vast territories to the pope. The exposé of the Donation was not intended by Valla to have the devastating force that Protestants attributed to it. He only demonstrated in a careful, scholarly way what others had long suspected. Using the most rudimentary textual analysis and historical logic, Valla proved that the document was filled with such anachronistic terms as *fief* and made references that were meaningless in the fourth century. In the same dispassionate way Valla also pointed out errors in the Latin Vulgate, still the authorized version of the Bible for the Roman Catholic church.

Such discoveries did not make Valla any less loyal to the church, nor did they prevent his faithful fulfillment of the office of Apostolic Secretary in Rome under Pope Nicholas V. Nonetheless, historical criticism of this type served those less loyal to the medieval church, and it was no accident that young Humanists formed the first identifiable group of Martin Luther's supporters.

Madonna and Child *by Giotto. Most historians consider Giotto to be the herald of modern Western art. The people in his painting seem strikingly real and alive.* [*National Gallery of Art, Washington, D.C., Samuel H. Kress Collection*]

CIVIC HUMANISM. Italian Humanists were exponents of applied knowledge; their basic criticism of traditional education was that much of its learning was useless. Education, they believed, should promote individual virtue and public service. This ideal inspired what has been called *civic Humanism,* by which is meant examples of Humanist leadership of the political and cultural life, the most striking instance of which was to be found in the city of Florence. There three Humanists served as chancellors: Colluccio Salutati (1331–1406), Leonardo Bruni (ca. 1370–1444), and Poggio Bracciolini (1380–1459). Each used his rhetorical skills to rally the Florentines against the aggression of Naples and Milan. Bruni and Poggio also wrote adulatory histories of the city. Another accomplished Humanist scholar, Leon Battista Alberti (1402–1472), was a noted architect and builder in the city.

On the other hand, many Humanists became clubbish and snobbish, an intellectual elite concerned only with pursuing narrow, antiquarian interests and writing pure, classical Latin in the quiet of their studies. It was in reaction against this elitist trend that the Humanist historians Niccolò Machiavelli (1469–1527) and Francesco Guicciardini (1483–1540) adopted the vernacular and made contemporary history their primary source and subject matter.

Renaissance Art

In Renaissance Italy, as in Reformation Europe, the values and interests of the laity were no longer subordinated to those of the clergy. In education, culture, and religion the laity assumed a leading role and established models for the clergy to imitate. This was a development due in part to the church's loss of its international power during the great crises of the late Middle Ages. But it was also encouraged by the rise of national sentiment, the creation of competent national bureaucracies staffed by the laity rather than clerics, and the rapid growth of lay education during the fourteenth

and fifteenth centuries. Medieval Christian values were adjusting to a more this-worldly spirit. Men and women began again to appreciate and even glorify the secular world, secular learning, and purely human pursuits as ends in themselves.

This new perspective on life is prominent in the painting and sculpture of the high Renaissance—the late fifteenth and early sixteenth centuries, when Renaissance art reached its full maturity. Whereas medieval art tended to be abstract and formulaic, Renaissance art was emphatically concerned with the observation of the natural world and the communication of human emotions. Renaissance artists also attempted to give their works a greater rational (chiefly mathematical) order, a symmetry and proportionality that did justice pictorially to their deeply held belief in the harmony of the universe. The interest of Renaissance artists in ancient Roman art was closely allied to an independent interest in humanity and nature.

Renaissance artists had the advantage of new technical skills developed during the fifteenth century. In addition to the availability of oil paints, two special techniques were perfected: that of using shading to enhance naturalness (chiaroscuro) and that of adjusting the size of figures so as to give the viewer a feeling of continuity with the painting (linear perspective). These techniques permitted the artist to "rationalize" space and paint a more natural world. The result was that, when compared with their flat Byzantine and Gothic counterparts, Renaissance paintings were filled with energy and life and stood out from the canvas in three dimensions.

The new direction was signaled by Giotto (1266–1336), the father of Renaissance painting. An admirer of St. Francis of Assisi, whose love of nature he shared, Giotto painted a more natural world than his Byzantine and Gothic predecessors. Though still filled with religious seriousness, his work was no longer so abstract and unnatural a depiction of the world. The painter Masaccio (1401–1428) and the sculptor Donatello (1386–1466) continued to portray the world around them more literally and

David, *by Donatello* (1386–1466). *This was the first freestanding nude statue sculpted since ancient Rome. Compare Donatello's treatment of David as a young, somewhat delicate youth with Michelangelo's more heroic portrayal of the same theme on page 345.* [*SCALA*]

naturally. The heights were reached by the great masters of the high Renaissance: Leonardo da Vinci (1452–1519), Raphael (1483–1520), and Michelangelo Buonarroti (1475–1564).

LEONARDO DA VINCI. More than any other person in the period, Leonardo exhibited the Renaissance ideal of the universal person. He was a true master of many skills. One of the greatest painters of all time, he was also a military engineer for Ludovico il Moro in Milan, Cesare Borgia in Romagna, and the French king Francis I. Leonardo advocated scientific experimentation, dissected corpses to learn anatomy, and was an accomplished, self-

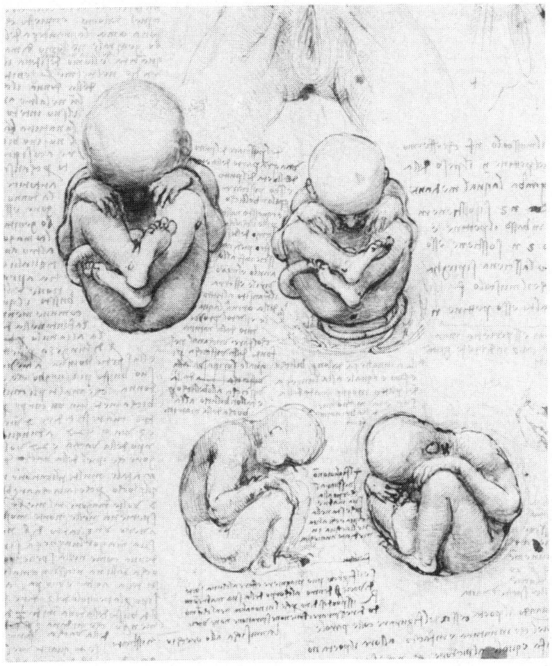

Leonardo da Vinci's drawing of the human fetus. Renaissance artists and scientists, in contrast to medieval artists, began to base their portrayal of the human body on the actual study of it. [The Royal Library, Windsor Castle, by gracious permission of HM the Queen]

A Contemporary Description of Leonardo

Giorgio Vasari (1512–1574), friend and biographer of the great Renaissance painters, sculptors, and architects, described Leonardo's versatility as actually a handicap, as it prevented him from dwelling on one pursuit sufficiently.

The richest gifts are occasionally seen to be showered, as by celestial influence, upon certain human beings; nay, they sometimes supernaturally and marvelously gather in a single person—beauty, grace, and talent united in such a manner that to whatever the man thus favored may turn himself, his every action is so divine as to leave all other men far behind. . . . This was . . . the case of Leonardo da Vinci . . . who had . . . so rare a gift of talent and ability that to whatever subject he turned his attention . . . he presently made himself absolute master of it. . . .

He would without doubt have made great progress in the learning and knowledge of the sciences had he not been so versatile and changeful. The instability of his character led him to undertake many things, which, having commenced, he afterwards abandoned. In arithmetic, for example, he made such rapid progress in the short time he gave his attention to it, that he often confounded the master who was teaching him. . . . He also commenced the study of music and resolved to acquire the art of playing the lute . . . singing to the instrument most divinely. . . .

Being also an excellent geometrician, Leonardo not only worked in sculpture but also in architecture; likewise he prepared . . . designs for . . . entire buildings. . . . While only a youth, he first suggested the formation of a canal from Pisa to Florence by means of certain changes . . . in the river Arno. He made designs for mills, fulling machines, and other engines run by water. But as he had resolved to make painting his profession, he gave the greater part of his time to drawing from nature.

James Harvey Robinson (Ed.), *Readings in European History,* Vol. 1 (Boston: Athenaeum, 1904), pp. 535–536.

The Mona Lisa, *by Leonardo. This is perhaps the most famous painting in Western art. It reveals Leonardo's mastery at conveying inner moods through complex facial features.* [*Art Resource*]

taught botanist. His inventive mind foresaw such modern machines as airplanes and submarines. Indeed, the variety of his interests was so great that it tended to shorten his attention span, so that he was constantly moving from one activity to another. His great skill in conveying inner moods through complex facial features can be seen in the most famous of his paintings, the *Mona Lisa,* as well as in his self-portrait.

RAPHAEL. Raphael, an unusually sensitive man whose artistic career was cut short by his premature death at thirty-seven, was apparently loved by contemporaries as much for his person as for his work. He is famous for his tender madonnas, the best known of which graced the monastery of San Sisto in Piacenza and is now in Dresden. Art historians praise his fresco *The School of Athens,* a grandly conceived portrayal of the great masters of Western philosophy, as one of the most perfect examples of Renaissance technique. It depicts Plato and Aristotle surrounded by the great philosophers and scientists of antiquity, who are portrayed with features of Raphael's famous contemporaries, including Leonardo and Michelangelo.

MICHELANGELO. The melancholy genius Michelangelo also excelled in a variety of arts and crafts. His eighteen-foot godlike sculpture *David,* which long stood majestically in the great square of Florence, is a perfect example of the Renaissance artist's devotion to harmony, symmetry, and proportion, as well as his extreme glorification of the human form. Four different popes commissioned works by Michelangelo, the most famous of which are the frescoes for the Sistine Chapel, painted during

Vasari Describes the Magic of Raphael's Personality

There was among his many extraordinary gifts one of such value and importance that I can never sufficiently admire it and always think thereof with astonishment. This was the power accorded him by heaven of bringing all who approached his presence into harmony, an effect . . . contrary to the nature of our artists. Yet all . . . became as of one mind once they began to labor in the society of Raphael, and they continued in such unity and concord that all harsh feelings and evil dispositions became subdued and disappeared at the sight of him. . . . This happened because all were surpassed by him in friendly courtesy as well as in art. All confessed the influence of his sweet and gracious nature. . . . Not only was he honored by men, but even by the very animals who would constantly follow his steps and always loved him.

James Harvey Robinson (Ed.), *Readings in European History,* Vol. 1 (Boston: Athenaeum, 1904), pp. 536–537.

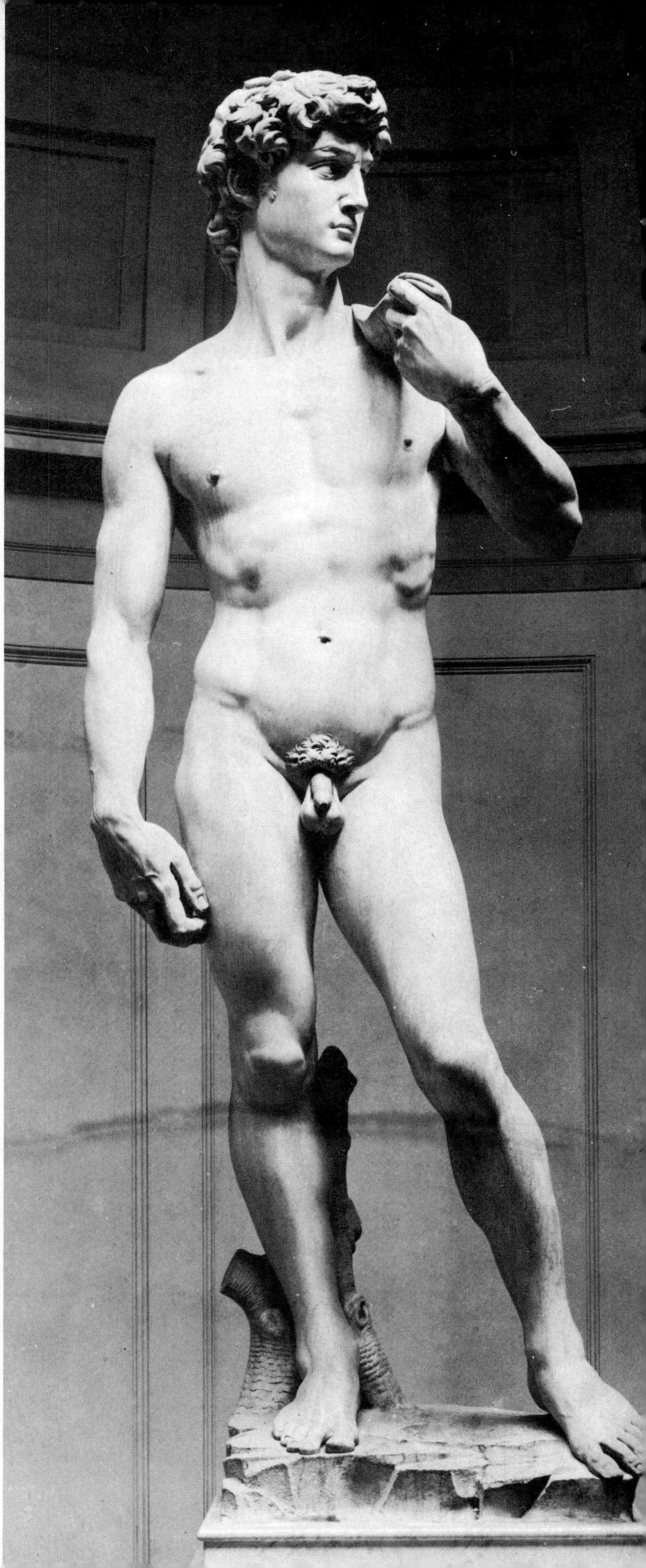

David, *by Michelangelo. Executed on a much larger scale than Donatello's, this statue has been one of the most popular sculptures in the world, since Michelangelo carved it between* 1501 *and* 1504. *Many consider it the symbol of the Italian Renaissance.* [*Art Resource*]

the pontificate of Pope Julius II (1503–1513), who also set Michelangelo to work on his own magnificent tomb. The Sistine frescoes originally covered 10,000 square feet and involved 343 figures, over half of which exceeded 10 feet in height. But it is their originality and perfection as works of art that impress most. This labor of love and piety, painted while Michelangelo was lying on his back or stooping, took four years to complete and left Michelangelo partially crippled. A man of incredible energy and endurance who lived to be ninety, Michelangelo insisted on doing almost everything himself and permitted his assistants only a few of the many chores involved.

Moses, *by Michelangelo. Originally intended for the tomb of Pope Julius II* (1503–1513), *this statue is now in the Church of St. Peter in Chains in Rome. The horns on Moses' head symbolize divine inspiration.* [*Art Resource*]

The Sistine Chapel in the Vatican, painted by Michelangelo during the pontificate of Julius II (1503–1513). The frescoes on the ceiling and the Last Judgement *on the wall behind the altar are considered the supreme masterpiece of Renaissance painting.* [*Art Resource*]

His later works are more complex and suggest deep personal changes within the artist himself. They mark, artistically and philosophically, the passing of high Renaissance painting and the advent of a new style known as *mannerism,* which reached its peak in the late sixteenth and early seventeenth centuries. A reaction against the simplicity and symmetry of high Renaissance art, which also found expression in music and literature, mannerism made room for the strange and even the abnormal and gave freer reign to the subjectivity of the artist. It derived its name from the fact that it permitted the artist to express his own individual perceptions and feelings, to paint, compose, or write in a "mannered" or "affected" way. Tintoretto (d. 1594) and especially El Greco (d. 1614) became its supreme representatives.

Michelangelo's Inability Ever to Be Satisfied with His Work

According to Vasari, Michelangelo was such an extreme perfectionist that he found fault in everything he did and frequently abandoned his sculptures and paintings before they were completed.

Michelangelo worked . . . almost every day at a group of four figures [in St. Peter's in Rome], but he broke up the block at last, either because it was found to have numerous veins, or was excessively hard and caused the chisel to strike fire, or because his judgment was so severe that he could never content himself with anything that he did. . . . Few of the works undertaken in his manhood were ever entirely completed, those finished being the productions of his youth. . . . He would himself often remark that if he were really permitted to satisfy himself in the works [he was commissioned] to produce, he would give little or nothing of it to public view. And the reason for this is obvious. He had advanced to such an extent of knowledge in art that the very slightest error could not exist in any figure without his immediate discovery; and having found such after the work had been given to view, he would never attempt to correct it, but would commence some other production, believing that a like failure would not happen again. This was, as he often declared, the reason why the number of pictures and statues finished by his hand was so small.

James Harvey Robinson (Ed.), *Readings in European History,* Vol. 1 (Boston: Athenaeum, 1904), pp. 540–541.

The Transport of the Body of St. Mark, *by Tintoretto (d.* 1594). *This was painted between* 1562 *and* 1566 *for the Doge of Venice (St. Mark is the patron saint of Venice). Tintoretto's paintings were immensely popular, and his influence helped to stimulate the painting of northern Europe in the late sixteenth and early seventeenth centuries.* [*Alinari*]

Italy's Political Decline: The French Invasions (1494–1527)

The Treaty of Lodi

As a land of autonomous city-states, Italy's peace and safety from foreign invasion, especially from invasion by the Turks, had always depended on internal cooperation. Such cooperation had been maintained during the last half of the fifteenth century, thanks to a carefully constructed political alliance known as the Treaty of Lodi (1454–1455). The terms of the treaty brought Milan and Naples, long traditional enemies, into alliance with Florence. These three stood together for decades against Venice, which was frequently joined by the Papal States to create an internal balance of power that also made possible a unified front against external enemies.

Around 1490, following the rise to power of the Milanese despot Ludovico il Moro, hostilities between Milan and Naples resumed. The peace made possible by the Treaty of Lodi ended in 1494 when Naples, supported by Florence and the Borgia Pope Alexander VI (1492–1503), prepared to attack Milan. Ludovico made what proved to be a fatal response to these new political alignments: he appealed for aid to the French. French kings had ruled Naples from 1266 to 1435, before they were driven out by Duke Alfonso of Sicily. Breaking a wise Italian rule, Ludovico invited the French to reenter Italy and revive their dynastic claim to Naples. In his haste to check his rival, Naples, Ludovico did not recognize sufficiently that France also had dynastic claims to Milan, nor did he foresee how insatiable the French appetite for Italian territory would become once French armies had crossed the Alps.

Charles VIII's March Through Italy

The French king Louis XI had resisted the temptation to invade Italy, while nonetheless keeping French dynastic claims in Italy alive. His successor, Charles VIII (1483–1498), an eager youth in his twenties, responded to Ludovico's call with lightning speed. Within five months he had crossed the Alps (August 1495) and raced as conqueror through Florence and the Papal States into Naples. As Charles approached Florence, the Florentine ruler, Piero de' Medici, who had allied with Naples against Milan, tried to placate the French king by handing over Pisa and other Florentine possessions. Such appeasement only brought about Piero's forced exile by a population that was revolutionized at this time by the radical preacher Girolamo Savonarola (1452–1498). Savonarola convinced a majority of the fearful Florentines that the French king's advent was a long-delayed and fully justified divine vengeance on their immorality.

Charles entered Florence without resistance and, thanks to Savonarola's flattery and the payment of a large ransom, spared the city a threatened destruction. Savonarola continued to rule Florence for four years after Charles's departure. The Florentines proved, however, not to be the stuff theocracies are made of. Savonarola's puritanism and antipapal policies made it impossible for him to survive indefinitely. This was especially true after the Italian cities reunited and the ouster of the French invader, whom Savonarola had praised as a godsend, became national policy. Savonarola was imprisoned and executed in May 1498.

Charles's lightning march through Italy also struck terror in non-Italian hearts. Ferdinand of Aragon, whose native land and self-interests as king of Sicily now became vulnerable to a French-Italian axis, took the initiative to create a counteralliance: the League of Venice, formed in March 1495, with Venice, the Papal States, and the Emperor Maximilian I joining Ferdinand against the French. The stage was set for a conflict between France and Spain that would not end until 1559.

Ludovico il Moro meanwhile recognized that he had sown the wind; having desired a French invasion only so long as it weakened his enemies, he now saw Milan threatened by the whirlwind of events that he had himself created. In reaction he joined the League of Venice, and this alliance was able to send Charles into retreat by May. Charles remained thereafter on the defensive until his death in April 1498.

Pope Alexander VI and the Borgia Family

The French returned to Italy under Charles's successor, Louis XII (1498–1515), this time assisted by a new Italian ally, the Borgia pope, Alexander VI (1492–1503). Alexander, probably the most corrupt pope who ever sat on the papal throne, openly promoted the political careers of the children he had had before he became pope, Cesare and Lucrezia, as he placed the efforts of the powerful Borgia family to secure a political base in Romagna in tandem with papal policy there.

In Romagna several principalities had fallen away from the church during the Avignon papacy, and Venice, the pope's ally within the League of Venice, continued to contest the Papal States for their loyalty. Seeing that a French alliance could give him the opportunity to reestablish control over the region, Alexander took steps to secure French favor. He annulled Louis XII's marriage to Charles VIII's sister so that Louis could marry Charles's widow, Anne of Brittany—a popular political move designed to keep Brittany French. The pope also bestowed a cardinal's hat on the archbishop of Rouen, Louis's favorite cleric. But most important, Alexander agreed to abandon the League of Venice, a withdrawal of support that made the league too weak to resist a French reconquest of Milan. In exchange, Cesare Borgia received the sister of the king of Navarre, Charlotte d'Albret, in marriage, a union that greatly enhanced Borgia military strength. Cesare also received land grants from Louis XII and the promise of French military aid in Romagna.

All in all it was a scandalous tradeoff, but one that made it possible for both the French king and the pope to realize their ambitions

Isabella d'Este *by the Venetian painter Titian* (1477–1576). *Titian was the most popular portrait painter of the age, patronized by the richest and most influential people in Europe. Isabella d'Este, the Duchess of Mantua, a small state in northern Italy, was one of the greatest patrons of the Renaissance. Her court was a major center for artists, musicians, and humanists. She also became the sister-in-law of Lucrezia Borgia, when Lucrezia married Isabella's brother Alfonso, Duke of Ferrara in* 1502. [*Kunsthistorisches Museum, Vienna*]

within Italy. Louis successfully invaded Milan in August 1499. Ludovico il Moro, who had originally opened the Pandora's box of French invasion, spent his last years languishing in a French prison. In 1500 Louis and Ferdinand of Aragon divided Naples between them, while the pope and Cesare Borgia conquered the cities of Romagna without opposition. Alexander awarded his victorious son the title "duke of Romagna."

Pope Julius II

Cardinal Giuliano della Rovere, a strong opponent of the Borgia family, became Pope Julius II (1503–1513). He suppressed the Borgias and placed their newly conquered lands in Romagna under papal jurisdiction. Julius came to be known as the "warrior pope" because he brought the Renaissance papacy to a peak of military prowess and diplomatic intrigue. Shocked, as were other contemporaries by this thoroughly secular papacy, the Humanist Erasmus (1466?–1536), who had witnessed in disbelief a bullfight in the papal palace during a visit to Rome, wrote a popular anonymous satire entitled *Julius Excluded from Heaven.* This humorous account purported to describe the pope's unsuccessful efforts to convince Saint Peter that he was worthy of admission to heaven.

Pope Julius II (1503–1513), *by Raphael in about 1511.*

Assisted by his powerful allies, Pope Julius succeeded in driving the Venetians out of Romagna in 1509, thereby ending Venetian claims in the region and fully securing the Papal States. Having realized this long-sought papal goal, Julius turned to the second major undertaking of his pontificate: ridding Italy of his former ally, the French invader. Julius, Ferdinand of Aragon, and Venice formed a second Holy League in October 1511, and within a short period Emperor Maximilian I and the Swiss joined them. By 1512 the league had the French in full retreat, and they were soundly defeated by the Swiss in 1513 at Novara.

The French were nothing if not persistent. They invaded Italy still a third time under Louis's successor, Francis I (1515–1547). French armies massacred Swiss soldiers of the Holy League at Marignano in September 1515, revenging the earlier defeat at Novara. The victory won from the pope the Concordat of Bologna in August 1516, an agreement that gave the French king control over the French clergy in exchange for French recognition of the pope's superiority over church councils and his right to collect annates in France. This was an important compromise that helped keep France Catholic after the outbreak of the Protestant Reformation. But the new French entry into Italy also led to the first of four major wars with Spain in the first half of the sixteenth century: the Habsburg–Valois wars, none of which France won.

Niccolò Machiavelli

The period of foreign invasions made a shambles of Italy. The same period that saw Italy's cultural peak in the work of Leonardo, Raphael, and Michelangelo also witnessed Italy's political tragedy. One who watched as French, Spanish, and German armies wreaked havoc on his country was Niccolò Machiavelli (1469–1527). The more he saw, the more convinced he became that Italian political unity and independence were ends that justified any means. A Humanist and a careful student of

Machiavelli Discusses the Most Important Trait for a Ruler

Machiavelli believed that the most important personality trait of a successful ruler was the ability to instill fear in his subjects.

Here the question arises; whether it is better to be loved than feared or feared than loved. The answer is that it would be desirable to be both but, since that is difficult, it is much safer to be feared than to be loved, if one must choose. For on men in general this observation may be made: they are ungrateful, fickle, and deceitful, eager to avoid dangers, and avid for gain, and while you are useful to them they are all with you, offering you their blood, their property, their lives, and their sons so long as danger is remote, as we noted above, but when it approaches they turn on you. Any prince, trusting only in their words and having no other preparations made, will fall to his ruin, for friendships that are bought at a price and not by greatness and nobility of soul are paid for indeed, but they are not owned and cannot be called upon in time of need. Men have less hesitation in offending a man who is loved than one who is feared, for love is held by a bond of obligation which, as men are wicked, is broken whenever personal advantage suggests it, but fear is accompanied by the dread of punishment which never relaxes.

Niccolò Machiavelli, *The Prince* (1513), trans. and ed. by Thomas G. Bergin (New York: Appleton-Century-Crofts, 1947), p. 48.

Major Political Events of the Italian Renaissance (1375–1527)

The Ciompi Revolt in Florence	1378–1382
Medici rule in Florence established by Cosimo de' Medici	1434
Treaty of Lodi allies Milan, Naples, and Florence (in effect until 1494)	1454–1455
Charles VIII of France invades Italy	1494
Savonarola controls Florence	1494–1498
League of Venice unites Venice, Milan, the Papal States, the Holy Roman Empire, and Spain against France	1495
Louis XII invades Milan (the second French invasion of Italy)	1499
The Borgias conquer Romagna	1500
The Holy League (Pope Julius II, Ferdinand of Aragon, Emperor Maximilian, and Venice) defeat the French	1512–1513
Machiavelli writes *The Prince*	1513
Francis I leads the third French invasion of Italy	1515
Concordat of Bologna between France and the papacy	1516
Sack of Rome by imperial soldiers	1527

ancient Rome, Machiavelli was impressed by the deliberate and heroic acts of ancient Roman rulers, what Renaissance people called *Virtù*. Stories of the unbounded patriotism and self-sacrifice of the old Roman citizenry were his favorites, and he lamented the absence of such traits among his compatriots. Machiavelli's romanticization of the ancient Romans caused his interpretation of both ancient and contemporary history to be somewhat exaggerated. His Florentine contemporary, Francesco Guicciardini, who was a more sober historian and was less given to idealizing antiquity, wrote truer chronicles of Florentine and Italian history.

The juxtaposition of what Machiavelli believed the ancient Romans had been with the failure of contemporary Romans to realize such high ideals made him the famous cynic we know in the popular epithet *Machiavellian*. Only an unscrupulous strongman, he concluded, using duplicity and terror, could impose order on so divided and selfish a people; the moral revival of the Italians required an unprincipled dictator.

It has been argued that Machiavelli wrote *The Prince* in 1513 as a cynical satire on the way rulers actually did behave and not as a serious recommendation of unprincipled despotic rule. To take his advocacy of tyranny literally, it is argued, contradicts both his earlier works and his own strong family tradition of republican service. But Machiavelli seems to have been in earnest when he advised rulers to discover the advantages of fraud and brutality. He apparently hoped to see a strong ruler emerge from the Medici family, which had captured the papacy in 1513 with the pontificate of Leo X (1513–1521). At the same time, the Medici family retained control over the powerful territorial state of Florence—a situation similar to that of Machiavelli's hero Cesare Borgia and his father Pope Alexander VI, who had earlier brought factious Romagna to heel by placing secular family goals and religious policy in tandem. *The Prince* was pointedly dedicated to Lorenzo de' Medici, duke of Urbino and grandson of Lorenzo the Magnificent.

Whatever Machiavelli's hopes may have been, the Medicis were not destined to be Italy's deliverers. The second Medici pope, Clement VII (1523–1534), watched helplessly as Rome was sacked by the army of Emperor Charles V in 1527, also the year of Machiavelli's death.

Suggested Readings

Margaret Aston, *The Fifteenth Century: The Prospect of Europe* (1968). Crisp social history, with pictures.

Hans Baron, *The Crisis of the Early Italian Renaissance*, Vols. 1 and 2 (1966). A major work, setting forth the civic dimension of Italian Humanism.

Bernard Berenson, *Italian Painters of the Renaissance* (1957).

Jacob Burckhardt, *The Civilization of the Renaissance in Italy* (1867). The old classic that still has as many defenders as detractors.

Wallace K. Ferguson, *Europe in Transition 1300–1520* (1962). A major survey that deals with the transition from medieval to Renaissance society.

Myron Gilmore, *The World of Humanism* 1453–1517 (1952). A comprehensive survey, especially strong in intellectual and cultural history.

J. R. Hale, *Renaissance Europe: The Individual and Society,* 1480–1520 (1971). Many-sided treatment of social history.

Denys Hay, *Europe in the Fourteenth and Fifteenth Centuries* (1966). Many-sided treatment of political history.

David Herlihy, *The Family in Renaissance Italy* (1974).

Johan Huizinga, *The Waning of the Middle Ages: A Study of the Forms of Life, Thought, and Art in France and the Netherlands in the Dawn of the Renaissance* (1924). A classic study of "mentality" at the end of the Middle Ages.

De Lamar Jensen, *Renaissance Europe: Age of Recovery and Reconciliation* (1981).

Ruth Kelso, *Doctrine of the Lady of the Renaissance* (1978).

Paul O. Kristeller, *Renaissance Thought: The Classic, Scholastic, and Humanist Strains* (1961). A master shows the many sides of Renaissance thought.

Harry A. Miskimin, *The Economy of Early Renaissance Europe* 1300–1460 (1969). Shows interaction of social, political, and economic change.

Heiko A. Oberman, *The Harvest of Medieval Theology* (1963). A demanding synthesis and revision.

Peter Partner, *Renaissance Rome,* 1500–1559: *A Portrait of a Society* (1976). Detailed and comprehensive.

Edouard Perroy, *The Hundred Years' War,* trans. by W. B. Wells (1965). The most comprehensive one-volume account.

J. B. A. Pocock, *The Machiavellian Moment: Florentine Political Thought and the Atlantic Republican Tradition* (1975). Traces the influence of Florentine political thought.

Yves Renovard, *The Avignon Papacy* 1305–1403, trans. by D. Bethell (1970). Standard narrative.

Quentin Skinner, *The Foundations of Modern Political Thought I: The Renaissance* (1978). Broad survey, very comprehensive.

Matthew Spinka, *John Huss's Concept of the Church* (1966).

J. W. Thompson, *Economic and Social History of Europe in the Later Middle Ages* 1300–1530 (1958). A bread-and-butter account.

Brian Tierney, *Foundations of the Conciliar Theory* (1955). Important study showing the origins of conciliar theory in canon law.

Brian Tierney, *The Crisis of Church and State* 1050–1300 (1964). Part IV provides the major documents in the clash between Boniface VIII and Philip the Fair.

Walter Ullmann, *Origins of the Great Schism* (1948). A basic study by a controversial interpreter of medieval political thought.

Charles T. Wood, *Philip the Fair and Boniface VIII* (1967). Excerpts from the scholarly debate over the significance of this confrontation.

H. B. Workman, *John Wyclif,* Vols. 1 and 2 (1926). Dated but still standard.

Philip Ziegler, *The Black Death* (1969). Highly readable journalistic account.

Luther and the Wittenberg reformers, painted about 1543 *by Lucas Cranach the Younger* (1515–1586). *Luther stands to the left behind the dominating figure of the Elector John Frederick of Saxony* (1532–1547). *The electors of Saxony were the first princely patrons of the Reformation. Their support protected Luther from the hostility of pope and emperor.* [*Toledo Museum of Art; gift of Edward Drummond Libbey*]

10

The Age of Reformation

IN THE SECOND DECADE of the sixteenth century there began in Saxony in Germany a powerful religious movement that rapidly spread throughout northern Europe, deeply affecting society and politics as well as the spiritual lives of men and women. Attacking what they believed to be burdensome superstitions that robbed people of both their money and their peace of mind, Protestant reformers led a broad revolt against the medieval church. In a relatively short span of time hundreds of thousands of people from all social classes set aside the beliefs of centuries and adopted a more simplified religious practice.

The Protestant Reformation challenged aspects of the Renaissance, especially its tendency to follow classical sources in glorifying human nature and its loyalty to traditional religion. Protestants were more impressed by the human potential for evil than by the inclination to do good and encouraged parents, teachers, and magistrates to be firm disciplinarians. On the other hand, Protestants also embraced many Renaissance values, especially in the sphere of educational reform and particularly with regard to training in ancient languages. Like the Italian Humanists, the Protestant reformers studied ancient languages and went directly to the original sources; only for them this meant the study of the Hebrew and Greek Scriptures and the consequent challenge of traditional institutions on the authority of the Bible.

We are, however, getting well ahead of our story. The road to the Reformation was long in preparation. As the Protestant ethic influenced an entire age, it was also itself born out of changes in European society beyond those within the purely religious and ecclesiastical spheres.

For Europe the late fifteenth and the sixteenth centuries were a period of unprecedented territorial expansion and ideological experimentation. Permanent colonies were established within the Americas, and the exploitation of the New World's human and seemingly endless mineral resources was begun. The American gold and silver imported into Europe spurred scientific invention and a weapons industry and touched off an inflationary spiral that produced a revolution in prices by century's end. The new bullion also helped create international traffic in African slaves, who were needed in ever-increasing numbers to work the mines and the plantations of the

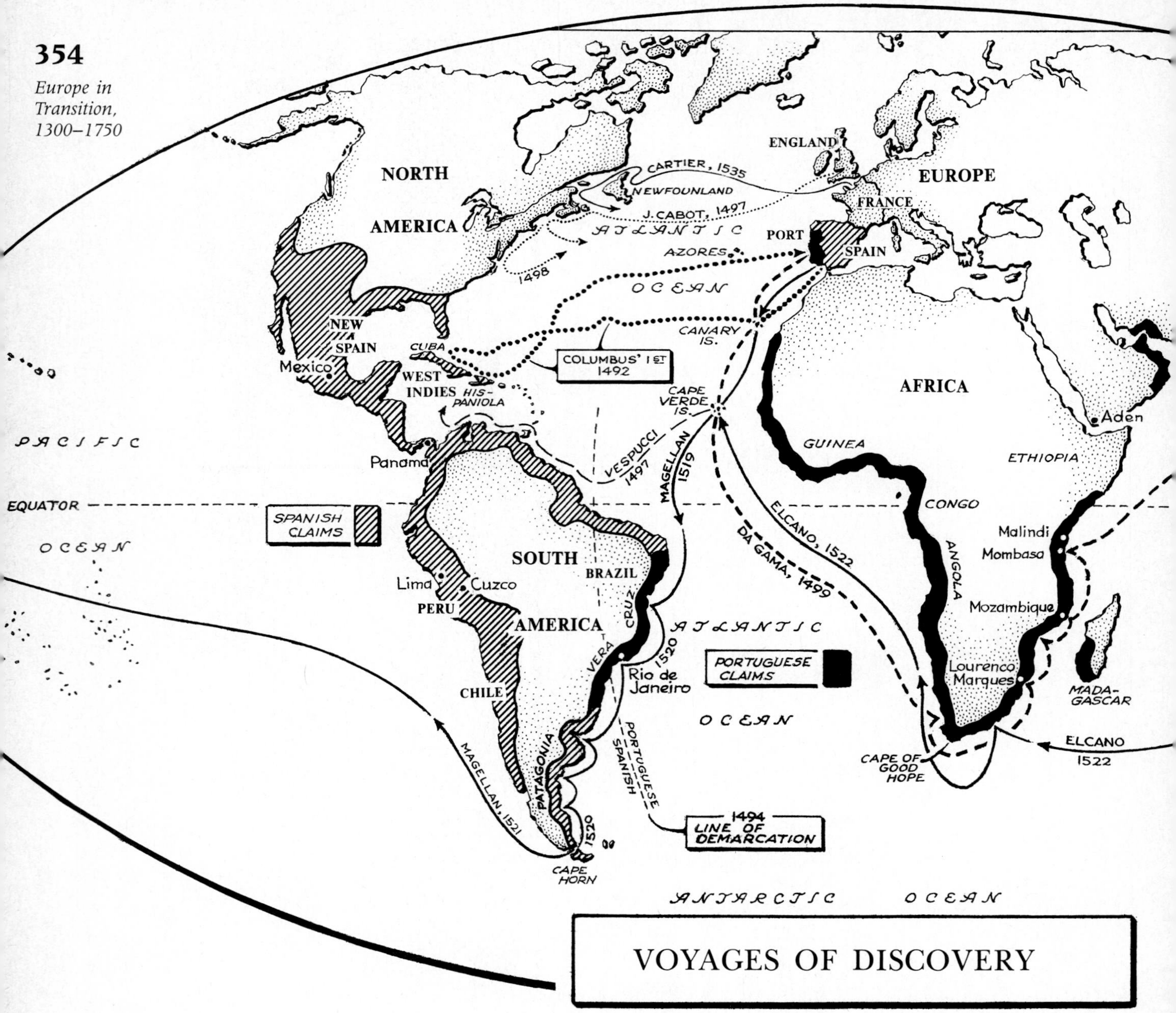

VOYAGES OF DISCOVERY

New World as replacements for faltering natives. This period further saw social engineering and political planning on a large scale as newly centralized governments were forced as never before to develop long-range economic policies, a practice that came to be known as *mercantilism*.

The late fifteenth and sixteenth centuries also marked the first wide-scale use of the printing press, an invention greatly assisted by the development of a process of cheap paper manufacture and publishers eager to exploit a fascinating new technology. Printing with movable type was invented by Johann Guttenberg (d. 1468) in the mid-fifteenth century in the German city of Mainz. Residential colleges and universities had greatly expanded in northern Europe during the fourteenth and fifteenth centuries, and there was a growing literate public in the cities eager to possess and read books. The new technology also made propaganda possible on a massive scale, as thousands of inexpensive pamphlets could now be rapidly produced and disseminated.

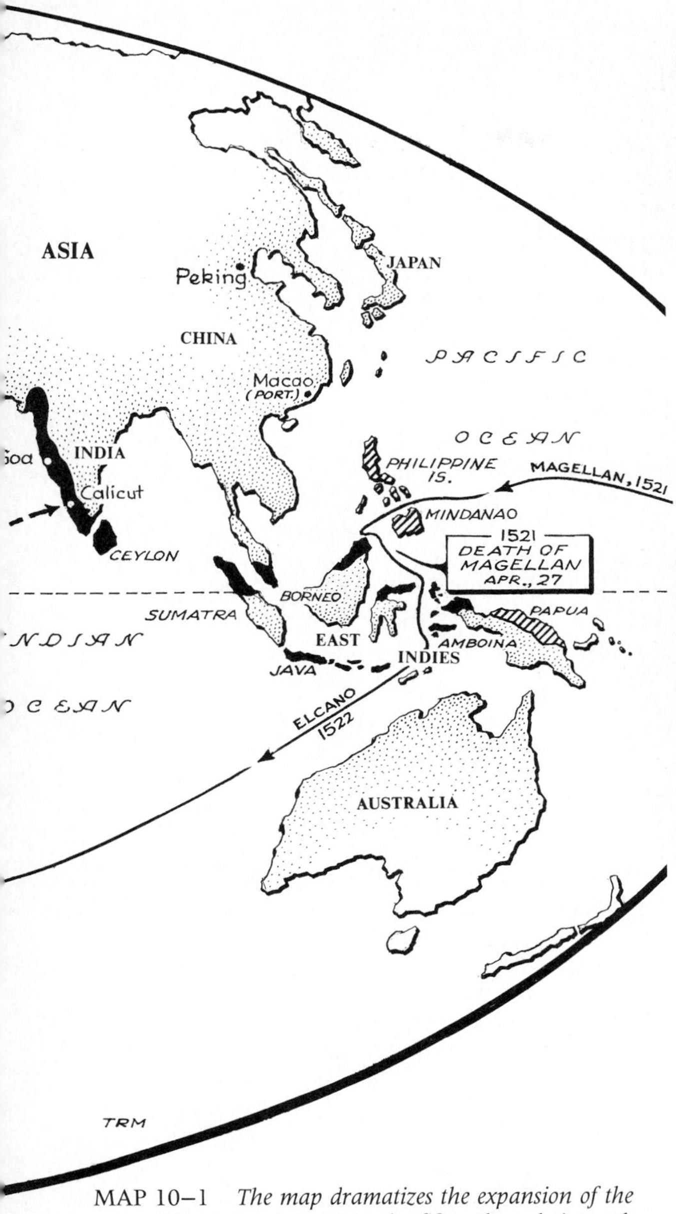

MAP 10–1 *The map dramatizes the expansion of the area of European interest in the fifteenth and sixteenth centuries. Not until today's "space age" has a comparable widening of horizons been possible.*

Hypothetical reconstruction of the printing press of Johannes Gutenberg of Mainz (in what is now West Germany). Between about 1435 and 1455, Gutenberg worked out the complete technology of making individual rectangular metal types, composing the type into pages held together by pressure, and printing from those on an adaptation of the wooden standing press with ink of lampblack mixed with oil varnish. This new technology for the first time made it possible to manufacture numerous identical copies of written works and was basic to the intellectual development of the West. [Gutenberg-Museum, Mainz]

Voyages of Discovery and of Empire and Changes in Society

Spices, Gold, and Silver

On the eve of the Reformation the geographical as well as the intellectual horizons of Western people were broadening. The fifteenth century saw the beginning of western Europe's global expansion and the transference of commercial supremacy from the Mediterranean and the Baltic to the Atlantic seaboard. Mercenary motives, reinforced by traditional missionary ideals, inspired Prince Henry the Navigator (1394–1460) to sponsor the Portuguese exploration of the African coast. His main object was the gold trade, which for centuries had been an Arab monopoly. By the last decades of the fifteenth century gold from Guinea was entering Europe by way of Portuguese ships calling at the port cities of Lisbon and Antwerp, rather than by Arab land routes. Antwerp became the financial center of Europe, a commercial crossroads where the enterprise and derring-do of the Portuguese and the Spanish met the capital funds of the German banking houses of Fugger and Welser.

The rush for gold quickly expanded into a rush for the spice markets of India. In the fifteenth century the diet of most Europeans was a dull combination of bread and gruel, cabbage, turnips, peas, lentils, and onions, together with what meat became available during seasonal periods of slaughter. Spices, especially pepper and cloves, were in great demand both to preserve and to enhance the taste of food. Bartholomew Dias (d. 1500) opened the Portuguese empire in the East when he rounded the Cape of Good Hope at the tip of Africa in 1487. A decade later, in 1498, Vasco da Gama (d. 1524) reached the coast of India. When he returned to Portugal, he brought with him a cargo worth sixty times the cost of the voyage. In subsequent years the Portuguese established themselves firmly on the Malabar Coast with colonies in Goa and Calcutta and successfully challenged the Arabs and the Venetians for control of the European spice trade.

Detail of a portrait of Christopher Columbus by Sebastiano del Piombo (1485–1547). It shows Columbus, who died in 1506, late in life. [Metropolitan Museum of Art, New York; gift of J. Pierpont Morgan, 1900]

While the Portuguese concentrated on the Indian Ocean, the Spanish set sail across the Atlantic. They did so in the hope of establishing a shorter route to the rich spice markets of the East Indies. Rather than beating the Portuguese at their own game, however, Christopher Columbus (1451–1506) discovered the Americas instead.

Amerigo Vespucci (1451–1512) and Ferdinand Magellan (1480–1521) demonstrated that these new lands were not the outermost territory of the Far East, as Columbus died believing, but an entirely new continent that opened on the still greater Pacific Ocean. Magellan died in the Philippines.

The Spanish Empire in the New World

Columbus's voyage of 1492 marked, unknowingly to those who undertook and financed it, the beginning of more than three centuries of Spanish conquest, exploitation, and administration of a vast American empire. That imperial venture, which created the largest and longest lived of all the great mercantile trading blocs, produced important results for the cultures of both the European and the American continents. The gold and silver extracted from its American possessions financed Spain's major role in the religious and political conflicts of the age and contributed to European inflation in the sixteenth century. In large expanses of both South and North America, Spanish government set an imprint of Roman Catholicism, economic dependence, and hierarchical social structure that has endured to the present day. Spanish economic and social influences came to dominate because the early explorers conquered the existing Indian civilizations and imposed their own.

A Conquered World

Mistaking the islands where he landed for the East Indies, Columbus called the native peoples whom he encountered *Indians.* That name persisted even after it had become clear that a new continent had been discovered. These native peoples had migrated onto the American landmass many thousands of years before the European voyages of discovery. They had come from Asia, probably across the Bering Straits, and by 9000 B.C. lived in various kinds of communities all the way from Alaska to the southernmost sections of South America. In what is today considered Latin America, these Indian peoples had established very high civilizations by approximately A.D. 500. The most famous of these is the Mayan civilization centered in present-day Guatemala and the Yucatán peninsula of Mexico. The Mayans built large cities in which stood immense pyramids. They also achieved very considerable skills in mathematics and astronomy. This remarkable civilization fell into decay and dissolution around the year A.D. 1000 and was an extinguished civilization when the Spanish arrived.

The two major Indian peoples whom the Spanish explorers and conquerors encountered were the Aztecs in Mexico and the Incas in Peru. Both were relative newcomers to political power and had established themselves through the conquest of other Indian tribes. Both were very rich, and their conquest promised the greedy Spanish the possibility of large quantities of gold.

The forebears to the Aztecs whom the Spanish encountered in the early sixteenth century had arrived in the Valley of Mexico early in the twelfth century. They had been forced by other tribes to live on marginal land as a subservient people. Over the years, the Aztecs became highly skilled in military matters. In 1428, under the leadership of a new chief named

Columbus Reports His Discovery of the Entrance to Paradise

During his third voyage, Columbus reached the mouth of the Orinoco River in Venezuela. He believed he was in the East Indies, where, according to tradition, Adam and Eve had first trod the earth. Columbus believed that he had now come upon the very entrance into Paradise. In October 1498 he wrote of this discovery to his patrons, Ferdinand and Isabella, monarchs of Spain.

I have already described my ideas concerning this hemisphere and its form [he believed it to be pear-shaped]. I have no doubt that if I could pass below the equinoctial line, after reaching the highest point . . . I should find a much milder temperature and a variation in the stars and in the water. Not that I suppose that elevated point to be navigable, nor even that there is water there; indeed, I believe it is impossible to ascend to it, because I am convinced that it is the spot of the earthly paradise, whither none can go but by God's permission. . . .

I do not suppose that the earthly paradise is in the form of a rugged mountain, as the descriptions of it have made it appear, but that it is on the summit of the spot, which I have described as being in the form of the stalk of a pear. The approach to it . . . must be by constant and gradual ascent, but I believe that . . . no one could ever reach the top. I think also that the water I have described may proceed from it, though it be far off, and that stopping at the place which I have just left, it forms this lake. There are great indications of this being the terrestrial paradise, for its site coincides with the opinion of the holy and wise theologians whom I have mentioned. Moreover, the other evidences agree . . . for I have never read or heard of fresh water coming in so large a quantity in close conjunction with the water of the sea. The idea is also corroborated by the blandness of the temperature. If the water of which I speak does not proceed from the earthly paradise, it seems to be a still greater wonder, for I do not believe that there is any river in the world so large or so deep.

The Renaissance and the Reformation 1300–1600, ed. by Donald Weinstein (New York: Free Press, 1965), pp. 138–139.

A sixteenth-century Aztec depiction of the Spanish conquest of Mexico.

Itzcoatl, they allied with two other tribes and rebelled against their rulers in Atzcapotzalco. That rebellion opened a period of Aztec conquest that reached its climax just after 1500. Their last ruler in this age of conquest was Montezuma. The Aztecs governed a large number of smaller tribes in a particularly harsh manner. Not surprisingly, they demanded payment of labor and tribute from the conquered tribes. However, they also demanded and received thousands of captives each year to be sacrificed to their gods. The Aztecs believed that the gods must literally be fed with human bodies to guarantee continuing sunshine and soil fertility. These policies meant that the Aztecs were surrounded by various "allied" tribes who felt no loyalty; rather, they felt a terror from which they wished to be liberated.

In 1519, Hernán Cortés landed on the coast of Mexico with a force of about six hundred men. He opened communication with tribes nearby and then with Montezuma. The Aztec chief lived in the capital city of Tenochtitlán (modern Mexico City), which was located on an island in the center of a lake and is said to have somewhat resembled Venice as a city built on water. Montezuma initially believed Cortés to be a god. Aztec religion contained the legend of a priest named Quetzalcoatl who had been driven away four centuries earlier and had promised to return in the very year in which Cortés arrived. Montezuma initially attempted to appease Cortés with gifts of gold, which only whetted the appetites of the Spanish. After several weeks of negotiations and the forging of alliances with subject tribes, Cortés's forces marched on Tenochtitlán, conquered it, and imprisoned Montezuma, who later died under unexplained circumstances. The Aztecs—under a new leader, Cuauhtémoc—attempted to drive the Spanish out, but the Aztecs were eventually defeated by late 1521 after great loss of life. Cortés proclaimed the Aztec Empire to be New Spain.

The second great Indian civilization to experience Spanish conquest was that of the Incas. Located in the highlands of Peru, the Incas were simply the most recent Indian rulers of the region. Like the Aztecs, they had commenced their own conquests in the early fifteenth century. By the early sixteenth century, the Incas ruled several million Indians. They were not as numerous a people as the Aztecs, nor did they possess so large a military organization. Instead, they compelled conquered tribes to fight for them. They carried out this policy by richly rewarding successful warriors and by treating well the conquered tribes who aided them. They also required the conquered peoples to speak Quechua, their own unwritten language. They created a relatively large bureaucracy that helped them to make use of forced labor to build roads, to farm land, and to construct their great cities, such as Cuzco and Machu Picchu. By the time the Spanish arrived, the Incas, whose chief was Atahualpa, were engaged in civil war among their own political elite.

In 1531, largely inspired by Cortés's example in Mexico, Francisco Pizarro sailed from Panama and landed on the western coast of the South American continent to undertake a campaign against the Inca Empire, about which he knew relatively little. His force included about two hundred men armed with guns and swords and equipped with horses, the military power of which the Incas did not understand. In late 1531, Pizarro lured Atahualpa into a conference, where he captured the chief and in the process killed several thousand Indians. The imprisoned Atahualpa then attempted to ransom himself by having a vast horde of gold transported from all over Peru to Pizarro. Needless to say, Pizarro refused to release his captive. After finding he could not use Atahualpa as a puppet ruler, Pizarro had him publicly executed in 1533. Further Indian insurrections took place, with some Inca factions seeking to ally themselves with the Spanish against other factions. The Spanish conquerors also fought among themselves, and effective royal control was not established until the late 1560s.

The conquests of Mexico and Peru stand among the most dramatic and brutal stories in modern western history. One civilization armed with advanced weapons subdued, in a remarkably brief time, two advanced, powerful peoples. But beyond the drama and bloodshed, these conquests, along with lesser ones of smaller groups of Indians, marked a fundamental turning point in the development of western civilization. Never again in the Americas would there be any real possibility that Indian civilizations and their values would produce any significant impact or influence. The Spanish and the Indians did make certain accommodations to each other, but there was never any doubt about which culture held the upper hand. European values, religion, economic goals, and language would dominate, and no group that retained Indian religion, language, or values would be part of the dominant culture or the political power elite. In that sense, the Spanish conquests of the early sixteenth century were the beginning of the process whereby South America (in this context including portions of the southwest United States, Mexico, and Central America) was transformed into Latin America.

The Economy of Exploitation

Almost from the earliest moments of discovery and conquest, the native peoples of America and their lands were drawn into the Atlantic economy and the world of competitive European commercialism. The Spanish set out for America in search of wealth, and they displayed little hesitation in exploiting their unexpected newfound opportunities. For the Indians of Latin America and somewhat later the blacks of Africa, that drive for gain meant various arrangements of forced labor.

There were three major components in the colonial economy of Latin America: mining, agriculture, and shipping. Each of them involved either labor or servitude or a relationship of dependence of the New World economy on that of Spain.

The early *conquistadores* ("conquerors") were primarily interested in gold, but by the middle of the sixteenth century, silver mining provided the chief source of metallic wealth. The great mining centers were Potosí in Peru and somewhat smaller sites in northern Mexico. The Spanish crown was particularly interested in mining because it received one fifth (the *quinto*) of all mining revenues. For this reason, the crown maintained a monopoly over the production and sale of mercury, which was required in the silver-mining process. Silver mining flourished in terms of extracting wealth for the Spanish until the early seventeenth century, when the industry underwent a recession because of lack of new investment and the increasing costs involved in deeper mines. Nonetheless silver never lost predominance during the colonial era, and its production by forced labor for the benefit of Spaniards and the Spanish crown epitomized the wholly extractive economy that stood at the foundation of colonial life.

The major rural and agricultural institution of the Spanish colonies was the *haciendas.* These were large landed estates owned by persons originally born in Spain *(peninsulares)* or persons of Spanish descent born in America *(creoles).* The establishment of haciendas represented the transfer of the principle of the large unit of privately owned land, which was characteristic of Europe and especially of Spain, to the New World setting. Such estates would become one of the most important features of Latin American life and, in the century after independence, one of the most controversial. Laborers on the hacienda usually stood in some relation of formal servitude to the owner. They were rarely free to move from the services of one landowner to another. There were two major products of the hacienda economy: foodstuffs for mining areas and urban centers and leather goods used in vast quantities on mining machinery. Both farming and ranching thus stood subordinate to the mine economy. However, like mining, the agricultural economy was wholly commercial in nature.

In the West Indies, the basic agricultural unit was the plantation. On Cuba, Hispaniola, Puerto Rico, and other islands, the labor of black slaves from Africa produced sugar to supply what seemed to be the insatiable demand for the product in Europe.

The final major area of economic activity in the Spanish colonies was the variety of service occupations pursued in the cities. These included the governmental bureaucracy, the legal profession, and shipping. These practi-

A Contemporary Describes Forced Indian Labor at Potosí

The Potosí range in Peru was the site of the great silver-mining industry in the Spanish Empire. The vast amount of wealth contained in the region became legendary almost as soon as mining began there in the 1540s. Indians, most of whom were forced laborers working under the *mita* system of conscription, did virtually all of the work underground. This description, written by a Spanish friar in the early seventeenth century, portrays both the large size of the enterprise and the harsh conditions that the Indians endured. At any one time, only one third of the 13,300 conscripted Indians were employed. The labor force was changed every four months.

According to His Majesty's warrant, the mine owners on this massive range have a right to the mita [conscripted labor] of 13,300 Indians in the working and exploitation of the mines, both those which have been discovered, those now discovered, and those which shall be discovered. It is the duty of the Corregidor [municipal governor] of Potosí to have them rounded up and to see that they come in from all the provinces between Cuzco over the whole of El Collao and as far as the frontiers of Tarija and Tomina. . . .

. . . The mita Indians go up every Monday morning to the locality of Guayna Potosí which is at the foot of the range; the Corregidor arrives with all the provincial captains or chiefs who have charge of the Indians assigned them, and he there checks off and reports to each mine and smelter owner the number of Indians assigned him for his mine or smelter; that keeps him busy till 1 P.M., by which time the Indians are already turned over to these mine and smelter owners.

After each has eaten his ration, they climb up the hill, each to his mine, and go in, staying there from that hour until Saturday evening without coming out of the mine; their wives bring them food, but they stay constantly underground, excavating and carrying out the ore from which they get the silver. They all have tallow candles, lighted day and night; that is the light they work with, for as they are underground, they have need of it all the time. . . .

These Indians have different functions in the handling of the silver ore; some break it up with bar or pick, and dig down in, following the vein in the mine; others bring it up; others up above keep separating the good and the poor in piles; others are occupied in taking it down from the range to the mills on herds of llamas; every day they bring up more than 8,000 of these native beasts of burden for this task. These teamsters who carry the metal do not belong to the mita, but are mingados—hired.

Antonio Vázquez de Espinosa, *Compendium and Description of the Indies* (ca. 1620), trans. by Charles Upson Clark (Washington, D.C.: Smithsonian Institution Press, 1968), p. 62, quoted in Helen Delpar (Ed.), *The Borzoi Reader in Latin American History* (New York: Alfred A. Knopf, 1972), pp. 92–93.

tioners were either *peninsulares* or *creoles*, with the former dominating more often than not. The rules they enforced, interpreted, or shipped by were those set by institutions of the Spanish government to realize the goals of a competitive mercantile empire.

All of this extractive and exploitive economic activity required labor, and the Spanish in the New World had decided very early that the Indian population would supply the labor. A series of social devices was used to draw Indians into the economic life imposed by the Spanish.

The first of these was the *encomienda*. This was a formal grant of the right to the labor of a specific number of Indians for a particular period of time. An *encomienda* usually involved a few hundred Indians but might grant the right to the labor of several thousand. *Encomienda* as an institution persisted in some parts of Latin America well into the seventeenth century but generally stood in decline by the middle of the

The great silver mine at Potosí in Peru, as depicted in a drawing of 1584. *Potosí was a veritable mountain of silver from which pack trains of llamas carried the ore to the refinery shown in the foreground.* [*Hispanic Society of America*]

sixteenth. The Spanish monarchs feared that the holders of *encomienda* were attempting to become a powerful independent nobility in the New World. The Spanish government was also persuaded by appeals on humanitarian grounds against this particular kind of exploitation of the Indians. The land grants that led to the establishment of haciendas were one means whereby the crown continued to use the resources of the New World for patronage without directly impinging on the Indians.

The passing of the *encomienda* led to a new arrangement of labor servitude, the *repartimiento*. This device required adult male Indians to devote so many days of labor annually to Spanish economic enterprises. In the mines of Peru, the *repartimiento* was known as the *mita,* and in some cases, Indians did not survive their days of labor rotation. The actual limitation of labor time led some Spanish managers to use their workers in an extremely harsh manner, under the assumption that more fresh workers would soon be appearing on the scene.

The eventual shortage of workers and the crown's pressure against extreme versions of forced labor led to the use of free labor. Here again, however, the freedom was more in appearance, and dependence and subservience were the reality. Free Indian laborers were required to purchase goods from the landowner or mine owner. They became indebted and were never able to pay off the debt. This situation was known as *debt peonage* and continued in different forms in Latin America long after the wars of liberation.

Black slavery was the final mode of forced or subservient labor in the New World. Both the Spanish and the Portuguese had used African slaves in Europe. They were used throughout Latin America at one time or another, but the sugar plantations of the West Indies were the major center of slavery.

The conquest and the economy of exploitation and forced labor (and the introduction of European diseases) produced extraordinary demographic consequences for the Indian population. By the early seventeenth century, the Indians were dying off in huge numbers. Estimates of the Pre-Columbian population of America have generated major controversies. Conservative estimates put the Indian population at the time of Columbus's discovery at well over fifty million. In New Spain (Mexico) alone, the decline in population was probably from approximately twenty-five million to less than two million. Whatever the exact figures, there was and is no doubt that the Indian population encountered by the *conquistadores* largely vanished and, with it, the easy supply of labor that they had exploited.

Jacob Fugger ''the Rich'' (1459–1525) *with his chief accountant. As bankers to the Habsburgs, the Fuggers became immensely wealthy.* [*Robert-Viollet*]

Rise in Prices and the Development of Capitalism

The influx of spices and precious metals into Europe from the Spanish Empire was not an unmixed blessing. It contributed to a steady rise in prices during the sixteenth century that created an inflation rate estimated at 2 per cent a year. The new supply of bullion from the Americas joined with enlarged European production to increase greatly the amount of coinage in circulation, and this increase in turn fed inflation. Fortunately the increase in prices was by and large spread over a long period of time and was not sudden. Prices doubled in Spain by mid-century, quadrupled by 1600. In Luther's Wittenberg the cost of basic food and clothing increased almost 100 per cent between 1519 and 1540. Generally wages and rents remained well behind the rise in prices.

The new wealth enabled governments and private entrepreneurs to sponsor basic research and expansion in the printing, shipping, mining, textile, and weapons industries—the growth industries of the Age of Reformation. There is also evidence of mercantilism or large-scale government planning in such ventures as the French silk industry and the Habsburg–Fugger development of mines in Austria and Hungary.

In the thirteenth and fourteenth centuries capitalist institutions and practices had already begun to develop in the rich Italian cities (one may point to the Florentine banking houses of Bardi and Peruzzi). Those who owned the means of production, either privately or corporately, were clearly distinguished from the workers who operated them. Wherever possible, monopolies were created in basic goods. High interest was charged on loans—actual, if not legal, usury. And the "capitalist" virtues of thrift, industry, and orderly planning were everywhere in evidence—all intended to permit the free and efficient accumulation of wealth.

The late fifteenth and the sixteenth centuries saw the maturation of such capitalism together with its peculiar social problems. The new wealth and industrial expansion raised the expectations of the poor and the ambitious and heightened the reactionary tendencies within the established and wealthy classes. This effect, in turn, greatly aggravated the traditional social divisions between the clergy and the laity, the higher and the lower clergy, the urban patriciate and the guilds, masters and journeymen, and the landed nobility and the agrarian peasantry.

Such social divisions may indirectly have prepared the way for the Reformation by making many people critical of traditional institutions and open to new ideas—especially those that seemed to promise a greater degree of freedom and equality.

The far-flung transactions created by the new commerce increased the demand for lawyers and bankers. The Medicis of Florence grew very rich as bankers of the pope, as did the Fuggers of Augsburg as bankers of the Habsburg rulers. The Fuggers lent Charles I of Spain over 500,000 florins to buy his election as Holy Roman Emperor in 1519, and they later boasted that they had created the emperor. But those who paid out their money also took their chances. Both the Fuggers and the Medicis were later bankrupted by popes and kings who defaulted on their heavy debts.

The Northern Renaissance

The scholarly works of northern Humanists created a climate favorable to religious and educational reforms on the eve of the Reformation. Northern Humanism was initially stimulated by the importation of Italian learning through such varied intermediaries as students who had studied in Italy, merchants, and the Brothers of the Common Life (an influential lay religious movement that began in the Netherlands and permitted men and women to live a shared religious life without making formal vows of poverty, chastity, and obedience). The northern Humanists, however, developed their own distinctive culture. They tended to come from more diverse social backgrounds and to be more devoted to religious reforms than their Italian counterparts. They were also more willing to write for lay audiences as well as for a narrow intelligentsia.

Erasmus

The most famous of the northern Humanists was Desiderius Erasmus (1466–1536), the reputed "prince of the Humanists." Erasmus gained fame as both an educational and a religious reformer. Earning his living by tutoring when patrons were in short supply, Erasmus prepared short Latin dialogues for his students that were intended to teach them how to speak and live well, inculcating good manners and language by encouraging them to imitate what they read. These dialogues were published under the title *Colloquies* and grew in number and length in consecutive editions, coming also

Erasmus of Rotterdam (1466–1536) *painted by Hans Holbein the Younger in* 1523. *Erasmus influenced all of the reform movements of the sixteenth century. He was popularly said to have "laid the egg that Luther hatched."* [*Kunstmuseum, Basel*]

to embrace anticlerical dialogues and satires on popular religious superstition. Erasmus collected ancient and contemporary proverbs, as well, which he published under the title *Adages*, beginning with about eight hundred examples and increasing his collection to over five thousand in the final edition of the work. Among the sayings that the *Adages* popularized are such common modern expressions as "to leave no stone unturned" and "where there is smoke, there is fire."

Erasmus aspired to unite the classical ideals of humanity and civic virtue with the Christian ideals of love and piety. He believed that disciplined study of the classics and the Bible, if begun early enough, was the best way to reform both individuals and society. He summarized his own beliefs with the phrase *philosophia Christi*, a simple, ethical piety in imitation of Christ. He set this ideal in starkest contrast to what he believed to be the dogmatic, ceremonial, and factious religious practice of the later Middle Ages. What most offended him about the Scholastics, both those of the late Middle Ages and, increasingly, the new Lutheran ones, was their letting doctrine and disputation overshadow humble piety and Christian practice.

To promote his own religious beliefs, Erasmus labored to make the ancient Christian sources available in their original versions, for, he believed, only as people drank from the pure, unadulterated sources could moral and religious health result. He edited the works of the Church Fathers and made a Greek edition of the New Testament (1516), which became the basis for his new, more accurate Latin translation (1519).

These various enterprises did not please church authorities, who were unhappy with both Erasmus's "improvements" on the Vulgate, Christendom's Bible for over a thousand years, and his popular anticlerical satires. At one point in the mid-sixteenth century all of Erasmus's works were placed on the *Index of Forbidden Books*. Erasmus also received Luther's unqualified condemnation for his views on the freedom of human will. Still,

Erasmus Describes the "Philosophy of Christ"

Although Erasmus called his ideal of how people should live the "philosophy of Christ," he found it taught by classical authors as well. In this selection he comments on its main features, with obvious polemic against the philosophy of the Scholastics.

This kind of philosophy [the philosophy of Christ] is located more truly in the disposition of the mind than in syllogisms. Here life means more than debate, inspiration is preferable to erudition, transformation [of life] a more important matter than intellectual comprehension. Only a very few can be learned, but all can be Christian, all can be devout, and—I shall boldly add—all can be theologians. Indeed, this philosophy easily penetrates into the minds of all; it is an action in special accord with human nature. What else is the philosophy of Christ, which he himself calls a rebirth, than the restoration of human nature . . . ? Although no one has taught this more perfectly . . . than Christ, nevertheless one may find in the books of the pagans very much which does agree with it. There was never so coarse a school of philosophy that taught that money rendered a man happy. Nor has there ever been one so shameless that fixed the chief good in vulgar honors and pleasures. The Stoics understood that no one was wise unless he was good. . . . According to Plato, Socrates teaches . . . that a wrong must not be repaid with a wrong, and also that since the soul is immortal, those should not be lamented who depart this life for a happier one with the assurance of having led an upright life. . . . And Aristotle has written in the Politics *that nothing can be a delight to us . . . except virtue alone. . . . If there are things that belong particularly to Christianity in these ancient writers, let us follow them.*

The *Paraclesis* in *Christian Humanism and the Reformation: Desiderius Erasmus*, ed. and trans. by John C. Olin (New York: Harper, 1965), pp. 100–101.

Erasmus's didactic and scholarly works became basic tools of reform in the hands of both Protestant and Catholic reformers.

Humanism in Germany

Peter Luder (d. 1474) and Rudolf Agricola (1443–1485) brought Italian learning to Germany. Agricola, the father of German Humanism, spent ten years in Italy. Like later German Humanists, he aspired to outdo the Italians in classical learning, thereby adding a nationalist motivation to German scholarship. Conrad Celtis (d. 1508), the first German poet laureate, and Ulrich von Hutten (1488–1523), a fiery knight, were exponents of romantic cultural nationalism. The life and work of Von Hutten especially illustrate the union of Humanism, German nationalism, and Luther's religious reform. A poet who admired Erasmus and attacked Scholasticism and bad Latin, von Hutten was also a member of the fading landed nobility who aspired to a revival of ancient German virtue—he died in 1523 in a hopeless knights' revolt against the princes. He was also an advocate of religious reform who attacked indulgences and published an edition of Valla's exposé of the Donation of Constantine.

THE REUCHLIN AFFAIR. The *cause célèbre* that brought von Hutten onto the historical stage and unified many reform-minded German Humanists was the Reuchlin affair. Johann Reuchlin (1455–1522) was Europe's foremost Christian authority on Hebrew and Jewish learning. He had written the first reliable Hebrew grammar by a Christian scholar and was personally attracted to Jewish mysticism. Around 1506 a converted Jew named Pfefferkorn, supported by the Dominican Order in Cologne (the city that was known as "the German Rome"), began a movement to suppress Jewish writings. When Pfefferkorn attacked Reuchlin, many German Humanists, in the name of academic freedom and good scholarship, not for any pro-Jewish sentiment, rushed to Reuchlin's defense. The controversy, which lasted several years, produced one of the great satires of the period, the *Letters of Obscure Men* (1515), a merciless satire on the narrowness and irrelevance of monks and Scholastics, particularly those in Cologne, written by Crotus Rubeanus and Ulrich von Hutten. When Luther came under attack after his famous ninety-five theses against indulgences in 1517, many German Humanists tended to see in his plight a repetition of the Scholastic attack on Reuchlin; religious reform and academic freedom were again at stake. Although, following Erasmus's lead, many of these same men ceased to support Luther when the revolutionary direction of his theology became clear, German Humanists formed the first identifiable group of Luther's supporters, and many young Humanists became Lutheran pastors.

Humanism in England

Humanists also promoted basic educational and religious reforms in England and France. English scholars and merchants and visiting Italian prelates brought Italian learning to England. The Oxford lectures of William Grocyn (d. 1519) and Thomas Linacre (d. 1524) and the Cambridge lectures of the visiting Erasmus (1510–1513), who worked on his Greek edition of the New Testament while in England, marked the scholarly maturation of English Humanism. John Colet (1467–1519), after 1505 dean of St. Paul's Cathedral, became renowned for his sermons and commentaries on the New Testament and his patronage of Humanist studies for the young. Like the other English Humanists, only more so, he stressed the relevance of Scripture to the problems of religious reform.

The best known of early English Humanists was Thomas More (1478–1535), a close friend of Erasmus. It was while visiting More that Erasmus wrote his most famous work, *The Praise of Folly,* an amusing and profound exposé of human self-deception. More's *Utopia* (1516), a criticism of contemporary society, still rivals the plays of Shakespeare as the most-read sixteenth-century English work. *Utopia* depicted an imaginary society based on reason and tolerance that had overcome social and political injustice by holding all property and goods in common and by requiring all to earn their bread by the sweat of their own brow.

A bureaucrat under Henry VII, More became one of Henry VIII's most trusted diplomats, succeeding Cardinal Wolsey as lord chancellor in 1529. More resigned that position in May 1532 because he could not in good conscience support the king's break with the papacy and his pretension to being head of the English church "so far as the law of Christ allows." More's repudiation of the Act of Supremacy (1534) and his refusal to recognize the king's marriage to Anne Boleyn led to his execution in July 1535.

Thomas More (1478–1535) by Hans Holbein the Younger, painted in 1527. The English statesman and author was beheaded by Henry VIII for his refusal to recognize the king's sovereignty over the English church. [*The Frick Collection*]

Although More remained staunchly Catholic, Humanism in England, as in Germany, played an important role in preparing the way for the English Reformation. A circle of English Humanists, under the direction of Henry VIII's minister Thomas Cromwell, translated and disseminated, to the king's advantage, such pertinent works as Marsilius of Padua's *Defender of Peace,* a work that exalted the sovereignty of rulers over popes and therefore had been condemned by the church, and writings of Erasmus that urged church reform.

Humanism in France

It was through the French invasions of Italy that Italian learning penetrated France, traffic in books and ideas going hand in hand with the transport of men and matériel to and fro. Guillaume Budé (1468–1540), an accomplished Greek scholar, and Jacques Lefèvre d'Etaples (1454–1536) were the leaders of French Humanism. Lefèvre's two main works—the *Quincuplex Psalterium,* five Latin versions of the psalms arranged in parallel columns, and a translation and commentary on Saint Paul's Epistle to the Romans—not only exemplified the new critical scholarship but also influenced the theology of Martin Luther. French Humanism had two powerful political patrons: Guillaume Briçonnet (1470–1533), after 1516 the bishop of Meaux, and Marguerite d'Angoulême (1492–1549), sister of Francis I and the future queen of Navarre, who made her own reputation as a writer. The future Protestant reformer John Calvin was a product of this native reform circle. Calvin was the first of three major vernacular writers with Humanist backgrounds who created the modern French language. The others were the physician François Rabelais (1494–1553), an ex-Franciscan and Benedictine monk whose *Gargantua* and *Pantagruel* satirized his age, and the skeptical essayist Michel de Montaigne (1533–1592), who ridiculed the authoritarian Scholastic mind.

Humanism in Spain

Whereas in Germany, England, and France Humanism prepared the way for Protestant reforms, in Spain it entered the service of the Catholic church. Here the key figure was Francisco Jiménez de Cisneros (1437–1517), a confessor to Queen Isabella, and after 1508 Grand Inquisitor—a position from which he was able to enforce the strictest religious orthodoxy. Jiménez was a conduit for Humanist scholarship and learning. He founded the University of Alcalá near Madrid in 1509, printed a Greek edition of the New Testament, and translated many religious tracts that aided clerical reform and control of lay religious life. His greatest achievement, taking fifteen years to complete, was the *Complutensian Polyglot Bible,* a six-volume work that placed the Hebrew, Greek, and Latin versions of the Bible in parallel columns. Such scholarly projects and internal church reforms joined with the repressive measures of Ferdinand and Isabella to keep Spain strictly Catholic throughout the Age of Reformation.

Religious Life

Popular Religious Movements and Criticism of the Church

The Protestant Reformation could not have occurred without the monumental crises of the medieval church during the "exile" in Avignon, the Great Schism, the conciliar period, and the Renaissance papacy. For increasing numbers of people the medieval church had ceased also to provide a viable religious piety. There was a crisis in the traditional teaching and spiritual practice of the church among many of its intellectuals and laity. Between the secular pretensions of the papacy and the dry teaching of Scholastic theologians, laity and clerics alike began to seek a more heartfelt, idealistic, and—often, in the eyes of the pope—increasingly heretical religious piety. The late Middle Ages were marked by independent lay and clerical efforts to reform local religious practice and by widespread experimentation with new religious forms.

A variety of factors contributed to the growth of lay criticism of the church. In the cities the laity were far more knowledgeable about the world and those who controlled their lives. The laity traveled widely—as soldiers, pilgrims, explorers, and traders. New postal systems and the printing press increased the information at their disposal. The new age of books and libraries raised literacy and heightened curiosity. Laypeople were increasingly in a position to take the initiative in shaping the cultural life of their communities.

From the Albigensians, Waldensians, Beguines, and Beghards in the thirteenth century to the Lollards and Hussites in the fifteenth, lay religious movements shared a common goal of religious simplicity in imitation of Jesus. Almost without exception they were inspired by an ideal of apostolic poverty in religion; that is, all wanted a religion of true self-sacrifice like that of Jesus and the first disciples. The laity sought a more egalitarian church, one that gave the members as well as the head of the church a voice, and a more spiritual church, one that lived manifestly according to its New Testament model.

The Modern Devotion. One of the most constructive lay religious movements in northern Europe on the eve of the Reformation was that of the Brothers of the Common Life, or what came to be known as the *Modern Devotion.* The brothers fostered the religious life outside formal ecclesiastical offices and apart from formal religious vows. Established by Gerard Groote (1340–1384) and centered at Zwolle and Deventer in the Netherlands, the brother and (less numerous) sister houses of the Modern Devotion spread rapidly throughout northern Europe and influenced parts of southern Europe as well. In these houses clerics and laity came together to share a common life, stressing individual piety and practical religion. Lay members were not expected to take special religious vows or to wear special religious dress, nor did they abandon their ordinary secular vocations.

The brothers were also active in education. They worked as copyists, sponsored many religious and a few classical publications, ran hospices for poor students, and conducted schools for the young, especially for boys preparing for the priesthood or a monastic vocation. As youths, Nicholas of Cusa, Johannes Reuchlin, and Desiderius Erasmus were looked after by the brothers. Thomas à Kempis (d. 1471) summarized the philosophy of the brothers in what became the most popular religious book of the period, the *Imitation of Christ,* a semimystical guide to the inner life intended primarily for monks and nuns, but widely appropriated by laity who also wanted to pursue the ascetic life.

The Modern Devotion has been seen as the source of Humanist, Protestant, and Catholic reform movements in the sixteenth century, although some scholars believe that it represented an individualistic approach to religion, indifferent and even harmful to the sacramental piety of the church. It was actually a very conservative movement. The brothers retained the old clerical doctrines and values, while placing them within the new framework of an active common life. They clearly met a need for a more personal piety and a better-informed religious life. Their movement appeared at a time when the laity were demanding good preaching in the vernacular and were even taking the initiative to endow special preacherships to ensure it. The Modern Devotion permitted laity to practice the religious life in the fullest, yet without having to surrender their life in the world.

Lay Control over Religious Life. On the eve of the Reformation, Rome's international network of church offices, which had unified Europe religiously during the Middle Ages, began to fall apart in many areas, hurried along by a growing sense of regional identity—incipient nationalism—and local secular administrative competence. The long-entrenched benefice system of the medieval church, which had permitted important ecclesiastical posts to be sold to the highest bidders and had left residency requirements in parishes unenforced, did not result in a vibrant local religious life.

The substitutes hired by nonresident holders of benefices, who lived elsewhere (mostly in Rome) and milked the revenues of their offices, often performed their chores mechanically and had neither firsthand knowledge of nor much sympathy with local needs and problems. Rare was the late medieval German town that did not have complaints about the maladministration, concubinage, and/or fiscalism of their clergy, especially the higher clergy (i.e., bishops, abbots, and prelates).

Communities loudly protested the financial abuses of the medieval church long before Luther published his famous summary of economic grievances in the *Address to the Christian Nobility of the German Nation*. The sale of indulgences, a practice that was greatly expanded on the eve of the Reformation and seemed now to permit people to buy release from religious punishment in purgatory both for their own and their deceased loved ones' sins, had also been repeatedly attacked before Luther came on the scene. Rulers and magistrates had little objection to and could even encourage the sale of indulgences as long as a generous portion of the income remained within the local coffers. But when an indulgence was offered primarily for the benefit of distant interests, as was the case with the Saint Peter's indulgence protested by Luther, resistance arose for strictly financial reasons, because their sale drained away local revenues.

Indulgences could not pass from the scene until rulers found new ways to profit from religion and a more effective popular remedy for religious anxiety was at hand. The Reformation provided the former by sanctioning the secular dissolution of monasteries and the confiscation of ecclesiastical properties. It held out the latter in its new theology of justification by faith.

City governments also undertook to improve local religious life on the eve of the Reformation by endowing preacherships. These were beneficed positions that provided for well-trained and dedicated pastors and regular preaching and pastoral care, which went beyond the routine performance of the Mass and traditional religious functions. In many instances these preacherships became platforms for Protestant preachers.

Magistrates also carefully restricted the growth of ecclesiastical properties and clerical privileges. During the Middle Ages special clerical rights in both property and person had come to be recognized by canon and civil law. Because they were holy places, churches and monasteries had been exempted from the taxes and laws that affected others. They were treated as special places of "sacral peace" and asylum. It was considered inappropriate for holy persons (clergy) to be burdened with such "dirty jobs" as military service, compulsory labor, standing watch at city gates, and other obligations of citizenship. Nor was it thought right that the laity, of whatever rank, should sit in judgment on those who were their shepherds and intermediaries with God. The clergy, accordingly, came to enjoy an immunity of place (which exempted ecclesiastical properties from taxes and recognized their right of asylum) and an immunity of person (which exempted the clergy from the jurisdiction of civil courts).

On the eve of the Reformation measures were passed to restrict these privileges and to end their abuses—efforts to regulate ecclesiastical acquisition of new property, to circumvent the right of asylum in churches and monasteries (a practice that posed a threat to the normal administration of justice), and to bring the clergy under the local tax code. Governments had understandably tired of ecclesiastical interference in what seemed to them to be strictly political spheres of competence and authority.

Martin Luther and German Reformation to 1525

Unlike France and England, late medieval Germany lacked the political unity to enforce "national" religious reforms during the late Middle Ages. There were no lasting Statutes of Provisors and *praemunire,* as in England, nor a Pragmatic Sanction of Bourges, as in France, limiting papal jurisdiction and taxation on a national scale. What happened on a unified national level in England and France occurred only locally and piecemeal within German territories and towns. As popular resentment of clerical immunities and ecclesiastical abuses, especially the selling of indulgences, spread among German cities and towns, an unorganized "national" opposition to Rome formed. German Humanists had long given voice to such criticism, and by 1517 it was pervasive enough to provide a solid foundation for Martin Luther's reform.

Luther (1483–1546) was the son of a successful Thüringian miner. He was educated in

Mansfeld; Magdeburg, where the Brothers of the Common Life were his teachers; and Eisenach. Between 1501 and 1505 he attended the University of Erfurt, where the nominalist teachings of William of Ockham and Gabriel Biel (d. 1495) prevailed within the Philosophical Faculty. After receiving his master of arts degree in 1505, Luther registered with the Law Faculty in accordance with his parents' wishes. But he never began the study of law. To the shock and disappointment of his family, he instead entered the Order of the Hermits of Saint Augustine in Erfurt on July 17, 1505. This decision had apparently been building for some time and was resolved during a lightning storm in which a terrified Luther, crying out to Saint Anne for assistance (Saint Anne was the patron saint of travelers in distress), promised to enter a monastery if he escaped death.

Ordained in 1507, Luther pursued a traditional course of study, becoming in 1509 a *baccalaureus biblicus* and *sententiarius,* that is, thoroughly trained in the Bible and the *Sentences* of Peter Lombard. In 1510 he journeyed to Rome on the business of his order, finding there justification for the many criticisms of the church he had heard in Germany. In 1511 he was transferred to the Augustinian monastery in Wittenberg, where he earned his doctorate in theology in 1512, thereafter becoming a leader within the monastery, the new university, and the spiritual life of the city.

Martin Luther (1483–1546), *painted in* 1521 *by Lucas Cranach the Elder* (1472–1553). [*Metropolitan Museum of Art, gift of Robert Lehman,* 1955]

Justification by Faith Alone

Reformation theology grew out of a problem common to many of the clergy and the laity at this time: the failure of traditional medieval religion to provide either full personal or intellectual satisfaction. Luther was especially plagued by the disproportion between his own sense of sinfulness and the perfect righteousness that medieval theology taught that God required for salvation. Traditional church teaching and the sacrament of penance proved to be of no consolation. Luther wrote that he came to despise the phrase "righteousness of God," for it seemed to demand of him a perfection he knew neither he nor any other human being could ever achieve. His insight into the meaning of "justification by faith alone" was a gradual process that extended over several years, between 1513 and 1518. The righteousness that God demands, he concluded, was not one that came from many religious works and ceremonies but was present in full measure in those who simply believed and trusted in the work of Jesus Christ, who alone was the perfect righteousness satisfying to God. To believe in Christ was to stand before God clothed in Christ's sure righteousness.

The Attack on Indulgences

An indulgence was a remission of the temporal penalty imposed by the priest on penitents as a "work of satisfaction" for their committed mortal sins. According to medieval theology, after the priest had absolved penitents of guilt for their sins, they still remained under an eternal penalty, a punishment God justly imposed on them for their sins. After absolution, however, this eternal penalty was said to be transformed into a temporal penalty, a manageable "work of satisfac-

Martin Luther Discovers Justification by Faith Alone

Many years after the fact, Martin Luther described his discovery that God's righteousness was not an active, punishing righteousness but a passive, transforming righteousness, which made those who believed in Him righteous as God Himself is righteous.

Though I lived as a monk without reproach, I felt that I was a sinner before God with an extremely disturbed conscience. I could not believe that he was placated by my satisfaction. I did not love, yes, I hated the righteous God who punishes sinners, and secretly, if not blasphemously, certainly murmuring greatly, I was angry with God, and said, ''As if, indeed, it is not enough, that miserable sinners, eternally lost through original sin, are crushed by every kind of calamity by the law of the decalogue, without having God add pain to pain by the gospel and also by the gospel threatening us with his righteousness and wrath!'' Thus I raged with a fierce and troubled conscience. Nevertheless, I beat importunately upon Paul at that place, most ardently desiring to know what St. Paul wanted.

At last, by the mercy of God, meditating day and night, I gave heed to the context of the words, namely, ''In it the righteousness of God is revealed, as it is written, 'He who through faith is righteous shall live''' [Romans 1:17]. There I began to understand that the righteousness of God is that by which the righteous lives by a gift of God, namely by faith. And this is the meaning: the righteousness of God is revealed by the gospel, namely, the passive righteousness with which merciful God justifies us by faith, as it is written, ''He who through faith is righteous shall live.'' Here I felt that I was altogether born again and had entered paradise itself through open gates. There a totally other face of the entire Scripture showed itself to me. Thereupon I ran through the Scriptures from memory. I also found in other terms an analogy, as, the work of God, that is, what God does in us, the power of God, with which he makes us strong, the wisdom of God, with which he makes us wise, the strength of God, the salvation of God, the glory of God.

And I extolled my sweetest word with a love as great as the hatred with which I had before hated the word ''righteousness of God.'' Thus that place in Paul was for me truly the gate to paradise.

Preface to the Complete Edition of Luther's Latin Writings (1545), in *Luther's Works,* Vol. 34, ed. by Lewis W. Spitz (Philadelphia: Muhlenberg Press, 1960) pp. 336–337.

tion'' that the penitent could perform here and now (for example, prayers, fasting, almsgiving, retreats, and pilgrimages). Penitents who defaulted on such prescribed works of satisfaction could expect to suffer for them in purgatory.

At this point indulgences came into play as an aid to a laity made genuinely anxious by a belief in a future suffering in purgatory for neglected penances or unrepented sins. In 1343 Pope Clement VI (1342–1352) had proclaimed the existence of a ''treasury of merit,'' an infinite reservoir of good works in the church's possession that could be dispensed at the pope's discretion. It was on the basis of this declared treasury that the church sold ''letters of indulgence,'' which covered the works of satisfaction owed by penitents. In 1476 Pope Sixtus IV (1471–1484) extended indulgences also to purgatory. Originally indulgences had been given only for the true self-sacrifice of going on a Crusade to the Holy Land. By Luther's time they were regularly dispensed for small cash payments (very modest sums that were regarded as a good work of almsgiving) and were presented to the laity as remitting not only their own future punishments, but also those of their dead relatives presumed to be suffering in purgatory.

In 1517 a Jubilee indulgence, proclaimed during the pontificate of Pope Julius II (1503–1513) to raise funds for the rebuilding of Saint Peter's in Rome, was revived and preached on the borders of Saxony in the territories of Archbishop Albrecht of Mainz. Albrecht was much in need of revenues because of the large debts he had incurred in order to hold, contrary to church law, three ecclesiastical appointments: the archbishoprics of Mainz and Magdeburg in addition to the bishopric of Halberstadt. The selling of the indulgence was a joint venture by Albrecht, the Augsburg banking-house of Fugger, and Pope Leo X, half the proceeds going to the pope and half to Albrecht and his creditors. The famous indulgence preacher John Tetzel (d. 1519) was enlisted to preach the indulgence in Albrecht's territories because he was a seasoned professional who knew how to stir ordinary people to action. As he exhorted on one occasion:

> Don't you hear the voices of your dead parents and other relatives crying out, "Have mercy on us, for we suffer great punishment and pain. From this you could release us with a few alms. . . . We have created you, fed you, cared for you, and left you our temporal goods. Why do you treat us so cruelly and leave us to suffer in the flames, when it takes only a little to save us?"[1]

When on October 31, 1517, Luther posted his ninety-five theses against indulgences, according to tradition, on the door of Castle Church in Wittenberg, he protested especially against the impression created by Tetzel that indulgences actually remitted sins and released the dead from punishment in purgatory—claims Luther believed went far beyond the traditional practice and seemed to make salvation something that could be bought and sold.

Election of Charles V

The ninety-five theses were embraced by Humanists and other proponents of reform. They made Luther famous overnight and prompted official proceedings against him. In April 1518 he was summoned to appear before the general chapter of his order in Heidelberg, and the following October he was called before the papal legate and general of the Dominican Order, Cardinal Cajetan, in Augsburg. As sanctions were being prepared against Luther, Emperor Maximilian I died (January 12, 1519), and this event, fortunate for the Reformation, turned all attention from heresy in Saxony to the contest for a new emperor.

The pope backed the French king, Francis I. However, Charles I of Spain, a youth of nineteen, succeeded his grandfather and became Emperor Charles V. Charles was assisted by both a long tradition of Habsburg imperial rule and a massive Fugger campaign chest, which

[1]*Die Reformation in Augenzeugen berichten,* ed. by Helmar Junghaus (Düsseldorf: Karl Rauch Verlag, 1967), p. 44.

A contemporary caricature of John Tetzel, the famous indulgence preacher. The last lines of the jingle read: "As soon as gold in the basin rings, right then the soul to heaven springs." It was Tetzel's preaching that spurred Luther to publish his ninety-five theses. [Staatliche Lutherhalle, Wittenberg]

Pope Leo X (1513–1521), *of the Medici family, with two cardinals, as painted about* 1517–1518 *by Raphael. Leo was pope when the reformation began and condemned Luther for heresy in* 1520. *[Alinari/SCALA]*

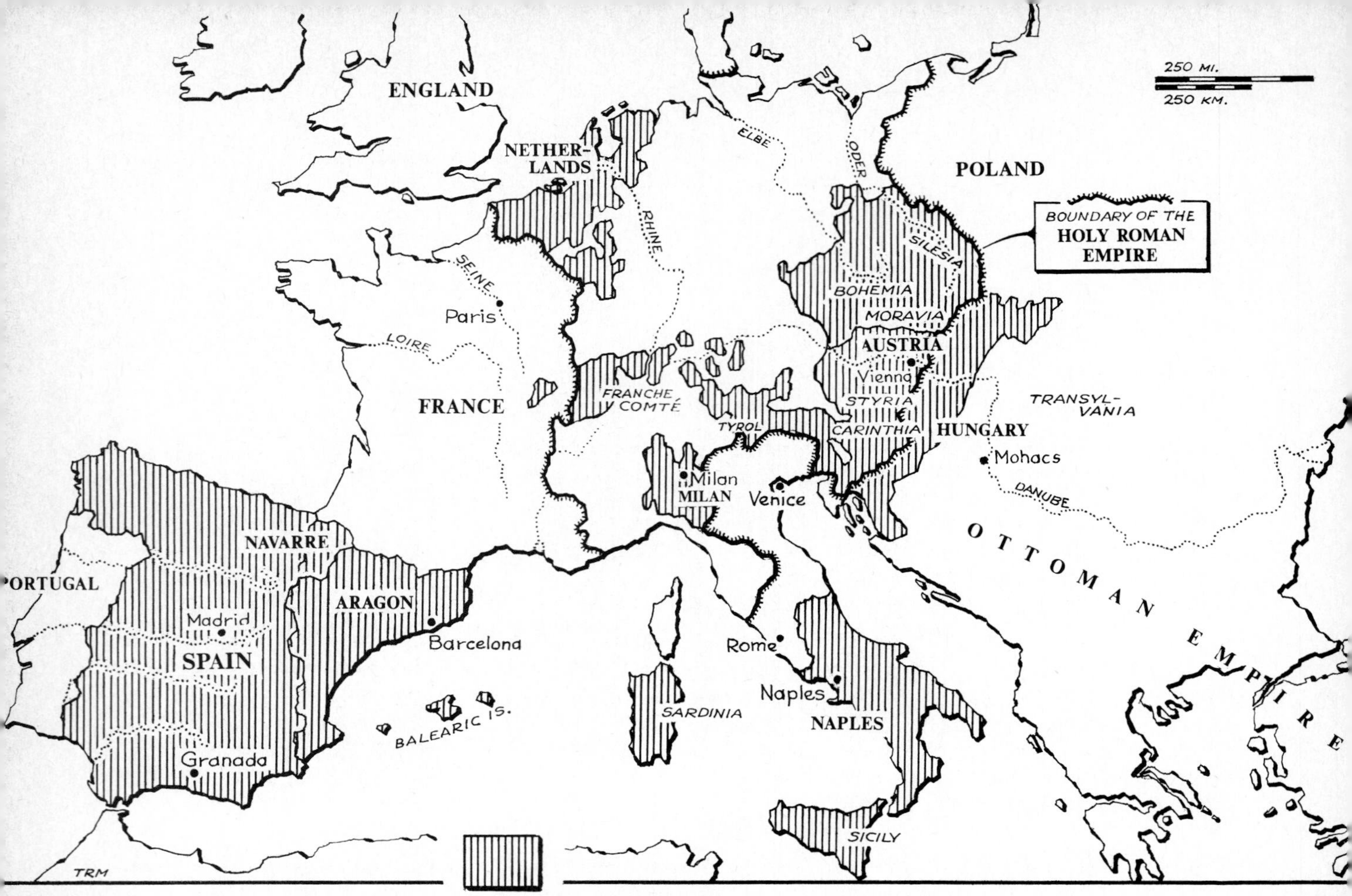

THE EMPIRE OF CHARLES V

MAP 10–2 *Dynastic marriages and simple chance concentrated into Charles's hands rule over the lands shown here, plus Spain's overseas possessions. Crowns and titles rained in on him; election in* 1519 *as emperor gave him new burdens and responsibilities.*

secured the votes of the seven electors. The electors, who traditionally enhanced their power at every opportunity, wrung new concessions from Charles for their votes. The emperor agreed to a revival of the Imperial Supreme Court and the Council of Regency and promised to consult with a diet of the empire on all major domestic and foreign affairs that affected the empire. These measures also helped the development of the Reformation by preventing unilateral imperial action against the Germans, something Luther could be thankful for in the early years of the Reformation.

Luther's Excommunication and the Diet of Worms

In the same month in which Charles was elected emperor, Luther entered a debate in Leipzig (June 27, 1519) with the Ingolstadt professor John Eck. During this contest Luther challenged the infallibility of the pope and the inerrancy of church councils, appealing, for the first time, to the sovereign authority of Scripture alone. All his bridges to the old church were burned when he further defended certain teachings of John Huss condemned by the Council of Constance. In 1520 Luther signaled his new direction with three famous pamphlets: the *Address to the Christian Nobility of the German Nation,* which urged the German princes to force reforms on the Roman church, especially to curtail its political and economic power in Germany; the *Babylonian Captivity of the Church,* which attacked the traditional seven sacraments, arguing that only two, Baptism and the Eucharist, were proper, and exalted the authority of Scripture, church councils, and secular princes over that of the pope;

and the eloquent *Freedom of a Christian*, which summarized the new teaching of salvation by faith alone. On June 15, 1520, the papal bull *Exsurge Domine* condemned Luther for heresy and gave him sixty days to retract. The final bull of excommunication, *Decet Pontificem Romanum*, was issued on January 3, 1521.

In April 1521 Luther presented his views before a diet of the empire in Worms, over which the newly elected Emperor Charles V presided. Ordered to recant, Luther declared that to do so would be to act against Scripture, reason, and his own conscience. On May 26, 1521, he was placed under the imperial ban and thereafter became an "outlaw" to secular as well as to religious authority. For his own protection friends hid him in Wartburg Castle, where he spent almost a year in seclusion, from April 1521 to March 1522. During his stay, he translated the New Testament into

A Catholic caricature of Martin Luther as a seven-headed monster. This picture served as the title page of a pamphlet by one of Luther's strongest Catholic critics, Johannes Cochlaeus.

Luther Calls on the German Nobility to Reform the Church

In his *Address to the Christian Nobility of the German Nation* (1520), Luther protested against the three "walls" of Rome that had prevented reform in the church by making the pope immune to corrective action on the basis of secular, biblical, and conciliar authority. In the following, Luther urges the nobility to tear down these walls.

The Romanists have with great dexterity built around themselves three walls, which hitherto have protected them against reform; and thereby is Christianity fearfully fallen.

In the first place, when the temporal power has pressed them hard [to reform], they have . . . maintained that the temporal power has no jurisdiction over them, that, on the contrary, the spiritual [power] is above the temporal.

Secondly, when it was proposed to admonish them from the Holy Scriptures they said, "It befits no one but the pope to interpret the Scriptures."

And, thirdly, when they were threatened with a council, they invented the idea that no one but the pope can call a council.

Thus have they secretly stolen our three rods so that they may go unpunished, and entrenched themselves safely behind these three walls in order to carry on all the knavery and wickedness that we now see. . . .

Now may God help us, and give us one of those trumpets that overthrew the walls of Jericho, so that we may also blow down these walls of straw and paper and . . . regain possession of our Christian rods for the chastisement of sin and expose the craft and deceit of the Devil.

James Harvey Robinson (Ed.), *Readings in European History*, Vol. 2 (Boston: Ginn and Co., 1906), p. 75.

German, using Erasmus's new Greek text, and he attempted by correspondence to oversee the first stages of the Reformation in Wittenberg.

Imperial Distractions: France and the Turks

The Reformation was greatly assisted in these early years by the emperor's war with France and the advance of the Ottoman Turks into eastern Europe. Against both adversaries Charles V, who also remained a Spanish king with dynastic responsibilities outside the empire, needed German troops, and to that end he promoted friendly relations with the German princes. Between 1521 and 1559 Spain (the Habsburg dynasty) and France (the Valois dynasty) fought four major wars over disputed territories in Italy and along their borders. In 1526 the Turks overran Hungary at the Battle of Mohacs, while in western Europe the French-led League of Cognac formed against Charles for the second Habsburg–Valois war. Thus preoccupied, the emperor agreed through his representatives at the German Diet of Speyer in 1526 that each German territory was free to enforce the Edict of Worms (1521) against Luther "so as to be able to answer in good conscience to God and the emperor." That concession, in effect, gave the German princes territorial sovereignty in religious matters and the Reformation time to put down deep roots. Later (in 1555) such local princely control over religion would be enshrined in imperial law by the Peace of Augsburg.

The Peasants' Revolt

In its first decade the Protestant movement suffered more from internal division than from imperial interference. By 1525 Luther had become as much an object of protest within Germany as was the pope. Original allies, sympathizers, and fellow travelers declared their independence from him.

Peasants plundering a German monastery in 1525. *The peasant revolt of* 1524–1525 *frightened both Protestant and Catholic rulers, who united to suppress the rising.* [*Bildarchiv Preussischer Kneturbesitz*]

German Peasants Protest Rising Feudal Exactions

In the late fifteenth and early sixteenth centuries German feudal lords, both secular and ecclesiastical, tried to increase the earnings from their lands by raising demands on their peasant tenants. As the personal freedoms of peasants were restricted, their properties confiscated, and their traditional laws and customs overridden, massive revolts occurred in southern Germany in 1525. Not a few historians, especially those of Marxist persuasion, see this uprising and the social and economic conditions that gave rise to it, as the major historical force in early modern history. The following, from Memmingen, in modern West Germany, is the most representative and well-known statement of peasant grievances.

1. It is our humble petition and desire . . . that in the future . . . each community should choose and appoint a pastor, and that we should have the right to depose him should he conduct himself improperly. . . .

2. We are ready and willing to pay the fair tithe of grain. . . . The small tithes [of cattle], whether [to] ecclesiastical or lay lords, we will not pay at all, for the Lord God created cattle for the free use of man. . . .

3. We . . . take it for granted that you will release us from serfdom as true Christians, unless it should be shown us from the Gospel that we are serfs.

4. It has been the custom heretofore that no poor man should be allowed to catch venison or wildfowl or fish in flowing water, which seems to us quite unseemly and unbrotherly as well as selfish and not agreeable to the Word of God. . . .

5. We are aggrieved in the matter of woodcutting, for the noblemen have appropriated all the woods to themselves. . . .

6. In regard to the excessive services demanded of us which are increased from day to day, we ask that this matter be properly looked into so that we shall not continue to be oppressed in this way. . . .

7. We will not hereafter allow ourselves to be further oppressed by our lords, but will let them demand only what is just and proper according to the word of the agreement between the lord and the peasant. The lord should no longer try to force more services or other dues from the peasant without payment. . . .

8. We are greatly burdened because our holdings cannot support the rent exacted from them. . . . We ask that the lords may appoint persons of honor to inspect these holdings and fix a rent in accordance with justice. . . .

9. We are burdened with a great evil in the constant making of new laws. . . . In our opinion we should be judged according to the old written law. . . .

10. We are aggrieved by the appropriation . . . of meadows and fields which at one time belonged to a community as a whole. These we will take again into our own hands. . . .

11. We will entirely abolish the due called Todfall *[that is, heriot or death tax, by which the lord received the best horse, cow, or garment of a family upon the death of a serf] and will no longer endure it, nor allow widows and orphans to be thus shamefully robbed against God's will, and in violation of justice and right. . . .*

12. It is our conclusion and final resolution, that if any one or more of the articles here set forth should not be in agreement with the Word of God, as we think they are, such article we will willingly retract.

Translations and Reprints from the Original Sources of European History, Vol. 2 (Philadelphia: Department of History, University of Pennsylvania, 1897).

Like the German Humanists, the German peasantry also had at first believed Luther to be an ally. The peasantry had been organized since the late fifteenth century against efforts by territorial princes to override their traditional laws and customs and to subject them to new regulations and taxes. Peasant leaders, several of whom were convinced Lutherans, saw in Luther's teaching about Christian freedom and his criticism of monastic landowners a point of view close to their own, and they openly solicited Luther's support of their political and economic rights, including their revolutionary request for release from serfdom. Luther and his followers sympathized with the peasants; indeed, for several years Lutheran pamphleteers made *Karsthans,* the burly, honest peasant who earned his bread by the sweat of his brow and sacrificed his own comfort and well-being for others, a symbol of the simple life that God desired all people to live. The Lutherans, however, were not social revolutionaries, and when the peasants revolted against their masters in 1524–1525, Luther, not surprisingly, condemned them in the strongest possible terms as "unchristian" and urged the princes to crush their revolt without mercy. Tens of thousands of peasants (estimates run between 70,000 and 100,000) had died by the time the revolt was put down.

For Luther, the freedom of the Christian was an inner release from guilt and anxiety, not a right to restructure society by violent revolution. Had Luther supported the Peasants' Revolt, he would have contradicted his own teaching and would probably also have ended any chance of the survival of his reform beyond the 1520s. Still, many believe that his decision greatly reduced the social impact of the Reformation.

Zwingli and the Swiss Reformation

Switzerland was a loose confederacy of thirteen autonomous cantons or states and allied areas (see Map 10.3). Some cantons (e.g., Zurich, Bern, Basel, and Schaffhausen) became Protestant, some (especially around the Lucerne heartland) remained Catholic, and a few other cantons and religions managed to effect a compromise. Among the preconditions of the Swiss Reformation were the growth of national sentiment occasioned by opposition to foreign mercenary service (providing mercenaries for Europe's warring nations was a major source of Switzerland's livelihood) and a desire for church reform that had persisted in Switzerland since the councils of Constance (1414–1417) and Basel (1431–1449).

The Reformation in Zurich

Ulrich Zwingli (1484–1531), the leader of the Swiss Reformation, had been humanistically educated in Bern, Vienna, and Basel. He was strongly influenced by Erasmus, whom he credited with having set him on the path to reform. He served as a chaplain with Swiss mercenaries during the disastrous Battle of Marignano in 1515 and thereafter became an eloquent critic of mercenary service. Zwingli believed that this service threatened both the political sovereignty and the moral well-being of the Swiss confederacy. By 1518 Zwingli was also widely known for opposition to the sale of indulgences and to religious superstition. In 1519 he entered the competition for the post of people's priest in the main church of Zurich. His candidacy was contested because of his acknowledged fornication with a barber's daughter, an affair he successfully minimized in a forcefully written self-defense. Actually his conduct was less scandalous to his contemporaries, who sympathized with the plight of the celibate clergy, than it may be to the modern reader. One of Zwingli's first acts as a reformer was to petition for an end to clerical celibacy and for the right of all clergy to marry, a practice that quickly became accepted in all Protestant lands.

From his new position as people's priest in Zurich, Zwingli engineered the Swiss Reformation. In March 1522 he was party to the breaking of the Lenten fast—an act of protest analogous to burning one's national flag today. Zwingli's reform guideline was very simple and very effective: whatever lacked literal support in Scripture was to be neither believed nor practiced. As had also happened with Luther, that test soon raised questions about such honored traditional teachings and practices as fasting, transubstantiation, the worship of saints, pilgrimages, purgatory, clerical celibacy, and certain sacraments. A disputation held on January 29, 1523, concluded with the city government's sanction of Zwingli's Scripture test. Thereafter Zurich became, to all intents and purposes, a Protestant city and the center of the Swiss Reformation. A harsh discipline was imposed by the new Protestant regime, making Zurich one of the first examples of a puritanical Protestant city.

The Marburg Colloquy

Landgrave Philip of Hesse (1504–1567) sought to unite Swiss and German Protestants in a mutual defense pact, a potentially significant political alliance. His efforts were spoiled, however, by theological disagreements between Luther and Zwingli over the nature of Christ's presence in the Eucharist. Zwingli

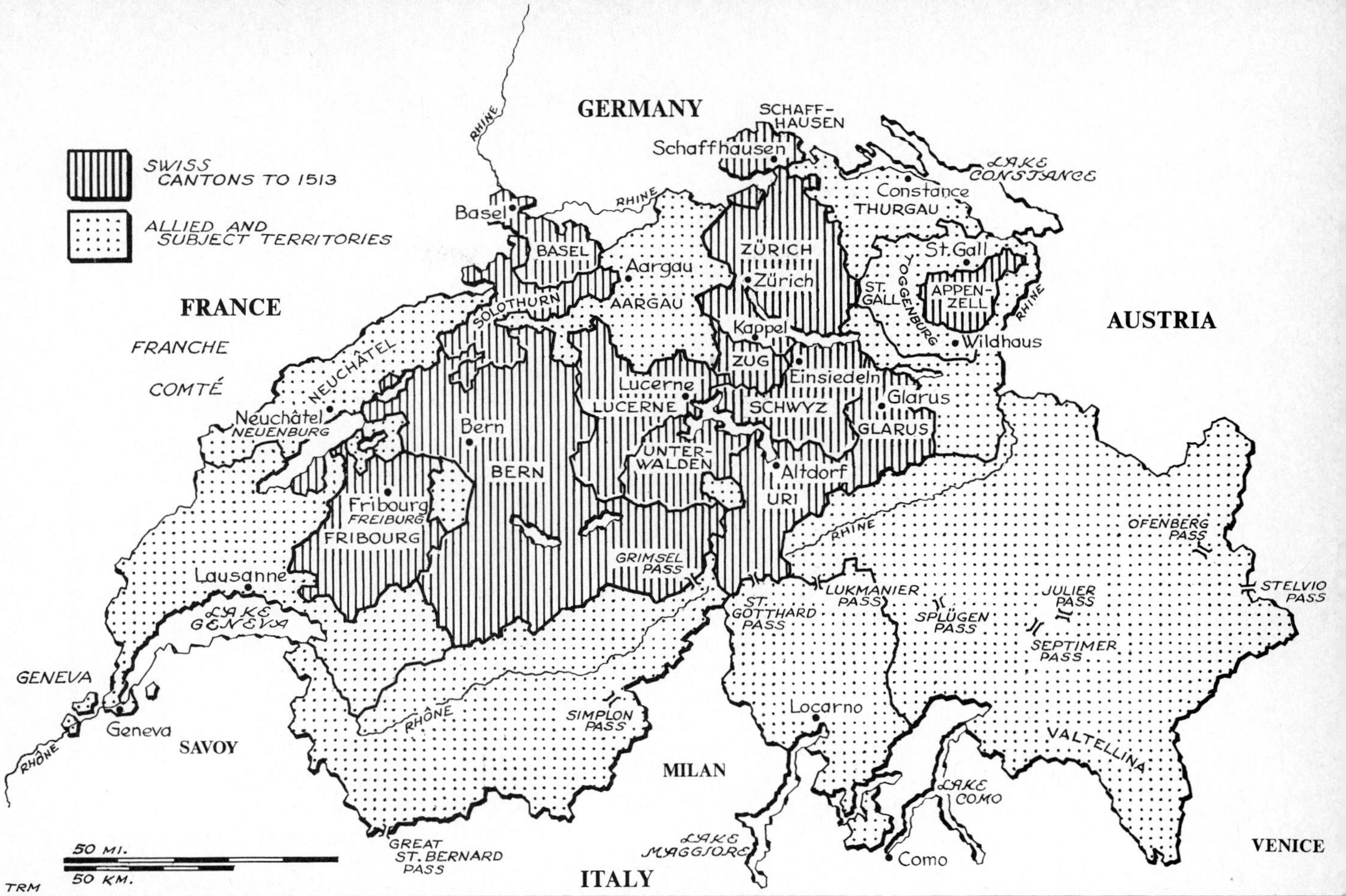

THE SWISS CONFEDERATION

MAP 10–3 *While nominally still a part of the Holy Roman Empire, Switzerland grew from a loose defensive union of the central "forest cantons" in the thirteenth century to a fiercely independent association of regions with different languages, histories, and, finally, religions.*

maintained a symbolic interpretation of Christ's words, "This is my body"; Christ, he argued, was only spiritually, not bodily, present in the bread and wine of the Eucharist. Luther, to the contrary, insisted that Christ's human nature could share the properties of his divine nature; hence, where Christ was spiritually present, he could also be bodily present, for his was a special nature. Luther wanted no part of an abstract, spiritualized Christ. Zwingli, on the other hand, feared that Luther had not broken sufficiently with medieval sacramental theology.

Philip of Hesse brought the two Protestant leaders together in his castle in Marburg in early October 1529, but they were unable to work out their differences on this issue. Luther left thinking Zwingli a dangerous fanatic. Although cooperation between the two sides did not cease, the disagreement splintered the Protestant movement theologically and politically. Separate defense leagues formed, and semi-Zwinglian theological views came to be embodied in the *Confessio Tetrapolitana,* a confession of faith prepared by the Strasbourg reformers Martin Bucer and Caspar Hedio for presentation to the Diet of Augsburg (1530) as an alternative to the Lutheran *Augsburg Confession.*

Swiss Civil Wars

As the Swiss cantons divided between Protestantism and Catholicism, civil wars began.

Zwingli Lists the Errors of the Roman Church

Religious argument can become confusing. A clear summary of issues is often helpful—both to the disputants and to interested bystanders. Before the first Zurich Disputation (1523), which effectually introduced the Protestant Reformation in Zurich, the reformer Zwingli prepared such a summary of the new Evangelical truths and the errors of the Roman church, known as the *Sixty-Seven Articles.* Here are some of them.

All who consider other teachings equal to or higher than the Gospel err, and they do not know what the Gospel is.

In the faith rests our salvation, and in unbelief our damnation; for all truth is clear in Christ.

In the Gospel one learns that human doctrines and decrees do not aid in salvation.

That Christ, having sacrificed himself once, is to eternity a certain and valid sacrifice for the sins of all faithful, wherefrom it follows that the Mass is not a sacrifice, but is a remembrance of the sacrifice and assurance of the salvation which Christ has given us.

That God desires to give us all things in his name, whence it follows that outside of this life we need no [intercession of the saints or any] mediator except himself.

That no Christian is bound to do those things which God has not decreed, therefore one may eat at all times all food, wherefrom one learns that the decree about cheese and butter [i.e., fasting from such foods at certain times of the year] is a Roman swindle.

That no special person can impose the ban upon [i.e., excommunicate] anyone, but the Church, that is, the congregation of those among whom the one to be banned dwells, together with their watchman, i.e., the pastor.

All that the so-called spiritual [i.e., the papal church] claims to have of power and protection belongs to the lay [i.e., the secular magistracy], if they wish to be Christians.

Greater offense I know not than that one does not allow priests to have wives, but permits them to hire prostitutes.

Christ has borne all our pains and labor. Hence whoever assigns to works of penance what belongs to Christ errs and slanders God.

The true divine Scriptures know naught about purgatory after this life.

The Scriptures know no priests except those who proclaim the word of God.

Ulrich Zwingli (1484–1531): *Selected Works,* ed. by Samuel M. Jackson (Philadelphia: University of Pennsylvania Press, 1972), pp. 111–117.

There were two major battles, both at Kappel, one in June 1529 and a second in October 1531. The first ended in a Protestant victory, which forced the Catholic cantons to break their foreign alliances and to recognize the rights of Swiss Protestants. During the second battle Zwingli was found wounded on the battlefield and was unceremoniously executed, his remains scattered to the four winds so that his followers would have no relics to console and inspire them. The subsequent treaty confirmed the right of each canton to determine its own religion. Heinrich Bullinger (1504–1575), who was Zwingli's protégé and later married his daughter, became the new leader of the Swiss Reformation and guided its development into an established religion.

Anabaptists and Radical Protestants

The moderate pace and seemingly low ethical results of the Lutheran and Zwinglian reformations discontented many people, among them some of the original co-workers of Luther and Zwingli. Many desired a more rapid and thorough implementation of primitive Christianity—that is, a more visible moral transformation—and accused the major reformers of going only halfway. The most important of these radical groups were the Anabaptists, the sixteenth-century ancestors of the modern Mennonites and Amish. The Anabaptists were especially distinguished by their rejection of infant baptism and their insistence on only adult baptism (*anabaptism* derives from the Greek word meaning "to rebaptize"), believing that baptism as a consenting adult conformed to Scripture and was more respectful of human freedom.

Conrad Grebel and the Swiss Brethren

Conrad Grebel (1498–1526), with whom Anabaptism originated, performed the first adult rebaptism in Zurich in January 1525. Initially a coworker with Zwingli and an even greater biblical literalist, Grebel broke openly with Zwingli after a religious disputation in October 1523 in which Zwingli supported the city government's plea for a gradual removal of traditional religious practices. The alternative of the Swiss Brethren, as Grebel's group came to be called, was set forth in the *Schleitheim Confession* of 1527. This document distinguished Anabaptists not only by their practice of adult baptism but also by their refusal to go to war, to swear oaths, and to participate in the offices of secular government. Anabaptists physically separated from society to form a more perfect community in imitation of what they believed to be the example of the first Christians. Because of the close connection between religious and civic life in this period, such separatism was viewed by the political authorities as a threat to basic social bonds.

The Anabaptist Reign in Münster

At first, Anabaptism drew its adherents from all social classes. But as Lutherans and Zwinglians joined with Catholics in opposition to the Anabaptists and persecuted them within the cities, a more rural, agrarian class came to make up the great majority. In 1529, rebaptism became a capital offense throughout the Holy Roman Empire. It has been estimated that between 1525 and 1618 at least one thousand and perhaps as many as five thousand men and women were executed for rebaptising themselves as adults. Brutal measures were universally applied against nonconformists after Anabaptist extremists came to power in the German city of Münster in 1534–1535. Led by two Dutch emigrants, a baker, Jan Matthys of Haarlem, and a tailor, Jan Beukelsz of Leiden, the Anabaptist majority in this city forced Lutherans and Catholics either to convert or to emigrate. As the Lutherans and Catholics left, Münster transformed itself into an Old Testament theocracy, replete with charismatic lead-

The siege of Munster in 1534–1535. A joint Catholic-Protestant army recaptured the city from the Anabaptists led by Jan of Leiden. [Bilderchiv Foto Marburg]

ers and the practice of polygamy. The outside world was deeply shocked. Protestant and Catholic armies united to crush the radicals, and the skeletons of their leaders long hung in public view as a warning to all who would so offend traditional Christian sensitivities. After this episode, moderate, pacifistic Anabaptism became the norm among most nonconformists. The moderate Anabaptist leader Menno Simons (1496–1561), the founder of the Mennonites, set the example for the future.

Spiritualists

In addition to the Anabaptists there were radicals known as *Spiritualists.* These were mostly isolated individuals distinguished by their disdain of all traditions and institutions. They believed that the only religious authority was God's spirit, which spoke here and now to every individual. Among them were several former Lutherans: Thomas Müntzer (d. 1525), who had close contacts with Anabaptist leaders in Germany and Switzerland and died as a leader of a peasants' revolt; Sebastian Franck (d. 1541), a free-lance critic of all dogmatic religion who proclaimed the religious autonomy of every individual soul; and Caspar Schwenckfeld (d. 1561), a prolific writer and wanderer after whom the Schwenckfeldian Church is named.

Antitrinitarians

A final group of radical Protestants was the Antitrinitarians, exponents of a commonsense, rational, and ethical religion. Chief among this group were the Spaniard Michael Servetus (1511–1553), executed in 1553 in Geneva for "blasphemies against the Holy Trinity," and the Italians Lelio (d. 1562) and Faustus Sozzini (d. 1604), the founders of Socinianism. These thinkers were the strongest opponents of Calvinism (to be discussed later), especially its belief in original sin and predestination, and have a deserved reputation as defenders of religious toleration.

Political Consolidation of the Lutheran Reformation

The Diet of Augsburg

Charles V, who spent most of his time on politics and military maneuvers outside the empire, especially in Spain and Italy, returned to the empire in 1530 to direct the Diet of Augsburg, a meeting of Protestant and Catholic representatives assembled for the purpose of imposing a settlement of the religious divisions. With its terms dictated by the Catholic emperor, the diet adjourned with a blunt order to all Lutherans to revert to Catholicism. The Reformation was by this time too firmly established for that to occur, and in February 1531 the Lutherans responded with the formation of their own defensive alliance, the Schmalkaldic League. The league took as its banner the *Augsburg Confession,* a moderate statement of Protestant beliefs that had been spurned by the emperor at the Diet of Augsburg. In 1538 Luther drew up a more strongly worded Protestant confession known as the *Schmalkaldic Articles.* Under the leadership of Landgrave Philip of Hesse and Elector John Frederick of Saxony, the league achieved a stalemate with the emperor, who was again distracted by renewed war with France and the ever-resilient Turks.

The Expansion of the Reformation

In the 1530s German Lutherans formed regional consistories, judicial bodies composed of theologians and lawyers, which oversaw and administered the new Protestant churches. These consistories replaced the old Catholic episcopates. Under the leadership of Philip Melanchthon, the "praeceptor of Germany," educational reforms were enacted that provided for compulsory primary education, schools for girls, a Humanist revision of the traditional curriculum, and catechetical instruction of the laity in the new religion.

The Reformation also dug in elsewhere. Introduced into Denmark by Christian II (ruled 1513–1523), Danish Lutheranism throve under Frederick I (1523–1533), who joined the Schmalkaldic League. Under Christian III (1536–1559), Lutheranism became the state religion, and the Wittenberg preacher Johannes Bugenhagen arrived to organize the Danish Lutheran church.

In Sweden, Gustavus Vasa (1523–1560), supported by a Swedish nobility greedy for church lands, confiscated church property and subjected the clergy to royal authority at the Diet of Vesteras (1527).

In politically splintered Poland, Lutherans, Anabaptists, Calvinists, and even Antitrinitarians found room to practice their beliefs, as

The Diet of Augsburg, 1530. *Charles V is enthroned beneath the canopy. The principal German princes are seated around him.* [*Bulloz*]

Poland, primarily because of the absence of a central political authority, became a model of religious pluralism and toleration in the second half of the sixteenth century.

REACTION AGAINST PROTESTANTS: THE INTERIM. Charles V made abortive efforts in 1540–1541 to enforce a compromise agreement between Protestants and Catholics. As these and other conciliar efforts failed, he turned to a military solution. In 1547 imperial armies crushed the Protestant Schmalkaldic League. John Frederick of Saxony was defeated in April 1547, and Philip of Hesse was taken captive shortly thereafter.

The emperor established puppet rulers in Saxony and Hesse and issued as imperial law the *Augsburg Interim,* a new order that Protestants everywhere must readopt old Catholic beliefs and practices. There were a few cosmetic Protestant concessions, for example, clerical marriage (with papal approval of individual cases) and communion in both kinds (that is, bread *and* wine). Although the *Interim* met only surface acceptance within Germany, it forced many Protestant leaders into exile. The Strasbourg reformer Martin Bucer, for example, departed to England, where he played an important role in the drafting of the religious documents of the English Reformation during the reign of Edward VI. In Germany, Magdeburg became a refuge for perse-

Charles V (1500–1558), painted by Titian in 1548 after his armies had crushed the Protestant Schmalkaldic League. [The Prado, Madrid]

cuted Protestants and the center of Lutheran resistance.

The Peace of Augsburg

The Reformation was too entrenched by 1547 to be ended even by brute force. Maurice of Saxony, hand-picked by Charles V to rule Saxony, recognized the inevitability of Protestantism and shifted his allegiance to the Protestants. Confronted by fierce Protestant resistance and weary from three decades of war, the emperor was forced to relent. After a defeat by Protestant armies in 1552, Charles reinstated John Frederick and Philip of Hesse and guaranteed Lutheran religious freedoms in the Peace of Passau (August 1552), a declaration that effectively surrendered his lifelong quest for European religious unity.

The division of Christendom was made permanent by the Peace of Augsburg in September 1555. This agreement recognized in law what had already been well established in practice: *cuius regio, eius religio,* meaning that the ruler of a land would determine the religion of the land. Lutherans were permitted to retain all church lands forcibly seized before 1552. An "ecclesiastical reservation" was added, however, that was intended to prevent high Catholic prelates who converted to Protestantism from retaining their lands, titles, and privileges. Those discontented with the religion of their region were permitted to migrate to another.

Calvinism and Anabaptism were not recognized as legal forms of Christian belief and practice by the Peace of Augsburg. Anabaptists had long adjusted to such exclusion by forming their own separatist communities. Calvinists, however, were not separatists and could not choose this route; they remained determined not only to secure the right to worship publicly as they pleased but also to shape society according to their own religious convictions. While Anabaptists retreated and Lutherans enjoyed the security of an established religion, Calvinists organized to lead national revolutions throughout northern Europe in the second half of the sixteenth century.

The Rise of Russia

Although the Reformation pushed northward into Scandinavia and eastward into Poland, it was not to penetrate into Russia. There another kind of reform, one strictly political in nature, was under way, as the principality of Moscow evolved into a new kind of state under Ivan IV (1533–1584), better known as Ivan the Terrible. His reign displayed a pattern that would be repeated frequently, and often tragically, in later Russian history: early years of reform and solid accomplishment followed by a period of almost inexplicable tyranny.

Ivan came into his political inheritance at the age of three. Consequently, there was a long regency that witnessed numerous clashes among the boyars, or Russian nobles. The first key moment in his personal reign occurred in 1547, when at the age of sixteen he had himself crowned czar (the Russian equivalent of *Caesar* or *Kaiser*) rather than prince of Moscow.

During the opening years of his personal reign, Ivan IV consulted with the great boyars and other able advisers in a relationship of mutual trust. He worked toward formulating a revised law code and a mode of local government that would be responsive to the needs of the areas governed. He reorganized the army, and he established direct economic contact with western Europe. During the 1550s Ivan undertook successful military campaigns against the Ottomans in the south, the Tatars in the south and east, and for a time the Livonians in the northwest. It appeared that his reign would be well regarded at home and abroad.

Beginning in about 1560, however, a profound change took place in his personality. He began to mistrust his most honest advisers and believed that they were plotting against him. When his first wife died in 1560, he thought she had been poisoned by a conspiracy. In the late 1560s he created a set of boyars and officials who were personally loyal to him and an army also loyal to him alone. He loosed these troops, who always dressed in black and who were called the *oprichniki*, against anyone he regarded as an enemy. He imprisoned, tortured, and executed boyars without cause and without trial. In 1581 Ivan killed his own son. He himself died in 1584. While he had pursued this utterly irrational behavior at home, his military forces in Livonia had been defeated by both Sweden and Poland. His reign ended in domestic political turmoil and foreign military defeat.

John Calvin and the Genevan Reformation

In the second half of the sixteenth century Calvinism replaced Lutheranism as the dominant Protestant force in Europe. Calvinism was the religious ideology that inspired or accompanied massive political resistance in France, the Netherlands, and Scotland. It established itself within the Palatinate during the reign of Elector Frederick III (1559–1576). Believing strongly in both divine predestination and the individual's responsibility to reorder society according to God's plan, Calvinists became zealous reformers determined to transform and order society in such a way that men and women would act externally as they believed, or should believe, internally and were destined to live eternally. In a famous study, *The Protestant Ethic and the Spirit of Capitalism* (1904), the German sociologist Max Weber argued that this peculiar combination of confidence and self-disciplined activism produced an ethic that stimulated and reinforced the spirit of emergent capitalism, bringing Calvinism and later

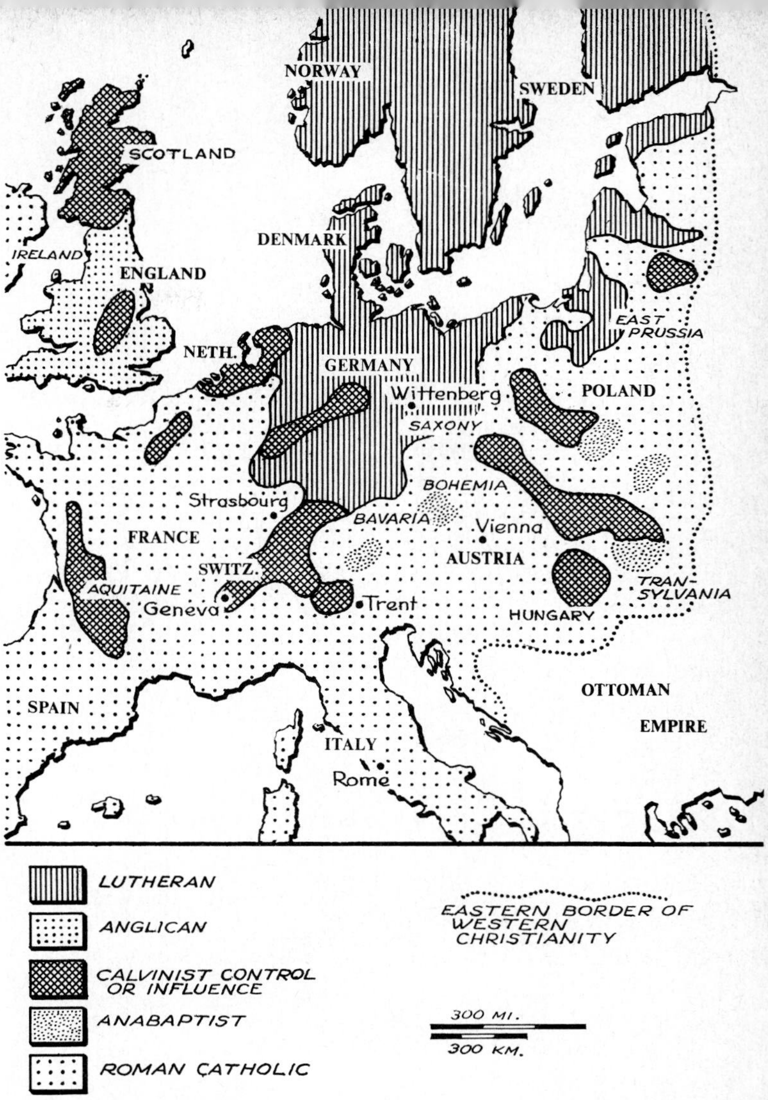

THE RELIGIOUS SITUATION ABOUT 1560

MAP 10–4 *By* 1560 *Luther, Zwingli, and Loyola were dead, Calvin near the end of his life, the English break from Rome fully accomplished, and the last session of the Council of Trent about to assemble. Here is the religious geography of Western Europe at this time.*

Puritanism into close association with the development of modern capitalist societies.

The founder of Calvinism, John Calvin (1509–1564), was born into a well-to-do family, the son of the secretary to the bishop of Noyon in Picardy. He received church benefices at age twelve, which financed the best possible education at Parisian colleges and a law degree at Orléans. Calvin associated with members of the indigenous French reform party, a group of Catholic Humanists led by Jacques Lefèvre d'Étaples and Marguerite d'Angoulême, the queen of Navarre after 1527. Although Calvin finally rejected this group as ineffectual, its members contributed to his preparation as a religious reformer. Their sincere but largely hortatory approach to reform was portrayed in Calvin's first published work, a commentary on Seneca's *De Clementia* in 1533.

It was probably in the spring of 1534 that Calvin experienced that conversion to Protestantism by which he said his "long stubborn heart" was "made teachable" by God—a personal model of reform he would later apply to the recalcitrant citizenry of Geneva. His mature theology stressed the sovereignty of God over all creation and the necessity of man's conformity to His will. In May 1534 he dramatically surrendered the benefices he had held for so long and at such profit and joined the Reformation.

The French Reformer and Protestant theologian John Calvin (1509–1564). *Between* 1540–1564, *Calvin made Geneva a Protestant theocracy.* [*Public and University Library of Geneva*]

Political Revolt and Religious Reform in Geneva

Whereas in Saxony religious reform paved the way for a political revolution against the emperor, in Geneva a political revolution against the local prince-bishop laid the foundation for the religious change. Genevans successfully revolted against the House of Savoy and their resident prince-bishop in the late 1520s. Assisted by the Swiss city-states of Fribourg and Bern, the Genevans drove out the prince-bishop in August 1527, and the city councils assumed his legal and political powers. In late 1533 Bern dispatched the Protestant reformers Guillaume Farel (1489–1565) and Antoine Froment (1508–1581) to Geneva. In the summer of 1535, after much internal turmoil, the Protestants triumphed, and the traditional Mass and other religious practices were removed. On May 21, 1536, the city voted officially to adopt the Reformation: "to live according to the Gospel and the Word of God . . . without . . . any more masses, statues, idols, or other papal abuses."

Calvin and Farel. Calvin arrived in Geneva after these events, in July 1536. He might not have come to Geneva at all had the third Habsburg–Valois war not forced him to detour there. Calvin was actually en route to a scholarly refuge in Strasbourg, in flight from Protestant persecution in France, when the war forced him to turn sharply south to Geneva. Farel successfully pleaded with him to stay and assist the Reformation, threatening Calvin with divine vengeance if he turned away from this task.

Before a year had passed, Calvin had drawn up articles for the governance of the new church as well as a catechism to guide and discipline the people, both of which were presented for approval to the city councils in early 1537. Because of the strong measures proposed to govern Geneva's moral life, the reformers were suspected by many of desiring to create a "new papacy." Their orthodoxy was attacked, and Geneva's powerful Protestant ally, Bern, which had adopted a more moderate Protestant reform, pressured Geneva's magistrates to restore the traditional religious ceremonies and holidays abolished by Calvin and Farel. Both within and outside Geneva, Calvin and Farel were perceived as going too far too fast. In February 1538 the four syndics (the chief magistrates of the city) chosen in the annual election turned against Calvin and Farel. Two months later the defiant reformers were exiled from the city.

Calvin went to Strasbourg, a model Protestant city, where he became pastor to the French exiles there. During his long stay in Strasbourg, Calvin wrote biblical commentaries and a second edition of his masterful *Institutes of the Christian Religion,* which many consider the definitive theological statement of the Protestant faith. Calvin also married and participated in the ecumenical discussions urged on Protestants and Catholics by Charles V. Most important, he learned from the Strasbourg reformer Martin Bucer how to implement the Protestant Reformation successfully.

CALVIN'S GENEVA. In 1540 Geneva elected syndics who were both favorable to Calvin and determined to establish full Genevan political and religious independence from Bern. They knew Calvin would be a valuable ally in the latter project and invited him to return. This he did in September 1540, never to leave the city again. Within months of his new arrival, new ecclesiastical ordinances were implemented that provided for cooperation between the magistrates and the clergy in matters of internal discipline. Following the Strasbourg model, the Genevan church was organized into four offices: (1) pastors, of whom there were five; (2) teachers or doctors to instruct the populace in and to defend true doctrine; (3) elders, a group of twelve laymen chosen by and from the Genevan councils and empowered to "oversee the life of everybody"; and (4) deacons to dispense church goods and services to the poor and the sick.

Calvin and his followers were motivated above all by a desire to transform society mor-

Theodore Beza Describes John Calvin's Final Days

Calvin's ceaseless labor to make Geneva a bulwark of Protestantism left him an ill and worn-out man at fifty-five. He remained nonetheless a model of discipline to the end. The following description comes from an admiring biography by Calvin's successor, Theodore Beza.

On the 6th of February, 1564, . . . he delivered his last sermon. . . . From this period he taught no more in public, except that he was carried at different times, until the last day of March, to the meeting of the congregation, and addressed them in a few words, His diseases, contracted by incredible labours of mind and body, were various and complicated. . . . He was naturally of a spare and feeble frame, tending to consumption. During sleep he seemed almost awake, and spent a great part of the year in preaching, teaching, and dictating. For at least ten years . . . the only food he [had taken] was at supper, so that it is astonishing how he could so long escape consumption. He frequently suffered from migraine, which he cured only by fasting, so as occasionally to refrain from food for thirty-six hours. But by overstraining his voice and . . . by an immoderate use of aloes, he suffered from hemorrhoids, which degenerated into ulcers, and five years before his death he was occasionally attacked by a spitting of blood. [He also suffered from] gout in the right leg, frequently returning pains of colic, and stone, which he had only felt a few months before his death. . . . The physicians neglected no remedies, and he observed the directions of his medical attendants with a strictness which none could surpass. . . . Though tormented by so many diseases, no one ever heard him utter a word unbecoming a man of bravery, much less a Christian. Only lifting up his eyes to heaven, he used to say, "How long, O Lord!" for even in health he often had this sentence on his lips, when he spoke of the calamities of his brethren, with whose sufferings he was both day and night more afflicted than with any of his own. When admonished and entreated by us to forbear, at least in his sickness, from the labour of dictating, or at least of writing, "What, then," he said, "would you have my Lord find me idle when he cometh?"

Theodore Beza, *The Life of John Calvin,* trans. by Francis Gibson (Philadelphia: Westminster, 1836), pp. 78–79.

ally. Faith, Calvin taught, did not sit idly in the mind but conformed one's every action to God's law. The "elect" should live in a manifestly God-pleasing way, if they were truly God's elect. In the attempted realization of this goal, Calvin spared no effort. The consistory became Calvin's instrument of power. This body was composed of the elders and the pastors and was presided over by one of the four syndics. It enforced the strictest moral discipline, meting out punishments for a broad range of moral and religious transgressions—from missing church services (a fine of 3 sous) to fornication (six days on bread and water and a fine of 60 sous)—and, as time passed, increasingly for criticism of Calvin and the consistory. Calvin ridiculed his opponents as undisciplined "Libertines."

Among the many personal conflicts in Geneva that gave Calvin his reputation as a stern moralist, none proved more damaging than his active role in the capture and execution of the Spanish physician and amateur theologian Michael Servetus in 1553. After 1555, the city's syndics were all devout Calvinists, and Geneva became home to thousands of exiled Protestants who had been driven out of France, England, and Scotland. Refugees (more than five thousand), most of them utterly loyal to Calvin, came to make up over one third of the population of Geneva. From this time until his death in 1564, Calvin's position in the city was greatly strengthened and the syndics were very cooperative.

Catholic Reform and Counter-Reformation

Sources of Catholic Reform

The Protestant Reformation did not take the medieval church completely by surprise. There were much internal criticism and many efforts at internal reform before there was a Counter-Reformation in reaction to Protestant successes. Before the Reformation ambitious proposals had been set forth to bring about the long-demanded reform of the church in head and members. One of the boldest attempts came on the eve of the Fifth Lateran Council (1513–1517), the last reform council before the Reformation, and was drafted by two Venetian monks, Tommaso Giustiniani and Vincenzo Quirini. Their program went so far as to call for a revision of the *Corpus Juris Canonici,*

A Protestant caricature of the pope: As Christ ascends, the pope plunges into Hell. [*Reproduced by permission of the Trustees of the British Museum*]

the massive body of church law that authorized papal practices and ensured papal prerogatives. Sixteenth-century popes, ever mindful of how the councils of Constance and Basel had stripped the pope of his traditional powers, quickly squelched such efforts to bring about basic changes in the laws and institutions of the church. High Renaissance popes preferred the charge given to the Fifth Lateran Council in the keynote address by Giles of Viterbo, the superior general of the Hermits of Saint Augustine: "Men are to be changed by, not to change, religion." The Fifth Lateran Council remained a regional council completely within the pope's control and brought about no significant reforms. The very month after its adjournment Martin Luther posted his ninety-five theses.

As the Fifth Lateran Council suggests, the most important reform initiatives did not always issue from the papal court. Catholic reformers were found within a variety of self-motivated lay and clerical movements. Two important organizations that brought reform-minded clergy and laity together were the Modern Devotion (already discussed) and the Oratory of Divine Love. The latter, founded in Rome in 1517, was an exclusive informal organization of earnest laity and clergy who were both learned and deeply committed to traditional religious devotion. Like that of Erasmus, whose religious writings the members admired, their basic belief was that inner piety and good Christian living, not theological arguments and disputations, were the surest way to reform the church.

Many new religious orders also sprang up in the sixteenth century to lead a broad revival of piety within the church. The first of these was the Theatines, an elitist order, founded in 1524 to groom devout and reform-minded leaders at the higher levels of the church hierarchy. One of the cofounders was Bishop Gian Pietro Carafa, the future Pope Paul IV. Another new order, whose mission pointed in the opposite direction, was the Capuchins. Authorized by the pope in The 1528, they sought to return to the original ascetic and charitable ideals of Saint Francis and became very popular among the ordinary people, to whom they directed their ministry. The Somaschi, who became active in the mid-1520s, and the Barnabites, founded in 1530, endeavored to repair the moral, spiritual, and physical damage done to people in war-torn areas of Italy. The members of the new order of Ursulines, founded in 1535, established convents in Italy and France for the religious education of girls from all social classes and became very influential. Another new religious order, the Oratorians, officially recognized in 1575, was an elite group of secular clerics, who devoted themselves to the promotion of religious literature and church music. Among their members was the great Catholic hymnist and musician Giovanni Palestrina (1526–1594).

In addition to these lay and clerical movements the Spanish mystics Saint Teresa of Avila (1515–1582) and Saint John of the Cross (1542–1591) revived and popularized the mystical piety of medieval monasticism.

Ignatius of Loyola and the Jesuits

Of the various reform groups, none was more instrumental in the success of the Counter-Reformation than the Society of Jesus, the new order of Jesuits, organized by Ignatius of Loyola in the 1530s and officially recognized by the church in 1540. The society grew within the space of a century from its

Ignatius of Loyola (1491–1556), *founder of the Society of Jesus.* [*Bradley Smith*]

Ignatius of Loyola's "Rules for Thinking with the Church"

As leaders of the Counter-Reformation, the Jesuits attempted to live by and instill in others the strictest obedience to church authority. The following are some of the eighteen rules included by Ignatius in his *Spiritual Exercises* to give pious Catholics positive direction. These rules also indicate the Catholic reformers' refusal to compromise with Protestants.

In order to have the proper attitude of mind in the Church Militant we should observe the following rules:

1. Putting aside all private judgment, we should keep our minds prepared and ready to obey promptly and in all things the true spouse of Christ our Lord, our Holy Mother, the hierarchical Church.

2. To praise sacramental confession and the reception of the Most Holy Sacrament once a year, and much better once a month, and better still every week. . . .

3. To praise the frequent hearing of Mass. . . .

4. To praise highly the religious life, virginity, and continence; and also matrimony, but not as highly. . . .

5. To praise the vows of religion, obedience, poverty, chastity, and other works of perfection and supererogation. . . .

6. To praise the relics of the saints . . . [and] the stations, pilgrimages, indulgences, jubilees, Crusade indulgences, and the lighting of candles in the churches.

7. To praise the precepts concerning fasts and abstinences . . . and acts of penance. . . .

8. To praise the adornments and buildings of churches as well as sacred images. . . .

9. To praise all the precepts of the church. . . .

10. To approve and praise the directions and recommendations of our superiors as well as their personal behaviour. . . .

11. To praise both the positive and scholastic theology. . . .

12. We must be on our guard against making comparisons between the living and those who have already gone to their reward, for it is no small error to say, for example: 'This man knows more than St. Augustine'; 'He is another Saint Francis, or even greater.' . . .

13. If we wish to be sure that we are right in all things, we should always be ready to accept this principle: I will believe that the white that I see is black, if the hierarchical Church so defines it. For I believe that between . . . Christ our Lord and . . . His Church, there is but one spirit, which governs and directs us for the salvation of our souls.

The Spiritual Exercises of St. Ignatius, trans. by Anthony Mottola (Garden City, N.Y.: Doubleday, 1964), pp. 139–141.

original ten members to more than fifteen thousand members scattered throughout the world, with thriving missions in India, Japan, and the Americas.

The founder of the Jesuits, Ignatius of Loyola (1491–1556), was a truly heroic figure. A dashing courtier and caballero in his youth, he began his spiritual pilgrimage in 1521 after he had been seriously wounded in the legs during a battle with the French. During a lengthy and painful convalescence, he passed the time by reading Christian classics. So impressed was he with the heroic self-sacrifice of the church's saints and their methods of overcoming mental anguish and pain that he underwent a profound religious conversion; henceforth, he, too, would serve the church as a soldier of Christ.

After recuperating, Ignatius applied the lessons he had learned during his convalescence to a program of religious and moral self-discipline that came to be embodied in the *Spiritual Exercises*. This psychologically perceptive devotional guide contained mental and emotional exercises designed to teach one absolute spiritual self-mastery over one's feelings. It taught that a person could shape his or her own behavior, even create a new religious self, through disciplined study and regular practice.

Whereas in Jesuit eyes Protestants had distinguished themselves by disobedience to church authority and religious innovation, the exercises of Ignatius were intended to teach good Catholics to deny themselves and submit without question to higher church authority and spiritual direction. Perfect discipline and self-control were the essential conditions of such obedience. To these was added the enthusiasm of traditional spirituality and mysticism—a potent combination that helped counter the Reformation and win many Protestants back to the Catholic fold, especially in Austria and Bavaria and along the Rhine.

The Council of Trent (1545–1563)

The broad success of the Reformation and the insistence of the Emperor Charles V forced Pope Paul to call a general council of the church to define religious doctrine. In anticipation Pope Paul appointed a reform commission, chaired by Caspar Contarini (1483–1542). Contarini, a member of the Oratory of Divine Love, was open to many reforms (his critics even described him as "semi-Lutheran"), and his committee consisted of some very liberal Catholic clergy. Their report, presented to the pope in February 1537, bluntly criticized the fiscality and simony of the papal Curia as the primary source of the church's loss of esteem. This report was so critical, in fact, that Pope Paul attempted unsuccessfully to suppress its publication. Protestants reprinted and circulated it as justification of their criticism.

The long-delayed council of the church met in 1545 in the imperial city of Trent in northern Italy. There were three sessions, spread over eighteen years, with long interruptions due to war, plague, and imperial and papal politics. The council met from 1545 to 1547, from 1551 to 1552, and from 1562 to 1563, a period that spanned the careers of four different popes.

Unlike the general councils of the fifteenth century, Trent was strictly under the pope's control, with high Italian prelates very prominent in the proceedings. Initially four of the five attending archbishops and twenty-one of the twenty-three attending bishops were Italians. Even at its final session in 1562, over three quarters of the council fathers were Italians. Voting was limited to high churchmen; university theologians, the lower clergy, and the laity were not permitted to share in the council's decisions.

The council's most important reforms concerned internal church discipline. Steps were taken to curtail the selling of church offices and other religious goods. Many bishops who resided in Rome rather than within their dioceses were forced to move to their appointed seats of authority. Trent strengthened the authority of local bishops so that they could effectively discipline popular religious practice. The bishops

Progress of Protestant Reformation on the Continent

Fifth Lateran Council fails to bring about reform in the church	1513–1517
Luther posts 95 theses against indulgences	1517
Charles I of Spain elected Holy Roman Emperor (as Charles V)	1519
Luther challenges authority of pope and inerrancy of church councils at Leipzig Debate	1519
Papal bull excommunicates Luther for heresy	1521
Diet of Worms condemns Luther	1521
Luther translates the New Testament into German	1521–1522
Peasants' Revolt in Germany	1524–1525
The *Schleitheim Confession* of the Anabaptists	1527
Marburg Colloquy between Luther and Zwingli	1529
Diet of Augsburg fails to settle religious differences	1530
Formation of Protestant Schmalkaldic League	1531
Anabaptists assume political power in city of Münster	1534–1535
Calvin arrives in Geneva	1536
Jesuits, founded by Ignatius of Loyola, recognized as order by pope	1540
Luther dies	1546
Armies of Charles V crush Schmalkaldic League	1547
Augsburg *Interim* outlaws Protestant practices	1548
Peace of Augsburg recognizes rights of Lutherans to worship as they please	1555
Council of Trent institutes reforms and responds to the Reformation	1545–1563

The Council of Trent in session. The Council met in three separate sessions over an eighteen-year period beginning in 1545 and formed the Catholic response to the theological divisions of the later Middle Ages and to the Protestant Reformation. This painting is possibly by the Venetian painter Titian (1477–1576). [*Musées du Louvre, Paris. Cliche des Musées Nationaux*]

were also subjected to new rules that required them not only to reside in their dioceses, but also to be highly visible by preaching regularly and conducting annual visitations. Trent also sought to give the parish priest a brighter image by requiring him to be neatly dressed, better educated, strictly celibate, and active among his parishioners. To this end Trent also called for the construction of a seminary in every diocese.

Not a single doctrinal concession was made to the Protestants, however. In the face of Protestant criticism the Council of Trent gave a ringing reaffirmation to the traditional Scholastic education of the clergy; the role of good works in salvation; the authority of tradition; the seven sacraments; transubstantiation; the withholding of the Eucharistic cup from the laity; clerical celibacy; the reality of purgatory; the veneration of saints, relics, and sacred images; and the granting of letters of indulgence. The council resolved medieval Scholastic quarrels in favor of the theology of Saint Thomas Aquinas, further enhancing his authority within the church. The strongest resistance was thereafter offered by the church to groups like the Jansenists, who strongly endorsed the medieval Augustinian tradition, a source of alternative Catholic as well as many Protestant doctrines.

Rulers initially resisted Trent's reform decrees, fearing a revival of papal political power within their lands. But with the passage of time and the pope's assurances that religious reforms were his sole intent, the new legislation took hold and parish life revived under the guidance of a devout and better-trained clergy.

The Church in Spanish America

Roman Catholic priests had accompanied the earliest explorers and the conquerors of the Indians. Because of internal reforms within the Spanish church at the turn of the sixteenth century, these first clergy tended to be imbued with many of the social and religious ideals of Christian Humanism. They believed that they could foster Erasmus's concept of the "philosophy of Christ" in the New World. Consequently these missionary priests were filled with zeal not only to convert the Indians to Christianity but also to bring to them learning and civilization of a European kind.

A very real tension existed between the early Spanish conquerors and the mendicant friars who sought to minister to the Indians. Without conquest, the church could not convert the Indians, but the priests often deplored the harsh labor conditions imposed on the native peoples. During the first three quarters of a century of Spanish domination, priests were among the most eloquent and persuasive defenders of the rights of Indians.

By far the most effective and outspoken of these clerics was Bartolomé de Las Casas, a Dominican. He contended that conquest was not necessary for conversion. One result of his campaign was new royal regulation of conquest after 1550. Another result was the emergence of the "Black Legend," which portrayed all Spanish treatment of Indians as unprincipled and inhumane. Advocates of this position drew heavily on Las Casas's writings. Although substantially true, the "Black Legend," nonetheless somewhat exaggerated the case against Spain. Many of the Indian rulers of other Indian tribes had also been exceedingly cruel, as witnessed by the Aztec demands for human sacrifice.

By the end of the sixteenth century, the church in Spanish America had become largely an institution upholding the colonial status quo. On numerous occasions, individual priests did defend the communal rights of Indian tribes, but the colonial church also prospered as the Spanish elite prospered. The church became a great landowner through crown grants and through bequests from Catholics who died in the New World. The monasteries took on an economic as well as a spiritual life of their own. Whatever its concern for the spiritual welfare of the Indians, the church remained one of the indications that Spanish America was a conquered world. And those who spoke for the church did not challenge Spanish domination or any but the most extreme modes of Spanish economic exploitation. By the end of the colonial era in the late eighteenth century, the Roman Catholic church had become one of the most conservative forces in Latin America.

Bartolomé de Las Casas (1474–1566). *Las Casas was the most outspoken and effective defender of the Indians of the New World from Spanish exploitation.* [*Library of Congress*]

The English Reformation to 1533

The Preconditions of Reform

Late medieval England had a reputation for maintaining the rights of the crown against the pope. Edward I (d. 1307) had rejected efforts by Pope Boniface VIII to prevent secular taxation of the clergy. Parliament passed the first

Statutes of Provisors and *Praemunire* in the mid-fourteenth century curtailing payments and judicial appeals to Rome. The English Franciscan William of Ockham had defended the rights of royalty against Pope John XXII, and John Wycliffe had even sanctioned secular confiscation of clerical property in support of the principle of apostolic poverty. Lollardy, Humanism, and widespread anticlerical sentiment prepared the way religiously and intellectually for Protestant ideas, which began to enter England in the early 1520s.

In the early 1520s future English reformers met at the White Horse Inn in Cambridge to discuss Lutheran writings smuggled into England by merchants and scholars. One of these future reformers was William Tyndale (ca. 1492–1536), who translated the New Testament into English in 1524–1525, while in Germany. Published in Cologne and Worms, Tyndale's New Testament began to circulate in England in 1526, and thereafter the vernacular Bible became the centerpiece of the English Reformation. Cardinal Thomas Wolsey (ca. 1475–1530), the chief minister of King Henry VIII, and Sir Thomas More (1478–1535), Wolsey's successor, guided royal opposition to incipient Protestantism. The king himself defended the seven sacraments against Luther, receiving as a reward the title "Defender of the Faith" from Pope Leo X. Following Luther's intemperate reply to Henry's amateur theological attack, More wrote a lengthy *Response to Luther* in 1523.

The King's Affair. While Lollardy and Humanism may be said to have prepared the soil for the seeds of Protestant reform, it was King Henry's unhappy marriage that furnished the plough that truly broke it. Henry had married Catherine of Aragon (d. 1536), daughter of Ferdinand and Isabella of Spain, and the aunt of Emperor Charles V. By 1527 the union had produced no male heir to the throne and only one surviving child, a daughter, Mary. Henry was justifiably concerned about the political consequences of leaving only a female heir. People in this period believed it unnatural for women to rule over men: at best, a woman ruler meant a contested reign; at worst, turmoil and revolution. Henry even came to believe that his union with Catherine, who had numerous miscarriages and stillbirths, had been cursed by God, because before their marriage Catherine had been the wife of his brother, Arthur. Henry's father, King Henry VII, had betrothed Catherine to Henry after Arthur's untimely death in order to keep the English alliance with Spain intact. They were officially married in 1509, a few days before Henry VIII received his crown. Marriage to the wife of one's brother was prohibited by both canon and biblical law (see Leviticus 18:16, 20:21), and a special dispensation had been required from Pope Julius II before Henry married Catherine.

By 1527 Henry was thoroughly enamored of Anne Boleyn, one of Catherine's ladies in waiting, and determined to put Catherine aside and take Anne to wife. This he could not do in Catholic England without papal annulment of the marriage to Catherine. And therein lay a special problem. The year 1527 was also the year when soldiers of the Holy Roman Empire mutinied and sacked Rome, and the reigning pope, Clement VII, was at the time a prisoner of Charles V, Catherine's nephew. Even if this had not been the case, it would have been virtually impossible for the pope to grant an annulment of a marriage that had not only survived for eighteen years but had been made possible in the first place by a special papal dispensation, the king's denial of the latter's validity notwithstanding.

Cardinal Wolsey, who aspired to become pope, was placed in charge of securing the royal annulment. Lord Chancellor since 1515 and papal legate-at-large since 1518, Wolsey had long been Henry's "heavy" and the object of much popular resentment. When he failed to secure the annulment, through no fault of his own, he was dismissed in disgrace in 1529. Thomas Cranmer (1489–1556) and Thomas Cromwell (1485–1540), both of whom harbored Lutheran sympathies, thereafter became the king's closest advisers. Finding the way to a papal annulment closed, Henry's new advisers struck a different course: Why not simply declare the king supreme in English spiritual affairs as he was in English temporal affairs? Then the king himself could settle the king's affair.

The Reformation Parliament

In 1529 Parliament convened for what would be a seven-year session that earned it the title the "Reformation Parliament." During this period, it passed a flood of legislation that harassed and finally placed royal reins on the clergy. In January 1531 the clergy in Convocation (a legislative assembly representing the

The Family of Henry VIII, *by Lucas de Heere* (1534–1584). *This allegorical painting depicts the Tudor succession. To Henry's right stands his Catholic daughter Mary,* (1553–1558) *and her husband Philip II of Spain. They are accompanied by Mars, the god of war. Henry's son, Edward VI,* (1547–1553) *is kneeling at the King's left. Elizabeth I* (1558–1603) *is shown standing in the foreground attended by Peace and Plenty.* [*Sudely Castle, The Walter Morrison Collection*]

English clergy) publicly recognized Henry as head of the church in England "as far as the law of Christ allows." In 1532 the Act of Supplication of the Commons Against the Ordinaries was passed, a list of grievances against the church ranging from alleged indifference to the needs of the laity to an excessive number of religious holidays. In the same year Parliament passed the Submission of the Clergy, effectively placing canon law under royal control and thereby the clergy under royal jurisdiction. The Act in Conditional Restraint of Annates further gave the English king the power to withhold from Rome these lucrative "first fruits" of new ecclesiastical appointments.

In January 1533 Henry wed the pregnant Anne Boleyn, with Thomas Cranmer officiating. In February 1533 the Act for the Restraint of Appeals made the king the highest court of appeal for all English subjects. In March 1533 Cranmer became archbishop of Canterbury and led the Convocation in invalidating the king's marriage to Catherine. In 1534 Parliament ended all payments by the English clergy and laity to Rome and gave Henry sole jurisdiction over high ecclesiastical appointments. The

Act of Succession in the same year made Anne Boleyn's children legitimate heirs to the throne, and the Act of Supremacy declared Henry "the only supreme head in earth of the church of England." Refusal to recognize these two acts brought the execution of Thomas More and John Fisher, bishop of Rochester—events that made clear the king's determination to have his way regardless of the cost. In 1536 came the first Act for Dissolution of Monasteries, which affected only the smaller ones; three years later a second act dissolved all English monasteries and turned their endowments over to the king.

WIVES OF HENRY VIII. Henry's domestic life proved to lack the consistency of his political life. In 1536 Anne Boleyn was executed for adultery, and her daughter, Elizabeth, was declared illegitimate. Henry had four further marriages. His third wife, Jane Seymour, died in 1537 shortly after giving birth to the future Edward VI. Henry wed Anne of Cleves sight unseen on the advice of Cromwell, the purpose being to create by the marriage an alliance with the Protestant princes. Neither the alliance nor Anne—whom Henry found to have a remarkable resemblance to a horse—proved worth the trouble; the marriage was annulled by Parliament, and Cromwell was dismissed and eventually executed. Catherine Howard, Henry's fifth wife, was beheaded for adultery in 1542. His last wife, Catherine Parr, a patron of Humanists and reformers, for whom Henry was the third husband, survived him to marry still a fourth time—obviously she was a match for the English king.

MAIN EVENTS OF THE ENGLISH REFORMATION

Reformation Parliament convenes	1529
Parliament passes the Submission of the Clergy, an act placing Canon law and the English clergy under royal jurisdiction	1532
Henry VIII weds Anne Boleyn; Convocation proclaims marriage to Catherine of Aragon invalid	1533
Act of Succession makes Anne Boleyn's children legitimate heirs to the English throne	1534
Act of Supremacy declares Henry VIII "the only supreme head of the church of England"	1534
Thomas More executed for opposition to Acts of Succession and Supremacy	1535
Publication of Coverdale Bible	1535
Henry VIII imposes the Six Articles, condemning Protestantism and reasserting traditional doctrine	1539
Edward VI succeeds to the throne under protectorships of Somerset and Northumberland	1547
First Act of Uniformity imposes *Book of Common Prayer* on English churches	1549
Mary Tudor restores Catholic doctrine	1553–1558
Elizabeth I fashions an Anglican religious settlement	1558–1603

THE KING'S RELIGIOUS CONSERVATISM. Henry's political and domestic boldness was not carried over to the religious front, although the pope did cease to be the head of the English church and English Bibles were placed in English churches. Despite his political break with Rome, the king remained decidedly conservative in his religious beliefs, and Catholic doctrine remained prominent in a country seething with Protestant sentiment. Despite his many wives and amorous adventures, Henry absolutely forbade the English clergy to marry and threatened any clergy who were twice caught in concubinage with execution. The Ten Articles of 1536 prescribed Catholic doctrine with only mild Protestant concessions. Angered by the growing popularity of Protestant views, even among his chief advisers, Henry struck directly at them in the Six Articles of 1539. These reaffirmed transubstantiation, denied the Eucharistic cup to the laity, declared celibate vows inviolable, provided for private masses, and ordered the continuation of auricular confession. Protestants referred to the articles as the "whip with six stings." Although William Tyndale's English New Testament grew into the Coverdale Bible (1535) and the Great Bible (1539) and the latter was mandated for every English parish during Henry's reign, England had to await Henry's death before it could become a genuinely Protestant country.

The Protestant Reformation Under Edward VI

When Henry died, his son and successor, Edward VI (1547–1553), was only ten years old. Edward reigned under the successive regencies of Edward Seymour, who became the duke of Somerset (1547–1550), and the earl of Warwick, who became known as the duke of Northumberland (1550–1553), during which time England fully enacted the Protestant Reformation. The new king and Somerset corresponded directly with John Calvin. During Somerset's regency, Henry's Six Articles and laws against heresy were repealed, and clerical marriage and communion with cup were sanctioned.

In 1547 the chantries, places where endowed masses had traditionally been said for the dead, were dissolved. In 1549 the Act of Uniformity imposed Thomas Cranmer's *Book of Common Prayer* on all English churches. Images and altars were removed from the churches in 1550. Still more radical Protestant reforms were carried out by the duke of Northumberland. After Charles V's victory over the German princes in 1547, German Protestant leaders had fled to England for refuge, and several directly assisted the completion of the English Reformation, Martin Bucer prominent among them. The Second Act of Uniformity, passed in 1552, imposed a revised edition of the *Book of Common Prayer* on all English churches. A forty-two-article confession of faith, also written by Thomas Cranmer, was adopted, setting forth a moderate Protestant doctrine. It taught justification by faith and the supremacy of Holy Scripture, denied transubstantiation (although not real presence), and recognized only two sacraments.

All these changes were short-lived, however. In 1553 Catherine of Aragon's daughter, Mary, succeeded Edward (who had died in his teens) to the English throne and proceeded to restore Catholic doctrine and practice with a singlemindedness that rivaled that of her father. It was not until the reign of Anne Boleyn's daughter, Elizabeth (1558–1603), that a lasting religious settlement was worked out in England (to be discussed in Chapter 11).

The Social Significance of the Reformation in Western Europe

It was a common feature of the Lutheran, Zwinglian, and Calvinist reforms to work within the framework of reigning political power. Luther, Zwingli, and Calvin saw themselves and their followers as citizens of the world, subject to definite civic responsibilities and obligations. Their adjustments in this regard have led scholars to characterize them as "magisterial reformers," meaning not only that they were the leaders of the major Protestant movements but also that they succeeded by the force of the magistrate's sword. It was probably not a matter of compromising the principles of the Gospels and choosing the way of brute force, as some have argued. The reformers never contemplated a reform outside or against the societies of which they were members. They wanted a reform that took shape within the laws and institutions of the sixteenth century, and to that end they remained highly sensitive to what was politically and socially possible in their age.

Some scholars believe that these reformers were too conscious of the historically possible, that their reforms went forward with such caution that they not only changed late medieval society very little but actually encouraged acceptance of the sociopolitical status quo.

There was a very conservative side to the Reformation. On the other hand, by the end of the sixteenth century the Reformation had also brought about radical changes in the religious beliefs and practices of many people. As it developed, the Reformation eliminated or put severe restrictions on such traditional practices as mandatory fasting; auricular confession; the veneration of saints, relics, and images; indulgences; pilgrimages and shrines; vigils; weekly, monthly, and annual masses for the dead; the belief in purgatory; Latin worship services; the sacrifice of the Mass; numerous religious ceremonies, festivals, and holidays; the canonical hours; monasteries and mendicant orders; the sacramental status of marriage, extreme unction, confirmation, holy orders, and penance; clerical celibacy; clerical immunity from civil taxation and criminal jurisdiction; nonresident benefices; excommunication and interdict; canon law; episcopal and papal authority; and the traditional Scholastic education of the clergy. Some Protestant lands (Switzerland, for example) enacted more of these reforms, and more radically, than others (England, for example).

It may be argued that by the second half of the sixteenth century Protestant religion had become just as burdensome as medieval religion had ever been. As Protestants won power in cities and towns, they tended to use their new position to erect what critics called "new papacies." In its first decades, however, the

The Injustice of the Law. This woodcut by an unknown artist is entitled the Spider Web. In it the law is compared to a spider web, which easily catches the wealthy and the poor, who are seen hanging on the gallows and the wheel on the left, while permitting the rich and powerful to escape punishment for their crimes. Note the hole in the spider web made by the large bee, while the smaller bugs become hopelessly trapped. [From Max Geisberg, The German Single-Leaf Woodcut, 1500–1550, *edited by Walter L. Strauss. Hacker Art Books,* 1974. *Used by permission of Hacker Art Books.*]

Greed. The Power of Money, by Peter Spitzer. The caption reads: ''Were my mother a whore (she can be seen in bed with a man in the upper left corner) and my father a thief (he can be seen hanging on the gallows in the upper right corner), still, if I had a lot of money I would have no grief.'' [*From Max Geisberg,* The German Single-Leaf Woodcut, 1500–1550, *edited by Walter L. Strauss. Hacker Art Books,* 1974. *Used by permission of Hacker Art Books.*]

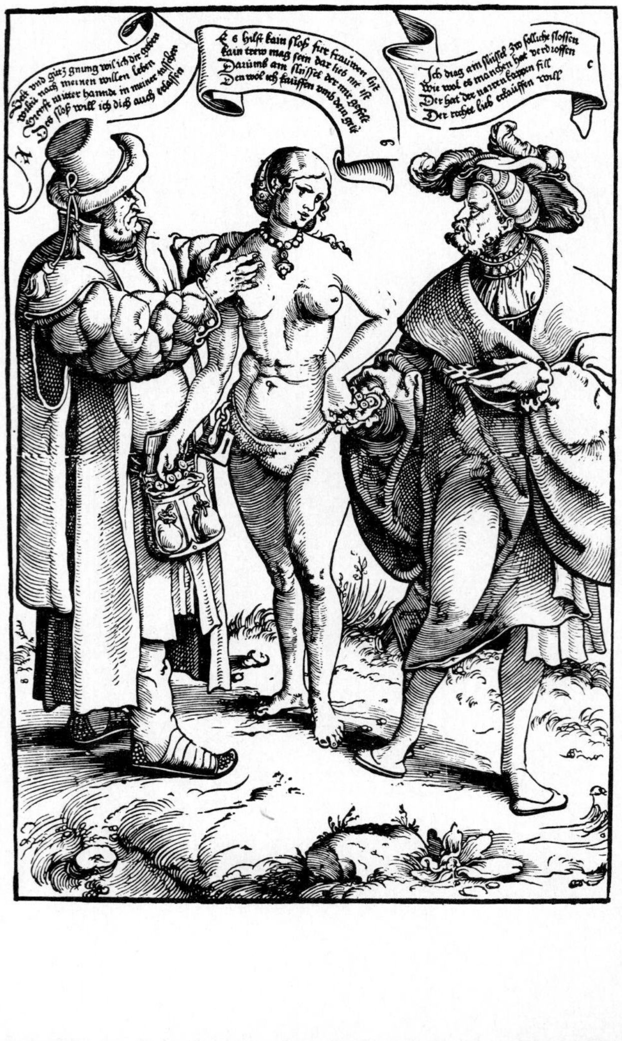

Adultery. The Chasity Belt, by H. Vogtherr gives one view—that of the wronged husband—of this age-old marital problem. Here a husband departing on a business trip has placed his wife, who does not love him, in a chastity belt. She takes his money, which he gladly gives her in exchange for promises of fidelity, to buy a key that will set her free to do as she pleases during his absence. [From Max Geisberg, The German Single-Leaf Woodcut, 1500–1550, *edited by Walter L. Strauss. Hacker Art Books,* 1974. *Used by permission of Hacker Art Books.*]

Failed Marriages. The Subservient Husband, by Hans Schaufelein. In the sixteenth century the husband who failed to rule his wife properly was thought to risk creating a shrew who would assume authority in the marriage. Note that in this woodcut the woman has the pocketbook and keys around her waist, for she has become master of the house. Her husband has been forced to do ''woman's work,'' which was considered a sure sign of a house no longer in order. [From Max Geisberg, The German Single-Leaf Woodcut, 1500–1550, *edited by Walter L. Strauss. Hacker Art Books,* 1974. *Used by permission of Hacker Art Books.*]

Tyranny. The Rabbits Catching the Hunters, by Georg Pencz. The rabbits, long brutalized by the hunters and their dogs, organize and then subject the hunters to the treatment the rabbits have long received from them. This woodcut is a warning to all tyrants that tyranny brings rebellion. [From Max Geisberg, The German Single-Leaf Woodcut, 1500–1550, *edited by Walter L. Strauss. Hacker Art Books,* 1974. *Used by permission of Hacker Art Books.*]

Old Age. A Peasant Couple by Christoph Amberger. The man is saying that he is now too old to hunt birds and must therefore depend on an owl to do his hunting. [From Max Geisberg, The German Single-Leaf Woodcut, 1500–1550, *edited by Walter L. Strauss. Hacker Art Books,* 1974. *Used by permission of Hacker Art Books.*]

Drunkenness. The Winebag and His Wheelbarrow, by Hans Weidt. Alcoholism was a very serious problem in the sixteenth century. It was caricatured by artists and railed against by Catholic and Protestant clergymen. [From Max Geisberg, The German Single-Leaf Woodcut, 1500–1550, *edited by Walter L. Strauss. Hacker Art Books,* 1974. *Used by permission of Hacker Art Books.*]

Reformation was presented and perceived by those who embraced it as a profound simplification of religious life. It was freeing precisely because it required less rather than more from those who wanted to be pious Christians and because it gave clearer focus to their ethical obligations.

The Reformation and Education

Another important cultural achievement of the Reformation was its implementation of many of the educational reforms of Humanism in the new Protestant schools and universities. Many Protestant reformers in Germany, France, and England were Humanists. Even when their views on church doctrine and humankind separated them from the Humanist movement, the Protestant reformers continued to share with the Humanists a common opposition to Scholasticism and a belief in the unity of wisdom, eloquence, and action. The Humanist program of studies, which provided the language skills to deal authoritatively with original sources, proved to be a more appropriate tool for the elaboration of Protestant doctrine than did Scholastic dialectic.

The connections between Humanism and the Reformation were recognized by the Catholic counterreformers. Ignatius of Loyola observed the way in which the new learning had been embraced by and served the Protestant cause. In his *Spiritual Exercises* he insisted that when the Bible and the Church Fathers were read directly, they be read under the guidance of the authoritative Scholastic theologians: Peter Lombard, Bonaventura, and Thomas Aquinas. The latter, Ignatius argued, being "of more recent date," had the clearer understanding of what Scripture and the Fathers meant and therefore should guide the study of the past.

When in August 1518 Philip Melanchthon (1497–1560), a young Humanist and professor of Greek, arrived at the University of Wittenberg, his first act was to implement curricular reforms on the Humanist model. In his inaugural address, entitled *On Improving the Studies of the Young,* Melanchthon presented himself as a defender of good letters and classical studies against "barbarians who practice barbarous arts." By the latter he meant the Scholastic theologians of the later Middle Ages, whose methods of juxtaposing the views of conflicting authorities and seeking to reconcile them by disputation had, he believed, undermined both good letters and sound biblical doctrine. Scholastic dominance in the universities was seen by Melanchthon as having bred contempt for the Greek language and learning and as having encouraged neglect of the study of mathematics, sacred studies, and the art of oratory. Melanchthon urged the careful study of history, poetry, and other Humanist disciplines.

Together Luther and Melanchthon completely restructured the University of Wittenberg's curriculum. Commentaries on Lombard's *Sentences* were dropped, as was canon law, and old Scholastic lectures on Aristotle were replaced by straightforward historical study. Students read primary sources directly, not by way of accepted Scholastic commentators. Candidates for theological degrees defended the new doctrine on the basis of their own exegesis of the Bible. New chairs of Greek and Hebrew were created. Luther and Melanchthon also pressed for universal compulsory education so that both boys and girls could reach vernacular literacy in the Bible.

In Geneva John Calvin and his successor, Theodore Beza, founded the Genevan Academy, which later evolved into the University of Geneva. This institution, created primarily for the purpose of training Calvinist ministers, pursued ideals similar to those set forth by Luther and Melanchthon. Calvinist refugees trained in the academy carried Protestant educational reforms to France, Scotland, England, and the New World. Through such efforts a working knowledge of Greek and Hebrew became commonplace in educated circles in the sixteenth and seventeenth centuries.

Some contemporaries decried what they saw as a narrowing of the original Humanist program as Protestants took it over. Erasmus, for example, came to fear the Reformation as a threat to the liberal arts and good learning, and Sebastian Franck pointed to parallels between Luther's and Zwingli's debates over Christ's presence in the Eucharist and such old Scholastic disputations as that over the Immaculate Conception of the Virgin.

Humanist culture and learning nonetheless remained indebted to the Reformation. The Protestant endorsement of the Humanist program of studies remained as significant for the Humanist movement as the latter had been for the Reformation. Protestant schools and universities consolidated and preserved for the modern world many of the basic pedagogical achievements of Humanism. There the *studia humanitatis,* although often as little more than a handmaiden to theological doctrine, found a permanent home, one that remained hospitable even in the heyday of Protestant Scholasticism.

The Reformation and the Changing Role of Women

The Protestant reformers took a positive stand on clerical marriage and strongly opposed monasticism and the celibate life. From this position they challenged the medieval tendency alternately to degrade women as temptresses (following the model of Eve) and to exalt them as virgins (following the model of Mary). Protestants opposed the popular antiwoman and antimarriage literature of the Middle Ages. They praised woman in her own right, but especially in her biblical vocation as mother and housewife. Although relief of sexual frustration and a remedy of fornication were motives behind Protestant promarriage arguments, and although motherhood and housewifery were considered woman's basic vocation, the reformers also viewed their wives as indispensable companions in their work, and this not solely because they took domestic cares off their husbands' minds. Luther, who married in 1525 at the age of forty-two, wrote of women:

> Imagine what it would be like without women. The home, cities, economic life, and government would virtually disappear. Men cannot do without women. Even if it were possible for men to beget and bear children, they still could not do without women.[2]

John Calvin wrote at the death of his wife:

> I have been bereaved of the best companion of my life, of one who, had it been so ordered, would not only have been the willing sharer of my indigence, but even of my death. During her life she was the faithful helper of my ministry.[3]

Such tributes were intended in part to overcome Catholic criticism of clerical marriage as a distraction from one's ministry. They were primarily the expression of a new value placed on the estate of marriage and family life. In opposition to the celibate ideal of the Middle Ages, Protestants stressed as no religious movement before them the sacredness of home and family, and this attitude contributed to a more respectful and sharing relationship between husbands and wives and between parents and children. The ideal of the companionate marriage—that is, of husband and wife as co-workers in a special God-ordained community of the family—led to an important expansion of the grounds for divorce in Protestant cities as early as the 1520s and ensured women an equal right to leave husbands who flagrantly violated the marriage contract. The new stress on companionship in marriage also worked indirectly to make contraception and planned parenthood a respectable choice for married couples, as it made husbands sensitive to the suffering and unhappiness that many pregnancies brought on their wives.

Protestant doctrines were as attractive to women as they were to men. Women who had been maligned as the concubines of priests came to know a new dignity as the "honorable wives" of Protestant ministers. Renegade nuns wrote exposés of the nunnery in the name of Christian freedom and justification by faith. Women in the higher classes, who were enjoying new social and political freedoms during the Renaissance, found in Protestant theology a religious complement to their greater independence in other walks of life.

Because of their desire to have women become pious housewives, Protestants also encouraged the education of girls to vernacular literacy, expecting them thereafter to model their lives on the Bible. Women came in the course of such study, however, to find in the Bible passages that made them the equals to men in the presence of God. Such education further gave them a role in the Reformation as independent authors. These may seem like small advances from a modern perspective, but they were significant, if indirect, steps in the direction of the emancipation of women.

Family Life in Early Modern Europe

Late Marriages. Between 1500 and 1800 men and women married at later ages than they had done in previous centuries. Men tended to be in their mid- to late twenties rather than in their late teens and early twenties, and women in their early to mid-twenties rather than in their teens. In sixteenth-century Nuremberg, the legal minimum age for marriage without parental permission was set at twenty-five for men and twenty-one for

[2] *Luther's Works,* Vol. 54: *Table Talk,* ed. and trans. by Theodore G. Tappert (Philadelphia: Fortress Press, 1967), p. 161.

[3] *Letters of John Calvin,* Vol. 2, trans. by J. Bonnet (Edinburgh: T. Constable, 1858), p. 216.

A sixteenth-century German family. This was a fairly comfortable household, as witnessed by the many toys and the maidservant. Note that the mother is nursing her youngest child herself. [*Bildarchiv Preussicher Kulturbesitz*]

women. The canonical or church-sanctioned age for marriage remained fourteen for men and twelve for women, and marriage could still occur at such young ages if the parents agreed. As it had done throughout the high and later Middle Ages, the church also recognized as valid the free, *private* exchange of vows between a man and a woman at these minimal ages. However, after the Reformation, which condemned such "clandestine" unions, the church increasingly required both parental agreement and public vows in church for a fully licit marriage, a procedure it had, in fact, always preferred.

The late marriage pattern, generally observable in western Europe and England, resulted primarily from the difficulty a couple had supporting themselves as an independent family unit. Such support had become difficult because of the large population increase that occurred in the fifteenth and early sixteenth centuries, when western Europe was recovering from the great plague. Larger families meant more heirs and a greater division of resources. In Germanic and Scandinavian countries, the custom of a fair sharing of inheritance among all male children worked both to delay marriages, as more got less, and to encourage independent family units, as children did not have to hang around the family home indefinitely and live off the charity of the eldest brother after the death of their parents, as more often happened in England where primogeniture (right of the first-born son to inherit all property) remained strong. Still, it took the average couple a longer time to prepare themselves materially for marriage. Many never married. An estimated 20 per cent of all women remained spinsters in the sixteenth century. Combined with the estimated 15 per cent who were unmarried widows, this made up to a sizable unmarried female population.

Marriage tended to be "arranged" in the sense that the male heads of the two families often met and discussed the terms of the marriage before they informed the prospective bride and bridegroom. However, it was rare for the two people involved not to know each other in advance or not to have a prior relationship. Parents did not force total strangers to live together, and children always had a legal right to protest and resist an unwanted marriage. A forced marriage was, by definition, invalid, and no one believed an unwanted marriage would last. The best marriage was one desired by both parties and supported by their families.

Later marriages meant marriages of shorter duration and contributed to more frequent remarriage. Later marriages also worked to slow overall population growth, although not by directly preventing older women from having as many children as younger women. Women who married later in life simply had children in more rapid succession, but with increased risk to health and life and hence with greater maternal mortality. As growing church condemnation confirms, delayed marriage increased fornication. It also raised the number of illegitimate children, as is testified by the rapid growth of orphanages and foundling homes between 1600 and 1800.

FAMILY SIZE. The early modern family was conjugal or nuclear; that is, it consisted of a father and a mother and two to four children who managed to live into adulthood. The average husband and wife had six to eight children, a birth about every two years. Of these, however, an estimated one third died by age five, and one half were gone by age twenty. Rare was the family, at any social level, that did not learn firsthand about infant mortality and child death. The Protestant reformer Martin Luther was typical. He married late in life (at forty-two, here atypical) and fathered six children, two of whom he lost, an infant daughter at eight months and another, more painfully, at thirteen years.

BIRTH CONTROL. Artificial birth control had existed since antiquity. (The ancient Egyptians used acidic alligator dung, and the use of sponges was equally old.) The church's frequent condemnation of *coitus interruptus* (male withdrawal before ejaculation) in the thirteenth and fourteenth centuries suggests that a "contraceptive mentality"—that is, a conscious and regular effort at birth control—may have developed in the later Middle Ages. Birth control was not, however, very effective, and for both historical and moral reasons the church firmly opposed it. During the eleventh century the church suppressed an extreme ascetic sect, the Cathars, that had practiced birth control, when not abstaining from sex altogether, on the grounds that to propagate the human species was to encase immortal souls in evil matter. But the church also turned against contraception on moral grounds. According to its most authoritative theologian, Saint Thomas Aquinas, a moral act must always aid and abet, never frustrate, the natural end of a creaturely process. In the eyes of Aquinas and his church, the natural end of sex could be only the production of children and their subsequent rearing to the glory of God within the bounds of holy matrimony and the community of the church.

Despite the church's official opposition on contraception, it is likely that more general Christian moral teaching actually reinforced a contraceptive mentality within the early modern family by encouraging men to be more sensitive husbands and fathers. As men identified emotionally with wives who suffered painful, debilitating, unwanted, life-threatening, serial pregnancies (the chances of dying in childbirth were about one in ten) and with hungry children in overcrowded families, Christian love may also have persuaded a father that *coitus interruptus* was a moral course of action.

WET NURSING. The church allied with the physicians of early modern Europe on another intimate family matter: the condemnation of upper-class women who put their newborn children out to wet nurses for as long as eighteen months. Wet nurses were women who had recently had a baby or were suckling a child of their own, and who, for a fee, agreed also to suckle another child. The practice appears to have greatly increased the risk of infant mortality inasmuch as an infant received a strange and shared milk supply from a woman who was not as healthy as its own mother and who often lived under less sanitary conditions. But nursing a child was a chore some upper-class women, and especially their husbands, found distasteful. Among women, vanity and convenience appear to have been motives for turning to wet nurses. For husbands even more was at stake in the practice. Because the church forbade sexual intercourse while a woman was lactating, and sexual intercourse was believed to spoil a lactating woman's milk (pregnancy, of course, ended her milk supply), a nursing wife often became a reluctant lover. In addition, nursing had a contraceptive effect (about 75 per cent effective). There is good evidence that some women prolonged nursing their children precisely in order to delay a new pregnancy—and loving husbands understood and cooperated in this primitive form of family planning. For other husbands, however, especially wealthy burghers and noblemen who desired an abundance of male heirs, nursing seemed to rob them of sex and offspring and to jeopardize the patrimony. Hence, their strong support of wet nursing.

LOVING FAMILIES? The early modern family had features that seem cold, unloving, even cruel. Not only did parents give infants to wet nurses, but later, when the children were between the ages of eight and thirteen, they sent them out of their houses altogether into apprenticeships or to employment in the homes and businesses of relatives, friends, or even mere acquaintances and strangers. The affective ties between spouses seem to have been as tenuous as those between parents and children. Widowers and widows sometimes remarried within three to six months of their spouse's death, occasionally within weeks, and marriages with extreme disparity in age—especially between old men and young women—also suggest low affection.

Love and affection, however, are as relative to time and culture as other values. A kindness in one historical period can be a cruelty in another; what sends a person to heaven in one culture may damn a person to hell in another culture. "What greater love," an early modern parent would surely have asked a modern critic, "can parents have for their children than to equip them to make their way vocationally in the world?" An apprenticed child was a child with a future. Because of primitive living conditions, contemporaries could also appreciate the purely utilitarian and humane side of marriage and wink at quick remarriages. On the other hand, marriages with extreme disparity in age were no more the norm in early modern Europe than was the practice of wet nursing, and they received just as much criticism and ridicule.

Suggested Readings

ROLAND H. BAINTON, *Erasmus of Christendom* (1960). Charming presentation.

CHARLES BOXER, *Four Centuries of Portuguese Expansion 1415–1825* (1961). Comprehensive survey by a leading authority.

OWEN CHADWICK, *The Reformation* (1964). Among the best short histories and especially strong on theological and ecclesiastical issues.

NORMAN COHN, *The Pursuit of the Millennium* (1957). Traces millennial speculation and activity from the Old Testament to the sixteenth century.

A. G. DICKENS, *The Counter Reformation* (1969). Brief narrative with pictures.

A. G. DICKENS, *The English Reformation* (1974). The best one-volume account.

A. G. DICKENS and JOHN M. TONKIN, *The Reformation in Historical Thought* (1985). The standard critical guide to the main developments of Reformation studies.

G. DONALDSON, *The Scottish Reformation* (1960). Dependable, comprehensive narrative.

H. OUTRAM EVENNETT, *The Spirit of the Counter Reformation* (1968). Essay on the continuity of Catholic reform and its independence from the Protestant Reformation.

JEAN-LOUIS FLANDRIN, *Families in Former Times* (1979). Family life in France.

C. GIBSON, *The Aztecs Under Spanish Rule: A History of the Indians of the Valley of Mexico* (1964). An exceedingly interesting book.

C. GIBSON, *Spain in America* (1966). A splendidly clear and balanced discussion.

HAROLD GRIMM, *The Reformation Era: 1500–1650* (1973). Very good on later Lutheran developments.

WERNER L. GUNDERSHEIMER (Ed.), *French Humanism 1470–1600* (1969). Collection of essays that both summarize and provoke.

L. HANKE, *Bartolomé de Las Casas: An Interpretation of His Life and Writings* (1951). A classic work.

JOYCE L. IRWIN (Ed.), *Womanhood in Radical Protestantism, 1525–1675* (1979). A rich collection of sources.

HUBERT JEDIN, *A History of the Council of Trent,* Vols. 1 and 2 (1957–1961). Comprehensive, detailed, authoritative.

DE LAMAR JENSEN, *Reformation Europe, Age of Reform and Revolution* (1981). Excellent, up-to-date survey.

WILBUR K. JORDAN, *Edward VI: The Young King* (1968). The basic biography.

F. KATZ, *The Ancient American Civilizations* (1972). An excellent introduction.

B. KEEN and M. WASSERMAN, *A Short History of Latin America* (1984). A good survey with very helpful biblographical guides.

ROBERT M. KINGDON, *Transition and Revolution: Problems and Issues of European Renaissance and Reformation History* (1974). Covers politics, printing, theology, and witchcraft.

ALAN MACFARLANE, *The Family Life of Ralph Josselin: A Seventeenth Century Clergyman* (1970).

JOHN F. MCNEILL, *The History and Character of Calvinism* (1954). The most comprehensive account and very readable.

E. W. MONTER, *Calvin's Geneva* (1967). Dependable sketch derived from authoritative studies.

STEVEN OZMENT, *Mysticism and Dissent* (1973). Treats dissenters from Lutheranism and Calvinism.

STEVEN OZMENT, *The Reformation in the Cities* (1975). An essay on why people thought they wanted to be Protestants.

STEVEN OZMENT, *The Age of Reform 1250–1550: An Intellectual and Religious History of Late Medieval and Reformation Europe* (1980).

STEVEN OZMENT, *When Fathers Ruled: Family Life in Reformation Europe* (1983). Provocative and revisionist.

J. H. PARRY, *The Age of Reconnaissance* (1964). A comprehensive account of explorations from 1450 to 1650.

R. R. POST, *The Modern Devotion* (1968). Currently the authoritative interpretation.

EUGENE F. RICE, JR., *The Foundations of Early Modern Europe 1460–1559* (1970). Broad, succinct narrative.

JASPAR G. RIDLEY, *Thomas Cranmer* (1962). The basic biography.

E. GORDON RUPP, *Patterns of Reformation: Oecolampadius, Karlstadt, Muntzer* (1969). Effort to demonstrate the variety within early Protestantism.

J. J. SCARISBRICK, *Henry VIII* (1968). The best account of Henry's reign.

QUENTIN SKINNER, *The Foundations of Modern Political Thought II: The Age of Reformation* (1978). A comprehensive survey that treats *every* political thinker and tract.

LEWIS SPITZ, *The Religious Renaissance of the German Humanists* (1963). Comprehensive and entertaining.

JAMES STAYER, *Anabaptists and the Sword* (1972).

LAWRENCE STONE, *The Family, Sex and Marriage in England 1500–1800* (1977). Controversial in some respects, but reigning view in most aspects of family history.

GERALD STRAUSS (Ed. and Trans.), *Manifestations of Discontent in Germany on the Eve of the Reformation* (1971). Rich collection of sources for both rural and urban scenes.

R. H. TAWNEY, *Religion and the Rise of Capitalism* (1947). Advances beyond Weber's arguments relating Protestantism and capitalist economic behavior.

ERNST TROELTSCH, *The Social Teaching of the Christian Churches,* Vols. 1 and 2, trans. by Olive Wyon (1960).

MAX WEBER, *The Protestant Ethic and the Spirit of Capitalism,* trans. by Talcott Parsons (1958). First appeared in 1904–1905 and has continued to stimulate debate over the relationship between religion and society.

FRANÇOIS WENDEL, *Calvin: The Origins and Development of His Religious Thought,* trans. by Philip Mairet (1963). The best treatment of Calvin's theology.

GEORGE H. WILLIAMS, *The Radical Reformation* (1962). Broad survey of the varieties of dissent within Protestantism.

The Crucifixion of St. Peter, *by Peter Paul Rubens* (1571–1640), *based on the tradition that St. Peter was crucified upside down. The intense energy of this painting expresses the aggressive self-confidence of the Counter-Reformation. In the late sixteenth century, Catholicism had been revived by the reforms of the Council of Trent and was moving to reclaim the allegiance of those territories that had been lost to the Protestant revolt.* [*Rheinisches Bildarchiv*]

11

The Age of Religious Wars

THE LATE SIXTEENTH CENTURY and the first half of the seventeenth century are described as an "age of religious wars" because of the bloody opposition of Protestants and Catholics across the length and breadth of Europe. The wars were fueled by both genuine religious conflict and bitter dynastic rivalries. In France, the Netherlands, England, and Scotland in the second half of the sixteenth century, Calvinists fought Catholic rulers for the right to govern their own territories and to practice their chosen religion openly. In the first half of the seventeenth century Lutherans, Calvinists, and Catholics marched against one another in central and northern Europe during the Thirty Years' War. And by the middle of the seventeenth century English Puritans had successfully revolted against the Stuart monarchy and the Anglican church.

In the second half of the sixteenth century the political conflict, which had previously been confined to central Europe and a struggle for Lutheran rights and freedoms, shifted to western Europe—to France, the Netherlands, England, and Scotland—and became a struggle for Calvinist recognition. War-weary German Lutherans and Catholics agreed to live and let live in the Peace of Augsburg (1555): *cuius regio, eius religio,* which means that he who controls the land may determine its religion. Lutheranism thereafter became a legal religion within the Holy Roman Empire. Non-Lutheran Protestants, however, were not recognized by the Peace of Augsburg: both sides scorned Anabaptists and other sectarians as anarchists, and Calvinists were not yet strong enough to demand legal standing.

If German Lutherans had reason to take quiet satisfaction, Protestants elsewhere obviously did not. The struggle for Protestant religious rights had intensified in most countries outside the empire by the mid-sixteenth century. The Council of Trent adjourned in 1563 committed to an international Catholic counteroffensive against Protestants to be led by the Jesuits. At the time of John Calvin's death in 1564, Geneva had become both a refuge for Europe's persecuted Protestants and an international school for Protestant resistance, producing leaders fully equal to the new Catholic challenge.

Genevan Calvinism and Catholicism as revived by the Council of Trent were two equally dogmatic, aggressive, and irreconcilable church systems. Although Calvinists looked like "new papists" to critics when they domi-

Self-portrait by Rembrandt van Rijn (1607–1669). [*The Frick Collection*]

nated cities like Geneva, they were firebrands and revolutionaries when, as minorities, they found their civil and religious rights denied. Calvinism adopted a presbyterian organization that magnified regional and local religious authority; boards of presbyters, or elders, representing the many individual congregations of Calvinists, directly shaped the policy of the church at large. By contrast, the Counter-Reformation sponsored a centralized episcopal church system, hierarchically arranged from pope to parish priest, which stressed absolute obedience to the person at the top. The high clergy—the pope and his bishops—not the synods of local churches, ruled supreme. Calvinism proved attractive to proponents of political decentralization in contest with totalitarian rulers, whereas Catholicism remained congenial to the proponents of absolute monarchy determined to maintain "one king, one church, one law" throughout the land.

The opposition between the two religions can be seen even in the art and architecture that each came to embrace. The Catholic Counter-Reformation found the Baroque style congenial. A successor to Mannerism, Baroque art is a grandiose, three-dimensional display of life and energy. Great Baroque artists like Peter Paul Rubens (1571–1640) and Gianlorenzo Bernini (1598–1680) were Catholics. Protestants by contrast seemed to opt for a simpler, restrained, almost self-effacing art and architecture, as can be seen in the English churches of Christopher Wren (1632–1723) and the gentle, searching portraits of the Dutch Mennonite Rembrandt van Rijn (1606–1669).

As religious wars engulfed Europe, the intellectuals perceived the wisdom of religious pluralism and toleration more quickly than did the politicians. A new skepticism, relativism, and individualism in religion became respectable in the sixteenth and seventeenth centuries. Sebastian Castellio's (1515–1563) pithy censure of John Calvin for his role in the execution of the Antitrinitarian Michael Servetus summarized a sentiment that was to grow in early modern Europe: "To kill a man is not to defend a doctrine, but to kill a man."[1] As a new skepticism greeted the failure of the great reform movements, the French essayist Michel de Montaigne (1533–1592) asked in scorn of the dogmatic mind: "What do I know?" The Lutheran Valentin Weigel (1533–1588), surveying a half century of religious strife in Germany, advised people to look within themselves for religious truth and no longer to churches and creeds.

Such views gained currency in larger political circles only by the most painful experiences. Where religious strife and its attendant civil war were best held in check, rulers tended to subordinate theological doctrine to political unity, urging tolerance, moderation, and compromise—even indifference—in religious matters. Such rulers came to be known as *politiques,* and the most successful among them was Elizabeth I of England. By contrast, rulers like Mary I of England, Philip II of Spain, and Oliver Cromwell, who tended to take their religion with the utmost seriousness and refused every compromise, did not in the long run achieve their political goals.

As we shall see, the wars of religion were both internal national conflicts and truly international wars. While Catholic and Protestant subjects struggled against one another for control of the crown of France, the Netherlands, and England, the Catholic governments of France and Spain conspired and finally sent

[1] *Contra libellum Calvini* (N.P., 1562), p. E 2 a.

The Ecstasy of St. Theresa, *by Gianlorenzo Bernini* (1598—1680), *in the church of Santa Maria della Vittoria in Rome. This statue of the saint in mystical rapture is part of a richly decorated altar. Like so much of the art of the Counter-Reformation, the altar was designed to dazzle and overawe the worshipper.* [*Art Resource*]

ABOVE: *The splendor of a Baroque church. This is the interior of the eighteenth-century cloister church at Ottobeuren in Bavaria, West Germany. The architect was Johann Michael Fischer. Note how the atmosphere is charged with energy and action.* [*Bettmann Archive.*]

LEFT: *The interior of St. Paul's Cathedral in London, by Sir Christopher Wren* (1632–1723). *Although elaborately decorated, the interior is subdued in effect.* [*Bettmann Archive.*]

armies against Protestant regimes in England and the Netherlands. The outbreak of the Thirty Years' War in 1618 made the international dimension of the religious conflict especially clear; before it ended in 1648, the war drew every major European nation directly or indirectly into its deadly net.

The French Wars of Religion (1562–1598)

Anti-Protestant Measures and the Struggle for Political Power

French Protestants came to be known as *Huguenots,* a term derived from Besançon Hugues, the leader of Geneva's political revolt against the House of Savoy in the 1520s, a prelude to that city's Calvinist Reformation in the 1530s. As early as the 1520s, however, the Sorbonne was vigilant against the Lutheran writings and doctrines that were circulating in Paris.

The capture of the French king Francis I by the forces of Charles V at the Battle of Pavia in 1525 provided a motive for the first wave of Protestant persecution in France. Hoping to pacify their Spanish conqueror, a fierce opponent of German Protestants, and to win their king's swift release, the French government took repressive measures against the native reform movement, led by Jacques Lefèvre d'Étaples and Bishop Briçonnet of Meaux, which had proved a seedbed of Protestant sentiment.

A second major crackdown came a decade later. When Protestants plastered Paris and other cities with anti-Catholic placards on October 18, 1534, mass arrests of suspected Protestants occurred. Government retaliation for this action drove John Calvin and other members of the French reform party into exile. In 1540 the Edict of Fontainebleau subjected French Protestants to the Inquisition. Henry II (1547–1559) established legal procedures against Protestants in the Edict of Chateaubriand in 1551. Save for a few brief interludes, the French monarchy remained a staunch Catholic foe of the Protestants until the ascension to the throne of Henry of Navarre in 1589.

The Habsburg–Valois wars (see Chapter 10) ended with the Treaty of Cateau-Cambrésis in 1559, and Europe experienced a moment of peace. But only a moment. The same year marked the beginning of internal French con-

The Battle of Pavia, 1525. *The French defeat at Pavia and the capture of Francis I by the Habsburg forces under Charles V provided a motive for the first wave of Protestant persecution in France.* [*SCALA/Art Resource*]

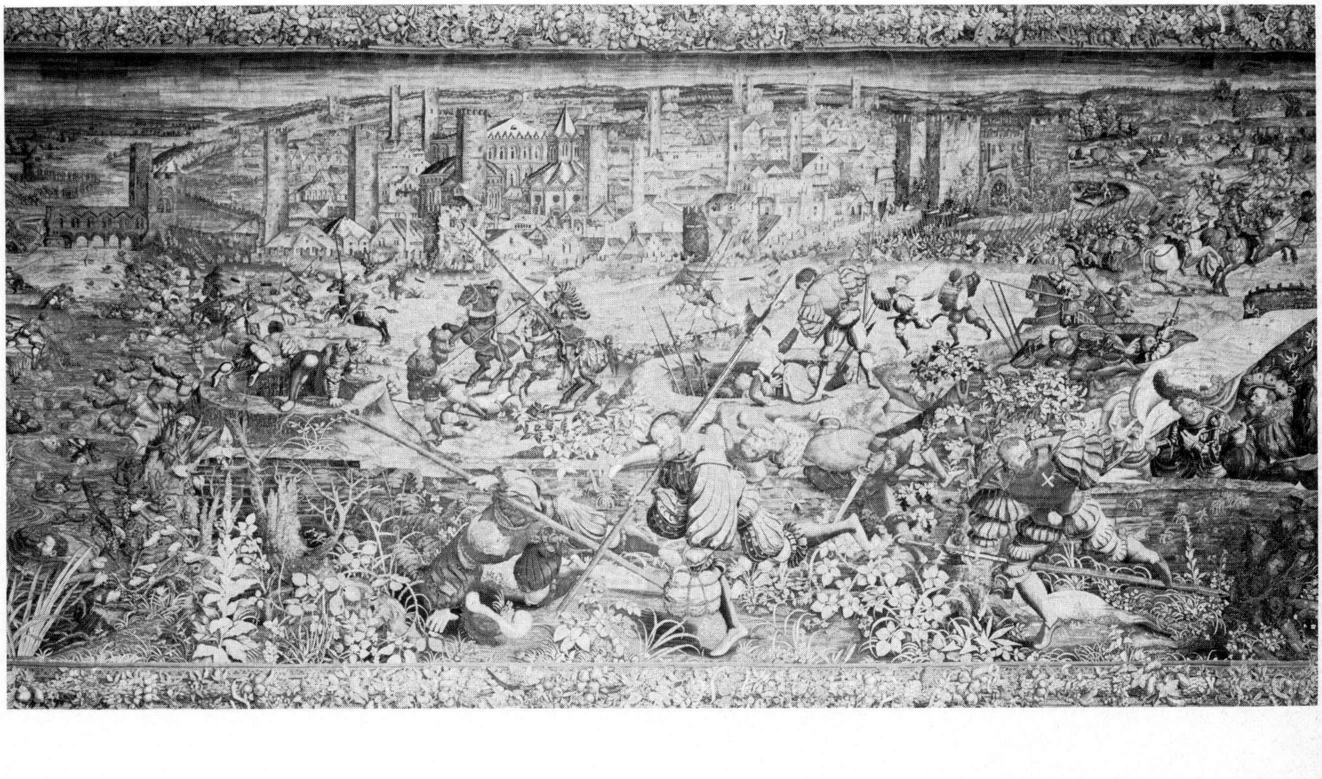

Diane de Poitiers, *by Francois Clouet* (1510–1572). *The mistress of Henry II of France, Diane* (1499–1566) *used her influence with the king to further the Catholic cause. After Henry's death in* 1559, *Diane was forced to retire to her country estates by Queen Catherine de' Medicis.* [*National Gallery of Art*]

flict and the shift of the European balance of power in favor of Spain. It began with an accident. During a tournament held to celebrate the marriage of his thirteen-year-old daughter, Elizabeth, to Philip II, the son of Charles V and heir to the Spanish Habsburg lands, the French king, Henry II, was mortally wounded. (A lance pierced his visor.) This unforeseen event brought to the throne Henry's sickly fifteen-year-old son, Francis II, under the regency of the queen mother, Catherine de Médicis. With the monarchy so weakened by Henry's death, three powerful families saw their chance to control France and began to compete for the young king's ear. They were the Bourbons, whose power lay in the south and west; the Montmorency-Chatillons, who controlled the center of France; and the Guises, who were dominant in eastern France.

The Guises were far the strongest and had little trouble establishing firm control over the young king. Francis, duke of Guise, had been Henry II's general, and his brothers, Charles and Louis, were cardinals of the church. Mary Stuart, Queen of Scots and wife of Francis II, was their niece. Throughout the latter half of the sixteenth century the name of Guise remained interchangeable with militant, reactionary Catholicism. The Bourbon and Montmorency-Chatillon families, in contrast, developed strong Huguenot sympathies, largely for political reasons. The Bourbon Louis I, prince of Condé (d. 1569), and the Montmorency-Chatillon Admiral Gaspard de Coligny (1519–1572) became the political leaders of the French Protestant resistance. They collaborated early in an abortive plot to kidnap Francis II from his Guise advisers in the Conspiracy of Amboise in 1560. This conspiracy was strongly condemned by John Calvin, who considered such tactics a disgrace to the Reformation.

Appeal of Calvinism

Often for quite different reasons ambitious aristocrats and discontented townspeople joined Calvinist churches in opposition to the Guise-dominated French monarchy. In 1561 over two thousand Huguenot congregations existed throughout France, although Huguenots were a majority of the population in only two regions. Dauphiné and Languedoc. Although they made up only about one fifteenth of the population, Huguenots were in important geographic areas and were heavily represented among the more powerful segments of French society. Over two fifths of the French aristocracy became Huguenots. Many apparently hoped to establish within France a principle of territorial sovereignty akin to that secured within the Holy Roman Empire by the Peace of Augsburg (1555). In this way Calvinism indirectly served the forces of political decentralization.

John Calvin and Theodore Beza consciously sought to advance their cause by currying favor with powerful aristocrats. Beza converted Jeanne d'Albert, the mother of the future Henry IV. The Prince of Condé was apparently converted in 1558 under the influence of his Calvinist wife. For many aristocrafts—Condé seems clearly to have been among them—Calvinist religious convictions were attractive primarily as aids to long-sought political goals. The military organization of Condé and

Coligny progressively merged with the religious organization of the French Huguenot churches, creating a potent combination that benefited both political and religious dissidents. Calvinism gave political resistance justification and inspiration, and the forces of political resistance made Calvinism a viable religious alternative in Catholic France. Each side had much to gain from the other. The confluence of secular and religious motives, although beneficial to aristocratic resistance and Calvinist religion alike, tended to cast suspicion on the religious appeal of Calvinism. Clearly religious conviction was neither the only nor always the main reason for becoming a Calvinist in France in the second half of the sixteenth century.

Catherine de Médicis and the Guises

Following Francis II's death in 1560, Catherine de Médicis continued as regent for her minor son, Charles IX (1560–1574). At a colloquy in Poissy she tried unsuccessfully to reconcile the Protestant and Catholic factions. Fearing the power and guile of the Guises, Catherine, whose first concern was always to preserve the monarchy, sought allies among the Protestants. In 1562, after conversations with Beza and Coligny, she issued the January Edict, a measure that granted Protestants freedom to worship publicly outside towns—although only privately within them—and to hold synods. In March this royal toleration came to an abrupt end when the duke of Guise surprised a Protestant congregation at Vassy in Champagne and proceeded to massacre several score—an event that marked the beginning of the French wars of religion (March 1562).

Had Condé and the Huguenot armies rushed immediately to the queen's side after this attack, Protestants might well have secured an alliance with the crown, so great was the queen mother's fear of Guise power at this time. But the hesitation of the Protestant leaders, due primarily to indecision on the part of Condé, placed the young king and the queen mother, against their deepest wishes, in firm Guise control, as cooperation with the Guises became the only alternative to capitulation to the Protestants.

During the first French war of religion, fought between April 1562 and March 1563, the duke of Guise was assassinated. It is a measure of the international character of the struggle in France that troops from Hesse and the Palatinate fought alongside the Huguenots. A brief resumption of hostilities in 1567–1568 was followed by the bloodiest of all the conflicts between September 1568 and August 1570. In this period Condé was killed and Huguenot leadership passed to Coligny—actually a blessing in disguise for the Protestants because Coligny was far the better military strategist. In the Peace of Saint-Germain-en-Laye (1570), which ended the third war, the crown, acknowledging the power of the Protestant nobility, granted the Huguenots religious freedoms within their territories and the right to fortify their cities.

Perpetually caught between fanatical Huguenot and Guise extremes, Queen Catherine had always sought to balance the one side against the other. Like the Guises, she wanted a Catholic France; she did not, however, desire a Guise-dominated monarchy. After the Peace of Saint-Germain-en-Laye the crown tilted manifestly toward the Bourbon faction and the Huguenots, and Coligny became Charles IX's

Catherine de' Medicis (1519–1589). *Catherine exercised enormous power in France during the reigns of her three sons Francis II* (1559–1560), *Charles IX* (1560–1574), *and Henry III* (1574–1589). [*Roger-Viollet*]

The Massacre of St. Bartholemew's Day, August 24, 1572, as depicted by the contemporary Protestant painter Francois Dubois. Three thousand Protestants were slaughtered in Paris, an estimated 20,000 others died throughout France. The massacre transformed the religious struggle in France from a conflict for political power to a war for survival between Protestants and Catholics. [*Museum of Lausanne*]

most trusted adviser. Unknown to the king, Catherine began at this time to plot with the Guises against the ascendant Protestants. As she had earlier sought Protestant support when Guise power threatened to subdue the monarchy, so she now sought Guise support as Protestant influence grew.

There was reason for Catherine to fear Coligny's hold on the king. Louis of Nassau, the leader of Protestant resistance to Philip II in the Netherlands, had gained Coligny's ear, and Coligny used his position of influence to win the king of France over to a planned French invasion of the Netherlands in support of the Dutch Protestants. Such a course of action would have placed France squarely on a collision course with mighty Spain. Catherine recognized far better than her son that France stood little chance in such a contest. She and her advisers had been much sobered in this regard by news of the stunning Spanish victory over the Turks at Lepanto in October 1571 (to be discussed later.)

The Saint Bartholomew's Day Massacre. When Catherine lent her support to the infamous Saint Bartholomew's Day Massacre of Protestants, she did so out of a far less reasoned judgment. Her decision appears to have been made in a state of near panic. On August 22, 1572, four days after the Huguenot Henry of Navarre had married the king's sister, Marguerite of Valois—still another sign of growing Protestant power—Coligny was struck down, although not killed, by an assassin's bullet. Catherine had apparently been party to this Guise plot to eliminate Coligny. After its failure she feared both the king's reaction to her complicity with the Guises and the Huguenot response under a recovered Coligny. Summoning all her motherly charm and fury, Catherine convinced Charles that a Huguenot coup was afoot, inspired by Coligny, and that only the swift execution of Protestant leaders could save the crown from a Protestant attack on Paris. On Saint Bartholomew's Day, 1572, Coligny and three thousand fellow Huguenots

Coligny's Death on Saint Bartholomew's Day

The following description of Coligny's murder by henchmen of the duke of Guise was written by an eyewitness to the Saint Bartholomew's Day Massacre, the statesman and historian Jacques-Auguste de Thou.

It was determined to exterminate all the Protestants, and the plan was approved by the queen. . . . The duke of Guise . . . was put in full command of the enterprise. . . . The signal to commence the massacre would be given by the bell of the palace, and the marks by which they [the Catholic Swiss mercenaries and the French soldiers who were to carry it out] should recognize each other in the darkness were a bit of white linen tied around the left arm and a white cross on the hat.

[As the massacre began] Coligny awoke and recognized from the noise that a riot was taking place. . . . When he perceived that the noise increased and that someone had fired an arquebus in the courtyard of his dwelling . . . , conjecturing what it might be, but too late, he arose from his bed and having put on his dressing gown said his prayers. . . . [Then] he said: "I see clearly that which they seek, and I am ready steadfastly to suffer that death which I have never feared. . . ."

Meanwhile the conspirators, having burst through the door of the chamber, entered, and [one named] Besme, sword in hand, demanded of Coligny, who stood near the door, "Are you Coligny?" Coligny replied, "Yes, I am he. . . ." As he spoke, Besme gave him a sword thrust through the body, and having withdrawn his sword, another thrust in the mouth, by which his face was disfigured. So Coligny fell, killed with many thrusts. Others have written that Coligny in dying pronounced . . . these words: "Would that I might at least die at the hands of a soldier and not [at those] of a valet. . . ."

Then the duke of Guise inquired of Besme from the courtyard if the thing were done, and when Besme answered him that it was, the duke replied that the Chevalier d'Angoulême was unable to believe it unless he saw it. . . . [So] they threw the body through the window into the courtyard, disfigured as it was with blood. When the Chevalier d'Angoulême, who could scarcely believe his eyes, had wiped away with a cloth the blood which overran the face and finally recognized him, some say he spurned the body with his foot . . . [and] said: "Cheer up my friends! Let us do thoroughly that which we have begun. The king commands it."

James Harvey Robinson (Ed.), *Readings in European History,* Vol. 2 (Boston: Ginn and Co., 1906), pp. 180–182.

were butchered in Paris. Within three days an estimated twenty thousand Huguenots were executed in coordinated attacks throughout France. It is a date that has ever since lived in infamy for Protestants.

Pope Gregory XIII and Philip II of Spain reportedly greeted the news of the Protestant massacre with special religious celebrations. Philip especially had good reason to rejoice, for the massacre ended for the moment any planned French opposition to his efforts to subdue his rebellious subjects in the Netherlands because France was now thrown into civil war. But the massacre of thousands of Protestants also gave the discerning Catholic world cause for new alarm. The event changed the nature of the struggle between Protestants and Catholics both within and beyond the borders of France. It was thereafter no longer an internal contest between Guise and Bourbon factions for French political influence, nor was it simply a Huguenot campaign to win basic religious freedoms. Henceforth, in Protestant eyes, it became an international struggle to the death for sheer survival against an adversary whose cruelty now justified any means of resistance.

Protestant Resistance Theory. Only as Protestants faced suppression and sure defeat did they begin to sanction active political resistance. At first, they tried to practice the biblical precept of obedient subjection to worldly authority (Romans 13:1). Luther had only grudgingly approved resistance to the emperor after the Diet of Augsburg in 1530. In 1550 Lutherans in the city of Magdeburg had published a highly influential defense of the right of lower authorities to oppose the emperor's order that all Lutherans return to the Catholic fold.

Calvin, who never faced the specter of total political defeat after his return to Geneva in 1541, had always condemned willful disobedience and rebellion against lawfully constituted governments as unchristian. But he also taught that lower magistrates, as part of the lawfully constituted government, had the right and duty to oppose tyrannical higher authority.

The exiled Scottish reformer John Knox, who had seen his cause crushed by Mary of Guise, the Regent of Scotland, and Mary I of England, had pointed the way for later Calvinists in his famous *Blast of the Trumpet Against the Terrible Regiment of Women* (1558). Knox declared that the removal of a heathen tyrant was not only permissible, but a Christian duty. He had the Catholic queen of England in mind.

After the great massacre of French Protestants on Saint Bartholomew's Day, 1572, Calvinists everywhere came to appreciate the need for an active defense of their religious rights. Classical Huguenot theories of resistance appeared in three major works of the 1570s. The first was the *Franco-Gallia* of François Hotman (1573), a Humanist argument that the representative Estates General of France historically held higher authority than the French king. The second was Theodore Beza's *On the Right of Magistrates over Their Subjects* (1574), which, going beyond Calvin's views, justified the correction and even the overthrow of tyrannical rulers by lower authorities. Finally, there was Philippe du Plessis Mornay's *Defense of Liberty Against Tyrants* (1579), an admonition to

Theodore Beza Defends the Right to Resist Tyranny

One of the oldest problems in political and social theory has been that of knowing when resistance to repression in matters of conscience is justified. Since Luther's day Protestant reformers, although accused by their Catholic critics of fomenting social division and revolution, had urged their followers to strict obedience to established political authority. After the 1572 Massacre of Saint Bartholomew's Day, however, Protestant pamphleteers urged Protestants to resist tyrants and persecutors with armed force. In 1574 Theodore Beza pointed out the obligation of rulers to their subjects and the latter's right to resist rulers who failed to meet the conditions of their office.

It is apparent that there is a mutual obligation between the king and the officers of a kingdom; that the government of the kingdom is not in the hands of the king in its entirety, but only the sovereign degree; that each of the officers has a share in accord with his degree; and that there are definite conditions on either side. If these conditions are not observed by the inferior officers, it is the part of the sovereign to dismiss and punish them. . . . If the king, hereditary or elective, clearly goes back on the conditions without which he would not have been recognized and acknowledged, can there be any doubt that the lesser magistrates of the kingdom, of the cities, and of the provinces, the administration of which they have received from the sovereignty itself, are free of their oath, at least to the extent that they are entitled to resist flagrant oppression of the realm which they swore to defend and protect according to their office and their particular jurisdiction? . . .

We must now speak of the third class of subjects, which though admittedly subject to the sovereign in a certain respect, is, in another respect, and in cases of necessity the protector of the rights of the sovereignty itself, and is established to hold the sovereign to his duty, and even, if need be, to constrain and punish him. . . . The people is prior to all the magistrates, and does not exist for them, but they for it. . . . Whenever law and equity prevailed, nations neither created nor accepted kings except upon definite conditions. From this it follows that when kings flagrantly violate these terms, those who have the power to give them their authority have no less power to deprive them of it.

Constitutionalism and Resistance in the Sixteenth Century: Three Treatises by Hotman, Beza, and Mornay, trans. and ed. by Julian H. Franklin (New York: Pegasus, 1969), pp. 111–114.

princes, nobles, and magistrates beneath the king, as guardians of the rights of the body politic, to take up arms against tyranny in other lands.

The Rise to Power of Henry of Navarre

Henry III (1574–1589), who was Henry II's third son and the last to wear the French crown, found the monarchy wedged between a radical Catholic League, formed in 1576 by Henry of Guise, and vengeful Huguenots. Neither group would have been reluctant to assassinate a ruler whom they considered heretical and a tyrant. Like the queen mother, Henry sought to steer a middle course, and in this effort he received support from a growing body of neutral Catholics and Huguenots, who put the political survival of France above its religious unity. Such *politiques* were prepared to compromise religious creeds as might be required to save the nation.

The Peace of Beaulieu in May 1576 granted the Huguenots almost complete religious and civil freedom. At this time, however, France was not ready for such sweeping toleration. Within seven months of the Peace of Beaulieu, the Catholic League forced Henry to return again to the illusory quest for absolute religious unity in France. In October 1577 the king issued the Edict of Poitiers, which truncated the Peace of Beaulieu, and once again circumscribed areas of permitted Huguenot worship. Thereafter Huguenot and Catholic factions quickly returned to their accustomed anarchical military solutions, the Protestants under the leadership of Henry of Navarre, now heir to the French throne.

In the mid-1580s the Catholic League, supported by the Spanish, became completely dominant in Paris. In what came to be known as the Day of the Barricades, Henry III attempted to rout the league with a surprise attack in 1588. The effort failed badly and the king had to flee Paris. Forced by his weakened position into unkingly guerrilla tactics, and also emboldened by news of the English victory over the Spanish Armada in 1588, Henry successfully plotted the assassination of both the duke and the cardinal of Guise. These assassinations sent France reeling once again. Led by still another Guise brother, Charles, duke of Mayenne, the Catholic League reacted with a fury that matched the earlier Huguenot response to the Massacre of Saint Bartholomew's Day. The king now had only one course of action: he struck an alliance with the Protestant Henry of Navarre in April 1589.

As the two Henrys prepared to attack the Guise stronghold of Paris, however, a fanatical Jacobin friar stabbed Henry III to death. Thereupon the Bourbon Huguenot Henry of Navarre succeeded the childless Valois king to the French throne as Henry IV (1589–1610). Pope Sixtus V and Philip II stood aghast at the sudden prospect of a Protestant France. They had always wanted France to be religiously Catholic and politically weak, and they now acted to achieve that end. Spain rushed troops to support the besieged Catholic League. Philip II apparently even harbored hopes of placing his eldest daughter, Isabella, the granddaughter of Henry II and Catherine de Médicis, on the French throne.

Direct Spanish intervention in the affairs of France seemed only to strengthen Henry IV's grasp on the crown. The French people viewed his right to hereditary succession more seriously than his espoused Protestant confession. Henry was also widely liked. Notoriously informal in dress and manner—a factor that made him especially popular with the soldiers—Henry also had the wit and charm to neutralize the strongest enemy in a face-to-face confrontation. He came to the throne as a *politique,* long weary with religious strife and fully prepared to place political peace above absolute religious unity. He believed that a royal policy of tolerant Catholicism would be the best way to achieve such peace. On July 25, 1593, he publicly abjured the Protestant faith and embraced the traditional and majority religion of his country. "Paris is worth a mass," he is reported to have said.

It was, in fact, a decision he had made only after a long period of personal agonizing. The Huguenots were understandably horrified by this turnabout and Pope Clement VIII remained skeptical of Henry's sincerity. But the majority of the French church and people, having known internal strife too long, rallied to the king's side. By 1596 the Catholic League was dispersed, its ties with Spain were broken, and the wars of religion in France, to all intents and purposes, had ground to a close.

The Edict of Nantes

On April 13, 1598, a formal religious settlement was proclaimed in Henry IV's famous Edict of Nantes, and the following month, on May 2, 1598, the Treaty of Vervins ended hos-

"Paris is worth a mass": Henry IV (1589–1610) *embraces Catholicism, July* 25, 1593, *from a contemporary print.* [*Roger-Viollet*]

Main Events of French Wars of Religion (1562–1598)

Treaty of Cateau-Cambrésis ends Habsburg–Valois wars	1559
Francis II succeeds to French throne under regency of his mother, Catherine de Médicis	1559
Conspiracy of Amboise fails	1560
Protestant worshipers massacred at Vassy in Champagne by the duke of Guise	1562
The Saint Bartholomew's Day Massacre leaves thousands of Protestants dead	1572
Assassination of Henry III brings Huguenot Henry of Navarre to throne as Henry IV	1589
Henry IV embraces Catholicism	1593
Henry IV grants Huguenots religious and civil freedoms in the Edict of Nantes	1598
Henry IV assassinated	1610

tilities between France and Spain. The Edict of Nantes recognized and sanctioned minority religious rights within what was to remain an officially Catholic country. In 1591 Henry IV had already assured the Huguenots of at least qualified religious freedoms. The Edict of Nantes made good that promise. This religious truce—and it was never more than that—granted the Huguenots, who by this time numbered well over one million, freedom of public worship, the right of assembly, admission to public offices and universities, and permission to maintain fortified towns. Most of the new freedoms, however, were to be exercised within their own towns and territories. Concession of the right to fortify their towns reveals the continuing distrust between French Protestants and Catholics. As significant as it was, the edict only transformed a long hot war between irreconcilable enemies into a long cold war. To its critics it had only created a state within a state.

A Catholic fanatic assassinated Henry IV in May 1610. Although Henry is remembered most for the religious settlement of the Edict of Nantes, it was he and his finance minister, the duke of Sully, who laid the foundations for the later transformation of France into the absolute state of Cardinal Richelieu and Louis XIV. It would be in pursuit of the political and religious unity that had escaped Henry IV that Louis XIV, calling for "one king, one church, one law," would revoke the Edict of Nantes in 1685 and force France and Europe to learn again by bitter experience the hard lessons of the wars of religion. Rare is the politician who has preferred to learn from the lessons of history rather than repeating its mistakes.

Henry IV Recognizes Huguenot Religious Freedom

By the Edict of Nantes (April 13, 1598) Henry IV recognized Huguenot religious freedoms and the rights of Protestants to participate in French public institutions. Here are some of its provisions.

We have by this perpetual and irrevocable Edict pronounced, declared, and ordained and we pronounce, declare and ordain:

Art. I. Firstly, that the memory of everything done on both sides from the beginning of the month of March, 1585, until our accession to the Crown and during the other previous troubles, and at the outbreak of them, shall remain extinct and suppressed, as if it were something which had never occurred. . . .

Art. II. We forbid all our subjects, of whatever rank and quality they may be, to renew the memory of these matters, to attack, be hostile to, injure or provoke each other in revenge for the past, whatever may be the reason and pretext . . . but let them restrain themselves and live peaceably together as brothers, friends, and fellow-citizens. . . .

Art. III. We ordain that the Catholic, Apostolic, and Roman religion shall be restored and re-established in all places and districts of this our kingdom and the countries under our rule, where its practice has been interrupted. . . .

. . . .

Art. VI. And we permit those of the so-called Reformed religion to live and dwell in all the towns and districts of this our kingdom and the countries under our rule, without being annoyed, disturbed, molested or constrained to do anything against their conscience, or for this cause to be sought out in their houses and districts where they wish to live, provided that they conduct themselves in other respects to the provisions of our present Edict. . . .

. . . .

Art. XXI. Books dealing with the matters of the aforesaid so-called Reformed religion shall not be printed and sold publicly, except in the towns and districts where the public exercise of the said religion is allowed. . . .

Art. XXII. We ordain that there shall be no difference or distinction, because of the aforesaid religion, in the reception of students to be instructed in Universities, Colleges, and schools, or of the sick and poor into hospitals, infirmaries, and public charitable institutions. . . .

. . . .

Art. XXVII. In order to reunite more effectively the wills of our subjects, as is our intention, and to remove all future complaints, we declare that all those who profess or shall profess, the aforesaid so-called Reformed religion are capable of holding and exercising all public positions, honours, offices, and duties whatsoever . . . in the towns of our kingdom . . . notwithstanding all contrary oaths.

Church and State Through the Centuries: A Collection of Historic Documents, trans. and ed. by S. Z. Ehler and John B. Morrall (New York: Biblo and Tannen, 1967), pp. 185–187.

Imperial Spain and the Reign of Philip II (1556–1598)

Pillars of Spanish Power

Until the English defeated his mighty Armada in 1588, no one person stood larger in the second half of the sixteenth century than Philip II of Spain. Philip was heir to the intensely Catholic and militarily supreme western Habsburg kingdom. The eastern Habsburg lands of Austria, Bohemia, and Hungary had been given over by his father, Charles V, to Philip's uncle, the Emperor Ferdinand I, and they remained, together with the imperial title, in the possession of the Austrian branch of the family. Populous and wealthy Castile gave Philip a solid home base. Additional wealth was provided by the regular arrival in Seville of bullion from the Spanish colonies in the New World. In the 1540s great silver mines had been opened in Potosí in present-day Bolivia and in Zacatecas in Mexico. These gave Philip the great sums needed to pay his bankers and mercenaries. He nonetheless never managed to erase the debts left by his father nor to finance his own foreign adventures fully. He later contributed to the bankruptcy of the Fuggers when, at the end of his life, he defaulted on his enormous debts.

The new American wealth brought dramatic social change to the peoples of Europe during the second half of the sixteenth century. As Europe became richer, it was also becoming more populous, especially in the economically and politically active towns of France, England, and the Netherlands, where populations had tripled and quadrupled by the early seventeenth century. Europe's population approached an estimated 100 million by 1600.

The combination of increased wealth and population triggered a serious inflation, a steady 2 per cent a year in much of Europe, with serious cumulative effects by midcentury. As there were more people and greater coinage in circulation, but less food and fewer jobs, wages stagnated while prices doubled and tripled in much of Europe. This was especially the case in Spain. Because the new wealth was concentrated in the hands of a few, the traditional gap between the "haves"—the

Philip II of Spain (1556–1598) *by Titian. Philip was the most powerful ruler of his time.* [*Alinari/Art Resource*]

propertied, privileged, and educated classes—and the "have-nots" greatly widened. Nowhere did the unprivileged suffer more than in Spain, where the Castilian peasantry, the backbone of Philip II's great empire, became the most heavily taxed people of Europe. Those who contributed most to making possible Spanish hegemony in Europe in the second half of the sixteenth century prospered least from it.

View of Toledo *by El Greco* (1541–1614). *Born Domenicos Theotocopoulos in Crete, El Greco (which means "The Greek" in Spanish) did most of his work in Italy and Spain. His depiction of Toledo, the religious capital of Spain, captures the brooding mysticism and intensity of the Spanish Counter Reformation.* [*Metropolitan Museum of Art. The H.O. Havemeyer Collection*]

A subjugated peasantry and wealth from the New World were not the only pillars of Spanish strength. Philip II shrewdly organized the lesser nobility into a loyal and efficient national bureaucracy. A reclusive man, he managed his kingdom by pen and paper rather than by personal presence. He was also a learned and pious Catholic, although some popes suspected that he used religion as much for political as for devotional purposes. That he was a generous patron of the arts and culture can be seen in his unique retreat outside Madrid, the Escorial, a combination palace, church, tomb, and monastery. Philip also knew personal sorrows. His mad and treacherous son, Don Carlos, died under suspicious circumstances in 1568—some contemporaries suspected that Philip had him quietly executed—only three months before the death of the queen.

During the first half of Philip's reign, attention focused almost exclusively on the Mediterranean and the Turkish threat, a constant European preoccupation. By history, geography, and choice, Spain had traditionally been Catholic Europe's champion against Islam. During the 1560s the Turks advanced deep into Austria, while their fleets dominated the Mediterranean. Between 1568 and 1570 armies under Philip's half-brother, Don John of Austria, the illegitimate son of Charles V, suppressed and dispersed the Moors in Granada. In May 1571 a Holy League of Spain, Venice, and the pope, again under Don John's command, formed to check Turkish belligerence in the Mediterranean. In what became the largest naval battle of the sixteenth century, Don John's fleet engaged the Ottoman navy under Ali Pasha off Lepanto in the Gulf of Corinth on October 7, 1571. Before the engagement ended, thirty thousand Turks had died and

The Escorial, Philip II's massive palace-monastery-mausoleum northwest of Madrid. Built between 1563 and 1584, the Escorial is a monument to the piety of the king. Philip had vowed to build the complex after the Spanish victory at Saint-Quentin over the French in 1577, which was won on St. Lawrence's day. Because the symbol of St. Lawrence is a grill—legend has it that he was martyred by being roasted alive—the Escorial's floor plan was designed to resemble a grill. [Editorial Photocolor Archives.]

The great battle of Lepanto (off the coast of Greece), October 7, 1541. *In this, the largest naval engagement of the sixteenth century, the Spanish and their Italian allies under Don John of Austria smashed the Turkish fleet and ended the Ottoman threat to the western Mediterranean.* [*National Maritime Museum, London*]

A sixteenth-century view of Genoa and its war fleet. Unlike its archrival Venice, Genoa tended to support Spanish policy in the Mediterranean. A large Genoese contingent fought under Don Juan at Lepanto. [*SCALA/Art Resource*]

ABOVE: *The mosque of Ottoman Sultan Suleiman the Magnificent (1520–1566) in Constantinople (modern Istanbul). It was built by Suleiman's architect Sinan at the height of the Ottoman Empire's glory. Like many Ottoman mosques, it was clearly inspired by neighboring Hagia Sophia built by Byzantine Emperor Justinian a thousand years earlier. [Turkish Government Tourism and Information Office. New York]*

LEFT: *St. Peter's in Rome was built in the sixteenth and seventeenth centuries replacing Emperor Constantine's early Christian Basilica of the fourth century on the probable site of the saint's tomb. The great church had many architects, among them Michelangelo, who designed the great dome. The vast piazza in front was designed by Bernini; note how the thrown-open arms extend to embrace pilgrims and draw them into the church. A portion of the pope's residence, the Vatican palace, is at the right center. [Fotocielo]*

over one third of the Turkish fleet had been sunk or captured. The Mediterranean for the moment belonged to Spain, and the Europeans were left to fight each other. Philip's armies also succeeded in putting down resistance in neighboring Portugal, which Spain annexed in 1580. The conquest of Portugal not only added to Spanish seapower but also brought the magnificent Portuguese overseas empire in Africa, India, and the Americas into the Spanish orbit.

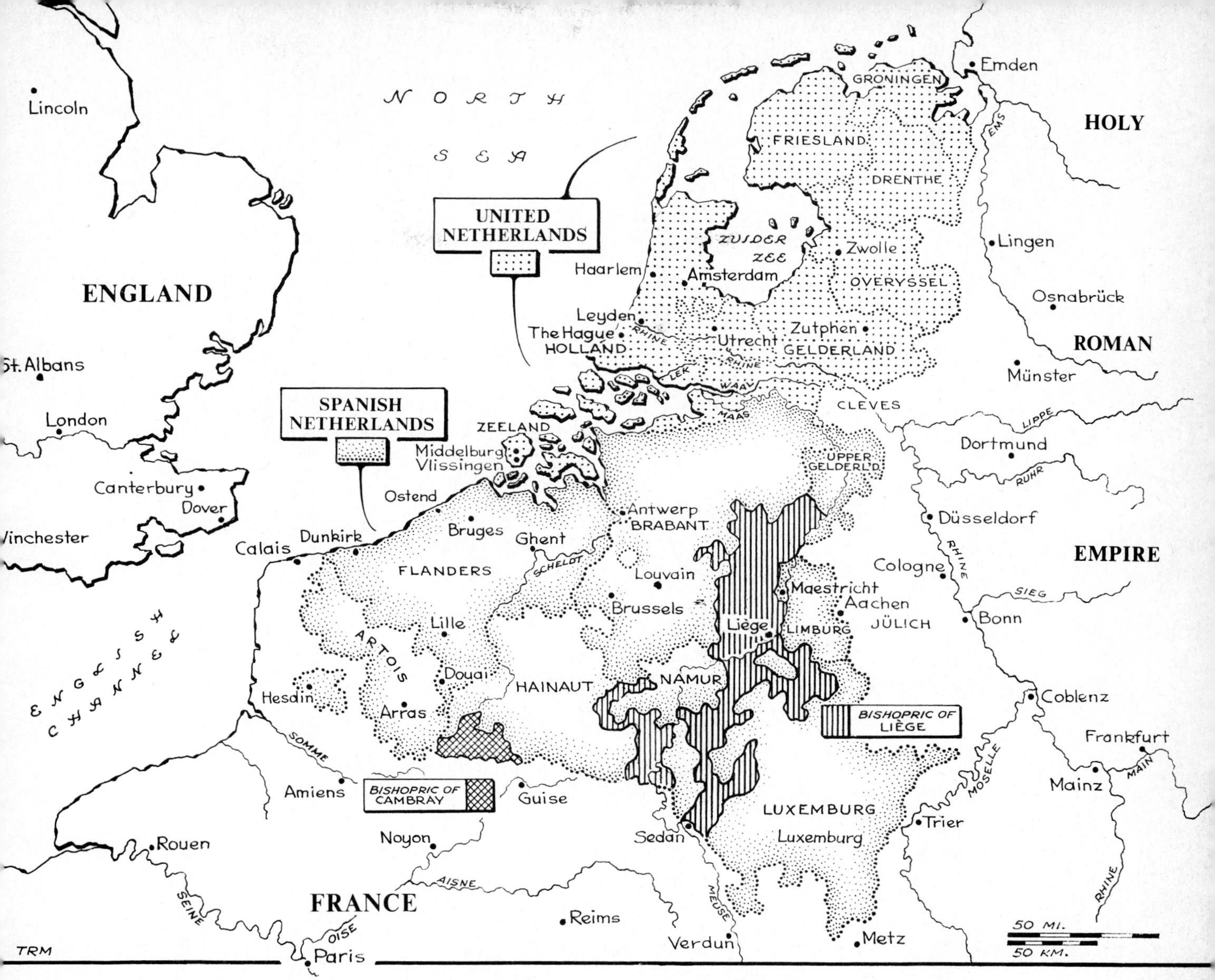

THE NETHERLANDS DURING THE REFORMATION

MAP 11–1 *The northern and southern provinces of the Netherlands. The former, the United Provinces, were mostly Protestant in the second half of the sixteenth century, while the southern, the Spanish Netherlands, made peace with Spain and remained largely Catholic.*

The Revolt in the Netherlands

The spectacular Spanish military success in southern Europe was not repeated in northern Europe. When Philip attempted to impose his will within the Netherlands and on England and France, he learned the lessons of defeat. The resistance of the Netherlands especially proved the undoing of Spanish dreams of world empire.

CARDINAL GRANVELLE. The Netherlands were not only the richest area of Philip's Habsburg kingdom, but of Europe as well. In 1559 Philip had departed the Netherlands for Spain, never again to return. His half-sister, Margaret of Parma, assisted by a special council of state, became regent in his absence. The council was headed by Philip's hand-picked lieutenant, the extremely able Antoine Perrenot (1517–1586), after 1561 Cardinal Granvelle. Granvelle hoped to check Protestant gains by internal church reforms, and he planned to break down the traditional local autonomy of the seventeen Netherlands provinces by stages and establish in its place a centralized royal government directed from Madrid. A politically docile and religiously uniform country was the objective.

The merchant towns of the Netherlands were, however, Europe's most independent; many, like magnificent Antwerp, were also Calvinist strongholds. By tradition and temperament the people of the Netherlands inclined far more toward variety and toleration than toward obeisant conformity and hierarchical order. Two members of the council of state formed a stubborn opposition to the Spanish overlords, who now sought to reimpose their traditional rule with a vengeance. They were the Count of Egmont (1522–1568) and William of Nassau, the Prince of Orange (1533–1584), known as "the Silent" because of his extremely small circle of confidants.

Like other successful rulers in this period, William of Orange was a *politique* who placed the Netherlands' political autonomy and well-being above religious creeds. He personally passed through successive Catholic, Lutheran, and Calvinist stages. In 1561 he married Anne of Saxony, the daughter of the Lutheran Elector Maurice and the granddaughter of the late Landgrave Philip of Hesse. He maintained his Catholic practices until 1567, at which time he turned Lutheran. After the Saint Bartholomew's Day massacre (1572), Orange became an avowed Calvinist.

In 1561 Cardinal Granvelle proceeded with a planned ecclesiastical reorganization of the Netherlands that was intended to tighten the control of the Catholic hierarchy over the

The Milch Cow, a sixteenth-century satirical painting depicting the Netherlands as a milk cow in whom all the powers are interested. Elizabeth of England is feeding the cow—England had long-standing commercial ties with Flanders; Philip II of Spain is attempting to ride her—Spain was trying to reassert its control over the country; William of Orange is trying to milk the animal—he had placed himself at the head of the anti-Spanish rebellion; and the King of France holds the cow's tail—France sought to profit from the rebellion at Spain's expense. [*Rijksmuseum, Amsterdam*]

country and to accelerate its consolidation as a Spanish ward. Orange and Egmont, organizing the Dutch nobility in opposition, succeeded in gaining Granvelle's removal from office in 1564, with Regent Margaret's blessing. But aristocratic control of the country after Granvelle's departure proved woefully inefficient, and popular unrest continued to grow, especially among urban artisans, who joined the congregations of radical Calvinist preachers in increasing numbers.

The Compromise. The year 1564 also saw the first fusion of political and religious opposition to Margaret's government. This opposition resulted from Philip II's unwise insistence that the decrees of the Council of Trent be enforced throughout the Netherlands. William of Orange's younger brother, Louis of Nassau, who had been raised a Lutheran, led the opposition, and it received support from the Calvinist-inclined lesser nobility and townspeople. A national covenant was drawn up called the *Compromise,* a solemn pledge to resist the decrees of Trent and the Inquisition. Grievances were loudly and persistently voiced, and when Margaret's government spurned the protesters as "beggars" in 1566, Calvinists rioted through the country. Louis called on French Huguenots and German Lutherans to send aid to the Netherlands, and a full-scale rebellion against the Spanish regency appeared imminent.

The Duke of Alba. The rebellion failed to materialize, however, because the Netherlands' higher nobility would not support it. Their shock at Calvinist iconoclasm and anarchy was as great as their resentment of Granvelle's more subtle repression. Philip, determined to make an example of the Protestant rebels, dispatched the duke of Alba to suppress the revolt. His army of ten thousand journeyed northward from Milan in 1567 in a show of combined Spanish and papal might. A special tribunal, known to the Spanish as the Council of Troubles and among the Netherlanders as the Council of Blood, reigned over the land. The counts of Egmont and Horn and several thousand suspected heretics were publicly executed before Alba's reign of terror ended.

The Spanish levied new taxes, forcing the Netherlands to pay for the suppression of its own revolt. One of these taxes, the "tenth penny," a 10 per cent sales tax, met such resistance from merchants and artisans that it remained uncollectable in some areas even after a reduction to 3 per cent. Combined persecution and taxation sent tens of thousands fleeing from the Netherlands during Alba's cruel six-year rule. Alba came to be more hated than Granvelle or the radical Calvinists had ever been.

The Duke of Alba (1507–1582). *His ruthless attempts to stamp out opposition in the Netherlands only inspired greater resistance by the Dutch.* [*Mas*]

Resistance and Unification. William of Orange was an exile in Germany during these turbulent years. He now emerged as the leader of a broad movement for the Netherlands' independence from Spain. The northern, Calvinist-inclined provinces of Holland, Zeeland, and Utrecht, of which Orange was the *stadholder,* or governor, became his base. As in France, political resistance in the Netherlands gained both organization and inspiration by merging with Calvinism.

The early victories of the resistance attest to the popular character of the revolt. A case in point is the capture of the port city of Brill by the "Sea Beggars." These men were an inter-

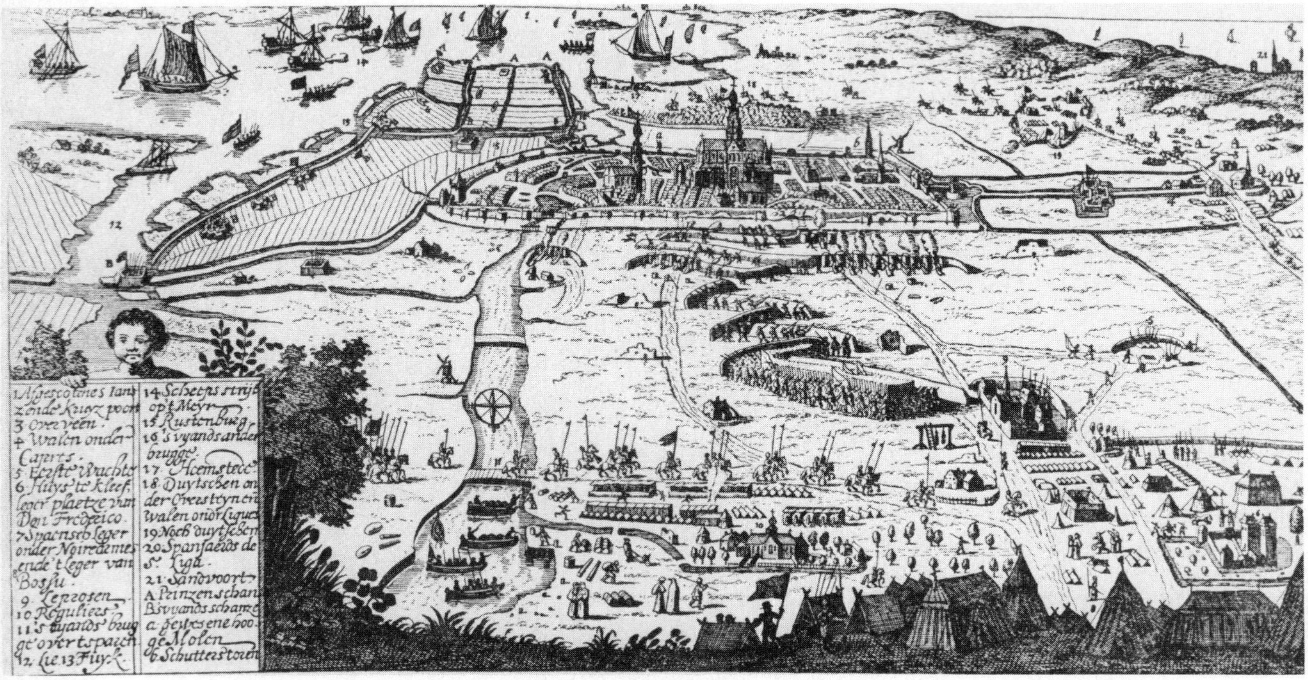

The siege of the Dutch city of Haarlem by Alba's army. The siege was a horrible example of the increasingly bloody struggle in the Netherlands. After resisting heroically for seven months (December 1572–June 1573), the city fell and all of the garrison and about 2000 inhabitants were slaughtered by the Spaniards. [Beschryvinge ende lof der stad Haerlem]

national group of anti-Spanish exiles and criminals, among them many Englishmen. William of Orange did not hesitate to enlist their services. Their brazen piracy, however, had forced Queen Elizabeth to disassociate herself from them and to bar their ships from English ports. In 1572 the Beggars captured Brill and other seaports in Zeeland and Holland. Mixing with the native population, they quickly sparked rebellions against Alba in town after town and spread the resistance southward. In 1574 the people of Leiden heroically resisted a long Spanish siege. The Dutch opened the dikes and flooded their country to repulse the hated Spanish. The faltering Alba had by that time ceded power to Don Luis de Requesens, who replaced him as commander of Spanish forces in the Netherlands in November 1573.

The Pacification of Ghent. The greatest atrocity of the war came after Requesens's death in 1576. Spanish mercenaries, leaderless and unpaid, ran amok in Antwerp on November 4, 1576, and they left seven thousand people dead in the streets. The event came to be known as the Spanish Fury.

These atrocities accomplished in four short days what neither religion nor patriotism had previously been able to do. The ten largely Catholic southern provinces (what is roughly modern Belgium) now came together with the seven largely Protestant northern provinces (what is roughly the modern Netherlands) in unified opposition to Spain. This union, known as the Pacification of Ghent, was accomplished on November 8, 1576. It declared internal regional sovereignty in matters of religion, a key clause that permitted political cooperation among the signatories, who were not agreed over religion. It was a Netherlands version of the territorial settlement of religious differences brought about in the Holy Roman Empire in 1555 by the Peace of Augsburg. Four provinces initially held out, but they soon made the resistance unanimous two months later by joining the all-embracing Union of Brussels in January 1577. For the next two years the Spanish faced a unified and determined Netherlands.

Don John, the victor over the Turks at Lepanto in 1571, had taken command of Spanish land forces in November 1576. He now experienced his first defeat. Confronted by unified Netherlands resistance, he signed the Perpetual Edict in February 1577, a humiliating treaty that provided for the removal of all Spanish troops from the Netherlands within twenty days. This withdrawal of troops not only gave the country to William of Orange but also effectively ended for the present whatever plans Philip may have had for using the Netherlands as a staging area for an invasion of England.

The Union of Arras and the Union of Utrecht. The Spanish, however, were nothing if not persistent. Don Juan and Alessandro Farnese of Parma, the regent Margaret's son, revived Spanish power in the southern provinces, where constant fear of Calvinist extremism had moved the leaders to break the Union of Brussels. In January 1579 the southern provinces formed the Union of Arras, and within five months they made peace with Spain. These provinces later served the cause of the Counter-Reformation. The northern provinces responded with the formation of the Union of Utrecht.

Netherlands Independence. Seizing what now appeared to be a last opportunity to break the back of Netherlands resistance, Philip II declared William of Orange an outlaw and placed a bounty of 25,000 crowns on his head.

Philip II Declares William of Orange an Outlaw (1580)

In the following proclamation the king of Spain accused William of Orange of being the "chief disturber of the public peace" and offered his captors, or assassins, generous rewards.

Philip, by the grace of God king of Castile, etc. to all to whom these presents may come, greeting:

It is well known to all how favorably the late emperor, Charles V, . . . treated William of Nassau. . . . Nevertheless, as everyone knows, we had scarcely turned our back on the Netherlands before the said William . . . (who had become . . . prince of Orange) began . . . by sinister arts, plots, and intrigues . . . to gain [control] over those whom he believed to be malcontents, or haters of justice, or anxious for innovations, and . . . above all, those who were suspected in the matter of religion. . . . With the knowledge, advice, and encouragement of the said Orange, the heretics commenced to destroy the images, altars, and churches. . . . So soon as the said Nassau was received into the government of the provinces, he began, through his agents and satellites, to introduce heretical preaching. . . . Then he introduced liberty of conscience . . . which soon brought it about that the Catholics were openly persecuted and driven out. . . . Moreover he obtained such a hold upon our poor subjects of Holland and Zeeland . . . that nearly all the towns, one after the other, have been besieged. . . .

Therefore, for all these just reasons, for his evil doings as chief disturber of the public peace . . . we outlaw him forever and forbid our subjects to associate with him . . . in public or in secret. We declare him an enemy of the human race, and in order the sooner to remove our people from his tyranny and oppression, we promise, on the word of a king and as God's servant, that if one of our subjects be found so generous of heart and so desirous of doing us a service and advantaging the public that he shall find the means of executing this decree and of ridding us of the said pest, either by delivering him to us dead or alive, or by depriving him at once of life, we will give him and his heirs landed estates or money, as he will, to the amount of twenty-five thousand gold crowns. If he has committed any crime, of any kind whatsoever, we will pardon him. If he be not noble, we will ennoble him for his valor; and should he require other persons to assist him, we will reward them according to the service rendered, pardon their crimes, and ennoble them too.

James Harvey Robinson (Ed.), *Readings in European History,* Vol. 2 (Boston: Ginn and Co., 1906), pp. 174–177.

The act predictably stiffened the resistance of the northern provinces. In a famous defiant speech to the Estates General of Holland in December 1580, known as the *Apology,* Orange publicly denounced Philip as a heathen tyrant whom the Netherlands need no longer obey. On July 22, 1581, the member provinces of the Union of Utrecht met in The Hague and formally declared Philip no longer their ruler. They turned in his stead to the French duke of Alençon, Catherine de Médicis's youngest and least satisfactory son, a man to whom the southern provinces had also earlier looked as a possible middle way between Spanish and Calvinist overlordship. All the northern provinces save Holland and Zeeland accepted Alençon as their "sovereign" (Holland and Zeeland distrusted him almost as much as they did Philip II), but with the understanding that he would be only a titular ruler. But Alençon, an ambitious failure, saw this as his one chance at greatness. When he rashly attempted to take actual control of the provinces in 1583, he was deposed and returned to France.

Spanish efforts to reconquer the Netherlands continued into the 1580s. William of Orange was assassinated in July 1584, to be succeeded by his seventeen-year-old son, Maurice (1567–1625), who, with the assistance of England and France, continued Dutch resistance. Fortunately for the Netherlands Philip II began at this time to meddle directly in French and English affairs. He signed a secret treaty with the Guises (the Treaty of Joinville in December 1584) and sent armies under Farnese into France in 1590. Hostilities with the English,

William of Orange Defends Himself to the Dutch Estates

Branded an outlaw by Philip II of Spain, the Protestant Dutch Prince William of Orange defended himself to his countrymen in an eloquent address known as the *Apology* (1581).

What could be more gratifying in this world, especially to one engaged in the great and excellent task of securing liberty for a good people oppressed by evil men, than to be mortally hated by one's enemies, who are at the same time enemies of the fatherland, and by their mouths to receive a sweet testimony to one's fidelity to his people and to his obstinate opposition to tyrants and disturbers of the peace? Such is the pleasure that the Spaniards and their adherents have prepared for me in their anxiety to disturb me. They have but gratified me by that infamous proscription by which they sought to ruin me. Not only do I owe to them this favor, but also the occasion to make generally known the equity and justice of my enterprises. . . .

My enemies object that I have "established liberty of conscience." I confess that the glow of fires in which so many poor Christians have been tormented is not an agreeable sight to me, although it may rejoice the eyes of the duke of Alba and the Spaniards; and that it has been my opinion that persecutions should cease in the Netherlands. . . .

They denounce me as a hypocrite, which is absurd enough. . . . As their friend, I told them quite frankly that they were twisting a rope to hang themselves when they began the barbarous policy of persecution. . . .

As for me personally . . . it is my head that they are looking for, and that they have vowed my death by offering such a great sum of money. They say that the war can never come to an end so long as I am among you. . . .

If, gentlemen, you believe that my exile, or even my death, may serve you, I am ready to obey your behests. Here is my head, over which no prince or monarch has authority save you. Dispose of it as you will for the safety and preservation of our commonwealth. But if you judge that such little experience and energy as I have acquired through long and assiduous labors, if you judge that the remainder of my possessions and of my life can be of service to you, I dedicate them to you and to the fatherland.

James Harvey Robinson, Readings in European History, Vol. 2 (Boston: Ginn and Co., 1906), pp. 177–179.

who had openly aided the Dutch rebels, also increased, gradually building toward the climax of 1588, when Philip's great Armada was defeated in the English Channel. These new Spanish fronts strengthened the Netherlands as Spain became badly overextended. Spanish preoccupation with France and England permitted the northern provinces to drive out all Spanish soldiers by 1593. In 1596 France and England formally recognized the independence of these provinces. Peace was not, however, concluded with Spain until 1609, when the Twelve Years' Truce gave the northern provinces their virtual independence. Full recognition came finally in the Peace of Westphalia in 1648.

England and Spain (1553–1603)

Mary I

Before Edward VI died in 1553, he agreed to a device to make Lady Jane Grey, the teen-age daughter of a powerful Protestant nobleman and, more important, the granddaughter on her mother's side of Henry VIII's younger sister Mary, his successor in place of the Catholic Mary Tudor (1553–1558). But popular support for the principle of hereditary monarchy was too strong to deprive Mary of her rightful rule. Popular uprisings in London and elsewhere led to Jane Grey's removal from the throne within days of her crowning, and she was eventually beheaded.

Once enthroned, Mary proceeded to act even beyond the worst fears of the Protestants. In 1554 she entered a highly unpopular political marriage with Prince Philip (later Philip II) of Spain, a symbol of militant Catholicism to English Protestants, and pursued at his direction a foreign policy that in 1558 cost England its last enclave on the Continent, Calais.

Mary's domestic measures were equally shocking and even more divisive. During her reign Parliament repealed the Protestant statutes of Edward and reverted to the strict Catholic religious practice of her father, Henry VIII. The great Protestant leaders of the Edwardian age—John Hooper, Hugh Latimer, Miles Coverdale, and Thomas Cranmer—were executed for heresy. Hundreds of Protestants either joined them in martyrdom (282 persons were burned at the stake during Mary's reign) or took flight to the Continent. These "Marian exiles," prominent among whom was the future leader of the Reformation in Scotland, John Knox, settled in Germany and Switzerland, forming especially large communities in Frankfurt, Strasbourg, and Geneva. There they worshiped in their own congregations, wrote tracts justifying armed resistance, and waited for the time when a Protestant counteroffensive could be launched in their homelands.

The execution of Thomas Cranmer (1489–1556), *Archbishop of Canterbury under Henry VIII and Edward VI. Cranmer was burned by Queen Mary Tudor* (1553–1558) *for his leading role in the English Reformation.* [*New York Public library*]

Elizabeth I

Mary's successor was her half-sister, Elizabeth I (1558–1603), the daughter of Henry VIII and Anne Boleyn, and perhaps the most astute politician of the sixteenth century in both domestic and foreign policy. Assisted by a shrewd adviser, Sir William Cecil (1520–1598; Lord Burghley after 1571), Elizabeth built a true kingdom on the ruins of Mary's reign. Between 1559 and 1563 she and Cecil guided a religious settlement through Parliament that prevented England from being torn asunder by religious differences in the sixteenth century, as the Continent was. A *politique* who subordinated religious to political unity, Elizabeth merged a centralized episcopal system, which she firmly controlled, with broadly defined Protestant doctrine and traditional Catholic ritual. In the resulting Anglican church inflexible extremes were not permitted in religion.

In 1559 an Act of Supremacy passed Parliament repealing all the anti-Protestant legislation of Mary Tudor and asserting Elizabeth's right as "supreme governor" over both spiritual and temporal affairs. An Act of Uniformity in the same year mandated a revised version of the second *Book of Common Prayer* (1552) for every English parish. The issuance of the Thirty-Nine Articles on Religion in 1563—which were a revision of Thomas Cranmer's original forty-two—made a moderate Protestantism the official religion within the Church of England.

CATHOLIC AND PROTESTANT EXTREMISTS. Elizabeth hoped to avoid both Catholic and Protestant extremism at the official level by pursuing a middle way. Her first archbishop of Canterbury, Matthew Parker (d. 1575), represented this ideal. But Elizabeth could not prevent the emergence of subversive Catholic and Protestant zealots. When she ascended the throne, Catholics were in the majority in England, and the extremists among them, encouraged by the Jesuits, plotted against her. They were also encouraged and later directly assisted by the Spanish, who were piqued both by Elizabeth's Protestant sympathies and by her refusal to follow the example of her half-

An Unknown Contemporary Describes Queen Elizabeth

No sixteenth-century ruler governed more effectively than Elizabeth of England (1558–1603), who was both loved and feared by her subjects. An unknown contemporary has left the following description, revealing not only her intelligence and shrewdness but also something of her tremendous vanity.

I will proceed with the description of the queen's disposition and natural gifts of mind and body, wherein she either matched or exceeded all the princes of her time, as being of a great spirit yet tempered with moderation, in adversity never dejected, in prosperity rather joyful than proud; affable to her subjects, but always with due regard to the greatness of her estate, by reason whereof she was both loved and feared.

In her later time, when she showed herself in public, she was always magnificent in apparel; supposing haply thereby that the eyes of her people (being dazzled by the glittering aspect of her outward ornaments) would not so easily discern the marks of age and decay of natural beauty; and she came abroad the more seldom, to make her presence the more grateful and applauded by the multitude, to whom things rarely seen are in manner as new.

She suffered not, at any time, any suitor to depart discontented from her, and though ofttimes he obtained not that he desired, yet he held himself satisfied with her manner of speech, which gave hope of success in the second attempt. . . .

Latin, French, and Italian she could speak very elegantly, and she was able in all those languages to answer ambassadors on the sudden. . . . Of the Greek tongue she was also not altogether ignorant. She took pleasure in reading of the best and wisest histories, and some part of Tacitus' Annals *she herself turned into English for her private exercise. She also translated Boethius'* On the Consolation of Philosophy *and a treatise of Plutarch,* On Curiosity, *with divers others. . . .*

It is credibly reported that not long before her death, she had a great apprehension of her own age and declination by seeing her face (then lean and full of wrinkles) truly represented to her in a glass, which she a good while very earnestly beheld; perceiving thereby how often she had been abused by flatterers (whom she held in too great estimation) that had informed her the contrary.

James Harvey Robinson (Ed.), *Readings in European History,* Vol. 2 (Boston: Ginn and Co. 1906), pp. 191–193.

Elizabeth I (1558–1603) *painted standing on a map of England in* 1592. *An astute politician in both foreign and domestic policy, Elizabeth was perhaps the most successful ruler of the sixteenth century.* [*National Portrait Gallery, London*]

sister Mary and take Philip II's hand in marriage. Elizabeth remained unmarried throughout her reign, using the possibility of a marriage alliance very much to her diplomatic advantage.

Catholic extremists hoped eventually to replace Elizabeth with Mary Stuart, Queen of Scots. Unlike Elizabeth, who had been declared illegitimate during the reign of her father, Mary Stuart had an unblemished claim to the throne by way of her grandmother Margaret, who was the sister of Henry VIII. Elizabeth acted swiftly against Catholic assassination plots and rarely let emotion override her political instincts. Despite proven cases of Catholic treason and even attempted regicide, however, she executed fewer Catholics during her forty-five years on the throne than Mary Tudor had executed Protestants during her brief five-year reign.

Elizabeth dealt cautiously with the Puritans, who were Protestants working within the national church to "purify" it of every vestige of "popery" and to make its Protestant doctrine more precise. The Puritans had two special grievances: (1) the retention of Catholic ceremony and vestments within the Church of England, which made it appear to the casual observer that no Reformation had occurred, and (2) the continuation of the episcopal system of church governance, which conceived of the English church theologically as the true successor to Rome, while placing it politically under the firm hand of the queen and her compliant archbishop.

Sixteenth-century Puritans were not separatists. Enjoying wide popular support and led by widely respected men like Thomas Cartwright (d. 1603), they worked through Parliament to create an alternative national church of semiautonomous congregations governed by representative presbyteries (hence, Presbyterians), following the model of Calvin and Geneva. Elizabeth dealt firmly but subtly with this group, conceding absolutely nothing that lessened the hierarchical unity of the Church of England and her control over it.

The more extreme Puritans wanted every congregation to be autonomous, a law unto itself, with neither higher episcopal nor presbyterian control. They came to be known as *Congregationalists.* Elizabeth and her second archbishop of Canterbury, John Whitgift (d. 1604), refused to tolerate this group, whose views on independence seemed to them to be patently subversive. The Conventicle Act of 1593 gave such separatists the option of either conforming to the practices of the Church of England or facing exile or death.

Deterioration of Relations with Spain. A series of events led inexorably to war between England and Spain, despite the sincerest desires on the part of both Philip II and Elizabeth to avoid a direct confrontation.

In 1567 the Spanish duke of Alba marched his mighty army into the Netherlands, which was, from the English point of view, simply a convenient staging area for a Spanish invasion of England. Pope Pius V (1566–1572), who favored a military conquest of Protestant England, "excommunicated" Elizabeth for heresy in 1570—a mischievous act that only encouraged both internal resistance and international intrigue against the queen. Two years later the piratical Sea Beggars, many of whom were Englishmen, occupied the port city of Brill in the Netherlands and aroused the surrounding countryside against the Spanish.

Following Don John's demonstration of Spain's awesome seapower at the famous naval battle of Lepanto in 1571, England signed a mutual defense pact with France. Also in the 1570s, Elizabeth's famous seamen, John Hawkins (1532–1595) and Sir Francis Drake (1545?–1596), began to prey regularly on Spanish shipping in the Americas. Drake's circumnavigation of the globe between 1577 and 1580 was one in a series of dramatic demonstrations of English ascendancy on the high seas.

After the Saint Bartholomew's Day massacre, Elizabeth's was the only bosom to which Protestants in France and the Netherlands could cleave. In 1585 she signed the Treaty of Nonsuch, which provided English soldiers and cavalry to the Netherlands. Funds that had previously been funneled covertly to support Henry of Navarre's army in France now flowed openly.

Mary, Queen of Scots. These events made a tinderbox of English-Spanish relations. The spark that finally touched it off was Elizabeth's reluctant but necessary execution of Mary, Queen of Scots (1542–1587).

Mary was the daughter of King James V of Scotland, and Mary of Guise and had resided in France from the time she was six years old. This thoroughly French and Catholic queen had returned to Scotland after the death of her husband, the French king Francis II, in 1561, there to find a successful, fervent Protestant Reformation that had won legal sanction the year before in the Treaty of Edinburgh (1560). As hereditary heir to the throne of Scotland, Mary remained queen by divine and human right. She was not intimidated by the Protestants who controlled her realm. She established an international French court culture, the gaiety and sophistication of which impressed many Protestant nobles, whose religion tended to make their lives exceedingly dour.

Mary was closely watched by the ever-vigilant eye of the Scottish reformer John Knox, who fumed publicly and always with effect against the queen's private Mass and Catholic practices, which Scottish law made a capital offense for everyone else. Knox won support in his role of watchdog from Elizabeth and Cecil. Elizabeth personally despised Knox and never forgave him for writing the *First Blast of the Trumpet Against the Terrible Regiment of Women,* a work aimed at provoking a revolt against Mary Tudor but published in the year of Elizabeth's ascent to the throne. Elizabeth and Cecil tolerated Knox because he served their foreign policy, never permitting Scotland to succumb to the young Mary and her French and Catholic ways.

In 1568 a public scandal forced Mary's abdication and flight to her cousin Elizabeth in England. Mary's reputed lover, the earl of Bothwell, was, with cause, suspected of having killed her legal husband, Lord Darnley. When a packed court acquitted Bothwell and he subsequently abducted Mary and married her, the outraged reaction from Protestant nobles forced Mary to surrender the throne to her one-year-old son, who became James VI of Scotland (and, later, Elizabeth's successor as King James I of England). Because of Mary's clear claim to the English throne, she remained an international symbol of a possible Catholic England. Her presence in England, where she resided under house arrest for nineteen years, was of constant discomfort to Elizabeth.

In 1583 Elizabeth's vigilant secretary, Sir Francis Walsingham, uncovered a plot against Elizabeth involving the Spanish ambassador Mendoza, a frequent companion of Mary Stuart. After Mendoza's deportation in January 1584, popular antipathy toward Spain and support for Protestant resistance in France and the Netherlands became massive throughout England.

In 1586 Walsingham uncovered still another plot against Elizabeth, the so-called Babington plot, (after Anthony Babington who was caught seeking Spanish support for an attempt on the Queen's life), and this time he had uncontestable proof of Mary's complicity. Elizabeth believed that the execution of a sovereign, even a dethroned sovereign, weakened royalty everywhere. She was also aware of the outcry that Mary's execution would create through-

The execution of Mary, Queen of Scots. [*Scottish National Portrait Gallery*]

out the Catholic world, and Elizabeth sincerely wanted peace with English Catholics. But she really had no choice in the matter and consented to Mary's execution on February 18, 1587. This event dashed all Catholic hopes for a bloodless reconversion of Protestant England. After the execution of the Catholic queen of Scotland, Pope Sixtus V (1585–1590), who feared Spanish domination almost as much as he abhorred English Protestantism, could no longer withhold public support for a Spanish invasion of England. Philip II ordered his Armada to make ready.

THE ARMADA. Spain's war preparations were interrupted in the spring of 1587 by Sir Francis Drake's successful shelling of the port city of Cadiz, an attack that inflicted heavy damage on Spanish ships and stores. After "singeing the beard of Spain's king," Drake raided the coast of Portugal, further incapacitating the Spanish. The success of these strikes forced the Spanish to postpone their planned invasion of England until the spring of 1588. On May 30 of that year, a mighty fleet of 130 ships bearing twenty-five thousand sailors and soldiers under the command of the duke of Medina-Sidonia set sail for England. But the day belonged completely to the English. The invasion barges that were to transport Spanish soldiers from the galleons onto English shores were prevented from leaving Calais and Dunkirk. The swifter English and Netherlands ships, assisted by what came to be known as an "English wind," dispersed the waiting Spanish fleet, over one third of which never returned to Spain.

The news of the Armada's defeat gave heart to Protestant resistance everywhere. Although Spain continued to win impressive victories in the 1590s, it never fully recovered from this defeat. Spanish soldiers faced unified and inspired French, English, and Dutch armies. By the time of Philip's death on September 13, 1598, his forces had been successfully rebuffed on all fronts. His seventeenth-century successors—Philip III (1598–1621), Philip IV (1621–1665), and Charles II (1665–1700)— were all inferior leaders who never knew responsibilities equal to Philip's. Nor did Spain ever again know such imperial grandeur. The French soon dominated the Continent, while in the New World the Dutch and the English progressively whittled away Spain's once glorious overseas empire.

Elizabeth died on March 23, 1603, knowing comparatively few national wounds and leaving behind her a strong nation, destined to become an empire on which the sun would not set.

The defeat of the Spanish Armada, a defeat from which Spain never fully recovered. [*The Worshipful Society of the Apothecaries of London*]

The Thirty Years' War (1618–1648)

Preconditions for War

FRAGMENTED GERMANY. In the second half of the sixteenth century Germany was an almost ungovernable land of about 360 autonomous political entities. There were independent secular principalities (duchies, landgraviates, and marches); ecclesiastical principalities (archbishoprics, bishoprics, and abbeys); numerous free cities; and castle regions dominated by knights. The Peace of Augsburg (1555) had given each a significant degree of sovereignty within its own borders. Each levied its own tolls and tariffs and coined its own money, practices that made land travel and trade between the various regions difficult, where not impossible. In addition, many of these little "states" were filled with great power pretensions. Political decentralization and fragmentation characterized Germany as the seventeenth century opened; it was not a unified nation like Spain, England, or even strife-filled France.

Germany had always been Europe's highway; during the Thirty Years' War it became its stomping ground. Europe's rulers pressed in on Germany both for reasons of trade and because some of them held lands or legal privileges within certain German principalities. German princes, in their turn, looked to import and export markets beyond German borders. They opposed any efforts to consolidate the Holy Roman Empire, lest their territorial rights, confirmed by the Peace of Augsburg in the principle *cuius regio, eius religio,* be overturned. German princes were not loath to turn to Catholic France or to the kings of Denmark and Sweden for allies against the Habsburg emperor. The latter's dynastic connections with Spain generated policies that were perceived to be against the best interests of the territorial states of the empire. Even the pope found political reasons for supporting Bourbon France against the menacing international Habsburg kingdom.

After the Council of Trent, Protestants in the empire gravely suspected the operation of an imperial and papal conspiracy to re-create the Catholic Europe of pre-Reformation times. The imperial diet, which was controlled by the German princes, demanded that the constitutional rights of Germans, as set forth in electoral agreements with the emperor since the mid-fourteenth century, be strictly observed, and it effectively countered every move by the emperor to impose his will in the empire. In the late sixteenth century the emperor ruled in the empire only to the degree to which he was prepared to use force of arms against his subjects.

RELIGIOUS DIVISION. Religious conflict accentuated the international and internal political divisions (see Map 11.2). During this period the population within the Holy Roman

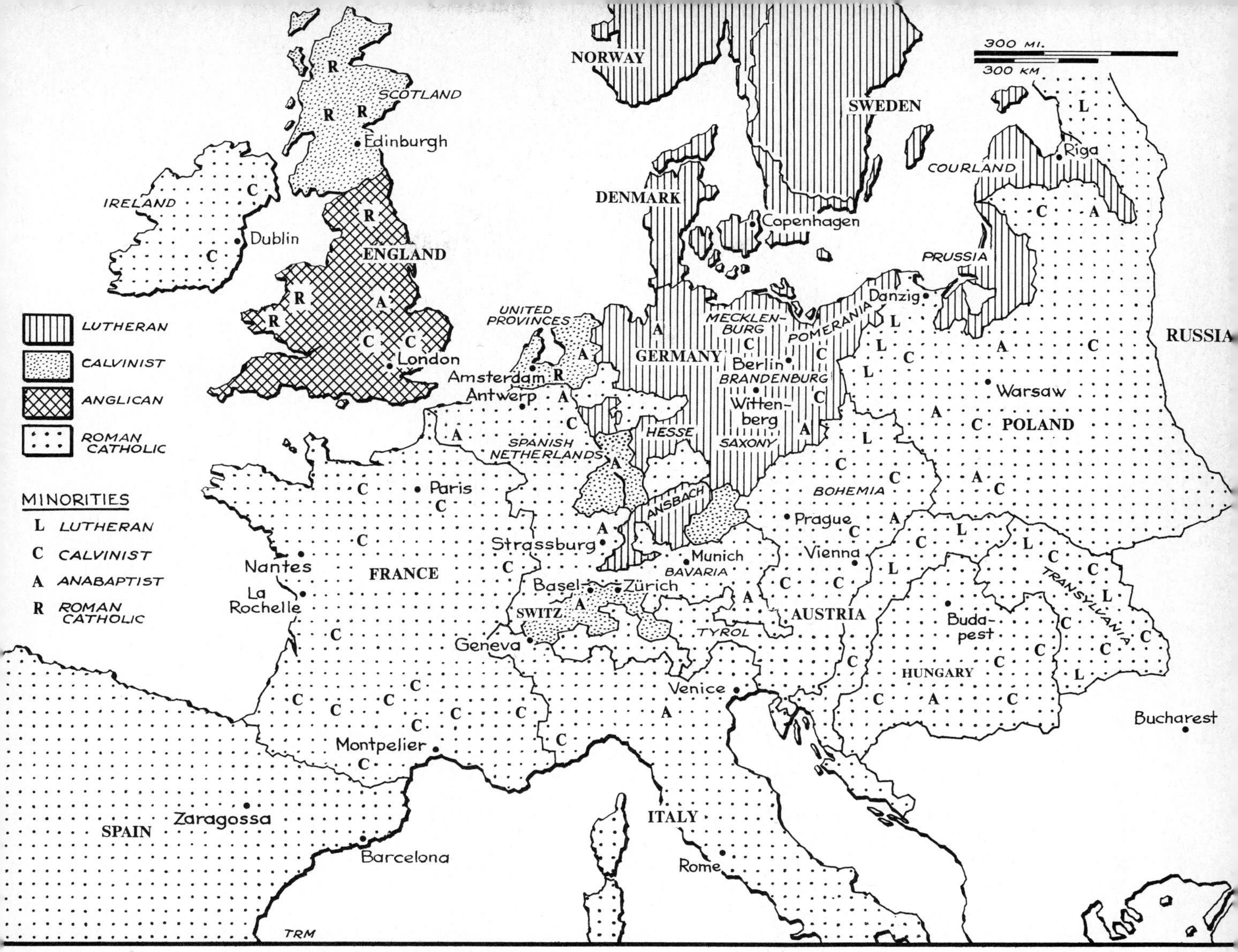

RELIGIOUS DIVISIONS ABOUT 1600

MAP 11–2 *By 1600 few could seriously expect Christians to return to a uniform religious allegiance. In Spain and southern Italy Catholicism remained relatively unchallenged, but note the existence of large religious minorities, both Catholic and Protestant, elsewhere.*

Empire was about equally divided between Catholics and Protestants, the latter having perhaps a slight numerical edge by 1600. The terms of the Peace of Augsburg (1555) had attempted to freeze the territorial holdings of the Lutherans and the Catholics. In the intervening years, however, the Lutherans had gained political control in some Catholic areas, as had the Catholics in a few previously Lutheran areas. Such territorial reversals, or the threat of them, only increased the suspicion and antipathy between the two sides.

The Lutherans had been far more successful in securing their rights to worship in Catholic lands than the Catholics had been in securing such rights in Lutheran lands, because the Catholic rulers, who were in a weakened position after the Reformation, had no choice but to make concessions to Protestant communities within their territories. Such communities remained a sore point. Also the Catholics wanted a strict enforcement of the "Ecclesiastical Reservation" of the Peace of Augsburg, which Protestants had made little effort to recognize; the Catholics demanded that all ecclesiastical princes, electors, archbishops, bishops,

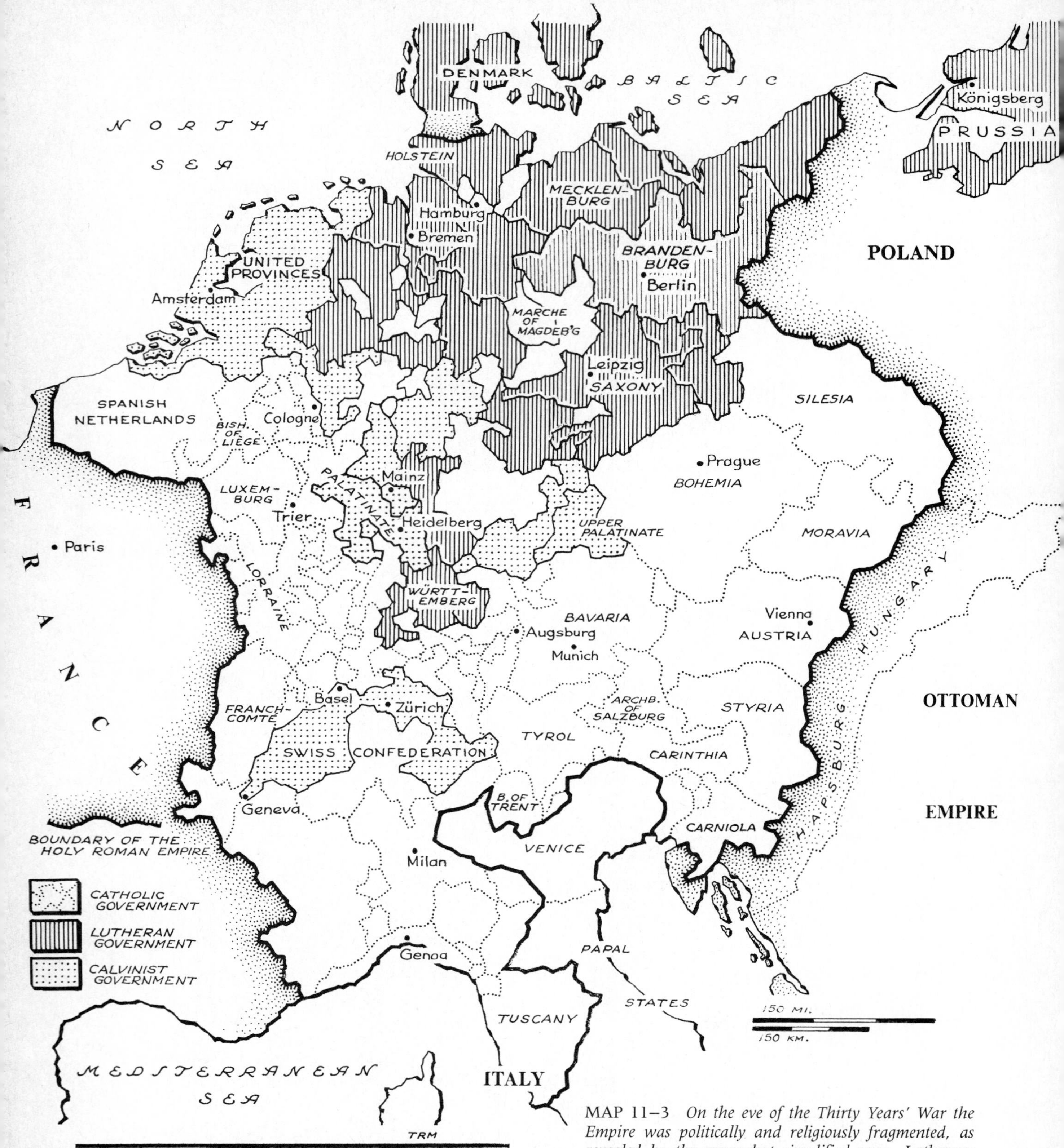

THE HOLY ROMAN EMPIRE ABOUT 1618

MAP 11–3 *On the eve of the Thirty Years' War the Empire was politically and religiously fragmented, as revealed by the somewhat simplified map. Lutherans dominated the north and Catholics the south, while Calvinists controlled the United Provinces and the Palatinate and were important in Switzerland and Brandenburg.*

and abbots who had deserted the Catholic for the Protestant side be immediately deprived of their religious offices and positions and that their ecclesiastical principalities be promptly returned to Catholic control. The Lutherans, and especially the Calvinists in the Palatinate, ignored this stipulation at every opportunity.

There was religious strife in the empire not only between Protestants and Catholics but also between liberal and conservative Lutherans and between Lutherans and the growing numbers of Calvinists. The last half of the sixteenth century was a time of warring Protestant factions within German universities. In addition to the heightened religious strife, the anxiety of religious people of all persuasions was increased by the challenge of the new scientific and material culture that was becoming ascendant in important intellectual and political circles. The age of religious wars was also an age of growing preoccupation with magic, mysticism, witchcraft, and the occult, as fears, doubts, and suspicions stampeded religious feeling.

CALVINISM AND THE PALATINATE. As elsewhere in Europe, Calvinism was the political and religious leaven within the Holy Roman Empire on the eve of the Thirty Years' War. Unrecognized as a legal religion by the Peace of Augsburg, Calvinism had established a strong foothold within the empire when Frederick III (1559–1576), a devout convert to Calvinism, had made it the official religion of his land on becoming Elector Palatine (ruler within the Palatinate) in 1559. Heidelberg became a German Geneva in the 1560s: both a great intellectual center of Calvinism and a staging area for Calvinist penetration into the empire. By 1609 Palatine Calvinists headed a Protestant defensive alliance that received outside support from Spain's sixteenth-century

A seventeenth-century Calvinist Church in the Palatinate. Note that all interior decoration has been removed—there is neither altar nor crucifix. [*German National Museum, Nuremberg*]

enemies: England, France, and the Netherlands. The Lutherans came to fear the Calvinists almost as much as they did the Catholics. Palatine Calvinists seemed to the Lutherans directly to threaten the Peace of Augsburg—and hence the legal foundation of the Lutheran states—by their bold missionary forays into the empire. The more religiously conservative Lutherans were also shocked by outspoken Calvinist criticism of the doctrine of Christ's real presence in the Eucharist. The Elector Palatine once expressed his disbelief in transubstantiation by publicly shredding the host and mocking it as a "fine God." To Lutherans, such religious disrespect and aggressiveness disgraced the Reformation.

MAXIMILIAN OF BAVARIA AND THE CATHOLIC LEAGUE. If the Calvinists were active within the Holy Roman Empire, so also were their Catholic counterparts, the Jesuits. Staunchly Catholic Bavaria, supported by Spain, became militarily and ideologically for the Counter-Reformation what the Palatinate was for Protestantism. From there the Jesuits launched successful missions throughout the empire, winning such major cities as Strasbourg and Osnabrück back to the Catholic fold by 1600. In 1609 Maximilian, duke of Bavaria, organized a Catholic League to counter a new Protestant alliance that had been formed in the same year under the leadership of the Calvinist Elector Palatine, Frederick IV (1583–1610). When the league fielded a great army under the command of Count Johann von Tilly, the stage was set, both internally and internationally, for the worst of the religious wars, the Thirty Years' War.

Four Periods of War

The war went through four distinguishable periods, and during its course it drew in every major western European nation—at least diplomatically and financially if not in terms of direct military involvement. The four periods were the Bohemian (1618–1625); the Danish (1625–1629); the Swedish (1630–1635); and the Swedish-French (1635–1648).

THE BOHEMIAN PERIOD. The war broke out in Bohemia after the ascent to the Bohemian throne in 1618 of the Habsburg Ferdinand, the archduke of Styria, who was also in the line of succession to the imperial throne. Educated by the Jesuits and a fervent Catholic, Ferdinand was determined to restore the traditional faith throughout Austria, Bohemia, and Poland—the eastern Habsburg lands.

No sooner had Ferdinand become king of Bohemia than he revoked the religious freedoms of Bohemian Protestants. These freedoms had been in force since 1575 and had even been recently broadened by Emperor Rudolf II (1576–1612) in his Letter of Majesty in 1609. The Protestant nobility in Prague responded to Ferdinand's act in May 1618 by literally throwing his regents out the window. The event has ever since been known as the "defenestration of Prague." The three officials feel fifty feet into a dry moat that, fortunately, was padded with manure, which cushioned their fall and spared their lives. When in the following year Ferdinand became Holy Roman Emperor as Ferdinand II, by the unanimous vote of the seven electors, the Bohemians defiantly deposed him in Prague and declared the Calvinist Elector Palatine, Frederick V (1616–1623), their overlord.

What had begun as a revolt of the Protestant nobility against an unpopular king of Bohemia thereafter escalated into an international war. Spain sent troops to Ferdinand, who found more immediate allies in Maximilian of Bavaria and the opportunistic Lutheran Elector John George I of Saxony (1611–1656). John George saw a sure route to territorial gain by joining in an easy victory over the weaker Elector Palatine. This was not the only time politics and greed would overshadow religion during this long conflict, although Lutheran-Calvinist religious animosity also overrode a common Protestantism. We shall find other instances of such conflicts.

Ferdinand's army under Tilly routed Frederick V's troops at the Battle of White Mountain in 1620. By 1622 Ferdinand had managed not only to subdue and re-Catholicize Bohemia but to conquer the Palatinate as well. While he and his allies enjoyed the spoils of these victories, the fighting extended into northwestern Germany as the duke of Bavaria pressed the conflict. Laying claim to land as he went, he continued to pursue Ernst von Mansfeld, one of Frederick's surviving mercenary generals, into the north.

THE DANISH PERIOD. The emperor's subjugation of Bohemia and the Palatinate and Maximilian's forays into northwestern Germany raised new fears that a reconquest and re-Catholicization of the whole empire now loomed. This was in fact precisely Ferdinand II's design. Encouraged by the English, the French, and the Dutch, the Lutheran King Christian IV (1588–1648) of Denmark, who already held territory within the empire as the duke of Holstein and was eager to extend Danish influence over the coastal towns of the North Sea, picked up the Protestant banner of resistance, opening the Danish period of the conflict (1625–1629). Christian's forces were not, however, up to the challenge. Entering Germany with his army in 1626, he was quickly humiliated by Maximilian and forced to retreat back into Denmark.

As military success made Maximilian stronger and more difficult to control, Ferdinand II sought a more pliant tool for his policies by hiring a powerful, complex mercenary, Albrecht of Wallenstein (1583–1634). Wallenstein was another opportunistic Protestant who had gained a great deal of territory by joining Ferdinand during the conquest of Bohemia. A brilliant and ruthless military strategist, Wallenstein not only completed Maximilian's work by bringing the career of the elusive Ernst von Mansfeld to an end but also penetrated into Denmark with an occupying army. By 1628 Wallenstein commanded a crack army of over 100,000 and became a law unto himself within the empire, completely outside the emperor's control. Pandora's box had now been fully opened.

Wallenstein broke Protestant resistance so successfully that Ferdinand issued the Edict of Restitution in 1629. This proclamation dramatically reasserted the Catholic safeguards of the

This Protestant broadsheet shows two monsters, wearing the papal crown and a cardinal's hat, spewing Catholic priests on the city of Augsburg. Under the Edict of Restitution (1629), *Augsburg was returned to Catholic jurisdiction.* [*British Library*]

Peace of Augsburg (1555). It reaffirmed the illegality of Calvinism—a completely unrealistic move in 1629—and it ordered the return of all church lands acquired by the Lutherans since 1552, an equally unrealistic mandate. Compliance with the latter demand would have involved the return of no less than sixteen bishoprics and twenty-eight cities and towns to Catholic allegiance. Although based on legal precedent and certainly within Ferdinand's power to command, the expectations of the edict were not adjusted to the political realities of 1629. It struck panic into the hearts of Protestants and Habsburg opponents everywhere, who now saw clearly the emperor's plan to recreate a Catholic Europe. Resistance quickly reignited.

THE SWEDISH PERIOD. Gustavus Adolphus of Sweden (1611–1632), a deeply pious king of a unified Lutheran nation, became the new leader of Protestant forces within the empire, opening the Swedish period of the war (1630–1635). He was handsomely bankrolled by two very interested bystanders: the French minister Cardinal Richelieu, whose foreign policy was to protect French interests by keeping Habsburg armies tied down in Germany, and the Dutch, who had not forgotten Spanish Habsburg domination in the sixteenth century. The Swedish king found ready allies in the electors of Brandenburg and Saxony and soon won a smashing victory at Breitenfeld in 1630. The Protestant victory at Breitenfeld so dramatically reversed the course of the war that it has been regarded as the most decisive, although far from the final, engagement of the long conflict.

One of the reasons for the overwhelming Swedish victory at Breitenfeld was the military genius of Gustavus Adolphus. The Swedish king brought a new mobility to warfare by having both his infantry and his cavalry master fire and charge tactics. At six deep, his infantry squares were smaller than the traditional ones, and he filled them with equal numbers of musketeers and pikemen. His cavalry also alternated pistol shot with sword charges. His artillery was lighter and more mobile in battle. Each unit of his army—infantry, cavalry, and artillery—had *both* defensive and offensive capability and could quickly change from one to the other.

Gustavus Adolphus died at the hands of Wallenstein's forces during the Battle of Lützen (November 1632)—a very costly engagement for both sides that created a brief standstill. Ferdinand had long been resentful of Wallenstein's independence, although he was the major factor in imperial success. In 1634 Ferdinand had Wallenstein assassinated. By that time Wallenstein had not only served his purpose for the emperor, but, ever opportunistic, he was even trying openly to strike bargains with the Protestants for his services. The Wallenstein episode is a telling commentary on this war without honor. Despite the deep religious motivations, greed and political gain were the real forces at work in the Thirty Years' War, and even allies that owed one another their success were not above treating each other as mortal enemies.

In the Peace of Prague in 1635 the German Protestant states, led by Saxony, reached a compromise agreement with Ferdinand. The Swedes, however, received continued support from France and the Netherlands. Desiring to maximize their investment in the war, they refused to join the agreement. Their resistance to settlement plunged the war into its fourth and most devastating phase, the Swedish-French period (1635–1648).

THE SWEDISH-FRENCH PERIOD. The French openly entered the war in 1635, sending men and munitions as well as financial subsidies. After their entrance the war dragged on for thirteen years, with French, Swedish, and Spanish soldiers looting the length and breadth of Germany—warring, it seemed, simply for the sake of warfare itself. The Germans, long weary of the devastation, were too disunited to repulse the foreign armies; they simply watched and suffered. By the time peace talks began in the Westphalian cities of Münster and Osnabrück in 1644, an estimated one third of the German population had died as a direct result of the war. It was the worst European catastrophe since the Black Death of the fourteenth century.

The Treaty of Westphalia

The Treaty of Westphalia in 1648 brought all hostilities within the Holy Roman Empire to an end. It rescinded Ferdinand's Edict of Restitution and firmly reasserted the major feature of the religious settlement of the Peace of Augsburg (1555), as the ruler of each land was again permitted to determine the religion of his land. The treaty also gave the Calvinists their long-sought legal recognition. The indepen-

The horror of the Thirty Years' War is captured in this painting by Jan Brueghel (1568–1625) *and Sebastien Vranx* (1573–1647). *During breaks in the actual fighting, marauding armies ravaged the countryside, destroying villages and massacring the rural population.* [*Kunsthistorisches Museum, Vienna*]

dence of the Swiss Confederacy and the United Provinces of Holland, long recognized in fact, was now proclaimed in law. And the treaty elevated Bavaria to the rank of an elector state. The provisions of the treaty made the German princes supreme over their principalities. Yet, as guarantors of the treaty, Sweden and France found many occasions to meddle in German affairs until the century's end, France to considerable territorial gain. Brandenburg-Prussia emerged as the most powerful north German state.

France and Spain remained at war outside the empire until 1659, when French victories forced on the Spanish the humiliating Treaty of the Pyrenees. Thereafter France became Europe's dominant power, and the once vast Habsburg kingdom waned.

By confirming the territorial sovereignty of Germany's many political entities, the Treaty of Westphalia perpetuated German division and political weakness into the modern period. Only two German states attained any international significance during the seventeenth century: Austria and Brandenburg-Prussia. The petty regionalism within the empire also reflected on a small scale the drift of larger European politics. In the seventeenth century, distinctive nation-states, each with its own political, cultural, and religious identity, reached maturity and firmly established the competitive nationalism of the modern world.

C. V. Wedgwood described the outcome of the Thirty Years' War:

> After the expenditure of so much human life to so little purpose, men might have grasped the essential futility of putting the beliefs of the mind to the judgment of the sword. Instead, they rejected religion as an object to fight for and found others. . . . The war

EUROPE IN 1648
SWEDISH DOMINIONS
BRANDENBURG-PRUSSIA
SPANISH MONARCHY
AUSTRIA HAPSBURGS
CHURCH LANDS
BOUNDARY OF THE EMPIRE
NORWAY
Bergen
Christiana
Stavanger
KINGDOM OF DENMARK AND NORWAY
SWEDEN
FINLAND
Reval
ESTONIA
Stockholm
LIVONIA
Riga
COURLAND
Memel
BALTIC SEA
Copenhagen
DENMARK
Danzig
EAST PRUSSIA
SCHLESWIG
HOLSTEIN
SCOTLAND
Edinburgh
Belfast
IRELAND
Dublin
Cork
York
ENGLAND
WALES
London
Bristol
Plymouth
NORTH SEA
ATLANTIC OCEAN
UNITED PROVINCES
SPANISH NETH.
Brussels
BRANDENBURG
Posen
POLAND
Warsaw
Breslau
SAXONY
SILESIA
Cracow
MINOR GERMAN STATES
HESSE
Prague
BOHEMIA
MORAVIA
HUNGARY
Pressburg
Budapest
Vienna
AUSTRIA
BAVARIA
HAPSBURG HUNGARY
Rouen
Reims
Paris
Orleans
Nantes
Tours
FRANCE
FRANCHE COMTÉ
SWITZ.
Lyons
SAVOY
Bordeaux
Toulouse
LANGUEDOC
AVIGNON
Marseilles
PIEDMONT
MILAN
PAR.
MOD.
Genoa
LUCCA
VENICE
Venice
Bologna
CROATIA
SLAVONIA
SAVA
Belgrade
BOSNIA
SERBIA
VEN.
Spalato
(VEN.)
REP. RAGUSA
MONTENEGRO
Cattaro (VEN.)
ALBANIA
ADRIATIC SEA
PAPAL STATES
TUSCANY
CORSICA (GEN.)
ITALY
Rome
Capua
Bari
Naples
SARDINIA (SP.)
KINGDOM OF THE TWO SICILIES
SICILY
León
NAVARRE
Burgos
Oporto
Salamanca
Saragossa
ARAGON
CASTILE
Madrid
Barcelona
PORTUGAL
Lisbon
Toledo
SPAIN
BALEARIC IS.
Cordova
Seville
Granada
Cadiz
MEDITERRANEAN
Tangier (PORT.)
Ceuta (SP.)
FEZ & MOROCCO
Algiers
ALGERIA
Tunis (OTT.)

MAP 11–4 *At the end of the Thirty Years' War Spain still had extensive possessions. Austria and Brandenburg-Prussia were prominent, the independence of the United Provinces and Switzerland was recognized, and Sweden held important river mouths in north Germany.*

solved no problem. Its effects, both immediate and indirect, were either negative or disastrous. Morally subversive, economically destructive, socially degrading, confused in its causes, devious in its course, futile in its result, it is the outstanding example in European history of meaningless conflict.[2]

Witchcraft and Witch-hunts in Early Modern Europe

Between 1400 and 1700 courts sentenced an estimated 70,000–100,000 people to death for harmful magic (*malificium*) and diabolical witchcraft. In addition to inflicting harm on their neighbors, these witches were said to attend mass meetings known as *sabbats,* to which they were believed to fly. They were also accused of indulging in sexual orgies with the Devil, who appeared at such gatherings in animal form, most often as a he-goat. Still other charges against them were cannibalism (they were alleged to be especially fond of small Christian children) and a variety of ritual acts and practices designed to insult every Christian belief and value.

Where did such beliefs come from? Their roots were in both popular and elite cultures, especially clerical culture.

In village societies, so-called cunning folk played a positive role in helping people cope with calamity. People turned to them for help when such natural disasters as plague and famine struck or when such physical disabilities as lameness or inability to conceive offspring befell either them or their animals. The cunning folk provided consolation and gave people hope that such natural calamities might be averted or reversed by magical means. In this way they provided an important service and kept village life moving forward.

Possession of magical powers, for good or ill, made one an important person within village society. Not surprisingly, claims to such powers seem most often to have been made by the

[2]In T. K. Rabb, *The Thirty Years' War: Problems of Motive, Extent and Effect* (Boston: D. C. Heath, 1964), pp. 18–19.

Four witches who were burned at the stake at Wittenberg in 1540. *The four were accused of commerce with the devil and of directing magic against their neighbors.* [*Hacker Art Books*]

people most in need of security and influence, namely, the old and the impoverished, especially single or widowed women. But witch beliefs in village society may also have been a way of defying urban Christian society's attempts to impose its laws and institutions on the countryside. From this perspective, village Satanism became a fanciful substitute for an impossible social revolt, a way of spurning the values of one's new masters. It is also possible, although unlikely, that witch beliefs in rural society had a foundation in local fertility cults, whose semipagan practices, designed to ensure good harvests, acquired the features of diabolical witchcraft under church persecution.

Popular belief in magic was the essential foundation of the great witch-hunts of the sixteenth and seventeenth centuries. Had ordinary people not believed that certain gifted individuals could aid or harm others by magical means, and had they not been willing to make accusations, the hunts could never have occurred. But the contribution of learned society was equally great. The Christian clergy also practiced magic, that of the holy sacraments, and the exorcism of demons had been one of their traditional functions within society. Fear of demons and the Devil, which the clergy actively encouraged, allowed them to assert their moral authority over people and to enforce religious discipline and conformity.

In the late thirteenth century the church declared that only its priests possessed legitimate magical power. Inasmuch as such power was not human, theologians reasoned, it had to come either from God or from the Devil. If it came from God, then it was obediently confined to and exercised only on behalf of the church. Those who practiced magic outside the church evidently derived their power from the Devil. From such reasoning grew accusations of "pacts" between non-Christian magicians and Satan. This made the witch-hunts a life-and-death struggle against Christian society's worst heretics and foes, those who had directly sworn allegiance to the Devil himself.

The church based its intolerance of magic outside its walls on sincere belief in and fear of the Devil. But attacking witches was also a way for established Christian society to extend its power and influence into new areas. To accuse, try, and execute witches was also a declaration of moral and political authority over a village or territory. As the "cunning folk" were local spiritual authorities, revered and feared by people, their removal became a major step in the establishment of a Christian beachhead in village society.

A good 80 per cent of the victims of witch-hunts were women, the vast majority between forty-five and sixty years of age and widowed. This fact has suggested to some that misogyny fueled the witch-hunts. Based in male hatred and sexual fear of women, and occurring at a time when women threatened to break out from under male control, witch-hunts, it is argued, were simply woman-hunts. Older women may, however, have been vulnerable for more basic social reasons. As a largely non-productive and dependent social group, ever in need of public assistance, older and widowed women became natural targets for the peculiar "social engineering" of the witch-hunts.

It may, however, be the case that gender played a purely circumstantial role. Because of their economic straits, more women than men laid claim to the supernatural powers that made them influential in village society. For this reason they found themselves on the front lines in disproportionate numbers when the church declared war against all who practiced magic without its blessing. Also the involve-

Why More Women Than Men Are Witches

The *Hammer of Witches* (1486), written by two Dominican monks, Heinrich Krämer and Jacob Sprenger, was sanctioned by Pope Innocent VIII as an official guide to the detection and punishment of witches. Here Krämer and Sprenger explain why the great majority of witches are women rather then men.

Why are there more superstitious women than men? The first [reason] is that they are more credulous; and since the chief aim of the devil is to corrupt faith, therefore he rather attacks them. . . . The second reason is that women are naturally more impressionable and ready to receive the influence of a disembodied spirit. . . . The third reason is that they have slippery tongues and are unable to conceal from their fellow-women those things which by evil arts they know; and since they are weak, they find an easy and secret manner of vindicating themselves by witchcraft. . . . [Therefore] since women are feebler both in mind and body, it is not surprising that they should come more under the spell of witchcraft. For as regards intellect, or the understanding of spiritual things, they seem to be of a different nature from men, a fact which is vouched for by the logic of the authorities, backed by various examples from the Scriptures. . . .

But the natural reason [for woman's proclivity to witchcraft] is that she is more carnal than a man, as is clear from her many carnal abominations. And it should be noted that there was a defect in the formation of the first woman, since she was formed from a bent rib, that is, a rib of the breast, which is bent as it were in a contrary direction to a man. And since through this defect she is an imperfect animal, she always deceives. . . .

As to her other mental quality, her natural will, when she hates someone whom she formerly loved, then she seethes with anger and impatience in her whole soul, just as the tides of the sea are always heaving and boiling. . . .

Truly the most powerful cause which contributes to the increase of witches is the woeful rivalry between married folk and unmarried women and men. This [jealousy or rivalry] is so even among holy women, so what must it be among the others . . . ?

Just as through the first defect in their intelligence they are more prone [than men] to abjure the faith, so through their second defect of inordinate affections and passions they search for, brood over, and inflict various vengeances, either by witchcraft or by some other means. Wherefore it is no wonder that so great a number of witches exist in this sex. . . . [Indeed, witchcraft] is better called the heresy of witches than of wizards, since the name is taken from the more powerful party [that is, the greater number, who are women]. Blessed be the Highest who has so far preserved the male sex from so great a crime.

Malleus Maleficarum, trans. by Montague Summers (Bungay, Suffolk: John Rodker, 1928), pp. 41–47.

ment of many of these women in midwifery associated them with the deaths of beloved wives and infants and thus made them targets of local resentment and accusations. Both the church and their neighbors were prepared to think and say the worst about these women. It was a deadly combination.

Why did the witch-hunts come to an end in the seventeenth century? Many factors played a role. The emergence of a new, more scientific worldview made it difficult to believe in the powers of witches. When in the seventeenth century mind and matter came to be viewed as two independent realities, words and thoughts lost the ability to affect things. A witch's curse was merely words. With advances in medicine and the beginning of insurance companies, people learned to rely on themselves when faced with natural calamity and physical affliction and no longer searched for supernatural causes and solutions. Witch-hunts also tended to get out of hand. Accused witches sometimes alleged that important townspeople had attended sabbats; even the judges could be so accused. At this point the trials ceased to serve the purposes of those who were conducting

A Confession of Witchcraft

A confession of witchcraft is here exacted from a burgomaster during a witch panic in seventeenth-century Bamberg in central Germany. The account, an official transcript, accurately describes the process by which an innocent victim was brought, step by step, to confession—from the confrontation with his accusers to the application of increasingly painful tortures. By at last concurring in the accusation (albeit reluctantly and only after torture), the victims were believed by their executioners to be saving the victims' souls as they lost their bodies. Having the victims' own confession may also have helped allay the executioners' consciences.

On Wednesday, June 28, 1628, was examined without torture Johannes Junius, Burgomaster at Bamberg, on the charge of witchcraft: how and in what fashion he had fallen into that vice. Is fifty-five years old, and was born at Niederwaysich in the Wetterau. Says he is wholly innocent, knows nothing of the crime, has never in his life renounced God; says that he is wronged before God and the world, would like to hear of a single human being who has seen him at such gatherings [as the witch sabbats].

Confrontation of Dr. Georg Adam Haan. Tells him to his face that he will stake his life on it, that he saw him, Junius, a year and a half ago at a witch-gathering in the electoral council-room, where they ate and drank. Accused denies the same wholly.

Confronted with Hopffens Elsse. Tells him likewise that he was on Haupts-moor at a witch-dance; but first the holy wafer was desecrated. Junius denies. Hereupon he was told that his accomplices had confessed against him and he was given time for thought.

On Friday, June 30, 1628, the aforesaid Junius was again without torture exhorted to confess, but again confessed nothing, whereupon, . . . since he would confess nothing, he was put to the torture, and first the

Thumb-screws *were applied [both hands bound together, so that the blood ran out at the nails and everywhere]. Says he has never denied God his Saviour nor suffered himself to be otherwise baptized [i.e., initiated into devilish rites]. Will again stake his life on it; feels no pain in the thumb-screws.*

Leg-screws. *Will confess absolutely nothing; knows nothing about it. He has never renounced God; will never do such a thing; has never been guilty of this vice; feels likewise no pain. Is stripped and examined; on his right side is found a bluish mark, like a clover leaf, is thrice pricked therein, but feels no pain and no blood flows out.*

Strappado *[the binding of the prisoner's hands behind the back, and pulling them up by a rope attached to a pulley, resulting in the slow dislocation of the shoulders]. Says he never renounced God; God will not forsake him; if he were such a wretch he would not let himself be so tortured; God must show some token of his innocence. He knows nothing about witchcraft. . . .*

On July 5, the above named Junius is without torture, but with urgent persuasions, exhorted to confess, and as last he . . . confesses.

Translations and Reprints from the Original Sources of European History, Vol. 3 (Philadelphia: University of Pennsylvania, 1912), pp. 23–24.

them. They not only became dysfunctional but threatened anarchy. Finally, the Reformation may have contributed to an attitude of mind that put the Devil in a more manageable perspective. Protestants ridiculed the sacramental magic of the old church as superstition and directed their faith to a sovereign God absolutely supreme over time and eternity. Even the Devil served God's purposes and acted only with His permission. Ultimately God was the only significant spiritual force in the universe. This belief made the Devil a less fearsome creature. "One little word can slay him," Luther wrote of the Devil in the great hymn of the Reformation, and he often joked outrageously about witches.

Suggested Readings

FERNAND BRAUDEL, *The Mediterranean and the Mediterranean World in the Age of Philip the Second,* Vols. 1 and 2 (1976). Widely acclaimed work of a French master historian.

NATALIE Z. DAVIS, *Society and Culture in Early Modern France* (1975). Essays on popular culture.

RICHARD DUNN, *The Age of Religious Wars* 1559–1689 (1979). Excellent brief survey of every major conflict.

J. H. ELLIOTT, *Europe Divided* 1559–1598 (1968). Direct, lucid narrative account.

G. R. ELTON, *England Under the Tudors* (1955). Masterly account.

JULIAN H. FRANKLIN, (Ed. and Trans.), *Constitutionalism and Resistance in the Sixteenth Century: Three Treatises by Hotman, Beza, and Mornay* (1969). Three defenders of the right of people to resist tyranny.

PIETER GEYL, *The Revolt of the Netherlands,* 1555–1609 (1958). The authoritative survey.

RICHARD KIECKHEFER, *European Witch Trials: Their Foundations in Popular and Learned Culture* 1300–1500 (1976).

ALAN KORS AND EDWARD PETERS (Eds.), *European Witchcraft,* 1100–1700 (1972).

CHRISTINA LARNER, *Enemies of God: The Witchhunt in Scotland* (1981).

JOHN LYNCH, *Spain Under the Hapsburg I:* 1516–1598 (1964). Political narrative.

J. RUSSELL MAJOR, *Representative Institutions in Renaissance France* (1960). An essay in French constitutional history.

GARRETT MATTINGLY, *The Armada* (1959). A masterpiece and novel-like in style.

J. E. NEALE, *The Age of Catherine de Medici* (1962). Short, concise summary.

JOHN NEALE, *Queen Elizabeth I* (1934). Superb biography.

THEODORE K. RABB (Ed.), *The Thirty Years' War* (1972). Excerpts from the scholarly debate over the war's significance.

JASPER G. RIDLEY, *John Knox* (1968). Large, detailed biography.

J. H. M. SALMON (Ed.), *The French Wars of Religion: How Important Were the Religious Factors?* (1967). Scholarly debate over the relation between politics and religion.

J. H. M. SALMON, *Society in Crisis: France in the Sixteenth Century* (1976).

ALFRED SOMAN (Ed.), *The Massacre of St. Bartholomew's Day: Reappraisals and Documents* (1974). Results of an international symposium on the anniversary of the massacre.

KEITH THOMAS, *Religion and the Decline of Magic* (1971).

C. V. WEDGWOOD, *The Thirty Years' War* (1939). The authoritative account.

C. V. WEDGWOOD, *William the Silent* (1944). Excellent political biography.

Louis XIV (1643–1715) was the dominant European monarch in the second half of the seventeenth century. His rule became the prototype of the modern centralized state. [*Giraudon*]

12

England and France in the Seventeenth Century

Constitutional Crisis and Settlement in Stuart England

BETWEEN 1603 AND 1715 England experienced the most tumultuous years of its long history. In this period Puritan resistance to the Elizabethan religious settlement merged with fierce parliamentary opposition to the aspirations to absolute monarchy of the Stuart kings. During these years no fewer than three foreigners occupied the English throne, and between 1649 and 1660 England was without a king altogether. Yet by the end of this century of crisis, England provided a model to Europe of limited monarchy, parliamentary government, and measured religious toleration.

James I

The first of England's foreign monarchs was James VI of Scotland (the son of Mary Stuart, Queen of Scots), who in 1603 succeeded the childless Elizabeth as James I of England. This first Stuart king inherited not only the crown but also a royal debt of almost one-half million pounds, a fiercely divided church, and a Parliament already restive over the extent of his predecessor's claims to royal authority. Under James each of these problems worsened. The new king utterly lacked tact, was ignorant of English institutions, and strongly advocated the divine right of kings, a subject on which he had written a book in 1598 entitled *A Trew Law of Free Monarchies*. He rapidly alienated both Parliament and the politically powerful Puritans.

The breach with Parliament was opened by James's seeming usurpation of the power of the purse. Royal debts, his own extravagance, and an inflation he could not control made it necessary for the king to be constantly in quest of additional revenues. These he sought largely by levying—solely on the authority of ill-defined privileges claimed to be attached to the office of king—new custom duties known as *impositions*. These were a version of the older such duties known as *tonnage* and *poundage*. Parliament resented such independent efforts to raise revenues as an affront to its power, and the result was a long and divisive court struggle between the king and Parliament.

As the distance between king and Parliament widened, the religious problems also worsened. The Puritans, who were prominent among the lesser landed gentry and within

Parliament, had hoped that James's experience with the Scottish Presbyterian church and his own Protestant upbringing would incline him to favor their efforts to "purify" the Anglican church. Since the days of Elizabeth the Puritans had sought to eliminate elaborate religious ceremonies and to replace the hierarchical episcopal system of church governance with a more representative presbyterian form like that of the Calvinist churches on the Continent. In January 1604 they had their first direct dealing with the new king. James responded in that month to a statement of Puritan grievances, the so-called Millenary Petition, at a special religious conference at Hampton Court. To the dismay of the Puritans the king firmly declared his intention to maintain and even enhance the Anglican episcopacy. "A Scottish presbytery," he snorted, "agreeth as well with monarchy as God and the devil. No bishops, no king." Nonconformists were clearly forewarned.

Both sides departed the conference with their worst suspicions of one another largely confirmed, and as the years passed, the distrust between them only deepened. It was during James's reign in 1620 that Puritan separatists founded Plymouth Colony in Cape Cod Bay in North America, preferring flight from England to Anglican conformity. The Hampton Court conference did, however, sow one fruitful seed. A commission was appointed to render a new translation of the Bible, a mission fulfilled in 1611 when the eloquent Authorized or King James Version of the Bible was published.

Though he inherited major political and religious difficulties, James also created special problems for himself. His court became a center of scandal and corruption. He governed by favorites, the most influential of whom was the duke of Buckingham, whom rumor made the king's homosexual lover. Buckingham controlled royal patronage and openly sold peerages and titles to the highest bidders—a practice that angered the nobility because it cheapened their rank. James's pro-Spanish foreign policy also displeased the English. In 1604 he concluded a much-needed peace with Spain, England's chief adversary during the second half of the sixteenth century. His subjects viewed it as a sign of pro-Catholic sentiment. James further increased suspicions when he attempted unsuccessfully to relax the penal laws against Catholics. The English had not forgotten the brutal reign of Mary Tudor and the acts of treason by Catholics during Elizabeth's reign. In 1618 James hesitated, not unwisely, to rush English troops to the aid of Protestants in Germany at the outbreak of the Thirty Years' War. This hesitation caused his loyalty to the Anglican church to be openly questioned by some. In the king's last years, as his health failed and the reins of government were increasingly given over to his son Charles and Buckingham, parliamentary power and Protestant sentiment combined to undo his pro-Spanish foreign policy, which had also failed to meet the king's own expectations. In 1624 England entered a continental war against Spain.

Charles I

Charles I (1625–1649) flew even more brazenly in the face of Parliament and the Puritans than did his father. Unable to gain adequate funds from Parliament for the Spanish war, Charles, like his father, resorted to extraparliamentary measures. He levied new tariffs and duties, attempted to collect discontinued taxes, and even subjected the English people to a so-called forced loan (a tax theoretically to be repaid), imprisoning those who refused to pay. Troops in transit to war zones were quartered in private English homes.

When Parliament met in 1628, its members were furious. Taxes were being illegally collected for a war that was going badly for England and that now, through royal blundering, involved France as well as Spain. Parliament expressed its displeasure by making the king's request for new funds conditional on his recognition of the Petition of Right. This major document of constitutional freedom declared that henceforth there should be no forced loans or taxation without the consent of Parliament, that no freeman should be imprisoned without due cause, and that troops should not be billeted in private homes. Though Charles agreed to the petition, there was little confidence that he would keep his word.

In August 1628 Charles's chief minister, Buckingham, with whom Parliament had been in open dispute since 1626, was assassinated. His death, while sweet to many, did not resolve the hostility between king and Parliament. In January 1629 Parliament further underscored its resolve to limit royal prerogative. It declared that religious innovations leading to "popery"—Charles's high-church policies were meant—and the levying of taxes without parliamentary consent were acts of treason. Perceiving that

Parliament Attacks Charles I's Royal Abuses of His Subjects

The tension between King Charles I (1625–1649) and Parliament had very few causes that did not go back to earlier reigns. The Petition of Right can, therefore, be seen as a general catalog of reasons for opposing arbitrary royal power. Specifically, angered by Charles and his levying of new taxes and other revenue-gathering devices, his coercion of freemen, and his quartering of troops in transit in private homes, Parliament refused to grant the king any funds until he rescinded such practices by recognizing the Petition of Right (June 7, 1628). Here is the Petition and the king's reply.

[The Lords Spiritual and Temporal, and Commons in Parliament assembled] do humbly pray your Most Excellent Majesty, that no man hereafter be compelled to make or yield any gift, loan, benevolence, tax, or such like charge, without common consent by Act of Parliament; and that none be called to make answer, or take such oath, or to give attendance, or be confined, or otherwise molested or disquieted concerning the same, or for refusal thereof; and that no freeman, in any such manner as is before-mentioned, be imprisoned or detained; and that your Majesty will be pleased to remove the said soldiers and mariners [who have been quartered in private homes], and that your people may not be so burdened in time to come; and that the foresaid commissions for proceeding by martial law, may be revoked and annulled; and that hereafter no commissions of like nature may issue forth to any person or persons whatsoever, to be executed as aforesaid, lest by colour of them any of your Majesty's subjects be destroyed or put to death, contrary to the laws and franchise of the land.

All which they most humbly pray of your Most Excellent Majesty, as their rights and liberties according to the laws and statutes of this realm.

[The King's reply: The King willeth that right be done according to the laws and customs of the realm; and that the statutes be put in due execution, that his subjects may have no cause to complain of any wrong or oppressions, contrary to their just rights and liberties, to the preservation whereof he holds himself as well obliged as of his prerogative.]

Samuel R. Gardiner, Ed. *The Constitutional Documents of the Puritan Revolution* (Oxford, England: Clarendon Press, 1889), pp. 4–5.

things were getting out of hand, Charles promptly dissolved Parliament and did not recall it again until 1640, when war with Scotland forced him to do so.

To conserve his limited resources, Charles made peace with France and Spain in 1629 and 1630, respectively. His chief minister, Thomas Wentworth (after 1640, earl of Stafford), instituted a policy known as *thorough*, that is, strict efficiency and administrative centralization in government. This policy aimed at absolute royal control of England and required for its success the king's ability to operate independently of Parliament. Every legal fund-raising device was exploited to the full. Neglected laws suddenly were enforced, and existing taxes were extended into new areas. An example of the latter tactic was the inland collection of "ship money." This tax normally was levied only on coastal areas to pay for naval protection, but after 1634 it was gradually applied to the whole of England, interior and coastal towns alike. A great landowner named John Hampden unsuccessfully challenged its extension in a close legal contest. Although the king prevailed, it was a costly victory, for it deepened the animosity toward him among the powerful landowners, who both elected and sat in Parliament.

Charles had neither the royal bureaucracy nor the standing army to rule as an absolute monarch. This became abundantly clear when he and his religious minister, William Laud (1573–1645; after 1633, the archbishop of Canterbury), provoked a war with Scotland. They tried to impose the English episcopal sys-

Charles I (1625–1649) *and his family. Both children in this painting became king. The future Charles II* (1660–1685) *is clasping his father's knee; the future James II* (1685–1688) *is in the arms of his mother, Queen Henrietta Marie, the daughter of Henry IV of France.* [*Metropolitan Museum of Art*]

tem and a prayer book almost identical to the Anglican *Book of Common Prayer* on the Scots as they had done throughout England. From his position within the Court of High Commission, Laud had already radicalized the Puritans by denying them the right to publish and preach.

Facing resistance from the Scots, Charles was forced to seek financial assistance from a Parliament that opposed his policies almost as much as it opposed the foreign invaders. Led by John Pym (1584–1643), Parliament refused even to consider funds for war until the king agreed to redress a long list of political and religious grievances. The result was the king's immediate dissolution of Parliament—hence its name, the Short Parliament (April–May 1640). When the Presbyterian Scots invaded England and defeated an English army at the battle of Newburn in the summer of 1640, Charles found himself forced to reconvene Parliament. This time it was on the latter's terms and for what would be a long and most fateful duration.

THE LONG PARLIAMENT. The landowners and the merchant classes represented by Parliament had resented the king's financial measures and paternalistic rule for some time. To this resentment was added fervent Puritan opposition. Hence the Long Parliament (1640–1660) acted with widespread support and general unanimity when it convened in November 1640. Both the earl of Stafford and Archbishop Laud were impeached by the House of Commons. Disgraced and convicted by a Parliamentary bill of attainder (a judgment of treason entailing loss of civil rights), Stafford was executed in 1641. Laud was imprisoned and later executed (1645). The Court of Star Chamber and the Court of High Commission, royal instruments of political and religious "thorough," respectively, were abolished. The levying of new taxes without consent of Parliament and the inland extension of ship money now became illegal. Finally, it was resolved that no more than three years should elapse between meetings of Parliament and that Parliament could not be dissolved without its own consent.

Marxist historians have seen in these measures a major triumph of the "bourgeoisie" over the aristocracy. But lesser aristocratic groups (the gentry) were actually divided between the parliamentary and royal camps, so more was obviously at issue than simple class warfare. The accomplishment of the Long Parliament was to issue a firm and lasting declaration of the political and religious rights of the many English people represented in Parliament, both high and low, against autocractic royal government.

There remained division within Parliament over the precise direction of religious reform. Both moderate Puritans (the Presbyterians) and extreme Puritans (the Independents) wanted the complete abolition of the episcopal system and the *Book of Common Prayer.* The majority Presbyterians sought to reshape England religiously along Calvinist lines, with local congregations subject to higher representative governing bodies (presbyteries). Independents wanted every congregation to be its own final authority. There was also a considerable number of conservatives in both houses who were determined to preserve the English church in its current form, although their numbers fell dramatically after 1642, when those who sympathized with the present Anglican church departed the House of Commons.

The division within Parliament was further intensified in October 1641, when a rebellion erupted in Ireland requiring an army to suppress it. Pym and his followers, loudly reminding the House of Commons of the king's past misdeeds, argued that Charles could not be trusted with an army and that Parliament should become the commander-in-chief of English armed forces. Parliamentary conservatives, who had winced once at Puritan religious reforms, winced thrice at this bold departure from English practice. On December 1, 1641, Parliament presented Charles with the "Grand Remonstrance," a more-than-200-article summary of popular and parliamentary grievances against the crown.

Charles saw the division within Parliament as a last chance to regain power. In January 1642 he invaded Parliament with his soldiers. He intended to arrest Pym and the other leaders, but they had been forewarned and managed to escape. Shocked by the king's action, a majority of the House of Commons thereafter passed the Militia Ordinance, a measure that gave Parliament control of the army. The die was now cast. For the next four years (1642–1646) civil war engulfed England.

Charles assembled his forces at Nottingham, and in August the civil war began. The main issues were whether England would be ruled by an absolute monarchy or by a parliamentary government and whether English religion would be conformist high Anglican and controlled by the king's bishops or cast into a more decentralized, presbyterian system of church governance. Charles's supporters, known as *Cavaliers*, were located in the northwestern half of England. The parliamentary opposition, known as *Roundheads* because of their close-cropped hair, had its stronghold in the southeastern half of the country. The nobility, identifying the power of their peerage with the preservation of the current form of the monarchy and the church, became prominent supporters of the king, whereas the townspeople supported the Parliamentary army.

Oliver Cromwell and the Puritan Republic

Two factors led finally to Parliament's victory. The first was an alliance with Scotland in 1643 consummated when John Pym persuaded Parliament to accept the terms of the Solemn League and Covenant, an agreement committing Parliament, with the Scots, to a presbyterian system of church government. The second was the reorganization of the parliamentary army under Oliver Cromwell (1599–1658), a middle-aged country squire of iron discipline and strong Independent religious sentiment. Cromwell and his "godly men" favored neither the episcopal system of the king nor the pure presbyterian system of the Solemn League and Covenant. They were willing to tolerate an established majority church, but only if it also permitted Protestant dissenters to worship outside it. The allies won the Battle of Marston Moor in 1644, the largest engagement of the war, and in June 1645 Cromwell's New Model Army, which fought with a disciplined fanaticism, decisively defeated the king at Naseby.

Though defeated militarily, Charles again took advantage of the deep divisions within Parliament, this time seeking to win the Presbyterians and the Scots over to the royalist side. But Cromwell's army firmly imposed its will. In December 1648 Colonel Thomas Pride physically barred the Presbyterians, who made up a majority of Parliament, from taking their seats. After "Pride's Purge," only a "rump" of fewer than fifty members remained. Though small in numbers, this Independent Rump Parliament had supreme military power within England. It did not hesitate to use this power. On January 30, 1649, after trial by a special court, it executed Charles as a public criminal and thereafter abolished the monarchy, the House of Lords, and the Anglican church. The revolution was consummated by events hardly contemplated at its outset.

From 1649 to 1660 England became officially a Puritan republic. During this period Cromwell's army conquered Ireland and Scotland, creating the single political entity of Great Britain. Cromwell, however, was a military man and no politician. He was increasingly frustrated by what seemed to him to be pettiness and dawdling on the part of Parliament. When in 1653 the House of Commons entertained a motion to disband the expensive army of fifty thousand, Cromwell responded by marching in and disbanding Parliament. He ruled thereafter as Lord Protector.

But his military dictatorship proved no more effective than Charles's rule had been and became just as harsh and hated. Cromwell's great

A Portrait of Oliver Cromwell

Statesman and historian Edward Hyde, the earl of Clarendon (1609–1674), was an enemy of Oliver Cromwell. However, his portrait of Cromwell, which follows, mixes criticism with grudging admiration for the Puritan leader.

He was one of those men whom his enemies cannot condemn without at the same time also praising. For he could never have done half that mischief without great parts of courage and industry and judgment. And he must have had a wonderful understanding of the natures and humours of men and a great dexterity in applying them . . . [to] raise himself to such a height. . . .

When he first appeared in the Parliament, he seemed to have a person in no degree gracious, no ornament of discourse, none of those talents which reconcile the affections of the standers-by; yet as he grew into his place and authority, his parts seemed to be renewed, as if he concealed faculties til he had occasion to use them. . . .

After he was confirmed and invested Protector . . . he consulted with very few . . . nor communicated any enterprise he resolved upon with more than those who were to have principal parts in the execution of it; nor to them sooner than was absolutely necessary. What he once resolved . . . he would not be dissuaded from, nor endure any contradiction. . . .

In all other matters which did not concern . . . his jurisdiction, he seemed to have great reverence for the law. . . . And as he proceeded with . . . indignation and haughtiness with those who were refractory and dared to contend with his greatness, so towards those who complied with his good pleasure, and courted his protection, he used a wonderful civility, generosity, and bounty.

To reduce three nations [England, Ireland, and Scotland], which perfectly hated him, to an entire obedience to all his dictates; to awe and govern those nations by an army that was not devoted to him and wished his ruin; this was an instance of a very prodigious address. But his greatness at home was but a shadow of the glory he had abroad. It was hard to discover which feared him most, France, Spain, or the Netherlands. . . . As they did all sacrifice their honour and their interest to his pleasure, so there is nothing he could have demanded that any of them would have denied him.

James Harvey Robinson (Ed.), *Readings in European History,* Vol. 2 (Boston: Ginn and Co., 1906), pp. 248–250.

An Account of the Execution of Charles I

Convicted of "high treason and other high crimes," Charles I was beheaded on January 30, 1649. In his last minutes he conversed calmly with the attending bishop and executioner, anxious only that the executioner not strike before he gave the signal.

To the executioner he said, "I shall say but very short prayers, and when I thrust out my hands—"

Then he called to the bishop for his cap, and having put it on, asked the executioner, "Does my hair trouble you?" and the executioner desired him to put it under his cap, which as he was doing by help of the bishop and the executioner, he turned to the bishop and said, "I have a good cause, and a gracious God on my side."

The bishop said, "There is but one stage more, which, though turbulent and troublesome, yet is a very short one. . . . It will carry you from earth to heaven . . . to a crown of glory. . . ."

Then the king asked the executioner, "Is my hair well?"

And taking off his cloak and George [the Order of the Garter, bearing a figure of Saint George], he delivered his George to the bishop. . . .

Then putting off his doublet and being in his waistcoat, he put on his cloak again, and looking upon the block, said to the executioner, "You must set it fast."

The executioner. *"It is fast, sir."*

King. *"It might have been a little higher."*

Executioner. *"It can be no higher, sir."*

King. *"When I put out my hands this way, then—"*

Then having said a few words to himself, as he stood with hands and eyes lifted up, immediately stooping down he laid his neck upon the block; and the executioner, again putting his hair under his cap, his Majesty, thinking he had been going to strike, bade him, "Stay for the sign."

Executioner. *"Yes, I will, as it please your Majesty."*

After a very short pause, his Majesty stretching forth his hands, the executioner at one blow severed his head from his body; which being held up and showed to the people, was with his body put into a coffin covered with black velvet and carried into his lodging.

His blood was taken up by divers persons for different ends; by some as trophies of the villainy; by others as relics of a martyr.

James Harvey Robinson (Ed.), *Readings in European History*, Vol. 2 (Boston: Ginn and Co., 1906), pp. 244–245.

army and foreign adventures inflated his budget to three times that of Charles. Trade and commerce suffered throughout England, as near chaos reigned in many places. Puritan prohibitions of such pastimes as theaters, dancing, and drunkenness were widely resented. Cromwell's treatment of Anglicans came to be just as intolerant as Charles's treatment of Puritans had been. In the name of religious liberty, political liberty had been lost. And Cromwell was unable to get along even with the new Parliaments that were elected under the auspices of his army. By the time of his death in 1658, a majority of the English were ready to end the Puritan experiment and return to the traditional institutions of government.

OPPOSITE: *The execution of Charles I, January 30, 1649. The king's portrait is on the upper left, Cromwell's on the upper right.* [*National Galleries of Scotland*]

Charles II and the Restoration of the Monarchy

The Stuart monarchy was restored in 1660 when Charles II (1660–1685), son of Charles I, returned to England amid great rejoicing. A man of considerable charm and political skill, Charles set a refreshing new tone after eleven years of somber Puritanism. His restoration returned England to the status quo of 1642, as once again a hereditary monarch

Cromwell disbands the House of Commons in 1653. *For the next six years, until his death in* 1659, *Cromwell ruled England as a dictator under the title of Lord Protector.* [*The Mansell Collection*]

sat on the throne and the Anglican church was religiously supreme.

Because of his secret Catholic sympathies the king favored a policy of religious toleration. He wanted to allow all persons outside the Church of England, Catholics as well as Puritans, to worship freely so long as they remained loyal to the throne. But the ultraroyalist Anglicans in Parliament decided otherwise. They did not believe patriotism and religion could be so disjointed. Between 1661 and 1665, through a series of laws known as the Clarendon Code, Parliament excluded Roman Catholics, Presbyterians, and Independents from the religious and political life of the nation. Penalties were imposed for attending non-Anglican worship services, strict adherence to the *Book of Common Prayer* and the Thirty-Nine Articles was required, and all who desired to serve in local government were made to swear oaths of allegiance to the Church of England. This trampling of Puritan sentiments did not go unopposed in Parliament, but the opposition was not strong enough to override the majority.

Under Charles II England stepped up its challenge of the Dutch to become Europe's commercial and business center. Navigation Acts were passed that required all imports into England to be carried either in English ships or in ships registered to the same country as the imports they carried. Because the Dutch were the original suppliers of hardly more than tulips and cheese, these laws struck directly at their lucrative role as Europe's commercial middlemen. A series of naval wars between England and Holland ensued. Charles also undertook at this time to tighten his grasp on the rich English colonies in North America and the Caribbean, many of which had been settled and developed by separatists who desired independence from English rule.

Although Parliament strongly supported the monarchy, Charles, following the habit of his predecessors, required greater revenues than Parliament appropriated. These Charles managed to get in part by increased customs. He also received French aid. In 1670 England and France formally allied against the Dutch in the Treaty of Dover. A secret portion of this treaty pledged Charles to announce his conversion to Catholicism as soon as conditions in England permitted, a declaration for which Louis XIV of

France promised to pay 167,000 pounds. (Such a declaration never came to pass.) Charles also received a French war chest of 250,000 pounds per annum.

In an attempt to unite the English people behind the war with Holland, and as a sign of good faith to Louis XIV, Charles issued a Declaration of Indulgence in 1672 suspending all laws against Roman Catholics and Protestant nonconformists. But again, the conservative Tory Parliament proved less generous than the king and refused to grant money for the war until Charles rescinded the measure. After Charles withdrew the declaration, Parliament passed the Test Act, which required all officials of the crown, civil and military, to swear an oath against the doctrine of transubstantiation—a requirement that no loyal Roman Catholic could honestly meet.

The Test Act was aimed in large measure at the king's brother, James, duke of York, heir to the throne and a recent, devout convert to Catholicism. In 1678 a notorious liar named Titus Oates swore before a magistrate that Charles's Catholic wife, through her physician, was plotting with Jesuits and Irishmen to kill the king so that James could assume the throne. The matter was taken before Parliament, where it was believed. In the ensuing hysteria, known as the *Popish Plot,* several people were tried and executed. In 1680–1681, riding the crest of anti-Catholic sentiment, opposition Whig members of Parliament, led by the earl of Shaftesbury (1621–1683), made an impressive but unsuccessful effort to enact a bill excluding James from succession to the throne.

More suspicious than ever of Parliament, Charles II turned again to increased customs revenue and the assistance of Louis XIV for extra income and was able to rule from 1681 to 1685 without recalling Parliament. In these years Charles suppressed much of his opposition, driving the earl of Shaftesbury into exile, executing several Whig leaders for treason, and bullying local corporations into electing members of Parliament submissive to the royal will. When Charles died in 1685 (after a deathbed conversion to Catholicism), he left James the prospect of a Parliament filled with royal friends.

James II and Renewed Fears of a Catholic England

James II (1685–1688) did not know how to make the most of a good thing. He alienated Parliament by insisting upon the repeal of the Test Act. When Parliament balked, he dissolved it and proceeded openly to appoint known Catholics to high positions in both his court and the army. In 1687 James issued a Declaration of Indulgence, which suspended all religious tests and permitted free worship. Local candidates for Parliament who opposed the declaration were removed from their offices by the king's soldiers and were replaced by Catholics. In June 1688 James went so far as to imprison seven Anglican bishops who had refused to publicize his suspension of laws against Catholics.

Under the guise of a policy of enlightened toleration, James was actually seeking to subject all English institutions to the power of the

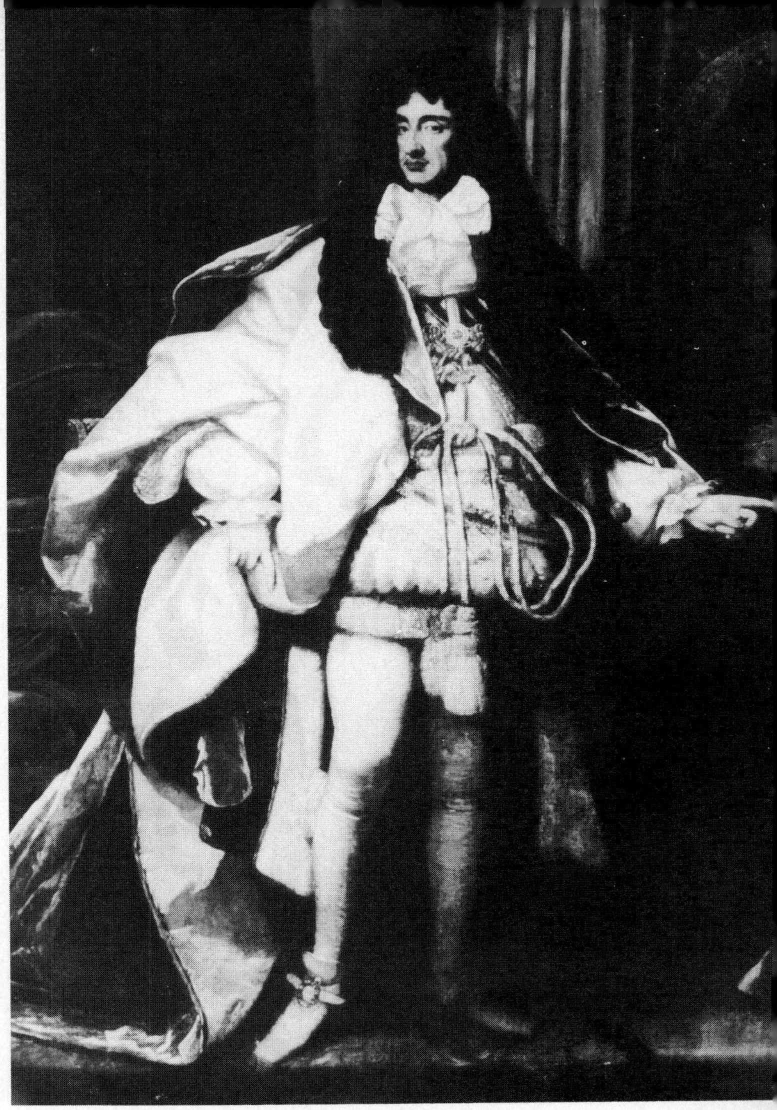

Charles II (1660–1685). *A man of considerable charm and political skill, Charles was a popular and astute ruler. [Robert Harding Picture Collection]*

England in the Seventeenth Century	
James VI of Scotland becomes James I of England	1603
Hampton Court Conference	1604
Publication of the Authorized or King James Version of the English Bible	1611
Charles I becomes English Monarch	1625
Petition of Right	1628
Charles I dissolves Parliament and embarks on eleven years of personal rule	1629
April–May Short Parliament	1640
November Long Parliament convenes	
Great Remonstrance	1641
Outbreak of the Civil War	1642
Charles I defeated at Naseby	1645
Pride's Purge	1648
Charles I executed	1649
Various attempts at a Puritan Commonwealth	1649–1660
Charles II restored to the English throne	1660
Secret Treaty of Dover between France and England	1670
Parliament passes the Test Act	1672
Popish Plot	1678
James II becomes king of England	1685
Glorious Revolution	1688
William and Mary come to the throne of England	1689
Act of Settlement provides for Hanoverian Succession	1701
Reign of Queen Anne, the last of the Stuarts	1702–1715

The Bill of Rights being read to William and Mary in 1688. *The ''Glorious Revolution'' established a limited monarchy. Henceforth, while English kings retained real power, they ruled by consent of Parliament and were subject to the law.* [*Department of the Environment, London*]

monarchy. His goal was absolutism, and even conservative, loyalist Tories could not abide this. The English had reason to fear that James planned to imitate the policy of Louis XIV, who in 1685 had revoked the Edict of Nantes (which had protected French Protestants for almost a century) and had returned France to Catholicism, where necessary, with the aid of dragoons. A national consensus very quickly formed against the monarchy of James II.

The direct stimulus for parliamentary action came when on June 20, 1688, James's second wife, a Catholic, gave birth to a son, a male Catholic heir to the English throne. The English had hoped that James would die without a male heir and that the throne would revert to his Protestant eldest daughter, Mary. Mary was the wife of William III of Orange, *stadholder* of the Netherlands, great-grandson of William the Silent, and the leader of European opposition to Louis XIV's imperial designs. Within days of the birth of a Catholic male heir, Whig and Tory members of Parliament formed a coalition and invited Orange to invade England to preserve ''traditional liberties,'' that is, the Anglican church and parliamentary government.

The ''Glorious Revolution''

William of Orange arrived with his army in November 1688 and was received without opposition by the English people. In the face of sure defeat James fled to France and the protection of Louis XIV. With James gone, Parliament declared the throne vacant and on its own authority proclaimed William and Mary the new monarchs in 1689, completing a successful bloodless revolution. William and Mary, in turn, recognized a Bill of Rights that limited the powers of the monarchy and guaranteed the civil liberties of the English privileged classes. Henceforth, England's monarchs would rule by the consent of Parliament and would be subject to law. The Bill of Rights also pointedly prohibited Roman Catholics from occupying the English throne. The Toleration Act of 1689 permitted worship by all Protes-

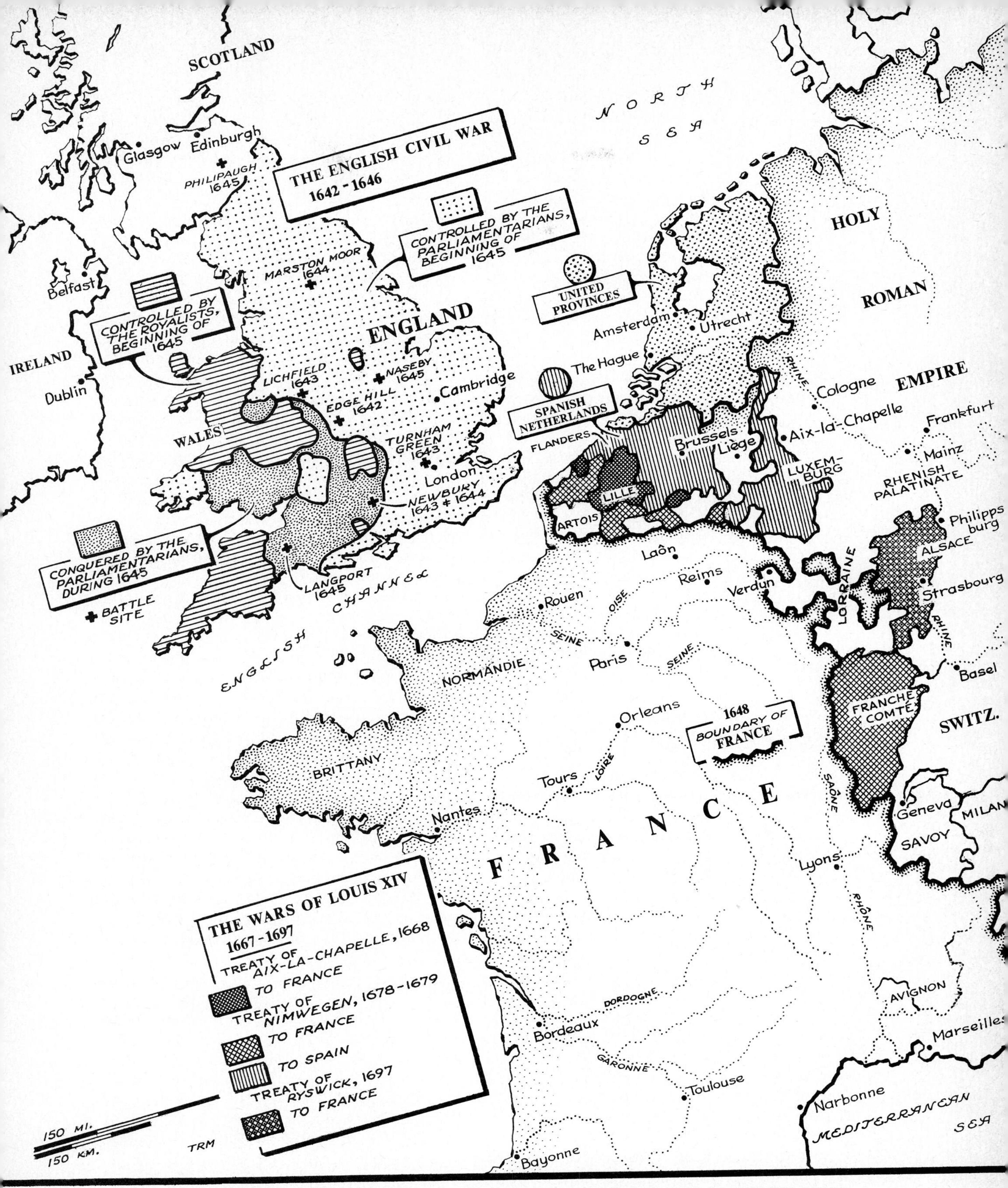

THE ENGLISH CIVIL WAR AND THE WARS OF LOUIS XIV

MAPS 12–1, 12–2 *In the English Civil War, 1645 was a crucial year; here the rapidly deteriorating Royalist position is shown. A bit later in France we see the territorial changes resulting from Louis XIV's first three major wars. The War of the Spanish Succession was yet to come.*

tants and outlawed Roman Catholics and antitrinitarians (those who denied the Christian doctrine of the Trinity).

The final measure closing the century of strife was the Act of Settlement in 1701. This bill provided for the English crown to go to the Protestant House of Hanover in Germany if Queen Anne (1702–1714), the second daughter of James II and the last of the Stuart monarchs, was not survived by her children. Consequently in 1714 the Elector of Hanover became King George I of England, the third foreign monarch to occupy the English throne in just over a century.

The "Glorious Revolution" of 1688 established a framework of government by and for the governed. It received classic philosophical justification in John Locke's *Second Treatise of Government* (1690), in which Locke described the relationship of a king and his people in terms of a bilateral contract. If the king broke that contract, the people, by whom Locke meant the privileged and powerful, had the right to depose him. Although it was, neither in fact nor in theory, a "popular" revolution such as would occur in France and America a hundred years later, the Glorious Revolution did establish in England a permanent check on monarchical power by the classes represented in Parliament.

Rise of Absolutism in France

Regional rights and a degree of religious diversity were recognized within the Holy Roman Empire, England, and the Netherlands during the seventeenth century. The assertion of local autonomy by the numerous member states and cities of the Holy Roman Empire made a strong central government there unthinkable. In England and the Netherlands centuries of parliamentary practice permitted regional freedoms to coexist with a strong central government.

Following the devastation of the Thirty Years' War, the Peace of Westphalia (1648) reaffirmed religious pluralism within the Holy Roman Empire. A degree of religious diversity, long a Netherlands tradition, received final confirmation also in England after decades of dogged Puritan resistance, when the Toleration Act of 1689 granted rights of worship to Protestant nonconformists.

Seventeenth-century France, in contrast, saw both representative government and religious pluralism crushed by the absolute monarchy and the closed Catholic state of Louis XIV (1643–1715). An aggressive ruler who sought glory (*la gloire*) in foreign wars, Louis subjected his subjects at home to "one king, one law, one faith."

Henry IV and Sully

The foundation was well laid for Louis's grand reign by his predecessors and their exceptional ministers. Henry IV (1589–1610; see Chapter 11) began in earnest the curtailment of the privileges of the French nobility necessary for the creation of a strong centralized state. His targets were the provincial governors and the regional *parlements*, especially the powerful Parlement of Paris, where a divisive spirit lived on. Here were to be found the old privileged groups, tax-exempt magnates whose sole preoccupation was to protect their self-interests. During Louis XIV's reign their activities came under the strict supervision of royal civil servants known as *intendants*, who implemented the king's will with remarkable success in the provinces.

Also during Henry IV's reign an economy more amenable to governmental regulation emerged after the long decades of religious and civil war. Henry and his finance minister, the duke of Sully (1560–1641), prepared the way for the mercantilist policies of Louis XIV and his minister Colbert by establishing government monopolies on gunpowder, mines, and salt. A canal system was begun to link the Atlantic and the Mediterranean by joining the Saône, the Loire, the Seine, and the Meuse rivers. An involuntary national labor force emerged with the introduction of a royal *corvée*, and this drafting of workers provided the labor to improve roads and the conditions of internal travel. Sully even dreamed of the political and commercial organization of the whole of Europe in a kind of common market.

Louis XIII and Richelieu

Henry IV was assassinated in 1610, and the following year Sully retired. Because Henry's successor, Louis XIII (1610–1643), was only nine years old when his father was assassinated, the task of governing fell to the queen mother, Marie de Médicis (d. 1642). Finding herself in a vulnerable position, she sought security abroad by signing a ten-year mutual defense pact with arch-rival Spain in the Treaty of Fontainebleau (1611), an alliance that also arranged for the later marriage of Louis XIII to the Spanish infanta as well as for the marriage of the queen's daughter Elizabeth to the heir to the Spanish throne. The queen sought internal security against the French nobility by promoting the career of Cardinal Richelieu (1585–1642) as the king's chief adviser, although Richelieu never became her pawn. Richelieu, loyal and shrewd, aspired to make France a supreme European power and he, more than any one person, was the secret of French success in the first half of the seventeenth century.

An apparently devout Catholic who also believed that the church best served both his own ambition and the welfare of France, Richelieu was strongly anti-Habsburg in politics. On the one hand, he supported the Spanish alliance of the queen and Catholic religious unity within France; on the other, he was determined to contain Spanish power and influence, even when that meant aiding and abetting Protestant Europe. It is an indication both of Richelieu's awkward political situation and of his diplomatic agility that he could, in 1631, pledge funds to the Protestant army of Gustavus Adolphus, while at the same time insisting that Catholic Bavaria be spared from attack and that Catholics in conquered countries be permitted to practice their religion.

At home Richelieu pursued his policies utterly without sentiment. Supported by the king, whose best decision was to let his chief minister make all the decisions of state, Richelieu stepped up the campaign against the separatist provincial governors and *parlements*. He made it clear to all that there was only one law, that of the king, and that none could stand above it. When disobedient noblemen defied his edicts, they were imprisoned and even executed. Louis XIV had Richelieu to thank for the fact that many of the French nobility became docile beggars at his court. Such treatment of the nobility won Richelieu much enmity, even from the queen mother, who was not always prepared to place the larger interests of the state above the pleasure of favorite princes. But the king let no criticism weaken his chief minister, not even that of his mother. The queen mother had largely ignored Louis during his youth—he was educated mostly at the hands of his falconer—and they remained estranged. This was doubtless a factor in the king's firm support of Richelieu when his mother became Richelieu's accuser.

Richelieu inspired the campaign against the Huguenots that would end in 1685 with Louis XIV's revocation of the Edict of Nantes. Royal armies conquered major Huguenot cities in 1629, and the subsequent Peace of Alais (1629) truncated the Edict of Nantes by denying Protestants the right to maintain garrisoned cities, separate political organizations, and independent law courts. Only Richelieu's foreign policy prevented the earlier implementation of the extreme intolerance of Louis XIV. In the same year that the independent political status of the Huguenots was rescinded, Richelieu also entered negotiations to make Gustavus Adolphus his counterweight to the expansion of Habsburg power within the Holy Roman Empire. By 1635 the Catholic soldiers of France were fighting openly with Swedish Lutherans against the emperor's army in the final phase of the Thirty Years' War.

Cardinal Richelieu, the mastermind behind French royal power in the seventeenth century. This striking triple portrait is by Philippe de Champaigne (1602–1674). [*Courtesy of the Trustees, The National Gallery, London*]

In the best Machiavellian tradition Richelieu employed the arts and the printing press to defend his actions and to indoctrinate the French in the meaning of *raison d'état* ("reason of state")—again setting a precedent for Louis XIV's elaborate use of royal propaganda and spectacle. It is one measure of Richelieu's success that France made substantial gains in land and political influence when the Treaty of Westphalia (1648) ended hostilities in the Holy Roman Empire and the Treaty of the Pyrenees (1659) sealed peace with Spain.

Young Louis XIV and Mazarin

Richelieu's immediate legacy, however, was strong resentment of the monarchy on the part of the French aristocracy and the privileged bourgeoisie. During the minority of Louis XIV, who was only five years old when Louis XIII died in 1643, the queen mother, Anne of Austria (d. 1666), placed the reins of government in the hands of Cardinal Mazarin (1602–1661), who continued Richelieu's determined policy of centralization. During his regency the long-building backlash occurred. Named after the slingshot used by street boys, the Fronde (1649–1652) was a series of widespread rebellions by segments of the French nobility and townspeople aimed at reversing the drift toward absolute monarchy—a last-ditch effort to preserve their local autonomy. These privileged groups saw their traditional position in French society thoroughly undermined by the crown's steady multiplication of royal offices, the replacement of local by "state" agents, and the reduction of their patronage.

The Parlement of Paris initiated the revolt in 1649, and the nobility at large soon followed. The latter were urged on by the influential wives of princes who had been imprisoned by Mazarin for treason. The many briefly triumphed over the one when Mazarin released the imprisoned princes in February 1651. He and Louis XIV thereafter entered a short exile (Mazarin leaving France, Louis fleeing Paris) and were unable to return to Paris until October 1652, when the inefficiency and near anarchy of government by the nobility made them very welcome. The period of the Fronde convinced a majority of the French that a strong king was preferable to the competing and irreconcilable claims of many regional magnates. After 1652 the French were ready to experiment in earnest with absolute rule.

Louis XIV presiding over the council of State. It was a maxim of French law that the king's wish was the law of the land. [*Giraudon*]

The World of Louis XIV

Unity at Home

Thanks to the forethought of Mazarin, Louis XIV was well prepared to rule France. The turbulent period of his youth seems also to have made an indelible impression. Louis wrote in his memoirs that the Fronde caused him to loathe "kings of straw" and made him determined never to become one. Indoctrinated with a strong sense of the grandeur of his crown, he never missed an opportunity to impress it on the French people. When the dauphin (the heir to the French throne) was born in 1662, for example, Louis appeared for the celebration dressed as a Roman emperor. Although his rule became the prototype of the modern centralized state, its inspiration remained a very narrow ideal of personal glory.

King by Divine Right

Reverence for the king and the personification of government in him had been nurtured in France since Capetian times. It was a maxim of French law and popular opinion that "the king of France is emperor in his realm," that the king's wish is the law of the land.

An important theorist for Louis's even grander concept of royal authority was the devout tutor of the dauphin, Bishop Jacques-Bénigne Bossuet (1627–1704). An ardent champion of the Gallican Liberties—the traditional rights of the French king and church in matters of ecclesiastical appointments and taxation—Bossuet defended what he called the "divine right of kings." He cited the Old Testament example of rulers divinely appointed by and answerable only to God. As medieval popes had insisted that only God could judge a pope, so Bossuet argued that none save God could sit in judgment on the king. Although kings remained duty-bound to reflect God's will in their rule—and in this sense Bossuet considered them always subject to a higher authority—as God's regents on earth they could not be bound to the dictates of mere princes and parliaments. Such were among the assumptions that lay behind Louis XIV's alleged declaration: *''L'état, c'est moi''* (''I am the state'').

Jacques-Benigne Bossuet, Bishop of Meaux. Called the ''Eagle of Meaux,'' Bossuet was an eloquent advocate of the ''divine right of kings'' and a strong defender of the autonomy of the French church against the Pope. This portrait by Hyacinthe Rigaud is in the Louvre. [*Giraudon*]

Bishop Bossuet Defends the Divine Right of Kings

The revolutions of the seventeenth century caused many to fear anarchy far more than tyranny, among them the influential French bishop Jacques-Bénigne Bossuet (1627–1704), the leader of French Catholicism in the second half of the seventeenth century. Louis XIV made him court preacher and tutor to his son, for whom Bossuet wrote a celebrated *Universal History.* In the following excerpt Bossuet defends the divine right and absolute power of kings, whom he depicts as embracing in their person the whole body of the state and the will of the people they govern and, as such, as being immune from judgment by any mere mortal.

The royal power is absolute. . . . The prince need render account of his acts to no one. ''I counsel thee to keep the king's commandment, and that in regard of the oath of God. Be not hasty to go out of his sight; stand not on an evil thing for he doeth whatsoever pleaseth him. Where the word of a king is, there is power; and who may say unto him, What doest thou? Whoso keepeth the commandment shall feel no evil thing'' [Eccles. 8:2–5*]. Without this absolute authority the king could neither do good nor repress evil. It is necessary that his power be such that no one can hope to escape him, and finally, the only protection of individuals against the public authority should be their innocence. This confirms the teaching of St. Paul: ''Wilt thou then not be afraid of the power? Do that which is good'' [Rom.* 13:3*].*

God is infinite, God is all. The prince, as prince, is not regarded as a private person: he is a public personage, all the state is in him; the will of all the people is included in his. As all perfection and all strength are united in God, so all the power of individuals is united in the person of the prince. What grandeur that a single man should embody so much! . . .

Behold an immense people united in a single person; behold this holy power, paternal and absolute; behold the secret cause which governs the whole body of the state, contained in a single head: you see the image of God in the king, and you have the idea of royal majesty. God is holiness itself, goodness itself, and power itself. In these things lies the majesty of God. In the image of these things lies the majesty of the prince.

From *Politics Drawn from the Very Words of Holy Scripture,* in James Harvey Robinson (Ed.), *Readings in European History,* Vol. 2 (Boston: Ginn and Co., 1906), pp. 275–276.

Versailles

The palace court at Versailles on the outskirts of Paris became Louis's permanent residence after 1682. It was a true temple to royalty, architecturally designed and artistically decorated to proclaim the glory of the Sun King, as Louis was known. A spectacular estate with magnificent fountains and acres of orange groves, it became home to thousands of aristocrats, royal officials, and servants. Although its physical maintenance and new additions, which continued throughout Louis's lifetime, consumed over half his annual revenues—around five million livres a year—Versailles paid political dividends well worth the investment.

Life at court was organized around the king's daily routine. During his rising and dressing, nobles whispered their special requests in Louis's ear.

After the morning mass, which Louis always observed, there followed long hours in council with the chief ministers, assemblies from which the nobility was carefully excluded. Louis's ministers and councilors were handpicked townsmen, servants who owed everything they had to the king's favor and who served him, for that reason, faithfully and without question. There were three main councils: the Council of State, a small group of four or five who met thrice weekly to rule on all matters of state, but especially on foreign affairs and war policy; the Council of Dispatches, which regularly assessed the reports from the *intendants* in the towns and provinces, a boring business that the king often left to his ministers; and finally, the Council of Finances, which handled matters of taxation and commerce.

Members of the royal court spent the afternoons hunting, riding, or strolling about the lush gardens. Evenings were given over to planned entertainment in the large salons (plays, concerts, gambling, and the like), followed by supper at 10:00 P.M.

Even the king's retirement became a part of day's spectacle. Fortunate nobles held his night candle as they accompanied him to his bed.

Although only five feet four inches in height, the king had presence and was always engaging in conversation. An unabashed ladies' man, he encouraged the belief at court that it was an honor to lie with the king. Married to the Spanish Infanta Marie Thérèse for political reasons in 1660, he kept many mistresses.

OPPOSITE: *Versailles as it appeared in 1668 in a painting by Pierre Patel the Elder (1605–1676). The central building is the hunting lodge built for Louis XIII earlier in the century; some of the first expansion undertaken by Louis XIV appears as wings. [Cliché des Musées Nationaux, Paris]*

BELOW: *A full view of Versailles as it appears today. Louis XIV vastly enlarged his father's hunting lodge into a palace estate beginning in 1661. It became not only the royal residence but the seat of the French government, a symbol of royal and national power, and the model for other monarchs. This photograph is from the opposite direction to Patel's painting; the coaches in his picture are arriving on the diagonal road at the top left of the photograph. [French Government Tourist Office, New York]*

After Marie's death in 1683 he settled down in secret marriage with one, Madame de Maintenon, and apparently became much less the philanderer.

All this ritual and play served the political purpose of keeping an impoverished nobility, barred by law from high government positions, busy and dependent so that they had little time to plot revolt. The dress codes and the high-stakes gaming at court contributed to the indebtedness and dependency of the nobility on the king. Court life was a carefully planned and successfully executed domestication of the nobility.

Suppression of the Jansenists

Like Richelieu before him, Louis believed that political unity required religious conformity. To that end he suppressed two groups of religious dissenters: the Catholic Jansenists, who were opponents of the Jesuits, and the Protestant Huguenots.

Although the king and the French church jealously guarded their traditional independence from Rome (the Gallican Liberties), the years following the conversion of Henry IV to Catholicism had seen a great influx of Catholic religious orders into France, prominent among which were the Jesuits. Because of their leadership at the Council of Trent and their close Spanish connections, Catherine de Médicis had earlier banned the Jesuits from France. Henry IV lifted the ban in 1603, with certain conditions: there was to be a limitation on the number of new colleges they could open; special licenses were required for activities outside their own buildings; and each member of the

Cornelis Jansen, Bishop of Ypres (1585–1638), *wrote that individuals could do nothing to contribute to their salvation unless they were assisted by divine grace. This teaching, which came to be called Jansenism, was condemned as heretical by the Church because it seemed to deny the doctrine of human free will.* [*Library of Congress*]

order was subjected to an oath of allegiance to the king. The Jesuits were not, however, easily harnessed. They rapidly monopolized the education of the upper classes, and their devout students promoted the religious reforms and doctrine of the Council of Trent throughout France. It is a measure of their success that Jesuits served as confessors to Henry IV, Louis XIII, and Louis XIV.

In the 1630s a group known as *Jansenists* formed an intra-Catholic opposition to both the theology and the political influence of the Jesuits. They were Catholics who adhered to the Augustinian tradition, out of which many Protestant teachings had also come. Serious and uncompromising in their religious doctrine and practice, the Jansenists opposed Jesuit teachings about free will. They believed with Saint Augustine that original sin dominated humankind so completely that individuals could do absolutely nothing good or contribute to their salvation unless they were first specially assisted by the grace of God. The namesake of the Jansenists, Cornelis Jansen (d. 1638), a Flemish theologian and the bishop of Ypres, was the author of a posthumously published book entitled *Augustinus* (1640), which assailed mainly Jesuit teaching on grace and salvation.

Jean du Vergier de Hauranne (1581–1643), the abbot of Saint-Cyran and Jansen's close friend, was instrumental in bringing into the Jansenist camp a Parisian family, the Arnaulds, who were prominent opponents of the Jesuits. The Arnauld family, like many other French people, believed that the Jesuits had been behind the assassination of Henry IV in 1610. Arnauld support added a strong political element to the Jansenists' theological opposition to the Jesuits. Jansenist communities at Port-Royal and Paris were dominated by the Arnaulds during the 1640s. In 1643 Antoine Arnauld published a work entitled *On Frequent Communion* in which he criticized the Jesuits for confessional practices that permitted the easy redress of almost any sin. The Jesuits, in turn, condemned the Jansenists as "crypto-Calvinists" in their theology.

On May 31, 1653, Pope Innocent X declared heretical five Jansenist theological propositions on grace and salvation. In 1656 the pope banned Jansen's *Augustinus*, and the Sorbonne censured Antoine Arnauld. In this same year Antoine's friend, Blaise Pascal (d. 1662), the most famous of Jansen's followers, published the first of his *Provincial Letters* in defense of Jansenism. A deeply religious man, Pascal tried to reconcile the "reasons of the heart" with growing seventeenth-century reverence for the clear and distinct ideas of the mind. He found Jesuit moral theology to be not only lax and shallow, but also a rationalized approach to religion that did injustice to religious experience.

In 1660 Louis permitted the enforcement of the papal bull *Ad Sacram Sedem* (1656), which banned Jansenism, and he closed down the Port-Royal community. Thereafter Jansenists either capitulated by signing retractions or went underground. At a later date (1710) the French king lent his support to a still more thorough purge of Jansenist sentiment. With the fall of the Jansenists went any hope of a Catholicism broad enough to attract the Huguenots.

Revocation of the Edict of Nantes

Since the Edict of Nantes, a cold war had existed between the great Catholic majority (nine tenths of the French population) and the Protestant minority. Despite their respectable numbers, about 1.75 million by the 1660s, the Huguenots were in decline in the second half of the seventeenth century. Government harassment had forced the more influential members to withdraw their support. Officially the French Catholic church had long denounced Calvinists as heretical and treasonous and had supported their persecution as both a pious and a patriotic act. Following the Peace of Nijmegen in 1678–1679, which halted for the moment Louis's aggression in Europe, Louis launched a methodical government campaign against the French Huguenots in a determined effort to unify France religiously. He hounded the Huguenots out of public life, banned them from government office, and excluded them from such professions as printing and medicine. Subsidies and selective taxation also be-

Louis XIV Revokes the Edict of Nantes

Believing that a country could not be under one king and one law unless it was also under one religious system, Louis XIV stunned much of Europe in October 1685 by revoking the Edict of Nantes, which had protected the religious freedoms and civil rights of French Protestants since 1598.

Art. 1. *Know that we . . . with our certain knowledge, full power and royal authority, have by this present, perpetual and irrevocable edict, suppressed and revoked the edict of the aforesaid king our grandfather, given at Nantes in the month of April,* 1598, *in all its extent . . . together with all the concessions made by [this] and other edicts, declarations, and decrees, to the people of the so-called Reformed religion, of whatever nature they be . . . and in consequence we desire . . . that all the temples of the people of the aforesaid so-called Reformed religion situated in our kingdom . . . should be demolished forthwith.*

Art. 2. *We forbid our subjects of the so-called Reformed religion to assemble any more for public worship of the above-mentioned religion. . . .*

Art. 3. *We likewise forbid all lords, of whatever rank they may be, to carry out heretical services in houses and fiefs . . . the penalty for . . . the said worship being confiscation of their body and possessions.*

Art. 4. *We order all ministers of the aforesaid so-called Reformed religion who do not wish to be converted and to embrace the Catholic, Apostolic, and Roman religion, to depart from our kingdom and the lands subject to us within fifteen days from the publication of our present edict . . . on pain of the galleys.*

Art. 5. *We desire that those among the said [Reformed] ministers who shall be converted [to the Catholic religion] shall continue to enjoy during their life, and their wives shall enjoy after their death as long as they remain widows, the same exemptions from taxation and billeting of soldiers, which they enjoyed while they fulfilled the function of ministers. . . .*

. . . .

Art. 8. *With regard to children who shall be born to those of the aforesaid so-called Reformed religion, we desire that they be baptized by their parish priests. We command the fathers and mothers to send them to the churches for that purpose, on penalty of a fine of* 500 *livres or more if they fail to do so; and afterwards, the children shall be brought up in the Catholic, Apostolic, and Roman religion. . . .*

. . . .

Art. 10. *All our subjects of the so-called Reformed religion, with their wives and children, are to be strongly and repeatedly prohibited from leaving our aforesaid kingdom . . . or of taking out . . . their possessions and effects. . . .*

. . . .

The members of the so-called Reformed religion, while awaiting God's pleasure to enlighten them like the others, can live in the towns and districts of our kingdom . . . and continue their occupation there, and enjoy their possessions . . . on condition . . . that they do not make public profession of [their religion].

Church and State Through the Centuries: A Collection of Historic Documents, trans. and ed. by S. Z. Ehler and John B. Morrall (New York: Biblo and Tannen, 1967), pp. 209–213.

came weapons to encourage their conversion to Catholicism. In 1681 Louis further bullied Huguenots by quartering his troops in their towns. The final stage of the persecution came in October 1685, when Louis revoked the Edict of Nantes. In practical terms the revocation meant the closing of Protestant churches and schools, the exile of Protestant ministers, the placement of nonconverting laity in galleys as slaves, and the ceremonial baptism of Protestant children by Catholic priests.

The revocation of the Edict of Nantes became the major blunder of Louis's reign. Thereafter he was viewed throughout Protestant Europe as a new Philip II, intent on a Catholic reconquest of the whole of Europe, who must be resisted at all costs. Internally the revocation of the Edict of Nantes led to the voluntary emigration of over a quarter million French, who formed new communities and joined the French resistance movement in England, Germany, Holland, and the New World. Thousands of French Huguenots served in the army of Louis's arch foe, William III of the Netherlands, later King William III of England. Those who remained in France became an uncompromising guerrilla force. But despite the many domestic and foreign liabilities created for France by the revocation of the Edict of Nantes, Louis, to his death, considered it his most pious act, one that placed God in his debt.

Louis XIV revoking the Edict of Nantes in 1685. [*Bulloz*]

War Abroad

War was the normal state of affairs for seventeenth-century rulers and for none more than for Louis XIV, who confessed on his deathbed that he had "loved war too much." Periods of peace became opportunities for the discontented in town and countryside to plot against the king; war served national unity as well as "glory." By the 1660s France was superior to any other nation in administrative bureaucracy, armed forces, and national unity. It had a population of nineteen million, prosperous farms, vigorous trade, and much taxable wealth. By every external measure Louis was in a position to dominate Europe.

LOUVOIS, VAUBAN, AND COLBERT. The great French war machine became the work of three ministers: Louvois, Vauban, and Colbert. The army, which maintained a strength of about a quarter of a million, was the creation of Michel le Tellier and his more famous son, the marquis of Louvois (1641–1691), Louis's war minister from 1677 to 1691 and a superior military tactician.

Before Louvois the French army had been an amalgam of local recruits and mercenaries, uncoordinated groups whose loyalty could not always be counted on. Louvois disciplined the French army and made it a respectable profession. He placed a limit on military commissions and introduced a system of promotion by merit, policies that brought dedicated fighting men into the ranks. Enlistment was for four years and was restricted to single men. The pay was good and regular. *Intendants*, the king's ubiquitous civil servants, carried out regular inspections, monitoring conduct at all levels and reporting to the king.

What Louvois was to military organization, Sebastien Vauban (1633–1707) was to military engineering. He perfected the arts of fortifying and besieging towns. He also devised the system of trench warfare and developed the concept of defensive frontiers that remained basic military tactics through World War I.

War cannot be successful without financing, and here Louis had the guidance of his most brilliant minister, Jean-Baptiste Colbert (1619–1683). Colbert worked to centralize the French economy with the same rigor that Louis had worked to centralize the French government. He put the nation to work under state supervision and carefully regulated the flow of imports and exports through tariffs. He created new

Jean-Baptiste Colbert (1619–1683). *His policies transformed France into a major industrial and commercial power.* [*Giraudon*]

national industries and organized factories around a tight regimen of work and ideology. Administrative bureaucracy was simplified, unnecessary positions were abolished, and the number of tax-exempt nobles was reduced. Colbert also increased the *taille* on the peasantry, the chief source of royal wealth. Although the French economy continued to be a puppet controlled by many different strings, more of these strings were now in the hand of the king than had been the case in centuries past. This close government control of the economy came to be known as *mercantilism*. Its aim was to maximize foreign exports and the internal reserves of bullion, the gold and silver necessary for making war. Modern scholars argue that Colbert overcontrolled the French economy and cite his "paternalism" as a major reason for French failures in the New World. Be that as it may, Colbert's policies unquestionably transformed France into a major industrial and commercial power, with foreign bases in Africa, India, and the Americas from Canada to the Caribbean.

THE WAR OF DEVOLUTION. Louis's first great foreign adventure was the War of Devolution (1667–1668). It was fought, as still a later and greater war would be, over Louis's claim to a Spanish inheritance through his wife, Marie Thérèse (1638–1683). According to the terms of the Treaty of the Pyrenees (1659), Marie had renounced her claim to the Spanish succession on condition that a 500,000-crown dowry be paid to Louis within eighteen months of the marriage, a condition that was not met. When Philip IV of Spain died in September 1665, he left all his lands to his sickly four-year-old son by a second marriage, Charles II (1665–1700), and explicitly excluded his daughter Marie from any share. Louis had always harbored the hope of turning the marriage to territorial gain and had argued even before Philip's death that Marie was entitled to a portion of the inheritance.

Louis had a legal argument on his side, which gave the war its name. He maintained that because in certain regions of Brabant and Flanders, which were part of the Spanish inheritance, property "devolved" to the children of a first marriage rather than to those of a second, Marie had a higher claim than Charles II to these regions. The argument was not accepted—such regional laws could hardly bind the king of Spain—but Louis was not deterred from sending his armies, under the viscount of Turenne, into Flanders and the Franche-Comté in 1667. In response to this aggression England, Sweden, and the United Provinces of Holland formed the Triple Alliance, a force sufficient to bring Louis to peace terms in the Treaty of Aix-la-Chapelle (1668).

INVASION OF THE NETHERLANDS. In 1670 England and France became allies against the Dutch by signing the Treaty of Dover, a move that set the Stuart monarchy of Charles II on a new international course. With the departure of the English from its membership, the Triple Alliance crumbled. This left Louis in a stronger position to invade the Netherlands for a second time, which he did in 1672. This second invasion was aimed directly at Holland, the organizer of the Triple Alliance in 1667 and the country held accountable by Louis for foiling French designs in Flanders. Louis had been mightily offended by Dutch boasting after the Treaty of Aix-la-Chapelle; cartoons like one depicting the sun (Louis was the "Sun King") eclipsed by a great moon of Dutch cheese cut the French king to the quick. It was also clear that there could be no French acquisition of land in the Spanish Netherlands, nor European hegemony beyond that, until Holland was neutralized.

Louis's successful invasion of the United Provinces in 1672 brought the downfall of Jan and Cornelius De Witt, Dutch statesmen whom the Dutch public blamed for the French success. In their place came the twenty-seven-year-old Prince of Orange, destined after 1689 to become King William III of England. Orange was the great-grandson of William the Silent, who had repulsed Philip II and dashed Spanish hopes of dominating the Netherlands in the sixteenth century.

Orange proved to be Louis's undoing. This unpretentious Calvinist, who was in almost every way Louis's opposite, galvanized the seven provinces into a fierce fighting unit. In 1673 he united the Holy Roman Emperor, Spain, Lorraine, and Brandenburg in an alliance against Louis, "the Christian Turk," a menace to the whole of western Europe, Catholic and Protestant alike. Subsequent battles saw the loss of Louis's ablest generals, Turenne and Condé, in 1675, whereas the defeat of the Dutch fleet by Admiral Duquesne established French control of the Mediterranean in 1676. The Peace of Nimwegen, signed with different parties in successive years (1678, 1679), ended the hostilities of this second war. The settlements were not unfavorable to France—Spain, for example, surrendered the Franche-Comté—but France still fell far short of the European empire to which Louis aspired.

The League of Augsburg. Between the Treaty of Nimwegen and the renewal of full-scale war in 1689, Louis restlessly probed his perimeters. The army was maintained at full strength. In 1681 it conquered the free city of Strasbourg, setting off the formation of new defensive coalitions against Louis. The League of Augsburg, created in 1686 to resist French expansion into Germany, grew by 1689 to include the Emperor Leopold; Spain; Sweden; the United Provinces; the electorates of Bavaria, Saxony, and the Palatinate; and the England of William and Mary. That year saw the beginning of the Nine Years' War (1689–1697) between France and the League of Augsburg. For the third time stalemate and exhaustion forced the combatants into an interim settlement. The Peace of Ryswick in September 1697 became a personal triumph for William of Orange, now William III of England, and the Emperor Leopold, as it secured Holland's borders and thwarted Louis's expansion into Germany. During this same period England and France fought for control of North America in what came to be known as King William's War (1689–1697).

War of the Spanish Succession: Treaties of Utrecht–Rastadt. After Ryswick, Louis, who seemed to thrive on partial success, made still a fourth attempt to realize his grand design of French European domination, this time assisted by an unfore-

An Appraisal of Louis XIV

In his history of the reigns of the first three Bourbon kings, written in 1746, the duc de Saint Simon (1675–1755), an army officer and public official during Louis XIV's reign, left the following highly critical portrait of Louis as a king smitten by vanity.

Louis XIV's vanity was without limit or restraint; it colored everything and convinced him that no one even approached him in military talents, in plans and enterprises, and in government. Hence, those pictures and inscriptions in the gallery at Versailles which disgust every foreigner; those opera prologues that he himself tried to sing; that flood of prose and verse in his praise for which his appetite was insatiable; those dedications of statues copied from pagan sculpture, and the insipid and sickening compliments that were continually offered to him in person and which he swallowed with unfailing relish; hence, his distaste for all merit, intelligence, education, and, most of all, independence of character and sentiment in others; his mistakes of judgment in matters of importance; his familiarity and favor reserved entirely for those to whom he felt himself superior in acquirements and ability; and, above everything else, a jealousy of his own authority which determined and took precedence over every other sort of justice, reason, and consideration whatever.

James Harvey Robinson (Ed.), *Readings in European History*, Vol. 2 (Boston: Ginn and Co., 1906), pp. 286–287.

The siege of Tournai in 1709 during the War of the Spanish Succession. Tournai, a fortress city on the border between France and the Spanish Netherlands, had been captured by the French in 1667. Here it is beseiged by the English and Imperial forces under Marlborough and Prince Eugene. Under the terms of the Treaty of Utrecht (1713), France ceded Tournai to Austria. This 1709 engraving is by P. Mortier. [BBC Hulton Picture Library]

seen turn of events. On November 1, 1700, Charles II of Spain, known as "the Sufferer" because of his genetic deformities and lingering illnesses, died. Both Louis and the Austrian Emperor Leopold had claims to the Spanish inheritance through their grandsons: Louis by way of his marriage to Marie Thérèse and Leopold through his marriage to her younger sister, Margaret Thérèse. Although the dauphin had the higher blood claim, it was assumed that the inheritance would go to the grandson of the emperor. The French raised the specter of a belligerent Habsburg kingdom threatening the whole of Europe should Spain come under the imperial crown. Marie Thérèse, however, had renounced any right to the Spanish inheritance in the Treaty of the Pyrenees (1659).

The nations of Europe feared a union of the French and Spanish crowns more than they did a union of the imperial and Spanish crowns. Indeed, they determined that the former alliance should not occur. Hence, before Charles's death, negotiations began to partition the inheritance in such a way that the current balance of power would be maintained.

Charles II upset all plans by leaving the entire Spanish inheritance to Philip of Anjou, Louis's grandson. At a stroke the Spanish inheritance had fallen to France. Although Louis had been party to the partition agreements in

The Reign of Louis XIV (1643–1715)

Peace of Westphalia reaffirms religious pluralism in Holy Roman Empire	1648
The Fronde, a revolt of nobility and townsmen against confiscatory policies of the crown	1649–1652
Jansenism declared a heresy by the pope	1653
Treaty of Pyrenees ends hostilities between France and Spain	1659
Louis XIV enforces papal ban on Jansenists	1660
War of Devolution fought over Louis's claims to lands in Brabant and Flanders by virtue of his Spanish inheritance through his wife	1667–1668
The Triple Alliance (England, Sweden, and the United Provinces) repels Louis's army from Flanders and forces the Treaty of Aix-la-Chapelle	1668
Treaty of Dover brings French and English together against the Netherlands	1670
France invades the United Provinces	1672
Peace of Nimwegen ends French wars in United Provinces	1678–1679
Louis XIV revokes Edict of Nantes	1685
Nine Years' War between France and League of Augsburg, a Europe-wide alliance against Louis XIV	1689–1697
Peace of Ryswick ends French expansion into Holland and Germany	1697
England, Holland, and Holy Roman Emperor resist Louis's claim to the Spanish throne in the War of Spanish Succession	1702–1714
Treaty of Utrecht between England and France	1712
Treaty of Rastadt between Spain and France	1714

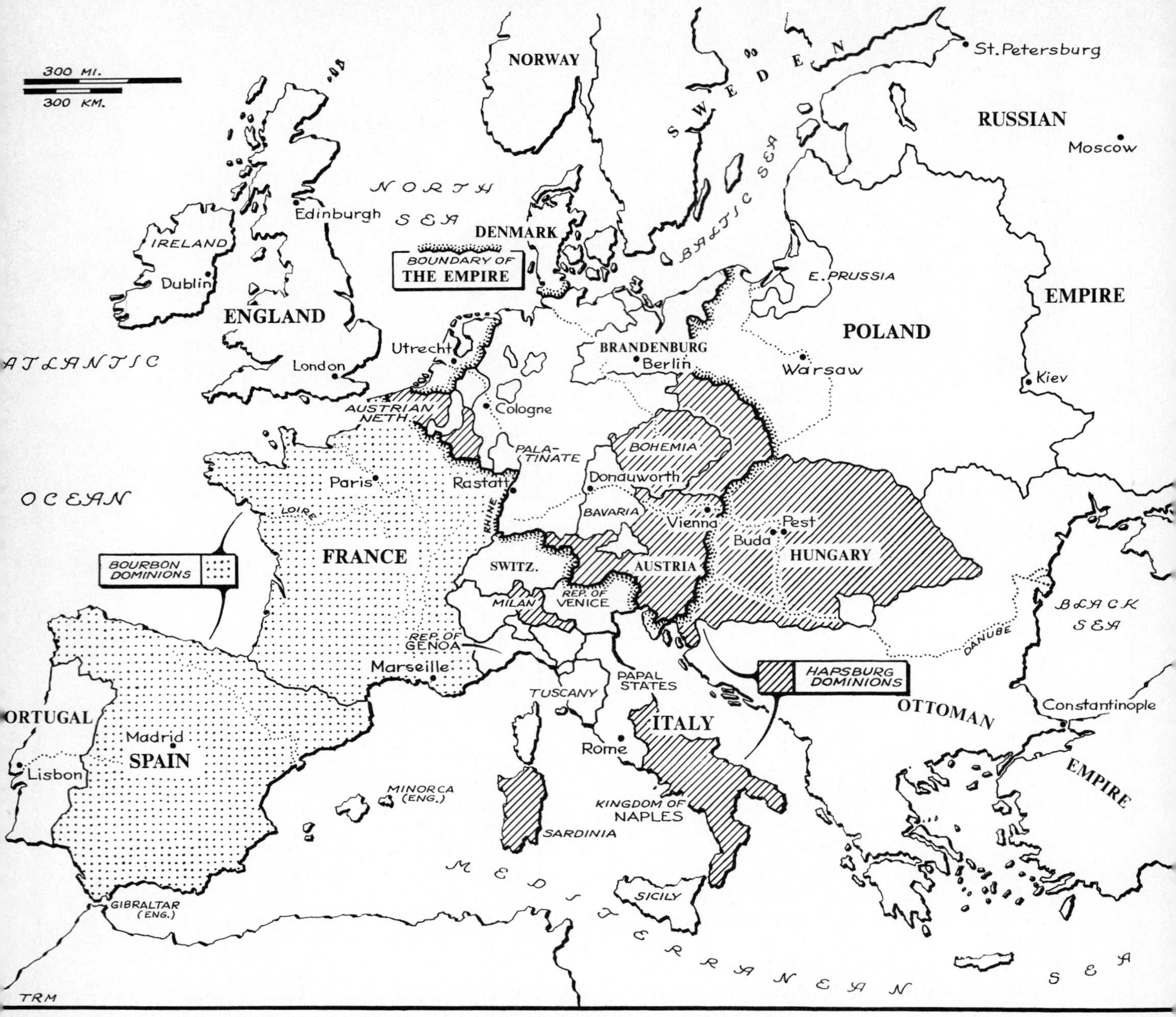

EUROPE IN 1714

MAP 12–3 *The War of the Spanish Succession ended in the year before the death of the aged Louis XIV. By then France and Spain, although not united, were ruled by members of the Bourbon family, and Spain had lost her non-Iberian possessions. Austria had continued to grow.*

advance of Charles's death, he now saw God's hand in Charles's will and chose to enforce its terms fully rather than abide by those of the partition treaty. Philip of Anjou moved to Madrid and became Philip V of Spain, and Louis, in what was interpreted as naked French aggression, sent his troops once again into Flanders, this time to remove Dutch soldiers from Spanish territory in the name of the new French king of Spain. He also declared Spanish America open to French ships.

In September 1701 the Grand Alliance of England, Holland, and the Holy Roman Emperor formed against Louis. Its intent was to preserve the balance of power by once and for all securing Flanders as a neutral barrier between Holland and France and by gaining for the emperor his fair share of the Spanish inheritance. After the formation of the alliance Louis increased the stakes of battle by recognizing the son of James II of England as James III, king of England.

Once again total war enveloped western Europe as the twelve-year War of the Spanish Succession (1702–1714) began. France, for the first time, went to war with inadequate finances, a poorly equipped army, and mediocre military leadership. The English had advanced weaponry (flintlock rifles, paper cartridges, and ring bayonets) and superior tactics (thin, maneuverable troop columns rather than the traditional deep ones). John Churchill, the duke of Marlborough, who succeeded William of Orange as military leader of the alliance, bested Louis's soldiers in every major engagement. Marlborough routed French armies at Blenheim in August 1704 and on the plain of Ramillies in 1706—two decisive battles of the war. In 1708–1709 famine, revolts, and uncollectable taxes tore France apart internally. Despair pervaded the French court. Louis wondered aloud how God could forsake one who had done so much for Him.

Though ready to make peace in 1709, Louis could not bring himself to accept the stiff terms of the alliance, which included the demand that he transfer all Spanish possessions to the emperor's grandson Charles and remove Philip V from Madrid. An immediate result of this failure to come to terms was a clash of forces at Malplaquet (September 1709), which left carnage on the battlefield unsurpassed until modern times.

France finally signed an armistice with England at Utrecht in July 1712 and concluded hostilities with Holland and the emperor in the Treaty of Rastadt in March 1714. This agreement confirmed Philip V as king of Spain. It gave England Gibraltar, which made England thereafter a Mediterranean power, and won Louis's recognition of the House of Hanover's right of accession to the English throne.

Politically the eighteenth century would belong to England as the sixteenth had belonged to Spain and the seventeenth to France. Although France remained intact and quite strong, the realization of Louis XIV's ambition had to await the rise of Napoleon Bonaparte. On his deathbed on September 1, 1715, a dying Louis fittingly warned the dauphin not to imitate his love of buildings and his liking for war.

When one looks back on Louis's reign, the grandeur and power of it still remain undimmed by his glory-seeking and military ambitions. One remembers not only a king who loved war too much, but also one who built the palace of Versailles and brought a new majesty to France; a king who managed the French aristocracy and bourgeoisie at court and controlled a French peasantry that had all too many just grievances; a king who raised up skilled and trustworthy ministers, councillors, and *intendants* from the middle classes; and a king who created a new French empire by expanding trade into Asia and colonizing North America.

Suggested Readings

MAURICE ASHLEY, *The Greatness of Oliver Cromwell* (1966). Detailed biography.

TREVOR ASTON (Ed.), *Crisis in Europe* 1560–1660 (1965). Essays by major scholars focused on social and economic forces.

PETER BURKE, *Popular Culture in Early Modern Europe* (1978). A journalistic romp.

WILLIAM F. CHURCH (Ed.), *The Greatness of Louis XIV: Myth or Reality?* (1959). Excerpts from the scholarly debate over Louis's reign.

C. H. FIRTH, *Oliver Cromwell and the Rule of the Puritans in England* (1900). Old but still very authoritative work.

WILLIAM HALLER, *The Rise of Puritanism* (1957). Interesting study based largely on Puritan sermons.

CHRISTOPHER HILL, *The Century of Revolution* 1603–1714 (1961). Bold, imaginative synthesis by a controversial master.

W. H. LEWIS, *The Splendid Century* (1953). Focuses on society, especially in the age of Louis XIV.

MICHAEL MACDONALD, *Mystical Bedlam: Madness, Anxiety and Healing in Seventeenth Century England* (1981).

DAVID OGG, *Europe in the Seventeenth Century* (1925). Among the most authoritative syntheses.

STUART E. PRALL, *The Puritan Revolution: A Documentary History* (1968). Comprehensive document collection.

LAWRENCE STONE, *The Causes of the English Revolution* 1529–1642 (1972). Brief survey stressing social history and ruminating over historians and historical method.

G. R. R. TREASURE, *Seventeenth Century France* (1966). Broad, detailed survey of entire century.

MICHAEL WALZER, *The Revolution of the Saints: A Study in the Origins of Radical Politics* (1965). Effort to relate ideas and politics that depicts Puritans as true revolutionaries.

C. V. WEDGWOOD, *Richelieu and the French Monarchy* (1950). Fine biography.

JOHN B. WOLF, *Louis XIV* (1968). Very detailed political biography.

Galileo Galilei (1564–1642), *the Florentine whose observations through a telescope showed the inaccuracy of the Ptolemaic assumption that the earth was the center of the universe and laid the foundations of modern astronomy.* [*Library of Congress*]

13

New Directions in Science and Thought in the Sixteenth and Seventeenth Centuries

The Scientific Revolution

New Departures

THE SIXTEENTH AND SEVENTEENTH CENTURIES witnessed a sweeping change in the scientific view of the universe. An earth-centered picture of the universe gave way to one in which the earth was only another planet orbiting about the sun. The sun itself became one of millions of stars. This transformation of humankind's perception of its place in the larger scheme of things led to a vast rethinking of moral and religious matters as well as of scientific theory. At the same time, the new scientific concepts and the methods of their construction became so impressive that subsequent knowledge in the Western world has been deemed correct only as it has approximated knowledge as defined by science. Perhaps no single intellectual development proved to be more significant for the future of European and Western civilization.

The process by which this new view of the universe and of scientific knowledge came to be established is normally termed the *Scientific Revolution*. However, care must be taken in the use of this metaphor. The word *revolution* normally denotes fairly rapid changes in the political world, involving large numbers of people. The Scientific Revolution was not rapid, nor did it involve more than a few hundred human beings. It was a complex movement with many false starts and many brilliant people with wrong as well as useful ideas. It took place in the studies and the crude laboratories of thinkers in Poland, Italy, Bohemia, France, and Great Britain. It stemmed from two major tendencies. The first, as illustrated by Nicolaus Copernicus, was the imposition of important small changes on existing models of thought. The second, as embodied by Francis Bacon, was the desire to pose new kinds of questions and to use new methods of investigation. In both cases, scientific thought changed the current and traditional opinions in other fields.

Nicolaus Copernicus

Copernicus (1473–1543) was a Polish astronomer who enjoyed a very high reputation throughout his life. He had been educated in Italy and corresponded with other astronomers throughout Europe. However, he had not been known for strikingly original or unorthodox thought. In 1543, the year of his death, Coper-

Copernicus Ascribes Movement to the Earth

Copernicus published *De Revolutionibus Orbium Caelestium (On the Revolutions of the Heavenly Spheres)* in 1543. In his preface, which was addressed to Pope Paul III, he explained what had led him to think that the earth moved around the sun and what he thought were some of the scientific consequences of the new theory. The reader should note how important Copernicus considered the opinions of the ancient writers who had also ascribed motion to the earth. This is a good example of the manner in which familiarity with the ancients gave many Renaissance writers the self-confidence to criticize medieval ideas.

I may well presume, most Holy Father, that certain people, as soon as they hear that in this book about the Revolutions of the Spheres of the Universe I ascribe movement to the earthly globe, will cry out that, holding such views, I should at once be hissed off the stage. . . .

So I should like your Holiness to know that I was induced to think of a method of computing the motions of the spheres by nothing else than the knowledge that the Mathematicians [who had previously considered the problem] are inconsistent in these investigations.

For, first, the mathematicians are so unsure of the movements of the Sun and Moon that they cannot even explain or observe the constant length of the seasonal year. Secondly, in determining the motions of these and of the other five planets, they use neither the same principles and hypotheses nor the same demonstrations of the apparent motions and revolutions. . . . Nor have they been able thereby to discern or deduce the principal thing—namely the shape of the Universe and the unchangeable symmetry of its parts. . . .

I pondered long upon this uncertainty of mathematical tradition in establishing the motions of the system of the spheres. At last I began to chafe that philosophers could by no means agree on any one certain theory of the mechanism of the Universe, wrought for us by a supremely good and orderly Creator. . . . I therefore took pains to read again the works of all the philosophers on whom I could lay hand to seek out whether any of them had ever supposed that the motions of the spheres were other than those demanded by the [Ptolemaic] mathematical schools. I found first in Cicero that Hicetas [of Syracuse, fifth century B.C.*] had realized that the Earth moved. Afterwards I found in Plutarch that certain others had held the like opinion. . . .*

Thus assuming motions, which in my work I ascribe to the Earth, by long and frequent observations I have at last discovered that, if the motions of the rest of the planets be brought into relation with the circulation of the Earth and be reckoned in proportion to the circles of each planet, not only do their phenomena presently ensue, but the orders and magnitudes of all stars and spheres, nay the heavens themselves, become so bound together that nothing in any part thereof could be moved from its place without producing confusion of all the other parts of the Universe as a whole.

As quoted in Thomas S. Kuhn, *The Copernican Revolution: Planetary Astronomy in the Development of Western Thought* (New York: Vintage Books, 1959), pp. 137–139, 141–142.

nicus published *On the Revolutions of the Heavenly Spheres.* Because he died near the time of publication, the fortunes of his work are not the story of one person's crusade for progressive science. Copernicus's book was "a revolution-making rather than a revolutionary text."[1] What Copernicus did was to provide an intellectual springboard for a complete criticism of the then-dominant view of the position of the earth in the universe.

At the time of Copernicus the standard explanation of the earth and the heavens was that associated with Ptolemy and his work entitled the *Almagest* (A.D. 150). There was not just one Ptolemaic system; rather, several versions had been developed over the centuries by commentators on the original book. Most of these systems assumed that the earth was the

[1]Thomas S. Kuhn, *The Copernican Revolution: Planetary Astronomy in the Development of Western Thought* (New York: Vintage, 1959), p. 135.

center of the universe. Above the earth lay a series of crystalline spheres, one of which contained the moon, another the sun, and still others the planets and the stars. This was the astronomy found in such works as Dante's *Divine Comedy.* At the outer regions of these spheres lay the realm of God and the angels. Aristotelian physics provided the intellectual underpinnings of the Ptolemaic systems. The earth had to be the center because of its heaviness. The stars and the other heavenly bodies had to be enclosed in the crystalline spheres so that they could move. Nothing could move unless something was actually moving it. The state of rest was natural; motion was the condition that required explanation.

Numerous problems were associated with this system, and these had long been recognized. The most important was the observed motions of the planets. Planets could be seen moving in noncircular patterns around the earth. At certain times the planets actually appeared to be going backward. The Ptolemaic systems explained these strange motions primarily through *epicycles.* An epicycle is an orbit upon an orbit, like a spinning jewel on a ring. The planets were said to make a second revolution in an orbit tangent to their primary orbit around the earth. Other intellectual but nonobservational difficulties related to the immense speed at which the spheres had to move around the earth. To say the least, the Ptolemaic systems were cluttered. However, they were effective explanations as long as one assumed Aristotelian physics and the Christian belief that the earth rested at the center of the created universe.

Copernicus's *On the Revolutions of the Heavenly Spheres* challenged this picture in the most conservative manner possible. It suggested that if the earth were assumed to move about the sun in a circle, many of the difficulties with the Ptolemaic systems would disappear or become simpler. Although not wholly eliminated, the number of epicycles would be somewhat fewer. The motive behind this shift away from the earth-centered universe was to find a solu-

Two seventeenth-century armillary spheres, astronomical devices composed of rings that represent the orbits of important celestial bodies. The top one was built on the Copernican model, the bottom sphere reflects the much more complicated Ptolemaic universe. [*Museum of the History of Science, Oxford, England*]

tion to the problems of planetary motion. By allowing the earth to move around the sun, Copernicus was able to construct a more mathematically elegant basis for astronomy. He had been discontented with the traditional system because it was mathematically clumsy and inconsistent. The primary appeal of his new system was its mathematical aesthetics: with the sun at the center of the universe, mathematical astronomy would make more sense. A change in the conception of the position of the earth meant that the planets were actually moving in circular orbits and only seemed to be doing otherwise because of the position of the observers on earth.

Except for the modification in the position of the earth, most of the other parts of Copernicus's book were Ptolemaic. The path of the planets remained circular. Genuine epicycles still existed in the heavens. His system was no more accurate than the existing ones for predicting the location of the planets. He had used no new evidence. The major impact of his work was to provide another way of confronting some of the difficulties inherent in Ptolemaic astronomy. This work did not immediately replace the old astronomy, but it did allow other people who were also discontented with the Ptolemaic systems to think in new directions.

Copernicus's concern about mathematics provided an example of the single most important factor in the developing new science. The key to the future development of the Copernican revolution lay in the fusion of mathematical astronomy with further empirical data and observation, and mathematics became the model to which the new scientific thought would conform. The new empirical evidence helped to persuade the learned public.

Tycho Brahe and Johannes Kepler

The next major step toward the conception of a sun-centered system was taken by Tycho Brahe (1546–1601). He actually spent most of his life opposing Copernicus and advocating a different kind of earth-centered system. He suggested that the moon and the sun revolved around the earth and that the other planets revolved around the sun. However, in attacking Copernicus, he gave the latter's ideas more publicity. More important, this Danish astronomer's major weapon against Copernican astronomy was a series of new naked-eye astronomical observations. Brahe constructed the most accurate tables of observations that had been drawn up for centuries.

When Brahe died, these tables came into the possession of Johannes Kepler (1571–1630), a German astronomer. Kepler was a convinced Copernican, but his reasons for taking that position were not scientific. Kepler was deeply influenced by Renaissance Neoplatonism and its honoring of the sun. These Neoplatonists were also determined to discover mathematical harmonies in those numbers that would support a sun-centered universe. After much work Kepler discovered that to keep the sun at the center of things, he must abandon the Copernican concept of circular orbits. The mathematical relationships that emerged from a consideration of Brahe's observations suggested that the orbits of the planets were elliptical. Kepler published his findings in 1609 in a book entitled *On the Motion of Mars.* He had solved the problem of planetary orbits by using Copernicus's sun-centered universe and Brahe's empirical data.

Kepler had, however, also defined a new problem. None of the available theories could explain why the planetary orbits were elliptical. That solution awaited the work of Sir Isaac Newton.

Galileo Galilei

From Copernicus to Brahe to Kepler there had been little new information about the heavens that might not have been known to Ptolemy. However, in the same year that Kepler published his volume on Mars, an Italian scientist named Galileo Galilei (1564–1642) first turned a telescope on the heavens. Through that recently invented instrument he saw stars where none had been known to exist, mountains on the moon, spots moving across the sun, and moons orbiting Jupiter. The heavens were far more complex than anyone had formerly suspected. None of these discoveries proved that the earth orbited the sun, but they did suggest the complete inadequacy of the Ptolemaic system. It simply could not accommodate itself to all of these new phenomena. Some of Galileo's colleagues at the university of Padua were so unnerved that they refused to look through the telescope. Galileo publicized his findings and arguments for the Copernican system in numerous works, the most famous of which was his *Dialogues on the Two Chief Systems of the World* (1632). This book brought down on him the condemnation of the

Galileo Discusses the Relationship of Science and the Bible

The religious authorities were often critical of the discoveries and theories of sixteenth- and seventeenth-century science. For many years religious and scientific writers debated the implications of the Copernican theory in the reading of the Bible. For years before his condemnation by the Roman Catholic church in 1633, Galileo had contended that scientific theory and religious piety were compatible. In his *Letter to the Grand Duchess Christiana* (of Tuscany) written in 1615, Galileo argued that God had revealed truth in both the Bible and physical nature and that the truth of physical nature did not contradict the Bible if the latter were properly understood.

The reason produced for condemning the opinion that the earth moves and the sun stands still is that in many places in the Bible one may read that the sun moves and the earth stands still. . . .

With regard to this argument, I think in the first place that it is very pious to say and prudent to affirm that the holy Bible can never speak untruth—whenever its true meaning is understood. But I believe nobody will deny that it is often very abstruse, and may say things which are quite different from what its bare words signify. . . .

This being granted, I think that in discussions of physical problems we ought to begin not from the authority of scriptural passages, but from sense-experiences and necessary demonstrations; for the holy Bible and the phenomena of nature proceed alike from the divine Word, the former as the dictate of the Holy Ghost and the latter as the observant executrix of God's commands. It is necessary for the Bible, in order to be accommodated to the understanding of every man, to speak many things which appear to differ from the absolute truth so far as the bare meaning of the words is concerned. But Nature, on the other hand, is inexorable and immutable; she never transgresses the laws imposed upon her, or cares a whit whether her abstruse reasons and methods of operation are understandable to men. For that reason it appears that nothing physical which sense-experience sets before our eyes, or which necessary demonstrations prove to us, ought to be called in question (much less condemned) upon the testimony of biblical passages which may have some different meaning beneath their words. For the Bible is not chained in every expression to conditions as strict as those which govern all physical effects; nor is God any less excellently revealed in Nature's actions than in the sacred statements of the Bible. . . .

From this I do not mean to infer that we need not have an extraordinary esteem for the passages of holy Scripture. On the contrary, having arrived at any certainties in physics, we ought to utilize these as the most appropriate aids in the true exposition of the Bible and in the investigation of those meanings which are necessarily contained therein for these must be concordant with demonstrated truths. I should judge the authority of the Bible was designed to persuade men of those articles and propositions which, surpassing all human reasoning, could not be made credible by science, or by any other means than through the very mouth of the Holy Spirit. . . .

But I do not feel obliged to believe that the same God who has endowed us with senses, reason, and intellect has intended to forgo their use and by some other means to give us knowledge which we can attain by them.

Discoveries and Opinions of Galileo, trans. and ed. by Stillman Drake (Garden City, N.Y.: Doubleday Anchor Books, 1957), pp. 181–183.

Roman Catholic church. He was compelled to recant his opinions. However, he is reputed to have muttered after the recantation, *''E pur si muove''* (''It [the earth] still moves'').

Galileo's discoveries and his popularization of the Copernican system were of secondary importance in his life work. His most important achievement was to articulate the concept of a universe totally subject to mathematical laws. More than any other writer of the cen-

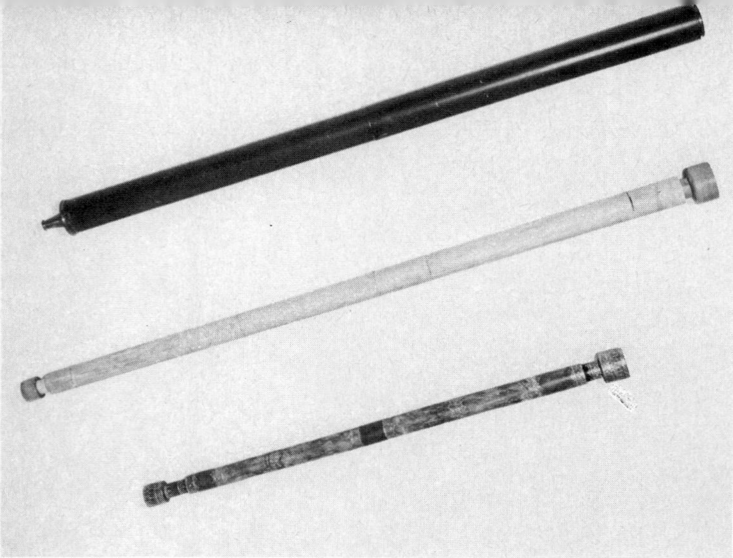

LEFT-*Telescopes built by Galileo. His astronomical observations had revolutionary intellectual and theological implications.* [*Science Museum, London*]

BELOW-*Galileo's drawing of his method for measuring the heights of lunar mountains* (1611). [*Ann Ronan Picture Library and E.P. Goldschmidt and Co., Ltd.*]

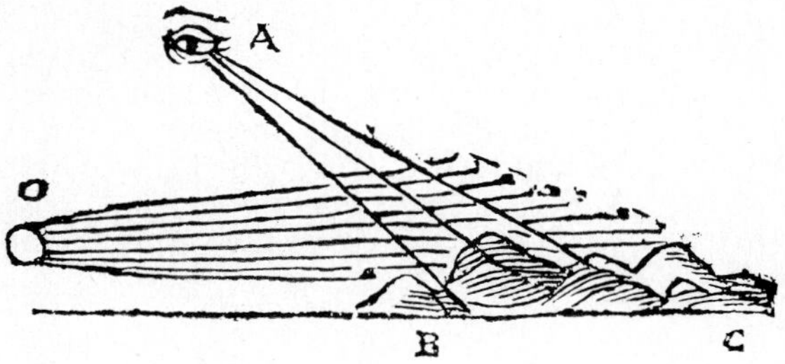

tury he argued that nature in its most minute details displayed mathematical regularity. He once wrote:

> Philosophy is written in that great book which ever lies before our eyes—I mean the universe—but we cannot understand it if we do not first learn the language and grasp the symbols in which it is written. This book is written in the mathematical language, and the symbols are triangles, circles, and other geometrical figures, without whose help it is impossible to comprehend a single word of it; without which one wanders through a dark labyrinth.[2]

The universe was rational; however, its rationality was not that of Scholastic logic but of mathematics. Copernicus had thought that the heavens conformed to mathematical regularity; Galileo saw this regularity throughout all physical nature. He believed that the smallest atom behaved with the same mathematical precision as the largest heavenly sphere.

Galileo's thought meant that a world of quantity was replacing one of qualities. Mathematical quantities and relationships would henceforth increasingly be used to describe nature. Color, beauty, taste, and the like would be reduced to numerical relationships. And eventually social relationships would be envisioned in a mathematical model. Nature was cold, rational, mathematical, and mechanistic. What was real and lasting in the world was what was mathematically measurable. Few intellectual shifts have wrought such momentous changes for Western civilization.

[2]Quoted in E. A. Burtt, *The Metaphysical Foundations of Modern Physical Science* (Garden City, N.Y.: Anchor-Doubleday, 1954), p. 75.

René Descartes

No writer of the seventeenth century more fully adopted the geometric spirit of contemporary mathematics than René Descartes (1596–1650). He was a gifted mathematician who invented analytic geometry, and he was the author of major works on numerous scientific topics. However, his most important contribution was to scientific method. He wanted to proceed by deduction rather than by empirical observation and induction.

In 1637 Descartes published a *Discourse on Method* in which he attempted to provide a basis for all thinking founded on a mathematical model. He published the work in French rather than in Latin because he wanted it to have wide circulation and application. He began by saying that he would doubt everything except those propositions about which he could have clear and distinct ideas. This approach rejected all forms of intellectual authority except the conviction of his own reason. He concluded that he could not doubt his own act of thinking and his own existence. From this base he proceeded to deduce the existence of God. The presence of God was important to Descartes because God was the guarantor of the correctness of clear and distinct ideas. Because God was not a deceiver, the ideas of God-given reason could not be false.

Descartes believed that this powerful human reason could fully comprehend the world. He divided existing things into mind and body. Thinking was the characteristic of the mind, extension of the body. Within the material

René Descartes (1596–1650). *Descartes believed that because the material world operated according to mathematical laws it could therefore be understood by the exercise of human reasoning.* [*Giraudon*]

world, mathematical laws reigned supreme. These could be grasped by the human reason. Because the laws were mathematical, they could be deduced from each other and constituted a complete system. The world of extension was the world of the scientist, whereas the mind was related to theology and philosophy. In the material world there was no room for spirits, divinity, or anything nonmaterial. Descartes had separated mind from body in order to banish the former from the realm of scientific speculation. He wanted to resurrect the speculative use of reason, but in a limited manner. It was to be applied only to the mechanical and mathematical realm of matter.

Descartes's emphasis on deduction and rational speculation exercised broad influence. Well into the eighteenth century European thinkers appealed to Descartes's method, which moved from broad intellectual generalizations to specific phenomena. The method then attempted to see how the phenomena could be interpreted so as to mesh with the generalization. However, that method was eventually overcome by the force of scientific induction, whereby the observer or scientist began with observations of empirical data and then attempted to draw generalizations from those observations. The major champion of the inductive method during the early seventeenth century had been Francis Bacon.

Francis Bacon

Bacon (1561–1626) was an Englishman of almost universal accomplishment. He was a lawyer, a high royal official, and the author of histories, moral essays, and philosophical discourses. Traditionally he has been regarded as the father of empiricism and of experimentation in science. Much of this reputation is unearned. Bacon was not a scientist except in the most amateur fashion. His accomplishment was setting a tone and helping to create a climate in which other scientists worked. In books such as *The Advancement of Learning* (1605), the *Novum Organum* (1620), and the *New Atlantis* (1627), Bacon attacked the Scholastic belief that most truth had already been discovered and only required explanation, as well as the Scholastic reverence for intellectual authority in general. He believed that Scholastic thinkers paid too much attention to tradition and to knowledge achieved by the ancients. He urged contemporaries to strike out on their own in search of a new understanding of nature. He wanted seventeenth-century

Sir Francis Bacon, Viscount St. Albans (1561–1626). *By teaching that knowledge should proceed inductively, Bacon became a major champion of the scientific method.* [*National Portrait Gallery, London*]

Europeans to have confidence in themselves and their own abilities rather than in the people and methods of the past. Bacon was one of the first major European writers to champion the desirability of innovation and change.

Bacon believed that human knowledge should produce useful results. In particular, knowledge of nature should be brought to the aid of the human condition. Those goals required the modification or abandonment of Scholastic modes of learning and thinking. Bacon contended, "The [Scholastic] logic now in use serves more to fix and give stability to the errors which have their foundation in commonly received notions than to help the search after truth."[3] Scholastic philosophers could not escape from their syllogisms to examine the foundations of their thought and intellectual presuppositions. Bacon urged that philoso-

[3]Quoted in Franklin Baumer, *Main Currents of Western Thought,* 4th ed. (New Haven, Conn.: Yale, 1978), p. 281.

Bacon Attacks the Idols that Harm Human Understanding

Francis Bacon wanted the men and women of his era to have the courage to change the way in which they thought about physical nature. In this famous passage from the *Novum Organum* (1620) Bacon attempted to explain why people had such difficulty in asking new questions and seeking new answers. His observations may still be relevant to the manner in which people form and hold their opinions in our own day.

The idols and false notions which are now in possession of the human understanding, and have taken deep root therein, not only so beset men's minds that truth can hardly find entrance, but even after entrance is obtained, they will again in the very instauration of the sciences meet and trouble us, unless men being forewarned of the danger fortify themselves as far as may be against their assaults.

There are four classes of Idols which beset men's minds. To these for distinction's sake I have assigned names,—calling the first class Idols of the Tribe; *the second,* Idols of the Cave; *the third,* Idols of the Marketplace; *the fourth,* Idols of the Theatre.

. . . .

The Idols of the Tribe have their foundation in human nature itself; and in the tribe or race of men. For it is a false assertion that the sense of man is the measure of things. On the contrary, all perceptions as well as the sense as of the mind are according to the measure of the individual and not according to the measure of the universe. And the human understanding is like a false mirror, which, receiving rays irregularly, distorts and discolours the nature of things by mingling its own nature with it.

The Idols of the Cave are the idols of the individual man. For every one (besides the errors common to human nature in general) has a cave or den of his own, which refracts and discolours the light of nature; owing either to his own proper and peculiar nature; or to his education and conversation with others; or to the reading of books, and the authority of those whom he esteems and admires. . . .

There are also Idols formed by the intercourse and association of men with each other, which I call Idols of the Marketplace, on account of the commerce and consort of men there. For it is by discourse that men associate; and words are imposed according to the apprehension of the vulgar. And therefore the ill and unfit choice of words wonderfully obstructs the understanding. . . .

Lastly, there are Idols which have immigrated into men's minds from the various dogmas of philosophies, and also from wrong laws of demonstration. These I call Idols of the Theatre; because in my judgment all the received systems are but so many stage plays, representing worlds of their own creation after an unreal and scenic fashion.

Francis Bacon, *Essays, Advancement of Learning, New Atlantis, and Other Pieces,* ed. by Richard Foster Jones (New York: Odyssey, 1937), pp. 278–280.

The microscope was the telescope's companion as a major optical invention of the seventeenth century. Several people, including Galileo, had a hand in its development, but the greatest progress was made by the Dutchman Anton von Leeuwenhoek (1632–1723) and the Englishman Robert Hooke (1635–1703). Hooke designed this microscope in 1670. [IBM Gallery of Science and Art]

BELOW-*Another optical aid: spectacles. Spectacles date from at least the fourteenth century and were becoming common during the later 1500s. Here we see a spectacle pedlar selling his wares. Spectacles were selected by trial and error, not made to prescription. [The Mansell Collection]*

phers and investigators of nature examine the evidence of their senses before constructing logical speculations. In a famous passage he divided all philosophers into "men of experiment and men of dogmas." He observed:

> The men of experiment are like the ant, they only collect and use; the reasoners resemble spiders, who make cobwebs out of their own substance. But the bee takes a middle course: it gathers its material from the flowers of the garden and of the field, but transforms and digests it by a power of its own. Not unlike this is the true business of philosophy.[4]

By directing scientists toward an examination of empirical evidence, Bacon hoped that they would achieve new knowledge and thus new capabilities for humankind.

Bacon compared himself with Columbus plotting a new route to intellectual discovery. The comparison is significant, because it displays the consciousness of a changing world that appears so often in writers of the late sixteenth and early seventeenth centuries. They were rejecting the past not from simple hatred but rather from a firm understanding that the world was much more complicated than their medieval forebears had thought.

Neither Europe nor European thought could remain self-contained. There were not only new worlds on the globe but also new worlds of the mind. Most of the people in Bacon's day, including the intellectuals, thought that the best era of human history lay in antiquity. Bacon dissented vigorously from that point of view. He looked to a future of material improvement achieved through the empirical examination of nature. His own theory of induction from empirical evidence was quite

[4]Quoted in ibid., p. 288.

MAJOR WORKS OF THE SCIENTIFIC REVOLUTION

On the Revolutions of the Heavenly Spheres (Copernicus)	1543
The Advancement of Learning (Bacon)	1605
On the Motion of Mars (Kepler)	1609
Novum Organum (Bacon)	1620
Dialogues on the Two Chief Systems of the World (Galileo)	1632
Discourse on Method (Descartes)	1637
Principia Mathematica (Newton)	1687

Sir Isaac Newton, discoverer of the mathematical and physical laws governing the force of gravity. Newton believed that religion and science were compatible and mutually supportive. To study nature was to gain a better understanding of the Creator. [*New York Public Library Picture Collection*]

unsystematic, but his insistence on appeal to experience influenced others whose methods were more productive. His great achievement was persuading increasing numbers of thinkers that scientific thought must conform to empirical experience.

Bacon gave science a progressionist bias. Science was to have a practical purpose and the goal of human improvement. Some scientific investigation does possess this character. Much pure research does not. However, Bacon linked in the public mind the concepts of science and material progress. This was a powerful idea and has continued to influence Western civilization to the present day. It has made science and those who can appeal to the authority of science major forces for change and innovation. Thus, though not making any major scientific contribution himself, Bacon directed investigators of nature to a new method and a new purpose.

Isaac Newton

Isaac Newton (1642–1727) drew on the work of his predecessors and his own brilliance to solve the major remaining problem of planetary motion and to establish a basis for physics that endured more than two centuries. The question that continued to perplex seventeenth-century scientists who accepted the theories of Copernicus, Kepler, and Galileo was how the planets and other heavenly bodies moved in an orderly fashion. The Ptolemaic and Aristotelian answer had been the crystalline spheres and a universe arranged in the order of the heaviness of its parts. Numerous unsatisfactory theories had been set forth to deal with the question.

In 1687 Newton published *The Mathematical Principles of Natural Philosophy,* better known by its Latin title of *Principia Mathematica.* Much of the research and thinking for this great work had taken place more than fifteen years earlier. Newton was heavily indebted to the work of Galileo and particularly to the latter's view that inertia could exist in either a state of motion or a state of rest. Galileo's mathematical bias permeated Newton's thought. Newton reasoned that the planets and all other physical objects in the universe moved through mutual attraction. Every object in the universe affected every other object through gravity. The attraction of gravity explained why the planets moved in an orderly rather than a chaotic manner. He had found that "the force of gravity towards the whole planet did arise from and was compounded of the forces of gravity towards all its parts, and towards every one part was in the inverse proportion of the squares of the distances from the part."[5] Newton demonstrated this relationship mathematically. He made no attempt to explain the nature of gravity itself.

[5]Quoted in A. Rupert Hall, *From Galileo to Newton, 1630–1720* (London: Fontana, 1970), p. 300.

Newton was a great mathematical genius, but he also upheld the importance of empirical data and observation. He believed, in good Baconian fashion, that one must observe phenomena before attempting to explain them. The final test of any theory or hypothesis for him was whether it described what could actually be observed. He was a great opponent of Descartes's rationalism, which he believed included insufficient guards against error. As Newton's own theory of universal gravitation became increasingly accepted, the Baconian bias also became more fully popularized.

With the work of Newton the natural universe became a realm of law and regularity.

Newton Sets Forth Rules of Reasoning in Philosophy

Philosophy was the term that seventeenth-century writers used to describe the new science. In this passage from his *Principia Mathematica* (1687) Isaac Newton laid down what he regarded as the fundamental rules for scientific reasoning. The reader should notice the importance he placed on experimental evidence and his desire to find rules or regularities that exist throughout the natural order.

Rule I. We are to admit no more causes of natural things than such as are both true and sufficient to explain their appearances.

To this purpose the philosophers say that Nature does nothing in vain, and more is in vain when less will serve; for Nature is pleased with simplicity, and affects not the pomp of superfluous causes.

Rule II. Therefore to the same natural effects we must, as far as possible, assign the same causes.

As to respiration in a man and in a beast; the descent of stones in Europe and in America; the light of our culinary fire and of the sun; the reflection of light in the earth, and in the planets.

Rule III. The qualities of bodies, which admit neither intension nor remission of degrees, and which are found to belong to all bodies within the reach of our experiments, are to be esteemed the universal qualities of all bodies whatsoever.

For since the qualities of bodies are only known to us by experiments, we are to hold for universal all such as universally agree with experiments and such as are not liable to diminution can never be quite taken away. We are certainly not to relinquish the evidence of experiments for the sake of dreams and vain fictions of our own devising. . . . We no other way know the extension of bodies than by our senses, nor do these reach it in all bodies; but because we perceive extension in all that are sensible, therefore we ascribe it universally to all others also. That abundance of bodies are hard, we learn by experience; and because the hardness of the whole arises from the hardness of the parts, we therefore justly infer the hardness of the undivided particles not only of the bodies we feel but of all others. That bodies are impenetrable, we gather not from reason, but from sensation. . . .

Lastly, if it universally appears, by experiments and astronomical observations, that all bodies about the earth gravitate towards the earth, and that in proportion to the quantity of matter which they severally contain; . . . we must, in consequence of this rule, universally allow that all bodies whatsoever are endowed with a principle of universal gravitation. . . .

Rule IV. In experimental philosophy we are to look upon propositions collected by general induction from phaenomena as accurately or very nearly true, notwithstanding any contrary hypotheses that may be imagined, till such time as other phaenomena occur, by which they may either be made more accurate, or liable to exceptions.

This rule must follow, that the argument of induction may not be evaded by hypotheses.

Introduction to Contemporary Civilization in the West, 3rd ed., Vol. 1 (New York: Columbia University Press, 1960), pp. 850–852.

Spirits and divinities were no longer necessary to explain its operation. Thus the Scientific Revolution liberated human beings from the fear of a chaotic or haphazard universe. Most of the scientists were very devout people. They saw the new picture of physical nature as suggesting a new picture of God. The Creator of this rational, lawful nature must also be rational. To study nature was to come to a better understanding of that Creator. Science and religious faith were not only compatible but mutually supporting. As Newton wrote, "The main Business of Natural Philosophy is to argue from Phaenomena without feigning Hypothesis, and to deduce Causes from Effects, till we come to the very first Cause, which certainly is not mechanical."[6]

This reconciliation of faith and science allowed the new physics and astronomy to spread rapidly. At the very time when Europeans were finally tiring of the wars of religion, the new science provided the basis for a view of God that might lead away from irrational disputes and wars over religious doctrine. Faith in a rational God encouraged faith in the rationality of human beings and in their capacity to improve their lot once liberated from the traditions of the past. The Scientific Revolution provided the great model for the desirability of change and of criticism of inherited views. Yet at the same time the new science caused some people to feel that the mystery had been driven from the universe and that the rational Creator was less loving and less near to humankind than the God of earlier ages.

Writers and Philosophers

The end of the sixteenth century saw weariness with religious strife and incipient unbelief as many no longer embraced either old Catholic or new Protestant absolutes. Intellectually as well as politically the seventeenth century was a period of transition, one already well prepared for by the thinkers of the Renaissance, who had reacted strongly against medieval intellectual traditions, especially those informed by Aristotle and Scholasticism.

Even as they sought to find a purer culture before the Middle Ages in pagan and Christian antiquity, however, Humanists and Protestants continued to share much of the medieval vision of a unified Christendom. Few wanted to embrace the secular values and preoccupations of the growing scientific movement, which found its models in mathematics and the natural sciences, rather than in the example and authority of antiquity. Some strongly condemned the work of Copernicus, Kepler, and Galileo, whose theories seemed to fly in the face of commonsense experience as well as to question hallowed tradition.

The thinkers of the Renaissance and the Reformation nonetheless paved the way for the new science and philosophy, both by their attacks on tradition and by their own failure to implement radical reforms. The Humanist revival of ancient skepticism proved an effective foundation for attacks on traditional views of authority and rationality in both religion and science. Already such thinkers as the Italian Pico della Mirandola (1463–1494), the German Cornelius Agrippa of Nettisheim (1486–1535), and the Frenchman François Rabelais (1494–1553) had questioned the ability of reason to obtain certitude. Sebastian Castellio (1515–1563), Michel de Montaigne (1533–1592), and Pierre Charron (1541–1603) had been as much repelled by the new Calvinist religion as John Calvin had been by medieval religion. It was in the wake of such criticism that René Descartes developed a more modest, yet surer, definition of rationality as the tool of the new scientific philosophy.

The writers and philosophers of the seventeenth century were aware that they lived in a period of transition. Some embraced the new science wholeheartedly (Hobbes and Locke), some tried to straddle the two ages (Cervantes, Shakespeare, and Milton), and still others ignored or opposed the new developments that seemed mortally to threaten traditional values (Pascal and Bunyan). As a group these thinkers helped to make the transition from medieval to modern times by clarifying the intellectual issues involved. In literature, religious thought, and political theory, they established the national landmarks and struck the new directions in Western thought.

Miguel de Cervantes Saavedra (1547–1616)

Spanish literature of the sixteenth and seventeenth centuries reflects the peculiar religious and political history of Spain in this period. Spain was dominated by the Catholic church. Since the joint reign of Ferdinand and Isabella (1479–1504) the church had received

[6]Quoted in Baumer, p. 323.

the unqualified support of reigning political power. Although there was religious reform in Spain, a Protestant Reformation never occurred, thanks largely to the entrenched power of the church and the Inquisition.

The second influence was the aggressive piety of Spanish rulers. The intertwining of Catholic piety and Spanish political power underlay the third major influence on Spanish literature: preoccupation with medieval chivalric virtues—in particular, questions of honor and loyalty. The novels and plays of the period almost invariably focus on a special decision involving a character's reputation as his honor or loyalty is tested. In this regard Spanish literature may be said to have remained more Catholic and medieval than that of England and France, where major Protestant movements had occurred. Two of the most important Spanish writers in this period became priests (Lope de Vega and Pedro Calderón de la Barca), and the one generally acknowledged to be the greatest Spanish writer of all time, Cervantes, was preoccupied in his work with the strengths and weaknesses of religious idealism.

Cervantes was born in Alcalá, the son of a nomadic physician. Having received only a smattering of formal education, he educated himself by insatiable reading in vernacular literature and immersion in the "school of life." As a young man he worked in Rome for a Spanish cardinal. In 1570 he became a soldier and was decorated for gallantry in the Battle of Lepanto (1571). While he was returning to Spain in 1575, his ship was captured by pirates, and Cervantes spent five years as a slave in Algiers. On his release and return to Spain, he held many odd jobs, among them that of a tax collector. He was several times imprisoned for padding his accounts. He began to write his most famous work, *Don Quixote,* in 1603, while languishing in prison.

The author of Don Quixote, *Miguel de Cervantes Saavedra* (1547–1616), *generally acknowledged to be the greatest Spanish writer.* [*Library of Congress*]

The first part of *Don Quixote* appeared in 1605. If, as many argue, the intent of this work was to satirize the chivalric romances so popular in Spain, Cervantes nonetheless failed to conceal his deep affection for the character he created as an object of ridicule, Don Quixote. The work is satire only on the surface and has remained as much an object of study by philosophers and theologians as by students of Spanish literature. Don Quixote, a none-too-stable middle-aged man, was presented by Cervantes as one driven mad by reading too many chivalric romances. He finally comes to believe that he is an aspirant to knighthood and must prove by brave deeds his worthiness of knightly rank. To this end he acquires a rusty suit of armor, mounts an aged steed (named Rozinante), and chooses for his inspiration a quite unworthy peasant girl, Dulcinea, whom he fancies to be a noble lady to whom he can, with honor, dedicate his life.

Don Quixote's foil in the story—Sancho Panza, a clever, worldly-wise peasant who serves as his squire—is an equally fascinating character. Sancho Panza watches with bemused skepticism, but also with genuine sympathy, as his lord does battle with a windmill (which he mistakes for a dragon) and repeatedly makes a fool of himself as he gallops across the countryside. The story ends tragically with Don Quixote's humiliating defeat by a well-meaning friend, who, disguised as a knight, bests Don Quixote in combat and forces him to renounce his quest for knighthood. The humiliated Don Quixote does not, however, come to his senses as a result. He returns sadly to his village to die a shamed and broken-hearted old man.

Throughout *Don Quixote* Cervantes juxtaposed the down-to-earth realism of Sancho Panza with the old-fashioned religious idealism of Don Quixote. The reader perceives that Cervantes admired the one as much as the other and meant to portray both as representing attitudes necessary for a happy life. If they are to be truly happy, men and women need dreams, even impossible ones, just as much as they need a sense of reality.

Don Quixote as imagined by the nineteenth-century French artist Honoré Daumier (1808–1879). *Cervantes' novel has delighted readers for four centuries.* [*Giraudon*]

William Shakespeare (1564–1616)

Shakespeare, the greatest playwright in the English language, was born in Stratford-on-Avon, where he lived almost all of his life except for the years when he wrote in London. There is much less factual knowledge about him than one would expect of such an important figure. Shakespeare married in 1582 at the early age of eighteen, and he and his wife, Anne Hathaway, had three children (two were twins) by 1585. He apparently worked as a schoolteacher for a time and in this capacity acquired his broad knowledge of Renaissance learning and literature. The argument of some scholars that he was an untutored natural genius is highly questionable. His own learning and his enthusiasm for the education of his day are manifest in the many learned allusions that appear in his plays.

Shakespeare enjoyed the life of a country gentleman. There is none of the Puritan distress over worldliness in his work. He took the new commercialism and the bawdy pleasures of the Elizabethan Age in stride and with amusement. The few allusions to the Puritans that exist in his works appear to be more critical than complimentary. In matters of politics, as in those of religion, he was very much a man of his time and not inclined to offend his queen.

That Shakespeare was interested in politics is apparent from his history plays and the references to contemporary political events that fill all his plays. He seems to have viewed government simply, however, through the character of the individual ruler, whether Richard III or Elizabeth Tudor, not in terms of ideal systems or social goals. By modern standards he was a political conservative, accepting the social rankings and the power structure of his day and demonstrating unquestioned patriotism.

Shakespeare knew the theater as one who participated in every phase of its life—as a playwright, an actor, and a part owner of a theater. He was a member and principal dramatist of a famous company of actors known as the King's Men. During the tenure of Edmund Tilney, who was Queen Elizabeth's Master of Revels during the greater part of Shakespeare's active period (1590–1610), many of Shakespeare's plays were performed at court. The queen enthusiastically patronized plays and pageants.

Elizabethan drama was already a distinctive form when Shakespeare began writing. Unlike

The English dramatist and poet, William Shakespeare. This engraving by Martin Droeshout appears on the title page of the collected edition of his plays published in 1623 and is probably as close as we shall come to knowing what he looked like. [*New York Public Library*]

French drama of the seventeenth century, which was dominated by the court and classical models, English drama developed in the sixteenth and seventeenth centuries as a blending of many extant forms, ranging from classical comedies and tragedies to the medieval morality play and contemporary Italian short stories. In Shakespeare's own library one could find Holinshed's and other English chronicles; the works of Plutarch, Ovid, and Vergil, among other Latin authors; Arthurian romances and popular songs and fables; the writings of Montaigne and Rabelais; and the major English poets and prose writers.

Two contemporaries, Thomas Kyd and Christopher Marlowe, especially influenced Shakespeare's tragedies. Kyd (1558–1594) was the author of the first dramatic version of *Hamlet* and a master at weaving together motive and plot. The tragedies of Marlowe (1564–1593) set a model for character, poetry, and style that only Shakespeare among the English playwrights of the period surpassed. Shakespeare's work was an original synthesis of the best past and current achievements. He mastered the psychology of human motivation and passion and had a unique talent for psychological penetration.

Shakespeare wrote histories, comedies, and tragedies. *Richard III* (1593), a very early play, stands out among the examples of the first genre, although some historians have criticized as historically inaccurate his patriotic depiction of Richard, the foe of Henry Tudor, as an unprincipled villain. Shakespeare's comedies, although not attaining the heights of his tragedies, surpass in originality his history plays. Save for *The Tempest* (1611), his last play, the

This 1596 sketch of the interior of the Swan Theater in London by Johannis de Witt, a Dutch visitor, is the only known contemporary view of an Elizabethan playhouse. In this kind of setting the plays of Marlowe, Shakespeare, Jonson, and their fellows were first seen. [*University Library, Utrecht*]

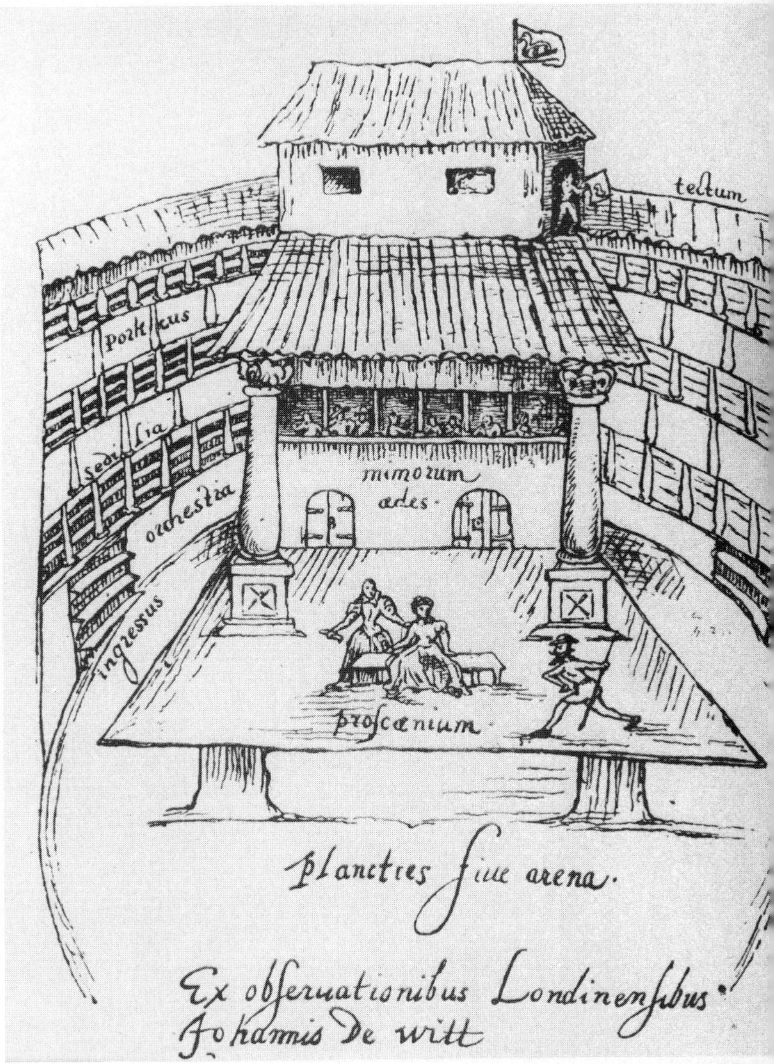

comedies most familiar to modern readers were written between 1598 and 1602: *Much Ado About Nothing* (1598–1599), *As You Like It* (1598–1600), and *Twelfth Night* (1602).

The tragedies are considered his unique achievement. Four of these were written within a three-year period: *Hamlet* (1603), *Othello* (1604), *King Lear* (1605), and *Macbeth* (1606). The most original of the tragedies, *Romeo and Juliet* (1597), transformed an old popular story into a moving drama of "star-cross'd lovers." Both Romeo and Juliet, denied a marriage by their factious families, die tragic deaths. Romeo, finding Juliet and thinking her dead after she has taken a sleeping potion, poisons himself. Juliet, awakening to find Romeo dead, stabs herself to death with his dagger.

Throughout his lifetime and ever since, Shakespeare has been immensely popular with both the playgoer and the play reader. As Ben Jonson, a contemporary classical dramatist who created his own school of poets, aptly put it in a tribute affixed to the First Folio edition of Shakespeare's plays (1623): "He was not of an age, but for all time."

The English writer and poet John Milton in an engraving by William Faithorne—one of the few authentic contemporary likenesses of him. [*Library of Congress*]

John Milton (1608–1674)

John Milton was the son of a devout Puritan father. Educated at Saint Paul's School and then at Christ's College of Cambridge University, he became a careful student of Christian and pagan classics. In 1638 he traveled to Italy, where he found in the lingering Renaissance a very congenial intellectual atmosphere. The Phlegraean Fields near Naples, a volcanic region, later became the model for hell in *Paradise Lost,* and it is suspected by some scholars that the Villa d'Este provided the model for paradise in *Paradise Regained.* Milton remained throughout his life a man more at home in the Italian Renaissance, with its high ideals and universal vision, than in the strife-torn England of the seventeenth century.

A man of deep inner conviction and principle, Milton believed that standing a test of character was the most important thing in an individual's life. This belief informed his own personal life and is the subject of much of his literary work. An early poem, *Lycidas,* was a pastoral elegy dealing with one who lived well but not long, Edward King, a close college friend who tragically drowned. In 1639 Milton joined the Puritan struggle against Charles I and Archbishop Laud. Employing his literary talents as a pamphleteer, he defended the presbyterian form of church government against the episcopacy and supported other Puritan reforms. After a month-long unsuccessful marriage in 1642 (a marriage later reconciled), he wrote several tracts in defense of the right to divorce. These writings became a factor in Parliament's passage of a censorship law in 1643, against which Milton wrote an eloquent defense of the freedom of the press, *Areopagitica* (1644).

Until the upheavals of the civil war moderated his views, Milton believed that government should have the least possible control over the private lives of individuals. When Parliament divided into Presbyterians and Independents, he took the side of the latter, who wanted to dissolve the national church altogether in favor of the local autonomy of individual congregations. He also defended the execution of Charles I in a tract on the *Tenure of Kings and Magistrates.* After his intense labor on this tract his eyesight failed. Milton was totally blind when he wrote his acclaimed masterpieces.

Paradise Lost, completed in 1665 and published in 1667, is a study of the destructive qualities of pride and the redeeming possibilities of humility. It elaborates in traditional Christian language and concept the revolt of

Satan in heaven and the fall of Adam on earth. The motives of Satan and all who rebel against God intrigued Milton. His proud but tragic Satan, one of the great figures of all literature, represents the absolute corruption of potential greatness.

In *Paradise Lost* Milton aspired to give England a lasting epic like that given Greece in Homer's *Iliad* and ancient Rome in Vergil's *Aeneid.* In choosing biblical subject matter, he revealed the influence of contemporary theology. Milton tended to agree with the Arminians, who, unlike the extreme Calvinists, did not believe that all worldly events, including the Fall of Man, were immutably fixed in the eternal decree of God. Milton shared the Arminian belief that human beings must take responsibility for their fate and that human efforts to improve character could, with God's grace, bring salvation.

Perhaps his own blindness, joined with the hope of making the best of a failed religious revolution, inclined Milton to sympathize with those who urged people to make the most of what they had, even in the face of seemingly sure defeat. That is a manifest concern of his last works, *Samson Agonistes,* which recounts the biblical story of Samson, and *Paradise Regained,* the story of Christ's temptation in the wilderness, both published in 1671.

John Bunyan (1628–1688)

Bunyan was the English author of two classics of sectarian Puritan spirituality: *Grace Abounding* (1666) and *The Pilgrim's Progress* (1678). A Bedford tinker, his works speak especially for the seventeenth-century working people and popular religious culture. Bunyan received only the most basic education before taking up his father's craft. He was drafted into Oliver Cromwell's revolutionary army in 1644 and served for two years, although without seeing actual combat. The visionary fervor of the New Model Army and the imagery of warfare abound in Bunyan's work.

After the restoration of the monarchy in 1660, Bunyan went to prison for his fiery preaching and remained there for twelve years. Had he been willing to agree to give up preaching, he might have been released much sooner. But Puritans considered the compromise of one's beliefs a tragic flaw, and Bunyan steadfastly refused all such suggestions.

During this period of imprisonment Bunyan wrote his famous autobiography, *Grace Abounding.* It is both a very personal statement and a model for the faithful. Like *The Pilgrim's Progress,* Bunyan's later masterpiece, *Grace Abounding* expresses Puritan piety at its most fervent. Puritans believed that individuals could do absolutely nothing to save themselves, and this made them extremely restless and introspective. The individual believer could only trust that God had placed her or him among the elect and try each day to live a life that reflected such a favored status. So long as men and women struggled successfully against the flesh and the world, they had presumptive evidence that they were among God's elect. To falter or to become complacent in the face of temptation was to cast doubt on one's faith and salvation and even to raise the specter of eternal damnation.

This anxious questing for salvation was the subject of *The Pilgrim's Progress,* a work unique in its contribution to Western religious symbolism and imagery. The story of the journey of Christian and his friends Hopeful and Faithful to the Celestial City, it teaches that one must deny spouse, children, and all earthly security and go in search of "Life, life, eternal life." During the long journey, the travelers must resist the temptations of Worldly-Wiseman and Vanity Fair, pass through the Slough of Despond, and endure a long dark night in Doubting Castle, their faith being tested at every turn. Bunyan later wrote a work tracing the progress of Christian's opposite, *The Life and Death of Mr. Badman* (1680), the story of a man so addicted to the bad habits of Restoration society, of which Bunyan strongly disapproved, that he journeyed steadfastly not to heaven but to hell.

MAJOR WORKS OF SEVENTEENTH-CENTURY LITERATURE AND PHILOSOPHY

King Lear (Shakespeare)	1605
Don Quixote, Part I (Cervantes)	1605
Leviathan (Hobbes)	1651
Provincial Letters (Pascal)	1656–1657
Paradise Lost (Milton)	1667
Ethics (Spinoza)	1677
The Pilgrim's Progress (Bunyan)	1678
Treatises of Government (Locke)	1690
An Essay Concerning Human Understanding (Locke)	1690

The loss of national unity during the Puritan struggle against the Stuart monarchy and the Anglican church took its toll on English literature and drama during the seventeenth century. In 1642 the Puritans had closed the theaters of London. They were reopened after the Restoration of Charles II in 1660, and drama revived following the long Puritan interregnum.

Literary thought thereafter became less experimental and adopted proven classical forms, as a new movement to subject reality to the strict rules of reason began. During the so-called Augustan Age, from John Dryden (1631–1700) to Alexander Pope (1688–1744), writers turned away from the universal ideals and the transcendental concerns of the Elizabethans and the Puritan divines. As in France, where the French comedy writer Molière (1622–1673) is the outstanding example, English writers tried to please the royal court and aristocracy by turning to more earthy and popular topics.

Blaise Pascal (1623–1662)

Pascal, a French mathematician and a physical scientist widely acclaimed by his contemporaries, surrendered all his wealth to pursue an austere, self-disciplined life. Torn between the continuing dogmatism and the new skepticism of the seventeenth century, he aspired to write a work that would refute both the Jesuits, whose casuistry (i.e., arguments designed to

Pascal Meditates on Human Beings As Thinking Creatures

Pascal was both a religious and a scientific writer. Unlike other scientific thinkers of the seventeenth century, he was not overly optimistic about the ability of science to improve the human condition. Pascal believed that science and philosophy would instead help human beings to understand their situation better. In these passages from his *Pensées (Thoughts),* he discussed the uniqueness of human beings as the creatures who alone in all the universe are capable of thinking.

339

I can well conceive a man without hands, feet, head (for it is only experience which teaches us that the head is more necessary than feet). But I cannot conceive man without thought; he would be a stone or a brute.

344

Reason commands us far more imperiously than a master; for in disobeying the one we are unfortunate, and in disobeying the other we are fools.

346

Thought constitutes the greatness of man.

347

Man is but a reed, the most feeble thing in nature; but he is a thinking reed. The entire universe need not arm itself to crush him. A vapour, a drop of water suffices to kill him. But, if the universe were to crush him, man would still be more noble than that which killed him, because he knows that he dies and the advantage which the universe has over him; the universe knows nothing of this.

All our dignity consists, then, in thought. By it we must elevate ourselves, and not by space and time which we cannot fill. Let us endeavour, then, to think well; this is the principle of morality.

348

A thinking reed—*It is not from space that I must seek my dignity, but from the government of my thought. I shall have no more if I possess worlds. By space the universe encompasses and swallows me up like an atom; by thought I comprehend the world.*

Blaise Pascal, *Pensées and The Provincial Letters* (New York: Modern Library, 1941), pp. 115–116.

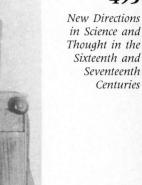

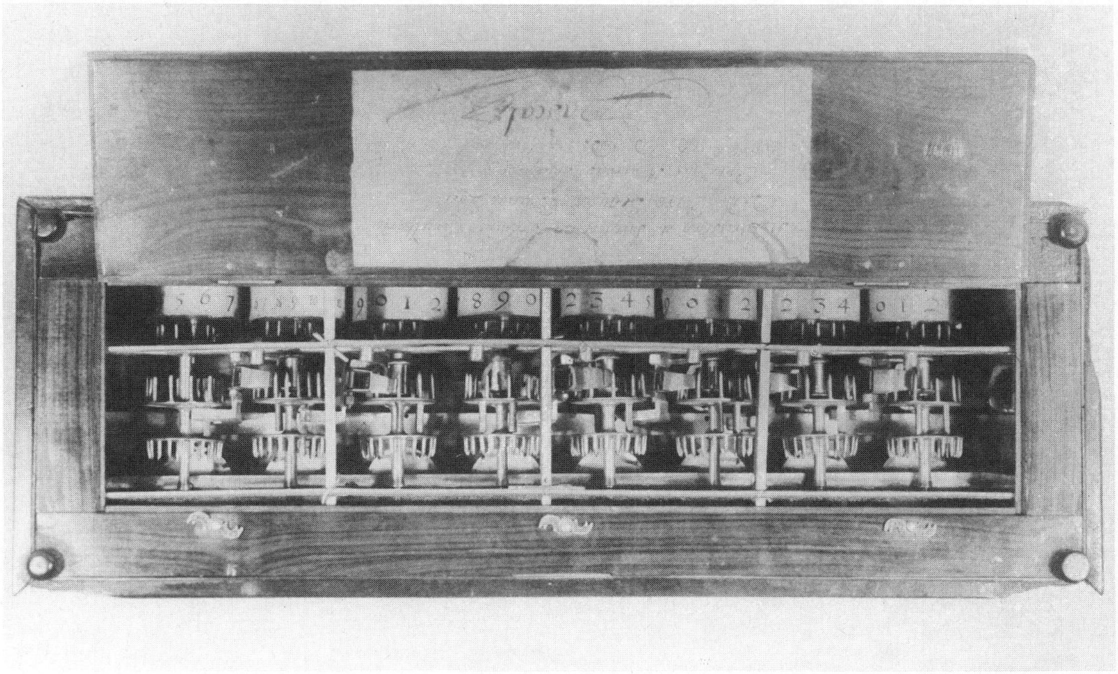

Pascal invented this adding machine, the ancestor of all mechanical calculators, about 1644. *It has eight wheels with ten cogs each, corresponding to the numbers 0–9. The wheels move forward for addition, backward for subtraction.* [*Musee des Techniques, Paris*]

minimize and even excuse sinful acts) he considered a distortion of Christian teaching, and the skeptics of his age, who either denied religion altogether (atheists) or accepted it only as it conformed to reason (deists). Such a definitive work was never realized, and his views on these matters exist only in piecemeal form. He wrote against the Jesuits in his *Provincial Letters* (1656–1657), and he left behind a provocative collection of reflections on humankind and religion that was published posthumously under the title *Pensées.*

Pascal allied himself with the Jansenists, seventeenth-century Catholic opponents of the Jesuits. His sister was a member of the Jansenist community of Port-Royal near Paris. The Jansenists shared with the Calvinists Saint Augustine's belief in human beings' total sinfulness, their eternal predestination by God, and their complete dependence on faith and grace for knowledge of God and salvation.

Pascal believed that reason and science, although attesting to human dignity, remained of no avail in matters of religion. Here only the reasons of the heart and a "leap of faith" could prevail. Pascal saw two essential truths in the Christian religion: that a loving God, worthy of human attainment, exists, and that human beings, because they are corrupted in nature, are utterly unworthy of God. Pascal believed that the atheists and the deists of the age had spurned the lesson of reason. For him rational analysis of the human condition attested humankind's utter mortality and corruption and exposed the weakness of reason itself in resolving the problems of human nature and destiny. Reason should rather drive those who truly heed it to faith and dependence on divine grace.

Pascal made a famous wager with the skeptics. It is a better bet, he argued, to believe that God exists and to stake everything on his promised mercy than not to do so, because if God does exist, everything will be gained by the believer, whereas the loss incurred by having believed in Him should He prove not to exist is by comparison very slight.

Convinced that belief in God improved life psychologically and disciplined it morally, regardless of whether or not God proved in the end to exist, Pascal worked to strengthen traditional religious belief. He urged his contemporaries to seek self-understanding by "learned ignorance" and to discover humankind's

Even before Pascal's day, of course, there was a tradition of elaborate mechanical devices throughout Europe. For example, by 1500, *there were public clocks in practically every town. One of the most famous is the astronomical clock of Strasbourg cathedral in France, which presents a parade of allegorical figures every day at noon.* [*French Government Tourist Office, New York*]

The Glockenspiel, or clock performance, occurring hourly at the Munich city hall, is another ingenious time-keeping device. [*German Information Center, New York*]

greatness by recognizing its misery. Thereby he hoped to counter what he believed to be the false optimism of the new rationalism and science.

Baruch Spinoza (1632–1677)

The most controversial thinker of the seventeenth century was Baruch Spinoza, the son of a Jewish merchant of Amsterdam. Spinoza's philosophy caused his excommunication by his own synagogue in 1656. In 1670 he published his *Treatise on Religious and Political Philosophy,* a work that criticized the dogmatism of Dutch Calvinists and championed freedom of thought. During his lifetime both Jews and Protestants attacked him as an atheist.

Spinoza's most influential writing, the *Ethics,* was published after his death in 1677. Religious leaders universally condemned it for its apparent espousal of pantheism. God and nature were so closely identified by Spinoza that little room seemed left either for divine revelation in Scripture or for the personal immortality of the soul, denials equally repugnant to Jews and to Christians. The *Ethics* was a very complicated work, written in the spirit of the new science as a geometrical system of definitions, axioms, and propositions. Spinoza divided the work into five parts, which dealt with God, the mind, emotions, human bondage, and human freedom.

The most controversial part of the *Ethics* deals with the nature of substance and of God. According to Spinoza, there is but one substance, which is self-caused, free, and infinite, and God is that substance. From this definition it follows that everything that exists is in God and cannot even be conceived of apart from Him. Such a doctrine is not literally pantheistic because God is still seen to be more than the created world that He, as primal substance, embraces. It may perhaps best be described as *panentheism:* the teaching that all that is is within God, yet God remains more than and beyond the natural world. Nonetheless, in Spinoza's view, statements about the natural world are also statements about divine nature. Mind and matter are seen to be extensions of the infinite substance of God; what transpires in the world of humankind and nature is a necessary outpouring of the divine.

Such teaching seemed to portray the world as eternal and human actions as unfree and inevitable. Jews and Christians have traditionally condemned such teachings because they deny the creation of the world by God in time and destroy any voluntary basis for personal reward and punishment.

Spinoza found enthusiastic supporters, however, in the nineteenth-century German philosopher Georg Wilhelm Friedrich Hegel and in romantic writers of the same century, especially Johann Wolfgang von Goethe and Percy Bysshe Shelley. Modern thinkers who are unable to accept traditional religious language and doctrines have continued to find in the teaching of Spinoza a congenial rational religion.

Thomas Hobbes (1588–1679)

Thomas Hobbes was incontestably the most original political philosopher of the seventeenth century. The son of a clergyman, he was educated at Oxford University. Although he never broke with the Church of England, he came to share basic Calvinist beliefs, especially the low view of human nature and the ideal of a commonwealth based on a covenant, both of which found eloquent expression in Hobbes's political philosophy.

An urbane and much-traveled man, Hobbes enthusiastically supported the new scientific movement. He worked as tutor and secretary to three earls of Devonshire over a fifty-year period. During the 1630s he visited Paris, where he came to know Descartes, and after the outbreak of the Puritan Revolution in 1640, he lived as an exile in Paris until 1651. In 1646 Hobbes became the tutor of the Prince of Wales, the future Charles II, and remained on good terms with him after the restoration of the Stuart monarchy. Hobbes also spent time with Galileo in Italy and took a special interest in the works of William Harvey (1578–1657). Harvey was a physiologist famed for the discovery of how blood circulated through the body; his scientific writings influenced Hobbes's own tracts on bodily motions. Hobbes became an expert in geometry and optics. He was also highly trained in classical languages, and his first published work was a translation of Thucydides' *History of the Peloponnesian War,* the first English translation of this work, which is still reprinted today.

The English Civil War made Hobbes a political philosopher. In 1651 his *Leviathan* appeared. Written as the concluding part of a broad philosophical system that analyzed physical bodies and human nature, the work established Hobbes as a major European thinker. Its subject was the political consequences of human passions and its originality lay in (1) its making natural law, rather than common law (i.e., custom or precedent), the basis of all positive law and (2) its defense of a representative theory of absolute authority against the theory of the divine right of kings. Hobbes maintained that statute law found its justification only as an expression of the law of nature and that political authority came to rulers only by way of the consent of the people.

Hobbes viewed humankind and society in a thoroughly materialistic and mechanical way. Human beings are defined as a collection of material particles in motion. All their psychological processes begin with and are derived from bare sensation, and all their motivations are egoistical, intended to increase pleasure and minimize pain. The human power of reasoning, which Hobbes defined unspectacularly as a process of adding and subtracting the consequences of agreed-upon general names of things, develops only after years of concentrated industry. Human will Hobbes defined as simply "the last appetite before choice."

Despite this mechanistic view of human beings, Hobbes believed they could accomplish much by the reasoned use of science. All was contingent, however, on the correct use of that greatest of all human creations, one compounded of the powers of most people: the commonwealth, in which people are united by their consent in one all-powerful person.

The key to Hobbes's political philosophy is a brilliant myth of the original state of humankind. According to this myth, human beings in the natural state are generally inclined to a "perpetual and restless desire of power after power that ceases only in death."[7] As all people desire and, in the state of nature, have a natural right to everything, their equality breeds enmity, competition, diffidence, and desire for glory begets perpetual quarreling—"a war of every man against every man."[8] As Hobbes put it in a famous summary:

> In such condition there is no place for industry, because the fruit thereof is uncertain; and consequently no culture of the earth; no navigation nor use of the commodities that may be imported by sea; no commodious building; no instruments of moving and removing such things as require much force; no knowledge of the face of the earth; no account of

[7]*Leviathan Parts I and II,* ed. by H. W. Schneider (Indianapolis: Bobbs-Merrill, 1958), p. 86.

[8]Ibid., p. 106.

Non est potestas Super Terram quæ Comparetur ei Iob. 41. 24.

The famous title-page illustration for Hobbe's Leviathan. *The ruler is pictured as absolute lord of his lands, but note that he incorporates the mass of individuals whose self-interests are best served by their willingness to accept him and cooperate with him.*

time; no arts; no letters; no society; and, which is worst of all, continual fear and danger of violent death; and the life of man solitary, poor, nasty, brutish, and short.[9]

Whereas earlier and later philosophers saw the original human state as a paradise from which humankind had fallen, Hobbes saw it as a corruption from which only society had delivered people. Contrary to the views of Aristotle and Christian thinkers like Thomas Aquinas, in the view of Hobbes human beings are not by nature sociable, political animals; they are self-centered beasts, laws unto themselves, utterly without a master unless one is imposed by force.

According to Hobbes, people escape the impossible state of nature only by entering a social contract that creates a commonwealth tightly ruled by law and order. They are driven to this solution by their fear of death and their desire for "commodious living." The social contract obliges every person, for the sake of peace and self-defense, to agree to set aside personal rights to all things and to be content with as much liberty against others as he or she would allow others against himself or herself. All agree to live according to a secularized version of the golden rule: "Do not that to another which you would not have done to yourself."[10]

Because words and promises are insufficient to guarantee this state, the social contract also establishes the coercive force necessary to com-

[9]Ibid., p. 107.

[10]Ibid., p. 130.

pel compliance with the covenant. Hobbes believed that the dangers of anarchy were always far greater than those of tyranny and conceived of the ruler as absolute and unlimited in power, once established in office. There is no room in Hobbes's political philosophy for political protest in the name of individual conscience, nor for resistance to legitimate authority by private individuals—features of the *Leviathan* criticized by contemporary Catholics and Puritans alike. To his critics, who lamented the loss of their individual liberty in such a government, Hobbes pointed out the alternative:

> The greatest that in any form of government can possibly happen to the people in general is scarce sensible in respect of the miseries and horrible calamities that accompany a civil war or that dissolute condition of masterless men, without subjection to laws and a coercive power to tie their hands from rapine and revenge.[11]

It is puzzling why Hobbes believed that absolute rulers would be more benevolent and less egoistic than all other people. He simply placed the highest possible value on a strong, efficient ruler who could save human beings from the chaos attendant on the state of nature. In the end it mattered little to Hobbes whether this ruler was Charles I, Oliver Cromwell, or Charles II, each of whom received Hobbes's enthusiastic support, once he was established in power.

John Locke (1632–1704)

Locke has proved to be the most influential political thinker of the seventeenth century. His political philosophy found expression in the Glorious Revolution of 1688–1689. Although he was not as original as Hobbes, his political writings became a major source of the later Enlightenment criticism of absolutism, and they gave inspiration to both the American and the French revolutions.

Locke's sympathies lay with the Puritans and the Parliamentary forces that challenged the Stuart monarchy. His father fought with the Parliamentary army during the English Civil War. Locke read deeply in the works of Francis Bacon, René Descartes, and Isaac Newton and was a close friend of the English physicist and chemist Robert Boyle (1627–1691). Some view Locke as the first philosopher to synthesize the rationalism of Descartes and the experimental science of Bacon, Newton, and Boyle.

Locke was for a brief period strongly influenced by the political views of Hobbes. This influence changed, however, after his association with Anthony Ashley Cooper, the earl of Shaftesbury. In 1667 Locke moved into Shaftesbury's London home and served him as physician, secretary, and traveling companion. A zealous Protestant, Shaftesbury was considered by his contemporaries a radical in both religion and politics. He organized an unsuccessful rebellion against Charles II in 1682. Although Locke had no part in the plot, both he and Shaftesbury were forced to flee to Holland after its failure.

Locke's two most famous works are the *Essay Concerning Human Understanding* (1690), completed during his exile in Holland, and the *Two Treatises of Government* (1690). In the *Essay Concerning Human Understanding* Locke stressed the creative function of the human mind. He believed that the mind at birth was a blank tablet. There are no innate ideas; all knowledge is derived from actual sensual experience. Human ideas are either simple (that is, passive receptions from daily experience) or complex (that is, products of sustained mental exercise). What people know is not the external world in itself but the results of the interaction of the mind with the outside world. Locke also denied the existence of innate moral norms. Moral ideals are the product of humankind's subjection of their self-love to their reason—a freely chosen self-disciplining of natural desires so that conflict in conscience may be avoided and happiness attained. Locke also believed that the teachings of Christianity were identical to what uncorrupted reason taught about the good life. A rational person would therefore always live according to simple Christian precepts. Although Locke firmly denied toleration to Catholics and atheists—both were considered subversive in England—he otherwise sanctioned a variety of Protestant religious practice.

Locke wrote *Two Treatises of Government* during the reign of Charles II. They oppose the argument that rulers are absolute in their power. According to the preface of the published edition, which appeared after the Glorious Revolution, the treatises were written "to justify to the world the people of England, whose love of their just and natural rights, with their resolution to preserve them, saved

[11] Ibid., p. 152.

John Locke Explains the Sources of Human Knowledge

An Essay Concerning Human Understanding (1690) may be the most influential philosophical work ever written in English. Locke's most fundamental idea, which is explicated in the passage below, is that human knowledge is grounded in the experiences of the senses and in the reflection of the mind on those experiences. He rejected any belief in innate ideas. His emphasis on experience led to the wider belief that human beings are creatures of their environment. After Locke, numerous writers argued that human beings could be improved if the environment in which they lived were reformed.

Let us then suppose the mind to be, as we say, white paper void of all characters, without any ideas. *How comes it to be furnished? Whence comes it by that vast store which the busy and boundless fancy of man has painted on it with an almost endless variety? Whence has it all the materials of reason and knowledge? To this I answer, in one word, from* experience; *in that all our knowledge is founded, and from that it ultimately derives itself. Our observation, employed either about* external sensible objects, or about the internal operations of our minds perceived and reflected on by ourselves, is that which supplies our understanding with all the materials of thinking. *These two are the fountains of knowledge, from whence all the ideas we have, or can naturally have, do spring.*

First, our senses, *conversant about particular sensible objects, do* convey into the mind *several distinct* perceptions *of things, according to those various ways wherein those objects do affect them. And thus we come by those* ideas we *have of* yellow, white, heat, cold, soft, hard, bitter, sweet, *and all those which we call sensible qualities. . . . This great source of most of the* ideas *we have, depending wholly upon our senses, and derived by them to the understanding, I call SENSATION.*

Secondly, the other fountain from which experience furnisheth the understanding with ideas *is the* perception of the operations of our own minds *within us, as it is employed about the* ideas *it has got. . . . And such are* perception, thinking, doubting, believing, reasoning, knowing, willing, *and all the different actings of our own minds. . . . I call this REFLECTION, the* ideas *it affords being such only as the mind gets by reflecting on its own operations within itself. . . . These two, I say, viz. external material things as the objects of SENSATION, and the operations of our own minds within as the objects of REFLECTION, are to me the only originals from whence all our* ideas *take their beginnings. . . .*

The understanding seems to me not to have the least glimmering of any ideas *which it doth not receive from one of these two.*

John Locke, *An Essay Concerning Human Understanding,* Vol. 1 (London: Everyman's Library, 1961), pp. 77–78.

the nation when it was on the brink of slavery and ruin."[12] Locke rejected particularly the views of Sir Robert Filmer and Thomas Hobbes.

Filmer had written a work entitled *Patriarcha, or the Natural Power of Kings* (published in 1680), in which the rights of kings over their subjects were compared with the rights of fathers over their children. Locke devoted his entire first treatise to a refutation of Filmer's argument, maintaining not only that the analogy was inappropriate, but that even the right of a father over his children could not be construed as absolute and was subject to a higher natural law. Both fathers and rulers, Locke argued, remain bound to the law of nature, which is the voice of reason, teaching that "all mankind [are] equal and independent, [and] no one ought to harm another in his life,

[12]*The Second Treatise of Government,* ed. by T. P. Peardon (Indianapolis: Bobbs-Merrill, 1952), Preface.

health, liberty, or possessions,"[13] inasmuch as all human beings are the images and property of God. According to Locke, people enter into social contracts, empowering legislatures and monarchs to "umpire" their disputes, precisely in order to preserve their natural rights, not to give rulers an absolute power over them. Rulers are rather "entrusted" with the preservation of the law of nature and transgress it at their peril:

> Whenever that end [namely, the preservation of life, liberty, and property for which power is given to rulers by a commonwealth] is manifestly neglected or opposed, the trust must necessarily be forfeited and the power devolve into the hands of those that gave it, who may place it anew where they think best for their safety and security.[14]

From Locke's point of view, absolute monarchy is "inconsistent" with civil society and can be "no form of civil government at all."

Locke's main differences with Hobbes stemmed from the latter's well-known views on the state of nature. Locke believed that the natural human state was one of perfect freedom and equality. Here all enjoyed, in unregulated fashion, the natural rights of life, liberty, and property. The only thing lacking in the state of nature was a single authority to give judgment when disputes inevitably arose because of the natural freedom and equality possessed by all. Contrary to the view of Hobbes, human beings in their natural state were creatures not of monomaniacal passion but of extreme goodwill and rationality. And they did not surrender their natural rights unconditionally when they entered the social contract; rather, they established a means whereby these rights could be better preserved. The state of warfare that Hobbes believed characterized the state of nature emerged for Locke only when rulers failed in their responsibility to preserve the freedoms of the state of nature and attempted to enslave people by absolute rule, that is, to remove them from their "natural" condition. Only then did the peace, goodwill, mutual assistance, and preservation in which human beings naturally live and socially ought to live come to an end and a state of war emerge.

[13] Ibid., Ch. 2, sects. 4–6, pp. 4–6.

[14] Ibid., Ch. 13, sect. 149, p. 84.

Suggested Readings

V. M. Brittain, *Valiant Pilgrim: The Story of John Bunyan and Puritan England* (1950). Illustrated historical biography.

K. C. Brown, *Hobbes Studies* (1965). A collection of important essays.

Herbert Butterfield, *The Origins of Modern Science 1300–1800* (1949). An authoritative survey.

John Caird, *Spinoza* (1971). Intellectual biography by a philosopher.

Norman F. Cantor (Ed.), *Seventeenth Century Rationalism: Bacon and Descartes* (1969).

Cervantes, *The Portable Cervantes,* ed. and trans. by Samuel Putnam (1969).

Hardin Craig, *Shakespeare: A Historical and Critical Study with Annotated Texts of Twenty-one Plays* (1958).

Maurice Cranston, *Locke* (1961). Brief biographical sketch.

J. Dunn, *The Political Thought of John Locke; An Historical Account of the "Two Treatises of Government"* (1969). An excellent introduction.

Manuel Duran, *Cervantes* (1974). Detailed biography.

Galileo Galilei, *Discoveries and Opinions of Galileo,* ed. and trans. by Stillman Drake (1957).

A. R. Hall, *The Scientific Revolution 1500–1800: The Formation of the Modern Scientific Attitude* (1966). Traces undermining of traditional science and rise of new sciences.

Thomas Hobbes, *Leviathan. Parts I and II,* ed. by H. W. Schneider (1958).

Margaret Jacob, *The Newtonians and the English Revolution* (1976). A controversial book that attempts to relate science and politics.

T. E. Jessop, *Thomas Hobbes* (1960). Brief biographical sketch.

H. Kearney, *Science and Change 1500–1700* (1971). Broad survey.

Alexander Koyre, *From the Closed World to the Infinite Universe* (1957). Treated from perspective of the historian of ideas.

Thomas S. Kuhn, *The Copernican Revolution* (1957). A scholarly treatment.

Peter Laslett, *Locke's Two Treatises of Government,* 2nd ed. (1970). Definitive texts with very important introductions.

John D. North, *Isaac Newton* (1967). Brief biography.

Alan G. R. Smith, *Science and Society* (1973). A readable, well-illustrated history of the Scientific Revolution.

E. M. W. Tillyard, *Milton* (1952). Brief biographical sketch.

Richard S. Westfall, *Never at Rest: A Biography of Isaac Newton* (1981). A new and very important major study.

Louis XV in coronation robes, painted by Hyacinthe Rigaud in 1730. Although by no means unintelligent, Louis was lazy and pleasure-loving, and his scandalous private life lessened respect for the French monarchy. [Josse/Art Resource]

14

The Waxing and Waning of States (1686–1740)

THE LATE SEVENTEENTH and early eighteenth centuries witnessed significant shifts of power and influence among the states of Europe. Nations that had been strong lost their status as significant military and economic units. Other countries, which had in some cases figured only marginally in international relations, came to the fore. Great Britain, France, Austria, Russia, and Prussia emerged during this period as the powers that would dominate Europe until at least World War I. The establishment of their political and economic dominance occurred at the expense of Spain, the United Netherlands, Poland, Sweden, and the Ottoman Empire. Equally essential to their rise was the weakness of the Holy Roman Empire after the Treaty of Westphalia (1648).

The successful competitors for international power were those states that in differing fashions created strong central political authorities. Farsighted observers in the late seventeenth century already understood that in the future those domains that would become or remain great powers must imitate the political and military organization of Louis XIV. Monarchy alone could impose unity of purpose on the state. The turmoil of seventeenth-century civil wars and aristocratic revolts had impressed people with the value of the monarch as a guarantor of minimum domestic tranquillity. Imitation of French absolutism involved other factors besides belief in a strong monarchy. It usually required building a standing army, organizing an efficient tax structure to support the army, and establishing a bureaucracy to collect the taxes. Moreover the political classes of the country, especially the nobles, had to be converted to a sense of duty and loyalty to the central government that was more intense than their loyalty to other competing political and social institutions.

The waning powers of Europe were those whose leaders failed to achieve such effective organization. They were unable to employ their political, economic, and human resources to resist external aggression or to overcome the forces of domestic dissolution. The internal and external failures were closely related. If a state failed to maintain or establish a central political authority with sufficient power over the nobility, the cities, the guilds, and the church, it could not raise a strong army to defend its borders or its economic interests. More often than not, the key element leading to success or failure was the character, personality, and energy of the monarch.

The Maritime Powers

In western Europe, Britain and France emerged as the dominant powers. This development represented a shift of influence away from Spain and the United Netherlands. Both the latter countries had been quite strong and important during the sixteenth and seventeenth centuries, but they became negligible during the course of the eighteenth century. However, neither disappeared from the map. Both retained considerable economic vitality and influence. The difference was that France and Britain attained so much more power and economic strength.

Spain

Spanish power had depended on the influx of wealth from the Americas and on the capacity of the Spanish monarchs to rule the still largely autonomous provinces of the Iberian peninsula. The economic life of the nation was never healthy. Except for wool Spain had virtually no exports with which to pay for its imports. Instead of promoting domestic industries, the Spanish government financed imports by using the gold and silver mined in its New World empire. This external source of wealth was not certain because the treasure fleets from the New World could be and sometimes were captured by pirates or the navies of other nations. The political life of Spain was also weak. Within Castile, Aragon, Navarre, the Basque provinces, and other districts, the royal government could not operate without the close cooperation of strong local nobles and the church. From the defeat of the Spanish Armada in 1588 to the Treaty of the Pyrenees in 1659, Spain experienced a series of foreign policy reverses that harmed the domestic prestige of the monarchy. Furthermore, between 1665 and 1700 the physically malformed, dull-witted, and sexually impotent Charles II was monarch. Throughout his reign the local provincial estates and the nobility increased their power. On his death the War of the Spanish Succession saw the other powers of Europe contesting the issue of the next ruler of Spain.

The Treaty of Utrecht (1713) gave the Spanish crown to Philip V (1770–1746), who was a Bourbon and the grandson of Louis XIV. The new king should have attempted to consolidate his internal power and to protect Spanish overseas trade. However, his second wife, Elizabeth Farnese, wanted to use Spanish power to carve out interests for her sons on the Italian peninsula. Such machinations diverted government resources and allowed the nobility and the provinces to continue to assert their privileges against the authority of the monarchy. Not until the reign of Charles III (1759–1788) did Spain possess a monarch concerned with efficient administration and internal improvement. By the third quarter of the century the county was better governed, but it could no longer compete effectively in power politics.

The Netherlands

The demise of the United Netherlands occurred wholly within the eighteenth century. After the death of William III of England in 1702, the various local provinces successfully prevented the emergence of another strong *stadtholder*. Unified political leadership therefore vanished. During the earlier long wars of the Netherlands with Louis XIV and England, naval supremacy slowly but steadily had passed to the British. The fishing industry declined, and the Dutch lost their technological superiority in shipbuilding. Countries between which Dutch ships had once carried goods now came to trade directly with each other. For example, the British began to use more and more of their own vessels in the Baltic traffic with Russia. Similar stagnation overtook the Dutch domestic industries, such as textile finishing, paper making, and glass blowing. The disunity of the provinces and the absence of vigorous leadership hastened this economic decline and prevented action that might have slowed or halted it. What saved the United Netherlands from becoming completely insignificant in European matters was their continued dominance of the financial community. Well past the middle of the century their banks continued to provide loans and financing for European trade.

France After Louis XIV

Despite its military losses in the War of the Spanish Succession, France remained a great power. It was less strong in 1715 than in 1680, but it still possessed a large population, an advanced if troubled economy, and the administrative structure bequeathed it by Louis XIV. Moreover, even if France and its resources had been badly drained by the last of Louis's wars, the other major states of Europe emerged from the conflict similarly debilitated. What the country required was a period of economic recovery and consolidation, wiser political leadership, and a less ambitious foreign policy. It did enjoy a period of recovery, but the quality of its leadership was at best indifferent. Louis XIV was succeeded by his five-year-old great-grandson Louis XV (1715–1774). The young boy's uncle, the duke of Orléans, became regent and remained so until 1720. The regency further undermined the already faltering prestige of the monarchy.

The duke of Orléans was a gambler, and for a time he turned over the financial management of the kingdom to John Law (1621–1729), a Scottish mathematician and fellow gambler. Law believed that an increase in the paper money supply would stimulate the postwar economic recovery of the country. With the permission of the regent he established a bank in Paris that issued paper money. Law then organized a monopoly on trading privileges with the French colony of Louisiana in North America.

The Mississippi Company also assumed the management of the French national debt. The company issued shares of its own stock in exchange for government bonds, which had fallen sharply in value. In order to redeem large quantities of bonds, Law encouraged speculation in Mississippi Company stock. In 1719 the price of the stock rose handsomely. However, smart investors took their profits by selling their stock in exchange for money from Law's bank. Then they sought to exchange the currency for gold. To make the second transaction, they went to Law's bank, but that institution lacked sufficient gold to redeem all the money brought to it.

In February 1720 all gold payments were halted in France. Soon thereafter Law himself fled the country. The Mississippi Bubble, as the affair was called, had burst. The fiasco brought disgrace on the government that had made Law its controller general. The Mississippi Company was later reorganized and functioned quite profitably, but fear of paper money and speculation marked French economic life for the rest of the century.

The duke of Orléans made a second departure that also lessened the power of the monarchy. He attempted to draw the French nobility once again into the decision-making

The Amsterdam Exchange. By the mid-seventeenth century, when this picture was painted, Amsterdam had replaced the cities of Italy and south Germany as the leading banking center of Europe. Amsterdam retained this position until the late eighteenth century. [*Museum Boymans-van Beuningen, Rotterdam*]

John Law (1621–1729). The collapse of his bank in 1720 damaged both the French economy and the prestige of the government. [*Library of Congress*]

The impending collapse of Law's bank engendered a financial panic throughout France, as desperate investors, such as these shown here in the city of Rennes, sought to exchange their paper currency for gold and silver before the bank's supply of precious metals was exhausted. [*Musee de Bretagne, Rennes*]

processes of the government. Louis XIV had downgraded the nobility and had filled his ministries and bureaucracies with persons of nonnoble families. The regent was seeking to restore a balance. He adopted a system of councils on which the nobles were to serve along with the bureaucrats. However, the years of noble domestication at Versailles had worked too well, and the nobility seemed to lack both the talent and the desire to govern. The experiment failed.

The failure of the great French nobles to function as satisfactory councilors did not mean that they had surrendered their ancient ambition to assert their rights, privileges, and local influence over those of the monarchy. The chief feature of French political life from this time until the French Revolution was the attempt of the nobility to impose its power on the monarchy. The most effective instrument in this process was the *parlements,* or courts dominated by the nobility. The French *parlements* were very different institutions from the English Parliament. These French courts, the most important of which was the Parlement of Paris, did not have the power to legislate. Rather, they had the power to recognize or not to recognize the legality of an act or law promulgated by the monarch. By long tradition their formal approval had been required to make a royal law valid. Louis XIV had often overridden stubborn, uncooperative *parlements.* However, in another of his many major political blunders, the duke of Orléans had formally approved the reinstitution of the *parlements'* power to allow or disallow laws. Thereafter the growing financial and moral weakness of the eighteenth-century monarchy allowed these aristocratic judicial institutions to reassert their authority. This situation meant that for the rest of the century until the revolution the *parlements* became natural centers for aristocratic resistance to royal authority.

By 1726 the chief minister of the French court was Cardinal Fleury (1653–1743). He was the last of those great churchmen who had so loyally and effectively served the French monarchy. Like his seventeenth-century predecessors, the cardinals Richelieu and Mazarin, Fleury was a realist. He understood the political ambition and incapacity of the nobility and worked quietly to block their undue influence. Fleury was also aware of the precarious financial situation in which the wars of Louis XIV had left the royal treasury.

The cardinal, who was seventy-three years

Saint-Simon Shows the French Nobility's Incapacity to Govern

The regent under the young Louis XV hoped that France's nobility might assume an active role in government in place of the passive role assigned to them by Louis XIV. This plan involved displacing many nonnoble bureaucrats and others who were regarded as noble by virtue of holding office rather than by virtue of noble birth ("nobles of the robe"). As described by the duke of Saint-Simon (1675–1755), the plan failed because the real nobles proved unequal to their new duties.

The design was to begin to put the nobility into the ministry, with the dignity and authority befitting them, at the expense of the high civil servants and nobles of the robe, and by degree and according to events to guide affairs wisely so that little by little those commoners would lose all those administrative duties that are not purely judicial . . . in order to submit to the nobility all modes of administration. The difficulty was the ignorance, the frivolity, and the lack of diligence of the nobility who were accustomed to being good for nothing except getting killed, succeeding at war only by seniority, and romping around for the rest of the time in the most mortal uselessness. As a result they were devoted to idleness and disgusted with all knowledge outside war by their conditioned incapacity for being able to provide themselves with anything useful to do. It was impossible to make the first step in this direction without overturning the monster that had devoured the nobility, the controller general and the secretaries of state.

Duc de Saint-Simon, *Memories,* trans. by Frank M. Turner, cited in John Lough, *An Introduction to Eighteenth Century France* (New York: David MacKay, 1964), pp. 135–136.

old when he came to office, was determined to give the country a period of peace. He surrounded himself with generally able assistants who attempted to solve the financial problems. Part of the national debt was repudiated. New industries enjoying special privileges were established, and new roads and bridges were built. On the whole the nation prospered, but Fleury was never able to draw from the nobles or the church sufficient tax revenues to put the state on a stable financial footing.

Fleury died in 1743, having unsuccessfully attempted to prevent France from intervening in the war then raging between Austria and Prussia. All of his financial pruning and planning had come to naught. Another failure must also be credited to this elderly churchman. Despite his best efforts he had not trained Louis XV to become an effective monarch. Louis XV possessed most of the vices and almost none of

Cardinal Fleury (1653–1743), *tutor and chief minister from* 1726 *to* 1743 *of Louis XV. He gave France a period of peace and prosperity, but was unable to solve the long-term financial problems of the state.* [*Bulloz*]

Madame de Pompadour (1721–1764), *the mistress of Louis XV. A woman of beauty, cultivation, and taste, she was a notable patroness of artists, craftsmen, and writers. This portrait, which captures her grace and elegance, is by Francois Boucher* (1703–1770), *one of her favorite painters.* [*National Galleries of Scotland*]

the virtues of his great-grandfather. He wanted to hold on to absolute power but was unwilling to work the long hours required. He did not choose many wise advisers after Fleury. He was tossed about by the gossip and intrigues of the court nobles. His personal life was scandalous. His reign became more famous for his mistress, Madame de Pompadour, than for anything else. Louis XV was not an evil person but a mediocre one. And in a monarch, mediocrity was unfortunately often a greater fault than vice.

Despite this political drift France remained a great power. Its army at mid-century was still the largest and strongest military force on the Continent. Its commerce and production expanded. Its colonies produced wealth and spurred domestic industries. Its cities grew and prospered. The wealth of the nation waxed as the absolutism of the monarchy waned. France did not lack sources of power and strength, but it did lack the political leadership that could organize, direct, and inspire its people.

Great Britain: The Age of Walpole

In 1713 Britain had emerged as a victor over Louis XIV, but the nation required a period of recovery. As an institution the British monarchy was not in the degraded state of the French monarchy, but its stability was not certain. In 1714 the Hanoverian dynasty, designated by the Act of Settlement (1701), came to the throne. Almost immediately George I (1714–1727) confronted a challenge to his new title. The Stuart pretender James Edward (1688–1766), the son of James II, landed in Scotland in December 1715. His forces marched southward but met defeat less than two months later.

Although militarily successful against the pretender, the new dynasty and its supporters saw the need for consolidation. During the seventeenth century England had been one of the most politically restive countries in Europe. The closing years of Queen Anne's reign (1702–1714) had seen sharp clashes between the political factions of Whigs and Tories over the coming Treaty of Utrecht. The Tories had urged a rapid peace settlement and after 1710 had opened negotiations with France. During the same period the Whigs were seeking favor from the Elector of Hanover, who would soon be their monarch. His concern for his domains in Hanover made him unsympathetic to the Tory peace policy. In the final months of Anne's reign, some Tories, fearing loss of power under the waiting Hanoverian dynasty, opened channels of communication with the Stuart pretender; and a few even rallied to his losing cause.

Under these circumstances it was little wonder that George I, on his arrival in Britain, clearly favored the Whigs and proceeded with caution. Previously the differences between the Whigs and the Tories had been vaguely related to principle. The Tories emphasized a strong monarchy, low taxes for landowners, and firm support of the Anglican church. The Whigs supported monarchy but wanted Parliament to retain final sovereignty. They tended to favor urban commercial interests as well as the prosperity of the landowners. They encouraged a policy of religious toleration toward the Protestant nonconformists in England. Socially both groups supported the status quo. Neither was organized like a modern political party. Organizationally, outside of Parliament, each party consisted of political networks based on local political connections and local economic influence. Each group acknowledged a few spokesmen on the national level who articulated positions and principles. However, after the Hanoverian accession and the eventual Whig success in achieving the firm confidence of George I, the chief difference for almost forty years between the Whigs and the Tories was that one group did have access to public office and patronage and the other did not. This early Hanoverian proscription of Tories from public life was one of the most prominent features of the age.

The political situation after 1715 had at first remained in a state of flux, until Robert Walpole (1676–1745) took over the helm of government. This Norfolk squire had been active in the House of Commons since the reign of Queen Anne, and he had served as a cabinet minister. What gave him special prominence under the new dynasty was a British financial scandal similar to the French Mississippi Bubble.

Management of the British national debt had been assigned to the South Sea Company, which exchanged government bonds for company stock. As in the French case, the price of the stock flew high, only to crash in 1720 when prudent investors sold their holdings and took their speculative profits. Parliament intervened and, under Walpole's leadership, adopted measures to honor the national debt. To most contemporaries Walpole had saved the financial integrity of the country and, in so doing, had proved himself a person of immense administrative capacity and political ability.

Sir Robert Walpole (1676–1745) *left, shown talking to the Speaker of the House of Commons. Walpole, who dominated British political life from* 1721 *to* 1742, *is considered the first prime minister of Britain.* [*The Mansell Collection*]

George I gave Walpole his full confidence. For this reason Walpole has often been regarded as the first prime minister of Great Britain and the originator of the cabinet system of government. However, unlike a modern prime minister, he was not chosen by the majority of the House of Commons. His power largely depended on the goodwill of George I and later of George II (1727–1760). Walpole generally demanded that all of the ministers in the cabinet agree on policy, but he could not prevent frequent public differences on policy. The real source of Walpole's power was the combination of the personal support of the king, his ability to handle the House of Commons, and his iron-fisted control of government patronage. To oppose Walpole on either minor or more substantial matters was to risk the almost certain loss of government patronage for oneself, one's family, or one's friends. Through the skillful use of patronage Walpole bought support for himself and his policies from people who wanted to receive jobs, appointments, favors, and government contracts. Such corruption supplied the glue of political loyalty.

Walpole's favorite slogan was "*Quieta non movere*" (roughly, "Let sleeping dogs lie"). To that end he pursued a policy of peace abroad and promotion of the status quo at home. In this regard he and Cardinal Fleury were much alike. The structure of the eighteenth-century British House of Commons aided Walpole in his pacific policies. It was neither a democratic nor a representative body. Each of the counties elected two members. But if the more powerful landed families in a county agreed on the candidates, there was no contest. Other members were elected from units called *boroughs,* of which there were a considerable variety. There were many more borough seats than county seats. A few were large enough for elections to be relatively democratic. However, most boroughs had a very small number of electors. For example, a local municipal corporation or council of only a dozen members might have the legal right to elect a member of Parliament. In Old Sarum, one of the most famous corrupt or "rotten" boroughs, the Pitt family for many years simply bought up those pieces of property to which a vote was attached and thus in effect owned a seat in the House of Commons. Through proper electoral management, which involved favors to the electors, the House of Commons could be controlled.

The structure of Parliament and the manner in which it was elected meant that the government of England was dominated by the owners of property and by especially wealthy nobles. They did not pretend to represent people and districts or to be responsive to what would later be called public opinion. They regarded themselves as representing various economic and social interests, such as the West Indian interest, the merchant interest, or the landed interest. These owners of property were suspicious of an administrative bureaucracy controlled by the crown or its ministers. For this reason they or their agents served as local government administrators, judges, militia commanders, and tax collectors. In this sense the British nobility and other substantial landowners actually did govern the nation. And because they regarded the Parliament as the political sovereign, there was no absence of central political authority and direction. Consequently the supremacy of Parliament provided Britain with the kind of unity that elsewhere in Europe was sought through the institutions of absolutism.

British political life was genuinely more free than that on the Continent. There were real limits on the power of Robert Walpole. Parliament could not be wholly unresponsive to popular political pressure. Even with the ex-

Lady Mary Wortley Montagu Gives Advice on Election to Parliament

In this letter of 1714 Lady Mary Wortley Montagu discussed with her husband the various paths that he might follow to gain election to the British House of Commons. Note the emphasis she placed on knowing the right people and on having large amounts of money to spend on voters. Eventually her husband was elected to Parliament in a borough that was controlled through government patronage.

You seem not to have received my letters, or not to have understood them: you had been chose undoubtedly at York, if you had declared in time; but there is not any gentleman or tradesman disengaged at this time; they are treating every night. Lord Carlisle and the Thompsons have given their interest to Mr Jenkins. I agree with you of the necessity of your standing this Parliament, which, perhaps, may be more considerable than any that are to follow it; but, as you proceed, 'tis my opinion, you will spend your money and not be chose. I believe there is hardly a borough unengaged. I expect every letter should tell me you are sure of some place; and, as far as I can perceive you are sure of none. As it has been managed, perhaps it will be the best way to deposit a certain sum in some friend's hands, and buy some little Cornish borough: it would, undoubtedly, look better to be chose for a considerable town; but I take it to be now too late. If you have any thoughts of Newark, it will be absolutely necessary for you to enquire after Lord Lexington's interest; and your best way to apply yourself to Lord Holdernesse, who is both a Whig and an honest man. He is now in town, and you may enquire of him if Brigadier Sutton stands there; and if not, try to engage him for you. Lord Lexington is so ill at the Bath, that it is a doubt if he will live 'till the elections; and if he dies, one of his heiresses, and the whole interest of his estate, will probably fall on Lord Holdernesse.

'Tis a surprize to me, that you cannot make sure of some borough, when a number of your friends bring in so many Parliament-men without trouble or expense. 'Tis too late to mention it now, but you might have applied to Lady Winchester, as Sir Joseph Jekyl did last year, and by her interest the Duke of Bolton brought him in, for nothing; I am sure she would be more zealous to serve me, than Lady Jekyl.

Lord Wharncliffe (Ed.), *Letters and Works of Lady Mary Wortley Montagu,* 3rd ed., Vol. 1 (London, 1861), p. 211.

tensive use of patronage many members of Parliament maintained independent views. Newspapers and public debate flourished. Free speech could be exercised, as could freedom of association. There was no large standing army. Tories barred from political office and Whig enemies of Walpole could and did voice their opposition to his policies, as would not have been possible on the Continent.

For example, in 1733 Walpole presented to the House of Commons a scheme for an excise tax that would have raised revenue somewhat in the fashion of a modern sales tax. The public outcry in the press, on the public platform, and in the streets was so great that he eventually withdrew the measure. What the English regarded as their traditional political rights raised a real and potent barrier to the power of the government. Again in 1739, the public outcry over the Spanish treatment of British merchants in the Caribbean pushed Britain into the War of Jenkins's Ear, which Walpole opposed and deplored.

Walpole's ascendancy, which lasted until 1742, did little to raise the level of British political morality, but it brought the nation a kind of stability that it had not enjoyed for well over a century. Its foreign trade grew steadily and spread from New England to India. Agriculture improved its productivity. All forms of economic enterprise seemed to prosper. The navy became stronger. As a result of this political stability and economic growth, Great Britain became a European power of the first order and stood at the beginning of its era as a world power. Its government and economy during the next generation became a model for all progressive Europeans.

France and Great Britain in the Early Eighteenth Century

Treaty of Utrecht ends the War of the Spanish Succession	1713
George I becomes king of Great Britain and thus establishes the Hanoverian dynasty	1714
Louis XV becomes King of France	1715
Regency of the duke of Orléans in France	1715–1720
Mississippi Bubble bursts in France and South Sea Bubble bursts in Great Britain	1720
Robert Walpole dominates British politics	1720–1742
Cardinal Fleury serves as Louis XV's chief minister	1726–1743
George II becomes king of Great Britain	1727
Excise bill crisis in Britain	1733
War of Jenkins's Ear begins between England and Spain	1739

Central and Eastern Europe

The major factors in the shift of political influence among the maritime nations were naval strength, economic progress, foreign trade, and sound domestic administration. The conflicts among them occurred less in Europe than on the high seas and in their overseas empires. These nations already existed in well-defined geographical areas with established borders. Their populations generally accepted the authority of the central government.

The situation in central and eastern Europe was rather different. Except for the cities on the Baltic, the economy was agrarian. There were fewer cities and many more large estates populated by serfs. The states in this region did not possess overseas empires. Changes in the power structure normally involved changes in borders, or at least in the prince who ruled a particular area. Military conflicts took place at home rather than overseas. The political structure of this region, which lay largely east of the Elbe River, was very "soft." The almost constant warfare of the seventeenth century had led to a habit of temporary and shifting political loyalties. The princes and aristocracies of small states and principalities were unwilling to subordinate themselves voluntarily to a central monarchical authority. Consequently the political life of the region and the kind of state that emerged there were different from those of western Europe.

Beginning in the last half of the seventeenth century, eastern and central Europe began to assume the political and social contours that would characterize it for the next two hundred years. After the Peace of Westphalia the Austrian Habsburgs recognized the basic weakness of the position of Holy Roman Emperor and began a new consolidation of their power. At the same time the state of Prussia began to emerge as a factor in north German politics and as a major challenger to Habsburg domination of Germany. Most important, Russia at the opening of the eighteenth century rose to the status of a military power of the first order. These three states (Austria, Prussia, and Russia) achieved their new status largely as a result

A series of four Hogarth etchings satirizing an English parliamentary election. In a savage indictment of the notoriously corrupt English electoral system, Hogarth shows the voters going to the polls after having been bribed and intoxicated with free gin. (Note that voting was public. The secret ballot was not introduced in England until 1872.) The fourth etching, Chairing the Member, shows the triumphal procession of the victorious candidate, which is clearly turning into a brawl. [Metropolitan Museum of Art]

WE MUST

of the political decay or military defeat of Sweden, Poland, and the Ottoman Empire.

Sweden: The Ambitions of Charles XII

Under Gustavus Adolphus II (1611–1632), Sweden had played an important role as a Protestant combatant in the Thirty Years' War. During the rest of the seventeenth century Sweden had consolidated its control of the Baltic, preventing Russian possession of a Baltic port and permitting Polish and German access to the sea only on Swedish terms. The Swedes also possessed one of the better armies in Europe. However, Sweden's economy, based primarily on the export of iron, was not strong enough to ensure continued political success.

In 1697 Charles XII (1697–1718) came to the throne. He was headstrong, to say the least, and perhaps insane. In 1700 Russia began a drive to the west against Swedish territory. The Russian goal was a foothold on the Baltic. In the resulting Great Northern War (1700–1721), Charles XII led a vigorous and often brilliant campaign, but one that eventually resulted in the defeat of Sweden. In 1700 he defeated the Russians at the battle of Narva, but then he turned south to invade Poland. The conflict dragged on, and the Russians were able to strengthen their forces. In 1708 the Swedish monarch began a major invasion of Russia but became bogged down in the harsh Russian winter. The next year his army was decisively defeated at the battle of Poltava. Thereafter the Swedes could maintain only a holding action. Charles himself sought refuge with the Ottoman army and then eventually returned to Sweden in 1714. He was shot four years later while fighting the Norwegians.

The Great Northern War came to a close in 1721. Sweden had exhausted its military and economic resources and had lost its monopoly on the Baltic coast. Russia had conquered a large section of the eastern Baltic, and Prussia had gained a portion of Pomerania. Internally, after the death of Charles XII, the Swedish nobles were determined to reassert their power over that of the monarchy. They did so but then fell into quarrels among themselves. Sweden played a very minor role in European affairs thereafter.

The Ottoman Empire

At the southeastern extreme of Europe the Ottoman Empire lay as a barrier to the territorial ambitions of the Austrian Habsburgs and of Poland and Russia. The empire in the late seventeenth century still controlled most of the Balkan peninsula and the entire coastline of the Black Sea. It was an aggressive power that had for two centuries attempted to press its control further westward in Europe. The Ottoman Empire had probably made its greatest military impression on Europe in 1683, when it laid siege to the city of Vienna.

However, the Ottomans had overextended themselves politically, economically, and militarily. The major domestic political groups resisted any substantial strengthening of the central government in Constantinople. Rivalries for power among army leaders and nobles weakened the effectiveness of the government. In the outer provinces, such as Transylvania, Wallachia, and Moldavia (all parts of modern Romania), the empire depended on the goodwill of local rulers, who never submitted themselves fully to the imperial power. The empire's economy was weak, and its exports were primarily raw materials. Moreover the actual conduct of most of its trade had been turned over to representatives of other nations.

By the early eighteenth century the weakness of the Ottoman Empire meant that on the southeastern perimeter of Europe there existed an immense political vacuum. In 1699 the Turks concluded a treaty with their longtime Habsburg enemy and surrendered all pretensions of control over Hungary, Transylvania, Croatia, and Slavonia. From this time onward Russia also attempted to extend its territory and influence at the expense of the empire. For almost two hundred years the decay of the Ottoman Empire constituted a major factor in European international relations. The area always proved tempting to the major powers, but their distrust of each other and their conflicting rivalries, as well as a considerable residual strength on the part of the Turks, prevented the dismemberment of the empire.

Poland

In no other part of Europe was the failure to maintain a competitive political position so complete as in Poland. In 1683 King John III Sobieski (1674–1696) had led a Polish army to rescue Vienna from the Turkish siege. But following that spectacular effort, Poland became little more than a byword for the dangers of aristocratic independence. In Poland as nowhere else on the Continent, the nobility be-

A contemporary Dutch print views the 1683 *Turkish siege of Vienna from a remarkably revealing position in the hills west of the city. The scene shows the Turkish forces deciding to give up the summer-long attack; their commanders, the Ottoman Grand Vizier and the Pasha of Adrianople, lower left, and just beginning their flight. Polish and other Christian aid for the beleaguered Habsburg forces had arrived, and the battle was clearly going against the Turks. Never again did the weakened Muslim Ottoman Empire threaten the west. Note the Danube River toward the top, the elaborate zig-zag fortifications outside the walls, and bursts of artillery fire at several points. Most details inside the walled city are omitted, but the central cathedral and the imperial palace, toward the bottom, are shown. One unforeseen lasting social result of the siege was the boost given to coffee drinking by the Viennese discovery of coffee beans in the Turkish camps around the city.* [*British Museum*]

came the single most powerful political factor in the country. Unlike the British nobility and landowners, the Polish nobility would not even submit to a central authority of their own making. There was no effective central authority in the form of either a king or a parliament.

The Polish monarchy was elective, but the deep distrust and divisions among the nobility prevented their electing a king from among their own numbers. Sobieski was a notable exception. Most of the Polish monarchs came from outside the borders of the kingdom and were the tools of foreign powers. The Polish nobles did have a central legislative body called the *Sejm,* or Diet. It included only the nobles and specifically excluded representatives from corporate bodies, such as the towns. In the Diet, however, there existed a practice known as the *liberum veto,* whereby the staunch opposition of any single member could require the body to disband. Such opposition was termed *exploding the Diet.* More often than not, this practice was the work of a group of dissatisfied nobles rather than of one person. Nonetheless, the rule of unanimity posed a major stumbling block to effective government.

Government as it was developing elsewhere in Europe simply was not tolerated in Poland. Localism reminiscent of the Middle Ages continued to hold sway as the nobles used all their energy to maintain their traditional "Polish liberties." There was no way to collect sufficient taxes to build up an army. The price of this noble liberty was eventually the disappearance of Poland from the map of Europe during the last half of the eighteenth century.

John III Sobieski (1624–1696). *Elected king of Poland in* 1674, *Sobieski was a military hero in the wars against the Turks. However, he failed in his attempt to give Poland a strong, national monarchy.* [*EPA*]

The Habsburg Empire and the Pragmatic Sanction

The close of the Thirty Years' War marked a fundamental turning point in the history of the Austrian Habsburgs. Previously, in alliance with the Spanish branch of the family, they had hoped to dominate all of Germany politically and to bring it back to the Catholic fold. They had failed to achieve either goal, and the decline of Spanish power meant that in future diplomatic relations the Austrian Habsburgs were very much on their own. The Treaty of Westphalia permitted Protestantism within the Holy Roman Empire, and the treaty also recognized the political autonomy of more than three hundred corporate German political entities within the empire. These included large units (such as Saxony, Hanover, Bavaria, and Brandenburg) and also scores of small cities, bishoprics, principalities, and territories of independent knights.

After 1648 the Habsburg family retained firm hold on the title of Holy Roman Emperor, but the effectiveness of the title depended less on force of arms than on the cooperation that the emperor could elicit from the various political bodies in the empire. The Diet of the empire sat at Regensburg from 1663 until its dissolution in 1806. The Diet and the emperor generally regulated the daily economic and political life of Germany. The post-Westphalian Holy Roman Empire in many ways resembled Poland in its lack of central authority. However, unlike its Polish neighbor, the Holy Roman Empire was reorganized from within as the Habsburgs attempted to regain their authority and, as will be seen shortly, as Prussia set out on its course toward European power.

While establishing a new kind of position for their Austrian holdings among the German states, the Habsburgs began to consolidate their power and influence within their other hereditary possessions. These included, first, the Crown of Saint Wenceslas encompassing the kingdom of Bohemia (in modern Czechoslovakia) and the Duchies of Moravia and Silesia and, second, the Crown of Saint Stephen, which ruled Hungary, Croatia, and Transylvania. In the middle of the seventeenth century much of Hungary remained occupied by the Turks and was liberated only at the end of the century. In the early eighteenth century the family further extended its domains, receiving the former Spanish (thereafter Austrian) Netherlands, Lombardy in northern Italy, and the

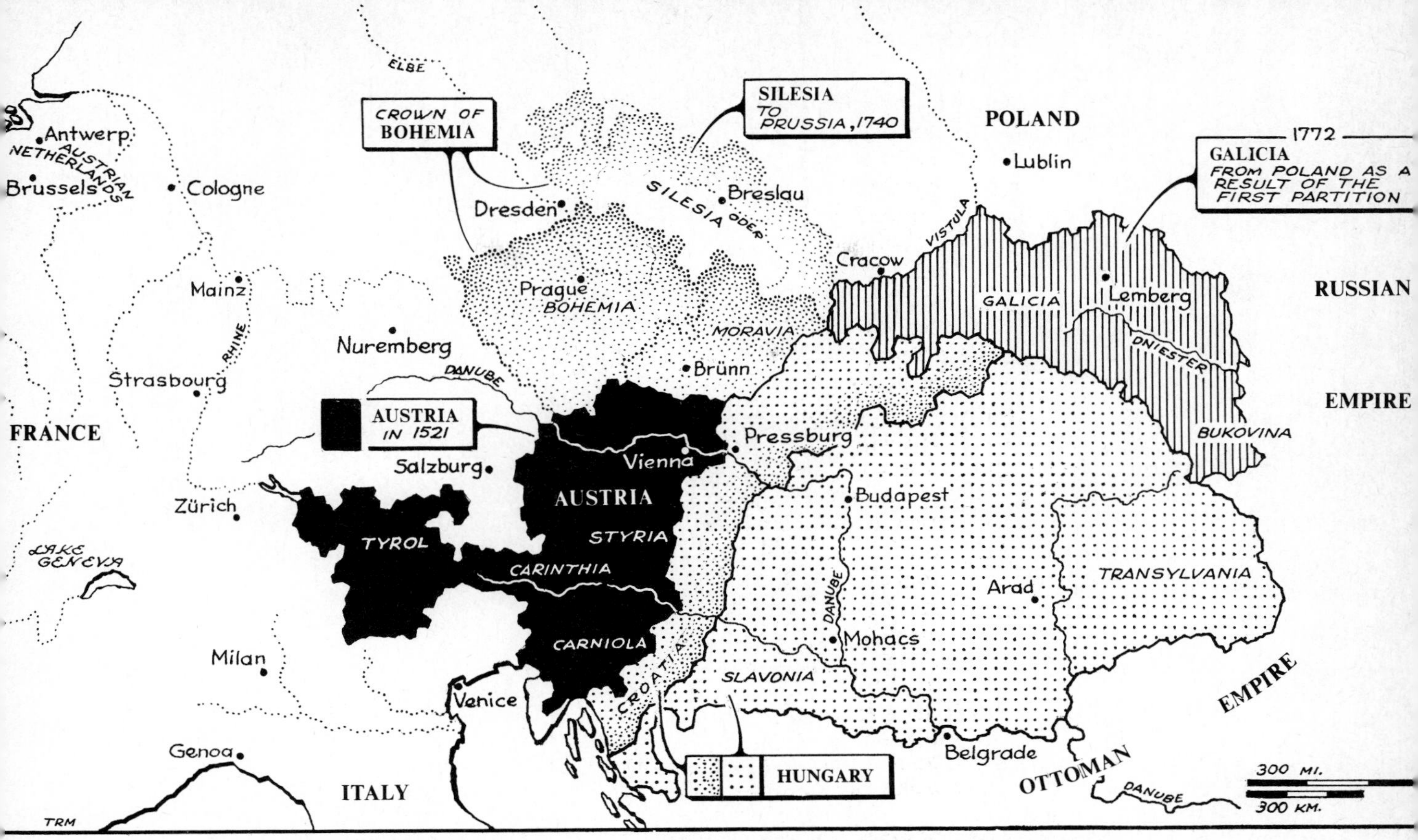

THE AUSTRIAN HAPSBURG EMPIRE, 1521–1772

MAP 14-1 *The Empire had three main units—Austria, Bohemia, Hungary. Expansion was mainly eastward: east Hungary from the Ottomans (17th century) and Galicia from Poland (1772). Meantime, Silesia was lost, but Hapsburgs retained German influence as Holy Roman Emperors.*

Kingdom of Naples in southern Italy through the Treaty of Utrecht in 1713. The Kingdom of Naples was lost relatively quickly and played no considerable role in the Habsburg fortunes. During the eighteenth and nineteenth centuries Habsburgs' power and influence in Europe would be based primarily on their territories located outside Germany.

In the second half of the seventeenth century and later the Habsburg confronted immense problems in these hereditary territories. In each they ruled by virtue of a different title and had to gain the cooperation of the local nobility. The most difficult province was Hungary, where the Magyar nobility seemed ever ready to rebel. There was almost no common basis for political unity among peoples of such diverse languages, customs, and geography. Even the Habsburg zeal for Roman Catholicism no longer proved a bond for unity as they continued to confront the equally zealous Calvinism of the Magyar nobles. Over the years the Habsburgs established various central councils to chart common policies for their far-flung domains. Virtually all of these bodies dealt with only a portion of the Habsburgs' holdings. Repeatedly they found themselves compelled to bargain with nobles in one part of Europe in order to maintain their position in another.

Despite all these internal difficulties Leopold I (1657–1705) rallied his domains to resist the advances of the Turks and to resist the aggression of Louis XIV. He achieved Ottoman recognition of his sovereignty over Hungary in 1699 and suppressed the long rebellion of his new Magyar subjects between 1703 and 1711. He also extended his territorial holdings over much of what is today Yugoslavia and western Romania. These southeastward extensions allowed the Habsburgs to hope to develop Mediterranean trade through the port of Trieste. The expansion at the cost of the Ottoman Empire also helped the Habsburgs to compensate for their loss of domination over the Holy Roman

Schonnbrunn Palace, outside Vienna. The Habsburg court migrated to this Austrian Versailles each spring, returning to Vienna only in the autumn. [*Shostal*]

Maria Theresa Discusses One Weakness of Her Throne

Scattered subjects of the multilingual Austrian Empire (Germans, Hungarians, Czechs, Slovaks, Slovenes, Croatians, Poles, and Romanians, for example) made impossible the unifying of the empire into a strong centralized monarchy. Maria Theresa, writing in 1745, explained how previous Habsburg rulers had impoverished themselves by attempting, with little success, to purchase the political and military support of the nobles in different provinces. The more privileges they gave the nobles, the more they were expected to give.

To return once again to my ancestors, these individuals not only gave away most of the crown estates, but absorbed also the debts of those properties confiscated in time of rebellion, and these debts are still in arrears. Emperor Leopold [1658–1705] *found little left to give away, but the terrible wars he fought no doubt forced him to mortgage or pawn additional crown estates. His successors did not relieve these burdens, and when I became sovereign, the crown revenues barely reached eighty thousand gulden. Also in the time of my forebears, the ministers received enormous payments from the crown and from the local Estates because they knew not only how to exploit selfishly the good will, grace, and munificence of the Austrian house by convincing each ruler that predecessor had won fame by giving freely but also how to win the ears of the provincial lords and clergy so that these ministers acquired all that they wished. In fact they spread their influence so wide that in the provinces they were more feared and respected than the ruler himself. And when they had finally taken everything from the sovereign, these same ministers turned for additional compensation to their provinces, where their great authority continuously increased. Even though complaints reached the monarch, out of grace and forebearance toward the ministers, he simply allowed the exploitations to continue. . . .*

This system gave the ministers such authority that the sovereign himself found it convenient for his own interests to support them because he learned by experience that the more prestige enjoyed by the heads of the provinces, the more of the sovereign's demands these heads could extract from their Estates.

Maria Theresa, *Political Testament*, cited in Karl A. Roider (Ed. and Trans.), *Maria Theresa* (Englewood Cliffs, N.J.: Prentice-Hall, 1973), pp. 32–33.

Empire. Strength in the East gave them greater political leverage in Germany. Leopold was succeeded by Joseph I (1705–1711), who continued his policies.

When Charles VI (1711–1740) succeeded Joseph, he added a new problem to the old chronic one of territorial diversity. He had no male heir, and there was only the weakest of precedents for a female ruler of the Habsburg domains. Charles feared that on his death the Austrian Habsburg lands might fall prey to the surrounding powers, as had those of the Spanish Habsburgs in 1700. He was determined to prevent that disaster and to provide his domains with the semblance of legal unity. To those ends, he devoted most of his reign to seeking the approval of his family, the estates of his realms, and the major foreign powers for a document called the *Pragmatic Sanction.*

This instrument provided the legal basis for a single line of inheritance within the Habsburg dynasty through Charles VI's daughter Maria Theresa (1740–1780). Other members of the Habsburg family recognized her as the rightful heir. The nobles of the various Habsburg domains did likewise after extracting various concessions from Charles. Consequently, when Charles VI died in October 1740, he believed that he had secured legal unity for the Habsburg Empire and a safe succession for his daughter. He had indeed established a permanent line of succession and the basis for future legal bonds within the Habsburg holdings, but he failed to protect his daughter from foreign aggression, either through the Pragmatic Sanction or, more important, by leaving her a strong army and a filled treasury. Less than two months after his death the fragility of the foreign agreements became all too apparent. In December 1740 Frederick II of Prussia invaded the Habsburg province of Silesia. Maria Theresa would now have to fight to defend her inheritance.

Prussia and the Hohenzollerns

The Habsburg achievement had been to draw together into an uncertain legal unity a collection of domains possessed by dint of separate feudal titles. The achievement of the Hohenzollerns of Brandenburg-Prussia was to acquire a similar collection of titular holdings and then to forge them into a centrally administered unit. In spite of the geographical separation of their territories and the paucity of their natural economic resources, they trans-

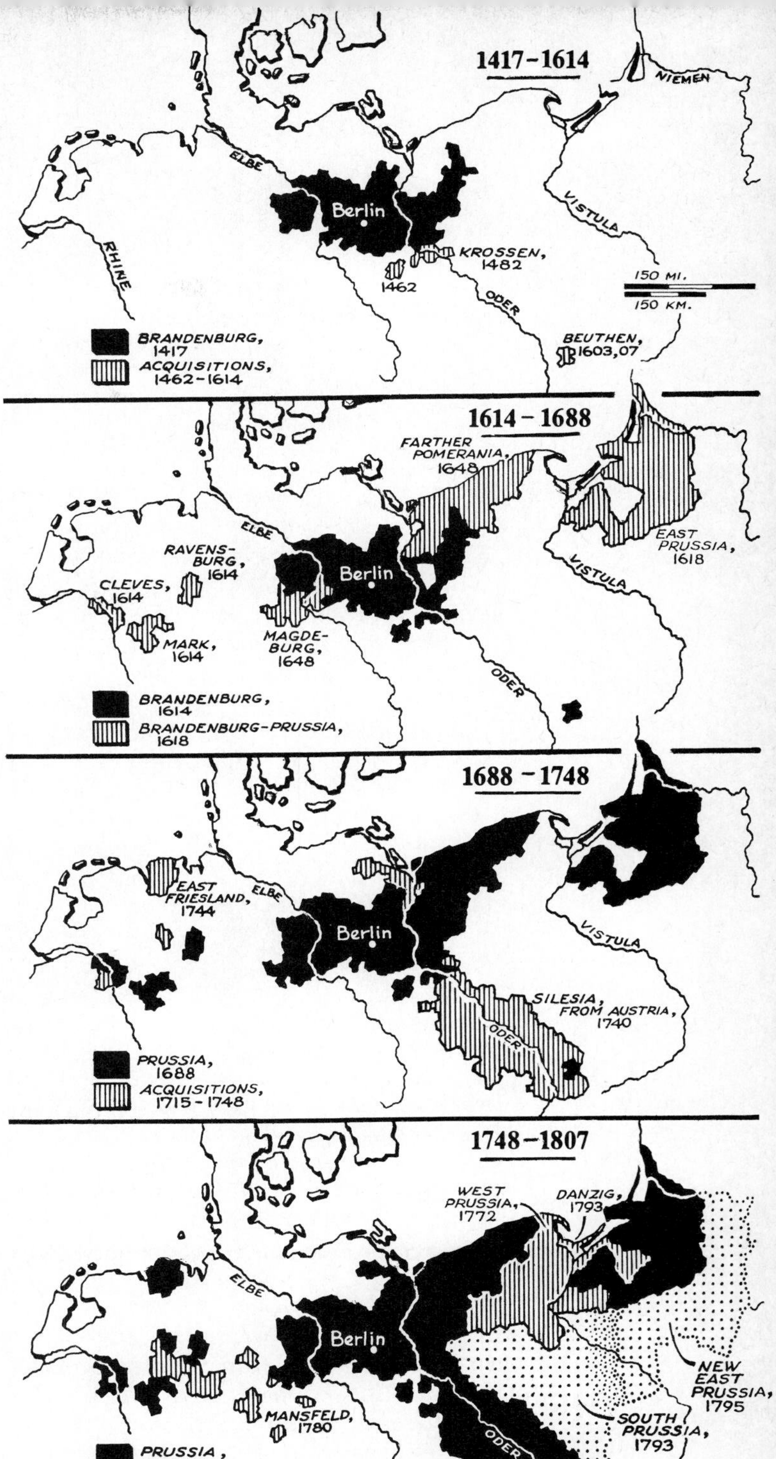

EXPANSION OF BRANDENBURG-PRUSSIA

MAP 14-2 *Seventeenth-century Brandenburg-Prussia expanded mainly by acquiring dynastic titles in geographically separated lands. Eighteenth-century expansion occurred through aggression to the east: Silesia seized in* 1740 *and various parts of Poland in* 1772, 1793, *and* 1795.

The Great Elector Welcomes Protestant Refugees from France

The Hohenzollern dynasty of Brandenburg-Prussia pursued a policy of religious toleration. The family itself was Calvinist, whereas most of its subjects were Lutherans. When Louis XIV of France revoked the Edict of Nantes in 1685, Frederick William, the Great Elector, seized on the opportunity to invite into his realms French Protestants. As his proclamation indicates, he was quite interested in attracting persons with productive skills who could aid the economic development of his domains.

We, Friedrich Wilhelm, by Grace of God Margrave of Brandenburg. . . .

Do hereby proclaim and make known to all and sundry that since the cruel persecutions and rigorous ill-treatment in which Our co-religionists of the Evangelical-Reformed faith have for some time past been subjected in the Kingdom of France, have caused many families to remove themselves and to betake themselves out of the said Kingdom into other lands, We now . . . have been moved graciously to offer them through this Edict . . . a secure and free refuge in all Our Lands and Provinces. . . .

Since Our Lands are not only well and amply endowed with all things necessary to support life, but also very well-suited to the reestablishment of all kinds of manufactures and trade and traffic by land and water, We permit, indeed, to those settling therein free choice to establish themselves where it is most convenient for their profession and way of living. . . .

The personal property which they bring with them, including merchandise and other wares, is to be totally exempt from any taxes, customs dues, licenses, or other imposts of any description, and not detained in any way. . . .

As soon as these Our French co-religionists of the Evangelical-Reformed faith have settled in any town or village, they shall be admitted to the domiciliary rights and craft freedoms customary there, gratis and without payment of any fee; and shall be entitled to the benefits, rights, and privileges enjoyed by Our other, native, subjects, residing there. . . .

Not only are those who wish to establish manufacture of cloth, stuffs, hats, or other objects in which they are skilled to enjoy all necessary freedoms, privileges and facilities, but also provision is to be made for them to be assisted and helped as far as possible with money and anything else which they need to realize their intention. . . .

Those who settle in the country and wish to maintain themselves by agriculture are to be given a certain plot of land to bring under cultivation and provided with whatever they need to establish themselves initially. . . .

C. A. Macartney (Ed.), *The Habsburg and Hohenzollern Dynasties in the Seventeenth and Eighteenth Centuries* (New York: Walker, 1970), pp. 270–273.

formed feudal ties and structures into bureaucratic ones. They subordinated every social class and most economic pursuits to the strengthening of the one institution that united their far-flung realms: the army. In so doing they made the term *Prussian* synonymous with administrative rigor and military discipline.

The rise of Prussia occurred within the German power vacuum created by the Peace of Westphalia. It is the story of the extraordinary Hohenzollern family, which had ruled the German territory of Brandenburg since 1417. Through inheritance the family had acquired the duchy of Cleves and the counties of Mark and Ravensburg in 1609, the duchy of East Prussia in 1618, and the duchy of Pomerania in 1637. Except for Pomerania, none of these lands was contiguous with Brandenburg. East Prussia lay inside Poland and outside the authority of the Holy Roman Emperor. All of the territories lacked good natural resources, and many of them were devastated during the Thirty Years' War. At Westphalia the Hohenzollerns lost part of Pomerania to Sweden but were compensated by receiving three more bishoprics and the promise of the archbishopric of Magdeburg when it became vacant, as it did in 1680. By the late seven-

Economically weak, with a small population, Prussia became an important state because it developed a large, well-trained army. The discipline for which Prussian troops were noted was the result of constant drill and harsh punishment. The parade-ground formation shown here was actually meant to be performed on the battlefield. The wooden horse (left) was used for punishment, not exercise. [*Bildarchiv Preussischer Kulturbesitz*]

teenth century the scattered Hohenzollern holdings represented a block of territory within the Holy Roman Empire second in size only to that of the Habsburgs.

Despite its size, the Hohenzollern conglomerate was weak. The areas were geographically separate, and there was no mutual sympathy or common concern among them, In each there existed some form of local noble estates that limited the power of the Hohenzollern prince. The various areas were exposed to foreign aggression.

The person who began to forge these areas and nobles into a modern state was Frederick William (1640–1688), who became known as the Great Elector. He established himself and his successors as the central uniting power by breaking the estates, organizing a royal bureaucracy, and establishing a strong army.

Between 1655 and 1660 Sweden and Poland engaged in a war that endangered the Great Elector's holdings in Pomerania and East Prussia. Frederick William had neither an adequate army nor the tax revenues to confront this foreign threat. In 1655 the Brandenburg estates refused to grant him new taxes; however, he proceeded to collect the required taxes by military force. In 1659 a different grant of taxes, originally made in 1653, elapsed; Frederick William continued to collect them as well as those he had imposed by his own authority. He used the money to build up an army, which allowed him to continue to enforce his will without the approval of the nobility. Similar processes of threats and coercion took place against the nobles in his other territories.

However, there was a political and social trade-off between the elector and his various nobles. These *Junkers,* or German noble landlords, were allowed almost complete control over the serfs on their estates. In exchange for their obedience to the Hohenzollerns, the *Junkers* received the right to demand obedience from their serfs. Frederick William also tended to choose as the local administrators of the tax structure men who would normally have been members of the nobles estates. In this fashion he co-opted potential opponents into his service. The taxes fell most heavily on the backs of the peasants and the urban classes. As the years passed, sons of *Junkers* increasingly dominated the army officer corps, and this practice became even more pronounced during the eighteenth century. All officials and army officers took an oath of loyalty directly to the elector. The army and the elector thus came to embody the otherwise absent unity of the state. The existence of the army made Prussia a valu-

Frederick William I of Prussia Demands Truthful Reports from His Royal Officials

On July 20, 1722, Frederick William I issued these orders to his civil servants in charge of Pomerania. He was deeply troubled by inaccuracies in the information being sent to him and to his officials in Berlin. He had no patience with lazy officials. He also intended to discourage officials from hiding bad news from him. Note in particular his concern with the collection of taxes and with all matters relating to the recruitment of troops into the army.

For some time past We have on various occasions remarked with particular displeasure that the reports rendered to Us, especially on matters concerning Our Provinces and towns, often contain statements that are unfounded, or, at least, not based on the necessary conscientious and mature examination of the true circumstances involved, and afterward, after closer scrutiny and examination, show that the event did not occur at all, or at any rate, not in the way in which it was represented, so that in the end We have not known what to believe, and what not. We wish therefore that this improper practice, which is directly contrary to the duty and obligations of Our servants, shall for the future cease absolutely, and no reports be rendered that do not rest on correct and truthful foundations and on mature precedent investigation of all and every attendant circumstance, as their authors have to answer for it before God, Us, and their consciences, under pain of Our extreme disfavor and most severe and active displeasure toward those who do not obey exactly this, Our express command. . . . Our most gracious intention remains, as before, that complete information should be rendered to Us periodically on everything that occurs in the country and the towns, and on the true situation, particularly when there is any deficit in the land tax or the town excise, or any incident in the commercial field; and similarly when, as often occurs in connection with recruiting and billeting, excesses have been committed—real, not hearsay, but actual demonstrable facts which have not been remedied by the commanding officers, to whom the complaints must, by regulation, be first addressed, detailed reports of all such and other similar cases must be sent to Us personally under seal, duplicates to be sent in every case to the General Commissariat of War. We hereby make known to you this, Our considered wish, and command you, not only yourselves to obey in the future, but also to make it known to the magistrates and other persons whom it may concern, in order that each one may safeguard himself against trouble and certain punishment.

C. A. Macartney (Ed.), *The Habsburg and Hohenzollern Dynasties in the Seventeenth and Eighteenth Centuries* (New York: Walker, 1970), pp. 298–299.

able potential ally and a state with which other powers needed to curry favor.

Yet, even with the considerable accomplishments of the Great Elector, the house of Hohenzollern did not possess a crown. The achievement of a royal title was one of the few state-building accomplishments of Frederick I (1688–1713). This son of the Great Elector was the least "Prussian" of his family during these crucial years. He built palaces, founded Halle University (1694), patronized the arts, and lived luxuriously. However, in 1700, at the outbreak of the War of the Spanish Succession, he put his army at the disposal of the Habsburg Holy Roman Emperor. In exchange for this loyal service the emperor permitted Frederick to assume the title of "King in Prussia." Thereafter Frederick became Frederick I, and he passed the much-desired royal title to his son Frederick William I in 1713.

Frederick William I (1713–1740) was both the most eccentric personality to rule the Hohenzollern domains and one of its most effective monarchs. After giving his father a funeral that matched the luxury of his life, Frederick William I immediately imposed policies of strict austerity. In some cases jobs were abolished, and in others salaries were lowered. His political aims seem to have been nothing else than the consolidation of an obedient, compliant bureaucracy and the expansion of the army. He initiated a policy of *Kabinett* government, which meant that lower officials submitted all relevant documents to him in his office, or *Kabinett*. Then he alone examined the papers, made his decision, and issued his orders. Frederick William I thus skirted the influence of ministers and ruled alone.

Frederick William organized the bureaucracy along the lines of military discipline. He united all departments under the *General-Ober-Finanz-Kriegs-und-Domänen-Direktorium*, which is more happily known to us as the *General Directory*. He imposed taxes on the nobility and changed most remaining feudal dues into money payments. He sought to transform feudal and administrative loyalties into a sense of duty to the monarch as a political institution rather than as a person. He once described the perfect royal servant as

> an intelligent, assiduous, and alert person who after God values nothing higher than his king's pleasure and serves him out of love and for the sake of honor rather than money and who in his conduct solely seeks and constantly bears in mind his king's service and interests, who, moreover, abhors all intrigues and emotional deterrents.[1]

Service to the state and the monarch was to become impersonal, mechanical, and, in effect, unquestioning.

The discipline that Frederick William applied to the army was little less than fanatical. During his reign the size of the military force grew from about thirty-nine thousand in 1713 to over eighty thousand in 1740. It was the third or fourth largest army in Europe, whereas Prussia ranked thirteenth in size of population. Rather than using recruiters, the king made each canton or local district responsible for supplying a certain number of soldiers.

After 1725 Frederick William always wore an officer's uniform. He built one regiment from the tallest soldiers he could find in Europe. Separate laws applied to the army and to civilians. Laws, customs, and royal attention made the officer corps the highest social class of the state. Military service attracted the sons of *Junkers*. In this fashion the army, the *Junker* nobility, and the monarchy became forged into a single political entity. Military priorities and values dominated Prussian government, society, and daily life as in no other state of Europe. It has often been said that whereas other nations possessed armies, the Prussian army possessed its nation.

Austria and Prussia in the Late Seventeenth and Early Eighteenth Centuries

Reign of Frederick William, the Great Elector	1640–1688
Leopold I rules Austria and resists the Turkish invasions	1657–1705
Turkish siege of Vienna	1683
Reign of Frederick I of Prussia	1688–1713
Peace treaty between Turks and Habsburgs	1699
Charles VI rules Austria and secures agreement to the Pragmatic Sanction	1711–1740
Frederick William I builds up the military power of Prussia	1713–1740
Maria Theresa succeeds to the Habsburg throne	1740
Frederick II violates the Pragmatic Sanction by invading Silesia	1740

[1]Quoted in Hans Rosenberg, *Bureaucracy, Aristocracy, and Autocracy* (Boston: Beacon Press, 1958), p. 93.

Although Frederick William I built the best army in Europe, he followed a policy of avoiding conflict. He wanted to drill his soldiers but not to order them into battle. Although Frederick William terrorized his family and associates and on occasion knocked out teeth with his walking stick, he was not a militarily aggressive monarch. The army was for him a symbol of Prussian power and unity, not an instrument to be used for foreign adventures or aggression. At this death in 1740 he passed to his son Frederick II (1740–1786; Frederick the Great) this superb military machine, but he could not pass to his son the wisdom to refrain from using it. Almost immediately on coming to the throne, Frederick II upset the Pragmatic Sanction and invaded Silesia. He thus crystallized the Austrian-Prussian rivalry for control of Germany that would dominate central European affairs for over a century.

Ivan the Terrible (1533–1584). *He was the first Muscovite ruler to call himself Tsar of Russia.* [*National Museum Copenhagen*]

The Entry of Russia into the European Political Arena

Though ripe with consequences for the future, the rise of Prussia and the new consolidation of Austrian Habsburg domains seemed to many at the time only one more shift in the long-troubled German scene. However, the emergence of Russia as an active European power constituted a wholly new factor in European politics. Previously Russia had been considered a part of Europe only by courtesy. Geographically and politically it lay on the periphery of Europe. Hemmed in by Sweden on the Baltic and by the Ottoman Empire on the Black Sea, the country had no warm-water ports. Its chief outlet to the west was Archangel on the White Sea, which was open to ships during only part of the year. There was little trade. What Russia did possess was a vast reserve of largely undeveloped natural and human resources.

The reign of Ivan the Terrible, which had begun so well and closed so frighteningly, was followed by a period of anarchy and civil war known as the *Time of Troubles.* In 1613, hoping to resolve the tension and end the uncertainty, an assembly of nobles elected as czar a seventeen-year-old boy named Michael Romanov (1613–1654). Thus began the dynasty that in spite of palace revolutions, military conspiracies, assassinations, and family strife ruled Russia until 1917.

Michael Romanov and his two successors, Alexis I (1654–1676) and Theodore III (1676–1682), brought stability and bureaucratic centralization to Russia. However, Russia remained militarily weak and financially impoverished. The bureaucracy after these years of turmoil still remained largely controlled by the boyars. This administrative apparatus was only barely capable of putting down a revolt of peasants and cossacks under Stepan Razin in 1670–1671. Furthermore, the government and the czars faced the danger of mutiny from the *streltsy,* or guards of the Moscow garrison.

Peter the Great

In 1682 another boy—ten years old at the time—ascended the fragile Russian throne as coruler with his half brother. His name was Peter (1682–1725), and Russia would never be the same after him. He and his ill half-brother, Ivan V, had come to power on the shoulders of the *streltsy,* who expected rewards from the persons they favored. Much violence and bloodshed had surrounded the disputed succession. Matters became even more confused when the boys' sister, Sophia, was named regent. Peter's followers overthrew her in 1689. From that date onward Peter ruled personally, although in theory he shared the crown with Ivan, until Ivan died in 1696. The

Peter the Great (1682–1725) *studying ship building in Holland. In* 1697, *the Tsar visited western Europe incognito to study the skills that he considered necessary for Russia to build a strong, modern state.* [*The Bettmann Archive*]

dangers and turmoil of his youth convinced Peter of two things. First, the power of the czar must be made secure from the jealousy of the boyars and the greed of the *streltsy.* Second, the military power of Russia must be increased.

Peter I, who became Peter the Great, was fascinated by western Europe, particularly its military resources. He was an imitator of the first order. The products and workers from the West who had filtered into Russia impressed and intrigued him. In 1697 he made a famous visit in rather weak disguises throughout western Europe. There he dined and talked with the great and the powerful, who considered this almost seven-foot-tall ruler both crude and rude. His happiest moments on the trip were spent inspecting shipyards, docks, and the manufacture of military hardware. He returned to Moscow determined by whatever means necessary to copy what he had seen abroad, for he knew that warfare would be necessary to make Russia a great power. The czar's drive toward westernization, though unsystematic, had four general areas of concern: taming the boyars and the *streltsy,* achieving secular control of the church, reorganizing the internal administration, and developing the economy. Peter pursued each of these goals with violence and ruthlessness.

He made a sustained attack on the Russian boyars. In 1698, immediately on his return from abroad, he personally shaved the long beards of the court boyars and sheared off the customary long, hand-covering sleeves of their shirts and coats, which had made them the butt of jokes throughout Europe. More important, he demanded that the nobles provide his state with their services.

In 1722 Peter published a Table of Ranks, which henceforth equated a person's social position and privileges with his rank in the bureaucracy or the army rather than with his position in the nobility. However, unlike the case in Prussia, the Russian nobility never became perfectly loyal to the state. They repeatedly sought to reassert their independence and their control of the Russian imperial court.

The *streltsy* fared less well than the boyars. In 1698 they had rebelled while Peter was on his European tour. When he returned and put

Bishop Burnet Looks Over a Foreign Visitor

In 1697 and 1698 Peter the Great of Russia toured western Europe to discover how Russia must change its society and economy in order to become a great power. As this description by Bishop Gilbert Burnet in England indicates, the west Europeans found the czar a curious person in his own right.

He came this winter over to England, and stayed some months among us. . . . I had good interpreters, so I had much free discourse with him; he is a man of a very hot temper, soon inflamed, and very brutal in his passion; he raises his natural heat, by drinking much brandy, . . . he is subject to convulsive motions all over his body, and his head seems to be affected with these; he wants not capacity, and has a larger measure of knowledge, than might be expected from his education, which was very indifferent; a want of judgment, with an instability of temper, appear in him too often and too evidently; he is mechanically turned, and seems designed by nature rather to be a ship-carpenter, than a great prince. This was his chief study and exercise, while he stayed here: he wrought much with his own hands, and made all about him work at the models of ships. . . . He was . . . resolved to encourage learning, and to polish his people, by sending some of them to travel in other countries, and to draw strangers to come and live among them. . . . After I had seen him often, and had conversed much with him, I could not but adore the depth of the providence of God, that had raised up such a furious man to so absolute an authority over so great a part of the world.

Bishop Burnet's History of His Own Time, Vol. 4 (Oxford, England: Clarendon Press, 1823), pp. 396–397.

down the revolt of these Moscow troops, he directed massive violence and brutality against both leaders and followers. There were private tortures and public executions, in which Peter's own ministers took part. Almost twelve hundred of the rebels were put to death, and their corpses long remained on public display to discourage future disloyalty.

Peter dealt with the potential political independence of the Russian Orthodox Church with similar ruthlessness. Here again, Peter had to confront a problem that had arisen in the turbulent decades that had preceded his reign. The Russian church had long opposed the scientific as well as the theological thought of the West. In the mid-seventeenth century a reformist movement led by Patriarch Nikon arose in the church. In 1667 certain changes had been introduced into the texts and the ritual of the church. These reforms caused great unrest because the Russian church had always claimed to be the protector of the ritual. The Old Believers, a group of Russian Christians who strongly opposed these changes, were condemned by the hierarchy, but they persisted in their opposition. Late in the century thousands of them committed suicide rather than submit to the new rituals. The Old Believers' movement represented a rejection of change and innovation; its presence discouraged the church hierarchy from making any further substantial moves toward modern thought.

In the future Peter wanted to avoid two kinds of difficulties with the Russian church. First, the clergy must not constitute a group within the state that would oppose change and westernization. Second, the hierarchy of the church must not be permitted to reform liturgy, ritual, or doctrine in a way that might again give rise to discontent such as that of the Old Believers. Consequently, in 1721, Peter simply abolished the position of patriarch of the Russian church. In its place he established a synod headed by a layman to rule the church in accordance with secular requirements. So far as transforming a traditional institution was concerned, this action toward the church was the most radical policy of Peter's reign. It produced still further futile opposition from the Old Believers, who saw the czar as leading the church into new heresy.

In his reorganization of domestic administration, Peter looked to institutions then used in Sweden. These were "colleges," or bureaus, composed of several persons rather than departments headed by a single minister. These colleges, which he imposed on Russia, were to look after matters such as the collection of taxes, foreign affairs, war, and economic matters. This new organization was an attempt to breathe life into the generally stagnant and inefficient administration of the country. In 1711 he created a central senate of nine members who were to direct the Moscow government when the czar was away with the army. The purpose of these and other local administrative reforms was to establish a bureaucracy that could collect and spend tax revenues to support an efficient army.

The economic development advocated by Peter the Great was closely related to his military needs. He encouraged the establishment of an iron industry in the Ural Mountains, and by mid-century Russia had become the largest iron producer in Europe. He sent prominent young Russians abroad to acquire technical and organizational skills. He attempted to attract west European craftsmen to live and work in Russia. Except for the striking growth of the iron industry, which later languished, all these efforts had only marginal success.

The goal of these internal reforms and political departures was to support a policy of warfare. Peter was determined to secure warm-water ports that would allow Russia to trade with the West and to have a greater impact of European affairs. This policy led him into wars with the Ottoman Empire and with Sweden. His armies commenced fighting the Turks in 1695 and captured Azov on the Black Sea in 1696. It was a temporary victory, for in 1711 he was compelled to return the port.

Peter had more success against Sweden, where the inconsistency and irrationality of Charles XII were no small aid. In 1700 Russia moved against the Swedish territory on the Baltic. The Swedish king's failure to follow up his victory at Narva in 1700 allowed Peter to regroup his forces and hoard his resources. In 1709, when Charles XII returned to fight Russia again, Peter was ready, and the Battle of Poltava sealed the fate of Sweden. In 1721, at the Peace of Nystad, which ended the Great Northern War, the Russian conquest of Estonia, Livonia, and part of Finland was confirmed. Henceforth Russia possessed warm-water ports and a permanent influence on European affairs.

At one point the domestic and foreign policies of Peter the Great literally intersected. This was at the spot on the Gulf of Finland where Peter founded his new capital city of Saint Petersburg (now Leningrad). There he built government structures and compelled his boyars to construct town houses. In this fashion he imitated those west European monarchs who had copied Louis XIV by constructing smaller versions of Versailles. However, the founding of Saint Petersburg went beyond the construction of a central court. It symbolized a new western orientation of Russia and Peter's determination to hold his position on the Baltic coast. He had begun the construction of the city and had moved the capital there in 1703, even before his victory over Sweden was assured.

Despite his notable success on the Baltic, Peter's reign ended with a great question mark. He had long quarreled with his only son, Alexis. Peter was jealous of the young man and fearful that he might undertake sedition. In 1718 Peter had his son imprisoned, and during

Rise of Russian Power

Reign of Ivan the Terrible	1533–1584
Time of Troubles	1584–1613
Michael Romanov becomes czar	1613
Peter the Great becomes czar as a boy	1682
Peter assumes personal rule	1689
Russia captures Azov on the Black Sea from the Turks	1696
European tour of Peter the Great	1697
Peter returns to Russia to put down the revolt of the *streltsy*	1698
The Great Northern War opens between Russia and Sweden; Russia defeated at Narva by Swedish Army of Charles XII	1700
Saint Petersburg founded	1703
Russia defeats Sweden at the Battle of Poltava	1709
Charles XII of Sweden dies	1718
Son of Peter the Great dies under mysterious circumstances in prison	1718
Peace of Nystad ends the Great Northern War	1721
Peter establishes a synod for the Russian church	1721
Peter issues the Table of Ranks	1722
Peter dies leaving an uncertain succession	1725

Peter the Great built St. Petersburg (now Leningrad) on the Gulf of Finland to provide Russia with better contact with Western Europe. He moved the capital there from Moscow in 1703. *This is an eighteenth-century view of the city.* [John R. Freeman]

this imprisonment the presumed successor to the throne died mysteriously. Thereafter Peter claimed for himself the right of naming a successor, but he could never bring himself to designate the person either orally or in writing. Consequently, when he died in 1725, there was no firmer policy on the succession to the throne than when he had acceded to the title. For over thirty years, once again soldiers and nobles would determine who ruled Russia. Peter had laid the foundations of a modern Russia, but he had failed to lay the foundations of a stable state.

Eighteenth-Century European States

By the second quarter of the eighteenth century the major European powers were not yet nation-states in which the citizens felt themselves united by a shared sense of community, culture, language, and history. They were still monarchies in which the personality of the ruler and the personal relationships of the great noble families exercised considerable influence over public affairs. The monarchs, except in Great Britain, had generally succeeded in making their power greater than the nobility's. However, the power of the aristocracy and its capacity to resist or obstruct the policies of the monarchs were not destroyed. In Britain, of course, the nobility had tamed the monarchy, but even there tension between nobles and monarchs would continue through the rest of the century.

In foreign affairs the new arrangement of military and diplomatic power established during the early years of the century prepared the way for two long-term conflicts. The first was a commercial rivalry for trade and overseas empire between France and Great Britain. During the reign of Louis XIV these two nations had collided over the French bid for dominance in

Europe. During the eighteenth century they dueled for control of commerce on other continents. The second arena of warfare was central Europe, where Austria and Prussia fought for the leadership of the states of Germany.

However, behind these international conflicts and the domestic rivalry of monarchs and nobles, the society of eighteenth-century Europe began to experience momentous change. The character and the structures of the society over which the monarchs ruled were beginning to take on some features associated with the modern age. These economic and social developments would, in the long run, produce transformations in the life of Europe beside which the state building of the early eighteenth-century monarchs paled.

Suggested Readings

M. S. ANDERSON, *Europe in the Eighteenth Century, 1713–1783* (1961). The best one-volume introduction.

T. M. BARKER, *Army, Aristocracy, Monarchy: Essays in War, Society and Government in Austria,* 1618–1780 (1982). Examines the intricate power relationships among these major institutions.

R. BROWNING, *Political and Constitutional Ideas of the Court Whigs* (1982). An excellent overview of the ideology of Walpole's supporters

F. L. CARSTEN, *The Origins of Prussia* (1954). Discusses the groundwork laid by the Great Elector in the seventeenth century.

A. COBBAN, *A History of Modern France,* 2nd ed., Vol. 1, (1961). A lively and opinionated survey.

L. COLLEY, *In Defiance of Oligarchy: The Tory Party,* 1714–60. (1982) An important study that challenges much conventional opinion about eighteenth-century British politics.

P. DUKES, *The Making of Russian Absolutism:* 1613–1801 (1982). An overview based on recent scholarship.

R. R. ERGANG, *The Potsdam Führer* (1941). The biography of Frederick William I.

R. J. W. EVANS, *The Making of the Habsburg Monarchy,* 1550–1700: *An Interpretation* (1979). Places much emphasis on intellectual factors and the role of religion.

S. B. FAY AND K. EPSTEIN, *The Rise of Brandenburg-Prussia to* 1786 (1937, rev. 1964). A brief outline.

F. FORD, *Robe and Sword: The Regrouping of the French Aristocracy After Louis XIV* (1953). An important book for political, social, and intellectual history.

G. P. GOOCH, *Maria Theresa and Other Studies* (1951). A sound introduction to the problems of the Habsburgs.

G. P. GOOCH, *Louis XV, The Monarchy in Decline* (1956). A discussion of the problems of France after the death of Louis XIV.

J. M. HITTLE, *The Service City: State and Townsmen in Russia,* 1600–1800 (1979). Examines the relationship of cities in Russia to the growing power of the central government.

H. HOLBORN, *A History of Modern Germany,* 1648–1840 (1966). The best and most comprehensive survey in English.

H. C. JOHNSON, *Frederick the Great and His Officials* (1975). An excellent recent examination of the Prussian administration.

R. A. KANN AND Z. V. DAVID, *The Peoples of the Eastern Habsburg Lands,* 1526–1918 (1984). The best overview of the subject.

V. K. KLYUCHEVSKY, *Peter the Great,* tr. by Liliana Archibald (1958). A standard biography.

D. MARSHALL, *Eighteenth-Century England* (1962). Emphasizes social and economic background.

R. K. MASSIE, *Peter the Great: His Life and His World* (1980). A good popular biography.

L. B. NAMIER AND J. BROOKE, *The History of Parliament: The House of Commons,* 1754–1790, 3 vols. (1964). A detailed examination of the unreformed British House of Commons and electoral system.

L. J. OLIVA (Ed.), *Russia and the West from Peter the Great to Khrushchev* (1965). An anthology of articles tracing an important and ambiguous subject.

J. B. OWEN, *The Eighteenth Century* (1974). An excellent introduction to England in the period.

J. H. PLUMB, *Sir Robert Walpole,* 2 vols. (1956, 1961). A masterful biography ranging across the sweep of European politics.

J. H. PLUMB, *The Growth of Political Stability in England,* 1675–1725 (1969). An important interpretive work.

N. V. RIASANOVSKY, *A History of Russia,* 3rd ed. (1977). The best one-volume introduction.

N. V. RIASANOVSKY, *The Image of Peter the Great in Russian History and Thought* (1985). Examines the ongoing legacy of Peter in Russian history.

P. ROBERTS, *The Quest for Security,* 1715–1740 (1947). Very good on the diplomatic problems of the period.

H. ROSENBERG, *Bureaucracy, Aristocracy, and Autocracy: The Prussian Experience,* 1660–1815 (1960). Emphasizes the organization of Prussian administration.

B. H. SUMMER, *Peter the Great and the Emergency of Russia* (1950). A brief, but well-organized discussion.

E. N. WILLIAMS, *The Ancien Régime in Europe* (1972). A state-by-state survey of very high quality.

A. M. WILSON, *French Foreign Policy During the Administration of Cardinal Fleury,* 1726–1743 (1936). The standard account.

J. B. WOLF, *The Emergence of the Great Powers, 1685–1715* (1951). A comprehensive survey.

Throughout Europe in the eighteenth century, the aristocracy dominated both society and government. This portrait of an English nobleman, Lord Willoughby de Brooke, and his family captures the elegance and luxury of aristocratic life. [*Michael Holford*]

Index

D

F

S